COLONEL HOUSE

COLONEL HOUSE

A BIOGRAPHY OF WOODROW WILSON'S SILENT PARTNER

CHARLES E. NEU

OXFORD

UNIVERSITY PRESS

OXFORD

UNIVERSITY PRESS

Oxford University Press is a department of the University of Oxford. It furthers the University's objective of excellence in research, scholarship, and education by publishing worldwide. Oxford is a registered trade mark of Oxford University Press in the UK and in certain other countries

Published in the United States of America by Oxford University Press
198 Madison Avenue, New York, NY 10016, United States of America

Library of Congress Cataloging-in-Publication Data
Neu, Charles E.
Colonel House: a biography of Woodrow Wilson's silent partner/Charles E. Neu.
pages cm
Includes bibliographical references and index.
ISBN 978–0–19–504550–5

1. House, Edward Mandell, 1858–1938. 2. Wilson, Woodrow, 1856–1924—Friends and associates. 3. Statesmen—United States—Biography. 4. United States—Foreign relations—1913–1921. 5. United States—Politics and government—1913–1921. 6. World War, 1914–1918—Peace. 7. Treaty of Versailles (1919) I. Title.
E748.H77N48 2015
973.91'3092—dc23
[B]
2014015227

1 3 5 7 9 8 6 4 2
Printed in the United States of America
on acid-free paper

For Sabina

Also by Charles E. Neu

An Uncertain Friendship: Theodore Roosevelt and Japan, 1906–1909

The Troubled Encounter: The United States and Japan

Co-editor, *The Wilson Era: Essays in Honor of Arthur S. Link*

Editor, *After Vietnam: Legacies of a Lost War*

America's Lost War: Vietnam, 1945–1975

Co-editor, *Artists of Power: Theodore Roosevelt, Woodrow Wilson, and Their Enduring Impact on U.S. Foreign Policy*

Contents

Prologue

A Great Adventure

Colonel Edward M. House led, by any measure—including his own—an extraordinary life, one as big as the limitless prairies of the Gulf Coastal Plain on which he spent his youth. He experienced the turbulence of post–Civil War frontier America and lived until the New Deal was fully enacted and World War II an inevitability. The mythology of that frontier and the heroic past of his state left a deep impression on him. After his father died on January 17, 1980, House left Cornell University and returned to Texas, where he married, pursued a variety of business activities, built an elegant mansion in Austin, and pondered his future. Though he later lived in New York and Boston's North Shore, went to Europe frequently, and became one of the most powerful Washington insiders in American political history, he was fundamentally a Texan.

When he had settled in Houston after his father's death in 1880, House realized that he would not duplicate the feats of Texans who had "molded a trackless wilderness into a great commonwealth." In 1885 he moved to Austin, both to escape the heat and humidity of Houston and to be closer to the political center of the state. He yearned for a political career and proceeded to build his own faction—"our crowd," as he called it—which would become a potent political machine and a powerful force in Texas politics. House proved an effective political operator—arguably one of the greatest in American political history—skilled in organizing and inspiring others by working largely behind the scenes, developing ties of loyalty and affection with his close associates and using patronage to rally party workers behind his candidates. From 1894 to 1906, House's protégés served as governors of Texas, all of them Democrats. One of these governors, James Stephen Hogg, bestowed the honorary title of "Colonel" on House, and three successive governors repeated the honor. The title stuck.

By the turn of the century House had grown tired of Texas politics and sought broader horizons. The energy and dynamism of New York fascinated him, and he began to spend more time there and on the North Shore of Boston. The first decade of the twentieth century became his "twilight years." Now in his fifties, House had a sense of time passing him by, and he began to fear that he would not be able to find a place on the national political stage. He waited for the "man and the opportunity," but the period from 1896 to 1912 was one of Republican ascendancy, and no Democratic leader emerged who could win the presidency. During these years House daydreamed, traveled to Europe, and wrote a novel of the future, *Philip Dru: Administrator,* in which the hero (featuring many of House's characteristics) achieved a sweeping transformation of American life.

Colonel House's moment came on November 24, 1911, when he met Woodrow Wilson, the governor of New Jersey and a leading candidate for the Democratic nomination for president. Only a few weeks after they met, House and Wilson were exchanging all kinds of confidences. Early in their friendship House asked Governor Wilson if he realized how short a time they had known one another. Wilson replied: "My dear friend, we have known one another always."[1]

They formed what would become, with Wilson's election to the presidency in November 1912, one of the most famous friendships in American political history. Although Wilson had a close marriage and a warm and happy family life, he often felt lonely and depressed, and yearned for male companionship. House appeared at the right time with a combination of personal and political qualities that appealed to Wilson. He had a gentle, deferential manner and was willing to offer assurances of affection and support. And House's own apparently fragile health, especially his need to avoid warm weather, elicited the president's sympathy and concern.

And in Wilson, House found a leader who embodied his moral and political values and who could move the American people toward larger goals. In the winter of 1912–1913 House joined a small circle of intimates around the president who were dedicated to advancing his presidency and to maintaining his physical health and emotional stability.

House realized that if he was to remain close to the president, he would need the help of well-placed associates, and he reached back to his Texas past. Partly through his efforts, three friends, Albert S. Burleson, Thomas Watt Gregory, and David F. Houston, entered Wilson's cabinet, and the two senators from Texas, Morris Sheppard and Charles Allen Culberson, labored to move Wilson's legislative program through the upper chamber.

Wilson's presidency therefore marked the emergence of Texans as a powerful force in the national Democratic Party. Indeed, House would live to see Texans achieve a dominant position in Congress during the New Deal years and no doubt would have been pleased to see, in the second half of the twentieth century and beyond, the rise of Texas into a kind of superstate, one whose leaders would play a prominent role in national and world affairs.

In the Wilson administration, House became a high-level political intermediary, one who took on all sorts of tasks that Wilson—who was a solitary figure—found distasteful. Working out of a small study in his New York apartment, he filled his days with conferences and phone calls. House was a patient, crafty, and sometimes cynical political infighter. He was not a deeply read man and nothing like the intellectual equal of Wilson. His great strength, and contribution to Wilson's presidency, was in the intangible realm of human relations. House patiently sifted through people and issues and helped rally various constituencies behind Wilson's legislative program.

House's role as a personal adviser, with no official position, fit well with the migratory pattern of his life. He and the president never saw that much of each other, since House spent winters in New York and summers on Boston's North Shore, and took long trips to Europe. When he visited Washington he rarely stayed for more than two or three days. Despite their long separations, however, the two men kept in close contact through a steady stream of letters and occasional phone calls.

It was, in fact, House's assessment of events in Europe that proved most decisive and in which he was to exert the deepest influence on Wilson's presidency. In May 1913, he had traveled to Europe and returned there in May 1914. During this second trip he became alarmed by the atmosphere in the capitals of Europe, convinced that he had witnessed "jingoism run stark mad."[2] After World War I erupted in August, House concentrated on diplomacy and quickly became the president's closest foreign policy adviser. He was the first member of the administration to inform himself about the complexity of the struggle and the dangers and opportunities it posed for the United States. In 1915, 1916, and 1917 he returned to Europe as the president's personal representative, sending back vivid and detailed letters full of valuable information about every phase of the war. As the Great War lengthened and its devastation grew, House and Wilson realized the damage it was inflicting on Western Civilization and hoped to devise some way to end it that would place the United States at the center of a new world order.

House became the key figure in these American mediation efforts, establishing close ties with British leaders and developing a mediation scheme that would either bring about a pro–Allied settlement or bring American entry into the war on the side of the Allies. While he was a resourceful and imaginative diplomat, his analysis of wartime politics was erratic. He relied heavily on personal contacts, often missing the larger historical forces that shaped the policies of the warring powers. Yet the president nonetheless relied on House as his principal emissary.

In December 1915, however, Wilson remarried, and his new wife, Edith, was very different from his first wife Ellen, who had died only a few months earlier, in August 1914. Edith was obsessive about her husband, critical of all of his advisers, and convinced from the start that House was, as she wrote to her husband, "not a very strong character."[3] The president, who had always viewed House as a counselor rather than a statesman, gradually pulled back from the relationship. House still remained, however, a key figure in Wilsonian diplomacy, traveling to Europe in November 1918 to conduct armistice negotiations with the Allies. Both men were convinced that out of the chaos of the war a new community of nations would emerge based on a sweeping reconstruction of the international order.

As the war progressed and as his experience grew, moreover, House gradually moved out of Wilson's shadow. He came to know most of the leaders in Berlin, London, and Paris, and by the end of 1918 had concluded that it would be best if the president stayed home or made only a brief, symbolic visit to Europe, leaving House to head the American delegation and to hammer out a peace settlement with the Allies. The president, however, viewed the peace conference as the culmination of his life; he had no intention of staying in Washington. As the Paris Peace Conference unfolded, differences appeared between the president and his counselor, who was more willing to concede to British, French, and Italian demands for a victor's peace. House's emphasis on people rather than ideas, along with his growing prominence, led Wilson to withdraw his confidence yet further. There was no open break or confrontation, but after the president left France on June 28, 1919, he would never see his counselor again.

House often reflected on his relationship with Wilson and on the extraordinary seven years during which they held power. He lived to see, during the New Deal years, Harry Hopkins draw close to Franklin

D. Roosevelt, but only after House's death in March 1938 and the outbreak of war in Europe did Hopkins become an important emissary to Joseph Stalin and Winston Churchill. Hopkins's role, however, was different from that of House. He actually lived in the White House for three and a half years and "never made the mistake," Robert Sherwood noted in his famous biography of Roosevelt and Hopkins, "of Colonel Edward M. House. . . of assuming he knew the President's mind better than the President did."[4] In contrast to Wilson, FDR enjoyed being around people and formed a large, shifting group of advisers. In fact, his approach foreshadowed that of presidents in the postwar decades. As the United States emerged as a global power and became engaged in a protracted Cold War, presidents turned to a broad range of advisers to help guide them through perilous times. They now sat at the apex of a sprawling national security bureaucracy and presided over what seemed an endless series of wars and international crises. From their perspective, the relationship between House and Wilson seemed almost quaint, a relic of a distant era of American innocence.

Throughout the Wilson years House worried about his place in history. Since he had no official position (just as Hopkins did not, after he became FDR's foreign emissary), he feared that his contribution—so intangible in so many ways—might be lost. To ensure that this did not happen, he began to keep a diary in which he recorded his impressions of people and his version of events, especially the many long conversations he had with Wilson. Most evenings, unless he was ill or traveling, House would dictate the day's events to his faithful private secretary, Fanny Denton, and eventually his diary, which he started on September 25, 1912, would total nearly 3,000 pages.

House's diary is a remarkable resource for his biographer. It also presents certain perils, as it forces that biographer to run the risk of seeing things too much from his point of view. In the pages that follow I have tried to keep in mind the subjective nature of House's account, testing it against other accounts—when they exist—and also testing the plausibility—given what I know from other sources—of his version of events. Fortunately, House's efforts to influence posterity often appear, after the passage of so many years, fairly transparent. As English prime minister David Lloyd George, who knew him well, remarked, "It is perhaps to his credit that he was not nearly as cunning as he thought he was."[5]

House had good reason to worry about his historical reputation; during the 1920s and 1930s he and his protégés engaged in a series of quarrels with Wilson's defenders about who was responsible for the triumphs and failures of Wilson's presidency. These quarrels, however, were misleading, since Wilson and House had never been antagonists. They shared the same beliefs and aspirations and formed an unusual partnership. House helped to make possible Wilson's achievements and deserves credit—how much this book will explore—for the fact that Wilson's legacy would endure, casting a long shadow over the twentieth and twenty-first centuries.

Wilson took office more than one hundred years ago, and his presidency would take place during a crucial period of reform, war, and revolution. House was at the center of these events, a shrewd observer of human foibles, and a study of his life will deepen our understanding of the American response to unprecedented challenges at home and abroad. House and Wilson lived in a world—now largely gone—of slow trains and long ocean voyages, of leisurely conversations, of letters and elaborate diaries, of diplomatic missions that lasted for months instead of days, and of an American government so small in scale that the president typed many of its diplomatic notes.

In the pages that follow I have sought to capture some of this lost world, and to convey to the reader House's anxieties and aspirations and a sense of the rhythms of his life, of the family and friends that he relied on over the years. House's life and career took place against a backdrop of great events. Over the many years that I have worked on this biography I have drawn on an enormous volume of material—including the voluminous House collection at Yale and documents scattered in archives throughout the country. I was fortunate to have begun this study at a time when both of House's daughters were still alive, as were many others who remembered him. House knew that he had led a fortunate life, blessed with many friends, an adoring family, and longevity. Wilson once remarked that "Providence did not remove a man until his work was finished."[6] He was wrong about his own life, but right about the life of his primary counselor. House lived for fourteen years after Wilson's death in 1924, giving him the opportunity to enjoy his role as elder statesman, to look after his historical reputation, and to conclude before his death on March 28, 1938, that the dreams of his youth, begun in Texas three quarters of a century earlier, had been fulfilled.

PART I

The Texas Years,
1858–1912

I

A Spacious Youth

It was hard to tell, approaching from the Gulf of Mexico, where the ocean ended and the land began. Only a thick streak of white foam served as a line of demarcation between the sea, the sand, and the green prairie grass, stretching to far horizons. Covered with lush vegetation, pine forests, and prairie, the semi-tropical Gulf Coastal Plain was a land of magnificent vistas. It was also a land swept by hurricanes, ravaged by yellow fever, malaria, and torrential rains.[1] Those who came to know it could look beyond the verdant façade and understand the ways in which the flat, open land and the dense, moist heat challenged, and most often defeated, the men who sought to tame it.

Toward the close of the 1830s Texas was still a distant outpost beyond the American frontier. Initially a province of Mexico, it had undergone a revolution and a war for independence and had become a Republic in 1836. Texas therefore drew a special breed of settlers who sought both to escape from past misfortunes and to grasp the unique opportunities this raw new nation afforded.[2]

Thomas William House, however, left no record of his own dreams, of what visions of the future led him to leave England for America and eventually to settle in Texas. Born in Somersetshire, England, on March 3, 1814, House ran away from home as a child, went to sea, and in May 1835 arrived in New York. Supporting himself as a baker, he met the proprietor of the famed St. Charles Hotel in New Orleans and accepted a job in that establishment. Restless and ambitious, in late 1837 or early 1838 he moved to Houston, where he established the firm of House and Loveridge, bakers and confectioners.[3]

In the late 1830s, about 30,000 people lived in Texas, in a small settled area within an arc of 100 miles from Galveston Island. Galveston was the hub, possessing a fine natural harbor, and served as the port of entry for both people and goods into Texas. San Antonio lay on the western edge of the frontier, while Houston lay fifty miles inland. Founded in 1836, Houston's shrewd promoters hoped that it would dominate its hinterland by serving as a transshipment point. The rich bottomlands of the Brazos and Trinity rivers produced a wide variety of agricultural products, particularly cotton and sugar, and soon long trains of wagons pulled by oxen arrived in Houston, where the goods were transferred to shallow-draft boats for the journey to Galveston. The early economic development of the region depended on water transportation, for the few roads that existed were impassable during periods of heavy rain. But the narrow, twisting channel of Buffalo Bayou, while superior to surrounding rivers, left much to be desired. Fallen trees and other debris so obstructed its upper reaches that a trip from Galveston to Houston took three days. Buffalo Bayou was a primitive but vital link to the sea.[4]

Travelers had a mixed reaction to this raw frontier town. Some were struck by the wildflowers and magnolias covering the steep banks of Buffalo Bayou and marveled at the vast prairies and pine forests surrounding Houston. Others were oppressed by the heat, by the deep black mud that engulfed the town during the rainy season, and by the clouds of dust that blew through its streets during periods of dryness. They feared the diseases that bred on the flat, wet coastal plain and in the sluggish bayous, particularly the epidemics of yellow fever that regularly swept through the city. Houston was filled with southerners and European immigrants seeking economic gain and adventure on the Texas frontier. In 1838, one visitor called it "the greatest sink of dissipation and vice that modern times have ever known."[5]

House turned out to be a resourceful entrepreneur whose business expanded with the young city. Initially confined to baking and the making of candy, he sold the first ice cream in Houston and gradually broadened the range of his activities. As early as 1840 he accepted deposits and loaned money to customers, and in 1853, he entered the grocery and dry goods business on a large scale. T. W. House and Company soon became the largest wholesale business in Texas. House also invested in local real estate, acquired farmland near Houston, purchased and exported cotton (which he shipped to Liverpool), and traveled widely, buying goods in Boston, New Orleans, and New York. A leading merchant and wealthy citizen, he was an active promoter of railroads and various public works projects, and his large homes in Galveston and Houston were a testament to his success and status.[6]

In the 1850s, House was involved with the growth of both Galveston and Houston. Galveston by then had acquired a polished, cosmopolitan quality, with its elegant mansions, broad boulevards, shell-covered streets, and rows of handsome cast iron and brick commercial buildings. In contrast, Houston was dominated by aggressive merchants who struggled to make it the hub of the region's economy. More energetic and far-sighted than their counterparts in Galveston, this merchant elite, as early as 1839, organized a company to remove obstructions in Buffalo Bayou and made Houston the center of the small railroad network that was spreading through the Texas Gulf Coast. On the eve of the Civil War, Galveston was still larger, with 7,307 people to Houston's 4,800, but the future belonged to the more vigorous inland port.[7]

The withdrawal of Texas from the Union and the outbreak of the Civil War brought new challenges to the merchants of the Gulf Coast. During most of the war Texas prospered, but the blockade of the Confederacy, along with the occupation of Galveston in 1862 by Union troops, forced a readjustment of trade patterns. Precious shipments of cotton went south across the Rio Grande to Matamoros, Mexico, and enterprising merchants—such as House—brought back weapons and civilian goods. In 1863, Confederate forces recaptured Galveston, and the "Queen City" now became a major center for blockade runners. Allying with several experienced captains, House funded daring attempts to slip through the cordon of Union ships. He cooperated with the Confederate government but never apparently had much faith in it; nor did he share the enthusiasm of most Texans for the Confederate cause. Avoiding Confederate paper money, House amassed $300,000 in gold in England and thus, at the end of the conflict, was in a strong financial position.[8]

In 1840, House had married Mary Elizabeth Shearn, the daughter of a business associate, and from 1844 to 1858 she bore eight children, the last of whom, Edward Mandell, was born on July 26, 1858, and named after a Boston friend of his father. Edward came of age during the Civil War and Reconstruction. He remembered vividly the excitement of wartime Galveston—his father climbing to the cupola of his mansion, "a large red brick white-pillared Colonial house with orange groves and oleanders," to count Union warships; the swashbuckling captains who, in their swift side-wheelers, sought to outrun enemy ships at night; and the nighttime stillness broken by the booming of guns and the sky aglow with rockets and Roman candles. Edward knew his father's captains, saw their battered ships at the docks in Galveston, and walked along the island's long, flat beaches, observing the Union flotilla in the distance. As he recalled years later, his "first impressions of life were of human conflict."[9]

Texas was spared the destruction inflicted on other Confederate states, since the fighting took place far from its borders. But the collapse of the Confederacy brought uncertainty and outbreaks of violence. In Houston, trade came to a halt, freedmen flowed from the bottomlands and crowded the city's streets, and in May 1865 looting by Confederate soldiers forced local citizens to form a voluntary guard. Fire bells warned of a riot and called heavily armed citizens—including T. W. House—from their homes to enforce the peace. Union troops soon restored order, but Edward never forgot the tense atmosphere and the dramatic stand of his father, shotgun in hand, daring anyone to enter his store.[10]

In the years after the Civil War, T. W. House's commercial empire continued to expand. He shifted the center of his business activities from Galveston to Houston and in 1872 paid $100,000 in gold for a large plantation southeast of Houston, 8,753 acres of rich land bordered by the Brazos River and Oyster Creek near Arcola Junction. Although he had owned land near Houston before 1872, this purchase represented a major expansion of his agricultural interests and solidified his position as one of the leading entrepreneurs of Texas.[11]

Arcola Plantation supplied many of its own needs and was the home of black laborers who worked its fields. Young Edward adored Arcola, with all its varied sights and sounds. He rode through the fields of corn, cotton, and sugar cane, camping in the Brazos bottom, moving beyond his family's land to the "beautiful but limitless prairies to the west of Houston."[12] He had a privileged youth, full of movement, excitement, and space—of big skies, distant horizons, and a sense of the limitless possibilities of life.

His youth also had a darker and more dangerous side, for violence permeated the atmosphere of post–Civil War Texas. Boys grew up with guns and horses, with gunfighters as their heroes, and in Houston groups of boys roamed the streets, swearing and chewing tobacco, armed with pistols and knives.[13] Edward rode and shot as early as he could remember, and on two occasions nearly killed a friend. "Death," he recalled, "was our playmate." Fascinated by the violence and the local code of honor, Edward studied the behavior of Arcola's workers and, in the evening, listened around the fireside as his father and his friends told tales of "daring deeds" in the past.[14]

Of Edward's six brothers, one, Charles James, died in 1850, well before Edward was born, while the other five—Thomas William Jr., John, Charles Shearn, James, and George—were three to twelve years older than he was. Two brothers were distant figures, but three were companions who helped to shape his personality. T. W. Jr. was a sober youth with strong literary and religious inclinations, while Charles was a self-indulgent connoisseur of wine and food. James, John, and George, however, were all close to Edward and admired by him. James or "Jimmie," six years his senior, led the neighborhood gang and awed Edward with his ambition, physical courage, and dominating personality. John, ten years older, was also a "hero" of young Edward, for he was an expert sportsman and rifle and pistol shot, who took his younger brother on camping expeditions and displayed great skill as an outdoorsman as well an indifference to physical danger. Intense admiration and rivalry bound Edward to both Jimmie and John, and he clearly had to struggle to find a place within his large, tumultuous family. Of all his brothers, Edward loved George, only three years older, the most, and as an old man thought of him often.[15]

However, of the three brothers Edward admired most, only one, John, lived well into adulthood. On March 10, 1968, Jimmie, a few days short of his sixteenth birthday, died of a brain concussion received in a fall from a trapeze, and on June 4, 1876, "Georgie" died from an unspecified illness at the age of twenty. Edward grew up with a strong sense of loss, aware that two of his brothers had died leaving their promise unfulfilled.[16]

Even those children who lived into adulthood were acutely conscious of their own encounters with death. T. W. Jr. accidentally shot himself and, after weeks of uncertainty, survived, but he was left with a long, sunken scar on one side of his face.[17] Edward was luckier. At the age of eleven or twelve, he recalled, when he was a "strong and sturdy little ruffian" he was swinging on a rope that broke, and in the fall he hit a carriage wheel. While he recovered from what was likely a concussion he never regained full strength, becoming susceptible to malaria. As he put it in his reminiscences, "My fighting, pony racing, mischief loving days in Texas were over."[18] Despite injury and illness, Edward would go on to lead an active life, though he transformed a boyhood accident into a seminal event in his life history, one that he would use over the years to escape the unpleasant heat of Texas and Washington and to avoid the oppressive routine of public office.

On January 28, 1870, Edward's mother, Mary Shearn House, died of tuberculosis after a long illness. He was only eleven and did not retain any vivid memories of his mother. A frequent visitor to the House home, Mary Ann McDowall, remembered her as a "lovely woman, gentle, refined and kind. . . loved and honored by everyone."[19] Perhaps she helped to soften conflicts within her large, active family, but T. W. House was clearly the dominant parent, and he sought to mold the careers of his children. He insisted that his oldest son, T. W. Jr., abandon his desire to become a clergyman in the Church of England and return to Texas to help carry on the family business, and he arranged for John to manage his plantation at Arcola. His clashes with Jimmie were frequent and unpleasant, and he also worried about Edward's "ruffian" behavior.[20] In the decade between his wife's death and his own, in 1880, he was particularly concerned about the development and education of his youngest son.

T. W. House had always wanted the best education for his children, sending most of them to England for a portion of their schooling. Except for a six-month stay at Bath—which seems not to have left much of an impression—Edward attended Houston Academy, where he remembered doing little "except to get into mischief and fight other boys of my age that undertook to challenge my leadership." In 1872, his father decided to send him East to school, and in February 1873 Edward and his boyhood friend, Paul Cruger, began the long and arduous trip to Amelia County, Virginia. When the two boys arrived at the railway station they had to hire a wagon to reach the Harrison School, which was some fifteen miles away. Like most academies in the post–Civil War era, the Harrison School had become a marginal institution, with only a handful of boys and primitive facilities. Edward never forgot his initial "depression" and recalled that "a more desolate, lonely spot no homesick boy ever saw." The school consisted of only two buildings—the Harrison residence and, about 200 yards away, the schoolhouse and dormitory. Edward and Paul were given a "small, bare room" on the third floor, and were so disappointed that in the autumn of 1873, T. W. House transferred them to Verulam Academy, about eight miles from Charlottesville. Verulam was, if anything, an even more marginal institution, with a thin larder and rugged living conditions. Both schools suffered from poor instruction and a small, unevenly prepared student body. Edward did not apply himself to his formal studies but enjoyed long conversations with the headmaster of Verulam, W. O. English, a graduate of the University of Virginia who had a wide range of knowledge and experience.[21] By the age of fifteen he had acquired what became a lifelong inclination of learning more from people than from books.

Edward adjusted with difficulty to the loneliness of school life and the boredom of classroom recitation from textbooks, but worse was the brutal hazing at both academies. As a newcomer he was singled out, awakened by blazing gunpowder on the floor of his room and alarmed by the extremes to which the rougher boys went. He held off the hazers by brandishing a large knife and pistol, but there was virtually open warfare among students. More than anything else, the beauty and openness of the land helped him to survive. At Verulam, Edward explored the nearby mountains, where he pursued his love of the outdoors.[22]

After two years at Verulam, Edward hoped to transfer to Yale University. His father knew President Noah Porter, and Edward believed he might be ready for Yale's sophomore class. He badly misjudged his own education, however. When Porter referred Edward to the rector of Hopkins Grammar School, William Cushing, in New Haven for an examination in Greek and Latin, he did so poorly that Cushing recommended no fewer than two years at Hopkins in preparation for Yale. Acutely disappointed, Edward journeyed to New Haven and enrolled at Hopkins in the autumn of 1875.[23]

William Cushing combined sternness with a sense of humor and taught the classics with rigor and imagination. In 1875, the school's 220 boys attended classes in one building at the corner of Wall and High Streets, while out-of-town students stayed at private boarding houses approved by the rector. By his own admission, Edward studied infrequently and crammed for examinations. During his first year his academic standing began at a respectable level, but it steadily declined until in May 1876 he ranked thirty-eight out of a class of thirty-nine. In June he skipped his final exams. Although Edward spent a second year in New Haven, he did not formally enroll at Hopkins, for he was absorbed in the presidential election of 1876 and the long crisis that followed it.[24]

Senator Oliver Perry Morton of Indiana, the father of one of Edward's classmates, was one of the leading candidates for the Republican nomination for the presidency,[25] but in June at the party's Cincinnati convention, Governor Rutherford B. Hayes of Ohio emerged victorious. The presidential campaign that followed between Hayes and Samuel J. Tilden of New York—two party regulars with reform inclinations—absorbed the nation as none had since 1860. With most of the South once again under Democratic control, the equilibrium between the two parties had been restored and many believed that Tilden would triumph. In fact, this appeared to be the case, for Tilden won a substantial popular majority and needed only one additional electoral vote to achieve victory. Success hinged on the fate of disputed electoral returns from three southern states that were still under Republican rule—Florida, Louisiana, and South Carolina. By claiming all of these votes, Republicans precipitated an unprecedented crisis in the winter of 1876–77. No constitutional machinery existed for choosing among the competing electoral slates and the winter was filled with threats of violence and bitter political rhetoric. In January, Congress finally created a special Electoral Commission, on which Morton served, to resolve the dispute. By a vote of 8 to 7 it seated all of the contested Republican electors and in effect elevated Hayes to the presidency by a margin of one electoral vote. Many Democrats, however, cried fraud, and angry debates broke out in Congress. Several informal agreements between Republican and Democratic leaders—apparently reached with Hayes's blessing—led to enough Democratic defections that the House on March 2, 1877, declared Hayes elected to the presidency. The election of 1876 marked the end of Reconstruction and the opening of a new, less ideological era of American politics.[26]

Ideological or not, the post–Civil War years were a time of intense interest in politics, of colorful parades and elaborate rites of victory and defeat. Edward and Oliver Morton, absorbed in public affairs and bored with their studies at Hopkins Grammar School, "gravitated together like magnet & steel and became inseparable friends." As the election of 1876 approached, they "abandon books for politics" and traveled frequently to New York and Washington. In New York they observed the activities at Democratic National Headquarters, and the more practical Edward had to restrain Oliver from spending all of their money and leaving nothing for the return trip to New Haven. In Washington they stayed with the Mortons and studied the stream of Republican leaders and followers to the senator's rooms, met President and Mrs. Ulysses S. Grant and members of the cabinet, and watched both the deliberations of the Electoral Commission and the debates in Congress.[27]

It was enormously exciting for a boy of eighteen to be at the center of a great national crisis and to receive firsthand impressions of the political leaders of the day. Edward was learning, he thought, in a "larger and more interesting school" than classrooms at Hopkins Grammar School and seemed far more interested—as he would be for his entire life—in the process rather than the substance of politics, fascinated with tactics and personalities.[28]

During his second year in New Haven, Edward gave up his intention to enter Yale. Given his undistinguished record at Hopkins Grammar School, he knew that Yale would probably not admit him in any event. Oliver Morton planned to attend Cornell, and another friend, Robert Morris, had gone there the year before and urged Edward to join him. He readily agreed to do so.[29]

Unlike Yale, which had resisted many of the postwar reforms in American higher education, Cornell embraced them. Opening in the fall of 1868, Cornell stirred the educational world with its exciting, controversial combination of traditional learning with utilitarian courses that would serve all the varied needs of American society. Non-sectarian and—perhaps even more revolutionary—coeducational, from the start it adopted the elective principle and placed far more reliance than most institutions of its day on the motivation of individual students to learn. President Andrew D. White was one of the great educational leaders of the time, a widely traveled, cosmopolitan man with a bold vision of the new university and a talent for assembling an outstanding faculty.[30]

When Edward arrived in the fall of 1877, 529 students attended Cornell, studying in a cluster of sturdy, rugged stone buildings, along with two more recent, elaborate Victorian gothic structures. Situated on Ezra Cornell's old East Hill farm, the campus was a remote and primitive place, swept by fierce winds and surrounded by hilly, forested country, and the village of Ithaca, whose unpaved streets, rows of white, Greek revival houses, and unpretentious commercial buildings, may have reminded Edward of his native Houston.[31]

Edward adjusted easily, enrolling in the literature program, pledging Alpha Delta Phi fraternity and, like most students in the late 1870s, living in Ithaca rather than on the campus. "The days ran swiftly at Cornell," he recalled. "I liked my companions, I liked the atmosphere and I enjoyed the wider opportunity to read and discuss what I read with those better informed than I." Absorbed in politics and in the social side of college, he only tolerated the academic side, ignoring the talented faculty, the forceful president, and the educational experiment of which he was a part. Edward sang in his fraternity quintet, joined several other social organizations, and relished the rituals and comradeship of his fraternity.[32] This included the occasional prank in which, with a combination of amusement and contempt, he would appeal to someone for help. "I used to ask questions and get minute instructions about how to do this or that thing, or how to play at games in which I was already more proficient than those who sought to teach me. In some instances I would gradually show my skill—in others I would do so at once much to the chagrin of my would be teachers."[33] He liked to conceal what he knew.

Occasionally Edward and his friends would ask "some boastful, arrogant, conceited boy" if he cared to join their secret society and subject him to severe hazing, as one degree proceeded to another. Edward and Oliver Morton also carried out what must have struck them as an exceptionally imaginative prank. As House later described it, they took a blindfolded candidate for a secret society "out on a rail-road track and tied him to a loose rail on a side track. We knew when the express train would come by and timed ourselves accordingly. When the whistle of the train was heard in the distance Morton said 'We had better begin to untie him.' I replied 'No, not just yet, there is plenty of time.' When the rumble became more distinct and the headlight of the engine could be seen, we would hurriedly get to work undoing the cord. The excitement grew intense, our fingers became all thumbs and we were unable to free him. We jumped back & the train rushed by. Cruel sport if you like, but one fascinating to a half-grown boy. The whole scheme was to frighten, not to hurt."[34]

Edward's days at Cornell drifted pleasantly by, and were full of comradeship, casual reading, and hunting in the surrounding countryside. Throughout his school years in Virginia, New Haven, and Ithaca, his father came East from June through October—the most oppressive months in Houston—and Edward was, he recalled, "my father's constant companion." Some summers he also returned to Texas. In the autumn of 1879, T. W. House became seriously ill and Edward went home to help look after him. For three months he sat with his father every other night. "My affection for him was such," he remembered, "that I wanted to care for him to the limit of my strength." Finally the family moved T. W. from his home in Houston to the Menger Hotel in San Antonio, where he would receive better medical attention and perhaps benefit from the dryer air. These efforts failed and on January 17, 1880, the great merchant died. Edward, his youngest son, was twenty-one.[35]

2

Searching for a Career

The death of T. W. House came as a tremendous blow to Edward. He had idolized his father, who had taught him that wealth should be a means to larger ends and left him so secure financially that he could pursue a political career. "He seemed to me then [in 1880], as he seems to me now," House wrote in 1916, "among the ablest men I have ever known. He was of that intrepid band that made Texas what she is today."[1]

T. W. House had lived during the heroic age of Texas history, when legendary figures such as Stephen F. Austin, Jim Bowie, Sam Houston, and William B. Travis had helped to carve a republic out of a wilderness, defying Mexicans and Indians, and had left a sacred tradition of revolution and independence.[2] By the early 1880s the frontier had been tamed and Texas was firmly a part of the nation; no challenges of a similar drama and magnitude seemed to exist for Edward House and his generation of Texans. Dreaming of future glory and yearning for a place in history, he needed time to absorb his father's death and decide on the path he would pursue.[3]

The senior House was one of the wealthiest men in Texas, leaving an estate of over one million dollars. His commercial empire included a mercantile and banking business centered in Houston, 250,000 acres of land scattered through sixty-three counties of Texas, along with stock in railways and other investments. His will provided that the estate must be held together for five years, after which time it was to be equally divided among his children, five of whom were still living. Mary, the eldest, had married and moved to San Marcos, about 200 miles northwest of Houston, while T. W. Jr., Charles, and John had all settled in Houston. Under the leadership of T. W. Jr., the four brothers shared the responsibilities of managing their father's enterprises. Initially Edward had no taste for business and tried to escape these new burdens.

Edward sought delay through a long, leisurely camping expedition with his friend Paul Cruger, one that lasted for weeks and carried them far up the Colorado River valley and beyond, deep into northwest Texas. Beginning in San Marcos, they rode through rolling plains, where wooded rivers and creeks wound through the sea of grass, up into the high plains, treeless and semi-arid, a land of boundless space and silence. This was wild and dangerous country, peopled by cattlemen and the remnants of defeated Indian tribes, and one traveled for days without seeing any sign of human habitation. Accompanied by a black servant and a wagon drawn by two mules, Edward sought anonymity. Unshaven and suntanned, he looked like an "uncivilized ruffian" and was able to roam through Texas without being recognized as a member of one of the state's most prominent families.[4]

Sometime in the spring of 1880 the two friends returned to Houston. Edward was still unready for the burdens that awaited him, and soon after his arrival he headed East for a reunion with his college friends.[5] The trip was cut short when T. W. Jr. asked that he come back to Texas and help with the management of his father's estate.

Edward's task was to inspect the family's land, scattered throughout Texas, and to decide which to sell and which to hold. He soon came to relish the independence of his work and the trips to sparsely settled parts of the state. Visits to the 64,000-acre family ranch near the Rio Grande were, he recalled, "filled with a certain exhilarating joy. The reckless freedom of the life, the campfires at night, sleeping under the skies, the soft dry air, the awakening at dawn, the riding with a free rein over the vast, undulating flower strewn prairies intoxicated the senses and stimulated the imagination. In the silent watches of the night and in the quieter moment of the day, I dreamed great dreams—many of which have since come true."[6]

Edward spent a year or so moving through the state, assessing the family's landholdings, but was still reluctant to settle into the family business. He dreamed of fame and glory far beyond what could be achieved in a business career in Texas, and fate intervened again to delay an acceptance of reality. Early in 1881 he met Loulie Hunter at a military ball in Houston. Her father, A. J. Hunter, had moved to Texas before the Civil War with his family and slaves and developed a substantial cotton plantation. Born in 1859, Loulie had been educated at a convent in San Antonio and at Hollins Institute in Virginia. She was a woman of charm and beauty, conscious of her place in life, and was a fitting partner for the youngest son of one of the leading families of Texas.[7] On August 4, 1881, Edward and Loulie were married. After the wedding they left on a year-long grand tour of Europe. They lingered in Florence, where Mona, their first child, was born, but left no record of their courtship and honeymoon, aside from two photographs.[8]

In the summer of 1882, Edward, Loulie, and Mona returned to Houston, where, he recalled, "I applied myself assiduously for a few years to business."[9] Edward continued to supervise the family's landholdings, buying and selling land and looking after the large ranch in South Texas, while John H. B. managed the Arcola Plantation and T. W. Jr. directed the family bank. In all areas, the family business thrived. At Arcola, black convicts helped to harvest the sugar cane, and during the 1880s, a cotton gin was purchased and a steam-powered sugar mill was constructed. Arcola sugar was of such a high quality that it won a prize at the World's Centennial Exposition in New Orleans. In 1883 a new House bank building opened on Main Street in Houston, an ornate three-story red stone structure built to celebrate the golden anniversary of T. W. House and Company in 1888. T. W. Jr. had twenty dollar gold souvenir coins minted for the occasion, while Edward wrote, on a card sent to friends of the family, that "to-day we are on the threshold of the second half century of our existence as a firm. From father to sons—from one generation to another, the principles and tradition of our house have remained unchanged."[10]

Yet even before House wrote these lines his father's inheritance was being divided among his surviving children. Although the four brothers continued to own much in common, as early as June 1884 extensive land transactions took place among them. The eldest, T. W. Jr., carried on his father's traditions. He became the dominant figure in the family bank and a leading citizen of Houston, where he served as alderman and promoted several local utilities as well as the deepening of the ship channel. When Edward returned from his honeymoon his brother was so well established that there was no real place for him in Houston, even if he had wanted to follow in his father's footsteps.[11]

Edward considered moving to San Antonio or Austin. San Antonio was close to the family ranch in South Texas, while Austin, at the edge of the Hill Country of Central Texas, was close to several large cotton plantations that he had inherited and was also the home of the state land office, where he conducted so much business. Its mild climate and beautiful setting contrasted sharply with Houston.[12] Unable "to keep my health" in Houston, Edward decided in 1885 to leave for the hills of Austin. The city offered more physical comfort and the more convenient pursuit of his business interests, and it was the political capital of the state. Austin promised a new beginning, where he could escape from the shadow of his father and older brother. Looking back in 1929, House speculated that "it may be that my entire life was changed by this move."[13]

For decades Austin had been a remote town, but the 1880s brought the completion of the great red-granite capitol, the founding of the University of Texas, the erection of elaborate mansions and of monumental public buildings, and the construction of a large dam across the Colorado River. The lake it formed wound through the hills for twenty-one miles and became an important part of the city's life. The dam's power brought dramatic improvements, such as electric streetcars and 150-foot-high towers that flooded the city with light at night. During the 1890s, Austin (with about 14,575 people) became the social and cultural center of the state, a provincial city but one of charm and vitality. It was the "Famous City of the Lone Star State," a fitting place for Edward to begin a new phase of his life and to continue his search for a career.[14]

In the autumn of 1885, when the House family moved to Austin, Mona was four and Janet, the second daughter, only a year and a half old. Edward was twenty-eight, and though a slight man, he had a look of intensity radiating from his face, with its prominent cheekbones, recessive chin, thick, closely cropped mustache, and black, already receding hair.[15] Edward and Loulie soon assumed a prominent place in the lively social life of the capital, appearing at ceremonial political events and entertaining Austin society. In February 1888 they gave a "Reception and 'Lotto'" of the "utmost elegance and polished finish," with Chinese lanterns hung from the ceilings along with fans and other Oriental objects. At 9 PM the lotto tables were arranged and House began calling numbers. The rooms filled with flowers, ornaments, and elegant guests all combined, reported the *Austin Statesman*, "to make a scene of rare and radiant loveliness, once to be seen, long to be remembered." Over the years other elaborate parties followed. Loulie gave a "German"—a party in which guests appeared with powdered hair—for her sister, Annie Hunter; on another occasion young ladies wore masks of old maids, auctioned themselves off to young men, and then removed their masks at an "evening masquerade" where the Houses "regaled their guests with all the delicacies that imported caterers and limitless expenditures could procure."[16]

Loulie was a gracious hostess who relished her social position. Newspaper accounts referred to her "dark beauty" and "queenly style," and praised her diamonds and magnificent, imported dresses. In 1885, when *Leslie's*

Weekly devoted a page to "types of Southern beauties—Prominent Society Women of Austin, Texas," Loulie and Annie were among the sixteen women included. She combined her love of society with warmth and kindness, organized French classes in her home, and was particularly concerned about Austin's unwed mothers. Her large domestic establishment included many servants, a carriage driver, and a French governess for the children.[17]

The House family soon became an extended one, as Loulie's sister Annie lived with the Houses until her marriage in 1896 and her brother, Clarence Hunter, helped with Edward's land transactions. Around 1890 Edward hired Frances B. Denton, called Fanny, then only eighteen, as his personal secretary. Her father, Dr. A. N. Denton, was the son of a famous Texas patriot and superintendent of the state Lunatic Asylum; Edward considered him a close friend and the greatest psychiatrist in Texas. Saddened by the death of her fiancé and troubled by an unstable family, Fanny may have sought through her employment both security and an entrée into a larger world. A striking woman, with an oval face, broad mouth, and brown, pulled-back hair, she was high-spirited and independent and gradually became Edward's confidante as well as virtually a member of the family.[18] Edward was sensitive to all the nuances of family life, concerned about the romances of Annie and Fanny, and affectionate with his children, who came to refer to him as "popsie." Over the years rumors circulated in Austin that Fanny was Edward's "mistress." There is no surviving written evidence that confirms such a relationship, and Frances Denton Miller, who lived with her "Aunt Fan" for three years, dismissed these rumors. "Aunt Fan," she recalled, "was a most Victorian woman who was terribly strict in her morals and so innocent . . . . You can't mistake real innocence about certain things."[19]

Edward acquired a deep and abiding love for Austin and the land around it. He often rode through the city on horseback, meticulously dressed in a riding suit and boots, sometimes with a six-shooter strapped around his waist, and occasionally he ranged beyond the city into the Hill Country to the northwest, with its limestone bluffs and ridges and cool, clean streams shaded with cedar and wild oak. Austin would always remain his legal address; even after he left, his stationery would bear the imprint "E. M. House, Austin, Texas."[20]

During the late 1880s and early 1890s, Edward was absorbed in his varied and demanding business affairs, in farming, ranching, money-lending, and land speculation. He watched over the large family ranch in south Texas, where he hired a skilled manager and occasionally visited. From his new location in Austin he could supervise more carefully the cotton plantations that he and Loulie had inherited and also intensify his land speculations. The general trend of Texas land prices was upward, although there were, of course, fluctuations, which increased the opportunities for profits. The House brothers bought and sold land together and among themselves, developing a well-defined set of procedures. T. W. Jr. handled the notes from these sales while Edward negotiated the transaction, always using local agents. His chief collaborator was T. F. Pinckney, who worked in the General Land Office in Austin and had an impressive knowledge of the Texas public domain. Most of the land for sale was in the western part of the state, but it was possible for a clever investigator to discover choice parcels in central and east Texas. Pinckney located and surveyed these parcels; Edward supplied the capital for their purchase. These land sales generated much cash and also interest income from vendors' lien notes. He was prospering, selling inherited land that did not yield a good return, buying and selling new lands, and improving his cotton plantations.[21]

Soon after moving to Austin Edward bought a whole block of land on West Avenue, at the summit of one of the city's highest hills and began to plan for a home of his own. During one of his stays in New York, he noticed the Brooklyn Savings Bank, designed by Frank Freeman, a prominent New York architect strongly influenced by Henry Hobson Richardson. As Edward wrote Freeman in 1901, "I will never forget my delight when I first saw the Brooklyn Savings Bank Building. It was so different from anything that I had ever seen and was so chaste and beautiful that the memory has been with me ever since." He commissioned Freeman to design his Texas home. On January 29, 1891, construction began and on April 25 Janet and Mona laid the cornerstone, surrounded by a few family friends gathered for the occasion. House entertained the workmen with cake and wine and placed within the cornerstone a box containing photographs and memorabilia reflecting the wealth and social position of the family.[22]

In late June 1892, the House family moved into the new home, which immediately became one of the great mansions of Austin. It was a sophisticated design, a version of a shingle-style house that could have been built by a wealthy Easterner. The vertical thrust of the two large chimneys broke the strong, horizontal lines of the house, and the massive roof was full of small gables and turrets with pointed pinnacles. The first floor, chimneys, and the supporting columns of the porch were built of rough blocks of red sandstone. On the south side a covered portico shielded arriving guests from the hot sun, while on the north side the porch running along the front of the house widened into a large veranda overlooking the garden. Both the exterior and interior of the house combined elegance and informality.[23]

Edward spared no expense in the construction of his mansion. Behind the sandstone facing were structural brick walls two feet thick, and sumptuous, expensive materials were used throughout the interior. The light, inlaid oak floors and paneling contrasted dramatically with the dark mahogany staircase, which swept upward to the second floor. The interior was filled with thick stained glass, chandeliers from Paris, full-length plate glass mirrors, and fireplaces bordered with illustrated, hand-made tiles imported from France and Germany. The house was a showpiece, the only shingle-style house ever built in the city. It sat on a whole block, with a garden and stables nearby, and provided spectacular views of Austin and the hills beyond. Edward was justifiably proud of his home and always believed, Mona wrote, that "it was the most beautiful home he ever saw."[24]

A popular and prominent businessman, during his early years in Austin Edward met many new people, some of whom became close friends. Perhaps the most fascinating of these new friends was William J. "Bill" McDonald, captain of Company B of the Texas Rangers, whose animal cunning had carried him through many encounters with death and whose exploits had made him a legend in the state. Slender and blue-eyed, six feet tall with mutton chop whiskers, McDonald embodied a frontier code of conduct that he summed up in the phrase, "No man in the wrong can stand up against a fellow that's in the right and keeps on acoming." McDonald was colorful and daring, a good talker with a gift for epigrams and an instinct for showmanship and self-promotion. He cultivated newspapermen and politicians and became the most widely known of the four Ranger captains. Edward felt a spiritual kinship with McDonald, becoming his friend and promoter.[25]

During his early years in Austin, Edward was absorbed in his family, the planning and construction of his new home, and his varied business activities. Inevitably, however, he met the leading political figures of Texas and was drawn into the political ferment of the capital city. In 1892, it was his friendship with James Stephen Hogg that led him to take the "plunge" into state politics.[26]

Hogg represented a new generation of Texas politicians, whose members had not fought in the Civil War and who were less bound by tradition than older Democrats. In 1886, he became attorney general, and four years later won his first term as governor. Over six feet tall and weighing 250 pounds, he had enormous energy and a commanding presence, a charismatic quality that allowed him to gather diverse groups behind his political banner. His booming voice, originality, and gift for picturesque phrases made him a feared opponent on the stump, one who knew how to talk to Texas farmers and who understood the anxieties and aspirations of many Texans. He combined these political gifts with a shrewd and intelligent understanding of the issues of the day and with a keen realization of the need for the Democratic Party to chart a middle path if it was to retain power.[27]

Of all the ex-Confederate states, Texas was perhaps the least southern, more a hybrid of the South and West, with a more fluid society, fewer African Americans, and a rapidly expanding population. Radical Reconstruction had been less severe there than in other parts of the South, and in 1874 Democrats had regained control of the state's government. During the late 1870s and 1880s that control was not seriously challenged, despite the persistence of a small, black-dominated Republican Party and a strong third-party tradition. Democratic leaders presided over a loosely organized coalition of businessmen, landowners, and Anglo-American farmers of southern background, all of whom were reasonably well satisfied with the distribution of wealth and power in Texas.[28]

Many Texans, however, drew few benefits from the established order, and during the 1880s their numbers and depth of their discontent dramatically increased. Labor unrest erupted in the Great Southwestern strike of 1886, when strikers in Texas engaged in pitched battles with troops and special deputies. Farmers were affected by drought, the lack of credit, the falling price of cotton, and the rising price of land, all of which brought an increase in tenantry. Marginal groups, along with those that were prosperous, felt the ominous presence of out-of-state forces—banks, railways, land companies, monopolies—that dominated the state's economy in often arbitrary and inscrutable ways. By the end of the 1880s, anxiety was pervasive through all segments of Texas society.[29]

The appearance of the Farmers' Alliance was the most striking indication of this anxiety. Founded in Texas in 1877, during the 1880s it spread rapidly throughout the West and South. Thousands of farmers and their families streamed to camp meetings, where orators denounced the status quo and sketched a vision of a brighter and more egalitarian future. Texas produced a galaxy of leaders who developed bold programs that would advance their self-interest. In 1887, Texans opened a Farmers' Alliance Exchange in Dallas, designed as a cooperative marketing and purchasing organization; in 1890 they adopted the sub-treasury plan, an innovative commodity credit corporation; and in general they advocated policies that would expand the scope of federal responsibilities. At the close of the 1880s Texas was in ferment, as farmers experimented with radical ideas and new organizations, and widespread restlessness brought challenges to the old social and political order.[30]

In 1890, Hogg swept into office on this wave of discontent, making railway regulation the key issue of the campaign. Suspicious of federal power, Hogg was willing to use state power aggressively and pushed through the legislature a railway commission, an alien land law aimed at foreign syndicates, and laws regulating public and railway securities. Sensitive to the electorate's mood, he assailed forces outside of Texas and sought, through his rhetoric and actions, to hold together the Texas Democratic Party. As economic conditions deteriorated and the reform impulse intensified, however, many farmers felt that Hogg's conservative, entrepreneurial bent was too strong and wanted to move beyond his modest readjustments of Texas society. These farmers broke with the Hogg administration and the Democratic Party and laid plans to run their own candidate for governor on the Populist ticket in 1892. Within the party, more traditional Democrats, including bankers, land agents, railway men, and businessmen, were uneasy over Hogg's assertion of state power and resentful of his flamboyant rhetoric. In 1892, they decided to challenge the governor for control of the Democratic Party, choosing as their candidate George Clark, a business lobbyist, railway attorney, and campaign manager of former Texas governors. Rallying behind the slogan "Turn Texas Loose," Clark and his supporters charged that Hogg's rhetoric and legislation were driving capital out of the state and damaging its economy.[31]

In 1892, the Democratic Party was, therefore, in disarray, locked in a bitter, internecine quarrel, and whatever faction emerged victorious at the Democratic convention would confront angry Populists in the general election. The campaign of 1892 combined high drama and real divisions over the shape of Texas society; it was natural for Edward to become involved in it. Drawn to Hogg's vivid personality and intrigued by the organizational challenges of the campaign, Edward and his friend Dr. Richard Swearingen shared the task of managing the governor's reelection effort.[32]

Although he had supported Hogg's legislation, Edward seemed distant from the passions of the 1892 campaign. He was fascinated with the machinery of Texas politics and eager to exploit it for his candidate's benefit. Texas was a vast state, with many different regions and groups, each of which had to be given special consideration. The key to the nomination, however, lay in mastering the loosely run system of selection. Democratic leaders in each county could choose to call conventions at any time for the purpose of selecting delegates to the state convention, a system that encouraged irregularities and enhanced the power of local leaders. Edward sought to build a network of support among influential local Democrats, one that would allow him to assess the situation in each county accurately and to arrange for early conventions in those where Hogg was strong. He created a bandwagon effect that brought wavering politicians to the governor's side.[33]

Edward also concentrated on special groups that voted in blocks, such as African Americans in the eastern part of the state and Mexican Americans in the southern portions along the Rio Grande. Both factions paid local "fluence" men and, when that failed, used violence and intimidation to get their voters to the county conventions. In south Texas, it was necessary to create alliances with powerful lawyers and landowners who served as patrons for Mexican Americans and could deliver their votes. Clark was more successful in appealing to both groups than was Hogg, but the governor's record as a reformer, along with his superior organization and powerful speeches on the stump, carried him into the lead as the summer progressed. In mid-August, when the Democratic convention gathered in Houston, Hogg possessed two-thirds of the delegates. It took forceful measures, however, to prevent Clark and his followers from packing a convention that nearly erupted in violence.[34]

The gubernatorial campaign of 1892 was a bitter, three-way race, for Clark refused to accept the convention's verdict and launched an independent campaign, while the Populists nominated Thomas L. Nugent of Fort Worth. Hogg ran on a platform that supported free silver and a graduated income tax, but he rejected more extreme Populist demands. Recognizing the closeness of the campaign, Hogg and his managers used state patronage to strengthen their organization, intensified their efforts to reach every corner of the state with literature and speakers, and sought to portray the governor's opponents as irresponsible extremists. They attacked Clark for his alliance with the black-dominated Republican Party, led by Norris Wright Cuney, referring to the "Three C's—Clark, Cuney, and the Coons," and attempted to place the stigma of destroying white solidarity on Clark. They also courted the black vote, organizing Hogg Clubs and emphasizing the governor's opposition to lynching. Hogg dismissed the Populists as "poisoned from disappointed ambition, mad with the world in general, chimerical in political convictions, shifting in party name." At the end of the long, tumultuous campaign, Hogg prevailed with a plurality of the vote. But it was, as House remembered, "a bitter fight and the wounds lasted many years."[35]

Hogg's reelection as governor brought a new role for House. On July 20, 1893, the governor recognized his valued political associate by commissioning House a lieutenant colonel on his staff, and gradually the press and others began to refer to "Colonel House" rather than "Ed House." House visited the governor's office daily, performing useful political tasks, advising on questions of patronage and serving as a middleman between Hogg and various people and groups. Newspaper reporters quickly noticed the closeness of the two men. One remarked that "Governor Hogg and chaperone, Mr. Ed House, returned from Dallas," while another described House as "the accomplished gentleman who plays Pythias to the executive Damon and who always accompanies his excellency in his pleasure jaunts."[36]

House was the junior partner in this relationship, and during Hogg's second term he served his political apprenticeship, learning more about the political diversity and peculiarities of the state. But his ability to influence Hogg, either on matters of strategy or substance, was limited.[37]

House had enormous affection and admiration for Hogg, and years later he romanticized the governor and his legacy, ranking him "as the foremost Texan," even ahead of Sam Houston. Hogg was, House recalled, "the most original man I have ever met," "a great politician of wonderful force," "a dominating personality." He also felt, however, some ambivalence about Hogg, a man who "presented a rough exterior," and who had a "limited education and about some things was very ignorant . . . . He talked a great deal of nonsense at times, and was apt to be misled by it."[38]

During Hogg's second term, deteriorating economic conditions pulled more farmers away from their allegiance to the Democratic Party as Populist orators continued to dwell on its failures and corruption. Democratic leaders now recognized the seriousness of the Populist challenge and the need to put their own house in order. In March 1894, the Hogg and Clark factions held a harmony meeting, agreeing to set aside their differences during the campaign. With neither Hogg nor Clark running for governor in 1894, the leading candidate soon became Charles Allen Culberson, the son of a prominent Democratic congressman who had served as Hogg's attorney general. Although he had been a vigorous defender of Hogg's reform legislation in the courts, Culberson was more conservative, less committed to silver coinage—a Populist staple—and less hostile to the administration of President Grover Cleveland. Handsome, reserved, urbane, he nonetheless lacked Hogg's self-confidence and colorful political style, as well as his sensitivity to the waves of discontent sweeping through the state. He was an ideal candidate for an ambitious political operator such as Colonel House.[39]

Although critical of Culberson's indecisiveness, House was impressed with his "fine analytical mind" and agreed to manage his campaign. Initially Culberson's position seemed strong, but his neglect of Hogg, along with his friendliness toward the Clark faction and ambiguity on the silver issue, worried the governor and some of his followers. In June, John H. Reagan, a former United States senator, chairman of the railway commission, and elder statesman of the Democratic Party, entered the race for the nomination. Reagan's eminence and clear identification with the silver wing posed a serious threat to Culberson's candidacy.[40]

Throughout Culberson's 1894 gubernatorial campaign, House played, for the only time in his political career, an active, public role. As in 1892, he sought to reach every precinct and county in the state and to tie his cause to influential local men.[41] Emphasizing the key role of personal contacts in the success of the campaign, he also began to build his own organization, a core of associates in Austin who shared his conservative political views and pragmatic approach to politics and who helped carry the burdens of campaign management. This group eventually became known as "our crowd."[42]

Culberson was a more malleable candidate than Hogg, more subject to moments of doubt and more in need of reassurance. House sought to quiet his fears and to emphasize the progress of the campaign, and he and his lieutenants also prodded him, analyzing his strengths and weaknesses. By early July, Culberson was in the lead over Reagan.[43] His youth, early start, and superb organization all worked in his favor, and by mid-August the Culberson forces were in a dominant position when the Democratic convention convened in Dallas. House carefully planned strategy for the convention and personally called to order the caucus of Culberson delegates.

House's attempts to reconcile the silver and gold wings of the party failed, and eventually the convention endorsed the Cleveland administration and a compromise on monetary policy. Sensing defeat, and preferring Culberson to a more conservative candidate, Reagan withdrew, ensuring Culberson's overwhelming nomination. After the delegates dispersed, Culberson, Hogg, House, and their families traveled to Rockport, on the Texas Gulf Coast, where House sought to heal the wounds of the primary campaign and prepare for what was certain to be a tense, violent general election.[44]

In 1894, the Populists again nominated Thomas L. Nugent, but this time they were better organized and made gains among voters in east Texas, as well as sweeping large areas of north and west Texas. The Populist challenge was so strong that Culberson now warmly endorsed silver coinage, but his shifting views on the money question and his failure to join Hogg in opposition to Cleveland's use of troops in the Pullman strike weakened his campaign. Culberson benefited, however, from the strong support of Hogg and from the exertions of a desperate Democratic organization that was willing to use bribery, intimidation, and ballot box stuffing to retain its hold on the reins of power. The Populist vote jumped from 24 percent in 1892 to 35 percent in 1894, but Culberson nonetheless won with a plurality.[45]

The election of 1894 was a triumph for the rejuvenated Texas Democratic Party as well as for the manager of the Culberson campaign, Colonel Edward M. House. Although only thirty-six, he was now widely recognized as the mastermind of Culberson's victory and as a powerful force in Texas politics.[46]

3

Creating "Our Crowd"

A s Culberson settled into his new office, House seemed to be everywhere, urging the governor and his family to live with him prior to
the inauguration, helping with plans for the inaugural ball, and dealing
with the nettlesome question of patronage. As House recalled, "I went
to his office at the Capitol nearly each day, went over his mail with him
and sometimes continued my work there until nightfall." He relished the
power that he now possessed. Hogg had been a major force in Texas politics
prior to his association with House; in contrast, House had played a key role
in elevating Culberson to the governorship and he soon became the dominant partner in the relationship.[1]

House enjoyed the companionship of the earnest, ambitious governor,
who was only thirty-nine, and Culberson's success was essential to his own.
Culberson's dependence, however, ran far deeper. He needed House not
only for his political skills but also as someone with whom he could share
the burdens of his life. Culberson was easily worn down by the strains of
campaigning and of holding office, and shared his doubts about a political
career with House, admitting that "often I feel an intense desire to quit
politics and again an ambitious moment comes." He loved the law but was
drawn to the glitter of politics. House's kindness and consideration touched
Culberson, and as early as February 1895 he wrote that "in my day I have
had many friends, but you have been more than any to me and I cherish you
accordingly."[2] During Culberson's years as governor the two men spent a
great deal of time together. Culberson still complained of House's absences,
emphasizing how "I would feel added confidence were you here." He
longed for intimacy with his elusive political adviser.[3]

Culberson dealt with the public side of politics, while House thrived on
all the private wheeling and dealing. Both had supported Hogg's reform
legislation but had no vision of moving beyond it, and both were eager

to avoid divisive national issues. Most of all, Culberson and House were determined to maintain their hold on the governorship in 1896.

As House's involvement in Texas politics grew, so too did his core of close political associates. The earliest members of "our crowd" were Thomas Watt Gregory and Frank Andrews, two industrious, conservative Austin lawyers who shared a deep attachment to House. "I would rather have... [Gregory] in a fight," House recalled, "than almost any man I have worked with unless, indeed, it is Frank Andrews." Throughout his life Andrews subordinated his own political interests to those of his friends, and even at the time House recognized the purity of Andrews's devotion to him. "None that know your friendship for me," he wrote in 1898, "can say that politics has failed to bring me its reward."[4]

The newer members of "our crowd" included James B. Wells, Albert Sidney Burleson, and Joe Lee Jameson. A Brownsville lawyer and land-owner, Wells was a Roman Catholic and the leader of a political machine that was the patron of Mexican Americans in south Texas. As a result, he controlled their vote and could invariably deliver several counties to the candidates of his choice. Wells had few firm convictions except his loyalty to the Democratic Party and his devotion to House. Burleson practiced law in Austin and served as a district attorney, until elected to Congress in 1898. An adroit operator and professional Democratic Party politician, Burleson was so absorbed in the world of political manipulation that he could seldom lift himself above it. Years later, House wrote that Burleson was "loyal, cou-rageous, and energetic, but he had too much of the partisan in his makeup to make him valuable in big undertakings." Nevertheless, Burleson was a valuable ally with an impressive mastery of Texas politics. Joe Lee Jameson was the youngest member of House's group, a former bookkeeper at one of the state's mental institutions who eventually became a state revenue agent. House consciously trained Jameson in the art of politics and regarded him as his right-hand man, as a political lieutenant "whose political sagacity was of real value."[5]

With the exception of Wells, all of these men were younger than House, and they combined energy and intelligence with a fascination with, like House, the machinery of politics. They conferred with him often and han-dled most of the innumerable details of political organization and cam-paigning. Wells and Jameson in particular moved through the shadowy world of Texas politics where the struggle for the African American and Mexican American vote took place. All looked to House for guidance and inspiration and formed lasting bonds of friendship with him. Wells vowed that "my shield will never go into the battle when it does not touch yours"; Jameson expected "to devote a goodly portion of my life trying to show my appreciation of your kindness"; and Andrews wrote that "words are therefore meaningless symbols compared to what I so deeply feel when I try to formulate sentences to express my sincere devotion and love for such unselfish friendship." It was the magnetism of House's personality that held together "our crowd."[6]

House had an unusual sensitivity to other people and had developed an uncanny ability to understand the needs and aspirations of his fellow men. His insight into others was in part intuition, in part the result of hard work. He spent much time assessing the forces and personalities of Texas politics. As his political style matured, he retreated to his home and spent less time in his office in downtown Austin, where Major Edward Sammons managed the details of his finances and business affairs. In the library, veranda, or private dining room of his mansion, with its aura of wealth and sophistication, House conferred with his intimates and courted aspiring politicians.[7]

From the start of his political career House avoided the limelight, leaving public honors and offices to others. During the twelve years he was active in Texas politics, he attended only three state conventions, in 1892, 1894, and 1896, and was the official chairman of a campaign committee only once, in 1894. His refusal to run for public office gave the appearance of selflessness, of being above the petty bickering and ambitions of others, and also kept him out of the eye of the political storm and allowed him to avoid many of the demands made on public officials. "Keep yourself as much in the background as possible," he advised his protégé Jameson, "and let everybody do the talking excepting yourself. Nothing ever kills a man's influence so quickly as to be too much in evidence."[8]

Operating largely behind the scenes, House developed his gifts for intrigue and manipulation that had emerged when he was a student at Cornell. He sought to avoid direct clashes or open antagonism, concealing his own position by working through others and encouraging even those he opposed or disliked to believe that he was their true friend. He urged Jameson to "make friends of your enemies and better friends of your old ones," and advised him to "consult with everyone who has any influence & make them feel that they are one of us . . . . No matter how very little they are in it, let them think they are very much so."[9]

House's close political associates were only a handful of men, the core of a large, shifting network of influential people scattered throughout the state. He understood the personal nature of Texas politics and the need to cement his political alliances with patronage. Despite low salaries, the clamor for state offices was loud, and at the beginning of each administration, House became absorbed in the task of rewarding faithful workers and in lessening the disappointments of those whose pleas were rejected. "Let all our friends know," he reminded Jameson, "that everybody will be taken care of in due time and that none will be overlooked." In order to sort through the list of applicants, House kept track of the services of his followers and punished those who had been slack in times of need. The failure to arrange a county convention at an early date or to go out on the stump to support House's candidate could doom the hopes of an applicant for office. Beneath the affable exterior, as well as his self-assured charisma, House had no illusions about the bonds of loyalty—he knew that the ability to reward the faithful was a key element of his political power.[10]

The Democrats knew that the party would face an even more serious contest in 1896 than in 1894. Economic conditions had continued their downward spiral, while the Populist Party had gained further strength. In early 1896 one politician warned Culberson that "a hard campaign is before us at best. There is no enthusiasm among democrats anywhere." Although some Democrats were disgruntled with Culberson's uninspired leadership, he had the support of most and easily won renomination. As Hogg wrote, Culberson "is making a splendid Governor. What else could he do than stand for 16 to 1; for an economical government, and for the enforcement of the laws?"[11]

In 1896, national events complicated the local struggle for power. William Jennings Bryan's nomination shifted control of the Democratic Party to the South and West and met with enthusiastic approval of most party leaders in Texas. The fusion of Democrats and Populists on the national level, however, did not work in Texas, where these two parties had been embattled since 1892. Distrust and bitterness ran deep on both sides; neither was willing to cooperate with the other. Texas Populists abandoned the national ticket and concentrated on the election of their candidate for governor, Jerome C. Kearby. Viewing the black vote as critical, they struck a bargain with Republicans, agreeing to support William McKinley for president in return for Republican votes for Kearby. The fusion between

Populists and Republicans, long feared by Democrats, had finally taken place.[12]

House was disappointed by Bryan's candidacy, with its emphasis on a stronger, more interventionist federal government. On the national level he was a traditional Democrat, an advocate of low tariffs, sound money—meaning a gold standard—and limited government. On the state level he had supported Hogg's legislation and identified with the reform wing of the party. He resented, however, the intrusion of the money question into state politics, an issue that complicated his quest for control and that forced him to subordinate his own beliefs to the interests of his faction. He hoped that the silver mania would soon pass away.[13]

In 1896, House, however, was uncharacteristically languid over the Populist challenge. In mid-August he attended the Democratic state convention in Fort Worth, but by the end of the month he had departed for the East, leaving the campaign under the leadership of the chairman of the state executive committee, J. W. Blake. Blake did little to rally the party, and ominous reports soon reached House in New York City. Although large and friendly crowds encouraged Culberson, in mid-September he warned House that "the fight is growing warm and unless all signs fail it will need close watching in many places. *It will in my judgment be a very serious contest.*" "You are," Culberson pleaded with his trusted adviser, "badly needed at the helm."[14]

In early October—a month before the election—House returned to direct what one Democratic Party worker labeled a "red hot fight." Bypassing the state chairman, he mobilized his close associates and rallied his friends throughout the state. Culberson was still alarmed, convinced that "They are making a desperate fight on me and in many places are really trying to elect all the state ticket except myself." House's reply to this letter has not survived, but the actions of his lieutenants indicate that he understood the closeness of the election and relied on traditional methods to win it. As Blake wrote House, "we must control the Negro vote as they hold the balance of power in this election as far as the Gov. is concerned, and you know what it requires to get this vote." What was required, of course, was money with which to pay local "fluence" men.[15]

Years later, House claimed that the money was used for absolutely legitimate purposes, but contemporary evidence does not bear this out. House's favorite legman, Jameson, wrote that "the Waco Negro Melton cost us nearly $40," while from south Texas Wells complained about the large sums

Republicans were spending in the counties under his control. "This election," he wrote House, "has already cost me over a thousand dollars and may be as much more." The practice of buying votes—both by Democrats and their opponents—was prevalent throughout House's years in Texas politics. Without it, Culberson might very well have lost the governorship in 1896.[16]

In the end, Texas was too diverse a state, the Democrats' hold on the voters too strong, and their resources too great, for the Populist challenge to succeed. Although Kearby pulled 44 percent of the vote, Culberson was reelected to a second term. But as one party worker wrote, "it was a hard fight. I don't want any more like it."[17]

House's absence during a critical state of Culberson's gubernatorial campaign reflected the changes that were taking place in the rhythms of his personal life. By the late 1880s House and his family had begun to spend a portion of each summer on the East Coast. Gradually the House family settled into a pattern of visits to New York City and long vacations on Boston's North Shore. Along a few miles of that rocky coastline, the elite of Boston summered, creating a cluster of exclusive communities—Beverly, Magnolia, Manchester, Pride's Crossing, Wenham—that became upper-class resorts. Their large homes had breathtaking views of the ocean, cool vistas stretching out across the rocks and water. There House gained relief from the heat of Texas and from the demands of politics, as well as the opportunity to escape from the provincialism of Austin and mingle with upper-class Bostonians, such as the noted entrepreneur, T. Jefferson Coolidge Jr.[18]

As the 1890s progressed, changes also occurred in the House family, as death claimed some members and others entered new stages of life. In 1893, House's niece Cora, only twenty, died of diphtheria, and three years later his brother Charles, only forty-seven, died of heart disease. On December 10, 1896, his sister-in-law Annie Hunter married Sidney E. Mezes, who taught philosophy at the University of Texas, and left the House home. Less than a year later, in September 1897, Mona, who was fifteen, departed for Hollins Institute in Virginia.[19] A slender girl of medium height, she lacked her mother's beauty but possessed wit, energy, and an unaffected, down-to-earth quality. During her youth in Texas she was a tomboy, riding through the hills around Austin on picnics and other outings and trying even her father's patience. James Stephen Hogg, who knew her well, could not see how college could improve "the plain, sensible, girl that she used to be when she leaped from rock to rock like a mountain goat, and skipped around the hillsides of Austin like a gazelle." Mona's departure, along with the lure of the North Shore, slowly pulled House away from Texas and the demands of his political career there.[20]

The election of 1896 marked the high tide of Populism, both in Texas and the nation. In Texas, the anxieties that peaked in that year began to recede, as economic conditions improved and as the Populist Party splintered under the pressures of fusion and defeat. The Populist surge of the decade had forced unity on the Democratic Party; after 1896, party discipline lessened and factionalism increased. One faction, led by House, controlled the governorship and was held together by patronage and personal loyalty. The other most powerful faction gathered around Joseph Weldon Bailey, who entered Congress in 1890 from a north Texas district and became, by the end of the decade, the most popular political figure in Texas. Unlike House, Bailey was a showman, volatile and flamboyant, an advocate of free silver and a supporter of Bryan. For all their differences, however, the two leaders respected each other's power and were eager to avoid a clash. They worked together and watched closely over the loose coalitions they led.[21]

In 1898, Culberson hoped to leave the governorship and enter the United States Senate; House was eager to promote his friend's political career and at the same time to tighten his grip on Texas politics. As the guardian of Culberson's political fortunes, House cleared the way for the governor's advancement, convincing at least one potential candidate to step aside. As it turned out, Culberson easily prevailed, beginning a long and undistinguished career in the Senate. Looking back, House claimed that he had "an extraordinary mind" and that, had it not been for his friend's indecisiveness, "he might possibly have been President of the United States." In fact, House cared far less about Culberson's competence than his loyalty and supported him long after alcoholism and Bright's disease (nephritis, or deterioration of the kidneys) made him "the sick man of the Senate."[22]

In 1898, it was the governorship that presented House with his greatest challenge. Culberson's obvious successor was Martin M. Crane who, as attorney general from 1894 to 1898, had vigorously enforced the state's anti-trust law and become the legitimate heir of the Hogg reform tradition. Crane had begun his campaign early and had built up a considerable following, he but had neither asked for nor received House's support. Instead, House had turned to another candidate, Congressman Joseph D. Sayers, a Confederate veteran who represented his Austin district in Congress.

A stiff, unimaginative man, Sayers had taken little interest in the broader currents of Texas politics and viewed the governorship as the crown to his long political career. Sayers had sought out House, and certainly the latter knew that the congressman, unlike Crane, would be heavily dependent on his managerial skills and knowledge of state politics.[23]

House knew that Sayers stood a good chance of winning the nomination. He was a respected free-silver Democrat who appealed to all segments of the party and who had substantial support among state officeholders and Texas congressmen. Moreover, he had the services of House's faction, the core of which remained intact, and unlike Crane he understood the personal nature of Texas politics. Crane might very well have survived his unwillingness to subordinate himself to House if only he had not alienated men who demanded far less of him. As Hogg summed up the situation to House, "He is a capable, honest, but impulsive fellow. . . every piece of advice I gave him was *unconditionally ignored*. So I did my duty without throwing mud on other gentlemen."[24]

As always, House proceeded with care, seeking to clear the way for Sayers and to pull together his friends into an effective organization. He convinced Sayers to support Bailey in his bid for the minority leadership in the House, and apparently assured Bailey that he would offer no opposition to his pursuit of a Senate seat in 1900. In return, Bailey endorsed both Culberson and Sayers. House selected Colonel L. L. Foster as president of the Sayers Campaign Committee and relied especially on Andrews and Jameson to look after the details of the campaign. Supplied with ample funds (from wealthy supporters such as his brother T. W. Jr.), House and his associates used their traditional technique of mobilizing local leaders and calling early conventions in those counties leaning toward Sayers. "There were," House recalled, "no single counties in Texas he [Crane] could call clearly his own, while there were many counties that could not be taken from Sayers."[25]

Sayers largely delegated his campaign to House. In the spring of 1898, as Spain and the United States headed toward war, Sayers felt he could not leave Washington and did not, in fact, return to Texas until late June. For a time House was apprehensive about his candidate's prolonged absence, but he and his friends soon came to relish the autonomy it gave them.[26] During the crucial stages of the campaign, House was fully in charge, responsible both for the organization and for the public defense of Sayers's record. The congressman, House told newspaper reporters, "was an ardent advocate of free silver and fought its battles in and out of Congress when most of his present critics were unknown, and before some of them knew the meaning of the phrase 'sixteen to one.' The men in charge of Sayers' affairs are rock-ribbed Hogg-Culberson-Bryan men."[27]

House's defense of Sayers was misleading, for he and his associates disliked Bryan and favored the gold standard. Frustrated by the free-silver craze, House wrote an anonymous editorial for the *Galveston News*, arguing that the real issue of the campaign should have been the industrial development of Texas. Instead, each candidate sought to prove that he was the most ardent friend of silver.[28]

By mid-May, Crane realized that his campaign was going badly and conceded defeat. Years later House vividly remembered his reaction to Crane's withdrawal. When the *Dallas News* called at midnight and asked for a statement, House replied that he would make one in the morning, then "lay awake for nearly an hour enjoying the victory and then went back to sleep." He had taken a mediocre candidate and outmaneuvered the opposition. It was a deeply satisfying experience.[29]

In mid-June, when Foster left the Sayers's organization to accept the presidency of Texas A & M College, House issued a circular announcing his resignation, assessing the state of the campaign, and mentioning that he would be "unavoidably absent from the State for several days." In fact, House planned to leave shortly for his summer vacation on the North Shore, much to the surprise of Sayers, who pleaded with his adviser to postpone his departure a week. By the end of June, however, House, confident that his friends could guide the campaign through to success, had left for Magnolia, one of the most exclusive resorts on Boston's Gold Coast.[30]

Even on the North Shore, however, House remained preoccupied with state politics. By mid-summer American victories in the Spanish-American War had raised the issue of territorial expansion, one that Texas Democrats would have to deal with in their state convention. Hogg had been swept up in the frenzy surrounding the war, but House seemed removed from the passions of the conflict and from the bitter controversy over the acquisition of the Philippines. He wrote letters to party leaders, seeking to discover a consensus, only to learn that none existed. As Hogg put it, the question of territorial expansion "is one of the hardest nuts to crack that has been thumped into the political arena within the last half century." As always, searching for a middle path, House composed a platform that proclaimed the Monroe Doctrine and called for the control of Cuba and Puerto Rico and the temporary possession of the Philippines. House asked, however, for more than most Texas Democrats were willing to take and eventually the convention endorsed more modest territorial goals.[31]

In early August delegates at the Galveston convention nominated Sayers by acclamation. With the collapse of the Populist Party, Democratic endorsement once again was tantamount to election, and Sayers conducted a leisurely campaign, winning an easy victory in November. His nomination and election were dramatic triumphs for House, a signal that, as Burleson boasted, "the 'machine' is stronger than ever." House and his friends were sure to play a major role in the new administration.[32]

Throughout the 1898 campaign, House was in poor health. He never fully explained the nature of his illness, although his correspondence in 1898 and 1899 is filled with references to it, and one incident suggests changes in his behavior. In September 1898, he wrote a letter, now lost, to Culberson, expressing doubts about his friend's devotion to him. Culberson was shocked, for House normally maintained tight control over his emotions. Your last letter, he replied, "is all nice and like you except its last sentence for which I think you owe me an apology. The idea that I will ever or can ever forget you! Without an exception you are the best, most unselfish and most valued friend I have or ever had and the very thought of such a thing as you suggest wounds me keenly."[33] Two months later an Austin newspaper reported that House "cannot stand worry" and that whenever someone attempted to call him, the operator replied that she could not make the connection because House was "suffering from nervous prostration and his physician has ordered that no bells be permitted to jingle within his hearing, as all noises of that character but retard his recovery."

Less than a year later House confirmed the seriousness of his illness.[34] "I believe that I am improving all the time," he wrote Andrews, "and I do not doubt that this winter will find me entirely well. I suppose that it will take a long while for me to altogether get over the recollection of my nervousness, but I feel sure that I can accomplish it." Gradually House's anxieties eased, but his restoration to full health seemed as elusive as the illness itself. In July 1899, he informed an old Austin friend that he was "well and strong once more," but as late as August 1901 he wrote that "I am just beginning to get on my feet again." House's memories of his "nervousness" were vivid and his fears of its recurrence great.[35]

The gubernatorial campaign of 1898, with all its risks and uncertainties, undoubtedly imposed a strain on House, as did his relationship with

Sayers. Although his power in Texas was at its peak, House knew that of the three governors he had supported, Sayers was by far the least impressive, a man who lacked the vision and exuberance of Hogg or the analytical precision of Culberson. House had supported Sayers out of necessity, not because any special rapport existed between the two men, and from the start he must have sensed that he might he unable to remain close to the new governor.[36]

Once in office, Sayers, apparently put off by House's reputation as a master manipulator, turned to others for advice. The governor quickly realized, however, that his long career in Congress had not prepared him for the maze of Texas politics, and he found himself "weary and heartsick" over the clamor for political preferment. Sayers had misjudged his own abilities and underestimated his dependence on House and his friends. Overwhelmed with more than 20,000 letters, he soon asked to confer with House at his elegant home at 1704 West Avenue. Over the course of an afternoon, House, with the help of Frank Andrews, gave Sayers his "opinion as to the best man for each office, as he mentioned it. He took my suggestions in every instance excepting one."[37]

House sought to become as indispensable for Sayers as he had been for Culberson. He helped with plans for the inaugural ball, read and criticized the governor's inaugural address, and warned Sayers peremptorily that his "intense independent nature" could lead to a break with Hogg, still a powerful figure in Texas politics. For a time the two men worked closely together, then drifted apart, and by the late summer of 1899 moved toward a reconciliation, as Sayers found himself far behind in his work and threatened with opposition to a second term. Once again House came to the governor's rescue, maneuvering successfully to prevent any challenge to Sayers's renomination.[38]

Sayers's reelection in November 1900 was never in doubt, and well before then House and his associates had begun to ponder the governor's successor in 1902. Inevitably House's name came to the forefront. His continuing triumphs in gubernatorial campaigns, along with the intense loyalty of his friends, created mounting pressure on him to enter the race. In late 1896 one businessman indicated the depth of this support when he wrote: "I have not taken off my coat in a political contest since I was 22 years old. But if this thing comes to pass [House running for governor], coat, shirt & all goes off and I stand stripped, greased, ready and eager for the fight." Wells warned that kingmakers inevitably lost their influence unless they became kings themselves, and pleaded with House to let him show his "confidence and love for him."[39]

House was not inclined to run for governor. Nonetheless he relished the attention he was receiving and hoped to use it to enhance his power. As long as his name was in the foreground, other candidates would be reluctant to declare and he and his friends would have more room to maneuver. They were unable, however, to resolve the question of Sayers's successor. Burleson had no doubt, he wrote House in July 1900, that "if your health will permit. . . you can be successfully landed two years from now," and outlined some of the regional deals that would be necessary to smooth the path for his friend's selection. House responded more decisively than he had in 1898, emphasizing the personal inconvenience the governorship would bring and concluding that "the crowd ought to center on me for the time being and then next Fall we can pick out our man and put him in throwing all the strength in a body."[40] Burleson agreed that House should serve as a stalking-horse but was reluctant to abandon him as a gubernatorial candidate. House would not reconsider his decision, but some ambiguity still remained in his mind, for he confided to Burleson that "if I were as strong and as vigorous as you I would enter the race with enthusiasm, and it would be my purpose to build up a strength throughout the length and breadth of our state which would be irresistible for years to come." But this was a fantasy that House lacked the will to achieve.[41]

No doubt the anxiety of sorting through his ambitions contributed to House's nervousness in 1898 and 1899. By 1900 he seems to have established his priorities and resolved on a course. House was no Theodore Roosevelt, who had overcome childhood illnesses, won the governorship of New York and the presidency, and become an advocate of the strenuous life. Instead, he would remain the leader of a faction, a behind-the-scenes wire-puller, although he continued to console himself with the thought that he could hold public office if only he desired to do so. But the price was too high; official responsibilities would alter the comfortable rhythms of his life and pull him back to Texas, with all its dense heat and political strife, at the very time he was enjoying society in New York and Boston. House feared the physical and psychological toll of public service, and the turmoil he experienced in 1898 and 1899 only strengthened his determination to continue the less stressful role of confidential adviser. Yet he knew, as Wells warned, that he could not dominate Texas governors forever.

4

The "Twilight Years"

During the 1890s, as House spun a web of connections beyond the confines of Texas, House thought of transferring his political skills from the state to the national level. He was not, however, ready for a major role in the Democratic Party, since he continued to identify with its conservative wing and disliked William Jennings Bryan's passion for free silver. He had to bide his time until the Great Commoner's crusade ran its course and the prospects for a centrist Democratic president improved.[1]

At the 1896 Democratic national convention Hogg was swept away by Bryan's "Cross of Gold" Speech—one of the greatest political stemwinders in American history—and became his ardent supporter. Even after the defeat of 1896, Hogg believed that Bryan might triumph four years later and maneuvered to bring his two friends together, to match Bryan's oratorical power with House's organizational skill and, in the process, to push House onto the national political stage. House was curious enough about Bryan, and ambitious enough for a larger role, to go along with Hogg's plan. In January 1897, Bryan lectured in Austin, where he was given an elaborate reception by Hogg and House as well as an elegant dinner at House's home. Attracted to Austin's mild climate and friendly atmosphere, during the winters of 1898–1899 and 1899–1900 Bryan and his family lived next door to the House mansion, which allowed House to take the measure of the man and his political philosophy.[2]

House quickly realized that he could never draw close to Bryan, who was too set in his ways and too emotionally self-sufficient. Moreover, by mid-summer 1900, House realized that the Republican ticket, led by William McKinley and Theodore Roosevelt, was formidable and almost certain to win. House was eager, as Hogg exhorted him, to *go to the front where you belong,* but he had no desire to interrupt his summer vacation and attach himself to a losing cause. The election confirmed his worst fears, and at the close of the year Culberson shared his gloomy prognosis with his close friend: "The Democratic Party nationally is in a bad way now—indeed it could scarcely be in worse shape." At the age of forty-two House realized that his entry on the national political stage was at least four years in the future.[3]

Whatever his national ambitions, House had first to deal with the shifting currents of Texas politics. The collapse of the Populist challenge, along with the general lethargy that spread across the Texas political scene in the early years of the new century, provided further opportunities for manipulation.[4] With Governor Sayers's second term due to end in 1902, House and his allies had to find a malleable successor if they were to retain their control of the governorship and their influence throughout the state. The first and second choice of "our crowd" declined to run, leaving House uncertain where to turn.[5]

In June 1901, House decided that Samuel W. Lanham, a Confederate veteran and longtime congressman, would do, and that his faction ought to put itself "in a position to take him up in the event that it becomes necessary." Conservative and colorless, Lanham, like Sayers, sought the governorship as the final honor of a long political career. Lanham was eager to run and willing to place his campaign in House's hands.

In the fall of 1901, House rallied "our crowd" behind Lanham and became more enthusiastic about the prospect of manipulating yet another governor. He did not expect "any great amount of pleasure out of Lanham's administration" but believed that "we may control him about as we have controlled the present incumbent and by about the same methods."[6]

House and his associates dominated Lanham's campaign. Except for a brief return to Texas in April, the congressman remained in Washington, while House moved to galvanize his faction. He sent Jameson on various errands, advanced his own funds to meet current expenses, and planned early conventions in those counties leaning toward Lanham. In late January 1902 Lanham's opponent suddenly withdrew, leaving him unopposed for the Democratic nomination. House was pleased, boasting that "the truth of it is the prestige of our crowd in Texas is such that anyone with normal intelligence hesitates to run up against the inevitable." He was also relieved, for with the demands of Lanham's campaign reduced, he would have more time for other activities.[7]

House and Burleson realized that the public was uninterested in the gubernatorial contest. In early April, when their candidate formally opened his campaign with a lackluster address, House commented, "He has managed to say nothing in a most convincing and masterly way." But they were ambivalent, pleased with Lanham's passivity and worried about its ultimate consequences. House wondered if a "clean administration" would be enough: "In my opinion we could *never stand another such administration* [like Sayers's] and go before the people with any hope of success." House, however, had tired of the turmoil of Texas politics; he had no agenda for reform that he could pass on to the new governor.[8]

Whatever excitement existed in the 1902 elections came prior to the Democratic convention in Galveston. Even during the primary campaign Lanham faced such weak opposition that House never had to fully mobilize his faction and had more time than usual to aid various congressional candidates. In the general election, Lanham won easily, receiving more than four times the vote of his Republican opponent. It was the sixth gubernatorial campaign that House had successfully managed.[9]

Well before the 1902 campaign House had begun to withdraw from Texas politics. His willingness to settle for Lanham instead of backing the far more colorful Wells was an indication of his inclination to follow the path of least resistance. As his stays in the East lengthened, House became impatient with the provincialism of Austin and of Texas politics. He had always cared more about personalities than causes, about the techniques rather than the substance of politics, and now he found himself advising dull, uninspiring men, whom he regarded with condescension if not contempt. Gradually he became bored by the very system he had helped to create, restlessly looking for broader horizons.[10]

As House's interest in politics waned, he became absorbed by the challenges of his business career and excited by the prospect of financial gain.[11] During the 1890s, House had bought and sold land, tended his cotton plantations, and in 1896 sold his one-third share in the family bank to his brother T. W. Jr., taking out $293,000 in notes, bonds, and real estate. By 1902, his land speculation had largely ended, though he continued to watch closely over his cotton plantations, especially the best of these, Monadale, which had come to House through the division of his father's estate. Located twenty-five miles northeast of Austin near Hutto, it consisted of over 1,200 acres of prime land, with deep, black soil. House invested heavily in Monadale, employing the best agricultural techniques of his day and gradually putting more and more land under cultivation. He chose capable farm managers, gave them generous wages and gifts, **and** took an interest in their lives and careers. But he also watched closely over every phase of his farming operations, following the price of cotton, deciding when to sell the crop, and sending detailed instructions to his manager even when absent from Texas. As a result of these efforts, his cotton lands became highly profitable.[12]

By the turn of the century, House was wealthier than ever, dreaming of new business enterprises and of even higher levels of prosperity. House's business acumen was respected, both by his friends in the East and by his political associates in Texas.[13] On January 10, 1901, a great geyser of oil broke through the ground at a salt dome called Spindletop, near Beaumont in the southeast corner of Texas. It took nine days to control this fabulous gusher, whose volume was so huge that the first well produced twice as much oil as the whole of Pennsylvania, then the leading oil-producing state. As news of the discovery spread, entrepreneurs rushed to Beaumont to stake out their claims and to begin the construction of the pipelines and refineries necessary to get the oil to market. House joined the stampede. By June 1901, he and Frank Andrews, with backing from investors, had formed a company for drilling and were making plans for a refinery. For $90,000, House and his associates purchased drilling rights in the streets and alleys of a surveyed town that covered two-thirds of the Spindletop field. It was an ingenious scheme, and the company they capitalized at one million dollars sold out its stock in less than thirty-six hours. In the end, however, legal difficulties prevented drilling on public thoroughfares and the plans for a refinery never materialized. Unlike his friend Hogg, House never cashed in on the great oil bonanza in Texas.[14]

In 1902, House's thoughts turned to another project—a railway that would link the Gulf Coast with the rich cotton country of central Texas. House had convinced his Boston friend Thomas Jefferson Coolidge Jr. to form a syndicate that would provide one and a half million dollars for the construction of the line. The syndicate managers, Coolidge informed House, "should not go into this for a moment except for the fact of our implicit confidence in you and yours." House excitedly informed Andrews that "my friends in Boston have decided to go in with us to the extent of half million as a starter and as much more as we want later on . . . . It looks a little as if the world and the fullness thereof will soon be ours."[15]

On October 17, 1902, the Trinity and Brazos Valley Railway Company was incorporated, with House as chairman of the board. The president,

Robert H. Baker, was a friend and business associate, and other positions were filled by House's brother, John; House's accountant, Edward M. Sammons; and the former manager of his cotton farms, William Malone. Although House and his associates lacked experience in railroad building, the company was staffed by reliable men, conservative in their promotion of the line. By mid-October 1903, the first twenty-six mile section was completed, and in January 1904, all seventy-eight miles from Cleburne to Mexia were opened. The Trinity and Brazos never went farther under House's leadership, for the spread of the boll weevil through Central Texas affected the cotton crop and lowered traffic on the new railroad.[16]

Despite the efforts of House and his associates, the line did not prove profitable, and by June 1904, House, with Coolidge's encouragement, was trying to sell the Trinity and Brazos to a larger system. Neither House nor his friends wished to be burdened with the day-to-day management of a small railroad. After negotiations with the railway magnate Edward H. Harriman failed, in late 1904 the Trinity and Brazos was sold to Benjamin F. Yoakum, the owner of the Frisco lines, who was piecing together a system that would directly connect Chicago and Mexico City. House's profit was $30,000. At a time when his interest in Texas politics was waning, he had found railway building a profitable and entertaining diversion.[17]

After Lanham's triumph in November 1902, House made some effort to control the new governor and to consolidate the influence of his faction, helping with patronage decisions and planning the inaugural ceremonies. Lanham reassured House of his "abiding gratitude for your many friendly offices" and told Burleson that he intended to rely on him and House as his "*closest advisers.*" But House never really tried to be such an adviser, and his connection with Lanham, while cordial, was more distant than with previous governors.[18]

As the primaries of 1904 approached, Lanham had no opposition for renomination, and House planned to leave for Europe in mid-June. In May he left Austin in such a hurry that he failed to see the governor before his departure; Lanham seemed unconcerned, complacent about his political position. Prior to his departure, House hastily drafted a platform and issued directives about the organization of the state convention. House wanted the convention to select Frank Andrews as the new chairman of the Democratic Executive Committee, as a reward for years of loyal and unobtrusive service. Burleson and Bailey, more sensitive to currents of state politics, doubted the wisdom of choosing a man who had served as an attorney and lobbyist for the Southern Pacific Railroad but gave way to House's insistence on an undivided front. Andrews easily won the convention's endorsement, and Lanham's renomination and reelection proved even less exciting than two years before.[19]

On May 10, 1904, shortly before House had left for New York, Joe Lee Jameson died at the age of thirty-three. House had rescued Jameson from obscurity, given him a position in the 1898 Sayers campaign and then a state office, and in 1902 had arranged to use Jameson full-time for political and business chores. Jameson's restless energy and zest for politics had been invaluable, as had his willingness to move along the underside of Texas politics. His death came as a terrible shock to his mentor; House wrote one friend that "No one will ever know how much I shall miss him." It was difficult for House to imagine an active role in state politics with Jameson gone.[20]

In 1904, House also had to worry about Culberson, whose Senate term expired that year. While his reelection was never seriously in doubt, he feared a possible challenge, and in February 1904 House gave a dinner for the senator to remind party leaders that he had "called the clans together" and that "our crowd" was solidly behind Culberson. Over the years the two men and their families had remained close, as they visited New York City and Magnolia and collaborated in state and national politics. In 1902 Culberson urged House to run for governor, expressing his "admiration of your character and wonderful intellectual poise," while House, as early as 1900, thought Culberson might move beyond the Senate, possibly to the vice-presidency or even the presidency itself.[21] In 1904 he discussed Culberson's selection as vice-president with the leading candidate for the nomination, Alton B. Parker (a New York lawyer and judge), speculating to his friend that if Parker "is nominated and elected you will be 'next.'" Culberson, however, was more cautious than House about the prospects of the Democratic Party; on national politics his judgments were more accurate and informed.[22] Yet Culberson remained dependent on House. "It is impossible to express how anxious I am to see you. . . you are very dear to me" Culberson confided to his friend, admitting in May 1900 that he had a "terrible case of the blues." Burdened with frequent depressions and an ill wife, Culberson allowed his expenses to exceed his income and wrestled with his ambivalence about politics, yearning for a spot on the Supreme

Court yet determined to seek reelection. His success in 1904 kept House's old and close friend near the center of national politics.[23]

Bryan's second defeat in 1900 left the Democratic Party in disarray. The Republicans had created a broad coalition that dominated the most urban and industrialized regions of the nation; the Democrats retained only isolated outposts of power, in the South and in some northern city machines, and lacked effective programs and national leaders. Bryan's loss had brought a swing to the right within the party, the formation of a loose conservative coalition that, as always, emphasized tariff reform, sound money, and a limited role for the federal government. As 1904 approached, Democratic conservatives united behind Alton B. Parker for president. With Parker's easy triumph, he and his managers were optimistic, determined to contrast his calmness and stability with the alleged combativeness and impetuosity of Theodore Roosevelt, who had become president after McKinley's assassination in September 1901. As it turned out, they badly underestimated the appeal of Roosevelt's personality and of his trust-busting policies, as well as the power and unity of the Republican Party, which ran a campaign that appealed to diverse groups of Americans and even made inroads into traditional centers of Democratic strength.[24]

Like many southern Democrats, House was pleased that the Gold Standard wing had regained control of the party and enthusiastically supported Parker. In mid-May 1904 he rushed off to New York, where he engaged in a flurry of political activity before leaving for Europe in mid-June, establishing close contacts with Parker's managers and seeking a solid pro-Parker delegation from Texas to the Democratic national convention in St. Louis. While he vacationed in Europe, House urged Burleson and Culberson to make certain that Texas Democrats supported Parker. "The issue is very clear in Texas," House informed Burleson. "All of our crowd have lined up for Parker, and the opposition to us have lined up against him, and if we do not instruct, it will be considered as much of a defeat for us as for Parker."[25]

House departed for his grand tour of Europe with a feeling of keen regret. "I could never," he complained, "have left at a more inopportune time." He urged Culberson to "see Governor Sheehan [Parker's close adviser] and have a talk with him about me. I would like for you to strain your imagination as far as your conscience will permit, and tell him what you think I know about politics."[26] At the Texas state convention the Parker forces were dominant, and in late September, after House returned from

Europe, Sheehan asked if House would go to Indiana and Wisconsin to supervise Parker's organization in those two states. By now, House knew that Parker's campaign was faltering and he declined to join the campaign staff. Shortly after Roosevelt's triumph, House assessed the situation in a letter to Hogg: "Today, in the shadow of our great defeat, I want to take my hat off to you, for you are the only man I know that understood the hold that Theodore Roosevelt had upon the American people." House finally realized that the nation was in an era of Republican ascendancy, one that could extend for years into the future.[27]

House had not been to Europe since he and Loulie honeymooned there in the winter of 1881–1882, and the excitement of his family ran high over the elaborate trip he had planned for the summer of 1904. House dared not delay it, for Loulie and Mona, he wrote an Austin friend, "are crazy to have her [Mona] presented at court . . . . I am opposed to the whole thing but what does one do with a lot of women." House also felt a need to get away. For several years, after his severe "nervousness" in 1898 and 1899, his health was much improved, but by the spring of 1904 he had suffered a partial relapse and hoped to recover during his European trip. House concluded that "if I come back entirely well it is worth all the trouble and money."[28]

In mid-June, the House family left on the SS Deutschland, along with Sidney and Nancy Mezes and old Austin friends, Judge and Mrs. Thomas S. Maxey. Mona was presented at the Court of St. James, like many socially prominent American women. She remarked afterward that "all that kept her eyes from coming out on little sticks was her wonderful self-control"— and after a brief stay in London the House party proceeded to travel in style through many countries, including England, Germany, Italy, Sweden, and Switzerland. While House studied the programs of European reformers, Janet, the second daughter (who was seventeen), worried that the adults had not enjoyed the trip as much as she had, in part because of the heat—which bothered her father—and in part because of their tendency to want to do different things and to go different places.[29]

In mid-September, House and his family returned to New York, lingering there until late December. Hogg complained that "your prolonged stay in New York is just a little odd, to say the least," but House was unapologetic and not at all pleased to be back in Texas. All sorts of matters had piled up during his seven and one half month absence, and he found himself "busy now all the time with politics, business and other people's troubles."

While the weather was glorious and Austin looked better than he had ever seen it, House had hardly returned before he was anticipating his annual migration to Magnolia.[30]

The pull of the East was strengthened by the attachments that Mona and Janet were forming there. In April 1905, Mona turned twenty-three, Janet eighteen; both had made formal debuts and adored the upper-class social life of Boston and New York. They enjoyed summers at Magnolia; there Mona shone at social events at the fashionable Oceanside Hotel, a large, rambling structure with a sweeping view of the sea, where the Houses stayed for many summers.[31] Janet attended the exclusive Miss Spence's School in New York and often visited her wealthy friends, commenting on butlers, automobiles, theater parties, and beautiful homes. While House was close to both his daughters, his relationship with Janet was special. "Tell her of my love for her," he wrote his personal secretary Fanny Denton, "and let her know she is my inspiration and my hope." Austin offered less and less for all the members of the House family.[32]

On August 10, 1905, the *Boston Herald* reported the engagement of Mona House and Randolph Tucker. It had been a whirlwind courtship; the two had known each other for only a few weeks before their engagement. Mona, the *Herald* continued, "is a slender girl of medium height, fair-haired, with blue eyes and inherits the grace and gentleness of her handsome mother, who is one of the most distinguished hostesses in the South." Randolph was twenty-six, tall and athletic, the son of a wealthy Boston banker. He had left Harvard after one year, traveled abroad, and then worked his way up to one of the top positions in a Boston bond house. When Randolph came to talk to House about the engagement, House listened quietly, then asked, his future son-in-law remembered, if any insanity ran in the Tucker family. On December 19, 1905, Mona and Randolph were married at St. David's Episcopal Church in Austin, and after the ceremony an elaborate reception was held at the House mansion. Mona and Randolph, accompanied by their bridal party, had traveled in a private railway car from Boston to Austin, and after their marriage went on to Mexico City for their honeymoon.[33] House had difficulty accepting the sudden loss of his oldest daughter. For a time he was cool toward Randolph, but he finally relaxed and became good friends with his son-in-law.[34]

House was also unsettled by the death of family and friends. In 1902, his brother-in-law Clarence Hunter died, "at a time," House recalled, "[when] I needed him most"; in 1904, his brother John's wife followed him, and on February 21, 1905, John, one of the heroes of his youth, died at the age of fifty-six. Of House's five brothers, only the eldest, T. W. Jr., still lived. Early in 1905, Hogg was seriously injured in a train collision, and a long illness ensued. House worried about the condition of his political mentor and reassured him that "it is seldom that a day goes by but that I think of you and wonder how you are getting along." Hogg may never have read this letter, for on March 3, 1906, a few days after it was written, he died. More than any other late nineteenth-century Texan, Hogg had inspired House. He had been bold, colorful, and fun to be with. Now he was gone.[35]

Even before Hogg's death, House was preoccupied with his own mortality. "If I should die before you," he wrote Fanny on August 26, 1905, "it is my wish that you have access to and absolutely free use of all my personal and political letters, documents and copying books and other papers relating to my quasi-public career to the end that you may make notes therefrom and copies thereof. It is my wish that you use these notes and copies in the way and for the purposes which I have stated to you verbally and which you fully understand." Given the mass of these papers and the twenty-year time span they covered, House left her in his will the interest for life on $20,000 at 6 percent, so that she would have the leisure to complete what was apparently conceived of as a large project. Although he was only forty-seven, House worried about establishing his place in the history of his state.[36]

In 1906, Lanham's second term as governor ended, but House displayed little interest in the selection of his successor or in the state elections of that year. It was the first time in fourteen years that he had not played an active role in a gubernatorial election. Some of House's associates backed Judge Charles K. Bell, a Fort Worth lawyer and former attorney general, but he faced a strong challenge from Thomas M. Campbell, whom they had defeated for the Democratic nomination in 1902. A carrier of the Hogg reform tradition, Campbell spoke out against machine politics and corporate power. In July he won the Democratic nomination.[37]

House had been unwilling to lead his faction into the battle against Campbell. Newspapers reported that his poor health forced him to stay out of the fight, but in fact he knew that the contours of Texas politics were changing and did not care to deal with the new procedures, new faces, and new issues coming to the fore. In October 1906, Culberson warned that "there is great unrest in the state and there is 'no telling' what may happen in a few years."[38] Reformers within the Democratic Party wanted better public services and more governmental regulation of business, along with a general purification of Texas society—favoring prohibition of alcohol and electoral reform, for example. By 1905 they had pushed two election laws through the legislature that outlawed a variety of fraudulent practices and that replaced the old system of county conventions with one statewide Democratic primary. Battles within the Texas Democratic Party would now be fought on different terms. House had no wish to recast his faction in order to master the new progressive politics in Texas. Instead, he clung to the hope, forlorn as it was, that he would somehow enter the national political arena.[39]

While House was drawing away from Texas politics, his business interests in the state remained substantial and continued to absorb much of his time. In 1905, John left an estate valued at one million dollars, mostly in land, which was split between his two surviving brothers. After the sale of the Trinity and Brazos Railway, House sought, unsuccessfully, to interest Thomas Jefferson Coolidge in new railway projects, and he invested in various enterprises, particularly the newly opened Union Bank and Trust Company in Houston. In 1906, he sold the Hunter farm near San Marcos, claiming that the land was worn out, and he was willing to sell Janet Farm, too, if offered $25,000.[40] Of all his farms, he took the greatest pride in Monadale, which produced an exceptionally high quality cotton and a profit of approximately $17,500 a year. By 1906, the manager of Monadale, E. J. Barkley, was restless, tired of farming, and considering another occupation. Urging Barkley to stay, House assured him that Monadale would remain under the control of "me and mine."[41]

In 1896, House had sold his share of T. W. House and Company, one of the largest private banks in the state, in part because of his displeasure over the management of the family firm. He had urged T. W. Jr. to apply for a national charter—which would have forced a tightening of procedures—but his brother had refused to do so, and the bank's fortunes declined as new, more dynamic Houston banks drew away its business and as members of the city's financial community lost confidence in T. W. Jr.'s leadership. He ran his bank loosely, covering too many large overdrafts, loaning money too generously, and keeping too many funds in non-liquid assets. Even so, Houstonians were stunned when T. W. House and Company, caught in the panic of 1907, closed its doors. Most assumed that it would soon reopen, but its creditors forced the famous establishment into bankruptcy, refusing to give T. W. Jr. time to convert a portion of the bank's large assets into cash. Over the next three years, bankruptcy trustees sold off those assets, including the bank building in Houston and nearby Arcola

Plantation. T. W. Jr., who was sixty-one in 1907, was left with nothing but his home in Houston.[42]

The currency shortage of the bank was $35,000, and it is possible that House, given his own large assets and his contacts with financiers in the East, might have been able to raise enough cash to keep T. W. House and Company solvent. He never tried, however, and the company that his father had built up into one of the great financial institutions of Texas passed into history.[43]

After Sidney E. Mezes had married Loulie's sister Nancy in 1896, House acquired a brother-in-law with a cosmopolitan background. A tall, lean man of dark complexion, "with a smile that lit up the earth," Mezes had studied at the University of California, Berkeley, and Harvard, and in 1894 had joined the Department of Philosophy at the University of Texas. He had traveled and studied in Europe, and undoubtedly the close friendship he formed with House helped to broaden the latter's horizons and to convince him that the state's universities should be kept out of politics. In 1902, when the presidency of Texas A & M fell vacant, House maneuvered to find a distinguished educator to fill it. After Mezes declined, he turned to David F. Houston, a political scientist who was dean of the Faculty of the University of Texas. Three years later Houston returned to Austin as president, and when he left in 1908 to lead Washington University in St. Louis, Mezes succeeded him. If House had a hand in Mezes's elevation, no record of his efforts remains, but his hopes for his gentle, cultivated friend were great.[44]

During these "twilight years," House established a migratory rhythm that took him away from Texas for all but four or five months of the year. In 1905 and 1906 he did not travel to Europe, but in 1907 he spent May in New York and June in Magnolia, and he left for Europe in late June, returning in September. He then lingered in New York, leaving for Texas in late December. With Mona and Randolph now in Boston, and with his first grandchild, Jane, born on November 3, 1907, House was inclined to stay in the East through Christmas. In 1908, his pattern of travel was very similar. He had come to relish his annual trips to Europe, urging his friends to join him even if it meant paying a portion of their expenses. The glamour of passage across the Atlantic appealed to House, for on these trips he could mingle with the socially prominent and also marvel at ocean liners such as the *SS Lusitania* and *SS Mauretania*, technological wonders of their era that set a new standard of luxury at sea.[45]

On July 28, 1908, House was fifty years old, traveling in Europe as he watched from afar still another presidential campaign. After Parker's defeat four years earlier, William Jennings Bryan had visited Austin, where House urged him not to run in 1908. Although he seemed to acquiesce, Bryan soon became a candidate and easily won the Democratic nomination. Bryan believed that this time he had a good chance to win, given the effects of the panic of 1907 and the fact that he faced William Howard Taft rather than Theodore Roosevelt. The Republicans were less united than in 1904, and early in the race it seemed as if Bryan was ahead. In September and October, however, the Republican effort began to build up momentum, and as the campaign neared its end it was clear to most political observers that Taft would triumph. The only question was the size of his victory.[46]

House kept his distance from Bryan's last presidential effort. As early as April 1908, House wrote that he had "no notion of getting deeper into the Bryan campaign than is pleasant," and in mid-July he left for Europe. After his return he speculated that Bryan had some chance of winning, but by the end of October he realized that the Great Commoner "will be badly beaten again." He consoled himself with the thought that Culberson had a good chance for the nomination in 1912. Bryan's defeat meant that House would have to endure "another period of waiting and discouragement" and it was by no means certain, even with Bryan finally eliminated as a presidential candidate, that the Democrats could win in 1912.[47]

Still another Democratic presidential defeat—the fourth in a row—deepened House's discontent. As a youth he had dreamed great dreams, but despite all of his achievements in Texas, the reality fell far short of his hopes. At the age of fifty, his career in Texas politics had come to an end while a career in national politics seemed unlikely to replace it. In the early years of the twentieth century he had sought to busy himself making money, and after 1904 found travel in Europe a pleasant distraction. But neither the pursuit of wealth nor European tours allowed House to escape from the disparity between what he was and what he had dreamed of becoming, or to quiet fears of stagnation, of a life that would offer no new challenges or adventures.

Like many others of the day, House sought solace in spiritualism, with its belief in a life beyond death and in communication with spirits through human mediums. It was an undemanding, optimistic faith, one that lacked philosophical depth and that had long sought to establish its legitimacy as an empirical science. House became a fellow of the American Society of

Psychological Research, an organization dedicated to the scientific investigation of mental powers that seemed to defy normal explanation, and as
early as 1901 he was following closely debates over the question of life after
death in the pages of *Harper's Magazine*.[48] In August 1908, while traveling in
France, House read an article in *Harper's* by a leading psychic researcher, Sir
Oliver Lodge, and communicated his excitement to Fanny Denton: "He
[Lodge] counts telepathy as quite proven—and you and I know it is—and
he also believes that their [*sic*] is a conscious hereafter and that this too
will be proven. It is a great promise that is now held out to us, and death is
robbed of its sting. How fine it will be for us to have another trial in another
field of endeavor. You and I will work it out together and what a joy it will
be in the working." Full of doubts about the future, House believed he and
Fanny would find fulfillment in life after death.[49]

5

"The Man and the Opportunity"

In the summer of 1909, Edward, Loulie, and their companions traveled leisurely from London to Paris, and then on to Monte Carlo, Vienna, Budapest, Hamburg, and Baden-Baden. From Monte Carlo, House reported to his Austin friend David Harrell that "there is a lot doing always to amuse one. Races, polo, pigeon shooting, fencing, concerts, grand opera, etc.," and he listed the many American friends he encountered as he moved from place to place.[1]

Despite his long absences from Texas, House remained interested in land transactions there and considered a variety of business opportunities ranging from a bond company to a cotton-seed oil mill. But his grip was loosening on even his most prized properties, and by early 1908 he was willing to consider the sale of his 1,215 acre farm Monadale.[2] House preferred selling the farm rather than finding a new manager, but he also sought to convince Barkley to stay, or to join him in the purchase of another farm or in other ventures in which they could both make a handsome profit. House patiently listened to his manager's discontents and plans for the future, as his desire to leave farm management for a different career waxed and waned. Finally, in March 1911 the two men decided to put the farm on the market for $175,000. House was in no hurry to sell such a productive property as long as Barkley stayed on.[3]

In 1906, the sale of Monadale had been unthinkable; two years later it was very much on House's mind. So, too, was the sale of his Austin mansion. In April 1909, he confided to Harrell that he would have sold his Austin home "at any time since Mona married [in December 1905] but I do not want to offer it for sale." If anyone asked Harrell about its possible purchase, he was to respond that it cost $75,000 to build but could be bought for much less.

As with Monadale, however, House was in no rush, reasoning that selling 1704 West Avenue would still leave him with the task of building a "smaller and less costly house." Ever so slowly, he was severing his ties with Texas.[4]

House also continued his withdrawal from Texas politics. He watched from a distance as Governor Thomas M. Campbell, elected without his support in 1906, pushed a series of reform measures through the legislature and won reelection in 1908. As the progressive impulse peaked in Texas, it became intertwined with prohibitionist sentiment and with a growing desire among many reformers to place the liquor question at the top of their political agenda. The conflict between those who wanted statewide prohibition and those who were content with the local option confused previous political alignments and led politicians as different as Campbell and Culberson to complain to House about the chaotic condition of state politics.[5]

During his stay in Texas in early 1910, however, House was primarily concerned about the political fate of Culberson, who faced a campaign for a third term for Senate. Culberson's failing health, or "nervous condition," prevented him from returning to Texas, but House once again rallied support for his candidacy and reassured his old friend of the warm feelings toward him in the state. As always, Culberson was deeply grateful for House's personal and political support, informing him that "no man ever had a finer friend than you have been to me."[6] Culberson's early declaration, along with the aid of House and some of the members of "our crowd," ensured the senator's reelection, although one political observer complained of Culberson's long absences from the state and observed that "he has been in a comatose state for five years, and he ought to resign."[7]

By 1910, however, Texas politics was a sideshow for House, as he cultivated a broad range of friendships in Boston and New York City and searched for a promising Democratic presidential candidate. For a time he thought that William J. Gaynor, the colorful and independent mayor of New York, might be destined for a national political career, but Gaynor seemed uninterested in seeking higher office, and by early 1911 House, offended by what he viewed as the mayor's refusal to take his advice, "wiped Gaynor from my political slate, for I saw he was impossible."[8]

As Gaynor's prospects faded, House turned to Woodrow Wilson, one of a group of new Democratic governors who had won office in the Democratic landslide in the midterm elections in November 1910. Even before his election as governor, Wilson's national prominence as president of Princeton had led some influential Democrats to think of him as presidential material on a wider scale. Once in office, Wilson pushed a series of reform measures through the New Jersey legislature, gaining the attention of Democrats across the country. In May 1911, he went on his first campaign tour; in July, a Woodrow Wilson Headquarters was opened in New York City. By September Wilson's drive for the presidency was well under way.[9]

House was in no rush to join the Wilson bandwagon. For a time he toyed with Culberson's nomination, but reluctantly gave up on this because of the senator's ill-health and southern background. In February he wrote a letter to George Harvey, the editor of *Harper's Weekly* and one of Wilson's early presidential supporters, assessing the situation in Texas and emphasizing the importance of William Jennings Bryan's support. As House had planned, on March 1 Harvey forwarded his letter to Wilson, describing the writer as "an exceptionally able man, well-to-do financially and, I think sound politically." It was Wilson's first introduction to House. Later in March, House also encouraged two influential friends, Edward S. Martin of *Life Magazine* and Walter Hines Page, editor of *World's Work*, to praise him as an "eminent and effectual" politician when they visited Wilson in Trenton.[10]

Beyond these preliminary moves, House quietly watched the situation in Texas and in the national Democratic Party crystallize in the spring and early summer of 1911. Texas Democrats, like those across the nation, were looking for a fresh face to lead the party to victory in 1912. One leading Texas progressive, Thomas B. Love, was attracted to Wilson soon after his election as governor of New Jersey and began promoting Wilson's candidacy among Democrats in Texas. Gradually the Wilson movement in Texas gathered momentum and on August 7, 1911, Wilson supporters met in Austin to organize the Woodrow Wilson State Democratic League. Despite the impressive turnout, Wilson's backers realized that many conservative Democrats who controlled the party machinery favored Governor Judson Harmon of Ohio for the nomination. It would take a determined effort to carry Texas for Wilson in May 1912.[11]

House had hoped that one of the most loyal members of "our crowd," Thomas Watt Gregory, would lead the new organization, but Gregory had to settle for the vice-presidency while the presidency went to Love. Gregory's new position, however, allowed House to employ him as an intermediary with Wilson. On September 4, Gregory, at House's urging, wrote Wilson in his official capacity, informing the governor of the activities of his supporters in Texas and enclosing a brief and bland letter from House to Gregory formally joining the Wilson movement in Texas. Gregory asserted that he and House had been discussing Wilson's candidacy for almost a year, claimed inaccurately that House "has been for years one of Mr. Bryan's most trusted advisers," and went on to describe House as "the most influential private citizen in our State." A meeting between Wilson and House would, he suggested, be arranged by mutual friends in the near future.[12]

The support of House and his associates strengthened the Wilson movement in Texas by adding a group of experienced, professional politicians to its ranks. House had not, however, engaged himself directly with either Wilson or his campaign; he had simply positioned himself within the Wilson movement in Texas so that, should Wilson's candidacy continue to gather momentum, he and his friends could eventually claim some reward.[13]

While House dabbled in state and national politics, he was absorbed in fantasies of power. During his travels in Europe he enjoyed entertaining his family and friends with elaborate descriptions of how, if he was the German Kaiser, he would fight a European war. In mid-September 1911, a letter revealed that he and Sidney Mezes also relished a game in which they rewarded each other with important political positions. House informed his brother-in-law that he would "probably decline" his offer of a senatorship, given his dislike of the "limelight and... of being bound down to the irksome tasks which necessarily surround the position." House reminded Mezes that during his years in Texas politics positions were scarce and that he was held to a "strict accounting" following political success. "But I have," he informed his friend, "found it a delightful diversion in National politics. There are so many splendid offices within the gift of the President that it is exhilarating to make ambassadors, consuls and members of the Cabinet." House closed his letter by turning "to more serious and less humorous things," describing a leisurely automobile tour of the Berkshires that would end in New York City late in September.[14]

As House settled into the Gotham Hotel for his fall stay in New York, he sought to draw closer to the inner circle of the Wilson campaign. On October 19, he finally met the two leaders of the Wilson for president drive, William F. McCombs and William Gibbs McAdoo, and soon undertook a variety of political chores.[15] At the end of October, House concluded that the Wilson organizers had "done a great deal more effective work than we had any idea of"; he seemed pleased with the progress of the campaign and read with interest Gregory's enthusiastic description of Wilson's performance and reception at the Texas State Fair. After a long conversation with Wilson, Gregory concluded that "he is one of the very few great men which this country has produced." The feelings of House's trusted lieutenant were running far ahead of those of his longtime mentor.[16]

House realized, of course, that he soon must meet the candidate himself but was determined to arrange the right sort of meeting at the right time.[17] As House waited for his opportunity, he continued to emphasize his alleged influence over Bryan and to advise McCombs that Wilson should make a big tariff speech. Although in fact Bryan had not committed himself to any candidate, House assured McCombs on November 18 that he had convinced Bryan that the other candidates had eliminated themselves from the race and that "barring mistakes Governor Wilson will be nominated beyond a question of a doubt."[18] In mid-November 1911, however, House still had serious doubts about Wilson. He did not believe that any of his opponents were equal to the job, but wrote his old friend David F. Houston, now the chancellor of Washington University, that "I do not know that Wilson is but I am very sure that with your help he can get up a speech that will attract the attention of the country and will place him in the popular mind as the exponent of Tariff Reform and the antagonist of President Taft." House had still not committed himself to Wilson and his campaign for the presidency.[19]

House had waited patiently for Wilson to take the initiative for a meeting, and on November 24, 1911, his patience was rewarded when McCombs called to ask if the candidate could see him at 4:00 PM at the Gotham Hotel.

Wilson left no account of their first encounter, but House recorded his impressions at the time and dwelled on the famous meeting in retrospect as well. The next day House shared his reaction with Mezes, excitedly reporting that he had had a "delightful visit" with Wilson and a "perfectly bully time." "From what I had heard," House continued, "I was afraid that he had to have his hats made to order [because of his inflated ego] but I saw not the slightest evidence of it. It is a pity that I cannot remain here as they want me to and see the thing through. It is just such a chance as I have always wanted for; never before have I found both the man and the opportunity. We talked as hard as we could for an hour and a half and he left reluctantly and only because he had an engagement and made as early a date to meet again as he could." House also noted that Wilson was not "the biggest man I have ever met but he is one of the pleasantest and I would rather play with him than any prospective candidate I have seen." The key reason for this conclusion, he informed Culberson, was that "I think he is going to be a man that one can advise with some degree of satisfaction. This you know you could never do with Mr. Bryan." After over a decade of waiting for "the man and the opportunity," House had, at long last, found a presidential candidate he believed he could influence and who also seemed likely to win the Democratic nomination.[20]

At the end of their first meeting, both men simultaneously suggested a second, and on the evening of November 29, House and Wilson dined together at the Gotham Hotel. If House left a contemporary record of their second conversation, it has not survived. Still, he later told his biographer Arthur Howden Smith that "our second meeting was even more delightful. We dined alone at the Gotham and talked together for hours. We talked about everything, I believe, and this time we could go into details and analyze our thoughts. It was remarkable. We found ourselves in agreement upon practically every one of the issues of the day. I never met a man whose thought ran so identically with mine."[21]

In 1916, House recalled that "a few weeks after we met and after we had exchanged confidences which men usually do not exchange except after years of friendship, I asked him if he realized that we had only known one another for so short a time. He replied 'My dear friend, we have known one another always.' And I think this is true."[22]

Whatever embellishments House later added to his memories of these early encounters with Wilson, the two men were unquestionably strongly drawn to one another. In late 1911, however, they had little time for further conversations; on December 9 House left New York for Texas. Two days before his departure he arranged a dinner with Wilson at the Gotham, where Houston discussed economic issues, particularly the tariff and currency reform. Reflecting on the evening, Houston concluded that "Wilson is the straightest thinking man in public life, and can say what he thinks better than any other man."[23]

Prior to his departure, House continued to play a useful if minor role in the Wilson campaign. He urged Wilson to abandon his opposition to the plan of Senator Nelson W. Aldrich (Republican, Rhode Island), for a centralized banking system and not to take a position on any specific measure, explaining to William Garrett Brown, an editorial writer for *Harper's*

Weekly, that Wilson was sound on financial issues and once in office would give them the highest priority.[24] At the urging of McCombs, House also continued to, as he put it, "nurse Bryan." In late November, Bryan had left for Jamaica, leaving House with the task of sending him newspaper clippings on the campaign. All the information that House forwarded emphasized the opposition of newspaper mogul William Randolph Hearst and Wall Street to Wilson's presidential ambitions.[25] By early December, House felt that he had "the situation well in hand at this end." "I have been able," he confided to his Texas farm manager, "to do him [Wilson] considerable service and he seems to appreciate it."[26]

By December 1911, Governor Harmon's candidacy was fading, but Wilson now faced a powerful challenge for the nomination from two influential congressmen, Representative Champ Clark of Missouri and Oscar W. Underwood of Alabama. House, however, remained confident of a Wilson victory, refusing to engage himself deeply in the formidable task of putting together a successful Wilson drive for the presidency. In late 1911, House dabbled on the fringes of the campaign, while McCombs grappled with the harsh realities of raising funds, creating a national organization, and forging alliances with Democratic state leaders.[27]

Nevertheless, McCombs and Wilson valued House's advice and wanted him to remain in New York. House, however, had other plans. In recent years he had stayed on the East Coast until after Christmas, but on December 9 he left New York for Texas via St. Louis, so that he could share the first half of the trip home with Houston.[28]

House parted from Houston in St. Louis in good health, but no sooner had he arrived in Austin, he remembered, that he "immediately fell ill with fever." It was not until February 1, 1912, that he reported that he was rapidly gaining in strength.[29] News of his new friend's illness brought a quick response from Wilson, who wrote on January 4, 1912, that "I hope with all my heart that before this reaches you, you will be out of your room and free from discomfort . . . . Pray, take care of yourself and be sure to get strong again." Toward the end of the month Wilson responded even more emotionally to news of House's improvement: "I have been very much distressed in thinking of your long illness, and it cheers me to think that you are now about to be released . . . . If you will permit me to say so, I have come to have a very warm feeling towards you, and hope that in years to come our friendship will ripen." House responded in kind: "Your kindly expressions as to our future relations touches me deeply for I have come to

have a regard for you that is akin to affection . . . . I regret that my recent illness has caused me to lag behind others in endeavor but I am rapidly gaining strength and I shall soon be doing my full share."[30]

Sick in Texas, House could do little to help Wilson's managers meet the
mounting troubles of his campaign. On January 7, 1912, the *New York Sun*
published a letter that Wilson had written in November 1907 to Adrian
H. Joline, a Princeton trustee, in which he wondered what could be done
to "knock Mr. Bryan once for all into a cocked hat." Wilson quickly apolo-
gized, containing much of the damage, but his managers remained deeply
concerned about Bryan's attitude toward his campaign. Later in the month
the growing tension between George Harvey and Wilson led to an open
break, while William Randolph Hearst launched a bitter anti-Wilson campaign across the country. Wilson's status as the front-runner was now being
challenged, as many southern Democrats rallied behind Underwood and
as Clark emerged as Wilson's most serious opponent for the nomination.
Clark was close to Bryan, had impressive progressive credentials, and also
had strong ties with state Democratic leaders. It looked as if Wilson's opponents had agreed on a division of territory in order to stop his nomination.[31]

House was complacent over the crisis of the Wilson campaign, but
Senator Culberson was more realistic about Wilson's growing political difficulties, warning his mentor on March 6 that "the opposition to Wilson
here [in Washington] is outspoken and bitter, so much so that unless he
makes a general sweep of things his nomination may be impossible under
the 2/3 rule." Even after Clark's March 15 victory in Kansas, House disagreed with Culberson's analysis. "I believe," he replied, "the Clark
strength has spent itself. No one regards him seriously and I also think that
what votes he gets will surely go to Wilson."[32]

No doubt House's judgment of rapidly shifting national political currents
suffered from his isolation in Texas and from his concentration on strength-
ening the Wilson movement there. As House, Burleson, and Gregory and
lesser members of "our crowd" joined the Wilson campaign in Texas,
they brought with them political experience and contacts throughout the
state. More interested in patronage than in progressivism, they improved
the organization of the Wilson forces, putting Judge Cato Sells in charge
of Wilson state headquarters in Dallas.[33] Sells and Gregory concentrated
on organizing Wilson supporters in each congressional district and, with
House's assistance, raised more money to finance their efforts. Well before
the end of March, when he left for New York, House and his lieutenants

were optimistic, convinced that Texas would send a solid Wilson delegation to the Democratic National Convention. House was so sure of the results in Texas that he did not believe Wilson needed to campaign there.[34]

By early April 1912, House was settled in New York, involved once again in the details of Wilson's national campaign. While he now realized that the opposition to Wilson had centered on Clark, he continued to believe that "nobody regards Clark seriously excepting as a means to defeat Wilson." He also realized, however, that "this is a very critical time and I shall watch with anxiety the results in Illinois, Nebraska and Pennsylvania." Clark's victory in Illinois on April 9 did not surprise House (although he was jolted by its size), and a few days later Wilson, as expected, carried Pennsylvania. Wilson's loss in Nebraska on April 17 convinced many Democrats that Clark was the leading candidate and that his nomination was inevitable. Even Wilson's most fervent supporters knew that his drive for the presidency had suffered serious setbacks.[35]

House now began to consider the possibility that Wilson would not win, or that the convention would be deadlocked. "If Wilson does not win," he speculated, "it will either be Clark or W. J. Bryan—probably the latter . . . . Wilson is the only man that can keep Bryan or Clark from being nominated." For a time he considered his old idea of pushing Culberson, and also continued his efforts to draw Bryan—who had quickly forgiven Wilson for his 1907 remarks—away from Clark toward Wilson and to discourage him from hoping for the nomination. He warned Bryan that the Republicans, whatever their current disarray, would come together after their convention in Chicago and that his only chance of achieving the presidency would be to wait four years, following a Democratic administration into office.[36]

Once back in New York, House renewed his ties with Wilson. In mid-April he attended the Jefferson Day Dinner, where both Wilson and Bryan spoke. Wilson, he reported to Mezes, "easily outclassed [Bryan] . . . . [He] spoke without notes in a well modulated voice and every sentence was clothed in the most eloquent and exact English. The trouble with him I suspect is that he talks over the heads of his audiences. In this respect Bryan is his superior but in no other." Despite the faltering of the Wilson movement, House's enthusiasm for Wilson as a person and as a candidate was growing stronger. "I feel sure," he wrote to Culberson, "if we could nominate and elect Governor Wilson that it would mean more for the country in general and the democrats in particular than anything that has happened within the last half century. He thinks as we do upon nearly all subjects and he has the courage and the diplomacy that would be necessary to formulate them into law."[37]

For a time in mid-April House and his allies in Texas were concerned about the situation there. While convinced that support for Wilson was overwhelming, they worried about the lack of "enthusiasm" among many of Wilson's followers and about how to get out the Wilson vote in such a large state. By late in the month, however, House and his allies had regained their confidence.[38] Wilson's overwhelming victory in precinct conventions on May 4 meant that his followers would dominate the county conventions on May 17 and the state convention on May 28 and 29, and that the Texas delegation to the Democratic national convention would be solidly for Wilson. "Our friends here," House wrote Burleson, "are delighted beyond measure, and the Texas crowd has materially increased its already very strong influence."[39]

Despite the triumph in Texas, in May the Wilson movement absorbed so many defeats that for a time it seemed likely to collapse. While Wilson's fortunes revived somewhat at the end of the month, most of his supporters were discouraged, realizing that Clark would enter the convention with substantially more delegates and that Wilson faced an uphill battle for the nomination. House, too, was pessimistic, noting that the combination against Wilson "is going to be too heavy to overcome unless we can manage to get the New York Delegation."[40] Uncertain what he should do, at the end of the month House informed Wilson that "I am not very well" and that he would soon retreat to the North Shore.[41] McCombs accompanied him to Beverly, Massachusetts, where the two men immersed themselves in convention strategy and were joined by two members of the Texas delegation, Gregory and Thad Thomson. All agreed on the need for binding the delegation together for a lengthy deadlock and for careful organization on the floor of the convention. "It looked to me," House recalled, "as if Wilson had a good chance, but nothing more."[42]

Faced with a highly volatile political situation, House decided to embark on his annual trip to Europe. On June 20, he informed Wilson that in five days he would sail for England on the SS Laconia. House reassured his new friend that he had "done everything that I could up to now to advise and to anticipate every contingency," and hoped that Wilson would permit him "to act as your friend in an advisory capacity." Wilson responded warmly, writing to "My dear Mr. House" that his letters "gave me additional proof of your thoughtful and admirable friendship." "I hope," he concluded, "that you will have a most refreshing voyage. It leaves me an empty feeling in my heart to have you away because it is good to know merely that you are within reach, but it would be selfish to ask you to stay."[43]

Wilson's acceptance of House's departure was not shared by his old friend and ally Culberson, who wrote that "I regret exceedingly that you will leave June 25th. It is my opinion that you ought to postpone your trip, for you can unquestionably be of *great service* to Wilson at Baltimore. *Do it!*" And two days later: "Put off your trip to Europe and take me with you *next year* when no Wilson campaign is on."[44]

Wilson would have been less forgiving, and Culberson even more insistent, had they known that three days before his departure, House wrote to Mary Bryan a last word before he left, promising "to return almost immediately" if her husband was nominated.[45] Uncertain about what would happen at the convention and unwilling to make a deep commitment to any candidate, on June 25 House departed on schedule for Europe.

By avoiding the convention, House could keep his options open. If Wilson won the nomination, he could claim that victory was inevitable and that he was not needed. If Wilson lost, he would avoid associating himself with a losing cause and possibly be in a position to advise the nominee. Beyond calculations of this sort, summer travel in Europe had become a relaxing and enjoyable routine that House was not about to give up. Even the sinking of the *SS Titanic* on April 15 did not deter him. Responding to Mezes's worries, House admitted that "I have known for a long time that the millionth chance would come and that some such accident would occur. The ocean is big therefore it has not come sooner. I have rushed through fogs too many times not to know that some day an accident would happen that would startle the world, at the same time we are committing ourselves to the *Mauretania* the speediest of them all."[46]

House missed one of the most exciting summers in modern American political history. The bitter Republican preconvention campaign came to a climax in Chicago, where on June 18 the convention itself opened. Once it became apparent that Taft would use his control of the party's machinery to gain the nomination, Roosevelt's followers walked out. With the Republicans badly split, and Roosevelt likely to run as a third party candidate, it seemed as if any candidate nominated by the Democrats could win.[47]

On the day House sailed, the Democratic convention opened in Baltimore. Wilson's cause seemed lost, for Clark entered the convention with a lead of over 200 delegates and, by the tenth ballot, secured over a majority of the convention votes. But the two-thirds rule, which House had wanted to abolish, allowed the Wilson forces to persevere and eventually to turn the tide. Led by loyal delegations from Texas—House's work, of course—and Pennsylvania, Wilson's supporters held firm and gradually eroded Clark's strength. Wilson's managers skillfully organized the convention floor, horse-traded with some Democratic party bosses, and struck a deal with Underwood to combine to put Wilson over the top. On July 2, on the forty-sixth ballot, Wilson finally won the Democratic nomination.[48]

One day out of Liverpool, House learned of Wilson's extraordinary triumph by telegram. If he felt excitement over Wilson's victory, or regret over having missed a remarkable convention, he did not record either at the time or later. Although House had promised Wilson that he would return if he won, he made no attempt to do so.[49] Instead he embarked on a leisurely tour of northern Europe, traveling through Sweden and Finland all the way to Moscow. Rather than resenting House's absence, Wilson remained solicitous about his friend's health: at the end of July House informed Wilson that he would sail for Boston on August 6, arriving on August 14. "I shall be unhappy," he reassured his friend, "until I can come in close touch with you," and he promised that from his arrival in Boston "until November every hour of my time will be devoted to your cause." He was confident that Wilson's "election seems as certain as anything political ever is, but it can be lost, and I think I see ways in which it may be."[50]

On his arrival in Boston, House put himself in touch, at a distance, with the political situation. But he delayed traveling to New York to visit Wilson's campaign headquarters. On August 18 House explained to Wilson that he had not been to New York because "the weather has been too warm for me to be of any service to the cause there."[51]

In part, House hesitated to engage himself with the Wilson campaign because of his long-standing fear of heat and of overexertion. But he also delayed because his youngest and closest daughter Janet (or "Boots" as he nicknamed her) planned to marry Gordon Auchincloss on September 14. A member of a prominent and wealthy New York City family, Auchincloss was a graduate of Groton School, Yale University, and Harvard Law School. He had met Janet on board the SS Lusitania in June 1909, and remembered vividly his first encounter with her father in London: "At luncheon one day at the Picadilly Hotel I met Mr. House for the first time. He scarcely said anything during the meal and disappeared directly afterward." By the time of the couple's engagement in November 1911, House approved of the match, confiding to Culberson that "we are all pleased for we think that he is about the cleanest and ablest young fellow we know." On September 14 Janet and Gordon were married by Endicott Peabody, the rector of Groton, at St. John's Episcopal Church in Beverly Farms. After a reception at House's summer home, where the young couple stood amid a profusion of flowers arranged in "the Italian garden style," they went to Poland Springs, New York, for their honeymoon. Both of House's daughters had now married into prominent East Coast families.[52]

By mid-August the presidential campaign of 1912 had begun to take shape. The founding of the Progressive Party on August 6 and Roosevelt's acceptance of its nomination meant that the real race for the presidency was between Wilson and Roosevelt and that Taft was out of the running. Since 1905 the Democratic Party had been gaining in strength, and if Wilson could hold on to the traditional Democratic vote, he was sure to win. But party lines were confused, both by the new Progressive Party and by a strong Socialist Party challenge led by Eugene V. Debs. At the start of the campaign Wilson was uncertain of the outcome, convinced that he could not match Roosevelt's personal magnetism.[53]

Wilson was worried, too, about the inexperience of some of the members of his inner circle and about the organization of the Democratic campaign. Both McCombs and McAdoo were political novices, and it was only with reluctance that Wilson appointed the volatile McCombs the director of his campaign. In early August, Democratic national headquarters was set up in New York City, but on August 12, McCombs, exhausted by the long struggle for the nomination, collapsed and retreated to the Adirondacks for a long rest. Until his return in mid-October, McAdoo managed the campaign while McCombs hovered in the background, ill, jealous, and quarrelsome. Despite the disruptions that McCombs caused, the Democrats gradually put together a well-financed, well-run campaign organization, with a branch in Chicago (where Burleson was prominent), one that cooperated with most of the party's state machines.[54]

Wilson's challenge, however, ran far beyond perfecting his political organization. He had to define campaign themes that would unify his party, appeal to the American people, and draw a distinction between his vision of the role of the federal government in American life and that of Theodore Roosevelt. Initially Wilson emphasized the tariff, new labor laws, banking and financial reform, and regulation of the trusts. In late August, stimulated by a conversation with the prominent progressive lawyer Louis D. Brandeis, he moved toward a more precise definition of what became known as the "New Freedom," one that was skeptical of great business enterprises and that emphasized the restoration of competition and the continual renewal of American society from below.[55]

On September 15 Wilson began a heavy schedule of traveling and speaking throughout the country. He and Roosevelt engaged each other in a far-ranging debate over the nature of political leadership and the power and purposes of the American government. The conflict between Wilson and Roosevelt, between the New Freedom and the New Nationalism (which called for the regulation of big business by a powerful federal agency), produced one of the most intense campaigns, on both a personal and intellectual level, that had ever occurred in American political history.

In the first half of October the Wilson campaign gained a momentum that it would retain until the end. Gradually pushed on the defensive, on October 14 Roosevelt was shot in the chest and seriously wounded by a deranged and unemployed New York saloon keeper in Milwaukee. He spent the rest of the month convalescing, realizing that the election was slipping beyond his grasp. By the end of the month it was clear that Wilson had retained his hold on the Democratic vote and that, given the split among Republicans, his triumph was inevitable.[56]

As House sought to pick up the threads of the campaign, he first confronted the breakdown of McCombs's health and the bitter quarrel between McCombs and McAdoo. Initially House was sympathetic with McCombs, and sought to lessen his suspicions and nourish his ambitions. House could not, however, get a first-hand impression of the McCombs-McAdoo quarrel or the situation at Democratic National Headquarters until he returned to New York. But not until mid-September, after Janet and Gordon's wedding, did he move into an apartment at 145 East 35 Street. He hoped a furnished apartment would be cheaper and more comfortable than a hotel.[57]

Once in New York, House focused intensively on the organization of the Democratic campaign. The election, he felt, was "in the bag" because of the split in the Republican Party, but he wanted to end the "jealousy and backbiting" at headquarters and maintain harmony among Democrats. Earlier, House had helped to prevent McCombs from resigning as chairman of the national committee, but as he became familiar with the situation his sympathy for McCombs faded. Visiting headquarters nearly every day, House began to complain about McCombs's treatment of McAdoo, worried that McCombs was "near a breakdown" and that "he grows more impossible every day"; House was amazed at his intemperate criticism of both McAdoo and Wilson. McCombs was, he concluded, "half crazed with jealousy." As the campaign progressed, House drew close to McAdoo and doubted that McCombs would have any place in the new Wilson administration.[58]

Wilson was delighted to have House back from his travels in Europe. During the fall, House saw Wilson often, conferring with him in New York or talking on the phone when Wilson was in Princeton. House confided to his close friend Frank Andrews that "my relations with him are closer than anyone knows. In writing to me he signs himself sometimes 'Gratefully yours' and other times 'Affectionately yours' and I believe that he feels it." Wilson once borrowed House's automobile, occasionally visited him in his apartment, and, ever solicitous of his friend's health, urged him "not to work too hard."[59]

House's most forceful advice came on October 15, after Roosevelt was shot and had to suspend his campaigning. Tired from his travels, Wilson wanted to rest, but McAdoo urged him to continue his efforts. House, however, told Wilson "to cancel all engagements until Roosevelt was able to get out again," reasoning that it was wiser to behave in a "generous" and "chivalrous" way toward Roosevelt. House's advice proved decisive in convincing Wilson to cut back temporarily his own engagements.[60]

On Election Day, November 5, House had dinner at the Plaza Hotel and waited for the returns to come in. In his diary he recorded the results in a matter-of-fact way, revealing no excitement over the culmination of years of waiting and dreaming: "By half past six o'clock it was evident that Wilson had won, so I sent him a telegram of congratulations. By seven o'clock returns were in enough to enable one to see that it was a Wilson landslide." Even at the moment of victory, House was overly optimistic, ignoring the fact that Wilson had won with a plurality, drawing fewer votes than Bryan in 1908, and that his prospects in four years would be dim if the Republicans healed their quarrels.[61] House, however, was thinking of the short run, about the success of the administration and what his role in it would be. In Texas, as the leader of "our crowd," he had focused on the acquisition of power, emphasizing personal loyalty, patronage, the deception of others, and the manipulation of the political system. As the new president's adviser, House realized that, to one extent or another, he would have to reinvent himself if he was to influence his intense, idealistic friend in the White House.[62]

6

The Ideal Society

In the decade before House met Woodrow Wilson, his political views underwent a transformation. While he recorded few of the details of this process, he clearly moved away from the narrow concerns of Texas party politics to an involvement with a broader range of national issues. The growing reform agitation across the nation affected House, who came to share the concern of many Americans over the corruption of the political process, the excesses of giant corporations, and the strains appearing in the nation's social fabric. He concluded that an extension of public authority and the use of expert knowledge were essential to ease the crisis in American life.[1]

Like many domestic reformers, House became a "cosmopolitan progressive," part of the movement, as one historian notes, "of politics and ideas throughout the North Atlantic world that trade and capitalism had tied together." He traveled to England and the continent of Europe, observing the ways in which the various governments confronted urban-industrial problems. House was particularly fascinated by developments in England, where the Liberal Party that came to power in late 1905 pledged to enact a program of advanced social legislation. Old age pensions came in 1908, and medical insurance for most wage earners and unemployment insurance for some in 1911. And House followed closely the extraordinary measures of Chancellor of the Exchequer David Lloyd George to modernize the British tax structure.[2]

In the summer of 1911, issues of reform were very much on House's mind. In June he informed one friend that Lloyd George "is working out the problems which are nearest my heart and that is the equalization of opportunity . . . . The income tax, the employers' liability act, the old age pension measure, the budget of last year and this insurance bill puts England well to the fore. We have touched these problems in America but lightly as yet but the soil is fallow."[3]

Back in Magnolia by late July, House followed closely the House of Representatives' investigation of the United States Steel Corporation and complained to Culberson that "the money trust was the most pernicious of all trusts." House was relieved that the federal government was finally "curbing and disintegrating the trusts," but he believed that "another and more stupendous form of monopoly is fattening itself upon the Nation." This was the "great money power," a group of "financial pirates [who] loot the ship that they themselves are in honor responsible for."[4]

Convinced that he lived in a "sordid and material" age, House talked and corresponded with his friends, especially David F. Houston, about what could be done. Houston was closely involved in House's intellectual efforts, sharing his interest in events in England and the continent. In early August 1911, Houston concluded that "England and Germany are doing many interesting things in a desirable socialistic direction. We shall follow slowly because of the newness of conditions here and the lack of pressure." In the summer and fall of 1911 he encouraged House to engage himself with ideas about government and reform and to find a form through which these ideas could be expressed.[5]

House's real purpose in returning so quickly to Texas in early December 1911 was to commit his thoughts to paper. While traveling from New York to St. Louis with Houston, the two men discussed the issues that a book should cover. Soon after House left for Texas, Houston wrote Mezes that House "has a vision, I should like to make him Dictator for a while. I think the first thing he would do would be to import Lloyd-George and make him Wilson's Prime Minister."[6]

House's illness delayed his immersion in this project, but by the end of January 1912 he was hard at work. After completing the manuscript on February 28, House gave it to Mezes, who was "good enough to say some nice things of it." The next day he wrote Houston, admitting that "it is not much of a novel," but arguing that only by casting his ideas in the form of fiction could he reach a large audience.[7]

At the end of March, House left Austin for New York, traveling via St. Louis so that he could confer with Houston about revisions to *Philip Dru*, named for its hero and principal character. Although Houston agreed with House's views and thought the book was "economically sound," he still wanted a serious work rather than a novel filled with romance, and urged House to deemphasize the role of Philip Dru and to make the revolution that Dru called for in this futuristic work "bloodless." Displeased with his suggestions, House decided, when he reached New York, to seek the advice of Harry P. Steger, the literary adviser of Doubleday, Page, and Company. Houston concurred, urging House to "get somebody that has much more aptitude as a novelist and as a popular writer than you or I have, to give the document the finishing touches."[8]

In early April, House turned the manuscript over to Steger, whom he paid to improve it. The revised manuscript arrived on June 25, 1912, the day House was sailing for England. On the voyage across the Atlantic House "worked assiduously" on *Philip Dru*, in mid-July returning the rewritten manuscript to Steger,[9] who was surprised at the "many great and radical changes" House had made. He now felt "superfluous" as a literary adviser. Nevertheless, Steger began to approach publishers but quickly ran into trouble. G. P. Putnam's Sons rejected House's story because it was "too heavily freighted with propaganda of a sociological nature to secure adequate attention from the fiction-reading public." Finally Steger advised House to pay B. W. Huebsch, a New York publisher, $1,500 to print 2,000 copies.[10]

After returning from Europe, House continued to follow the progress of his manuscript, but, absorbed in the Wilson campaign, he had no taste for further revisions, admitting to Houston that "it is not what it should be but I had no time to do it better."[11] Despite his other commitments, House rushed the manuscript through the press. On September 26 he made final revisions and mailed the completed text to the publisher. On October 27 he reviewed advertising with Steger and on October 31 received fifteen copies of *Philip Dru: Administrator, A Story of Tomorrow, 1920–1935*.[12]

Like most of the political, utopian novels that emerged in the decade and a half before the outbreak of World War I, *Philip Dru: Administrator* was a crudely written effort. Filled with clichés and wooden characters, it portrayed a dull, static utopia, one that emerged out of the violence that followed after social conditions had become intolerable. Utopian novels of the period offered varied visions of the future, but all contained a young hero who arose from obscurity to vanquish a great enemy. This "Young Knight" was idealistic and prophetic, and usually had at his side a rich young woman, a spiritual guide willing to carry out demeaning assignments. Both dedicated their lives to the overthrow of a political boss and to the cleansing of society. Once sweeping reforms were implemented, the young hero relinquished his dictatorial power and restored free elections.[13]

Aside from expressing House's ideas, *Philip Dru: Administrator* also served as a means of expressing his anxieties about the problems of industrial society. It revealed his yearnings for efficiency and control, and his belief that inspired leadership could solve the nation's problems. His utopia sought to allay fears about old age, death, aggression, and class conflict, and to portray a future filled with comfort and reconciliation.[14]

The novel begins a little ahead in the future, in 1920, when conditions in the United States have grown so bad that a civil war was impending. Dru, a young, idealistic army officer, assembles a large military force to overthrow the corrupt government in Washington. After routing the enemy army, Dru assumes the title of "Administrator of the Republic." He quickly puts in place a new world order, based on an Anglo-American understanding, but devotes the bulk of his efforts to a sweeping reform of American life. Drawing on advisers from England, France, and Germany, Dru enacts a series of reforms that would have pleased even William Jennings Bryan and that lead to a far more just and efficient society.

After seven years—a somewhat biblical number—Dru's dictatorship draws to a close. The government is running smoothly, the world is at peace, and Dru decides that it is time to withdraw from public service. With the great love of his life, Gloria Strawn, at his side, he is finally able to consummate the romance that, for reasons of state, he had deferred for years. Philip and Gloria travel to San Francisco, where they board the *Eaglet* and sail into the Pacific. "Where were they bound? Would they return? These were the questions asked by all, but to which none could give answer." The "effacement" of Philip Dru was complete[15]

The only two characters of any note in the novel are Philip Dru and the leader of the corrupt political machine, Senator Selwyn, both of whom embody different sides of House himself and whose lives become increasingly intertwined as the story progressed. Dru grows up on a Kentucky farm, the youngest and most loved of seven sons (House was the youngest of eight children). He is close to his father, a "sturdy farmer" who has sacrificed his own accumulation of wealth in order to help his children. Although Dru has no desire to kill others, he has always wanted to be a soldier, for within him lurked a "lust for action and battle." Physically he is a "lithe young Kentuckian," a man of "medium height, slender but toughly knit, and with a strong, but homely face." His eyes are "bright and hard," his voice "tense and vibrant," like a "deep-toned bell." Dru combines astonishing intellectual powers with remarkable discipline and self-control. Far-sighted, compassionate, ever-vigilant, with a "remarkable insight into character," Dru is a flawless leader, totally dedicated to the welfare of the nation.[16]

While House wished to keep the authorship of *Philip Dru* a secret, he could not resist telling a number of friends that he had written a novel of the future. In a long talk with McAdoo about his political beliefs, he told him of his authorship, and even sent a copy to the manager of Monadale, E. J. Barkley, informing him in "absolute confidence" that he had written the novel and that only three or four other people knew that he had done so.[17] But he also sent copies to T. C. Dunn, a Houston banker; to Henry C. Roberts, the London editor of *World's Work*; and to Gregory, Culberson, and Mary and William Jennings Bryan. And in working with Steger on the advertising for the book, House sought to stimulate and exploit the curiosity of readers about the identity of its author. Press releases stressed the fact that the author of *Philip Dru*, unlike the authors of most utopian novels, was "a man distinguished in political councils" who had filled the pages of his book with "facts known only to the inner circle of statecraft and finance." He was forced to remain anonymous because it would be "uncomfortable and unpleasant. . . to have his name known."[18]

It would not have taken a particularly discerning reader to have guessed the author of the novel. Aside from aspects of his own personality and experience embodied in Dru and Selwyn, House dropped a number of hints. When Selwyn strikes a deal with Governor Rockland to make him president, the two dine at Mandell House, where Selwyn (like House himself) merely tasted the wine, since he seldom did more. Selwyn's youngest daughter, like House's, is named Janet, while Dru in his leisure moments reads two of House's favorite authors, O. Henry and Sir Oliver Lodge.[19] House wished to cultivate mystery about the authorship of the novel but in the end to allow the persistent investigator to discover that he had written it.

The response of critics was mixed. Most reviewers found *Philip Dru* interesting and enjoyable and some predicted that it would have "a large popular appeal." Others complained about its amateurish quality, and *Book News Monthly* dismissed the love story as "absurd" and the whole novel as "unreal and pedantic." Most reviews were superficial, summarizing the plot without making any effort to analyze the novel's political ideas. The most thoughtful review was also the most devastating. Writing in the *New York Times*, Walter Lippmann, at the beginning of his journalistic career, described *Philip Dru* as "didactic," and claimed that "the author was quite incapable of producing a character or sustaining a plot." "Now, if the author," Lippmann continued, "is really a man of affairs, this is an extraordinarily interesting book. It shows how utterly juvenile a great man can be. If he is really an 'insider,' then we who are on the outside have very little to learn. If he is really an example of the far-seeing public man, then, in all sincerity, I say, God help this sunny land. The imagination is that of a romantic boy of 14 who dreams of what he would do if he had supreme power and nobody objected. But if *Philip Dru* is a projection of an anonymous great man, the only adequate comment is that of the girl whom Dru marries: 'How you do enthuse one, Philip.' "[20]

The response of House's friends was far more generous. Mezes regarded the novel as a "real success," Gregory noted its "tremendous originality" and its intellectual range, while Roberts predicted that it would have more of an impact than Edward Bellamy's 1888 masterpiece *Looking Backward*. Mary Bryan complimented House on his writing and reported that her husband, although he disliked the idea of revolution, commented favorably on the political reforms imposed by Philip Dru.[21]

House valued the judgments of his friends far more than those of popular critics. He was proud of his novel, insisting in 1916 "that most of it I stand upon as being both my ethical and political faith." He suggested that Roberts arrange for an English edition and sent out copies to labor leaders across the country.[22] It provided, after all, evidence of his transformation from a Texas political operator to a man of advanced progressive convictions, one who was familiar with reform measures in England and on the continent of Europe. It proved, in short, that he was a fit companion for Woodrow Wilson. In mid-November, just before Wilson left for Bermuda, House gave him a copy of *Philip Dru*.[23] The fact that House did so revealed how much he overvalued his own work, and how dimly he appreciated the newly elected president's literary and intellectual standards.

PART II

Wilson in Power, 1913–1914

7

"Our Crowd" Goes to Washington

In the fall of 1912, as the presidential campaign had intensified, House began to consult with his political allies and to think about the composition of a Democratic administration. He decided that David F. Houston ought to be offered a place in the cabinet, worried about what to do with William F. McCombs, whose vindictive behavior at Democratic National Headquarters had alienated Wilson, and learned that Albert S. Burleson and Thomas Watt Gregory expected substantial rewards for their support. Burleson asked House to push him for postmaster general, while Gregory, restless and worn down by his legal practice in Austin, sought either a judgeship of the United States Circuit Court of Appeals or the ambassadorship to Mexico.[1]

One member of "our crowd," Frank Andrews, urged House to think of himself. Convinced that his mentor's "political life has been one of self defacement [sic] and of self sacrifice," he urged his friend to accept a prominent position for the sake of his family and the nation. House was firm in his response: "I have seen so much of office holding and how empty and unsatisfactory such honors are, that I want none of them." He agreed, however, "that Governor Wilson would probably take pleasure in giving me what I desired, in the event he became President."[2]

As early as September 25 House had discussed with the future president one of the most difficult decisions he would have to make, where to place William Jennings Bryan. Wilson and House quickly agreed that "it would be best to make him [Bryan] Secretary of State, in order to have him in Washington and in harmony with the administration rather than outside and possibly in a critical attitude." Twice more before the election, House discussed key appointments with Wilson, but by October 30 they had second thoughts about putting Bryan in the cabinet. Apparently with Wilson's approval, House sought to exploit Mary Bryan's desire to be close to her daughter Ruth, who lived in London. Suggesting that Bryan take the ambassadorship to Great Britain, House disingenuously explained "how important it was to do away with all display," and reassured her that they would have enough money for the post.[3]

After Wilson's election, House waited patiently on patronage decisions, letting the president-elect set his own pace in the selection of his cabinet.[4]

On November 16, the day he sailed from New York for a vacation on Bermuda, Wilson and House again discussed appointments. Wilson wanted to give McCombs an ambassadorship "in order to get rid of him"— as House recorded—while House proposed McAdoo as secretary of the treasury and Burleson as postmaster general. The two men discussed James C. McReynolds, a Tennessee Democrat who practiced law in New York, for attorney general without reaching any conclusion, and once again pondered the fate of Bryan, and whether to make him secretary state or ambassador to Great Britain. Neither Wilson nor House wanted Bryan in the cabinet, but both knew that his goodwill and cooperation were essential for the success of the new administration.[5]

Wilson's departure for a month's vacation in Bermuda delayed the selection of his cabinet, since no decisions could be made in his absence. House, whose closeness to the new president was now apparent to office seekers, felt the pressure, for many Democrats saw him as the person through whom they could win a position. His years in Texas politics had accustomed him to dealing with those seeking political preferment, although the numbers of offices to be filled were far beyond anything he had ever experienced before. Nevertheless, House continued to meet with a range of individuals, collecting information and assessing personalities. "I am busy," he recorded in his diary on November 21, "getting up a list of Cabinet possibilities with data attached to send the President-elect."[6]

On November 25 House left for a two-day stay in Washington, where he conferred with party leaders, seeking "to harmonize differences and to find the 'lay of the land' in order to write Governor Wilson." The result was a long letter to Wilson in Bermuda, describing his efforts to appease Speaker of the House Champ Clark and other prominent Democrats and confirming his earlier judgment of a "strong disposition among Democratic Senators to line up and to back the administration." Wilson appreciated House's efforts, which proved, he wrote, "your thoughtfulness and friendship . . . . You can see so much more than other men do and report it so much better, always getting the right point."[7]

Wilson's disgust with McCombs, chairman of the Democratic National Committee, had left a vacuum in patronage matters which House had adroitly filled. On December 18, two days after Wilson's return from Bermuda, the two men lunched at House's apartment, where they deliberated over a variety of key positions. House advised firmness in dealing with McCombs, who "talked big but was a man of but little courage," discouraged the appointment of Louis D. Brandeis as attorney general, since he "was not fit for the place," and returned to the nagging problem of what to do with Bryan. Both the president and his counselor still had serious reservations about Bryan's fitness for office, but on December 21, Wilson, bowing to the inevitable, asked Bryan to be his secretary of state and had a long and "delightful" talk with him about political affairs. Wilson had finally filled his first cabinet position.[8]

House had proved extremely useful as a collector of information and as a tactful intermediary, and he knew that the Wilson now relied heavily on him. Even so, he had long planned to leave for Texas shortly before Christmas, but by December 1912 he was, whatever his momentary doubts and longings for escape, too close to the president-elect to be absent from Washington. With the process of cabinet selection entering a crucial phase, House dared not leave without imperiling his position as Wilson's most trusted adviser.[9]

By late 1912 House was promoting the aspirations of William G. McAdoo, Joseph P. Tumulty, and Albert S. Burleson, all of whom were seeking three of the most influential positions around the president. During the fall, as House had observed the workings of Democratic National Headquarters in New York, he had become acquainted with McAdoo. A tall, lean man, forty-nine years old, with a hawk-like nose, he radiated energy and ambition. In 1892, after his street railway company in Knoxville, Tennessee, had failed, he moved his family to New York, where he eventually achieved fame as the builder of the first railway tunnels under the Hudson River. As president of the Hudson and Manhattan Railway Company, McAdoo became a leading figure in the New York business community, but he never found a comfortable niche within it. His idealism and concern for social justice led to yearnings for something more than business success. An early Wilson supporter, he became, after McComb's breakdown, the driving force in Wilson's presidential campaign. By late September 1912, House appreciated the range of McAdoo's talents and realized that he might be destined for a large role in a new Democratic administration.[10]

During the campaign, House and McAdoo had long talks about the nation's social problems. House told McAdoo of *Philip Dru* before it was published, and once the book appeared in print, McAdoo greatly admired it. House became McAdoo's promoter, in part because he shared his ideals about social justice, in part because he shrewdly recognized that McAdoo needed him and that House could play an essential role in helping him maintain self-control and in achieving his tremendous ambitions.[11]

By the end of the campaign, McAdoo was "nervous and impatient," worn down by his exertions and by the constant tension with the volatile McCombs. As the process of choosing the cabinet dragged on, McAdoo visited House, or talked with him on the telephone, nearly every day, seeking advice and reassurance. McAdoo realized the one-sidedness of the friendship, observing to House that " 'I tell you everything I know and you never tell me anything.' " House did, however, keep McAdoo informed of the progress of Wilson's thought and when, on December 18, Wilson asked House if he thought McAdoo was "suited for the Treasury," that very evening House told McAdoo of the conversation.[12]

House continued to advise patience and restraint, and wrote that "The more I see of McAdoo the better I like him. He is a splendid fellow, whole-souled and generous without a tinge of envy and, with it all, he is honest and progressive. His thoughts are in line with my own." McAdoo's ordeal lasted until early February 1913, when Wilson finally offered him the position that he coveted, the secretaryship of the treasury.[13]

House also became involved in the quest of Joseph Tumulty to continue as Wilson's personal secretary. An Irish Catholic who had grown up above his father's grocery store in Jersey City, New Jersey, Tumulty, who was only thirty-three, had enjoyed ward politics as a youth, and after establishing a legal practice, had moved into state politics. As a member of the state assembly, he became a leader of the insurgent faction within the Democratic Party and met Wilson during his 1910 gubernatorial campaign. Tumulty traveled around the state with the candidate, introducing him to the intricacies of New Jersey politics. After Wilson's victory, he became the new governor's personal secretary, running his office and, most important, using patronage to advance his legislative agenda. Gregarious and hardworking, Tumulty was uncritically devoted to his chief and was a skilled political operator who knew how to deal with the many diverse people who sought the governor's attention. Given his success in New Jersey and his devotion to Wilson, he was the obvious choice for personal secretary. But Tumulty's New Jersey perspective and Catholic faith caused the president-elect to hesitate before making the appointment.[14]

During the campaign Tumulty had stayed in Trenton, managing New Jersey affairs, and he and House had not become well acquainted. Not until December 15 did Tumulty and House have a long talk, in the course of which Tumulty directly asked "if I thought his being a Catholic would be a bar to his appointment as Secretary to the President." House was impressed with the governor's secretary, recording in his diary: "He is bright and quick and seems honest . . . . He is very courageous and out-spoken." Three days later, when House asked Wilson if he had considered appointing Tumulty, the president-elect replied: "Yes, but the trouble with Tumulty is that he cannot see beyond Hudson County, his vision is so narrow." House did not dispute Tumulty's limitations but pointed out that "he had the political instinct which would be an essential asset" and wisely observed that "in making a selection it was like walking in the country—one could always imagine that something better was beyond, but upon reaching the given point the view was still in the distance like the rainbow."[15]

House continued to urge Tumulty's selection, assuring Ellen Wilson that once the appointment was made, the strong opposition to having a Catholic so close to the president would quickly fade away. House argued that Tumulty was "singularly fit," that he "knew all the ins and outs of his [Wilson's] public and private affairs," and that Wilson should be "loath to swap horses in crossing a stream." On January 25, 1913, Wilson finally gave Tumulty the position he craved; Tumulty telegraphed House: "God bless you."[16]

Of all those that House sought to place in Wilson's cabinet, Burleson proved the most difficult. One of the original members of "our crowd," since the early 1890s he and House had worked closely together to advance the interests of their faction in Texas politics. After the turn of the century, as House withdrew from Texas politics, Burleson remained in Congress, accumulating seniority. He joined the Wilson movement in Texas late but was a prominent member of the Texas delegation at the Baltimore convention, and during the 1912 presidential campaign, he worked effectively at the party's midwestern headquarters in Chicago. Burleson had a legitimate claim for some reward from the new administration.[17]

Burleson, who was forty-nine, was a poseur—a man of education and ability who acted and dressed like a crude rural politician. A consummate political operator, he was a party regular who was far more interested in power than in ideas. Burleson's extensive ties with Democrats in Congress and his fascination with the machinery of politics made him especially well qualified to use the vast patronage available to the postmaster general (around 56,000 appointments) to advance Wilson's legislative program.[18]

On November 16, House suggested to Wilson that he appoint Burleson as postmaster general, but Wilson preferred Josepheus Daniels, a North Carolina journalist who had directed publicity in New York Democratic Headquarters. Quick to counter, House replied that Daniels "was not aggressive enough and that the position needed a man who was in touch with Congress." Nothing was decided, but Burleson's quest for preferment remained undiminished. It would be strange, he told House, "if he 'could not run away with at least one ear of corn.' "[19]

Burleson was not to be easily denied, for soon after Wilson's decision not to appoint him he received a letter from Oscar W. Underwood, perhaps the most influential Democrat in the House, declaring that Burleson possessed the confidence of House Democrats and that he was their choice for postmaster general. And as House pointed out a few days later, Wilson needed some "rock-ribbed Democrats" in his cabinet to compensate for those appointees who had not voted for the Democratic national ticket for many years. By the end of January 1913, House reported that "Albert is on the map again and I think will land." Finally on February 23 Wilson relented. House's tenacity and patience had been rewarded; his old political ally would have a major role in dispensing patronage for the new administration.[20]

While House had spent a great deal of time promoting McAdoo, Tumulty, and Burleson, he also participated in the selection of many other officials. He pushed Houston as secretary of agriculture, Franklin K. Lane of California, a member of the Interstate Commerce Commission, as secretary of the interior, and James C. McReynolds as attorney general, and maneuvered to keep Brandeis out of the cabinet and to place Gregory either as ambassador to Mexico or as solicitor general.[21] Bryan blocked Gregory's appointment as ambassador, insisting that given the tangled history of Texas-Mexican relations, no Texan should serve in that post, while Gregory turned down the solicitor generalship. Finally he became a special counsel to the attorney general to prosecute the New Haven and

Hartford Railway.[22] House also remained entangled with the disappointments and strivings of McCombs, seeking to avoid an open break between him and the president. He alternated between sympathy and disgust toward McCombs, complaining on April 19 that "he is full of trouble as usual and drooled along for an hour about nothing." House tried to convince him to accept the ambassadorship to France, but McCombs could not decide what to do and in May left for Europe with his future undecided.[23]

Most of all, however, House sought to be of service to the president-elect, controlling the flow of information he received about prospective cabinet appointees and staying in close touch with him.

On January 8, 1913, House and Loulie traveled to Princeton, where the two couples dined together at the Princeton Inn. Wilson and House sat at one end of the table, their wives at another, so that the two men could confer over dinner, and after the meal, they retired to the living room for a long conference on cabinet appointments and other matters. When House noted the absence of Texans from the cabinet, Wilson replied: "'I want you to go in the Cabinet.'" House declined, but Wilson urged him to think about becoming a "member of his official family, that it seemed to coincide with the fitness of things."[24]

While House was pleased with the offer, he preferred to retain his autonomy "being a free lance. . . and to have a roving commission to serve wherever and whenever possible." He had never been tied down by an official position, and no doubt sensed that if he was to retain his influence with the president, a certain amount of distance was essential. The next day, back in New York, House thanked Wilson for a "memorable evening." "You can never know," he continued, "how deeply I appreciate your wanting me in your Cabinet."[25]

During his stay in Princeton, House urged Wilson to come to New York and spend the night at his apartment at 145 East 35th Street, where they could "talk undisturbed." On January 15, 1913, during a long talk with Ellen over patronage matters, House renewed the invitation, suggesting that he would send Loulie to Janet and Gordon Auchincloss's apartment so that the two men could have complete privacy. Ellen, who told House that "'Woodrow' valued my opinion more than that of any other man," must have approved the invitation, for two days later Wilson called, asking if he could spend the night with House and go to the theater. The two men assessed the political situation, enjoyed *Peg o' My Heart* at the Cort Theater, and talked until midnight. House sought to quiet Wilson's fears, assuring him "that he would make a great success; that it could not be otherwise; that his steadfastness of purpose; that the righteousness of his cause, would inevitably mean success." The next morning the two continued their conversation, agreeing that House should travel to Florida to talk with Bryan about currency reform and cabinet appointments. While both were pleased with his good-natured cooperation, House was to provide Bryan with information rather than really seek his advice.[26]

On January 24 Wilson was back in New York for the night. With the telephone disconnected, the president-elect and his counselor had a quiet dinner together, once again canvassing the political scene and attending the Little Theater to see a political drama, *Rutherford and Son*. Over sandwiches before bedtime, Wilson talked of his troubles at Princeton and of his broken friendship with philosophy professor John Grier Hibben, who had differed with him over controversies there—regarding eliminating the upper-class eating clubs and the control of the graduate school—and succeeded him as president. When the two men parted the next day, Wilson "expressed the keenest regret at my [House's] departure for Florida, but we agreed if he wanted me that I would return at a moment's notice."[27]

On January 27 House left for Miami, the booming subtropical city where the Bryans had relocated from Nebraska. There he consulted with the Great Commoner for five days before leaving for a vacation in St. Augustine. House went over Wilson's thinking about the cabinet and found that while Bryan offered some suggestions and was especially concerned about the attorney generalship, he was in a "delightful humor" and "is exceedingly anxious for your [Wilson's] success."[28]

House seems to have been more interested in Bryan's lifestyle than his views on cabinet positions. "The Bryans," he observed, "lead almost primitive lives in regard to their daily habits. They arise around six o'clock, have a light breakfast, lunch around eleven and supper or dinner around five or six o'clock, and I suppose are safely in bed by nine." Seeking to balance his condescension with some positive comments, House concluded that Bryan "is really a fine man, full of democratic simplicity, earnest, patriotic and of a fervently religious nature. Mrs. Bryan is the 'salt of the earth.' She has all the poise and good common sense which is lacking in her distinguished husband." House had little respect for Bryan's judgment of men and no intention of allowing him to play a major role in the new administration.[29]

During the remainder of February, after House's return from Florida, he and Wilson spent four more evenings in New York, settling the final composition of the cabinet and discussing a wide range of other topics. House was philosophical about the group of men that was emerging, observing that "there is not much material in the party from which to choose . . . . I think, in all the circumstances, we have done well." He was critical, however, of "the casual way in which the President-elect is making up his Cabinet. I can see no end of trouble for him in the future unless he proceeds with more care."[30]

On March 2 House left New York for Washington on what would become, over the next seven years, a familiar journey, traveling from Penn Station to Union Station, two structures that were, one historian notes, "twin symbols of the new imperial republic." Two days later he attended the inauguration, accompanied by Loulie and Janet and Gordon Auchincloss and Mona and Randolph Tucker. House did not observe the ceremony at the Capitol, where over 100,000 people gathered to witness the inauguration of the first Democratic president in two decades. Instead, he "loafed around" the Metropolitan Club, lunched at the White House, and stood for awhile on the president's reviewing stand in front of the White House. On March 8 he had a "delightful talk" with the president about the cabinet, one in which Wilson "laughingly told me of his estimate of each one and how they acted at the first meeting." Wilson suggested a "cipher between us," or nicknames for each member of the cabinet, so that he and House could write and talk about them without revealing their identities. Obviously Wilson planned to consult House often, and the two men agreed that it would be best if House "remained away from Washington."[31]

House was pleased with his efforts and optimistic about his role as a confidential adviser. Throughout March, April, and May, he participated in a wide variety of patronage decisions, traveling to Washington six times to consult with the president, while Wilson visited House once in New York. Appointments remained high on the agenda between the two men, for many ambassadors and lesser officials were yet to be named. During a visit on March 25 House promised to come the next week and stay longer, so that he and the president could make more decisions. Wilson was relying heavily on House in selecting officials and in dealing with members of his cabinet. House was eager to serve, and did so efficiently, but he was careful to travel to Washington only when Wilson urged him to do so.[32]

During the late winter and spring of 1913, House's longest stay in Washington ran from April 11 to 18. Earlier, at the president's request, he had spoken to some members of the cabinet who "had bothered him by

taking up his time in threshing out matters with him instead of bringing things to him in condensed form." On April 14, pleased with House's
efforts, Wilson "was generous and fine in his praise of my work. He
declared he did not know how he could do without me, and thanked me
again and again for what I am trying to do. He asked me to be always frank
and 'scold him' if I thought he was doing anything wrong." Worried that
Wilson "seemed depressed," House "tried to brace him by telling him that
everything was in splendid condition excepting himself." Wilson apparently laughed at this and "promised to give himself more time for recreation." Whatever his concern for Wilson's well-being, House left on the
midnight train for New York.[33]

During the process of cabinet-making, Wilson and House came to know
each other well. The president and his counselor (a term Wilson would later
use to describe House) were, however, an odd couple. Wilson was fifty-six,
two years older than House, and was taller and heavier, trim and vigorous,
with a "long-jawed, animated face" and a "magnificent, resonant voice,"
while House, Raymond Fosdick (Wilson's Princeton student who knew
both men well) remembered, was "a small, frail, courteous, bright-eyed
man with a gentle voice and winning manners."[34]

Fosdick for one thought Wilson "a prophet touched by fire," a brilliant,
intense man, a spellbinding orator whose ambition and sense of destiny had
carried him far. His moral and political vision inspired many Americans,
making him perhaps the most compelling figure of his day (although second,
some said, to Teddy Roosevelt). Wilson knew how to phrase national ideals
in lofty and inspiring words; he also was a bold party leader who knew how
to drive legislation through the Congress.[35] Wilson had paid a physical price
for his intensity, entering the White House in 1913 with a complex medical
history. He suffered from cerebral vascular disease, which may have appeared
as early as 1896, when he was only thirty-nine, and which brought a series
of strokes of varying intensity prior to 1913. Coupled with this progressive
disease, the nature of which Wilson never clearly understood, was a cluster of
other ailments, headaches, digestive troubles, lethargy, and depression, with
which he had to contend over the course of his life. Wilson compulsively
described the details of his various ailments to those he loved, and these discussions of illness formed a bond between him and his close friends.[36]

Despite a wonderful marriage and a warm, happy family life, Wilson was
highly vulnerable to emotional stress. He often felt lonely and sometimes

feared the loss of emotional control. Even so, he displayed an uncanny ability to translate these inner tensions into a language that had meaning for many Americans. "Now and again," the psychohistorian Erik H. Erikson once wrote, "an individual is called upon. . . to lift his individual patienthood to the level of a universal one and to try to solve for all what he could not solve for himself alone."[37] Many people loved Wilson and tried to help him through the difficulties of his life; the most important of these intimates was Ellen Axson Wilson, a widely read, reflective woman who sought to nurture her husband while fighting off her own melancholy moods. She was completely devoted to his career, offering shrewd advice and accepting his new political associates. She was a person, in short, with whom any friend of Wilson's had to deal.[38]

Ellen respected House's political skills and welcomed him into the Wilson family. All three of Woodrow's daughters, Margaret (twenty-seven), Jessie (twenty-six), and Eleanor (twenty-four), stayed with them in the White House, and the family sought to live in Washington as it had in Princeton. House liked the feminine atmosphere of the president's immediate family and the Wilsons' daily routine, with its emphasis on family meals and plain food. "The Wilsons," he noted approvingly after a dinner at the White House, "are living simply. We had fish, veal cutlets, rice, peas and potatoes, a simple lettuce salad and ice cream. It is a household in which there are no pretenses and where everything is in good taste." It was, in fact, a household similar to his own, although both of House's daughters were married and none of Wilson's were.[39]

Wilson was an unusually solitary figure for an American political leader, one who had little taste for day-to-day contacts with politicians and reporters and the constant intrusions of politics into his private life. With his election to the presidency, he faced political pressures far more intense than any he had experienced before, and also found himself more isolated in a personal sense than ever before as well. He was in need of advisers who could serve as buffers and who would carry out many tasks he found unpalatable. He was also in need of male companionship, since his long and close friendship with John Grier Hibben had ended in 1907.[40]

House appeared at the right time, with a combination of personal and political qualities that strongly appealed to Wilson. House's gentle, deferential manner, his lack of an assertive masculinity, put the president at ease. His own apparently fragile health elicited the president's sympathy and concern, and his frequent assurances of affection and esteem helped to satisfy one of Wilson's deepest needs. Moreover, House had impressive political skills that complemented those of the president. He was unusually gifted in drawing people out, estimating their abilities, and winning their confidence, without, as we've seen, offering the same in return. His many years in Texas politics had made him a patient and crafty political infighter, experienced in dispensing patronage and in attempting to maintain harmony among the many factions within the Democratic Party. During the winter of 1912—1913, House joined that circle of intimates around the president who were dedicated both to advancing his political career and to maintaining his physical health and emotional stability.[41]

In *Philip Dru* House had expressed his concern with the spiritual regeneration of the nation and his belief that inspired leadership could solve the nation's problems. Now he found in Wilson a leader who embodied his moral values and who could move the American people toward this larger goal. Thus House wanted the dominant theme in the president's public addresses to be that the "strong should help the weak, that the fortunate should aid the unfortunate, and that business should be conducted upon a higher and more humane plane." On February 13, when Wilson read to House his inaugural address, House thought it a "masterpiece of its kind. It is off the beaten track and is full of spirituality." At the close of the month, defending Wilson at a dinner with skeptical financial leaders, House claimed that he was a leader of exceptional moral and physical courage, one who sought "to raise the moral stamina of the Nation."[42]

For a man of allegedly frail health, House himself had displayed a remarkable degree of stamina during the winter of 1912—1913. He had worked long hours, beginning generally around 9:00 AM and often continuing late into the evening, screening applicants, collecting information, conferring with aspiring politicians, and advising the president. He made those many trips to Washington, where his schedule was equally arduous, and missed his annual winter stay in Texas. His only regular escape from the constant pressure of patronage and cabinet-making was evenings at the theater. Nevertheless, his health was remarkably good. Twice he complained that he was "worn out," and in early January he was in bed with a fever and cold for five days. All in all, however, he thrived on this intense political activity, excited by the fact that at last he was "playing a part on so large a stage."[43]

House realized, however, that the arrival of warm weather would bring a change in his routine, and as early as April 23 he warned Wilson that "the weather will soon begin to grow warm which warns me that I am not to see much more of you until the Autumn." Breaking away for his annual trip to Europe would provide a much-needed rest and also deflate the publicity that was beginning to worry him, especially an article in *Collier's Weekly* entitled, "The President's Silent Partner." House did not know how much Wilson would tolerate, and concluded that his growing fame was all the more reason to leave for Europe.[44]

Wilson was sympathetic with his friend's European journey, urging him not to worry "after you have once stepped on board." "I do not think you can ever know, my great and good friend," House wrote Wilson the day before he left, "how much I appreciate your kindness to me . . . . I shall believe that you will be successful in all your undertakings for, surely, no one is so well equipped as you to do what you have planned. My faith in you is as great as my love for you—more than that I cannot say." Wilson responded in kind, telegraphing House that "my affectionate thoughts go with you and my prayers for your strength, refreshment and happiness." On May 21, House sailed on the *SS Mauretania* for England.[45]

8

Foreign Horizons, 1913

During the winter of 1912–1913, as House joined the inner circle around the new president, his thoughts turned to his role in the administration's foreign policy. On January 22, 1913, he confided to his journalist friend Edward S. Martin that he wanted "to bring about a better understanding between England and Germany." House did not intend to take Secretary of State Bryan or the American ambassadors in Berlin or London into his confidence; he planned to "take messages directly from the President to the Ministers of State for Foreign Affairs in England, and to the Emperor in Germany."[1] Even before Wilson took office, House was planning a dramatic, confidential initiative that would make him the president's chief envoy abroad.

Shortly before his inauguration in March 1913, Wilson allegedly told a friend that "It would be an irony of fate if my administration has to deal chiefly with foreign affairs."[2] In fact, Wilson's remark was misleading, for in the previous decade and a half he had observed with care the increase in American power and the nation's growing involvement in world affairs. Once in office, he was prepared to transform the country's foreign as well as its domestic policy, determined, as one biographer writes, "to make it genuinely democratic, pacific, anti-imperialistic, free of the manipulations of big financial interests."[3] But on entering office—absorbed in his program of domestic reform—he had no specific plan to advance these goals; initially Wilson's foreign policy was reactive.

Wilson possessed an instinctive sense of the complexity of national life, and he proved, during his first year in office, to be a master of domestic politics. In foreign affairs, however, Wilson's faith in America's sacred mission often led—especially during his early years in office—to a confused, amateurish approach.[4] He saw little need for a foreign policy apparatus that would provide information about other governments and their objectives and that would include mechanisms for the execution of his policies. As one historian remarks, Wilson "relied heavily upon unofficial sources—either a random scattering of friends or an ill-equipped set of private emissaries—in deciding important matters of policy . . . . [He had] a powerful faith in the intuitive management of world affairs."[5]

While Wilson expected to dominate foreign policy, he had no choice—given the range of international issues confronted by the United States—but to share the burdens of diplomacy with a small foreign policy bureaucracy. During the winter of 1912–1913 he labored to fill a wide range of positions in the State Department and in American embassies and legations abroad. The Department of State in 1913 was still a small, quaint organization, understaffed and overworked, with a staff of only 213 people in Washington and fewer than 450 diplomats and consuls scattered abroad. While organizational changes under President Taft had improved its efficiency, it remained an organization appropriate for a second-rate power. Wilson had no awareness of the need for change and selected, in collaboration with Bryan and House, a mixture of amateurs and professionals to fill the Department's top positions. Wilson chose John Basset Moore, a noted authority on international law and diplomacy, as counselor, the most important officer in the Department under the secretary of state, while Bryan chose as first assistant secretary of state John E. Osborne, a close friend and former governor of Wyoming. And Wilson and House together decided that Dudley Field Malone—an intense, emotional Irishman who was the son-in-law of New York's senator James A. O'Gorman—should be the third assistant secretary of state. Malone, who dealt largely with the consular and diplomatic services, gave House an important link to the inner workings of the Department.[6]

Prior to his inauguration, Wilson had vowed to fill ambassadorships with men of the highest caliber, such as former Harvard president Charles W. Eliot, rather than "to the merely rich who were clamoring for them."[7] But he found that the pressure from party donors was relentless and that the Democratic Party, out of power for sixteen years, lacked a large pool of qualified men who could handle major positions abroad. Many of the best men the president sought out refused appointments, and he often had to compromise his principles and give major positions to wealthy contributors to the party. Throughout the winter of 1912–1913 House was Wilson's adviser on ambassadorial and ministerial appointments; those who aspired to serve abroad soon learned to seek him out for advice and preferment.[8]

Both Wilson and House understood the importance of the ambassador-ship to Great Britain, eventually settling on Walter Hines Page, a promi-nent publisher and old friend of the president. Page's appointment, along with that of the University of Wisconsin scholar Paul S. Reinsch to Beijing, were excellent choices, but other key positions were given to party faithful who were wealthy and mostly amateurs in diplomacy. Wilson sent James W. Gerard, a New York judge, member of Tammany Hall and a heavy con-tributor in 1912, to Berlin; Frederic C. Penfield, a former consul general in Egypt, to Vienna; Thomas Nelson Page, a second-rate novelist and leader of the Virginia Democratic Party, to Rome; Joseph E. Willard, another Virginia politician, to Madrid; and Henry Morgenthau, a New York finan-cier who directed the party's fund-raising efforts in 1912, to the Ottoman Empire.[9] In the case of France, Wilson finally, in September 1914 and after war had been declared, dispatched William G. Sharp, a wealthy former congressman with no diplomatic experience, to Paris. Page wrote that Sharp's appointment was living proof that "in whatever obscurity a man may be, he is hardly safe from an Ambassadorial appointment."[10]

Of all these ambassadors, Page was the only one with whom Wilson had a close personal relationship. Even in the case of Page, however, the presi-dent saw no need to give him any instructions on the eve of his departure for London. "I called again on the President to ask his instructions," Page wrote in his diary. "He had none . . . . [He] seemed to have in mind only this idea—that he wanted somebody in London whom he knew & upon whose judgment he could rely."[11] Neither Wilson nor House could imagine, in the spring of 1913, just how important these positions would soon become.

The president was interested in only the top layer of diplomatic appoint-ments, but House was also concerned with appointments to American legations (where ministers worked in less important countries), with the secretaries of embassies and legations (career diplomats who guided ama-teur ambassadors and ministers), and with the consular service, which had been reformed and put on a merit basis by Wilson's Republican predeces-sors. And House worked to limit the influence of Secretary of State Bryan, warning Wilson on March 8—four days after his inauguration—"to be careful concerning the recommendations Mr. Bryan made, because of his notoriously bad judgment in regard to men."[12]

Despite House's efforts, Bryan's influence was substantial. He had been a major figure in national politics for nearly two decades and had an impas-sioned following throughout the nation; his support was essential for the

success of Wilson's domestic agenda. Beyond political expediency, however, Wilson and Bryan shared many assumptions about America's role in
world affairs and agreed that most of the officers in the diplomatic service were either incompetent Republicans or members of a snobbish professional elite.[13] Bryan wanted a clean sweep of American representatives
abroad, replacing incumbents with men "fresh from the people." Wilson
realized that Bryan had debts to his followers and gave him a free hand with
many lesser appointments, but neither Wilson nor House would go as far
as Bryan wanted and both insisted on maintaining the integrity of the diplomatic and consular services. "Mr. Bryan," House wrote disapprovingly,
"is a spoilsman and is in favor of turning the republicans out and putting in
democrats."[14]

As the new administration settled in, Wilson nonetheless came to appreciate Bryan's loyalty and decency, and he worked out a rough division of
labor in which his secretary of state managed most issues dealing with Latin
America—with the exception of Mexico—and promoted his schemes for
world peace.[15] Eager to abolish warfare among nations, Bryan won the
president's approval to negotiate "cooling off" treaties with other governments, accords in which the signatories would agree to submit disputes
to a permanent commission for six months or one year.[16] From the start,
however, Bryan's tenure as secretary of state was controversial. Despite his
hard work, Bryan had little understanding of the requirements of the position and was disorganized both in his thoughts and in his routines. He
disregarded protocol, had poor relations with the press, and was soon criticized for continuing to accept payment for his lectures, for his refusal to
serve alcohol at diplomatic receptions ("grape juice diplomacy"), and for
his alleged neglect of his duties. The president would gradually lose faith in
Bryan and turn to others to conduct the diplomacy of his administration.[17]

Soon after taking office Wilson began to face challenges from abroad.
In China in 1911 revolutionaries had rebelled against the Manchu dynasty,
forcing the abdication of the emperor and creating in February 1912 a new
republican government under the leadership of Yuan Shih-k'ai, the former
commander in chief of the Imperial Army. On March 18, 1913, Wilson—
who felt "so keenly the desire to help China"—cut loose from the other
powers and withdrew from an international financial consortium that he
felt had imposed unjust terms on China.[18] "The awakening of the people of
China to a consciousness of their possibilities under free government," he
asserted, "is the most significant, if not the most momentous, event of our

generation."[19] He only dimly realized that the world was entering a new age and that his romantic, idealistic view of revolutionary forces in China and elsewhere would not provide an adequate guide for American policy.

In the spring of 1913 the California legislature, responding to fears of a growing Japanese influence in the state, moved toward the passage of legislation that would bar Japanese residents from owning real estate. Wilson and Bryan passively observed the developing crisis; they sympathized with the efforts of Californians to protect their society and actually encouraged the passage of a less overtly discriminatory alien land law. Wilson was reluctant to meddle in California's affairs, and in mid-April, when the lower house of the legislature approved an alien land bill, he only suggested a modification of its language. Later in the month he dispatched Bryan on a mission to Sacramento to urge delay and moderation. Bryan, however, had nothing to offer legislators, and on May 3, with the support of the progressive Republican governor Hiram W. Johnson, the alien land bill passed the California Senate and Assembly. The Japanese government's bitter protest jolted the president and secretary of state, who had never seriously considered the Japanese point of view, and set off a minor war scare in the United States. Wilson and Bryan dismissed the alarmist views of their military advisers and of some members of the cabinet, but their attempts to conciliate Japan failed, and the alien land controversy remained unresolved, embittering relations between the two nations.[20]

These early foreign policy decisions did not deeply engage House. He had never traveled to East Asia and had given even less thought than the president to China and Japan. House accepted Wilson's approach to revolution in China and was content to let Bryan labor in Sacramento to "disentangle the Japanese imbroglio." He dismissed his friend McAdoo's alarmist thoughts about a Japanese "dash for the Philippines, Hawaii and the Pacific Coast for a quick indemnity," and seemed puzzled that the Japanese "exhibited so much feeling" over the alien land legislation. Absorbed in America's relations with England and Germany, House seemed unconcerned about the growing tension between Japan and the United States.[21]

Wilson also had to confront a serious dispute with Great Britain. In the summer of 1912 Congress had given preferential treatment to American ships as they passed through the Panama Canal. At the end of the year the British government protested, claiming that the legislation discriminated against foreign shipping and that it violated a treaty between the United States and Great Britain. Wilson, along with other presidential candidates, had supported the tolls exemption during the campaign, but by early 1913 he had changed his mind, agreeing with House that "the clause should be repealed." Soon after his inauguration Wilson told Ambassador James Bryce that the United States would live up to its treaty obligations.[22] But with tariff and currency bills soon to be moving through Congress, the president would not be rushed, and not until January 1914 would he open a campaign to repeal the exemption provision.

By the time he took office in March 1913 Wilson faced chaos in Mexico, where the revolutionary government of Francisco I. Madero had been overthrown by federal troops led by General Victoriano Huerta. Huerta deposed Madero on February 18, 1913, murdered him, and had himself proclaimed the provisional president. A brutal, cunning man, Huerta hoped to forge an alliance with the Catholic Church, the wealthy classes, and the army, and return to the old pre-revolutionary social order. He failed to understand the revolution and the way in which it was spreading in waves across Mexican society.[23]

In late March, anti-Huertistas met in Guadalupe in northern Mexico to adopt a platform and to declare themselves the legitimate heirs of Madero's revolution. These "Constitutionalists" were led by their "First Chief," Venustiano Carranza, who proclaimed himself the provisional president of Mexico. In Morelas province, south of Mexico City, Emiliano Zapata led a peasant rebellion that demanded sweeping changes in the nation's rural society. Huerta lacked the military power to suppress these diverse revolutionary forces.[24]

Wilson took office amid this swirl of events, only a few weeks after Huerta had deposed Madero and seized power. The European powers had promptly recognized Huerta's government, and the new president faced strong pressure from the American ambassador in Mexico City—Henry Lane Wilson (who had conspired with Huerta to bring down Madero)—also to recognize new regime. John Bassett Moore, the State Department's counselor, urged recognition, as did the large American colony in Mexico City, which had hated Madero and believed that Huerta would restore order throughout the country.[25] The president, however, was not convinced of Huerta's legitimacy. Suspicious of the information provided by Ambassador Wilson and shocked by Huerta's coup and murder of Madero, he decided to delay recognition. He soon concluded that the Mexican dictator was presiding over a "government of butchers"; Huerta had overthrown a popular, constitutional government, and his regime lacked what

Wilson termed "constitutional legitimacy." The president, whose grasp of the reality of the revolution was hazy, assumed that all the factions would cooperate and that Huerta would, in effect, agree to remove himself from office. In early May, Wilson approved a scheme—one given to him by House—that would use American good offices to mediate between Huerta and the Constitutionalists and bring about fair, nationwide elections. House liked the idea of a presidential commission that would go "to Mexico and demand that the different factions unite sufficiently long to have an election and agree to abide by it."[26]

As the crisis in Mexico deepened in the early months of 1913, House followed events there closely, gathering information from American businessmen and journalists. The American businessmen with whom he visited urged the recognition of Huerta, warning that the failure of his regime would bring chaos. On May 2, when the president and House once again discussed Mexico, Wilson asked "whether I [House] thought intervention and war would be as bad as his Cabinet thought." House told him that he did not. He believed "that 50,000 men could do the work, but there would be considerable guerrilla warfare afterwards." Nor did House share Wilson's aversion to Huerta; he was concerned about maintaining order in one of the "waste places" of the earth so that the great powers could develop it.[27] His naïve nationalism was still uninformed by the messy reality of the great revolution south of the border.

When House and Loulie left for Great Britain on May 21, he was, he recorded, "very tired and slept a large part of the time during the voyage. I did but little and thought not at all."[28] His journey to London and Paris was in part a vacation, to recover from the long hours he had spent that winter helping to put together Wilson's administration, and in part an attempt to strengthen Anglo-American understanding and to lessen tension between Germany and Great Britain. In early February he had discussed with the president his idea of a "sympathetic understanding with England and Germany," but left no account of this conversation. On May 11, when House saw Wilson for the last time before his departure, he did not remind the president—who thought the trip abroad was essential for his friend's health—of the diplomatic purposes of his journey.[29] Whatever the reasons for House's reticence, he had not carefully prepared for his first mission to Europe.

For four days House rested in London, and on May 31 he traveled to Paris. During a leisurely thirteen-day stay there, House conferred with

Ambassador Myron T. Herrick, learning of the burdens and difficulties of an ambassadorial position in a major European capital. He also learned about the condition of the American consular service in Europe, concluding that "these posts are much more important than I realized." But he did not meet any leaders of the French government.[30]

On June 14, a well-rested House returned to London, where he and Loulie settled in for a more than three-week stay at the Stafford Hotel on St. James Place. The new American ambassador, Walter Hines Page, who had arrived on May 24, had already begun his ambassadorial duties. Page greeted his old friend effusively. A verbose and emotional man, Page told House of his social blunders and triumphs, of his worries over expenses, of his embarrassment over the shabby condition of the chancery of the American embassy (his place of work which the American government rented), and of his talks with Foreign Secretary Sir Edward Grey.[31]

Page and House, both ardent Anglophiles, also laid large if vague plans for the future, agreeing that they must formulate "some constructive policy that will make the President's administration and his [Page's] notable in the annals of this Embassy." While working to establish a special relationship with Page, House also continued his efforts to undermine the secretary of state. He confided to the new ambassador that "I did not believe that anyone outside of myself knew how thoroughly out of sympathy the President was with Mr. Bryan's excessive zeal for universal peace." House sought to establish himself as the president's primary foreign policy adviser.[32]

While House waited for a conference with the foreign secretary, he met with publishers, journalists, politicians, and aristocrats, discussing Liberal reforms, Irish home rule, labor conditions, and the personalities of leading politicians. Now that he was the president's adviser and special emissary, he easily expanded his network of friends and acquaintances in British society.[33]

On July 3, House's visit came to a climax when he and Page conferred with Grey over lunch at his home at 33 Eccleston Square. Page had set up the meeting, writing Grey that House "is 'the silent partner of President Wilson'—that is to say, he is the most trusted political adviser and the nearest friend of the President. He is a private citizen, a man without personal political ambition, a modest, quiet, even shy fellow . . . . But he is very eager to meet you."[34]

Grey had been foreign secretary since the Liberals assumed power in December 1905. A tall, melancholy country squire, his love of nature seemed greater than his love of politics, and he fled London on weekends to his fishing cottage on the river Itchen near Winchester. Prime Minister H. H. Asquith—absorbed in domestic affairs—gave Grey a free hand, and as his stay in office lengthened, the foreign secretary acquired great prestige at home and on the continent. He became a reassuring figure, noted for his candor and disinterestedness in dealing with foreign diplomats. But Grey's apparent straightforwardness hid an artful side; many Americans who fell under his spell missed the fact that he was an experienced political in-fighter with clear diplomatic priorities. Or, as two historians remark, he would "prove to be amazingly adroit in handling opposition and a master at silence and concealment."[35]

Grey had continued his predecessor's policy of ending Britain's international isolation, extending the Anglo-Japanese Alliance of 1902 and forming an entente with first France in 1904, then Russia in 1907. He assumed, along with most British leaders, "that Germany is our worst enemy and our greatest danger," and maneuvered to adjust the international balance of power so that Britain and its allies could contain rather than confront Germany. As part of this strategy, successive British governments had accepted America's dominance in the Western Hemisphere and had placed a high value on maintaining Anglo-American friendship.[36] Shortly before taking office, Grey had praised "the growing friendship and good feeling between ourselves and the United States." Over the years between this statement and his meeting with House in July 1913, this conviction had, if anything, deepened. Grey had favored Wilson—who had close ties with England—in the 1912 elections, and no doubt was eager to meet his confidential adviser.[37]

Grey appeared to open his mind to House, and soon the two men reached the issue that ostensibly was the purpose of House's mission—"the feeling between Germany and England." But this discussion quickly trailed off into vague generalities, and the two men proceeded to specific diplomatic controversies, discussing Japanese-American tension, the controversy over Panama tolls, and the turmoil in Mexico. On the first two issues, they covered familiar ground, but on Mexico House confused his own views with those of the president. House correctly emphasized Wilson's reluctance to intervene and his hope that the different factions would get together. But when Grey asked if the president "was opposed to any particular faction," House badly misstated Wilson's position, neglecting to mention the president's disgust with Huerta and claiming that the American government did not care which faction ruled, so long as order was maintained. House also minimized the difficulties of intervention, asserting that it would "not be as serious as most people thought." And continuing his efforts to undermine Bryan, he told Grey that "the President was not altogether *en rapport* with Mr. Bryan's peace plans."[38]

On July 8, House left Liverpool, arriving in Boston on the sixteenth. Fearful of the heat in New York and Washington, he traveled directly to his summer cottage at Beverly Cove, Massachusetts. He would not return to his apartment in New York until September 21 and would not see the president until he traveled to Washington in mid-October. During his stay in Paris and London, House wrote and telegraphed Wilson on a variety of matters, but gave him only a brief report on his conversation with Grey.[39] On his first trip abroad as the president's emissary, the vagueness of House's thoughts on international affairs, his misrepresentation of Wilson's position on Mexico, and his inability to follow through on his ideas, were all ominous portents for the future.[40]

9

The New Freedom

When Woodrow Wilson took office on March 4, 1913, the demand for domestic reform had reached a floodtide. In the years prior to his inauguration, the progressive movement—a varied and contradictory impulse—had swept across the nation, affecting both the Democratic and Republican parties and dominating the campaign of 1912. Americans in all walks of life, weary and impatient with society's ills, now searched for ways to come to grips with the waves of corporate growth, immigration, and industrialization that had fragmented the nation and threatened the values of democracy and opportunity. Most Americans now realized that only the federal government could deal with the problems of a continental nation.[1] Or, as Wilson declared in his inaugural address, the nation's mighty industrial achievements had come at a high human cost. The federal government, he promised, would now, under his leadership, "be put at the service of humanity, in safeguarding the health of the nation, the health of its men and its women and its children, as well as their rights in the struggle for existence."[2]

Soon after taking office, however, Wilson had to deal with a bitter controversy over race relations. Southern Democrats, who were in a majority in the cabinet and now in control of Congress, moved toward the segregation of African Americans in federal bureaus and agencies. Although the president had reached out to them during the campaign, he now allowed Burleson and McAdoo, who were in charge of the departments with the most black employees, to begin to segregate their workers and to remove black political appointees in the South. The segregation of federal departments brought strong protests from some northern Democrats, the National Association for the Advancement of Colored People, and the reformer Oswald Garrison Villard, the publisher of *The Nation* and the *New York Evening Post*. These protests, however, were ineffective, and during the Wilson years, as one historian remarks, civil servants were channeled "into a racially tiered system with less mobility and less money for black Washingtonians."

On this issue House offered no help to his friend in the White House. He had traditionally southern and paternalistic attitudes toward African Americans and in 1913 largely ignored the controversy, noting only that he and McAdoo discussed the "negro segregating question, about which Oswald Villard is raising so much foolish talk." House believed, as Philip Dru explains in the novel, that "we have placed his [the black man's] feet upon firm ground, and are leading him with helping hands along the road of opportunity."[3]

Nonetheless, Wilson fit House's model of an inspired progressive national leader. He was imperious and in command of the facts, with keen political instincts and an almost mystical identification with the American people; and he realized that the time was ripe to push through an ambitious agenda of domestic legislation. The Democratic Party, out of power for sixteen years, had a large majority in the House and a narrow one in the Senate; Democrats in the Congress were determined to prove that they could govern effectively, and most supported economic, political, and regulatory reform. In the years prior to Wilson's election, the party's tradition of states' rights and limited government had faded and Democrats had become what one historian terms "the party of reform."[4] Now, most Democrats were suspicious of great concentrations of wealth and power and had long supported tariff reduction, an income tax, banking and currency legislation, and stronger forms of corporate regulation. But their concept of change was limited; the New Freedom called for a restoration of conditions of equality and economic competition without the creation of a large federal government. The president's task was to work with Democrats in Congress, agree on an agenda, and then use party discipline and patronage to push through legislation. As he noted, members of his party followed him "because they see that I am attempting only to mediate their own thoughts and purposes . . . . They are using me; I am not driving them."[5]

Wilson moved first on tariff reform, calling a special session of Congress for April 7 that would run until the late summer of 1914. The next day, in a break with precedent, he addressed the Congress in person rather than have the clerk read his message. Convinced, like most members of his party, that the protective tariff was the mother of the trusts and that it was responsible for a sharp increase in the cost of living, the president rallied Democrats behind the Underwood Bill, which substantially reduced duties and included a modest income tax to make up for lost revenue. Wilson boldly led his party, going to the Capitol to consult with members of Congress and immersing himself in the details of the legislative battle. On May 8 the Underwood Bill passed the House by a lopsided margin, but in the Senate, where Democrats had only a majority of six, a united Republican opposition, along with a few Democratic defections, created some uncertainty about the outcome of the struggle. Throughout the summer, the president, who stayed in Washington, maneuvered to unify Democrats in the Senate and overcome Republican obstructionism. Finally on October 3, 1913, Wilson signed the Underwood Tariff Act. The president had achieved his first great legislative victory.[6]

Tariff reduction and banking and currency reform were closely linked, the core of the New Freedom; a lower tariff would free business from artificial restraints, while improvements in the banking and currency system would stabilize the economy and make credit available for economic expansion. For years, weaknesses in the nation's financial institutions had been widely recognized; they were decentralized and inflexible, unable to expand the money supply to meet seasonal needs or to prevent financial panics.[7] Banking and currency legislation, however, was far more difficult than a reduction of the tariff; the issues were complex and technical, powerful business and financial interests had diverse views, and popular passions ran deep in many parts of the country.[8]

After their triumph in November 1912, Wilson and Democratic Party leaders had debated ways to improve the nation's financial system and moved toward a new scheme of regional, reserve banks coordinated by a powerful Federal Reserve Board. This plan provided for the decentralization of credit—a key demand of progressives—but it left control of the board largely in the hands of private bankers. In May 1913, William Jennings Bryan objected, arguing passionately for public control of the reserve system and for the government issue of currency, while Louis D. Brandeis, a key adviser on domestic issues, and Secretary of the Treasury McAdoo convinced the president that attempts to appease the financial community would not succeed and that the government must manage the nation's money supply. Rethinking his position, on June 23, in another address to the Congress, Wilson put banking legislation on the agenda of the special session and declared that control of the banking system "must be public, not private, must be vested in the Government itself, so that the banks may be the instruments, not the masters, of business, and individual enterprise and initiative."[9]

During the winter of 1912–1913, House followed closely the currents of domestic reform. He strongly supported tariff reduction, congratulating the president on his tariff address to the Congress and urging him to push the Underwood Bill swiftly through the House and Senate.[10] House was far more concerned, however, about banking and currency legislation, talking with Wilson even before the November election and, after his triumph, sifting through proposals about the path to be taken. He conferred with prominent bankers, especially Paul Warburg, a partner in the investment firm of Kuhn, Loeb & Company; with Samuel Untermeyer, a New York lawyer who had been special counsel for the Pujo Committee (a House committee that probed the so-called money trust formed by Arsène Pujo of Louisiana); and with Democratic leaders in the House and Senate. By the end of November 1912, House decided that a powerful central bank largely under the control of bankers and businessmen provided the best solution.[11] House soon realized, however, that bankers could not be left in control of the new Federal Reserve Board, and that the president would have to accept a more decentralized system.[12] In meetings with New York bankers he defended the president's concessions to progressive Democrats, but on May 11, in his last meeting with Wilson before departing for Europe, he remained critical of Bryan. House believed that the government should "keep out of the banking business."[13]

During House's absence in Europe from May 21 to July 16 the Federal Reserve bill moved forward. Conservative bankers denounced it as a dangerous break from the past, tainted by, as one put it, the "slime of Bryanism," while agrarian Democrats in the House demanded more radical measures. The president made some concessions to bankers and, with Bryan's help, put down the revolt of southern and western Democrats.

In late August, House Democrats approved the Federal Reserve bill and made it a party measure. On September 18 it passed the lower chamber by a large margin.[14]

From London and Paris, House followed the progress of the bill with great interest. He continued to oppose government issue of the currency, but lost his patience with the "Wall Street bunch" and concluded that the bill, while flawed, was acceptable. On his return to the United States, he traveled directly to the North Shore, where he resumed his efforts to conciliate conservative opponents of the measure and to guarantee its passage.[15]

In the fall of 1913, the situation of the banking and currency bill in the Senate was confused. Most Democratic senators had closed ranks behind the president, but three of the seven who served on the Banking and Currency Committee joined with the Republican minority to conduct leisurely hearings in September and most of October. While frustrated by these tactics, Wilson consulted with Democratic leaders in the Senate and reached out to the three dissident Democrats on the committee.[16] During this delay, House continued to consult widely, confiding in his diary that "We are all getting our war paint on and will use all legitimate means to give the country the much needed currency reform."[17]

In early November the impasse on the committee was finally broken, and on December 19 a solid Democratic block, with one dissenter, defeated a substitute measure by a vote of 44 to 41 and then, with some Republican support, approved the Federal Reserve Act. On December 23 Wilson signed the bill, one which struck a delicate balance between private management and public supervision and which turned out to be the most enduring legislative achievement of his presidency. House was lavish in his praise, telegraphing the president that he had "carried to a successful conclusion the greatest measure of beneficent legislation that has been enacted during our generation and I need not tell you how happy I am to-day."[18] But House's role in this legislative drama, if measured by the standard set in *Philip Dru: Administrator*, had been disappointing. He had sided with conservative bankers, not with progressive reformers, and had therefore lagged behind the president and the more far-sighted members of his own party. Or perhaps, when writing his novel of the future, he had not carefully thought out his positions. In the first year of the New Freedom, House had emerged as a timid reformer.[19]

During the summer of 1913 the president stayed in Washington, leading Democratic forces in the Congress, while Ellen and his three daughters—Margaret, Jessie, and Eleanor—moved to Cornish, New Hampshire, living in a Georgian mansion with views across rolling meadows to the Connecticut River and enjoying the small colony of artists and musicians that resided there. "Here I am," Wilson wrote a friend, "marooned in the White House, alone in my majesty and discontent." The president would visit his beloved family only four times at its vacation retreat.[20]

While the president's family stayed in Cornish until mid-October, he pursued a solitary life in the White House. Wilson's navy doctor Cary Grayson moved in, as did Tumulty. The three men shared their meals, automobile rides, and games of golf, although Tumulty left on Sundays to spend time with his family. Wilson had of course known Tumulty since his campaign for the New Jersey governorship in 1910, but Grayson had joined the White House staff in March 1913. A young (he was only thirty-four), handsome, affable naval officer, Grayson had, on Taft's recommendation, become Wilson's personal physician. He monitored the president's health, putting him on a regular diet and a regime of daily exercise. Grayson also became one of the president's favorite companions.[21] In 1913, the president was fifty-six years old and appeared to be in good health. He seemed a physically fit man, with a round and firm neck and a quick gate. But in fact he suffered from frequent colds and digestive problems and from lingering blindness in his left eye (the result of a stroke in 1906). In April 1913, Wilson suffered a recurrence of pains in his right arm. Committed to maintaining the president's health, Grayson worried about a possible circulatory problem. But he was careful not to alarm the president and his family.[22]

By his first summer as president, Wilson's routines had crystallized; he organized his presidency, as one biographer remarks, "to preserve a central calm and to create a White House that was more of a sanctuary than a sounding board." Wilson rose at 8:00, ate breakfast at 8:30, and then went to his office, where from 9:00 to 10:00 he opened his mail and dictated replies. From 10:00 to 1:00 he received callers, who had to make an appointment through Tumulty (his only major staff assistant) and who were given only ten or fifteen minutes of the president's time. He lunched in the White House's private quarters with members of his family. At 2:00 or 2:30 he returned to his office for more work, but left by 4:00 to play golf with Grayson or take an automobile ride. Dinner was at 7:00 with family and sometimes a few friends, and then the president often went to the theater, or sang or read aloud from familiar books with his family or, if affairs of state pressed, worked in his study. Evenings at the White House were similar to evenings at Princeton. While Ellen and Woodrow engaged in some official entertaining, they made no attempt at cultural or intellectual patronage; they lived in the White House like a middle-class, intellectually and artistically inclined family that cherished its privacy and a small circle of relatives and friends. Rather than mingle with a wide range of people, the president spent many hours alone reading and thinking; his unusual solitude, while it concerned his advisers, gave him an inner calm and self-control that contributed to his remarkable political achievements.[23]

The president's inner circle consisted of his family and a few close friends, from whom he gained emotional sustenance, and from a group of political associates who assisted in advancing his domestic agenda. Tumulty, who had a warm relationship with the president and his family, tracked public opinion, gave political advice, helped draft speeches, and supervised relations with the press and Congress. Of the ten members of the cabinet, three stood out. Secretary of State Bryan played a crucial role, both in the conduct of diplomacy and as the leader of the progressive wing of the Democratic Party. Postmaster General Burleson, while personally conservative, used federal patronage to build support for the administration's policies in the Congress and the country. And Secretary of the Treasury McAdoo, the ablest man in the cabinet, was an advocate of expanded federal authority whose fierce drive for power led to clashes with other members of the administration. McAdoo's engagement to the president's youngest daughter, Eleanor, in March 1914, and their marriage in May, drew McAdoo deeper into the president's inner circle of advisers.[24]

In the unending struggle for preferment around the president, House had a unique position. He was both a close friend and a close adviser and, more than any of the others, could gain access to the president and influence his decisions. But from May 21 to July 8, House was in London and Paris, distant from the battles in Congress and from the constant maneuvering in Washington. Arriving on the SS *Laconia* in Boston on July 16, House motored to the North Shore, where he remained among the cool breezes and ocean vistas while the president suffered in the heat and humidity of Washington. House left the North Shore on September 19, arrived in New York on September 21, and did not see the president in Washington until the middle of October, a separation of nearly five months.[25]

During his long absence from Washington, various friends assured House of Wilson's continuing affection. His political legman Dudley Field Malone conveyed a message from the president, in which he stated that "Mr. House is my second personality. He is my independent self. His thoughts and mine are one," while his politically active friend Daisy Harriman reported that the president told her that "he had more confidence in my political judgment than he had in any man in the world."[26] On his return from Europe, House received a warm welcome from the White House, and in early September Wilson wrote that "I am fairly longing to see you." The president eagerly awaited the arrival of cool weather for a reunion with his counselor. In return, House was effusive in his compliments, congratulating him on his efficiency as a public man and reassuring him that "It is a splendid future that I see before you and God grant you strength to carry all your noble undertakings to completion."[27]

Once again the president tracked House's movements, and in late September House promised Wilson that he would soon travel to Washington. On October 14 he finally arrived for a two-night visit. But despite the president's wishes, House stayed with McAdoo rather than at the White House. The president, House noted in his diary, "greeted me very warmly, taking both hands to shake mine," and House learned from Grayson that Wilson "had a deep affection for me and often during the summer while I was gone he would say, 'my Grayson, but how I wish that dear fellow House was here.'" The two men discussed Wilson's health, the progress of banking and currency legislation, and relations with Mexico, but did not exchange the sort of intimacies that had marked many of their earlier meetings.[28]

Between this mid–October visit and the end of the year, House made up for lost time, making five trips to Washington, while Wilson traveled once to New York.[29] Only gradually did Wilson resume his earlier practice of confiding his deepest fears and feelings to House. On December 22, during his last visit of the year, House sought to encourage the president, speaking of his impressive political accomplishments. But Wilson was not easily reassured, for he worried about his early successes and said that "his Princeton experience hung over him sometimes like a nightmare; that he had wonderful success there, and all at once conditions changed and the troubles. . . were brought about. He seemed to fear that such a denouement might occur again." House could only point out that "there was a difference in dealing with the American people and a small clique of selfish millionaires." It was nearly midnight before the two men left the president's study for bed.[30]

House received a steady flow of political gossip from Burleson, Houston, McAdoo, and McReynolds, and he also sought to stay in touch with Bryan, the one member of the cabinet with a formidable following in the Democratic Party. House had been friendly with Bryan and his wife Mary for years, but after Bryan's appointment as secretary of state, House had, as we've seen, maneuvered to limit his influence with the president, often disparaging his judgment of men and his leadership of the State Department. There was, in fact, considerable duplicity in House's relationship with the secretary of state. With Bryan, as with others who sought his advice, House

radiated warmth and understanding, although in private he was often contemptuous of Bryan's abilities and lifestyle.[31]

In October, November, and December 1913, House and Bryan consulted
about a wide range of domestic and foreign policy issues. During one visit
to Washington, House stayed with the Bryans, enjoyed a family dinner
with them and their daughter Ruth, and accompanied a sick Bryan home
from the wedding of Francis Sayre and Wilson's daughter Jessie. Leaning
heavily on his old friend in their carriage, Bryan talked "of his life, of his
trials and of the future," expressing a "desire to die in harness and not to
live to a decrepit age." Early in December Bryan traveled to New York,
where House hosted a lunch at the Century Club "to introduce him to a
new element." Once again the two friends discussed personal matters, such
as Bryan's tendency "to take on flesh," his attempts to diet, and his political
future, and together rode the night train to Washington.[32]

While House pursued his ambivalent relationship with the secretary of
state, his admiration for the secretary of the treasury, or, as he called him,
"Chief," continued to grow. During the winter of 1912–1913 House had
grown close to McAdoo, and after his appointment watched with fascination McAdoo's emergence as the most forceful member of the cabinet. "For
five years," one biographer writes, "the Treasury resembled a giant battleship, constantly on the move and firing an endless barrage of new ideas and
projects into official Washington."[33] House and McAdoo often discussed
personal and political matters, and on August 17 McAdoo appeared off
Beverly, Massachusetts, in the revenue cutter *Androscoggin* to take House on
a cruise up the coast. That evening House concluded that McAdoo "has a
fine imagination, indomitable courage, and a touch of genius"; he believed
that McAdoo's energy, intellect, and progressive beliefs made him a man
of destiny. And House appreciated his friend's emotional dependence,
observing in late November that "He is as emotional as a woman. He said
he would rather be with me than any man in the world, and he acts as if he
meant it."[34]

Inevitably, House's intimacy with the president pulled him into controversies within his inner circle, particularly the growing tension between
McAdoo and Tumulty. Prior to Wilson's election, House had not known
Tumulty well, but in the aftermath of victory he had strongly urged his
appointment as the president's personal secretary. House anticipated that
he would be a valuable ally, but from the start he was uncertain of his loyalty, sensing that with Tumulty, in contrast with McAdoo, he did not have

any special rapport.[35] In fact, Tumulty was jealous of House's access to the president and sometimes tactless in dealing with others. After his return from Europe, House began hearing complaints from McAdoo and Grayson about the behavior of the president's secretary.[36] By the end of the year House had turned against Tumulty. "Tumulty talks too much," he complained in his diary. "The President desired a man of refinement and discretion and of broad vision. He has instead just the opposite and almost wholly at my instance . . . . Tumulty has good sense, but it is becoming warped by his growing egotism and jealousy concerning everyone near the President." And on January 22, 1914, during his last visit to Washington before leaving for Texas, he noted with pleasure news from Grayson that "there seems enough trouble brewing for Tumulty to drown him." House plotted Tumulty's downfall but concealed his animosity, knowing that he retained Wilson's affection and had daily access to his chief.[37]

In the meanwhile, throughout 1913 the bloody civil war in Mexico continued. Despite Wilson's and Bryan's efforts, Huerta desperately clung to power. For a time the United States pursued a policy of watchful waiting, but by late October Wilson contemplated more forceful measures, such as recognizing the Constitutionalists as belligerents so that they could obtain arms and ammunition, and possibly blocking Mexico's ports, cutting off revenues to Huerta's government. House encouraged Wilson's belligerency, praising him because "he was not only unafraid, but he did not look upon war in the same spirit as our Secretary of State, and he was not a man to be trifled with."[38]

Huerta's regime, however, endured, and by early 1914 Wilson decided that his only hope was to give the Constitutionalists diplomatic and moral support. House disliked recognizing the Constitutionalists but offered forceful advice: "I urged him to do what he could to settle the Mexican matter without intervention. I thought it would be the crowning glory of his administration if this could be brought about, and that it would add to his reputation throughout the world." After receiving assurances from Venustiano Carranza that his movement would respect foreign property rights, on January 31, 1914, the American government notified the powers that it was shifting its support to the Constitutionalists, lifting the embargo on the exportation of arms and ammunition into Mexico.[39] The president, with House's support, had dramatically changed American policy, in still another attempt to quiet the revolutionary whirlwind sweeping through Mexico.

House had last gone to Texas in the winter of 1911–1912, and his long absence from his home state had left his affairs there unsettled. But before leaving for Houston on January 30, 1914, he traveled to Washington twice, staying with Burleson during his first visit and at the White House during his second. During these two visits House consulted with Bryan, Burleson, Grayson, Houston, and McAdoo, discussing patronage, appointments to the new Federal Reserve Board, and Wilson's forthcoming anti-trust message to the Congress. During his second stay he had more contact with the president, one night talking with him until midnight. The next day, their official agenda completed, the two friends moved on to less urgent questions. As House recorded, "Whenever we have no governmental business to discuss, somehow or other, we drift into his life at Princeton and his troubles there, showing, as I have said before, how deeply the iron entered his soul." And Ellen, with whom House discussed family finances and other personal matters, thanked him "for 'being so good to us all.' "[40]

Just prior to House's departure for Texas, Wilson wrote that "it grieves me to see you go to even the distance of Texas. My thought and affection go with you. I thank God every day that I have so generous and disinterested a friend." Filled with renewed admiration for Wilson's political gifts, House replied, "I never forgot that but for you I should not have had the supreme joy that comes from effort in such a glorious cause." House knew that his fate could not be separated from that of Wilson.[41]

10

Reform and Intervention

On the long train ride home, House may have reflected on how many of his hopes had been realized since he had left for Texas almost two years earlier. Wilson had won the nomination and election, chosen House as his friend and confidential adviser, and pushed much of his reform agenda through Congress. Many of the dreams of House's "twilight years" had been fulfilled.

Within the new administration, House's native state had won a prominent position. Two Texans, Burleson and Houston, had joined Wilson's cabinet, and another member of "our crowd," Thomas Watt Gregory, would become attorney general in the summer of 1914. House and Burleson had funneled a stream of patronage to Texas, including the postmastership of Houston for House's older brother T. W. Jr. Texas Democrats had many reasons to be satisfied with Wilson's leadership.[1]

On his arrival in Houston on February 1, 1914, House found that "my friends and the town generally were after me." He declined all dinner invitations and left the next day for Galveston, but returned briefly on February 10 for a tour of his birthplace given by its prominent citizens. As House drove around he saw the many ways in which the "Bayou City" had been transformed since his days in Texas. In 1892, one Houstonian had complained that "Houston is the most dirty, slovenly, go-as-you please, vagabond appearing city of which I have knowledge," but by 1914 it had become a modern, prosperous community of around 80,000 people. The ship channel had finally been dredged to twenty-five feet, and Houston was a railway hub and a center for the cotton, lumber, and oil industries. It boasted substantial commercial buildings, miles of paved streets, an electric trolley system, and the beginnings of what would become important cultural institutions. It was clearly a city on the move.[2]

During his stay in Austin, Secretary of the Treasury McAdoo and Secretary of Agriculture Houston arrived to hold hearings on the location of the regional reserve banks. Bankers and businessmen from all over Texas poured into Austin to make the case for their hometowns, and House and Loulie gave a dinner party at 1704 West Avenue to honor their distinguished guests.[3] This was the last dinner that House would give in the imposing mansion that had been completed in 1892. On March 16, he sold the house that had been his home for over twenty years to a close friend, W. F. Ramsey, for $12,500 (far less than it had cost to build) and an unspecified amount of land and livestock in Cleburne, Texas.[4] It was the last home that House would ever own. Throughout the rest of his life he continued to rent an apartment in New York and a summer cottage in various North Shore villages. House left in place the furniture and other objects that adorned his large mansion. But he had to deal with his large collection of personal correspondence that went back thirty years. Rather than move it to New York, he and Fanny went "through thirty odd thousand old letters, culling out those that are to be saved and those that are to be burned." At a time when he was keeping a voluminous record of his political activities in Washington, he destroyed much of the record of his years in Texas politics.[5]

The main reason for House's trip to Texas was, as he readily admitted, to straighten out "my personal affairs which I have sadly neglected during the past two years." Prior to his involvement with Wilson and his administration, House had supplemented his regular income, but he no longer had the time or the inclination to do so. He noted in May 1913 that he had "spent twice as much last year" as my income, and in January 1914 was still worried about his personal finances. Part of the solution was the sale of 1704 West Avenue; the other part was to complete the sale of Monadale, despite his friendship with his longtime foreman, E. J. Barkley. From 1913 to 1916, House cut up his 1,215 acres into parcels ranging from 90 to 200 acres and sold them to various parties. Although Monadale had given House an income of $17,500 annually, it yielded an aggregate amount of $200,000, a very large sum for the time. But the sale of his mansion and of his prize farm left him with only scattered pieces of land in Texas and with far less personal involvement in the state.[6]

On March 20, House left Texas and arrived in Washington three days later for a two-night stay. During his long absence he had corresponded with the president and with others, but he was eager to catch up with affairs of state. House did not plan to stay at the White House, but during lunch with the president on his first day in Washington he found Wilson in a despondent mood, insisting that he send his bags over in the morning and spend another night so that they might have a "more connected talk." The second night, after dining alone, they retreated to the president's study, where they had "an old time business session." House was pleased with the results, as was Wilson, who wrote House after his departure that "It is delightful to have you so near again and to feel that we are in constant touch with each other."[7]

While House was in Washington, Ellen was ill and confined to her room. Neither the president nor his adviser realized that she suffered from Bright's disease, an infection of the kidney that would bring her death in early August 1914. During this visit House also received disturbing news about the president's condition. From the start of his relationship with Wilson, he had known that his friend's health was fragile. Now he learned from Grayson (who "tells me every thing concerning the President in the most minute detail in order to get my advice") that Wilson's medical problems were serious. Grayson, House recorded, "alarmed me somewhat by saying that the Philadelphia occulist, Dr. Swinehart [George E. de Schweinitz], who had had the President under his care for ten years or more, told him, Grayson, that there was some indication of the hardening of the arteries. The President does not know this, neither does any member of his family. It seems in 1905 the President had an almost complete breakdown at Princeton and it was uncertain whether he could resume his duties." House must have wondered how long his friend could survive the far greater stress of the presidency.[8]

In the early months of 1914 it seemed as if the New Freedom, like Wilson, had nearly reached its limits. The previous year had brought a reduction of the tariff, an income tax, and the creation of the Federal Reserve System. Only anti-trust legislation remained. On January 20, 1914, ten days before House had left for Texas, Wilson went before the Congress and asked for legislation—what would become known as the Clayton Bill—that would define and prohibit those practices that were in violation of the Sherman Antitrust Act. In the spring of 1914, as the struggle over the Clayton Bill progressed, Wilson, acting on the advice of Brandeis, shifted his ground, losing interest in the approach embodied in the Clayton Bill and moving toward the creation of a government agency, later known as the Federal Trade Commission, that would monitor the daily activities of big business and, through administrative regulation, assure the preservation of fair competition. In late September, Wilson signed the Trade Commission Act, and in mid-October a much-weakened Clayton Act. After a remarkable burst of legislation lasting only eighteen months, the New Freedom was complete.[9]

Some progressives, however, wanted more, urging on the president measures of social and economic reform, such as woman suffrage, the prohibition of child labor, a rural credit system, and stronger pro-union legislation. Other progressives had had enough reform and opposed projects for social amelioration or the creation of a more activist federal government. Wilson was cautious, partly because he had doubts about the wisdom of further reform measures, partly because he sensed that the reform impulse that had been on the rise for nearly a decade was beginning to recede. As one historian remarks, Wilson knew that he did not have "Roosevelt's instinct for self-dramatization, nor his hold on the popular imagination," and he was aware of the acute unrest and social conflict in many parts of the country. Finally, the president's advisers were also divided: Burleson, McReynolds, and Tumulty wanted to reassure frightened businessmen; Bryan and McAdoo wanted to press ahead with reform legislation. Buffeted by so many currents and cross-currents, Wilson decided to pursue a more cautious course, reaching out to business leaders and waiting until the congressional elections in November 1914 to test the mood of the nation.[10]

House had approved Wilson's anti-trust message to Congress on January 20, but he lost interest in the complicated disputes over anti-trust policy as various bills moved slowly through the Congress.[11] At times he seemed disturbed by the waning reform impulse, and he also worried about the political mood of the cabinet, complaining that Burleson, Garrison, and McReynolds were "leaning more and more toward conservatism . . . [while] the President and Mr. Bryan are about the only ones who are progressive, although Lane is so in certain directions and so is Houston, in spots."[12] House did not, however, urge further reforms on the president, accepting his conclusion that it was time to consolidate the gains of the New Freedom and to reassess the political landscape. In selecting members of the new Federal Reserve Board, Wilson rejected the advice of McAdoo, who wanted a progressive board that would work with him, and instead turned to House, who wanted a board that would win the confidence of the business community.[13] In the early months of 1914, House consulted widely among conservative banking circles, and in late April he and Wilson agreed on a board that would be representative of the nation's great financial and industrial interests.[14] When Wilson announced his nominees on May 4, many progressives were appalled, and the president, in the summer of 1914—while House was in Europe—had to fight a bitter and only partly successful battle in the Senate to win the confirmation of two of his most controversial choices.

In the late winter and spring of 1914, as Wilson struggled to complete the New Freedom, foreign policy remained a pressing concern, though not one to which he had devoted much attention. On January 26, Wilson finally took up the Panama tolls issue, seeking to build support in the Congress and among the public for the repeal of the exemption provision. In March the two Democratic Party leaders in the House, Champ Clark and Oscar W. Underwood, joined the opposition, and Wilson had to assert his leadership over Democratic ranks in the Congress and push through his repeal measure. In early June, with the Senate's passage of the Sims Bill, which repealed the exemption, the president had taken an important step in building Anglo-American understanding.[15]

The shifting currents of the Mexican revolution, however, remained the administration's most dangerous challenge abroad. By the end of January 1914, revolutionaries controlled more than half of Mexico and it seemed as if Carranza's most effective general, Francisco "Pancho" Villa and his powerful Division of the North, would soon sweep into Mexico City.[16] Despite diplomatic isolation and revolutionary advances, the Catholic Church, the propertied classes, and the officer corps rallied around Huerta's regime and the wily dictator clung to his hold on power. In March and April, Wilson searched for some way to intervene to bring Huerta down without risking a general war with Mexico.[17]

On April 9, however, an incident at the port city of Tampico, where Huerta's forces seized the crew of an American whaleboat, led the president to ask Congress for approval of punitive action. Armed with congressional consent, Wilson and his war council decided to seize the customs house at Veracruz and impound ammunition brought by a German steamer. On the late morning of April 21, American marines and sailors landed without opposition and occupied the customs house and other public buildings. Soon, however, the Mexican garrison opened fire, and until noon of the next day, when reinforced American forces overwhelmed the Mexican opposition, fierce fighting ensued. One hundred twenty-six Mexicans and nineteen Americans were dead. A wave of patriotism and anger swept through Mexico, and "First Chief" Carranza warned that the American invasion might "drag us into an unequal war . . . which until today we have desired to avoid." As events spun out of control, war with Mexico seemed certain.[18]

Wilson's advisers were divided. Secretary of War Lindley M. Garrison and army commanders wanted to start a general campaign against Mexico, including the dispatch of an expeditionary force from Veracruz to Mexico City; Bryan and Secretary of the Navy Josephus Daniels opposed sending American troops beyond Veracruz. Between April 22 and 25, Wilson decided to restrain the military and to accept mediation by Argentina, Brazil, and Chile. He was upset by the news of fighting and casualties, realized that he had blundered into hostilities and that the American public was divided, and feared that the Constitutionalist armies might join the anti-American tide sweeping through Mexico and bring clashes along the border. Wilson now abandoned his plan for large-scale military operations against Huerta and instead resolved to use the mediation effort to remove him from power and install a new, pro-American provisional government in Mexico City.[19] As Wilson struggled to gain control of the crisis, on April 26 House received a telegram from Grayson, urging him to come to Washington. House left the next morning, for he did "not like the President to be dependent upon Secretaries Bryan, Garrison, and Daniels as his war council. Garrison will do, but I cannot imagine worse advisers at this time than either Bryan or Daniels." But House and Wilson had only brief, indecisive discussions about Mexico and reached no firm conclusions. Wilson's acceptance of mediation the day before House arrived had eased the crisis and given the administration time to adjust its course in Mexico.[20]

After stopping in Washington on March 23 on his return from Texas, House saw the president four times before his departure for Europe on May 16, three times in Washington and once in New York. As House drew closer to the president, he continued to assess his strengths and weaknesses. He had no doubts about Wilson's intellectual gifts. "I am impressed," House wrote on April 17, "by the analytic qualities of his mind and the clearness with which he expresses his thoughts. I have come in contact with minds of greater initiative and imagination, but never one that had more analytical power and comprehension." But he complained about Wilson's reluctance to consult with his cabinet and with congressional leaders, and occasionally encouraged him, without success, to broaden his range of advisers.[21]

House continued to serve as a kind of companion for the president. The two men ate meals together, went to the theater, and wandered through the White House, studying various objects. House did not play golf, but he did agree to walk the links with Wilson, noticing that Grayson did not play "as well as he could." The president pressed House to conform to his routines, demanding that he sleep at the White House and lengthen his stays in Washington.[22] House was virtually a member of the Wilson family, forming close personal ties with Ellen and with Wilson's daughters and members of his extended family. Wilson's cousin Helen Bones told Loulie that " 'When Uncle Woodrow and the Colonel are together the families feel the country is safe, and that nothing can happen.' "[23]

During Wilson's May 11 visit to New York, where he marched in a procession in honor of the men who died at Veracruz and spoke at the Brooklyn Navy Yard, House worried about the president's safety. "I always," he revealed in his diary, "carry a six shooter when the President is with me for I feel I could be of more protection to him than the Secret Service . . . . I shoot quickly and accurately and without aim further than looking at the object." After returning from golf at the Piping Rock Club on Long Island, Wilson, House, and Grayson dined alone at House's apartment. After dinner, Grayson left and Wilson read aloud from the poems of two of his favorite English poets, Matthew Arnold and William Wordsworth. Only then did the two men turn to official business. They would not see each other again until the end of August.[24]

While House was away in Texas, his dissatisfaction with Tumulty continued. House's friend Hugh C. Wallace, a wealthy, well-connected businessman, reported that he heard "complaints and denunciation" of the "scrubby Irishman" and "gutter snipe" on all sides. House differed with Tumulty over patronage in New York, where Tumulty favored working with party regulars, and over the direction of the administration's domestic policies. On the surface, House's relations with the president's secretary remained cordial; beneath the surface, however, House worked to replace him. But on May 11, when House once again sought to measure the president's devotion to his secretary, he discovered that Wilson "seemed upset over the idea of losing Tumulty," a skilled political operator who had been at his side for many years.[25]

House also continued his ambivalent relationship with Bryan, discussing domestic and foreign affairs with the secretary of state but also maneuvering to limit his influence with the president. House listened to Bryan's

many critics within the administration, sometimes defending his contribution to Wilson's legislative program, sometimes portraying him as a spoils
man with "no patience with the civil service." When Bryan discovered
that House was promoting his protégé, William "Billy" Phillips, a career
diplomat and Boston Brahmin, for an administrative position in the State
Department, he complained that " 'I am certain Phillips is one of those
supercilious persons who will constantly be looking down upon me.' "
Nonetheless, House persisted in the advancement of his young friend, and
in February convinced Wilson to appoint Phillips third assistant secretary of state (replacing Dudley Field Malone, who had resigned to become
Collector of the Port of New York). He was determined to have an ally in a
key State Department position.[26]

McAdoo remained House's closest contact. Throughout the late winter
and spring of 1914, he and McAdoo, despite their differences over appointments to the Federal Reserve Board, remained close friends and political
allies. McAdoo's was a powerful progressive voice within the administration and was a valuable source of information on intrigues around the
president. And he remained emotionally dependent on House. On March
3, McAdoo wrote his absent friend with the news that he was going to
marry one of Wilson's daughters. "Miss Eleanor and I are engaged! The
'Governor' has consented and I am supremely happy. Isn't it wonderful?
The days of miracles are not yet over or she never would have accepted me."
McAdoo was euphoric. "I can only tell you," he confided to House, "that
I am in a state of ecstasy and I want you to share in the knowledge of my joy.
I can't write on any other topic tonight . . . . I miss you fearfully."[27]

For the next two months McAdoo, understandably, was preoccupied with his personal affairs. On March 27, McAdoo and House spent
a morning together in New York "selecting his trousseau [sic], in which
he shows as much enthusiasm as a boy," and in the evening Edward and
Loulie gave a dinner party for McAdoo and Eleanor at the Ritz Hotel. As
McAdoo pondered the implications of his forthcoming marriage, he realized that it would change his relationship with the president. "He begins
to see," House noted perceptively, "the other side of being the President's
son-in-law." On May 7, House traveled to Washington to attend McAdoo
and Eleanor's wedding in the White House, a late-afternoon service that
he found "simple and very beautiful." He knew, through Grayson, how
deeply Wilson felt about his favorite daughter's marriage (especially to a
man twenty-six years older) and how he "does not want her to leave him."

After the service, when McAdoo and Eleanor left the White House, all the wedding guests followed them to the South Porch except Wilson and House. House stayed with his friend, sensing that "he seemed to lack the heart to see the last of her. I think he loves her better than any member of his household."[28]

House continued to formulate his foreign policy ambitions. In early July 1913, during his stay in London, House had talked with British Foreign Secretary Sir Edward Grey, seeking to lay the groundwork for a future understanding between England and Germany. House's conversations with Grey were vague, but after his return to the United States in mid-July he began preparations for another trip to Europe. He cultivated German Ambassador Johann von Bernstorff and Austro-Hungarian Ambassador Constantin Dumba, and urged the new American ambassador to Germany, James W. Gerard, to "do something more than walk through the part."[29] House also drew closer to Walter Hines Page, the American ambassador to London, whose cooperation was essential if he was to form a special relationship with British leaders. House listened to Page's complaints about Bryan and the State Department, encouraged the president to read Page's long letters, and shared with Page his plans for a grand disarmament scheme in Europe and "a sympathetic alliance between the two great English speaking countries."[30] House's grandiose vision excited Page, who believed that "the English speaking fold must rule the world." "You have," he wrote House in early January 1914, "set my imagination on fire." Page helped House with housing in London, arranged for Loulie to be presented at Court, and prepared the way with British leaders for his next European mission. It was an odd partnership—Page, loud and assertive; House, quiet and unobtrusive—but in 1913 and 1914 the two seemed to share similar goals and joined together to reshape the international system.[31]

In early 1914, House accelerated his preparations for another diplomatic mission to Europe. On January 1, 1914, he lunched with Benjamin Ide Wheeler, president of the University of California, who had just returned from a trip to Germany, where he had "spent hours with him [the kaiser] and his family." House was pleased with the meeting, convinced that he received "nearly all the information I need regarding the Kaiser and his entourage." Wheeler was optimistic about House's prospects for an Anglo-German disarmament agreement, but warned that Grand Admiral Tirpitz would be an obstacle, and confided that he and the kaiser had agreed that a major conflict had been narrowly averted during the Balkan crisis of

March 1912–1913. As the historian Christopher Clark notes, "the conflicts in the Balkan theatre became tightly intertwined with the geopolitics of the European system."[32]

These rumblings of a European war, still faint in America, only added a sense of urgency to what House came to term his "Great Adventure."[33] However, he did not talk with the president about his plan for "international disarmament" and his proposed trip to Germany until mid-December 1913, when Wilson gave the project "his warm approval and cooperation." He returned to the subject during his visit to Washington in mid-April 1914, recording that the president "considered it of such vast importance that it was worth while to try." Armed with the president's approval, House decided to leave for Germany on May 16.[34]

When Wilson visited House in New York on May 11—their last conversation prior to House's departure—House asked the president to write a letter of farewell that would "show our relationship." Wilson quickly agreed, writing that "It is hard to say goodbye, but knowing what I do it is delightful to think of what awaits you on the other side, and it is particularly heartening to me to know that I have such a friend and spokesman."[35]

II

"The Great Adventure"

On May 16, 1914, Edward and Loulie, accompanied by their friends Hugh and Mildred Wallace, boarded the SS *Imperator* for their voyage to Cuxhaven, Germany. The dock was crowded with well-wishers witnessing the departure of the great liner, and House's cabin was filled with books, fruit, and flowers sent by friends. Two months and ten days shy of his fifty-sixth birthday, House was described by one journalist as "a slender, middle-aged man with a gray, close-cropped moustache, well-dressed, calm-looking." Once under way, he wrote excitedly to his confidante Fanny Denton, "I am ready for Berlin and the great adventure. No matter how unsuccessful, not even an Emperor can take from me the joy I have had in looking at the stars."[1]

After a "featureless voyage" with clear skies and summer seas, on May 24 House arrived in Berlin. He spent a week there, staying with Ambassador James W. Gerard at the "delightfully situated" American Embassy. Berlin was a bustling metropolis of four million people, the third largest city in Europe after London and Paris, and the political and economic center of the German empire. Over the years the emperor had ordered the destruction of much of the city's inner core in order to give what he termed a "dowdy wasteland" more of a sense of dignity and history. The result was the construction of great squares, modern boulevards, massive public buildings, and large monuments and heroic sculptures. It was in this rapidly changing city that House first encountered the leaders of Wilhelmine Germany.[2]

On the evening of May 26, Gerard brought together twenty-five German dignitaries for dinner at the American Embassy. The president's emissary was the center of attention, standing in the middle of the drawing room for two hours, talking with the leaders of the German government.[3] House spent the bulk of the evening conversing with Foreign Minister Gottlieb von Jagow and Grand Admiral Alfred von Tirpitz. He dismissed Jagow, a small, frail official of limited influence, as "in the second rank," a "clever diplomat without much personality." But Tirpitz, with his white, forked beard, bald head, and fierce gaze, was a formidable figure, one who had the ear of the kaiser (as Wilhelm II was popularly known) and a large following in the Reichstag and among the German people. He was the founder of the modern German navy, a believer in the battleship and in the command of the seas, convinced that Great Britain was Germany's "most dangerous" enemy.[4] With Jagow and Tirpitz, as well as with the other German leaders he would soon meet at Potsdam, House spoke of the "courage and charac- ter" of Wilson and drew a clear distinction between the president and his secretary of state. "I wanted," he recorded, "official Germany to know that if any international complications arose between our two countries, they would have to deal with a man of iron courage and inflexible will."[5]

House was, unsurprisingly, especially eager to engage Tirpitz, "the most forceful man in Germany, excepting the kaiser," "the quintessence of the war spirit." The grand admiral was blunt with House, insisting on the need for "the highest possible order of military and naval organization" in order to "put fear into the hearts of her [Germany's] enemies." Tirpitz and other German leaders, House noted, realized that Great Britain "holds the bal- ance of power" on the continent and wanted "England to detach herself from the Triple Entente and become neutral."[6] House pleaded with Tirpitz for arms limitation, warning of the dangers of his naval program. But the grand admiral had no interest in reassessing his belief in the importance of seapower for Germany; nor did he have any faith that an Anglo-German understanding could be reached. He was, House noted, "the most anti-English of any of the German officials with whom I talked."[7]

Tirpitz's belligerence shocked House. Two days later, reporting to the president on the encounter, he warned that "the situation is extraordinary. It is jingoism run stark mad. Unless someone acting for you can bring about a different understanding, there is some day to be an awful cataclysm. No one in Europe can do it. There is too much hatred, too many jealousies. Whenever England consents, France and Russia will close in on Germany and Austria." And in a prophetic conclusion, he told Wilson that maintain- ing the peace of Europe "is an absorbing problem, and one of tremendous consequence. I wish it might be solved and to the everlasting glory of your Administration and our American civilization."[8]

On June 1, House and Gerard set off for Potsdam for their much-anticipated meeting with Wilhelm II. Dressed in black evening dress ("like two black crows," the kaiser joked, a little maliciously), they were painfully out of place amid the splendor of the emperor's court. After entering the Palace, they realized that they were the only guests invited to the Schrippenfest, an elaborate ceremony led by the kaiser to honor the common soldiers of the German army, one that involved religious exercises, a parade, decorations, and a lunch in the famous Shell Hall (its walls consisted of sea shells set in plaster). House was pleased that he and Gerard were given the seats of honor, directly across from the emperor and empress and the royal family. Before and during lunch he talked with War Minister Erich von Falkenhayn and with Arthur Zimmermann, the undersecretary of state for Foreign Affairs. At the end of lunch, House was presented to the empress; then the kaiser summoned the two Americans and Zimmermann to the terrace, where, while the ambassador and undersecretary stepped back, House and the emperor fell into a "very animated" conversation for half an hour, "both of us talking at one another in quick succession."[9]

The kaiser, fond of sweeping generalities, denounced England's alliance with "semi-barbarous" "Latins and Slavs," asserted that "England, Germany, and the United States [were] . . . the only hope of advancing Christian civilization," and urged that all Western civilization "should stand together as against the Oriental race." He declared his friendship for England, insisted that Germany must have a large navy "commensurate with her growing power and importance," and "spoke of the impossibility of Great Britain being able to make a permanent and satisfactory alliance with either Russia or France." Joining in this *tour d'horizon*, House spoke of "the awakening of Japan," emphasized Germany's role in holding Russia "in check," and argued, as he had with Tirpitz, that Germany's enormous army and growing navy made an Anglo-German understanding impossible and threatened the peace of Europe. House believed that if only the naval race could be ended, the "community of interests between England, Germany, and the United States" could maintain the peace of the world.[10]

As their conversation drew to a close, House finally got to the purpose of his mission, explaining that he and the president had thought that an American might be able to mediate among the great powers. The next step, House continued, was to travel to London, where he would pursue his peace initiative with leaders of the British government. But he reassured the kaiser that he would proceed "cautiously" and, if he wished it, keep him informed. The kaiser "asked me to do this," suggesting that letters could reach him through Zimmerman in the Foreign Office. After the conversation ended, House and Gerard returned to Berlin.[11]

Confronted with the kaiser's charm and apparent moderation, House's earlier pessimism gave way to renewed hope. The day after his visit to Potsdam he left Berlin for Paris; once there, he urged Ambassador Page in London to "work quickly" and prepare the way for the next stage of his trip.[12] He also reported to the president on his talk with the kaiser, claiming that he had been successful and now planned to pursue a bold scheme (which he had not mentioned to the kaiser) to arrange a high-level meeting between himself, Grey, and Wilhelm II. And he wrote his journalist friend Edward Martin that "the great adventure about which I spoke to you is well under way and next week I take up the London end. So far, I have been successful beyond my expectations, but of course the end is nowhere in sight for the moment."[13]

House's belief that he might draw the kaiser into a summit meeting revealed how little he understood about the Byzantine workings of the German Reich. Wilhelm II had become emperor in 1888, when he was only twenty-nine, and by 1914 had ruled Germany for twenty-six years. He was a striking figure on the world stage, the very model of a warrior prince, with his withered left arm, brilliant uniforms, and "brushy mustache with extended, upturned points." On first impression, the kaiser seemed a dazzling personality, charming and conversant in many different subjects. But as one of his aides remarked, "Oh that he could reign so well as he can speak." Those who looked deeper realized that he was a flawed monarch—boastful, impetuous, restless, and self-centered. The kaiser was not, in short, completely in control of himself, and he lacked the emotional stability and self-confidence to rule effectively. His views often reflected those of the last strong person he had seen. As his uncle, Edward VII of England, remarked, Wilhelm II was a "splendid failure."[14]

The kaiser had, to be sure, sweeping authority in the foreign and military realms. He possessed the power to declare war, was the supreme commander of the armed forces, and received reports directly from the chief of the general staff and the chief of the naval staff. But Imperial Chancellor Theobald von Bethmann Hollweg, whom House had not met because of the death of Hollweg's wife, had wide executive powers and control over the Foreign Ministry and other civilian agencies. He and the emperor in effect split the responsibility for German foreign policy.[15] In the decades before the war, tension in Germany had mounted between the quasi-absolutist monarchical system and a society that was undergoing rapid urbanization and industrialization. The growing strength of the Social Democratic Party, which in the 1912 elections became the largest party in the popularly elected Reichstag, revealed the extent of the political impasse. As Bethmann Hollweg sought to stand above political parties and bypass the Reichstag, he became more and more dependent on non-parliamentary forces in the army, the court, and the bureaucracy. These conservative elites, alarmed by the leftward drift of German politics and fearful for the monarchical system, had no intention of allowing a gradual evolution into a parliamentary system of government. On the eve of World War I, domestic politics in Germany had reached an ominous deadlock, what one historian terms a "profound internal crisis."[16]

After his interview with the kaiser, House was eager to travel to Paris, where he and Loulie arrived on June 2. Edward, Loulie, and the Wallaces, now joined by Fanny, stayed at the Ritz Hotel. House spent a "quiet" week in Paris, declining all invitations to dinner and luncheons except those from Ambassador Herrick. He seemed uninterested in Paris, a city that for two centuries had had an important place in the American imagination and one that many, both Parisians and foreigners, regarded as the cultural capital of the world. "I was in Paris for a few days," he wrote his friend McAdoo, "but did nothing there worth while excepting to get you a necktie to match the suit I helped you select." Like the American novelist Henry James, House preferred life in London.[17]

House made no attempt to contact the leaders of the Third Republic, President Raymond Poincaré and Premier and Foreign Minister René Viviani. A cabinet crisis that followed the formation of Viviani's center-left government in May, along with the spectacular trial of the wife of the former premier Joseph Caillaux, Henriette Caillaux, who had shot and killed the editor of the newspaper Le Figaro, absorbed the French people and their leaders. House apparently concluded that discussions with Poincaré and Viviani would be impossible.[18]

Loulie and Mildred Wallace left Paris for London on June 3, six days before House followed them. Ambassador Page had arranged for them, along with his own wife, to be presented at court. One June 6, Loulie appeared before the king and queen dressed in a "Nile-green chiffon gown, embroidered with pearls and rhinestones." Her husband was relieved that he could stay behind and ponder the next phase of his "great adventure."[19]

When House crossed the Channel on June 9 he remained alarmed about the imminent prospect of war. He did not share the mood, so prevalent in European capitals in the spring and early summer of 1914, that no conflict among the great powers was on the horizon. Reporting on his visit to Germany, House informed Secretary of State Bryan that "I have never seen the war spirit so nurtured and so glorified as it is there." He was eager to pursue his peace plan on the more familiar terrain of London.[20]

After arriving in London, House, Loulie, and Fanny settled into the Berkeley Hotel on Belgrave Square for a stay that would last until their departure six weeks later. House enjoyed his life in London. With over seven million people, London was the largest and richest city in the world, the hub of a great empire, a royal seat, a cultural mecca, an international port, and a financial and commercial center. In contrast to Paris, it was an unplanned city, but it did have great public buildings such as the Foreign Office in Whitehall and the Palace of Westminster, and a vitality and cosmopolitanism that drew people to it.[21] House picked up where he had left off in the summer of 1913, renewing and expanding his contacts with the British ruling elite, meeting a long list of people who could provide insights into British politics and society.[22] He also renewed his friendship with Ambassador Page, who had now served over a year in London. House had kept the ambassador informed of his activities in Germany and, during their first lunch, the two men plotted their strategy in England. They would approach Foreign Secretary Grey first and "leave it to his judgment whether to bring in [Prime Minister] Asquith and the king." Page was extravagant in his praise of House, telling him that "he considered my work in Germany the most important done in this generation." The ambassador sought to advance House's agenda, although Page was also more realistic than House, doubting in mid-June that "the British government would be in a position to negotiate with Germany." In general, however, he was an enthusiastic partner, contemplating, as his biographer notes, "a central role for himself in pursuing the colonel's initiative."[23]

As House's stay lengthened, he started to grow irritated with Page, who seemed reluctant to accept the role of junior partner in pursuit of the "great adventure." House preferred to be alone with British leaders, explaining that they "will talk more freely and I will be more upon my mettle." He also noted in his diary several of Page's indiscretions, warning "how likely he is to get into trouble before his term of office expires." Despite these irritations, however, the ambassador remained an important part of House's diplomatic mission, and by July 1914, Page had decided, with House's encouragement, to stay on for another year.[24]

House arrived in London at the height of the social season, and at a time when a series of domestic crises confronted Asquith's Liberal cabinet. The government faced serious industrial unrest, an aggressive suffragette movement, controversies over the implementation of its social programs, and a bitter debate over Home Rule for Ireland that threatened, in the summer of 1914, to lead to civil war there. But House did not seem upset over the fact that, as he reported to the president, "I find here everything cluttered up with social affairs and it is impossible to work quickly." His "great adventure" had to wait until it could be fitted into the busy schedule of the foreign secretary.[25]

On June 17, over a week after his arrival, House had a two-hour lunch with Page, Grey, and his influential private secretary, William Tyrrell. Grey and House did most of the talking. House was convinced, he told Grey, that "French statesmen had given up all idea of revenge and of the recovery of Alsace and Lorraine." He now urged Britain to "permit Germany to aid in the development of Persia [present-day Iran]" and warned of "the militant war spirit in Germany and of the high tension of the people." He feared that "some spark might be fanned into a blaze. I thought Germany would strike quickly when she moved. That there would be no parley or discussions." Both men spoke of the "difficulties of bringing about negotiations [between England and Germany]. I suggested that the Kaiser, he and I meet at Kiel in some way, but this was not gone into further." Grey had somehow managed to slip away from House's risky proposal for a high-level conference.[26] In turn, the foreign secretary praised Wilson for the Panama Tolls repeal, explained the importance of a "good understanding" between Britain and Russia, and seemed intrigued by House's assertion—which Britain's entrance into World War I would soon validate—"that the time had come when England could protect herself no longer merely because of her isolated position," that she should, in fact, think of herself as a continental power.[27]

The results of this first meeting pleased House. He was impressed with how far he had advanced his peace plan in the last year and now saw himself affecting the fate of the world, convinced that "every government. . . may be more or less affected by the moves we are making."[28]

On June 24 House had his second lunch with Grey, one that included Tyrrell, Richard Haldane, the Lord Chancellor, and Lord Crewe, secretary of state for India. In a rambling two-hour discussion, the group covered "industrial conditions" in America and Europe and the situation in Mexico. House defended Wilson's Mexican policy and also brought up a proposal for "an understanding between the United States, Great Britain, Germany and France regarding the undeveloped countries of the earth." All agreed that House, Page, Tyrrell, and Spring-Rice should try to work out "something" to present to the president.[29]

In a report to Wilson written two days later, House noted that Grey had told him "that there was no written agreement between England, France and Russia and their understanding was one merely of sympathy and the determination to conserve the interests of one another." But House did not press his British friend about the nature of the Triple Entente or the extent of Britain's commitment to France. He now felt no sense of urgency in advancing his peace proposal.[30]

House's second lunch with Grey on June 24 was his last face-to-face encounter with the foreign secretary. As Grey became more elusive, he communicated with House through his private secretary. On July 3, House learned from Tyrrell that the foreign secretary would not give "any written message to the Kaiser," but he also learned from Page that Grey had talked with the German ambassador and "had sent messages direct to the Kaiser concerning the bringing about of a better understanding between the two countries, and the countries of Europe along the lines suggested by me."[31] Two days after his talk with Grey and his colleagues on June 26, House had gone to Chancellor of the Exchequer David Lloyd George's office for breakfast. The energetic, unconventional chancellor had led the way in moving Britain toward a welfare democracy since his appointment in 1908. Tyrrell, no doubt at Grey's urging, had warned House that Lloyd George was "an uneducated man, a man who reads not at all, but who obtained his information from others." House found Lloyd George a "most agreeable personality," but concluded that he was "lamentably ignorant of the workings of our governmental system."[32]

In early July, House joined Prime Minister Asquith and his wife Margot, along with nine other guests, for lunch at number ten Downing Street. Asquith, who would turn sixty-two in September, had served as prime minister since 1908 and had led the Liberal Party in a remarkable period of domestic reform. He was a swift worker who, in the ample time he set aside for relaxation, enjoyed golf, cards, alcohol, and feminine society, and who wore conventional clothes in a baggy and careless way. But his disheveled appearance was misleading, for he was a patient, wily leader who "ruled by postponement." He left the initiative to his ministers and especially gave his foreign secretary free rein in the conduct of diplomacy.[33]

Asquith appreciated House's importance, and after lunch he and his American guest talked privately for fifteen or twenty minutes. House was impressed with the prime minister, who had a "very keen and incisive mind and is one of the biggest men I have met on this side," and was pleased with the warm welcome he had received from the leaders of the Liberal government. As he wrote his friend Edward Martin, "the Great Adventure is progressing finely and my visit over here has justified itself."[34]

As House's proposal for an Anglo-German understanding and summit meeting stalled, he turned to his scheme for an agreement among the great powers for the development of the "waste places of the earth." The pursuit of this plan had not been a part of House's original mission, and only in a letter of July 4 did he explain it to Wilson. Convinced that the president would approve this initiative and "ask me to push it as far as possible," House confided to Mezes that "I am doing that anyway confident of his cooperation." House's willingness to exceed his instructions could one day lead to serious friction with the president.[35] Nonetheless, encouraged by Grey, House sought to find a way to move toward an understanding over the development of "weaker and undeveloped nations." After two discussions with Page and Spring-Rice, however, the three men decided that nothing more should be done until House returned to the United States and reported to the president.[36]

On June 28, 1914, a Serbian terrorist assassinated Archduke Franz Ferdinand, the heir to the Austro-Hungarian throne, in Sarajevo, the capital of the province of Bosnia. House made no mention of this event in his diary or in letters written at the time. But that evening his friend Daisy Harriman, who was visiting in London, recorded that "Colonel House was the only one [at the dinner party] who seemed gravely concerned about the assassination of the Austro-Hungarian heir-presumptive, in some little Bosnian town."[37]

The assassination of Franz Ferdinand set off a crisis that slowly gathered momentum. Leaders in Vienna, fearful for the survival of their sprawling, multi-national empire and convinced that they now had an opportunity to "settle accounts" with Serbia, were eager to attack that nation. They would end what Chief of the General Staff Franz Baron Conrad Hotzendorf termed "this foul peace which drags on and on." But they dared not move without the support of their ally in Berlin; only German backing could prevent Russian intervention—Russia being a staunch ally of the Serbs—and keep the crisis localized. On July 5, an Austrian diplomat dispatched to Berlin found Wilhelm II and his advisers in a bellicose mood. The kaiser assured the Austrian government that Russia was "in no way prepared for war" and promised that "should war between Austria-Hungary and Russia prove unavoidable," Germany would stand at its ally's side. Armed with this "blank cheque" from Berlin, officials in Vienna soon resolved on war against Serbia, a conflict that would hopefully end its expansionist agitation and leave Austria-Hungary the dominant political force in the Balkans. Despite German pressure for speedy action, however, Foreign Minister Leopold Berchtold and his colleagues were slow to resolve internal disputes and decide on the contents of their ultimatum to Belgrade, which was not delivered until the evening of July 23.[38]

German leaders, like their counterparts in Vienna, were concerned that time was running out for their nation. They felt Germany was in a precarious position, encircled by the Triple Entente and especially threatened in the east by Russia's growing economic and military strength. Russia, Chancellor Bethmann Hollweg warned, "grows and grows and weighs on us like a nightmare," while Chief of Staff Helmuth von Moltke argued that "to wait any longer meant a diminishing of our chances." Germany's army hierarchy was eager for war; Bethmann Hollweg and civilian leaders reasoned that the July crisis presented a unique opportunity for their beleaguered nation. If the Triple Entente powers stood aside and allowed Austria to punish Serbia, Germany and its ally would win a great diplomatic victory and weaken if not destroy the bond between France, Great Britain, and Russia. If, on the other hand, the crisis expanded into a general European war, they believed that Germany would emerge victorious and establish its hegemony on the continent of Europe. Their strategy was, as Bethmann Hollweg remarked, a "calculated risk," one that held out the hope of victory, as one historian remarks, "either on the field of battle or at the conference table."[39]

Throughout these deliberations in July, a brooding, fatalistic mood hung over leaders in Berlin and Vienna, as if they were being overwhelmed by historical forces beyond their control. At the height of the July crisis, Bethmann Hollweg reflected that "A fate beyond human power hangs over Europe and our *Volk*," while Emperor Franz Joseph asserted that "If we must go under, we better go under decently." Both governments preferred to strike now rather than watch the slow decline of their nation's position in Europe.[40]

Russia's rulers also felt that despite the impressive growth of their nation's economic and military strength in the years before the war its strategic position was imperiled. Leaders in St. Petersburg were suspicious of Germany's intentions and, all along the borderlands of Russia's vast empire, saw threats from hostile powers. In crises in the Balkans in 1909 and 1912–1913, Russia had been humiliated, and Austria's ultimatum to Serbia, if successful, would further erode Russia's standing as a great power. Members of Russia's ruling elite were also preoccupied with a fear of internal upheaval. Some conservatives argued that war would bring revolution, but Foreign Minister Sergei Sazonov rejected this analysis and warned the czar that if he failed to support Serbia he risked "revolution and the loss of his throne."

The July crisis also presented Russia with opportunities to assemble a powerful coalition and to fight a war that would enable the nation to realize some of its imperial ambitions. For the czar and his advisers, who were convinced that the Austro-Hungarian and Ottoman Empires were near collapse, war offered the prospect of gaining Austrian Galicia and, if Turkey became involved, winning control of Constantinople and the Straits. In the July crisis, Russia's rulers, one historian observes, "would not shrink from going to war to improve her precarious position in a hostile international environment."[41]

Russia's ally France played a secondary role in the July crisis. For decades, leaders of the Third Republic had been determined to regain Alsace and Lorraine, which they had lost to Germany during the humiliating war of 1870, prepare France for a new war with Germany, and regain their nation's position as a great power. The Russian alliance, which the French hoped would deter Germany through the threat of an unwinnable two-front war, was a key part of this policy, as were French attempts to draw Great Britain into a closer relationship. President Raymond Poincaré, who dominated the government, realized that if war came he could unify his country and gain British support only if France appeared to be on the defensive. On July 16, Poincaré and his inexperienced prime minister and foreign minister, René Viviani, sailed for Russia for a long-planned state visit. In talks with Russian officials in St. Petersburg they agreed that there must be no infringement of Serbia's sovereignty. Only on July 30, after Poincaré and Viviani returned to Paris, did they telegram St. Petersburg, warning Russian Foreign Minister Sazonov not to escalate the crisis. But Poincaré's belated attempt to restrain France's ally came too late; the Russian government had already decided on general mobilization. As one historian notes, "the preservation of the Entente was a more important objective in French foreign policy than the avoidance of war."[42]

By early August, Poincaré knew that France had no choice but to accept war with Germany. In a letter addressed to the Chamber of Deputies and the nation, he emphasized the peacefulness of France and proclaimed that "nothing will break the Union Sacrée in the face of the enemy." Most of the French people, although they faced war with a kind of grim resolve, agreed with their president that the conflict had been forced on France by brutal and unprovoked German aggression.[43]

For most of July, while the crisis simmered, Prime Minister Asquith and his ministers found it difficult to take its measure. As early as July 11 Grey conveyed to House through Ambassador Page that he "was much disturbed about the Russia-Austria-Serbia complication, and was afraid something serious might grow out of it," and on July 20, the day before House's departure, Grey sent another message through Tyrrell "that the Austria-Serbia situation was giving him grave concern."[44] But Grey did not expect the dispute to lead to a European war. Unaware of the determination of governments in Vienna and Berlin to risk a general war, the foreign secretary sought to find a way to mediate Austria's quarrel with Serbia.[45]

On July 24, after reading Austria's ultimatum to Serbia, Grey declared that it was "the most formidable document that was ever addressed from one state to another." Despite the drift toward war, many observers in Great Britain still saw their nation as detached from events on the continent. After a cabinet discussion of the Austrian ultimatum, Asquith wrote King George V that Europe was close to a major conflict, but that as far as Britain was concerned "Happily there seems to be no reason why we should be anything more than spectators."[46]

Grey felt differently from most of his cabinet colleagues. As early as 1903 he had warned of the German danger, and in 1911 he wrote of a "Napoleonic" threat to Europe in which Germany, if it became dominant on the continent, would eventually challenge Britain's maritime supremacy. During his years in office Grey had presided over the transformation of the Anglo-French Entente—which had begun as an attempt to settle quarrels outside of Europe—into what was a de facto defensive alliance, and he had assured the French, though not in writing, that Britain would help them resist German aggression. If Grey's views prevailed, Britain would not stand

aside if Germany launched a struggle for supremacy in Europe. But Grey's
fear of Germany, and his enthusiasm for the entente with France, were not
shared by the majority of the Liberal cabinet. It was by no means clear what
Britain's response would be to the outbreak of a continental war.[47]

By early July, House had more or less completed the British phase of his
"great adventure." He had lunched with Grey twice, met with Lloyd
George and Asquith, and realized that the foreign secretary would not join
him and the kaiser in a summit meeting at Kiel or even give him a written
message to forward to the German emperor. He lingered on in London
until July 21, apparently more concerned about the danger of civil war
in Ireland than about the standoff between Austria and Serbia (which he
continued to ignore in his diary and letters). On July 21, House departed
from Liverpool on board the SS *Franconia* and, after an uneventful voyage, reached Boston on July 29. On his arrival he learned that Austria had
declared war on Serbia at noon on July 28.[48]

Throughout his stay in Berlin, Paris, and London, House had written
Wilson often, reporting on his conversations with European statesmen and
giving his assessment of the situation there, and Page had reassured the
president that British leaders were "all charmed" by House, whose journey
to Europe was a "very substantial triumph." But Wilson seemed disengaged from House's mission; he did not press him for more precise information about great-power diplomacy. House letters from Paris gave the
president "a thrill of deep pleasure," while letters from London led him to
hope that House was "getting lots of fun and pleasure out of these things"
and to reassure him that "It is perfectly delightful to read your letters and to
realize what you are accomplishing. I have no comments except praise and
self-congratulation that I have such a friend." Even House's promise that
Wilson could become "the world figure of your time . . . the prophet of a
new day" did not appear to interest the president.[49]

After landing in Boston, House drove to Prides Crossing on the North
Shore, where he planned to spend the rest of the summer. The day after his
arrival, however, the Austrian declaration of war against Serbia led House
to write Wilson a long letter, defending his accomplishments in Europe
and claiming that, if war came, he would be in a unique position to undertake another mission to Europe.[50] House's self-serving letter underscored
both the strengths and weaknesses of his approach to the crisis in Europe.
As early as 1913 he had, alone among Wilson's advisers, recognized the

gathering storm clouds and through his two trips in 1913 and 1914 had sought to learn about the rivalries among the great powers, gotten to know their leaders, and tried to figure out how he and Wilson might ease the tension between Germany and Great Britain. But his preparations for high-level diplomacy had been careless, and during his "great adventure" he overemphasized person-to-person contacts, exaggerated his accomplishments, and engaged in wishful thinking rather than analyze the larger historical forces that shaped the behavior of British and German leaders. By late July 1914, on the eve of war, House had only begun his education in European politics and diplomacy.

PART III

The Great War, 1914–1917

12

America and World War I

The Austro-Hungarian declaration of war against Serbia on July 28 set off a chain reaction of mobilizations and declarations among the great powers. The German government, confronted with Russian mobilization and a two-front war, moved quickly to gain an edge over its enemies. On August 1, Germany declared war against Russia; on August 2, German patrols crossed the French frontier and Germany delivered a twelve-hour ultimatum to Belgium, demanding that its government give German troops free passage across its territory; and on August 3, Germany declared war against France. Officials in Berlin felt a combination of relief and excitement. In the Prussian War Office, one general recorded, "Everywhere beaming faces, shaking of hands in the corridors; one congratulates one's self for having taken the hurdle."[1]

As events spiraled out of control on the continent, the British government stood aside; within the cabinet there was no clear majority for war, even if Germany attacked France. But the German violation of Belgium's neutrality, long guaranteed by the great powers, united the cabinet, the Liberal Party, and the nation behind a British declaration of war against Germany on August 4. German policy, Grey told the cabinet, was "that of the great European aggressor, as bad as Napoleon." British leaders felt that their nation's security was at risk. If Britain did not intervene and Austria-Hungary and Germany won the conflict, the continental balance of power would be destroyed; if France and Russia prevailed while Britain stood aside, British interests both on the continent and on the borders of its empire would be imperiled. As one historian remarks, "British intervention on the side of the Entente offered a means both of appeasing and tethering Russia and of opposing and containing Germany." By midnight on August 4, five empires—Austria-Hungary, France, Germany, Great Britain, and Russia—were at war.[2] Millions of men mustered to the colors across the continent to take their place in the complex mobilization schemes that dispatched thousands of trains loaded with young men and horses and equipment to various fronts. House's friend Daisy Harriman, traveling from Carlsbad, Germany, to Paris, noted in her diary that "All afternoon we saw from the car-window interminable lines of troops marching, gray uniforms winding like a great writhing serpent over white roads between the yellow wheat and rye."[3]

Few Americans thought a great war would break out in Europe. A few, such as former diplomat Lewis Einstein, who published an article in the *National Review,* predicted a conflict among the great powers, but most Americans believed in the supremacy of law and reason. Secretary of State Bryan, one of the leaders of the prewar peace movement, caught the popular mood when he predicted in 1913 that there would be no more wars in his lifetime. He was pleased that by August 1914 he had secured the ratification of twenty cooling-off treaties (which required the signatories to delay going to war) between the United States and other nations.[4] As a result, during most of the summer of 1914 the State Department was in a somnolent mood. American diplomats took their normal vacations and had not been alarmed over the assassination of Franz Ferdinand on June 28. Ambassador Gerard had assured House, then still in England, on July 7 that Berlin "is as quiet as the grave." The outbreak of war surprised both the Department of State and American diplomats serving in Europe.[5]

The president was shocked by the eruption of what he termed "this incredible European catastrophe." In late May, House had, as we've seen, warned him of the rampant militarism in Germany, but during the remainder of his stay in Europe, House had himself lost his sense of urgency about the outbreak of war and as late as August 1 remained optimistic about the prospects for peace. "It is evident," House informed Wilson, "that England is laying a restraining hand upon France and is urging Germany to do the same with Austria."[6] On August 3, with Britain's declaration of war against Germany imminent, Wilson realized that House's prediction was wrong. Seeking to calm public opinion, the president held a press conference in which he emphasized the nation's aloofness from the conflict. The next day, against House's advice, Wilson sent a note to the European powers, informing them that he would "welcome the opportunity to act in the interest of European peace." Responding to the public's expectation that he make a peace move, Wilson explained to his "dear friend" that "I took the risk and sent the messages to the heads of the several countries. It can, at least, do no harm."[7]

House seemed genuinely stunned by the collapse of the balance of power in Europe. "The general European war," he wrote the day after Britain's declaration of war against Germany, "is of such staggering proportions and of such epoch making consequences that I have not attempted to keep the diary from day to day."[8] Speculating that the Allies would triumph, he reasoned that it would be in "the interest of England, America and civilization to have her [Germany's] integrity preserved, shorn however of her military and naval power." He now alerted Page in London and Gerard in Berlin to the possibility of an American peace move. If peace came quickly, House believed that it should be based on a guarantee of all the belligerents' territorial integrity and a general plan of disarmament. He hoped to end the conflict soon after it had begun.[9]

Throughout the summer of 1914, Ellen Wilson's health worsened. On July 23, as she faded, Cary Grayson moved into the room next to her bedroom while the president sat by her side until the early hours of the morning. On August 4, Grayson told Wilson to summon his daughters; two days later, his beloved wife died at 5 o'clock in the afternoon. "God has stricken me," Wilson wrote a friend, "almost beyond what I can bear." With the great love of his life dead, Wilson's private universe crumbled and for several weeks, as the war in Europe accelerated, he was nearly paralyzed with grief.[10]

The news of Ellen's death shook House. The day after she died, House wrote his friend, "I never dreamed that Mrs. Wilson was so mortally ill and her death leaves me unnerved and stunned. It only proves again how near to us the Angel of Death hovers." He reminded Wilson that he was the leader of a great nation in "an epoch making time" and urged him to show "splendid courage" in dealing with this personal tragedy.[11] Ellen's death intensified their desire to end their long separation; they had not seen each other since May 11. "I simply must see you soon and am thinking every day how to manage it," wrote the president. In late August, when Wilson left the heat of Washington for Harlakenden, the summer home that he and Ellen had rented near Cornish, New Hampshire, House decided to meet the president there. On August 29, House and his son-in-law Gordon Auchincloss left Boston's North Shore for Cornish, driving through a terrible rain and arriving the next morning.[12]

House was impressed with Harlakenden, with its sweeping view of the Connecticut River and its "comfortable and artistic" furnishings. It reminded him of an English country house. He stayed in the room that Ellen had occupied, one that shared a common bathroom with the president's bedroom. For two days, the two men renewed their friendship. The president read aloud, told "humorous stories" about golf, reminisced about his Princeton days, and asserted that "he had a great desire to be let alone after he left office." On the second afternoon of House's stay, Wilson's grief finally broke through to the surface and "he began to talk of Mrs. Wilson and of what her loss meant to him personally. Tears came into his eyes, and he said he felt like a machine that had run down, and there was nothing left in him worth while." Wilson also showed House "photographs of her, read poems written about her, and talked of her as freely as if she were alive." As always, House listened sympathetically, seeking to relieve his friend's grief and loneliness.[13]

The president and his adviser also discussed events in Europe. Curious about the personalities of European leaders, Wilson listened as House "told him of my experiences in Europe and gave him more of the details of my mission." While House did "most of the talking," the president also spoke "with deep feeling of the war," which he thought "would throw the world back three or four centuries." Wilson was "scornful of Germany's disregard of treaty obligations," "felt deeply the [German] destruction of Louvain [Belgium's leading university town]," and condemned Germany's role in the war, asserting that "German philosophy was essentially selfish and lacking in spirituality." Wilson and House also speculated about the future. The president believed that "if Germany won it would change the course of our civilization and make the United States a military nation"; he thought that "eventually there might be but two great nations in the world, Russia, on the one hand, and this country on the other." House concluded that "there would be three, China dominating Asia, Russia dominating Europe, and a part of Asia, and America dominating the Western world and perhaps the English speaking colonies." The president, with guidance from House, was now beginning to consider the way in which World War I might change the geopolitical landscape. House reminded Wilson that he would have the opportunity "few men had been given" to right the wrongs of the past and to lead the way toward a more humane world. Wilson was not hopeful, but House "tried to make him see that reforms were going forward with much more celerity than heretofore" and that public opinion, if properly mobilized, could become a powerful force for good.

Their last morning together both men planned to get up early, Wilson to play golf before departing for Washington, House to leave for the North Shore. The president rose half an hour earlier than he had to in order to give his friend the use of their common bathroom. "This illustrates," House recorded, ". . . his consideration for others and the simplicity of the man." It was, House concluded, "a pleasant and profitable visit and one which I shall long remember."[14]

During his stay abroad, House had tried to keep up with the struggle for preferment taking place around the president. Letters from McAdoo covered a wide range of issues and reminded the "Dear Colonel" "how much we all love you." "I miss you terribly," McAdoo confided to House, "& wish you would let me know when you are coming back." Letters from Hugh Wallace described intrigues—especially the activities of "Irish" (Tumulty)—and mentioned a conversation with the president, who "told me to give you his love." And letters from Gordon Auchincloss conveyed still more gossip from Washington, including reassurances that both McAdoo and Grayson remained House's loyal friends.[15]

Cary Grayson, who did not write House during his absence, spent far more time with Wilson than anyone else and monitored closely the president's physical and emotional health.[16] Grayson kept his absent "dear friend" informed about the trip to Rome, Georgia (where Ellen was buried), and about Wilson's continuing affection for him.[17] Finally on August 20, Grayson poured out his anxieties in a long letter and revealed the terrible strain that he had been under as Ellen's death approached. Grayson had been caught in a difficult position: he knew that Ellen was dying but dared not tell the president, who was in denial almost until the end. As the pressure mounted, Grayson wrote, "I longed for you many, many times. I went to our dear and true friend, McAdoo, and told him all."[18] At the end of August, Grayson had accompanied Wilson to Harlakenden. When House arrived, the young physician gave him "all the mischievous, petty, White House gossip. It seems impossible for the President to escape espionage concerning his most intimate personal affairs." Whatever House's reservations about this gossip, he collected as much of it as possible in order to remain Wilson's most influential adviser.[19]

During August, while House enjoyed the cool breezes at Pride's Crossing, a stream of visitors brought him up to date on affairs of state.[20] He especially worried about the fate of one of the original members of "our crowd," Thomas Watt Gregory, who had become a special assistant to Attorney General McReynolds to press anti-monopoly charges against the New York, New Haven, & Hartford Railroad. Once in Washington, Gregory impressed the president with his railway prosecution; in July 1914, after the death of Supreme Court justice Horace Harmon Lurton, House urged the president to move McReynolds to the high court and to appoint Gregory as his successor. While his fifty-two-year-old friend was torn by ambivalence,[21] House dismissed his friend's anxieties, and on August 10, during Gregory's visit to Prides Crossing, convinced him to accept the position if the president offered it. On August 19, Wilson sent Gregory's name to the Senate without consulting him. Gregory felt a fierce loyalty to the president, convinced that he "stands out before my vision as the most gigantic figure of the present," and also felt gratitude toward his "very best friend." "The mere knowledge of this fact [his friendship with House] has wonderfully comforted me in hours of pain & depression. Outside of my wife & children that friendship is by far my most valued possession."[22]

In August, House was also caught up with the vicissitudes of the Mexican revolution. During the summer of 1914, while he was in Europe, the mediation effort of Argentina, Brazil, and Chile had failed; American troops stayed in Veracruz, and Carranza's forces continued their advance on Mexico City. On July 15, Huerta finally resigned and left Mexico for exile in Europe; in mid-August Constitutionalist armies entered the capital city, followed a few days later by the first chief. Sitting tall and erect on a fine horse, Carranza rode through streets lined with cheering crowds and soldiers. It seemed as if the Mexican revolution had entered a more stable phase.[23] By the time Carranza and his armies occupied Mexico City, however, their star had begun to fade. His generals were divided and confused, and Constitutionalist authority was defied by Zapata and his agrarian revolutionaries in Morelos province, and by Pancho Villa and his powerful Division of the North in Chihuahua province. Villa, who appeared to welcome American guidance, convinced Wilson and Bryan that he was a genuine reformer and offered the best hope for the Mexican revolution. During his stay at Harlakenden, House talked with Wilson briefly about events in Mexico. They agreed that "Villa is the only man of force now in sight in Mexico." But House, absorbed in the war in Europe, gave little attention to the confused evolution of the Mexican revolution. In the fall, Villa continued to gather strength, Carranza withdrew from Mexico City, and observers in Washington concluded that Villa would soon establish military supremacy and become the new ruler of Mexico.[24]

Meanwhile, during the early weeks of the European war, German arms were triumphant everywhere. In the east, where German forces stood on the defensive, the numerically superior Russian army, which mobilized quicker than the German General Staff expected, poured into east Prussia. But after the German commander in the east was relieved, his successors, General Paul von Hindenberg and his chief of staff Erich Ludendorff, devised a bold gamble to outflank their enemy. By the end of the month, after dramatic victories at Tannenberg and Masurian Lakes, two Russian army corps were destroyed, two were badly mauled, and the surviving Russian soldiers fled back across the border. Hindenberg became the war's first hero.[25]

In the west, German forces crossed the border into Belgium, overwhelmed the great fortress at Liege, and on August 20 occupied Brussels. Now two German armies advanced in a broad band across the center of Belgium and soon swept west and southwest into France. They were carrying out the Schlieffen Plan, which called for a pincers movement to overwhelm Paris, with one army attacking from the west and another from the east. German prewar planners had calculated that once Paris fell, French resistance would collapse, Great Britain would withdraw from the war, and Germany would transfer its forces to the east and inflict a similar defeat on Russia. During the early weeks of the war it looked as if the German plan would succeed; the kaiser, sure victory was near, predicted that "within two weeks I will be able to send my troops home." Unable to halt the German advance, the French army and the British Expeditionary Force, which had reached the continent in mid-August, retreated toward the Marne River. On September 2 the French government left Paris for Bordeaux and tens of thousands of Parisians followed it to the south. The next day, elements of the German army reached the outskirts of Paris.[26]

On September 5, the Battle of the Marne began: 1,275,000 German troops faced 1,000,000 French and 125,000 British soldiers. Anglo-French forces now rallied to avoid a catastrophic defeat; German troops, worn down by weeks of marching and fighting in the blazing summer heat, were exhausted and at the end of their supply lines. After four days of combat, Germany armies began to pull back to avert a severe defeat and to prepare a line of fortifications on ground of their own choosing. The first phase of the war in the west was over. The German campaign plan, which had assumed a swift and decisive victory by the fortieth day of mobilization, had failed. After mid-September, the new German commander in the west, Erich von Falkenhayn, sought to prevent a stalemate by reinforcing his right wing and overrunning the Allies' left flank in Flanders, cutting off the cross-Channel supply lines of the British army. This race to the sea, the second decisive phase of the war in the west, lasted until late November, when the German offensive to break through to the North Sea and the channel coast failed. The war of rapid movement in the west now ended.

In south and central Europe, the Austro-Hungarian army soon proved to be a far less effective fighting force than its German ally. An Austro-Hungarian offensive against Serbia, launched on August 12, soon ended in defeat, while in late August Austro-Hungarian and Russian forces clashed along a 200-mile front in Galicia. The result was another Austro-Hungarian defeat, one that put Austrian Galicia in Russian hands and that left the Carpathian passes leading down to the Hungarian plain and to Budapest poorly defended. This ended the hopes of Austrian chief of staff Franz Baron Conrad Hotzendorf for a short, triumphant war.[27]

During the early months of the war, casualties had been heavy, as commanders on both sides, committed to offensive operations, discovered the difficulty of attacking positions defended by modern rifles, machine guns, and barbed wire. Throughout Europe armies became exhausted and short of supplies, confronting the possibility of a long war for which they were not prepared. On the Western Front they began to dig in, and gradually a parallel line of trenches emerged, separated by a no-man's-land of 200 to 1,000 yards that stretched from the North Sea to the frontier of Switzerland. At the end of the year the French army controlled only seventy-seven of the republic's ninety departments; the Germany army remained in occupation of areas that were vital to France's economy. As German troops dug deep beneath the surface and constructed a front line of formidable strength, they settled in for a long stay while their high command transferred elite units to the east. Neither the Allies nor the Central Powers had any plan for victory, and the war had spread beyond Europe, engulfing Africa, East Asia, and the Middle East. Five months after its outbreak, the struggle for supremacy in Europe had become a world war.[28]

Few Americans believed that the United States had any vital interest in the struggle or that it would ever be drawn into the conflict. But the president, worried about extremists on either side (in 1910 nearly one-third of Americans were foreign-born), on August 18 reminded his "fellow countrymen" that "the United States must be neutral in fact as well as in name during these days that are to try men's souls." He also soon realized that the war had had a dramatic impact on the nation, stranding 30,000 Americans on the continent and in Great Britain, bringing a stock market crisis, disrupting overseas markets, and ending the foreign demand for important American commodities such as copper and cotton. Only vigorous action by the president and Secretary of the Treasury McAdoo headed off panic and set in motion a variety of plans designed to protect the American economy from the disruptions brought by the European war.[29] The war also forced the president and his advisers to sort through the accumulation of treaties and precedents that defined relations among neutrals and belligerents and to work out a series of specific policies. Complex issues arose over loans to belligerents, the sale of munitions and other arms, and the definitions of blockade and contraband of war. In general, the American government wanted the largest possible freedom of trade with the belligerents, while the British government wanted to cut off the flow of supplies to the Central Powers. The president, preoccupied by domestic issues and depressed after the death of his wife, initially left most of the decisions about American neutrality to Secretary of State Bryan and to Robert Lansing, who had become counselor of the State Department in April 1914. After some early confusion, they moved the nation, with Wilson's increasing involvement, toward an acceptance of the British maritime system.[30]

Removed from these debates in Washington, House hoped to find a way to bring an end to the war. Through his trips to Europe in 1913 and 1914 he seemed the obvious agent for any American peace move. He knew, however, that Bryan desperately wanted to end the war. The Great Commoner sought to bring peace at any time on any terms and urged Wilson almost daily to take steps to stop the fighting. For a time, in early September, it seemed as if Bryan had taken over the American mediation effort.[31] But by September 16, when House arrived in New York, Bryan's efforts had floundered. A few days earlier Bryan left for a vacation in Asheville, North Carolina, and for the remainder of September and all of October he was away from Washington supporting Democratic candidates in the fall congressional campaign.[32]

As House pondered an American peace move, he began to have sustained contact with the two key ambassadors in Washington, Bernstorff and Spring-Rice. Bernstorff was an experienced career diplomat who had served in Washington since the summer of 1908. Proper and self-assured, he spoke perfect English and seemed to many American officials both suave and crafty. He knew the United States well, understood its enormous economic power, and from the start of the war urged his superiors in Berlin—with whom he had little influence—not to underestimate America's potential impact on the conflict.[33] Like his German antagonist, British ambassador Spring-Rice had a wide range of American connections. As a young man he had been stationed in Washington during the 1880s and 1890s, when he had become close friends with Theodore Roosevelt and Senator Henry Cabot Lodge. A witty, scholarly man, one journalist described him as "a neat, compact figure, [with a] gray suit, pale face, short-grizzled beard, and keen, kindly eyes behind steel-rimmed spectacles." Spring-Rice had arrived in Washington in March 1913, but soon became seriously ill and did not take up his duties until December of that year. While Spring-Rice was close to Grey, he was nervous, irritable, and highly patriotic, an erratic but often perceptive observer of the American scene.[34]

Two days after House arrived in New York, on September 18, he met with both ambassadors, eager to discuss with each the prospects for peace. Bernstorff agreed to meet with his British counterpart, but Spring-Rice would not agree to meet with his German adversary, insisting that "the time was not ripe for peace proposals." He reminded House that Britain could not begin secret negotiations without the approval of its allies. House was impressed with the British ambassador, who was, he observed, "quite different than Bernstorff, in that he is frank and honest, and is a high-minded scholarly gentleman." When House asked if he should go to Europe "at this time," Spring-Rice encouraged him to go "a little later, or. . . at the psychological time." And he urged House to travel to Germany first.

During this meeting House outlined in more detail than before his views on a "satisfactory outcome" to the European war. Germany, he thought, must indemnify Belgium, accept general disarmament, and agree to return Alsace to France. Poland should become an independent nation, the Austro-Hungarian empire should be dismantled, the Dardanelles should be open to all nations, and Russia should have an "open port" on the Baltic. House argued that "Britain should not take any big gamble in this conflict. If she could get disarmament and compensation for Belgium, she had better accept it and not risk the stupendous consequences of defeat." And if the Allies won and crushed Germany, "there would be no holding Russia back, and the past situation would hardly be less promising than the future." As the passions of war grew, House remained a voice of reason, urging a limited victory and a compromise peace. But caught between the resistance of the British ambassador and the optimism of his German counterpart, even a diplomat as resourceful as House could not discover a way to move forward.[35]

With his peace initiative stalled, House decided to travel to Washington, his first visit since early May. Arriving at Union Station late on the afternoon of September 27, he was met by McAdoo and his wife, Eleanor, who then joined him at the White House for dinner with the president. After dinner a large package of papers marked "urgent" arrived from the State Department, and the McAdoos and other members of the president's family left so that he and House could get "down to work." The package included a long letter of instruction from Counselor Lansing to Ambassador Page, directing him to protest Great Britain's refusal to accept the Declaration of London, a code of maritime warfare approved by an international conference held in London in 1908–1909. The Declaration consisted of an elaborate set of rules, favorable to neutral trade during wartime, that would have severely restricted Britain's ability to control trade with Germany. In late August the British government, which had never accepted the Declaration, had announced that it would make certain crucial modifications of it in order to pursue its economic warfare against Germany. With Bryan absent on the campaign hustings, Lansing had decided that the time had come for a strong assertion of American rights and a sweeping denunciation of the emerging British system of maritime warfare.[36]

House was taken aback by the severity of Lansing's language, which he found "exceedingly undiplomatic," and urged Wilson not to send the message. He immediately realized that the dispatch of such a note would bring a crisis in Anglo-American relations and disrupt his plans for American mediation of the war. Wilson agreed, telling Lansing to delay the dispatch of the letter and deciding that House should discuss the matter with Spring-Rice. "After this," he recorded, "we went to bed pretty tired and somewhat worried."[37]

After conferring with Spring-Rice, House rushed back to the White House, where he and the president agreed that Lansing should redraft and shorten his note. The new dispatch, sent to London on September 28, was briefer and used less forceful language, but still reaffirmed the American position. The president was, like House, eager to avoid a public controversy and to pursue negotiations in a friendly way. Throughout October the two governments sparred over the Declaration of London but failed to reach any agreement, and by the end of the month the United States tacitly accepted the British maritime system, reserving its right to protest.

Whatever American objections to British orders-in-council, they were based on international law and did not seriously harm American economic interests.[38]

House's main purpose in traveling to Washington, however, was to devise some plan to end the war. But neither he nor the president "could see exactly how he [Wilson] could inject himself into the foreign situation in regard to peace at this time." If the war ended in a stalemate, they thought a peace conference might meet in Washington, or that the United States might send a peace commission abroad. They agreed, House recorded with pleasure, "that I should keep the matter in my hands and advise him what was being done." House was now, so it seemed, firmly in control of the mediation effort and could make certain that it would not disrupt Anglo-American relations. House worried that the Allies would put off peace negotiations and that it would be necessary for the United States to pressure them. "This could be done," he assured the president, "indirectly through me so as not to make it quite official." House then informed Wilson of Bernstorff's assertion that Germany "was ready to discuss peace measures" and suggested that he ought to travel to London to discuss terms with British leaders. But Wilson discouraged a journey to London; his rejection of his peace mission irritated House, who now complained that the president was, as he wrote in his diary, "singularly lacking in appreciation of the importance of this European crisis. He seems more interested in domestic affairs, and I find it difficult to get his attention centered upon the one big question."[39]

Prior to House's departure for Washington, Grayson had unexpectedly appeared at his apartment in New York and stayed for dinner. As always, he brought news of the president and of the tensions within his inner circle of advisers. When House had left Cornish after his late August visit, Wilson, Grayson confided to him, had said: "I am thankful for such a friend. If there were more like him we would not need government." House also learned that the president suffered "from indigestion and he thought one cause of it was that McAdoo and Tumulty persisted in talking business to him during his meals." House accepted the unenviable task of urging his friend McAdoo to exercise restraint.[40]

House could not avoid the question of whether Wilson would run for a second term, a question that was complicated by uncertainties about the president's health. Still depressed by Ellen's death, Wilson freely shared his doubts with his counselor, claiming that "if he knew he would not have to stand for re-election two years from now, he would feel a great load had been lifted from him." House wondered what he could do with his life that would be so interesting; Wilson had no answer but "feared that the country would expect him to continue as he had up to now, which would be impossible." House did not believe that the nation expected additional domestic achievements, reminding his friend once again that he could add to his fame through a foreign policy that "would bring him world-wide recognition."[41]

Bryan's and McAdoo's presidential ambitions complicated the question of a second term. By September 1914, Bryan seemed reconciled to Wilson's renomination in 1916, but McAdoo, as House realized, was restless and ambitious. His great abilities had made him the most powerful member of the cabinet and, even before his marriage to Eleanor, he had enjoyed informal access to the president. During his stay in Washington, House informed McAdoo that "his chances [of becoming president] had materially lessened since he became the President's son-in-law," since the American people would not approve of "anything that looked like [a] succession." House reassured him that he had already become one of the greatest secretaries of the treasury in the nation's history, and argued that his best chance for winning the White House would be "by doing his job better than anyone had done it before."[42]

McAdoo's discontent, however, continued to disrupt Wilson's inner circle. On October 20, McAdoo told House that he had been offered the presidency of the Metropolitan Life Insurance Company, at a salary of $85,000. Torn by "conflicting desires," he asked House what he should do; he could not imagine staying in office six years longer, and if convinced that Wilson would run for a second term would take the Metropolitan Life offer. "McAdoo has the Presidential bee firmly fixed," as House put it, and believed Wilson would not run in 1916. "I did not tell him," he confided to his diary, "that I see every indication of this fact [that Wilson would run for reelection]. People in office often delude themselves, and I believe the President is in this state now. I am certain he would be a disappointed man if anything should arise to make a second term impossible."[43]

On November 4, Edward and Loulie traveled to Washington, where they arrived in time to join Woodrow and McAdoo and Eleanor for dinner. Immediately after dinner the president and his adviser retreated to the White House study, where House raised the subject of McAdoo's Metropolitan Life offer. House explained that McAdoo was worried about his health and upset by the fact that, if he stayed on, he had no chance to become president. Wilson sharply disagreed with House's willingness to see McAdoo leave the administration, arguing that his connection with a large financial institution would destroy any chance he had for the Democratic nomination. They discussed successors to McAdoo, but their differences over his political prospects remained unresolved and by mid-November, when McAdoo turned town the Metropolitan Life offer, the issues surrounding his political ambitions receded, for a time, into the background.[44]

After his return to America on July 29, House had focused on the possibility that he and Wilson might bring an end to the European war. Absorbed in great events on the world stage, his interest in domestic politics waned and he began to complain in his diary of the "usual political routine" that was of no great importance and that "need not be chronicled." He had tired of the burdens of patronage, lamenting that while he had tried to keep out of politics, "I seem doomed to the treadmill for awhile longer."[45]

House seemed uninterested in the fall congressional campaign. He stood on the sidelines as Burleson, Tumulty, and Thomas Pence of the Democratic National Committee moved to strengthen state organizations around the country, flooded the nation with a *Campaign Text Book* (which proclaimed "War in the East! Peace in the West! Thank God for Wilson!") and sent prominent Democrats to speak in states that were not secure for the party. Wilson, with neither the inclination nor the time to take to the stump, issued a letter on October 17 reviewing the achievements of his administration. Despite the emphasis of Democratic candidates on the peace theme, the tide of reform was ebbing and Republicans, more united than they were during the Bull Moose split, won a series of key states in the Northeast and Midwest. The Democrats made gains in the West and retained the solid South; the Democratic margin in the Senate increased by five seats while its margin in the House fell to thirty-four seats. Wilson and many progressives, however, were discouraged by what seemed a declining popular interest in reform and the reemergence of a united, conservative Republican Party. It looked as if the New Freedom had run its course.[46]

On election night House thought the returns "looked pretty bleak for the democrats"; but a few days later, after he had time to reflect on the results, he was more optimistic. On November 4, during his first meeting with Wilson after the elections, he found the president upset over

Democratic setbacks and concerned that he had suffered a loss of prestige both in the Congress and in Europe. "He seemed," House recorded, "thoroughly weary and heartsick, and it took my best endeavors to put him in a better frame of mind." As House pointed out, the outcome in the West had exceeded Democratic Party expectations and the administration, confronting a solid Republican Party for the first time, had retained control of the Congress. With Wilson heading the ticket in 1916, a second term for the president, with all the possibilities it offered House, seemed more than possible.[47]

13

The Search for Peace

As the war of rapid movement in the west ended, leaders in all the belligerent capitals of Europe gradually realized the grim scale of the struggle. They now confronted a savage war, with hand-to-hand fighting in cold and muddy trenches and terrible casualties inflicted by modern rifle, machine gun, and artillery fire. On November 10 the journalist Will Irwin, back from a visit to the war zone, gave House a vivid report on the fighting on the Western Front. Irwin, House recorded, described the modern battle as "a very drab affair. One looked into the distance miles away and saw little puffs of smoke and then heard, perhaps, the shriek of the shell, and nothing else. Everyone was hidden, and the lines stretched away hundreds of miles . . . . He said, usually in war soldiers entered with enthusiasm and with the expectation of coming through safely. But now, when they enlisted, it was to leave hope behind, and with the determination of going to their death."[1]

During the early months of the war the Asquith government operated largely as it had in the past. Asquith appointed General Sir Herbert Kitchner, who had acquired fame fighting Britain's colonial wars, as secretary of state for war, and also created a War Council and met the cabinet more often. But the prime minister's technique for managing the cabinet, his "well-established routine of authority," adequate in peacetime, was inadequate for wartime, when there was a need for quick decisions and a follow-through on policy; the conviction grew that the prewar methods of the Asquith government were inadequate for what would clearly be a long struggle.[2]

By September, the war plans of Great Britain, like those of every belligerent, were in disarray. The British Expeditionary Force had suffered reverses and taken heavy casualties; it was too small and poorly equipped for fighting on the Continent. British leaders now had to expand and rebuild their army and decide how to fight the war. Some generals and politicians felt the conflict would be won or lost on the battlefields of France; others wished to avoid, as First Lord of the Admiralty Winston Churchill put it, sending troops to "chew barbed wire in Flanders," and wanted to intensify economic pressure on the Central Powers or explore new fronts in Turkey and the Near East.[3]

With the outbreak of war, Foreign Secretary Grey had become, his biographer writes, "a symbol of the nation's probity and purpose." Convinced of the importance of American friendship, Grey patiently negotiated with Washington over the Declaration of London and resisted French and Russian demands for a more aggressive use of British naval power to sever Germany's supply lines. So long as Grey's position in the cabinet remained strong and the Asquith government retained the confidence of the country, the British government was sensitive to the needs of the American economy. The object of his diplomacy, Grey later wrote, was "to secure the maximum of blockade that could be enforced without a rupture with the United States."[4] At first, when he expected a short war and a quick peace, the foreign secretary welcomed American mediation efforts. But as a stalemate developed on the Western Front and as it became apparent that the war would extend into 1915, Grey realized that Great Britain's situation had become more complex. He now had to worry about disunity among Britain's major allies, France and Russia, and he also knew that as the war became longer and bloodier the terms on which the Allies would settle it grew more elaborate. Grey could no longer state that Britain's only peace terms would be reparations for Belgium and disarmament; leaders in Paris and St. Petersburg now talked about acquiring German and Austrian territory, while the need of the Allies to bring Greece, Italy, and Romania into the war required various territorial concessions. By late 1914, the possibility of an American peace move caused considerable alarm in London.[5]

In Germany the army's early triumphs sparked euphoria about a quick victory; even as the war in the west became what one historian describes as "a long, bloody halt in the mud," victories in the east obscured the seriousness of Germany's predicament. With the collapse of the Schlieffen Plan, Germany had no strategy for victory and faced an Allied coalition with command of the seas and superior economic resources. Germany's prospects in a long war were not encouraging.[6] As the war lengthened, however, enthusiasm for the conflict spread through a broad range of the German political spectrum. Political parties on the right and center formed vast dreams of territorial annexation, while on the left Social Democrats vowed to oppose demands for a German–dominated central Europe. Confronted with these bitter disagreements, Chancellor Bethmann Hollweg had little room for maneuver if he was to maintain the fragile political truce at home.[7]

Deepening divisions within his own government also constrained the chancellor. By mid-November, as the German army failed to outflank Allied forces in Flanders and as the war in the west became a stalemate, Chief of Staff Falkenhayn lost his faith in total victory; he urged a separate peace with Russia so that Germany could pursue the war against Britain, its "most dangerous opponent," to the bitter end. Falkenhayn's proposal alarmed Bethmann Hollweg, who denounced him as a "gambler" and an "execrable character." In early September, at the height of the Battle of the Marne, when German leaders imminently expected the entry of their armies into Paris, Bethmann Hollweg had drafted a war aims program that would have established German domination of central Europe "for all imaginable time." The German nation, he believed, required "rewards for its incredible sacrifice"; he had no plan for a compromise peace or for a return to the status quo ante bellum. Disappointed with Falkenhayn, Bethmann Hollweg turned to his commanders in the east, Hindenberg and Ludendorff, for assurances that the war was not lost, and sought to replace his faltering chief of the general staff. But the kaiser refused to dismiss Falkenhayn and the dispute remained unresolved, further paralyzing decision making within the German government.[8]

The influence of the kaiser, always erratic, also diminished as the war lengthened. Initially he had heady visions of victory and of the humiliation of the British, but increasingly he was out of his depth, unable to resolve bitter debates over strategy among his military advisers. He became an ill-informed and peripheral figure who traveled between the various fronts, visiting hospitals and reviewing his troops. Mostly he remained at his villa at Charleville, Luxembourg, where he could reach the Western Front easily and perform his imperial duties. The man who in peacetime had embodied so many imperial pretensions became in wartime the "shadow Kaiser."[9]

House's efforts to begin peace talks forced Bethmann Hollweg to clarify his views toward American mediation. When the Austrian foreign minister, Count Leopold Berchtold, asked the chancellor his views on House's scheme for peace and especially on his terms, the evacuation of Belgium and general disarmament, Bethmann Hollweg on November 23 dismissed

House's offer as impractical. The chancellor, unlike his ambassador in Washington, had no intention of seriously exploring an American mediation effort.[10]

Throughout November and December 1914, House kept in close touch with the president. Still depressed over the loss of Ellen, Woodrow leaned heavily on him for political advice and also for companionship and emotional support. During these two months House traveled to Washington five times, while Wilson visited him in New York twice. On November 4, when House and Loulie arrived at the White House for a four-night stay, they found Wilson in a fragile emotional state. After several difficult discussions, on their third evening together the two talked of "the trouble brewing between McAdoo and Tumulty," and House told the president that McAdoo thought Tumulty "too near the interests." Wilson, he recorded, "became flushed and excited and wanted to know if McAdoo had gone crazy." Wilson's pallor was disconcerting. "His face became grey and he looked positively sick. I was unable to lift him out of this depression before bedtime. He said he was broken in spirit by Mrs. Wilson's death, and was not fit to be President because he did not think straight any longer, and had no heart in the things he was doing. He asked if I had noticed it. I said I had not." Before House went to bed he "tried to brace him up by telling him what great work he had to do in foreign affairs, but it was useless."[11]

The next day Grayson told House that Wilson "had passed a wretched night," and that evening after dinner the president avoided retreating to his study, fearful that his counselor might bring up the McAdoo-Tumulty feud. But House, by now a practiced observer of the president's moods, avoided the subject and the two of them discussed German political philosophy and the writings of Edmund Burke and Walter Bagehot. At House's urging, Wilson read some poems, recited a few limericks, and went to bed, relaxed, around 10:30.[12]

The president also insisted that his adviser conform to Wilson's routines. He convinced House to accompany him to the golf course and asked him "to take a long automobile ride," but House was busy and declined to ride in an open car in the cold air. The next day House avoided going to church with the president "by having Loulie go" in his place. As House's visit ended on November 8, Wilson "insisted on our remaining longer, and asked me to come as often as I could." "I wish you could know," House wrote the president on his return to New York, "what a happy time I had with you during the past few days."[13]

On November 13, only six days after he had come back from Washington, House returned to his apartment from the theater to learn that the president would arrive at 6:00 AM the following morning and would expect to see him at 6:30 for breakfast. House had to stay up past midnight to prepare for the sudden presidential visit. The next day, after Wilson arrived with his daughter Margaret and Grayson, House took the president and his companions to the Piping Rock Club on Long Island for golf. Wilson, Grayson, and Gordon Auchincloss played golf, while House waited patiently in the clubhouse for their return.[14] In the evening, House and Wilson had a quiet dinner in his apartment, and at 9:00 PM, when their after-dinner talk was finished, the two took a walk from 57th Street to Seventh Avenue and down Seventh to Broadway. Once back at House's apartment, Wilson "began to tell me how lonely and sad his life was since Mrs. Wilson's death, and he could not help wishing when we were out tonight that someone would kill him. He has told me this before. His eyes were moist when he spoke of not wanting to live longer, and of not being fit to do the work he had in hand. He said he had himself so disciplined that he knew perfectly well that unless someone killed him, he would go on to the end doing the best he could."[15] The next day the two friends went to the Fifth Avenue Presbyterian Church, drove to Riverdale for lunch with Wilson's old Princeton friend Cleveland Dodge, and ended up at Pennsylvania Station so the president could catch a late afternoon train. House concluded that Wilson had "thoroughly enjoyed his two day diversion."[16]

As plans for peace moves and for a Pan American Pact (designed to transform relations with Latin America) matured, House traveled to Washington on December 16 for another four-day stay, an unusually long one for him. The president and his counselor quickly fell into their accustomed routine. During the day Wilson performed his regular duties, while House consulted with government officials. They conducted most of their business in the evening after dinner. Of the four dinners House ate at the White House, McAdoo was the only non-family member, with the exception of House, who sat at the president's table.[17]

By the second day of his stay, House was eager to leave, writing Fanny, "how disappointed I am that I am compelled to stay until at least Monday night!" On December 20, House told Wilson over lunch that he planned to take the 3:00 PM train back to New York. But Wilson asked him to remain until later in the day. In the afternoon, the president, his cousin Helen Bones, and House took a long drive and after dinner Wilson praised

House for all of his assistance. "He spoke," House recorded, "in feeling terms, and expressed again and again his gratitude for my assistance. He was fine enough to say that I had suggested two great things [American mediation of the war and the Pan American Pact], and the manner of doing them. I have never known him so appreciative or more affectionate." At 11:00, House left the White House and took the midnight train back to New York.[18]

In the fall of 1914 some Americans, primarily conservative Republicans in the East, had become concerned about the nation's lack of military preparedness. Led by Theodore Roosevelt and former Army Chief of Staff Leonard Wood, these "preparedness advocates" worried that the American army of 100,000 men was too small and too poorly equipped. They advocated the creation of a large conscript reserve army that would be trained and commanded by regulars and coordinated by a general staff. Preparedness leaders were impressed with the large standing armies of the continental European powers and wanted an American force that could project power overseas. As a start, they called for a special congressional investigation into the state of the nation's defenses.[19]

The weaknesses of the American army also worried House. On November 3 he talked with Wood about the creation of a national reserve force and learned that no American military officers had any experience "in the handling of large bodies of troops." The next day, during his stay at the White House, House raised the issue with the president. Wilson dismissed the need for "immediate action," arguing that "no matter how the great war ended, there would be complete exhaustion, and even if Germany won, she would not be in a condition to seriously menace our country for many years to come." In a rare open disagreement, House "combatted this idea," arguing that a victorious Germany would threaten American security. But the president was unconvinced and would not even agree to send Wood to Europe to observe the war. "The President," House lamented in his diary, "does not seem to fully grasp the importance of such matters."[20]

On November 25, when Wilson had passed through New York, House again spoke "of our unpreparedness and how impractical Mr. Bryan was. I urged the need of our having a large reserve force and he replied 'Yes, but not a large army,' an amendment which I accepted." It looked as if he and the president had reached an agreement. On December 8, however, in his second annual message to Congress, Wilson rejected the proposals of the advocates of preparedness. "We are," he told those assembled, "the champions of peace and of concord"; he refused to allow the nation to be "thrown off our balance by a war with which we have nothing to do, whose causes can not touch us, whose very existence affords us opportunities of friendship and disinterested service which should make us ashamed of any thought of hostility or fearful preparation for trouble." As he finished, many congressmen stood and cheered. The president had spoken; he would not allow any significant increases in the nation's army. Confronted with his friend's firm position, House backed away from his advocacy of a reserve force, reassuring Wilson that "You go far enough to satisfy any reasonable man and your reasons for not going further are. . . conclusive."[21]

Throughout the last two months of 1914, House followed the European war closely, looking for an opening for an American peace move and sharing his thoughts with the president. He identified with the Allied cause and idealized Grey, asking Page for a photograph of the foreign secretary that he could hang on his study wall next to that of the president. On November 8, House had told Wilson that when the Germans were pushed back to their own borders, "it would be advisable for me to go there and urge the Kaiser to ask him, the President, to mediate." Wilson, more realistic than his adviser, "thought the Kaiser would hesitate to admit defeat," but House nonetheless remained optimistic, noting that morale in Vienna was sagging and that the Austrian government might "be willing to treat with the Allies for peace separately from Germany." He also emphasized the German government's hostility toward America, arguing that "Germany would never forgive us for the attitude we have taken in the war, and if she is successful, she will hold us to account."[22]

On November 30, House wrote Wilson, advising him to make foreign policy the administration's highest priority. During House's December 3 visit to the White House, Wilson agreed, and now regretted Bryan's "unsuitability for the office of Secretary of State." Wilson speculated that Bryan might leave the cabinet over some policy disagreement; both the president and his adviser agreed that Bryan "had served his usefulness as Secretary of State" and hoped that he would "pleasantly take himself out of the Cabinet."[23]

On December 16, when House arrived at the White House, the president, he recorded, "spoke of my going abroad in order to initiate peace conversations. He desires me to take charge of it and to go whenever I think it advisable." The two men agreed that House would see the German ambassador the next day and explore the possibility of another mission to Berlin and London.[24] However, the main purpose of House's visit to Washington was to promote a Pan American Pact. Earlier, in late November, House had urged Wilson to renounce the policy of the " 'big stick' " and to give greater attention "to the welding together of the two Western Continent[s]." He now wanted him to promote a plan that "would serve as a model for the European Nations when peace is at last brought about." In previous years, leaders of the peace movement had promoted a hemispheric peace alliance; now House and Wilson advanced the idea as they pondered American mediation of the European war.[25] "I could see," House recorded, "that this excited his enthusiasm," and Wilson picked up a pencil and wrote out two articles, the first a "mutual guarantee of political independence under republican forms of government and mutual guarantees of territorial integrity," the second a mutual agreement that each government would control "the manufacture and sale of munitions of war." The president typed up the two articles and handed the document to House to use in his negotiations with the ambassadors of Argentina, Brazil, and Chile. He continued, however, to worry about offending Bryan's "sensibilities," and House agreed to explain to the secretary of state why he was handling the negotiations for the Pan American Pact. When House raised the subject with Bryan, he seemed unconcerned about his role and soon "drifted off into the question of [federal] patronage [in Nebraska]."[26]

This outline of a Pan American Pact represented the president's first thoughts on collective security, and he may have seen a connection between a covenant with the nations of Latin America and a settlement of the European war. By December 1914, Wilson's initial reaction to the war had receded and he had worked out an analysis of the causes and consequences of the conflict. In a December 14, 1914, interview with the *New York Times*, given off the record, Wilson argued that "I think that the chance of a just and equitable peace. . . will be happiest if no nation gets the decision by arms." Wilson now suggested that Germany was not alone in being responsible for the war and that the causes of the conflict were complex. While he still felt personal sympathy for the Allies and their cause, he had become fairly critical toward all the belligerents and now began to think more systematically about the future and how the United States might lead the way to a peace of reconciliation.[27] House quickly contacted the Argentine, Brazilian, and Chilean ambassadors in Washington, and found the first two enthusiastic about the possibility of a hemispheric agreement. Initially House believed he could "button up" a Pan American Pact early in 1915, but the Chilean government, locked in a border dispute with Peru, was not forthcoming. After House left for Europe in late January 1915, Bryan took charge of the negotiations and added more articles to the proposed pact. Eventually the negotiations floundered because of Latin American suspicions of American policies in Mexico and the Caribbean.[28]

While House pursued the elusive Pan American Pact, he also sought to advance the American mediation effort. On December 17 he discussed peace moves with Ambassador Bernstorff, who assured him that the German government was willing to consider a peace based on the evacuation of and indemnity for Belgium and "drastic disarmament." But House was suspicious of Bernstorff's reliability and asked him to secure confirmation of these terms from Undersecretary Zimmerman.[29] The ambassador's assurances put Foreign Secretary Grey in a difficult position. Grey believed that the German government was insincere and was trying to put the onus for the continuation of the war on the Allies. Rather than reveal the full extent of the Allies' territorial ambitions, however, he conveyed through Spring-Rice the impression that Britain, France, and Russia would be willing to consider peace on the basis of the restoration of Belgium and general disarmament. But the foreign secretary carefully hedged his message, stating that it was only an expression of "his personal attitude," not, by implication, the policy of his government. On December 20, when House told the president of Grey's dispatch, "He was much elated, and wanted to know whether I could go to Europe as early as the coming Saturday. I stated that I could go at any time. He said he needed me on two Continents . . . . He spoke in feeling terms, and expressed again and again his gratitude for my assistance." The president and his counselor were, however, out of touch with the growing intransigence of leaders in Berlin and London.[30]

On December 23, House returned to Washington to discuss with the president the prospects for American mediation. Wilson was so eager for news that, although House's train had not arrived until 6:45 PM, he "came to my room and kept me from dressing for a few minutes which delayed dinner." They decided that House should again see Ambassador Spring-Rice and ask him to urge Grey to "feel out the Allies as to Bernstorff's proposal." At 9:45 PM House met with the British ambassador at Billy Phillips's home. Spring-Rice had received the previous day another telegram from Grey, who was clearly trying to discourage an American peace move. The foreign secretary now revealed that he had not discussed peace terms with his own cabinet or with the Allies, and he warned that "there would be difficulties with France and Russia." Spring-Rice wanted to explore the nature of a peace settlement, but House thought such a discussion premature and argued that the conversations among the belligerents should initially focus on the restoration of Belgium and "an arrangement for a permanent settlement of European difficulties, including a reduction of armaments."

When House returned to the White House, he found Wilson "anxiously awaiting me." The president sat with House until "I had changed my clothes and was ready to say goodbye. He again expressed gratitude and affection for the trouble I had taken and the manner in which I was trying to serve." House did not reach Union Station until after midnight.[31]

December 25, 1914, was the first Christmas of the war. On the Western Front it was a cold, clear day, and on some sections of the front British, French, and German soldiers climbed out of their trenches and walked into no-man's-land, shaking hands and exchanging cap stars, badges, and other gifts.[32] In Washington Wilson celebrated Christmas at the White House with Margaret and Frank and Jessie Sayre. In New York, House, Loulie, Fanny Denton, Sidney and Nancy Mezes, and Gordon and Janet Auchincloss enjoyed what he termed a "delightful Christmas" at the Auchincloss's home. House knew that he had much to be grateful for. His first grandchild, Jane Tucker, had arrived on November 3, 1907; his second, Randolph Tucker, on November 6, 1914; his third, Louise Auchincloss, on December 3, 1914. Also, Mezes had accepted the presidency of the City College of New York and in mid-December had taken up his duties.[33]

But House also knew, midway through his fifty-seventh year, that time was passing and that as a new generation of his family arrived, an older one was departing. In the summer of 1914 he had learned that Ruth, his brother T. W.'s wife, was seriously ill; after her death in late October, House wrote his niece that "I can never think of your mother as dead for such a radiant, glorious personality can never die. She will be with us always as an inspiration and a benediction."[34]

On Christmas day, Wilson and House exchanged telegrams. "I wish," the president told House, "I could see brought into your life some happiness and blessing equal to those you have brought into mine by your wonderful friendship. You have kept faith and strength in me." House responded that "Your message has made the day a happy one for me. May God's blessings fall upon you and yours abundantly during the coming years." The two men had never been closer.[35]

In early December the president had given an interview to a reporter from the *Saturday Evening Post*. Wilson, the reporter noted, was kind and courteous, and gave the appearance of a healthy man who spent a lot of time outdoors. Complaining about the loneliness of the presidency, Wilson observed, "A President can have no intimates; because, no matter how unselfish those intimates may be at the beginning, inevitably they will seek to take advantage of that intimacy before the end." There is no reason to suppose that Wilson was thinking of his friendship with House. But he may have sensed that, however close the bond between them seemed at the end of 1914, their friendship would one day come to an end.[36]

14

London, Paris, Berlin

In late December 1914, Foreign Secretary Grey had called in Chandler Anderson, a legal adviser in the American embassy who was about to leave London to return to the United States, to ask him to inform President Wilson and House that the time had not come for peace overtures or even for a discussion of possible terms. At the end of the war, Grey suggested, the Allies, if they were in a position to do so, would insist on reparations for Belgium, the return of Alsace-Lorraine to France and an indemnity for France, and Russian control of Constantinople and the Dardanelles. And in early January 1915 Grey emphasized a further point in a dispatch to British ambassador Spring-Rice. Earlier, House had told the ambassador that the United States would not sign any postwar agreement for the preservation of the peace. "If this is so," Grey warned, "it is difficult to see how a durable peace can be secured without complete exhaustion of one side or the other." Grey did not believe that Germany was prepared to make peace on reasonable terms and reminded Spring-Rice that France and Russia needed to be consulted and that he "could not open discussions with them unless very sure of the ground respecting Germany's real disposition."[1]

On January 8, Spring-Rice conveyed Grey's line of reasoning to House, who, oddly enough, did not seem discouraged by the Allies' new conditions for peace. "It is now clearly up to us," he wrote Wilson, "to get something definite from Germany and then we can test the sincerity of Great Britain." House thought he might leave for Europe on January 30. However, he now lowered his estimate of Grey, recording that he thought him "absolutely trustworthy and a man of high character, but without ability of the first order."[2]

On January 12, 1915, House traveled to Washington for an overnight stay, his first of the New Year. McAdoo and Grayson met him at Union Station and drove him to the White House. Retreating to the president's study before dinner, the president and House decided that House should leave for Europe on January 30. They agreed that talks about a peace move had stalled and that House would have to confront British and German leaders to break the impasse. After dinner, much to House's surprise, Wilson read aloud from Alfred George Gardiner's *Prophets, Priests and Kings* and did not bring up the details of House's forthcoming mission; House could only conclude that "He evidently had confidence in my doing the work I came to Washington for, without his help."[3]

The next day, before dinner, Wilson and House discussed aspects of his forthcoming trip. The secretary of state's desire to go to Europe upset Wilson, who asserted that "if necessary he would allow Mr. Bryan to resign from the Cabinet before he would let him undertake such a delicate mission, for which he felt he was so unfitted." After dinner, Wilson and House worked out a code for their use in transatlantic cables and agreed that Wilson should write his emissary a letter of introduction. And the president reminded House that "You are the only one in the world to whom I can open my mind freely, and it does me good to say even foolish things and get them out of my system."[4]

The despair and depression that had descended on Woodrow after Ellen's death in early August was now lifting. On the second evening of House's stay, the president, House, McAdoo, Eleanor, and several relatives looked at a presidential portrait by the artist Stephen Seymour Thomas. Instead of standing in front of the painting, as Eleanor wished, her father "made all sorts of contortions, sticking his tongue in his cheek, twisting his mouth into different positions, rolling his eyes, dropping his jaw, and doing everything a clown would do at a circus. She tried composing his features with her hand, and whenever she would touch his chin he would let it drop on his shirtfront, and when she lifted it, he would raise his eyes to heaven." Everyone laughed. As the group started up the stairway to the president's study, Wilson and McAdoo went ahead. "McAdoo walked as bow-legged as his long legs could possibly be bowed, and the President not only walking bowlegged, but pigeon toed. In this way they walked up the entire flight, much to the amusement of the rest of us." No doubt Wilson's high spirits and renewed energy encouraged House, whose great ambitions could only be achieved if his friend stayed in office. But late on the evening of January 13, as Cary Grayson accompanied him to Union Station, House learned that "the President's kidneys were not acting as well as they should. There was nothing serious as yet, but he was watching him closely." Questions about Wilson's health, and his longevity, would not go away.[5]

On January 24, House once again traveled to Washington for an overnight stay to consult one last time with the president. Wilson asked his counselor to "'Let him [Grey] know that while you are abroad I expect to act directly through you and to eliminate all intermediaries.' He approved all I had in mind to say to Sir Edward and to the Germans. He said: 'There is not much for us to talk over for the reason we are both of the same mind and it is not necessary to go into details with you.'"[6] Wilson insisted that the government cover House's expenses, along with those of Loulie and Fanny. House had paid his own way on his trips to Europe in 1913 and 1914, but he felt unable to pay for such a long stay, which he anticipated would last six months, and wrote that the allocation of $4,000 "lifts a load from me." House also planned to have Gordon Auchincloss join him later as a confidential secretary. But Janet's ill health, and the offer of a law partnership from David Hunter Miller, forced Auchincloss to stay in New York.[7]

On January 25, after completing their after-dinner discussion, the president and his adviser said goodbye. House recorded the scene carefully for posterity: "The President's eyes were moist when he said his last words of farewell. He said: 'Your unselfish and intelligent friendship has meant much to me,' and he expressed his gratitude again and again, calling me his 'Most trusted friend.' He declared I was the only one in all the world to whom he could open his entire mind."

"I asked if he remembered the first day we met, some three and a half years ago. He replied, 'Yes, but we had known one another always, and merely came in touch then, for our purposes and thoughts were as one.'"

On the morning of January 30, 1915, Edward, Loulie, and Fanny boarded the SS *Lusitania*, at 30,395 tons the pride of the Cunard Line. This graceful, slender four-funnel vessel, launched in September 1907, reminded some observers of "a skyscraper adrift." With 2,200 passengers and a crew of 850, the *Lusitania* included impressive technical advances and lavish first-class accommodations. House would arrive in England in style.[8]

On the first two days of the voyage House enjoyed calm, summer seas; then a severe storm swept down from the north that "tossed [the *Lusitania*] about like a cork in the rapids." When House arrived in London he and his party were met by Ambassador Page, who accompanied them to the Hotel Washington on Curzon Street. House and Page then drove to the

American embassy, where they spent the entire afternoon discussing Anglo-American affairs. House was pleased with the mild, sunny weather and reassured Gordon Auchincloss that "We are both well and are altogether looking forward to the most interesting time of our lives."[9]

In the early months of 1915, the war on the Western Front remained stalemated; the huge armies assembled on both sides could not move forward more than a few hundred yards without sustaining heavy losses. Belligerent governments now prepared for a longer and bloodier conflict, mobilizing their people and economies, raising additional manpower, and seeking new allies. As the war grew longer and more violent, neither the Central Powers nor the Allies had any plan for victory; neither did they have any interest in peace. Leaders in Berlin viewed peace moves purely as a way of splitting the Allied coalition, while leaders in London and Paris believed that so long as Germany occupied French territory, it had more to gain from peace negotiations than did the Allied coalition.[10]

Initially the Allies lacked any unified strategy, and during the first half of 1915 they wasted their resources in a series of uncoordinated campaigns. France's commitment on the Western Front was far larger than Britain's, and General Joseph Joffre, the commander of French forces and the author of the "miracle of the Marne," was determined to expel the invader from French soil. Joffre resumed the offensive in early 1915, convinced that he could achieve a breakthrough and relieve the pressure on Russia.[11] In contrast, Lord Kitchener, who dominated British strategy, was reluctant to commit more troops to the Western Front and to undertake major offensives there. He and other British leaders, searching for a way to escape the stalemate, moved toward a campaign to attack the Dardanelles, one that would knock Turkey out of the war, open the trade route to Russia, draw Bulgaria, Greece, and Romania into the Allied coalition, and offer the prospect for large territorial gains. By mid-January 1915, the members of Asquith's war council liked the idea; as its secretary, Maurice Hankey, recorded, they "turned eagerly from the dreary vistas of a 'slogging match' on the Western Front to brighter prospects" in the eastern Mediterranean.[12]

In Germany, bitter disputes about strategy continued into the new year. Generals Hindenberg and Ludendorff pressed for a massive transfer of troops to the Eastern Front and promised, if they received sufficient resources, to end the war against Russia in 1915. Chief of Staff Falkenhayn took a more balanced view of the military challenges facing Germany. He was willing to go on the defensive in the west and to shift some resources to the east, but in the end he hoped to negotiate with Russia rather than destroy its armies. He also had to take swift action to prevent the collapse of Austro-Hungarian forces in Galicia and the Carpathians. While the generals argued over strategy, Chancellor Bethmann-Hollweg maneuvered to replace Falkenhayn and to maintain his authority. The German command system, however, lacked any central agency where political-military strategies could be resolved; instead, generals and politicians intrigued against one another and sought to win over the kaiser. But Germany's Supreme Commander was "depressed" and "upset," unable to restore order among his contentious subordinates.[13]

As frustration mounted in Germany over the stalemated war, the navy's high command turned to U-boats as a way to gain a role in the war and to break the deadlock. Only twenty-one were available, but they had scored some successes in the fall of 1914, and by early 1915 the U-boat fever had spread beyond the navy to the press and political parties. Initially Bethmann-Hollweg and his colleagues in the Foreign Office opposed a U-boat blockade of Britain, fearing the effect it would have on neutral nations, and in early January they convinced the kaiser to postpone the U-boat assault on merchant vessels. But as the pressure on the chancellor grew and as Germany's food stocks dwindled, Bethmann-Hollweg concluded that the diplomatic risks of U-boat warfare would be acceptable; on February 2 he told the navy to go ahead and one day later the kaiser approved a decree establishing a war zone in the waters surrounding Great Britain and Ireland. Beginning on February 18, German U-boats would seek to destroy enemy merchant ships found in this area. Since British ships sometimes flew neutral flags, the decree warned that neutral vessels should not enter the war zone. A new, more dangerous phase of the war had begun.[14]

On February 7, one day after his arrival in London, House met with Foreign Secretary Grey at 33 Eccleston Square. By early February 1915 the burdens of the war, just half a year old, weighed heavily on Grey. Asquith found his foreign secretary "most dolorous and despondent," while Grey admitted that he was "inhumanly busy & tired." A year earlier he had consulted several oculists and learned that he had an eye infection that would eventually end his ability to read. Faced with the inexorable decline of his eyes, Grey continued to work long hours in the Foreign Office. But he longed for a quieter life, immersed in nature, free from all of the stresses and strains of wartime diplomacy.[15] At their first meeting, which lasted three and a half hours, House recorded that Grey "talked with me as freely as

W [Wilson] does and I know the situation from the bottom up. As far as I could see, there were no reservations of any sort." House and Grey discussed the position of the Allies—less favorable than House had thought—and the details of a peace settlement, but in general each man took the measure of the other and sought to reestablish the rapport they had achieved in June and July 1914. A few days later House learned, through Grey's private secretary William Tyrrell, that the foreign secretary's "liking for me makes him hope that I will come to his home informally at any and all times. This end of the job," House confidently noted, "is secure if Washington does nothing to upset the apple cart."[16]

On February 10, House and Grey, at a lunch that included Page and Tyrrell, differed on several major issues. House believed that Germany "was in earnest about beginning peace parleys," while Grey thought that the German government was merely seeking an advantage over the Allies. Grey insisted that the United States should participate in a peace conference and in a postwar security system; House rejected any American participation, arguing that "we could not do so, that it was not only the unwritten law of our country, but also our fixed policy not to become involved in European affairs." He did agree, however, that after a peace agreement had been concluded, the United States would take part in a second convention defining the "principles of civilized warfare." House believed that his plan to regulate warfare in the future would "bring the president into playing a big part"; he would preside at a general convention of all neutral and belligerent nations that would determine "the rules of future warfare and the rights of neutrals."[17]

Prior to his departure, House and Wilson had agreed that the major purpose of his mission was to get peace discussions under way. Now Grey informed House that the Allies would not pursue peace talks until they had won some more convincing military victories; they would only listen to any proposals from the other side. Confronted with the foreign secretary's reluctance to negotiate, House quickly gave way, reassuring Grey that "I had no intention of pushing the question of peace." House was content to wait until an Allied spring offensive put Germany in a less "advantageous position." Without consulting the president, he had changed the character of his mission.[18] The foreign secretary was relieved to discover that Wilson's emissary was no zealot for peace, that he was a sympathetic friend who desired to strengthen Anglo-American friendship. In his memoirs, Grey remembered that "When House came to London after the outbreak of war our conversation almost at once became not only friendly but intimate. I found combined in him a rare degree the qualities of wisdom and sympathy. In the stress of war it was at once a relief, a delight, and an advantage to be able to talk with him freely . . . . House left me in no doubt from the first that he held German militarism responsible for the war. . . . He had a way of saying 'I know it' in a tone and manner that carried conviction both of his sympathy with, and understanding of, what was said to him."[19]

The question remained, however, about when House should leave London for Berlin. On February 12 he received a formal invitation from Undersecretary Zimmermann. House now seemed uncertain how to proceed.[20] Over lunch on February 17, House, Page, Grey, and Asquith discussed when he should go to Germany. The prime minister and foreign secretary urged House to delay his visit; they saw no point in pursuing peace as long as Germany seemed to be winning the war. House accepted their advice, writing Zimmermann that unless Germany was "ready to consider [the] evacuation of Belgium and a plan of permanent peace, there would be no use of my coming to Berlin." As House wrote Wilson, "As long as the military forces of Germany are successful as now, the militarists will not permit any suggestion of peace."[21]

In Berlin, Ambassador Gerard viewed the war from a different perspective. He believed that Germany "will win on land and probably get a separate peace from Russia, then get the same from France or overwhelm it and put a large force in Egypt, and perhaps completely blockade England." He urged the Allies to make a peace proposal immediately, before the U-boat blockade on February 18 inaugurated a new, more intense phase of the war.[22] Soon after receiving Gerard's letter House visited Grey and read it to him. Neither man shared the ambassador's sense of urgency, but the president, whose hopes for peace were stimulated by Gerard's dispatches, was growing impatient. "It will of course occur to you," he cabled his counselor, "that you can go too far in allowing the English government to determine when it is best to go to Germany, because they naturally desire to await some time when they have the advantage because of events in the field or elsewhere." Wilson thought it was important "to learn Germany's mind at the earliest possible moment."[23]

House insisted, however, that he delay his trip to Berlin for at least two weeks, when he though the Allied attack on the Dardanelles might be successful. He reminded Wilson that Germany refused to evacuate and indemnify Belgium and agree to a "permanent peace settlement," that France and

Russia were not willing to discuss peace proposals, and that if he went to Berlin immediately the president would "lose the sympathetic interest which England, and through her, the Allies, now feel in your endeavors." It would be much better, House urged the president, to stay in touch with Grey, "the one sane, big figure here," who would be "the dominant figure when the final settlement comes."[24] Confronted with his emissary's insistence on the hopelessness of American peace moves at this time, Wilson gave way. "I am, of course, content to be guided by your judgment as to each step." Like House, the president was unwilling to press peace proposals that might threaten Anglo-American understanding.[25]

By the end of February, House was finally prepared to travel to Berlin, and speculated that he would remain in Germany or on the Continent rather than return to England.[26] On March 7, four days before his departure for the Continent, House and Grey held a final conversation. Grey told House that the French government believed the Allies would win the war and would be able to impose peace terms on Germany. While he "did not know the mind of Russia," he reasoned that the government in St. Petersburg would be content with the control of Constantinople and the Straits. House was not, in fact, optimistic about an early end to the war. Privately he worried about the lack of a dominant political leader in either London or Berlin. Asquith and Grey both lacked "something of initiative, boldness and decision," while in Germany the leadership situation was "even more uncertain." "My main object now," he confided to Auchincloss in early March, "must be to mark time and not offend by overdoing." He believed that the Allied attack on the Dardanelles, if successful, would turn the tide against Germany and "the time will then be propitious for me to act." Certainly British leaders, now that they understood the depth of House's pro-Allied sympathies, no longer feared an American-led peace move. Peace talk, Asquith told Page in early March, was "the twittering of a sparrow in a tumult that shakes the world."[27]

During his long stay in London—nearly five weeks—House mingled, as in his earlier visits, with Britain's ruling elite. "I am lunching and dining," he reported to Auchincloss, "with someone of importance every day."[28] One of the high points of his stay came on March 4, when the Anglo-Irish statesman Horace Plunkett introduced him to Arthur Balfour, the former Conservative prime minister. After the Liberal landslide of January 1906 had left his party in the minority, Balfour had become the leader of the opposition in Parliament, but had resigned his position in 1911 in order to return to the study of philosophy and spend more time with his extended family. He remained, however, involved in high-level politics and, after the outbreak of war, joined the Asquith government's war council. Like Grey, Balfour had a deep belief in Anglo-American understanding; unlike the foreign secretary, he had no interest in a negotiated peace and urged a more energetic prosecution of the war. Balfour had grown up at the very apex of British society, a wealthy, aristocratic member of the leisured class whose interest in philosophy was as strong as his interest in politics. He was a handsome man, over six feet tall, with luminous eyes and a down-turned moustache. Charming, rich, and highly intelligent, he was described by contemporaries as "brilliant," "dazzling," and "resplendent," while his critics found him too detached from the problems that affected most of the British people. Or as Plunkett explained to House, "Balfour has the finest analytical mind in Great Britain, but he is too philosophical and too intellectual to deal with the ordinary man."[29]

Balfour and House talked of America's position in the war and of House's hopes for peace. As House explained his plans, Balfour "became enthusiastic" and got up and stood by the fire. His physical presence and the "quality of his mind" appealed to House, who felt that they "got along famously together." Balfour reminded House of Wilson, and House ranked him "along with the President and Mr. Asquith in intellectuality and this, to my mind, places him at the summit." Balfour was also drawn to House, telling Plunkett later that "he liked House immensely, and Wilson because he appreciated House. We agreed that House was not intellectually brilliant, but, what was far better, intellectually honest."[30]

As House moved through English ruling circles, the war seemed to be everywhere. At lunches and dinner parties he sometimes wearied of discussions of the conflict, but by early 1915 even members of the upper class were aware of the mounting death toll and preoccupied with the war. Grey's personal secretary, Tyrrell, had two sons in the war, and learned in mid-February that one had been killed. Worn down by illness and the strain of the war, he entered a sanitarium. "And so," House reflected, "death's harvest continues. I do not permit myself to think of these things for fear they will warp my judgment in dealing with the large questions which constantly confront me. I try to remain in every way as normal here as I would be in America."[31]

Throughout his stay in England House tried to keep in touch with the president, sending him long letters describing his impressions of British leaders, the course of the war, and progress in his plans for peace. In return, House received only short, unrevealing telegrams from the White House. Foreign affairs now overwhelmed Wilson; he could not focus only on events in Europe. As he wrote a friend, he was deluged with problems concerning "Japan, China, the Philippines, Mexico, Chile, San Domingo, Haiti, England, Germany, and Turkey . . . . It is often necessary for me to work far into the night to give them [these issues] prompt and careful attention."[32] News from the president's other associates was also sparse. Assistant Attorney General Samuel Huston Thompson reported that Wilson had described House as "a rare person and a remarkable character," while Grayson wrote that he "needs you more now than ever" and concluded that "physically, he is holding as well as could be expected in such trying circumstances."[33]

Despite the dearth of news from Washington, House was pleased with the autonomy the president had given him. A few days before he left London for Paris, Wilson cabled that "there is nothing special to report on this side, and you do not need instructions. Your admirable letters and telegrams keep me posted in just the right way." Wilson's faith in his friend and emissary seemed undiminished.[34]

News of the U-boat decree of February 4 shocked Wilson and Bryan, who were not aware of the debates within the German government and who learned of the measure when they read the morning newspaper. As Wilson, Bryan, and Lansing (counselor of the State Department) discussed the American response, they agreed that the United States had to make a protest, to protect both the president's domestic leadership and the economic and moral interests of the nation. On February 10, the American government dispatched a note to Berlin, one that firmly defended the nation's neutral rights and warned that the German government would be held "to a strict accountability" for the loss of American lives and property. But this protest, while popular at home, left many aspects of the administration's policy unclear. As the U-boat campaign progressed, Wilson and his advisers would have to define the meaning of "strict accountability" and decide if they should back up their demands with the threat of war.[35]

The German government's reply—which arrived in Washington on February 18—was so conciliatory that it encouraged Bryan to urge a compromise, in which Britain would allow Germany to import foodstuffs while Germany would abandon its war-zone decree. Wilson quickly agreed and on

February 20 the United States sent notes to Berlin and London. Germany's response was ambiguous, while British leaders never seriously considered accepting the modus vivendi. Asquith and Grey regarded the German war zone decree as largely a bluff and concluded that it would complicate American-German relations and allow Britain to intensify its blockade. Responding to the growing clamor within Britain for an intensification of economic warfare, on March 11 the foreign office issued a new order-in-council that imposed a complete blockade on Germany. After much deliberation, Wilson, Bryan, and Lansing decided to accept the new British system; by the end of March they had, in effect, adjusted to both Britain's and Germany's methods of naval warfare, while warning leaders in London and Berlin that they would be held to a strict accountability for the violation of American neutral rights. Or as Wilson wrote a friend, "together England and Germany are likely to drive us crazy, because it looks oftentimes as if they were crazy themselves, the unnecessary provocations they invent."[36]

On March 11, House, Loulie, and Fanny left London for Paris. House worried about crossing the Channel in wartime (which reminded him, he wrote, of running the Union blockade of Galveston during the Civil War), placing his diary and other papers in a safe deposit box in London, where, in case of an accident, Gordon Auchincloss would have access to them. On the day of House's crossing, however, the Channel was quiet, and the British government expedited the passage of its distinguished guest and arranged for a submarine destroyer to accompany his boat. House and his party arrived in Paris at 7:30 in the evening, where they were met by the new ambassador, William G. Sharp, and his staff and taken to the Hôtel de Crillon. House talked with Sharp, a wealthy former congressman from Ohio, until nearly midnight, and judged him "a level headed, plain, good hearted American of the Western small town type."[37]

House found Paris much more affected by the war than London. "The malevolent touch of war [in Paris]," he wrote, "shows itself in the faces of the women and the men. Half the shops are closed and the traffic in the streets is very light." France was, in fact, engaged in a desperate national struggle to expel German forces from its soil. After the outbreak of the war, the cabinet had been broadened and all political groups had rallied behind the spirit of union sacrée. By the early months of 1915 French political and military leaders were optimistic about the prospects for success on the Western Front and eager for the army to go on the offensive. They were unanimous in rejecting the idea of a compromise peace; only a decisive victory would ensure an end to the German threat.[38]

Two days after his arrival House traveled to the Quai d'Orsay, epicenter of French foreign policy, where he met the French foreign minister, Théophile Delcassé, "a small, polite, shrewd looking man." Before this meeting House realized that "the French not only want Alsace and Lorraine, but so much more that the two countries [France and Germany] are not within sight of peace." He now sought to avoid a confrontation, reassuring the foreign minister "that we [House and Wilson] knew this was not the right moment to discuss peace, but the President desired to let them know that his services were always open," and also wanted House to go to Berlin to find out "what was in the mind of Germany." Delcassé, in turn, was content with an exchange of diplomatic pleasantries, promising to tell House about French war aims when he returned to Paris from Berlin. Only through a third party did House let the foreign minister know that he believed "France is taking a big gamble in demanding peace terms that Germany will never accept unless the Allies reach Berlin." Given the balance of forces on the Western Front, the optimism of French leaders puzzled House. The French ruling classes, he realized, "do not desire peace, but [he believed] a large part of the people and the men in the trenches would welcome it."[39]

House sent Wilson detailed reports on his conversations with Delcassé. He claimed, inaccurately, that "France has at least tentatively accepted you as mediator and that, I think, is much," and also wrote the president that he was "pushing [for peace] just as hard as it is safe to do." Wilson seemed satisfied with his emissary's conciliatory approach to the French and the leisurely pace of his diplomacy; he made no comment on House's reports from Paris.[40]

After six days in Paris, the Houses and Fanny, accompanied by Lanier Winslow (Gerard's private secretary), left for Germany, traveling to Berlin by way of Switzerland. As their train passed within ten or twelve miles of the front lines, soldiers boarded it, pulled down the shades, and stationed themselves in the corridors so that no one could get out. On each side of the Swiss-German border the tracks had been pulled up, and House's party had to travel across the gap by automobile. On March 19 at 9:00 AM, House and his companions arrived in Berlin in a snowstorm. Later that morning he went to the Wilhelmstrasse for an appointment with Undersecretary Zimmermann.[41]

The reaction of the United States and of other neutrals to the U-boat decree had set off an intense debate within the German government. After the American denunciation of the decree, Ambassador Bernstorff had cabled that *"A mistake could have the most serious consequences,"* and Chancellor Bethmann-Hollweg and Foreign Minister Jagow quickly decided that the decree had been a mistake and must be suspended. In contrast, Admiral Tirpitz and other navy leaders pushed for full-scale U-boat warfare. In mid-February the irresolute kaiser sided with Bethmann-Hollweg, but the chancellor was aware of the growing clamor within Germany for the use of this new weapon. Unless confronted with an American threat of war, he would be tempted to appease his domestic critics.[42]

Before arriving in Berlin, House had decided that, rather than push for peace, he needed to build trust between German and American leaders and find some formula to break the Anglo-German impasse. He reassured Zimmermann that he "had no intention of pushing peace negotiations upon anyone," while the undersecretary confirmed the fact that "it was impossible for them [Germany] to make any peace overtures." House believed that he would have to wait for a decisive military victory by one side or another that would break the stalemate and open the door to peace.[43]

During his visit to Germany in 1914, House had met the kaiser but not the imperial chancellor; during this visit he failed to see the kaiser, but on March 27 he did at last talk with Bethmann-Hollweg.[44] Theobald von Bethmann-Hollweg, fifty-eight years old, was a tall, broad-shouldered Prussian aristocrat with a Vandyke beard who had served as imperial chancellor since 1909. He had grown up on Hohenfinow, a large estate thirty miles from Berlin. Intense and idealistic, with a passionate belief in the Prussian monarchy, he had risen through the civil service of Prussia and the Empire and had only reluctantly accepted the chancellorship. As he confided to a friend, "Only a genius or a man driven by ambition and lust for power can covet this post. I am neither. An ordinary man can only assume it when compelled by his sense of duty." He was similar to Grey in that the pressures of the war increased his distaste for power, and whenever possible he fled Berlin for the pleasures of his country estate.[45]

Bethmann-Hollweg was a professional bureaucrat, a deliberate, experienced administrator with, as one historian notes, "narrow intellectual and political horizons." He had known the kaiser for years and understood the politics of his court and of the imperial government. In small conferences or with individuals, Bethmann-Hollweg could be charming and convincing, but he lacked the skills or the vision for a broader kind of political leadership. As the war lengthened and casualties mounted, he became less decisive, agonizing over decisions because of what he termed a "deadening sense of responsibility." Bethmann-Hollweg had no solution for Germany's predicament; he could only maneuver among all of the contending domestic forces and hope that a military breakthrough would lead to a favorable peace.[46]

Late in the afternoon of March 27, House arrived at the chancellor's official residence. He found Bethmann-Hollweg "exceedingly cordial and delightful." House first summarized his efforts on behalf of peace since the beginning of the war, then declared that it was impossible "to discuss peace parleys now" and went on to outline his thoughts about the freedom of the seas. He now claimed that he intended to take up the idea with the British government and "fight it out with them." Bethmann-Hollweg was enthusiastic about House's plan and asked to be kept informed, but revealed nothing about his own thoughts or about divisions within the German government. House was, however, impressed with the chancellor. "I like him, I think," he wrote Auchincloss, "better than any of the officials I met in Germany, though they were all exceedingly cordial."[47]

During his nine days in Berlin, House mingled with a wide range of Germany's ruling elite. In all of these conversations House sought to promote German-American understanding and also explained that Wilson was not, like Bryan, in favor of peace at any price; the European belligerents would discover, if they challenged America, "that no one would maintain our rights more firmly than Woodrow Wilson." But House made no mention in his diary or letters of the quarrels within the German government over U-boat warfare; uninformed about this debate, he pursued a conciliatory approach when a more confrontational strategy might have alerted German leaders to the dangers of war with America.[48]

House was poorly informed about German politics in part because of Ambassador Gerard, whose confused, impetuous reports did little to enlighten Wilson or his emissary.[49] House seemed unconcerned, however, about Gerard's limitations as a diplomat, grateful that this ambassador, unlike Page, knew the part House expected him to play. "He has," House recorded, "been very considerate in not intruding himself in any of the conferences I have had with officials and with influential Germans." Gerard stayed in the background, making arrangements and waiting until House was ready to inform him about his diplomatic activities. One young

American diplomat attached to the embassy, Joseph C. Grew, was also impressed with Wilson's emissary and his wife. "A successful dinner," he recorded in his diary, "for Colonel and Mrs. House. Mrs. House is very pretty and charming and the Colonel is one of the most interesting men I have ever met; he is up to date on practically every subject."[50]

House felt that his visit to Germany had been a success and hoped that he had "sown some good seed and that they may bear fruit later." He found no evidence in Berlin of the strains of war. "No stores closed and no lack of people in the streets, and if the food supply is short it is not apparent." Peace did not seem on the horizon. He confided to Auchincloss that "It looks as if the slaughter will have to continue at least during the spring and summer. It is going to grow more and more bitter and the casualties will be something beyond anything known in history."[51]

House wrote Wilson long letters reporting on his conversations in Berlin. He now claimed that the German people (who had been given "an exaggerated idea of success"), not the government, were the major impediment to peace, and that he and Wilson would have to wait to push for peace until a crack appeared somewhere. In the meantime, House had accomplished "much of value here" and he assured the president, incorrectly, that "the warring nations have tentatively accepted you as their mediator." As House moved into the next stage of his journey, Wilson telegraphed that "I warmly admire the way in which you are conducting your conferences at each stage. You are laying the indispensable groundwork and sending me just the information I need."[52]

On the morning of March 28, House left Berlin for Switzerland, and after a night in Basel and another in Geneva, traveled by train to Nice. He lingered in the south of France for over a week, enjoying the warm, sunny weather, and finally reached Paris on the evening of April 10.[53] He soon informed Gregory that "As far as peace is concerned there is no rift in the clouds as yet and I see no prospect of my return [to the United States] before the Autumn." In the meantime, House was pleased with his accomplishments in Berlin, London, and Paris, convinced that "if the war ended tomorrow America and the President would be, I think, the most potent factors in the conventions to determine the permanent settlement."[54] He planned to leave for England soon and, after a few weeks there, travel to Russia via Holland, Denmark, Norway, and Sweden. House would "keep in touch with the situation in each belligerent country" and wait until one side or another had lost its confidence in victory.[55]

Three days after his arrival House met once again with Foreign Minister Delcassé. After listening to a summary of House's visit to Berlin, Delcassé explained that, while France had not wanted war, the nation was now determined "to make another such conflict impossible within several generations . . . . There was no chance of peace at the moment on any terms that Germany had in mind." Rather than ask on what terms France would end the struggle, House agreed with Delcassé's position and "told him the President was of the same mind." "I let him see," House recorded, "that it was not our purpose to push peace negotiations, but to let them come when the parties at interest were ready."[56]

On April 16, House had his first conference with President Raymond Poincaré at the Elysée Palace. Although warned that the French president could be "cold and austere," House received a warm welcome as he and Poincaré exchanged diplomatic niceties. House concluded from his interviews with both French leaders that, until the French people and their leaders had a better understanding of America and its president, any peace move would be premature.[57]

Twelve days later House crossed the Channel for the final part of his mission to Europe. Unlike his earlier trips in 1913 and 1914, the stakes were higher now; the great powers were engaged in a global war with no end in sight, one which threatened the breakdown of European civilization. But House had accomplished little on his journey through the belligerent capitals. Confronted with the intransigence of British, French, and German leaders, he had chosen a policy of conciliation rather than of confrontation and began to pursue the vague idea of rewriting the code of international behavior. He turned his gaze toward the future, neglecting the present, over-identifying with British leaders and ignoring the emergence of the submarine issue between Germany and the United States. Two days after House arrived in London, Page summed up his mission: "Peace-talk, therefore, is yet mere moonshine—House has been in Berlin, from London, thence to Paris, thence back to London again—from Nowhere (as far as peace is concerned) to Nowhere again."[58]

15

The Turn to War

When the House family and the ever-present Fanny arrived in London on the evening of April 28, 1915, they went to Ambassador Page's residence, where they planned to stay for a few days. Early the next morning, House left to find more permanent quarters, and soon rented a small house on Bolton Street, just off Piccadilly Circus and close to Green Park. "It is," he reported to Gordon Auchincloss, "charmingly furnished, very small, but plenty of room for us and for you and Janet and the baby if you come over." In mid-April House had planned to spend only a few weeks in England and then leave for Russia; now he intended "to remain in London indefinitely for I have cut out much of importance to do."[1]

Prior to House's return to London he had written Grey describing Germany's extensive peace terms; Grey had responded that "your news from Berlin is not encouraging: it reduced Bernstorff's peace talk at Washington to 'fudge.'"[2] Grey sought to discourage meddling by Wilson and his emissary, emphasizing the "moral wrong. . . done by Germany" and the "great divergence between the German estimate of the situation and that of the Allies." He knew that Britain's allies, France and Russia, were against neutral mediation of the war, while his subordinates in the Foreign Office had a low regard for American politicians and were wary of Wilsonian intervention. Grey's task was to listen patiently to House and remind him of the idealistic aspects of the Allied cause.[3]

Despite Grey's reservations, House was "pleased with the outlook" for his peace efforts and eager to see the foreign secretary. Two days after his arrival he and Grey lunched together and then retired to his library for "one of the most interesting and important conferences we have yet had." House focused on the details of the peace conference, explaining how he would draw upon his experience in organizing political conventions. Grey, preoccupied with the prosecution of the war, must have been puzzled by House's focus on a peace settlement. Rather than appear unreasonable, however, he promised to take up House's ideas with the cabinet and suggested that House also discuss them with leaders of the Conservative opposition. House left his two-hour talk with Grey encouraged, determined to consult "some of the best minds in England" on issues that would come before the peace conference and convinced that Grey's "mind and mine run nearly parallel and we seldom disagree. I know in advance, just as I know with the President, what his views will be on almost any subject . . . . It is. . . my good fortune that fate has given me two such friends as Woodrow Wilson and Edward Grey."[4]

In early May, House settled into his London routine, attending an endless round of lunches and dinner parties and consulting with a wide range of British leaders. At a dinner party on May 6, House revealed the extent of his identification with the British cause. When the conversation turned to whether Great Britain "was doing her full duty" in the war, House interrupted to praise the British contribution. Britain had not only "asserted her supremacy at sea" and "raised an enormous army," but had become "the only belligerent with a worldwide vision of the war and its consequences." "When Great Britain entered the war," House concluded, "every neutral country felt that Germany was doomed to defeat, and I was sure that Germany herself had the fear of God in her heart." Throughout his talk House was interrupted by cries of "'hear, hear,'" and when he finished, Balfour told him that "that is the most eloquent speech I have ever heard."[5]

The next morning, May 7, House and Grey drove together to visit the Royal Botanic Gardens at Kew. Once they had passed through the gates of Kew Gardens, their talk of the war ceased and they became absorbed in the beauty of the fresh, green English spring, discussing the birds and trees and the differences between spring in England and Texas. Grey reminded House of his failing eyesight, revealing that "unless he stops reading he will lose his sight to the extent of not being able to read again." The two men lingered so long in Kew Gardens that House arrived late at Buckingham Palace for his meeting with George V.[6]

In early May speculation was rife on both sides of the Atlantic that a German U-boat might sink one of the North Atlantic passenger liners. During their drive to Kew Gardens, House and Grey "spoke of the probability of an ocean liner being sunk, and I told him if this were done, a flame of indignation would sweep across America, which would in itself, probably carry us into the war."[7] On May 7, their fears became a reality. On a clear, warm, early summer afternoon, the U-20 spotted the SS *Lusitania* sailing on a straight course at eighteen knots off the southern coast of Ireland. At 2:10 PM it fired one torpedo that hit the great ship on the starboard side close to the bridge, causing a large explosion. Within eighteen minutes the *Lusitania* sank, carrying 1,198 of its 1,257 passengers to their deaths, including 128 Americans.[8]

The sinking of the *Lusitania* angered Page, whose daughter entered in her diary, "Ambassador violent for war." Now an advocate of American intervention, on May 8 he dispatched a telegram to Washington—after showing it to House—declaring that the United States must enter the war on the side of the Allies or forfeit the respect of the nations of Europe.[9]

House's reaction was similar to Page's. On May 9 he cabled the president, urging him to demand from the German government assurances that passenger liners would not be sunk. Two days later House remained convinced that war must come "unless Germany promises to ease her policy of making war upon non combatants." If Wilson did not issue a stern protest, he predicted that "her next act will probably be the sinking of an American liner." If war came, House urged Wilson to prepare so efficiently that the European belligerents—who thought that America would be slow to mobilize its resources—would be astonished at the speed with which American supplies flowed across the Atlantic. And he sympathized with the new burdens that had fallen on his friend in the White House. "My heart goes out to you at this time," he reassured the president, "as never before and I think of you every hour of the day and wish that I was by your side."[10]

The sinking of the *Lusitania* shocked Americans, who now began to understand the savageness of the Great War. Some pro-Allied extremists, convinced that Germany was an outlaw nation, urged American intervention; most Americans, however, while they wanted their government to express their moral indignation, hoped to avoid involvement in the conflict. As Ambassador Spring-Rice noted, there was "an intense desire to keep the peace."[11]

Initially the president retreated into himself, seeking to find his moorings and to reflect on the nature of the American response. On May 10, he broke his silence in a speech at Philadelphia, where he declared that "there is such a thing as a man being too proud to fight. There is such a thing as a nation being so right that it does not need to convince others by force that it is right." Wilson quickly realized, however, that he had gone too far in his Philadelphia address, and on May 11 read to his cabinet a draft note to Germany—a note he had composed on his own typewriter—affirming the right of American citizens to travel on the high seas and insisting that Germany spare the lives of noncombatants, disavow the commander of the U-20, and offer reparations. In effect, Wilson demanded that Germany abandon its U-boat campaign against merchantmen and passenger liners.[12] House, who had been "distressed" by the passivity of the president's Philadelphia speech, applauded his firm note to Berlin[13]

House was, in fact, now preoccupied with—even eager about—the possibility of American entry into the war, concluding that the torpedoing of the Lusitania had brought his efforts to end the conflict to a "standstill." On May 12 he finally met Lord Kitchener, the nation's most illustrious living soldier, the conqueror of the Sudan, who had spent most of his life abroad in Egypt, India, and South Africa. A tall, powerfully built man with a florid complexion and a bushy moustache, he was proud and autocratic, unaccustomed to delegating authority or to the give-and-take of the cabinet. On his acceptance of Asquith's offer of the war office, he remarked: "May God preserve me from the politicians."[14] From the start Kitchener was prescient on the big issues of the war. He believed that the conflict would last three years and that Britain would have to raise and equip an enormous New Army to fight on the Western Front. Kitchener also pushed hard to expand Britain's small prewar munitions industry. During the first winter of the war he was, Winston Churchill remembered, "All-powerful, imperturbable, reserved, he dominated absolutely our councils at this time." But by the spring of 1915, as the British war effort floundered, Kitchener's leadership became controversial. Britain's production of munitions, although vastly expanded, remained inadequate; Kitchener's organizational skills seemed flawed, and his relations with his cabinet colleagues, especially with Lloyd George, deteriorated. He remained, however, a popular hero, indispensable to the British war effort.[15]

On his arrival at York House, Kitchener's private residence, House received a cordial welcome from the secretary of state for war, who talked with him for nearly an hour. When House asked if American entry into the war would benefit the Allies, Kitchener walked up and down the room, repeating again and again that "it would greatly shorten the war and would save innumerable lives." Obviously relieved that the United States seemed on the brink of joining the Allies, Kitchener mentioned his earlier fear that "the President would try to intervene." House reassured him—in a remark he did not report to Wilson—that "the President would not intervene and would do nothing to embarrass any of the belligerents." The "frankness and cordiality" of Kitchener's reception pleased House, who found him a "forceful and able" leader. "Kitchener was not," he recorded, "the greatest intellect with which I have come in touch, but he has a manner indicating great reserve force, and if I were going 'tiger hunting' I would gladly have him as a companion."[16]

Two days later House discussed the course of the war, and the possibility of American entry, with the foreign secretary. Grey approved of Wilson's *Lusitania* note and agreed with Kitchener that the "effect [of American entry] would be immediate and decisive," but made no attempt to influence the decision of the American government. Grey confided to House that "there were almost none with whom he talked as he did to me," for most individuals were "surrounded by some invisible substance that enveloped them." He gave House one of his books and inscribed his name on the flyleaf. Grey's "high expression of friendship" touched House, who trusted both Grey and Balfour "implicitly." "Grey and Balfour," he concluded, "are two great gentlemen and I feel sure of their discretion."[17]

While House focused on the war in Europe, events in Mexico continued to spiral out of control, since none of the revolutionary factions seemed capable of uniting the country. In late January, Pancho Villa's troops withdrew from Mexico City and in early April, Venustiano Carranza's forces, under the leadership of General Alvaro Obregon, badly defeated Villa's Division of the North. But conditions in Mexico City—where 23,000 foreigners (including 2,500 Americans) lived—continued to deteriorate; the city was in chaos, ravaged by looting and food shortages. Wilson and Bryan, convinced that Carranza could never bring an end to the turmoil, were under both domestic and international pressure to impose order. They hoped to create a new government that all of the factions would support.[18]

Absorbed in his peace efforts in Berlin, London, and Paris, House paid little attention to events in Mexico. He found Mexico's revolution a tiresome distraction, especially after the sinking of the *Lusitania* and the crisis in German-American relations. House concluded that "we have about reached the limit of our forbearance" in Mexico and that some form of American intervention was the "only hope." He urged Wilson to cooperate with Argentina, Brazil, and Chile "in straightening out the affairs of that republic." They should create a new government in Mexico City and "compel the Mexican people to live under that Government, whether or no." House saw no reason to continue to tolerate disorder south of the border.[19]

By early May, the tide of military events seemed to be running against the Allies. British and French offensives on the Western Front had failed, German and Austro-Hungarian forces were pushing Russian troops out of the Carpathians and Galicia, and the Anglo-French military landings on the Gallipoli peninsula, from which the Allies had expected so much, soon ended in a deadly stalemate with Turkish forces. Gallipoli, Churchill's brother wrote from that front, "has become siege warfare as in France." The only good news for the Allies was Italy's agreement on April 26, in the Treaty of London, to enter the war.[20] These military failures, combined with the shell shortage on the Western Front—which the London Times revealed on May 14—crystallized the widespread feeling that Asquith's government was inadequate to meet the burdens of the war. Confronted with the first serious challenge to the Liberal Party's control of war policy, Asquith moved quickly to avoid bitter partisan warfare by giving senior places in a new coalition government to his Conservative Party rivals and by establishing a ministry of munitions. The prime minister juggled cabinet positions adroitly, keeping most of the key positions in Liberal hands, replacing Churchill at the Admiralty with Balfour and shifting Lloyd George to the new ministry of munitions. Some members of the new cabinet were sure to push for a fuller mobilization of men and resources and a more vigorous prosecution of the war.[21]

Although the agreement to form a coalition cabinet was announced on May 19, not until June 2 did House have a long talk with its rising star, David Lloyd George. Despite his friend Horace Plunkett's warning that Lloyd George was a "demagogue" and a "shifty lawyer," House was eager to take his measure. Lloyd George, fifty-two when House met him, was ten years younger than Asquith, a forceful, charming man with bright blue eyes and stylishly long hair, attractive to women and unconventional in his personal life (he maintained two households, one with his wife in Wales and another with his secretary and mistress, Francis Stevenson). Born in Wales, he had risen to power within the Liberal Party as a radical, outside the London establishment, and, as Asquith's chancellor of the exchequer, had played a major role in the enactment of the party's social reform legislation. Once Great Britain entered the war, Lloyd George turned his attention to wider strategic issues and became dissatisfied with Asquith's leadership, convinced that Britain's war effort could succeed only if there was a driving force at the top.[22] As Asquith's new minister of munitions, Lloyd George intended to provide this direction, transforming Britain into a war economy. He was vigorous and dynamic, an instinctive politician who had "a rare capacity," one biographer notes, "to project himself into the thoughts and feelings of others." Even those who thought Lloyd George cynical and opportunistic realized that he was a powerful force in the new coalition cabinet.[23]

House met with Lloyd George on his first day in his new quarters in Whitehall. He found him "full of energy and enthusiasm," critical of Kitchener and his War Ministry, and determined to increase rapidly Britain's production of artillery shells. House had complained earlier about the lack of forceful leaders in Asquith's cabinet; now he was convinced that Lloyd George would soon make something "happen in his department." Lloyd George, House concluded, was different from the other British politicians that he met, "more of the virile, aggressive type of American politician than any member of the Cabinet. He lacks the learning, the culture and the trustworthiness of his governmental associates, but he has something dynamic within him which his colleagues have not and which is badly needed in this great hour."[24]

While Wilson waited for a reply from Germany to his *Lusitania* note, he considered the possibility of a strong protest to Britain over its violation of American neutral rights. As the British blockade intensified, pressure mounted from Secretary of State Bryan and from some Democrats in Congress for a forceful American response, including a possible embargo on the shipment of arms and war supplies to the Allies. Wilson, hoping to avoid a formal protest, instructed both House and Page to raise with Grey the issue of British interference with neutral cargoes. The foreign secretary was sympathetic with American concerns and by the end of the month House and Page believed that the situation had improved. But House warned Wilson that while his position "with Germany and Great Britain is correct," he must remember that if the United States lost the "good will" of the Allies, it would not "figure at all in peace negotiations." Wilson did not dispute the advice. Keen on playing a major role in ending the war, he had no desire to provoke a crisis with Britain while America's relations with Germany hung in the balance.[25]

When House returned to England in late April, he had planned to linger in London for many months. He relished his life there—the mingling with Britain's cultural and social elite; the long, intimate conversations with

Balfour, Grey, and other political leaders; and the occasional weekends at a country house or expeditions outside of London.[26] The sinking of the *Lusitania* changed House's sense of the timing of his mission. Earlier he had hoped that the war would end by late summer; now he realized, with the American note of protest to Germany and with Germany's evasive reply of May 28, that the diplomatic standoff between the United States and Germany could lead to war. After reading the full text of Germany's note, House concluded "that war with Germany is inevitable" and decided to leave for home on June 5.[27] When House informed Wilson of his decision to return, the president let him decide where he could be of "better service." "You have been so invaluable to me over there," he telegraphed, "and can be of such great service to me here in these times of perplexity that I am at a loss to advise." It is not surprising that House felt the president "has been splendid in giving me a free hand."[28]

Other, more personal considerations also influenced House's decision. Grey's departure to the countryside for at least a month, where he hoped to rest his failing eyes, made staying in London less appealing. House was also eager to be reunited with "Boots," his daughter Janet, who had been slow, after the birth of her daughter Louise in December 1914, to regain her physical strength and emotional equilibrium. "I long," he wrote his son-in-law, "to be home in order to cheer dear Janet. I fear she loses heart at times." On the day House wired Wilson that he planned to return he had received a letter from Janet "telling how lonely she was." It was time to reunite his family.[29]

Before departing on June 5, House received disappointing news about the war. Ambassador Gerard wrote of the confidence and determination of German leaders, who were encouraged by recent military successes (especially on the Eastern Front), had no intention of restraining their U-boat commanders, and planned to keep Belgium and "extract great indemnities from other countries." Balfour reported on "a distinct feeling of depression in England," due to the shortage of high-explosive shells and Russia's military defeats, and on the lack of confidence among British leaders that the French could break through German lines. The Allies' military failures had cast a pall over their war effort.[30]

House also continued to think about the peace settlement. Lord Loreburn, a prominent Liberal, promised to draft a clause on the freedom of the seas for the peace convention, while Grey, writing from Fallodon in Northumberland, tried to focus House's thoughts on America's role in the "larger aspects of the peace," warning prophetically that "Germany is the peril to-day, but the peril will recur every century in Europe, if Europe is left to itself. And the peril now cannot be confined to one continent—the world is too closely knit together by modern inventions and conditions."[31]

Throughout his stay in London, House remained on good terms with Ambassador Page, who entertained him and Loulie often and helped with many practical matters. Beneath the surface cordiality, however, tensions simmered. House believed that Page was often indiscreet and, especially after the sinking of the *Lusitania*, too openly pro-British, while Page gradually realized that House was undercutting him and doubted the value of House's efforts to end the war. House claimed to like Page—"He is direct and without guile"—and sought to avoid offending "his sensibilities," but he excluded him from most of his talks with Grey and recruited the ambassador's secretary, Clifford Carver, to act as his personal agent. House conducted most of his diplomacy in Britain without Page's knowledge or involvement; only so long as Page was content to remain on the sidelines would relations between him and the president's emissary remain cordial.[32]

The Houses had "a restful and pleasant voyage" on the SS *St. Paul*, which sailed from Liverpool on June 5 and, until it left the war zone, was escorted by two fast destroyers. On arriving in New York on June 13, the House party boarded a revenue cutter before reaching the dock and then drove to the Auchincloss's summer home in Roslyn, Long Island. Janet, her husband recorded, "was . . . overjoyed to see her parents again" and that evening the House family had a happy reunion. As House told his son-in-law of the details of his trip, "he was very full of fight and. . . thought war was imminent between the United States and Germany." Convinced that the warlords of Germany were dominant, House's mind was filled with ambitious plans for a "stupendous" American war effort to counter them. In late April he had arrived in London full of plans for peace; in early June he left, as Page noted in his diary, "red-hot for war."[33]

16

American Interlude

House was at sea when on June 8, 1915, he learned of Bryan's resignation as secretary of state. For many months Bryan had felt that his stature within the administration had been eroding. The president, often working behind his back and ignoring his advice, clearly did not trust his judgment. In early June, when Wilson drafted his second, sterner, *Lusitania* note, he rejected Bryan's pleas for a conciliatory response and once again insisted that Germany abandon its U-boat campaign. Convinced that the president's note carried with it the risk of war, on June 7 Bryan told Wilson of his decision to resign, complaining "with a quiver in his voice and of his lips 'Colonel House has been Secretary of State, not I, and I have never had your full confidence.'" The next day, at a farewell luncheon with his friends, the Great Commoner announced that "I go out into the dark. The President has the Prestige and the Power on his side." Then he added, somewhat cryptically, "I have many friends who would die for me."[1]

Bryan's resignation raised a furor across the nation. Many Americans—given the widespread approval of Wilson's second *Lusitania* note—were puzzled by the reasons for his departure, and those who had long been hostile to Bryan now vented their fury at his abandonment of the administration. The *New York World* denounced his "unspeakable treachery," while Ambassador Page wrote that "of course he's a traitor: he always had a yellow streak, the yellow streak of a sheer fool." The president was simply relieved that Bryan was gone, though also realized that Bryan could now rally his large following against the administration's neutrality policies and possibly imperil his renomination and reelection in 1916.[2]

On June 13, House arrived in Roslyn in the midst of these stirring events. He had last seen Wilson on January 25, a few days before he left for Europe, but had no plans to travel to Washington. He both feared the early summer heat in the capital and wanted to get in touch with "the feeling in America which will make my talk with the President of more value."[3] The president, however, was eager to consult with House about Bryan's successor and on June 14 dispatched McAdoo to New York. Wilson, in fact, had few ideas about Bryan's replacement, dismissing Robert Lansing, who had been counselor since March 1914, as "not a big enough man."[4] But House had given the appointment more thought than Wilson. As House put it bluntly in a letter to the president: "I think the most important thing is to get a man without too many ideas of his own and one that will be entirely guided by you without unnecessary argument, and this, it seems to me, you will find in Lansing. I only met him once and then for a few minutes only, and while his mentality did not impress me unduly, at the same time I hope that you have found him able enough to answer the purpose indicated." In short, House urged Wilson to select someone who would look after the details of American diplomacy while he and the president made the big decisions. Wilson agreed with House's conclusions, offering Lansing the position on June 23.[5]

Since House would not risk a trip to Washington, Wilson decided to stop at Roslyn for a day on his way to vacation with his family at Cornish. After a separation of nearly five months, the president greeted House with "warmth and affection, placing both hands over mine." Then the two men drove from the Roslyn railway station to Gordon Auchincloss's summer cottage, where they "went on the terrace and began one of our most intimate conversations."[6]

In his meeting with the president, House exaggerated his accomplishments during his long stay in Europe, boasting that "I had left matters in such shape that there were people in each of the belligerent countries ready to notify me when it was thought I had best return." Wilson, House recorded, "seemed delighted with the work done and the good relations established in the different capitals." He was pleased that his counselor was back and would leave it to his judgment when the time was "propitious" to return to Europe.[7] The president and House also discussed Bryan and Lansing. Wilson had noticed "a change for the better even in the short time he [Bryan] had been out," while House, conceding that his antagonist "has imagination and has genius in certain directions," delivered a harsh judgment on the former secretary of state: "I replied that Mr. Bryan had never done any serious work in his life; that he was essentially a talker, and I believed if he had remained in the State Department two years longer and had been suppressed as he has been during the past two years, it would have killed him."[8] Both men agreed that Lansing would be a good replacement. Wilson had, House noted, "explained to Lansing our relations, and he did not believe we would have any trouble with him." But the president wanted House to invite Lansing to the North Shore for a talk. When House asked if he should tell the new secretary of state "the whole story regarding my European work," Wilson replied " 'No, not fully, but enough to get him to work in harmony with us.' "[9]

After his arrival in Roslyn, House had learned, through his talks with Gregory and McAdoo, that the president had fallen in love. Around March 20, when House was in Berlin, Wilson had met Edith Bolling Galt, a tall, shapely widow with grey eyes and dark hair. Vivacious and stylish, she had grown up in a genteel but impoverished Virginia family and had married Norman Galt, the owner of Washington's most prominent jewelry and fine silver store. After his death in 1908, she had taken over the management of the store and had led a quiet, affluent life, mingling with a small group of friends and taking frequent trips to Europe. Her beauty and warm, romantic temperament appealed to Wilson, and within a few weeks after their first meeting they were taking long drives and eating dinner together at the White House, retreating afterward to the president's study for private conversations. Although Edith was forty-two, sixteen years younger than the president, Wilson pressed his courtship. On May 4, less than two months after they had met, he declared his love and asked Edith to marry him. While she gently rebuffed him, he continued his pursuit, sending flowers every day to her house near Dupont Circle and writing a torrent of letters, some as long as twenty pages. "Here stands your friend," he wrote Edith on May 5, "a longing man, in the midst of a world's affairs—a world that knows nothing of the heart he has shown you and which would as lief break it as not . . . . Will you come to him some time, without reserve and make his strength complete?"[10]

At some point during their talk at Roslyn, Wilson told House that "Since you left I have met a delightful woman and I am thinking of asking her to marry me [Wilson had, in fact, already done so]. Do you believe I would lessen my influence with the American people by taking such a step? And when do you think I could do it?" Fortunately, House had been forewarned of the president's romance and quickly approved Wilson's plans for remarriage. He had long been worried about Wilson's longevity and now felt "that his health demands it [remarriage]." "I also feel," he recorded in his diary, "that Woodrow Wilson today is the greatest asset the world has. If he should die or become incapacitated, it is doubtful whether a right solution of the problems involved in this terrible conflict and its aftermath would be possible." But House did give Wilson one piece of (unwelcomed) advice, urging him to delay the marriage until the spring of 1916.[11]

After their long morning talk, they walked down a hill to call on one of Wilson's old college friends, ate lunch together, and then drove to the Piping Rock Country Club, where Wilson played golf with Grayson and Auchincloss. Before the president left Roslyn station on an evening train, House urged him to take a complete rest at Cornish and reminded him "of how much depended upon him and how anxious I was that he might maintain his health and strength." But Wilson was convinced "that Providence did not remove a man until his work was finished."[12]

The sinking of the *Lusitania* and the ensuing crisis with Germany had dramatically increased anti-war sentiment in the United States and brought widespread appeals for some sort of reasonable settlement. A few days after his return from England, House sensed the shift of opinion. An old Texas friend confirmed his judgment, writing that he was certain that "there is an overwhelming desire for peace, not perhaps at any price, but at most prices, which is altogether unprecedented in the history of this country." He warned that Wilson could win reelection in 1916 only with "the whole-hearted support of Mr. Bryan."[13]

As Wilson and House pondered the U-boat impasse with Germany, they received discouraging news about the course of the war in Europe. Ambassador Gerard believed that Germany was winning the war, an American diplomat in France noted the general "feeling of pessimism" in Paris, and Ambassador Page wrote of the "distinct wave of depression" in England. He found London a sad and lonely place, as people left the city and as the wounded returned from the Western Front.[14] Even some of House's British friends seemed discouraged. Lord Loreburn saw no hope for peace, despite the growing realization "that the war must end or Western Civilization may be submerged." Foreign Secretary Grey, back at work by the middle of July, did not believe the belligerents could agree on terms. He missed House's "presence in London," and already seemed nostalgic about his vacation in Northumberland. He found "the indifference of Nature to the war" reassuring, and on his return to the burdens of office in London felt as he imagined "wounded or invalided soldiers feel when the time comes for them to return to the trenches."[15]

In Berlin, Chancellor Bethmann Hollweg maneuvered among contending factions and sought to avoid a break with the United States. Leaders in the German Navy, convinced that the U-boat would bring decisive results, clamored for all-out warfare against Great Britain and found strong support from the public and from powerful blocs in the Reichstag. The chancellor lacked the power to force an abandonment of the U-boat and could only hope to appease his opponents, intriguing within the inner circle around the kaiser for concessions to the American government.[16] Confronted with Wilson's first *Lusitania* note, Bethmann Hollweg procrastinated and sought to strengthen his position. While Germany's formal reply to America's protest was evasive, the chancellor, with the support of Chief of Staff Falkenhayn, convinced the kaiser to forbid any U-boat attacks on large passenger ships. Confronted with Wilson's second *Lusitania* note, he once again outmaneuvered Navy leaders and carried the day. The German government made no specific concessions to American demands, but it did promise to do everything in its power to protect the lives of American citizens.[17]

After receiving Germany's reply to the second American note on July 10, House immediately drafted a vigorous response that he sent to the president, and the same day House poured out his frustrations over the president's inaction. Long an advocate of military preparedness, House now condemned Wilson's failure to realize "the gravity of our unprepared position." He was convinced that if the United States had built up a powerful war machine Germany would have been more circumspect and "we would be in a position today to enforce peace." House then broadened his critique, regretting in his diary Wilson's inability "to carry along more than one idea at a time." While House professed admiration for the president's "judgment, his ability, and his patriotism," he regretted that he lost so much time each summer. "From the first of May until the first of October," he lamented, "I see him practically not at all, and I find that I cannot stir him to action unless I am with him in person and undertake the prosecution largely myself." Forgetting that he had chosen to linger in Europe from late January to early June, and then to summer on the North Shore, he now cast himself as the indispensable adviser, standing at the ready.[18]

The president, "refreshed and renewed" by his vacation in Cornish, was unaware of House's discontents. He felt that House's draft reply to the German note was "very much along the lines of my own thought," and he was convinced that "the Germans *are* modifying their methods."

But Wilson was also more impressed than his adviser with the power of anti-war sentiment and now sought to narrow the disagreement with Germany, in effect accepting the U-boat campaign as long as submarines did not attack passenger ships without warning. The note that the United States dispatched to Berlin on July 21 still insisted on a disavowal and reparations for the sinking of the *Lusitania*, but the president did not intend to press hard on these issues; he seemed content to accept an impasse. At the end of July, when the German government made further concessions, it looked as if the most dangerous phase of the submarine controversy had passed.[19] House for his part seemed content with the president's response, convinced that he was in part responsible for its firmness. But he remained annoyed with Wilson. When his brother-in-law Sidney Mezes wrote that he liked the note, House responded that "Wilson flickered a little, but came up to the lick-log at the last."[20]

In June, Wilson had suggested that House confer with Secretary of State Lansing, but it was not until July 24 that Lansing and his wife arrived in Manchester for a two-day stay. The new secretary of state, fifty years old, was a compact, handsome man, formal in his dress and manners, with a carefully trimmed grey mustache. Lansing had married the daughter of John W. Foster, a distinguished American diplomat who had served as President Benjamin Harrison's secretary of state. Helped by his father-in-law's connections, he had turned to the practice of international law, spending more and more time in Washington and serving on more international arbitration cases than any other American lawyer. In April 1914, he had been an obvious choice to replace John Bassett Moore as counselor of the State Department.[21]

Given Bryan's frequent absences, Lansing, as counselor, had often run the department, and after the outbreak of the war the president had drawn on his expert legal knowledge in shaping American neutrality. Many people, including House and Wilson, were misled by Lansing's diffident exterior and tended to underrate the new secretary of state. He had a thorough understanding of the diplomatic process and a tough, disciplined mind, accustomed to dealing with complex questions of law and diplomacy.[22] Lansing thought of foreign policy in terms of strategy and power—firmly in the tradition of realpolitik—and, at the start of the war, concentrated on the perfection of American neutrality. By the early summer of 1915, however, he had concluded that German submarine warfare threatened America's economic and military security and that the United States must enter the struggle. On July 11, less than two weeks before he met with

House, Lansing wrote, in a private memorandum, that "only recently has the conviction come to me that democracy throughout the world is threatened by German aggression. We will have to cast aside our neutrality and become one of the champions of democracy."[23]

Soon after Lansing's mid-morning arrival at Manchester, House and the secretary of state went into "executive session." House was surprised that Wilson "had not talked with him [Lansing] more freely and given him fuller information concerning pending matters," and he proceeded to review the whole range of American foreign policy. House was pleased with his new partner, who was familiar with the machinery of the State Department and who seemed "energetic and ambitious to make a record." Soon after Lansing's departure, he wrote Auchincloss that "I had a delightful time with Lansing. We got along famously together and I am congratulating myself that I had the foresight to back him."[24]

With Lansing's appointment as secretary of state, House sought to increase his influence in the State Department, ridding it of "incompetent Democrats" and putting more of his protégés in key positions. In February 1914, he had secured the appointment of William Phillips as third assistant secretary of state; now he placed Frank Polk, the corporation counsel for New York, as counselor. The department, he warned the president, "is your most important instrument at present and everything should be done to perfect it so that your policies may be carried through in the shortest time and most efficient manner."[25]

On July 26, the day Lansing left Manchester, House turned fifty-seven. He did not mention his birthday in his diary, but on August 4 did note his thirty-fourth wedding anniversary. He and Loulie had married in 1881, when he was twenty-three and she was twenty-two—less than two years after his father's death and at a time when he was still managing a part of the family's business. Over the years, as House ascended to the national and international political stage, Loulie had been an elegant and charming hostess who deferred to the needs of his political career. While Fanny ran the household, renting houses, hiring and firing servants, soothing irate maids and chauffeurs, his "Dearest Loulie" remained a close companion.[26]

Despite the brevity of their meeting on June 24, as the summer progressed Wilson and House felt that they were back in touch with one another. "But I need not explain anything to you," Wilson wrote him on July 21. "You know as well as I do what my motives are, so soon as I form them."[27] On July 31, Grayson appeared at House's cottage and for nearly two hours poured out intimate details of Wilson's personal life. Grayson was upset by "the President's infatuation with Mrs. Norman Galt. It seems the President is wholly absorbed in this love affair and is neglecting practically everything else." House regretted that Wilson "had fallen in love at this time" and realized that "he will be criticized for not waiting longer after Mrs. Wilson's death." But he sympathized with the president's lack of privacy, noting in his diary that "There is someone to watch every turn and movement he makes."[28]

In June and July of 1915, as Wilson and Edith Galt spent weeks together at Cornish, their love deepened. "You are my ideal companion," Wilson declared, "the close and delightful *chum of my mind.* You are my perfect *playmate,"* while Edith wrote her "Sweetheart" that "There are no locked doors. . . but instead all the gates are flung wide, and a perfect flood of longing rushes to you."[29]

House, who had not yet met Edith, had no way of knowing that she was a different kind of person than Ellen Wilson. Ellen was a woman of learning and artistic talent, one with a keen insight into her husband's emotional needs and a wise tolerance of his political associates. She had welcomed House into her family, seeking his advice on both personal and political matters and thanking him, on one occasion, for "being too good to us all."[30] Edith was lively and stylish, but poorly educated and intolerant of the president's closest advisers. She was curious about his work, eager to be "taken into partnership" with him, and Wilson quickly obliged, writing that "I am so glad to share public matters with you—so anxious to share them with you." During the summer of 1915, when separated, Edith began receiving a "big envelope" nearly every day full of official documents, with notes of explanation written by the president. When together at Harlakenden, they would sit on the terrace overlooking the Connecticut River Valley while, Edith wrote, "you put one dear hand on mine, while with the other you turn the pages of history."[31]

Well before Edith and House met, Wilson sought to encourage a friendship between them. Writing to her on August 13, Wilson revealed that "I feel about your character and the disinterested loyalty of your friendship just as I have so often told you I felt about House. If I did not love you, I would still utterly trust you and cling to you and value your clear-sighted counsel, in which you would be *thinking for me,* as House does. You are talking nonsense. . . when you speak of wishing that you had the 'wisdom of a well-informed mind' in order that you might be a 'staff for me to lean on' . . . . That is not what I need. What I need is what you give me . . . . And the *capacity* of your mind is as great and satisfactory as that of any man I know." Rather than acknowledge Edith's limitations, Wilson equated her advice with that of one of his oldest and most experienced associates.[32]

Despite the president's efforts, however, Edith was not inclined to share her love for him with another person. Tumulty's "commonness" troubled her, and, after reading some of House's letters in the summer of 1915, she was also skeptical of his value. Or as she wrote: "I know I am wrong but I can't help feeling he is not a very *strong* character. I suppose it is in comparison to you, for really every other man seems like a dwarf when I put them by you in my thoughts. I know what a comfort and staff Col. House is to you Precious One and that your judgment about him is correct, but he does look like a weak vessel and I think that he writes like one very often."[33] Wilson responded with the fullest assessment of Tumulty and House that he ever wrote. He agreed with Edith that Tumulty lacked "our breeding," but pointed out that the majority of people with whom he had to deal were also common and that his longtime secretary "does understand them and know how to deal with them." Moreover, Tumulty was "absolutely devoted and loyal to me" and a shrewd judge of the opinion of "the man on the street." Any administration, Wilson concluded, required a diversity of talent if it was to grasp all the currents of national affairs.

"And, then," Wilson wrote to "My own Darling," "dear House,"

> About him, again, you are no doubt partly right. You have too keen an insight and too discerning a judgment to be wholly wrong, even in a snap judgment of a man you do not know! House *has* a strong character,—if to be disinterested and unafraid and incorruptible is to be strong. He has a noble and lovely character, too, for he is capable of utter self-forgetfulness and loyalty and devotion. And he is wise. He can give prudent and far-seeing counsel. He can find out what many men, of diverse kinds, are thinking about, and how they can be made to work together for a common purpose. He wins the confidence of all sorts of men, and wins it at once,—by deserving it. But you are right in thinking that intellectually he is not a great man. His mind is not of the first class. He is a counsellor, not a statesman . . . . We cannot require of every man that he should be everything. You are going to love House some day,—if only because he loves me and would give, I believe, his life for me,— and because he loves the country and seeks its real benefit and glory. I'm not afraid of the ultimate impression he will make on you,—because I know you and your instinctive love and admiration for whatever is true and genuine.

You must remember, dear little critic, that sweetness and *power* do not often happen together. You are apt to exact too much of others because of what you are yourself and mistakenly suppose it easy and common to be.[34]

Confronted with Wilson's remarkable assessment of House's strengths and weaknesses, Edith relented, but only slightly. "I am almost sorry," she quickly replied, "I wrote you what I did yesterday about Col. House, but I can no more keep things from you than I can stop loving you—and so you must forgive me. I know he is fine and true, but I don't think him vigorous and strong—am I wrong?"[35]

Throughout the summer of 1915 the situation in Mexico remained chaotic. While Venustiano Carranza's Constitutionalist faction gained strength, conditions in Mexico City remained bleak, with widespread looting and starvation. Not until August 3 did the forces of General Alvaro Obregon, his military commander, finally occupy the capital and end its long ordeal.[36]

By the time of his meeting with House on June 24, Wilson had decided that his policy of watchful waiting in Mexico would have to end. He complained about dealing with Carranza and agreed with his new secretary of state that the United States and Argentina, Brazil, and Chile should establish a provisional government, insist that all the factions support it, and provide the new government with recognition and financial aid. In early August, Lansing brought together Pan American diplomats in Washington, and on August 13 they appealed to the warring factions to endorse their plan. Pancho Villa and Emiliano Zapata agreed to accept this outside mediation, but Carranza refused. As late as early July, Wilson had endorsed Lansing's plan for a Pan American intervention, but as the summer progressed he backed away from this attempt to find a political solution to the Mexican revolution and telegraphed Lansing on August 11 that insisting on the elimination of Carranza's Constitutionalists "would be to ignore some very big facts." The president realized that his attempt to force his will on "the stiff-necked First Chief" had failed.[37]

On September 1, Carranza launched a military campaign against the remnants of Villa's Division of the North. His forces met with rapid success, shattering Villa's military power and undermining his political pretensions; now Carranza controlled much of Mexico. The president and secretary of state, confronted with Carranza's unyielding attitude and with his military successes, finally accepted the futility of their efforts to guide the revolution in Mexico. On October 19, the United States extended de facto recognition to Carranza's government.[38]

House's reaction to events in Mexico paralleled that of Wilson and Lansing. On June 24, during his talk with the president, he was eager for the United States to put its "moral and financial weight" back of a plan to impose order on Mexico. During the summer he became more involved with the administration's Mexican policy, collecting information on events there and urging Lansing to find a way to advance the "pacification" of that "unhappy people." Initially he hoped that Wilson would use a "firm hand," but as the summer progressed he discovered that "scarcely two suggestions agree" and seemed "perplexed as to what action to take." As Carranza gained in strength, House agreed with the president that General Obregon had become the "man of the hour" and that American recognition of the Constitutionalist regime was inevitable.[39]

During the summer of 1915, as negotiations dragged on with Germany, the controversy over the British seizure of American ships and cargoes continued. Popular resentment of the British blockade grew so intense that Wilson realized that the American government would have to take action soon. Wilson and House sought to avoid a dual crisis with Germany and Great Britain; but they also knew that they had to defend the nation's neutral rights.[40] While Wilson asserted that "we cannot long delay action," he also heeded his friend's warning that if the United States, in its shipping troubles with Britain, pressed too hard, "we would gain their eternal resentment."[41]

When Grey returned to London on July 13, he turned his attention to Anglo-American tensions, especially the crisis over the American export of cotton to Central Europe. The foreign secretary, caught between panic among American cotton producers in the South and domestic pressure to suppress the cotton trade, moved decisively to end the controversy. In late July he decided to put cotton on the contraband list, while maintaining its price by having the British government purchase all of the cotton that would normally have gone to Central Europe. When Ambassador Spring-Rice told House of the plan, he was enthusiastic, informing Wilson that the ambassador "confirmed my opinion as to the length Great Britain would go in the event you brought sufficient pressure." The plan's implementation in late August brought a steady rise in the price of cotton and the end of a serious issue in Anglo-American relations. And Grey's extraordinary efforts had diminished the urgency of an American protest over Great Britain's violation of American neutral rights.[42]

The continuing tension in Anglo-American relations, however, disturbed Ambassador Page, who remained an ardent interventionist and who objected to Lansing's litigious approach to the British government. House, whose ardor for American intervention had cooled after his return to the United States, tried to explain to Page the realities of American opinion. "Sir Edward and you cannot know," he wrote his friend in London, "the true situation here . . . . Today he [Wilson] is the most popular President since Lincoln, and it is not altogether because of his firmness to Germany, but more particularly because he has not involved us in war . . . . He [Wilson] sees the situation just as you see it and as I do, but he must necessarily heed the rocks."[43]

House realized, as he wrote the president, that "Page is in a blue funk." Once tension with Great Britain decreased, he thought, "it would be well to send for Page and let him have thirty or forty days in this country." Wilson agreed that his ambassador needed "a bath in American opinion; but is it wise to send for him just now, and is it not, after all, rather useful to have him give us the English view so straight?" Page's argumentative letters and his passionate embrace of the Allied cause had eroded his influence in Washington.[44]

On July 23 a Secret Service agent picked up a large briefcase left behind on an elevated train in New York by the commercial attaché of the German embassy. The next day the briefcase was delivered to Secretary of the Treasury McAdoo at his summer home in Maine. Its contents revealed a widespread German propaganda and sabotage campaign in the United States. Directed by the president to confer with Lansing and House, on August 10 McAdoo arrived at House's sanctuary on the North Shore to seek his advice. The president and his advisers decided to give the materials to the *New York World*, which published them from August 15 through August 23. The result was widespread public indignation over the vast German conspiracy and a diminishment of the faith of American leaders in the good will of the German government. "But I am sure," Wilson wrote House, "that the country is honeycombed with German intrigue and infected with German spies." House agreed, though he also realized that the publication of the documents would strengthen the president's hands "enormously" and would "weaken such agitators as Mr. Bryan and Hoke Smith [Democratic senator from Georgia]."[45]

As the American public absorbed the details of these activities, still another crisis erupted in German-American relations. Late on the morning of August 19, off the southern coast of Ireland, the U-24 torpedoed the White Star liner SS *Arabic*, outward bound from Liverpool. Of the 423 passengers and crew, forty-four died, including two American citizens. After Wilson learned of the sinking, he kept his regular schedule and tried to encourage the American public to remain calm. But the president was deeply upset. He knew that now he might have to break diplomatic relations with Germany, while also realizing that most Americans trusted his leadership and did not want war. His challenge was to maintain peace with honor.[46] The president was eager for a peaceful solution to the *Arabic* crisis, even if he knew as well that he must finally settle the issue of the safety of passenger liners in the war zone.

In Berlin, Chancellor Bethmann Hollweg and his advisers feared a break with the United States and understood that they must force the issue with the Navy, insisting that it conduct U-boat warfare against passenger ships according to the rules of cruiser warfare. On August 26, the chancellor, with the backing of Chief of Staff Falkenhayn, won the support of the emperor and soon instructed Ambassador Bernstorff that passenger liners would be sunk only after warning and the saving of human life. On September 1, the ambassador gave Secretary of State Lansing a pledge, which became known as the *Arabic* pledge, for the safety of passenger liners, although the German government did not disavow the sinking of the *Arabic*. Amid the public rejoicing over the triumph of Wilsonian diplomacy, it seemed for a brief time as if the long struggle to maintain American rights in the war zone had ended.[47] House joined in the praise of the president. "I wonder if you realize," he wrote him, "what a great diplomatic triumph you have achieved in your negotiations with Germany."[48]

This peaceful interlude, however, in German-American relations was short-lived. It was as if, as Ambassador Bernstorff reported to Berlin, "An evil star seems to hang over German-American negotiations on the submarine war." On September 4, only three days after the *Arabic* pledge, another liner, the SS *Hesperian,* was sunk by what appeared to be a torpedo. While the one American citizen aboard was unhurt, Wilson and Lansing were shocked that the *Arabic* pledge could be violated so quickly and were suspicious of German duplicity. Bethmann Hollweg and Foreign Secretary von Jagow now sought to convince the American government that Germany would stand by its pledges. In order to avoid future incidents, on September 18 they persuaded the kaiser to suspend U-boat operations in the English Channel and off the west coast of Great Britain. Wilson and Lansing welcomed Germany's conciliatory gestures; they were content to let the *Arabic* negotiations continue in regular diplomatic channels. House now seemed to agree with this approach. He concluded in his diary that "The fact that he [Wilson] has been so patient and has tried so hard to avoid war, gives the people confidence in his judgment."[49]

The sinking of the *Lusitania* and the ensuing crisis in German-American relations had given new life to the preparedness movement. At the end of 1914, Wilson had dismissed advocates of preparedness, including House, but by late May of 1915, impressed with the growing demand for greater military strength, the president called for a larger navy. Later in the summer he endorsed the War Department's training program at Plattsburg, New York, and elsewhere, and directed Secretary of the Navy Daniels and Secretary of War Garrison to work out plans for increases in both services. By early September, Wilson confirmed that when Congress convened in December, he would lead the fight for military expansion. He did not intend to advocate massive preparations for war; however, he would pursue "reasonable" preparedness, a program that was "very self-restrained and judicial."[50]

Despite Wilson's shift, House remained concerned about the weaknesses of the nation's military, and on August 7 he met with General Leonard Wood. The next day he conveyed Wood's thoughts to the president, urging him immediately to increase the size of the army, spread munitions factories across the country, begin a military training program for all young men, and send Wood to Europe to study the way the Allies conducted the war. "New conditions have arisen," House warned, "that seem to me to make it the part of wisdom to heed." The president's counselor also worried about "a possible outbreak" in the United States, one in which German agents would attempt "to blow up waterworks, electric light and gas plants, subways and bridges in cities like New York." Wilson shared this concern but, conscious of the powerful anti-war sentiment among many Americans, planned to move cautiously toward increases in the nation's military strength.[51]

As the summer drew to a close, both men were eager to meet again and to renew their friendship. Wilson felt "desperately lonely" (Edith was away visiting friends) and now began to anticipate his adviser's arrival. House promised that the "first cool spell" would find him in Washington.

On September 8 he left Manchester by car for Long Island, and arrived in Roslyn two days later. Wilson tracked his friend's southern migration, writing that "It's jolly that you are making your way in this direction. I am very eager to see you."[52] A mid-September heat spell kept House in Roslyn, and Wilson's desire to see him grew more urgent. "I wish with all my heart," he wrote, "that this heat *would* pass." Finally, on September 21, the weather turned and House telegraphed Wilson that he would leave for Washington the next day.

Before leaving, however, House saw Grayson in New York, who warned that "the President is anxious to have his engagement announced and is waiting for me to come in order to discuss it with me. Grayson says it is clearly up to me to decide this question." House knew that he faced a daunting task, reconciling the desires of a lovesick president with the political implications of an early marriage.[53]

17

The Lure of Peace

On September 22, 1915, House boarded the train at Pennsylvania Station for his first trip to the nation's capital since the end of January. When he arrived in the afternoon, the president was playing golf and House went to the Treasury Department to visit McAdoo. It was not until after dinner that he and the president took up Wilson's "most intimate personal affairs."[1]

Some Democratic leaders in Washington feared that the president's remarriage prior to November 1916 might hurt the party's prospects. Tumulty had already urged his chief to postpone the wedding until after the elections, and on September 18, four days before House arrived in Washington, McAdoo tried to find a way to approach his father-in-law. In an attempt to get him to discuss his plans, McAdoo told the president that he had received an anonymous letter from Los Angeles, informing him that Mary Allen Hulbert, (with whom Wilson had had a passionate flirtation prior to his presidency), was publicizing his letters.[2] Wilson did not respond to McAdoo's bait but was upset by the news of Mrs. Hulbert's apparent disloyalty and by its political implications. His first move was to go to Edith, confess his relationship, and ask for her forgiveness. After the initial shock of the revelation, Edith wrote that "this earthquake has left our love untouched." Wilson, filled with remorse over "the contemptible error and madness of a few months," now promised to consult with House over his romantic difficulties.[3]

After dinner at the White House, Wilson told House the story of his relationship with Mrs. Hulbert. According to the president, "there had never been anything between them excepting a platonic friendship, though afterward he had been indiscreet in writing her letters rather more warmly than was prudent." Wilson showed House some of the letters and "expressed the desire, if any trouble were to come to him because of this indiscretion, he would like it to come now, and he would not, in any circumstances, allow anyone to blackmail him." The president's "splendid courage" impressed House. Knowing that an anonymous letter did not really exist, he advised his friend "not to worry about it, for I was sure she was not showing his letters or attempting in any way to blackmail him." House was convinced that "no trouble was brewing" and that McAdoo was "entirely wrong" to engage in such "cruel" behavior. In short, he had managed both to reassure the president and to protect the secretary of the treasury.

The two then went on to discuss the timing of the announcement and other details concerning the wedding. They agreed upon the middle of October for the announcement and for the wedding to follow before the end of the year.[4] House believed, as he wrote in his diary, that if Wilson "does not marry, and marry quickly, I believe he will go into a decline."[5]

On September 23 the president, relieved that the path to his remarriage had finally been cleared, wrote Edith that "I had a *fine* talk with House last night, which cleared things wonderfully . . . . He is really a wonderful counselor . . . . I am sure that the first real conversation you have with him, about something definite and of the stuff of judgment, you will lose entirely your impression that he lacks strength. It is quiet, serene strength, but it is great and real. I am impatient to have you know him."[6] Indeed, that same day Wilson's new partner and his trusted adviser finally met over lunch at the White House. "She and I," House wrote in his diary, "became friends immediately," and they agreed to get together the next day for a private talk. On September 24, over late afternoon tea, Edith and House each sought to charm the other. Edith told him that Woodrow spoke of him with "affection" and had described their "first meeting and. . . the delight it was to find one whose mind ran parallel to his own upon public questions." House tried to captivate her with his vision of Wilson's future greatness, confiding that "if our plans carried true, the President would easily outrank any American that had yet lived." House found Edith "delightful and full of humor" and was pleased "to think the President will have her to cheer him in his loneliness."[7]

Edith now softened her earlier harsh judgment of House. "I did have," she wrote her "Dearest One," "such a nice talk with Col. House, and he is just as nice and fine as you pictured him, and his admiration for you is sufficient to establish my faith in his judgment and intelligent perceptions. I shall wait and tell you some of the things he said—and you will tell me honestly if he *liked* me."[8]

Woodrow's romance with Edith had already begun to change the dynamics within the president's inner circle of advisers. While House and Grayson had encouraged his early remarriage, Tumulty, with his conservative moral training and fears of the political repercussions, had disapproved. House had long been dissatisfied with Tumulty's role and now, sensing his opponent's vulnerability, moved to replace him as the president's personal secretary. Tumulty, House informed the president, "did not work well with other people . . . [and] that none of his, Wilson's close friends had been able to work with Tumulty since he had held office, and it was a serious handicap to the Administration." Nor could the garrulous Tumulty keep information confidential. Nonetheless the president was noncommittal about his secretary's fate, and Tumulty's failure to resign once again frustrated House's efforts to get rid of him.[9]

House was also concerned about McAdoo's behavior. The secretary of the treasury's clumsy attempt to manipulate Wilson over the supposed Hulburt letters had disturbed him, as did his quarrels with the members of the Federal Reserve Board. House had once been close to McAdoo, but since his marriage to Eleanor in May 1914, the two men had drifted apart. "McAdoo," House recorded in his diary, "had gotten pretty well from under my influence." In mid-December, three days before his father-in-law's wedding, House found McAdoo "depressed over his finances" and his position within the administration. McAdoo, House noted, "thinks Tumulty is working against him all the time and the President is listening to Tumulty, which indeed, is more or less true." House could only attempt to reassure his insecure friend.[10]

House was generally pleased with the results of his visit. Back in Roslyn, he wrote Wilson that "you can never know what a happy time I had in Washington. I feel that life will soon have a more splendid outlook for you and that your days of loneliness will be something of the past. I wish I could tell you too of my deep affection and of my appreciation of your confidence and friendship."[11]

As House contemplated another peace move, he watched closely the troubled prospects of the Allies. In early May, on the Eastern Front, where trench networks were less complete than in the west, German forces broke into open country, forcing a massive Russian retreat and capturing, by the end of the first year of the war, 1,740,000 Russian prisoners. On August 4, German troops occupied Warsaw, and by the end of September they had overrun most of Russian Poland and the Baltic coastline. German assistance kept the Austro-Hungarian army in the field, stabilizing the front in Galicia and allowing Hapsburg armies to repulse Italian assaults. On the Western Front, when French and British armies launched an offensive in late September to relieve pressure on Russia, they made little progress against the formidable German defensive belt.[12]

On more distant fronts the Allies also suffered one setback after another. At Gallipoli, British and French troops could not drive Turkish defenders from the high ground and found themselves bunched together disastrously in heavily shelled trenches. In December the Allies began the evacuation of their Mediterranean Expeditionary Force, one that was completed in early 1916. The year-long effort to reach Constantinople by sea and knock the Ottoman Empire out of the war had ended in an abysmal failure.[13] The success of the German offensive in the east allowed Austro-German-Bulgarian forces (Bulgaria had joined the Central Powers on September 6) to attack Serbia. They entered Belgrade on October 9, sending Serbian troops in a desperate retreat across Albania to the sea. By early November Germany had established a direct rail link between Berlin and Constantinople. The dispatch of an Anglo-French force to Salonika, Greece, which became a large Allied base, failed to prevent the collapse of Serbia.[14]

As the war intensified, a mood of resignation settled in among troops in the field and citizens at home, and leaders on both sides prepared for a longer war. The Central Powers, which occupied Belgium, Poland, Serbia, and part of France, realized that they had achieved impressive successes in 1915 and planned for a great offensive on the Western Front in 1916. The Allies, while discouraged by their failures in 1915, were far from broken. The fighting power of the Russian army had not been destroyed, the French army retained its aggressive spirit, and Kitchener's New Armies, when fully committed to the Western Front, offered the promise of a decisive breakthrough.[15]

During the fall of 1915, against the backdrop of the war in Europe, the president's courtship of Edith moved toward completion. On October 6 the White House announced the engagement of the president and Mrs. Norman Galt, "a woman of charm and pleasing personality," as Wilson had described her to House. "The old shadows are gone," an ecstatic Wilson wrote "My own precious Darling," "the old loneliness banished, the new joy let in like a great healing light."[16] Two days after the announcement, Woodrow and Edith arrived in New York for their first visit with House and Loulie. Edith and her companions stayed at the St. Regis Hotel, while the president joined House in his apartment, which had been turned into a sanctuary (the telephone was not allowed to ring, and Loulie moved in with Gordon and Janet Auchincloss). At Wilson's request he also had a prominent New York jeweler send thirteen engagement rings to his apartment so that the president and his fiancée could make a selection. House eagerly awaited their arrival. "You can never know," he wrote Wilson, "how happy I am that such great good fortune has come to you. I feel that a more splendid day has dawned, and that soon there will be no more lonely hours."[17]

As House, Wilson, and the president's party drove from Pennsylvania Station to 115 East 53 Street, the streets were lined with large crowds that enthusiastically cheered the president and his bride-to-be. For the remainder of the afternoon, Edward, Woodrow, Edith, her mother, and Helen Bones (Wilson's cousin) took a long drive. Finally, before dressing for dinner, Wilson learned that his counselor had been considering another peace move. Assuming that Germany might prevail, House argued that "we should do something decisive now—something that would either end the war in a way to abolish militarism or that would bring us in with the Allies to help them do it." He then went on to explain his plan for an American proposal, one that would have to be approved by the Allies in advance, that the war should end on the basis of "military and naval disarmament . . . . The Allies, after some hesitation, could accept our offer or demand, and if the Central Powers accepted, we would then have accomplished a master stroke in diplomacy. If the Central Powers refused to acquiesce, we could then push our insistence to a point where diplomatic relations would first be broken off, and later the whole force of our Government, and perhaps the force of every neutral, might be brought against them."

The president was understandably "startled" by House's bold plan, so full of risks and uncertainties. "He seemed," House wrote optimistically, "to acquiesce by silence. I had no time to push it further, for our entire conversation did not last longer than twenty minutes." That evening, after a dinner party and the theater, the two did not return to the subject; nor did they in the morning, when House continued to entertain Wilson and Edith and accompanied them to Pennsylvania Station for their 11:00 AM departure.[18]

On October 13, only four days after Wilson left New York, House arrived in Washington to explain his plan for American intervention to Secretary of State Lansing and to discuss it further with the president.

House told the secretary of state that "it would not do to permit the Allies to go down in defeat, for if they did, we would follow in natural sequence." Lansing agreed "absolutely." Not surprisingly House continued to find him a "satisfactory" secretary of state. "He is not," House continued, "a great man, but he is level headed, has courage and has a fairly correct knowledge of diplomatic procedure."[19]

The third day of his stay, October 15, Ambassador Spring-Rice handed House a letter from Foreign Secretary Grey assessing the prospects for peace. While Grey was careful to convey only his personal impressions to House—a more formal response would require consultation with the cabinet and Allies—he doubted that either side was ready for a peace proposal based on the elimination of militarism and navalism and a return to the status quo ante bellum. Britain would fight on, he asserted, until Belgium was restored, Alsace and Lorraine were returned to France, and Russia received an outlet to the sea. Grey was, however, hopeful that after the war the nations of the world would "band together to treat the maker of war as an enemy of the human race." Would the United States, he asked, support a postwar league of nations?[20]

Both Wilson and House were excited by the foreign secretary's ambiguous letter, concluding that "it gave much ground for hope." Wilson quickly assented to House's suggestion that he send his scheme for American intervention to Grey. That afternoon he returned to New York, where he dictated a letter and mailed it to the president for his approval. In his draft House outlined his plan for an Allied-approved American mediation effort that would either bring the war to an end or pave the way for American intervention. At a time selected by the Allies, House would go to London and, after reaching an understanding with British leaders, move on to Berlin, where he would try to convince the German government to accept the American peace proposal (concealing his agreement with the Allies). If Germany acquiesced, the war would end on favorable terms. "If the Central Powers were still obdurate, it would [Wilson added probably here] be necessary for us to join the Allies and force the issue."[21]

House's effort pleased the president, who made what he considered "one or two unimportant verbal changes." As he explained to House, "I do not want to make it inevitable quite that we should take part to force terms on Germany, because the exact circumstances of such a crisis are impossible to determine. The letter is altogether right. I pray God it may bring results." While House realized that the president's addition of the word "probably" was an important change in the document, he seemed unconcerned by Wilson's more cautious approach to American intervention.[22]

No doubt Wilson was in part attracted to House's peace plan because of growing domestic pressure to end the war. In early 1915, progressive internationalists, led by reformers such as Jane Addams, concluded that peace was essential for domestic reform and organized a Woman's Peace Party that developed a "program for constructive peace," one that included a "Concert of Nations" and that called for "continuous mediation" by neutral governments. After a tour of Europe in the spring of 1915, Addams had returned to the United States in mid-summer, received an enthusiastic welcome at a rally at Carnegie Hall, and met with Wilson, House, and Lansing to promote her plan for a new diplomacy in Europe. While the president and his advisers regarded Addams and her followers as naïve, they studied their program carefully and knew, as House wrote, that her following "is large and influential."[23]

The president also had to deal with those on the right of the political spectrum, who in June 1915 founded the League to Enforce Peace and elected former president William Howard Taft as its first president. It soon became the most influential part of the American peace movement. Dominated by conservative Republicans, the League to Enforce Peace called for American participation in a postwar league and coordinated its activities with the League of Nations Society in Great Britain. In contrast to Wilson and progressive internationalists, however, these conservatives were not interested in a stand-off in Europe. They believed that the defeat of Germany was essential for a lasting peace and envisaged a new postwar order based on an Anglo-American understanding.[24]

House's letter to Grey of October 17 arrived in London around November 8. It found the foreign secretary in no mood to talk of peace. Asquith's new coalition cabinet, formed in May, turned out to be a quarrelsome body, full of powerful personalities and incapable of making swift decisions on policy and strategy. By the summer of 1915 the debate within the cabinet over how to mobilize the nation had intensified, with one faction, led by Lloyd George, arguing for compulsory military service and a concentration of the nation's resources on the war effort. The other faction, led by Chancellor of the Exchequer Reginald McKenna and including Grey, argued that the nation should husband its resources for a long war and avoid dispatching a large conscript army to the Western Front.[25] By the fall of 1915, however, McKenna's assumptions—that France and Russia would fight most of the land war and that the British Empire was safe from a German attack—seemed unrealistic. Britain could not stand aloof from the continent without risking the breakup of the Allied coalition, while the Anglo-French failure at Gallipoli and Turkish successes in Mesopotamia threatened Britain's position in Egypt.[26] Asquith faced mounting pressure from France and Russia for the dispatch of more British troops to the Western Front, and he also faced a formidable domestic pressure for the escalation of the war. Conservatives, the influential Northcliffe press, and a "Ginger group" of Liberal MPs, including Lloyd George, all pressed for a more vigorous war effort.

The prime minister gradually gave way before the assault on his government's policies, putting Douglas Haig in charge of the British Expeditionary Force in France and William Robertson in command of the Imperial General Staff. But the dissatisfaction with Asquith's leadership remained intense. On December 20, Lloyd George, speaking before the House of Commons, expressed the widespread anger over the way in which opportunities had been missed, and warned that "unless we quicken our movements damnation will fall upon the sacred cause for which so much gallant blood has flowed."[27]

Grey had been on the losing side of these controversies. In the fall of 1915, his moderate approach to the war could no longer be sustained. By the end of the year he had lost his influence in the formation of blockade policy and was under attack for his conciliatory policies toward America. The strain of the war, and of his deteriorating eyesight, had taken their toll on the foreign secretary. "E. G.," one observer noted, "was never intended for the service of Mars."[28]

Grey's reply to House's proposal did not reach New York until late November. It was a discouraging letter. The foreign secretary focused on the vagueness of House's plan, pointing out that the Allies could not "commit themselves in advance to any proposition without knowing exactly what it was, and knowing that the United States of America were prepared to intervene and make it good if they accepted it." Britain, France, and Russia had prepared for a winter campaign, and Gray informed House that "the situation at the moment and the feelings here and among the Allies, and in Germany so far as I know, do not justify me in urging you to come." In short, another peace mission to Europe would not bring any results.[29] Grey was also upset over a stern American protest against Britain's interference with American ships and cargoes destined for neutral ports.

Once Wilson and Lansing had received the *Arabic* pledge from Germany, the secretary of state set to work on a challenge to the British maritime system. On November 5 Grey received a detailed indictment of Britain's "vexatious and illegal practices" and a strong affirmation of American neutral rights. While the note made no threats, it did undercut Britain's claim to exceptional international virtue and conveyed menacing possibilities for the future. If Britain, Grey informed House, accepted all of America's contentions, "we could not prevent Germany from trading, at any rate through neutral ports, as freely in time of war as in time of peace." He worried that the United States "might now strike the weapon of sea power out of our hands, and thereby ensure a German victory."[30]

On November 28, when Wilson and Lansing visited House in New York, the three men considered the next step. In a talk with Lansing, House impressed on the secretary of state "the necessity of the United States making it clear to the Allies that we considered their cause our cause, and that we had no intention of permitting a military autocracy [Germany] to dominate the world if our strength could prevent it." The secretary of state, who was as pro-Allies as House, readily agreed. Later in the afternoon of the same day, Wilson and House had a long discussion about his mediation proposal. It seems unlikely that House was as frank in expressing his pro-Allied sentiments in his talks with Wilson as he had been with Lansing. The president felt that "we should let the Allies know how our minds are running, but he did not think it could be done by a change of Ambassadors." Despite his reluctance to see House travel in the war zone, it seemed "the only way to properly accomplish what we had in mind."

Wilson took a casual approach to House's mediation scheme. He did not, House noted, want to put "our thoughts and intentions into writing. He would rather have them conveyed by word of mouth." In contrast, House preferred a written plan, since the negotiations he had in mind meant "the reversal of the foreign policy of this Government and no one can foresee the consequences." If the United States, in a historic departure, was to entangle itself in European alliances and alignments, it would have to proceed with great care.[31]

House was, however, in no hurry to leave for Europe. He was worried about Loulie's health; she was "nervous and run down" and taking a "rest cure" that would keep her in bed for several weeks. He was also concerned about his daughter Janet, who was recovering from an appendectomy. In a few days Horace Plunkett—whom House used as a go-between with the

British cabinet—would arrive from London with confidential information. House hoped that before his departure at the end of the month, he could persuade Grey to view his peace plan with a more open mind.[32]

Throughout the fall of 1915 Wilson had continued to advance his program for preparedness. In late October he received a plan for the expansion of the army from Secretary of War Garrison, one that included a modest increase in the size of the regular army and the creation of a new Continental Army, to be composed of citizen soldiers. Wilson believed that public opinion had shifted in favor of preparedness and on November 4, in a speech at the Manhattan Club in New York, he spoke "of the urgency and necessity of preparing ourselves to guard and protect the rights and privileges of our people."[33]

Many Republicans were dissatisfied with the president's program; they favored larger increases in the army and universal military training. The strongest reaction to the president's speech, however, came from reformers, who were concerned about economic and social justice at home and who denounced any attempt to turn the United States into a heavily armed nation. By mid-November Democrats from the South and West had rallied behind the House majority leader, Claude Kitchin of North Carolina; they were convinced that the Unites States had no stake in the quarrels of Europe and were passionately opposed to even the president's modest measures. Bryan led the attack, denouncing Wilson's program as "not only a menace to our peace and safety, but a challenge to the spirit of Christianity which teaches us to influence others by example rather than by exciting fear."[34] On December 7, the day after Congress convened, Wilson delivered his third annual message, once again insisting that it was "absolutely imperative now" to expand the army and navy. The president sought to rally his forces in the Congress, but it was clear that Wilson's program faced massive opposition within his own party.[35]

While House approved the president's advocacy of preparedness, his mind was now jumping ahead to the 1916 election. He urged Wilson to make "Americanism" the main theme of the campaign, worried about Bryan's attitude toward the administration, and fretted over the "lagging" organizational efforts of the Democratic National Committee. The political situation, he noted in early December, "is not encouraging because it lacks a certain cohesiveness, that is always dangerous."[36]

On December 14 the president summoned House to Washington. After breakfast they retreated to Wilson's study, where House "found the president not quite as belligerent as he was the last time we were together [November 28]. He seemed to think we would be able to keep out of the war." Given the gap between his views and those of the president, House was now inclined to delay his mission. He and Lansing agreed that it would be better to wait, since the diplomatic impasse with Germany and Austro-Hungary (over the sinking of the Italian liner *SS Ancona* on November 7) might draw the United States into the war and make American disputes with the Allies irrelevant.[37]

The president, however, overrode the hesitations of his counselor; he was dissatisfied with the performance of ambassadors on both sides of the Atlantic. Spring-Rice was a "highly excitable invalid" who "was not only incompetent, but also a mischief maker." He wanted House to secure his recall. Nor was Bernstorff "much more satisfactory." Wilson had concluded that Page was hopelessly pro-British and had also lost patience with Gerard.[38] "Who can fathom this [a report from Gerard]?" he asked Edith. "I wish they would hand this idiot his passports." Wilson insisted that House go immediately, reasoning that he could give the British government a much better sense of America's position, especially over Allied violations of American neutral rights.[39]

Beneath the surface, important differences existed between the president and his trusted adviser. House believed that the United States, one way or another, must see the Allies through to victory, and had already informed British leaders that it would do so. He saw his mission as a way to gain Allied acceptance of an American mediation effort and to prevent Germany's "military autocracy" from dominating the world. His secondary objective was to convince the British government to moderate its blockade.[40] In contrast, Wilson was less committed than his adviser to the Allied cause and more aware of the domestic pressures to stay out of war. Initially, after House returned to New York, Wilson wrote, "You need no instructions. You know what is in my mind and how to interpret it." This time House was not content with such vague instructions, asking his friend to give him "your impressions as to what to say in London and what to say in Berlin and how far I should go." The president responded at length. He and House agreed that the United States should "have nothing to do with local settlements,- territorial questions, indemnities, and the like,- but are concerned only in the future peace of the world and the guarantees to be given for that. The only possible guarantees are. . . (a) military and naval disarmament and (b) a league of nations to secure each nation against aggression and maintain the absolute freedom of the seas. If either party to the present war will let us say to the other that they are willing to discuss peace on such terms, it will clearly be our duty to use our utmost moral force to oblige the other party."[41]

House's primary task, however, was to convey to the British "the demand in the Senate for further, immediate, and imperative pressure on England and her allies." Wilson's instructions were clear. The United States would use only *moral* force to help end the war and House must press British leaders hard for relief from the blockade.[42]

During the fall of 1915 House had engaged in his own courtship of Edith Galt, trying to win her friendship and protect his access to the president. For her birthday he sent Edith "blood red roses," and also sought to have her portrait painted as a wedding gift to the president. But he worried about rumors of Wilson's "immoral" behavior and the political impact of Wilson's remarriage. And House was surely displeased when Edith told him that the president "had shown her some of my European correspondence."[43] House felt a growing resentment over Wilson's transference of affection to Edith and over the extent to which she was changing his relationship with the president. Late in November he complained in his diary that the president "is so engrossed with his fiancée that he is neglecting business."[44] Realizing that Edith had now become a part of Wilson's inner circle, on November 30 House drew her into his study after lunch and urged her to ignore the importunities of the Wilson's friends and "to let [sic] the President alone to think out his problems in the future as he has done in the past." House did not record Edith's reaction to this advice, but clearly he hoped that she would not disrupt his own role of confidential adviser.[45]

On December 15 House arrived in Washington for a final visit prior to his departure for Europe. It was only three days before the president's wedding. For half an hour Grayson plied him with "family and household matters." "I seem to be the receptacle," House complained in his diary, "for everything and everybody when I am in Washington. It is tiresome, though in a way, gratifying." After lunch Wilson showed him the diamond brooch he had gotten for Edith and other presents that had arrived for her. He and House ate dinner alone and afterward visited Edith at her home near Dupont Circle, where they "sat for half an hour in intimate personal conversation." "She expressed regret," House noted cryptically, "that we were going to Europe and also that I was not to be at the wedding. She said it did not seem right, but I made it clear that it would be an impossibility on account of the hurt feelings it would engender."[46]

In fact, House's decision not to attend the wedding is puzzling. He was not leaving for Europe until December 28; his explanation that his attendance was impossible because "of the hurt feelings it would engender" is unconvincing. The wedding was, to be sure, a small one, including only thirty-eight relatives and close friends, but House had a unique relationship with Wilson and had been instrumental in clearing away the obstacles to an early marriage. His refusal to attend the wedding revealed a curious insensitivity, for he disappointed both Edith and his friend the president. It is hardly surprising that, when House left Washington on the evening of December 15, Wilson's goodbye must have been so perfunctory that he did not bother to record it.[47]

On the eve of his departure for Europe House seemed untroubled by the instructions he had received from the president and by the ambiguity of his peace mission. "He clearly places the whole responsibility," he recorded, "back on my shoulders where I would gladly have it, for if I am to act, I wish to act with a free hand." "I am sure I need not tell you," House wrote Wilson, "how deeply I appreciate your confidence, your friendship and affection." Wilson responded from his honeymoon retreat in Hot Springs, Virginia, that "Our loving thoughts will follow you across the sea and in all your generous labors on the other side the good wishes that go with you from us are too many and too deep to express."[48]

18

The House–Grey
Memorandum

On December 28, 1915, the House contingent—House, Loulie, and Fanny—boarded the SS *Rotterdam*, as family and friends gathered to see them off and as reporters crowded around House, trying to get him to reveal the purpose of his mission. Gordon Auchincloss wrote his father-in-law, "I hated to see you go for you've been so wonderfully good and kind to me that I love you dearly and only wish I could do something in a way to show my appreciation." But House was glad they were away. "I need the rest," he confided in his diary. "I could not have stood it much longer in New York under the same circumstances."[1]

Aside from the stormy weather, with winds at moments reaching nearly hurricane force, House enjoyed his voyage across the Atlantic. The manager of the Holland American Line had upgraded his important passenger to a cabin deluxe, consisting of a sitting room, two bedrooms, and two baths; other passengers, especially Brand Whitlock, the American ambassador in Brussels, proved to be "congenial spirits." House arrived in London on the morning of January 6, 1916, rested and "better able to encounter the madness of Europe." He settled into rooms at the Ritz Hotel with a view of Green Park and relished the early spring-like weather, much milder than what he had left behind in New York. Within a few days he was booked for nearly every lunch and dinner until his departure for Paris on January 20. He planned to talk with "soldiers, sailors, politicians and editors, as I wished to cover the whole field."[2]

In London the mood was somber. Occasional Zeppelin attacks (gas-filled airships that cruised at a height of 10,000–15,000 feet) and raids by German airplanes reminded its citizens that the city was less than 100 miles from the Western Front. According to Ambassador Page, "a dense cloud of weariness hangs over all London."[3] Moreover, the stalemate on the Western Front, and defeats in other theaters of the war, had increased the dissatisfaction with Prime Minister Asquith and his government. The prime minister needed military successes to restore his waning prestige. Allied industrial production and military forces were rapidly increasing, and in a series of conferences at the end of 1915 British and French leaders agreed that the Western Front was the primary theater of operations, planning a large offensive there in the spring of 1916. As they intensified the nation's war effort, Asquith and his colleagues hoped for a victor's peace.[4] In mid-January, Foreign Secretary Grey told the cabinet's war committee that Britain must make a maximum military effort in 1916 because "if things remain as they are, I think that there will be a sort of general collapse and inconclusive peace next winter."[5]

The day of his arrival in London, January 6, House plunged into the British political scene, meeting Grey at 7:00 PM at his home at 33 Eccleston Square. House quickly turned to the main purpose of his mission, his plan for American mediation of the conflict "based upon a demand for the freedom of the seas and the curtailment of militarism." House believed that Wilsonian intervention—whether it led to a pro-Allied peace or American entry into the conflict—would be far better than if the United States drifted "into the war by breaking diplomatic relations with the Central Powers." Grey, not wishing to antagonize the president's emissary or reveal the disinterest of British leaders in American mediation, seemed sympathetic, and the two agreed that Arthur Balfour, who had entered Asquith's coalition cabinet in May 1915 as first lord of the admiralty, should be the next member of the cabinet that House would approach.[6]

Four days later House lunched with Grey and Balfour to discuss his mediation plan. He had first met Balfour in March 1915 and found him an appealing figure. But their conversation then had been general, obscuring Balfour's deep commitment to an Allied victory.[7] While Grey said little, Balfour confronted for the first time House's complex mediation scheme. The first lord, House recorded, was "not very constructive, but analytical and argumentative," skeptical of Wilson's ability to carry out a pro-Allied mediation. Looking beyond the end of the war, both Balfour and Grey "wanted to know how far you [Wilson] would be willing to enter into an agreement concerning European affairs." House assured them that the president would do so or, as he had told Grey earlier, "it was reasonably certain we [the United States] would enter some world agreement having for its object the maintenance of peace if a workable plan could be devised." Despite Balfour's obvious doubts, House reported to the president that his conference was "entirely satisfactory." His plan, he confidently told Wilson, was "to come to a tentative agreement with them [Balfour and Grey] before going to the Continent on the twentieth and let them bring their colleagues into line before I return."[8]

On January 12 Wilson telegraphed his emissary that now that difficulties with Germany had been resolved it was "imperative" for Great Britain to relax its blockade. That very day, over lunch with Grey and Minister of Blockade Lord Robert Cecil, House explained the president's domestic difficulties and urged concessions. Both men listened sympathetically, but emphasized the overwhelming demand in Britain for a stricter embargo of the Central Powers and pressure from France "to keep up the blockade in all its severity."[9]

On January 14, House joined Lloyd George, the dynamic minister of munitions, along with his confidant Lord Reading (the lord chief justice), for a wide-ranging conversation. Lloyd George emphasized the growth of Allied military power and anticipated a major Allied offensive in the summer. While the Allies would not make a decisive breakthrough, he did expect them to gain some military advantage and suggested that Wilson should intervene around September 1. Otherwise, "the war could go on indefinitely."[10]

As the conversation progressed, Lloyd George began to canvass the globe, suggesting that Germany must evacuate France and Belgium, that Poland should become an independent nation, and that the Ottoman Empire "must go." And he warned of the demands of Australia, New Zealand, and South Africa. Warming to these geopolitical speculations, House (ignoring Wilson's instructions not to discuss territorial aspects of a peace settlement) argued that Britain should eventually withdraw from Asia, giving Germany a freer hand there, and "concentrate on Africa, Australia and her other colonies outside of Asia." As in June 1915, Lloyd George impressed House with his energy and forcefulness. "His mind," he recorded, "acts quickly, largely upon impulse, and he lacks the slow reasoning of the ordinary British statesman." The minister of munitions was now part of an inner group in the cabinet that would deal with the issue of American mediation.[11]

The day after his expansive talk with Lloyd George, House met again with Balfour and Grey at 4 Carlton Gardens, the first lord's home near the

Houses of Parliament. House stood before "a large map of Southeastern Europe and Anatolia that was upon the wall" and told them of the way in which he and Lloyd George had divided the world and "of the extraordinary part he would have the President play." Lloyd George, however, had not discussed these matters with Balfour and Grey, who had mixed feelings about their cabinet colleague, labeling him "as brilliant and unstable. He jumps at conclusions quickly, but as quickly forms another." They were not convinced of his discretion and trustworthiness.

Once again the three men took up the issue of American mediation, "without reaching any definite conclusion." Balfour and Grey doubted the prudence of raising this issue with the cabinet or with Britain's allies, and, as before, House found the first lord argumentative, exploring the meaning of phrases such as "the freedom of the seas" and "the elimination of militarism" and asserting that the German government could not "be counted upon to keep any bargain or play any game fairly," as House noted in his diary. They left, as House wrote Wilson, "with the understanding that they should think the matter [American mediation] over and discuss it with the Prime Minister and Lloyd George and take it up with me when I returned from the Continent."[12]

Not until January 18, two days before his departure for Paris, did House lunch with Prime Minister Asquith and his wife Margo at Ten Downing Street. House was unimpressed with Asquith, and wished that Lloyd George "was Prime Minister with Sir Edward Grey as Foreign Minister, for I believe we could then do something. The Cabinet are all too conservative, and boldness is needed at this time."[13] Asquith's passivity disappointed House.

The next day House had a final conference with Grey, one in which the two men focused on which members of the cabinet to take into their confidence. Lloyd George, despite his unreliability, had to be included, as did Chancellor of the Exchequer McKenna, who had already learned of House's mediation plan. House reluctantly concluded that Ambassador Page would have to be told. He worried that Page would "retard rather than help" the negotiations, and also feared "that British conservatism will make improbable any real accomplishment."[14] Over the course of 1915 the American ambassador had become disillusioned with Wilson and his policies toward the belligerents. Page had no interest in American mediation of the war; he wanted a break with Germany and American entry into the conflict on the side of the Allies. He resented House's mission to Europe

1. House at the age of sixteen. (San Jacinto Museum of History Association.)

2. and 3. Edward and Loulie, on their honeymoon. They were married on
August 4, 1881, and, after the wedding, took a year-long grand tour of Europe.
They lingered in Florence, where Mona, their first child, was born. (San Jacinto
Museum of History Association.)

4. Fanny Denton, taken around 1890, when House hired her as his private secretary. She became House's confidante as well as virtually a member of the family, typing all of his letters, taking dictation for his diary, traveling with him to the North Shore and on trips to Europe, and managing his household affairs. (Author's collection.)

5. A House family portrait, taken around 1887, two years after the family moved to Austin. Standing, left to right, Loulie, Janet, and a nurse. Seated, left to right, Annie Hunter, House, and Mona. In 1896 Annie married Sidney Mezes. (PICB 04173, Austin History Center, Austin Public Library.)

6. Loulie Hunter House, taken around 1895, as an elegant young woman. During the House family's years in Austin, Loulie was a gracious hostess who relished her social position. Newspaper accounts referred to her "dark beauty" and "queenly style," and praised her diamonds and magnificent imported dresses. (Author's collection.)

RESIDENCE OF MR. E. M. HOUSE.

7. The House mansion at 1704 West Avenue, Austin, shortly after its completion in June 1892. It was designed by a prominent New York architect, Frank Freeman, and House spared no expense in the construction of his new home. The first floor, chimney, and supporting columns of the porch were built of rough blocks of red sandstone. (PICH 03293, Austin History Center, Austin Public Library.)

8. Mona House, taken around 1897, when she entered Hollins Institute. Governor James Stephen Hogg, who knew her well, liked her unaffected, down-to-earth quality. He could not imagine how college could improve "the plain, sensible, girl that she used to be when she leaped around the hillsides of Austin like a gazelle." (Hollins College Archives.)

9. A dapper-looking House around 1895, when he was deeply involved in Texas politics. (Author's collection.)

10. James Stephen Hogg, governor of Texas from 1890 to 1894. Drawn to Hogg's vivid personality and progressive vision, House became the manager of Hogg's campaign for reelection in 1892. It was the beginning of his career in Texas politics and the formation of "our crowd." (Hogg [Ima] Photograph Collection, di_07640, Dolph Briscoe Center for American History, University of Texas at Austin.)

11. Thomas Watt Gregory, one of the original members of "our crowd." Gregory was an Austin lawyer and leading Texas Democrat who formed a deep attachment to House. In August 1914 he became President Woodrow Wilson's attorney general. (Library of Congress Prints and Photographs Division Washington, D.C., LC-USZ62-86697.)

12. Albert Burleson, another early member of "our crowd." Burleson was elected to Congress in 1898 and served in the House until 1913, when Wilson appointed him postmaster general. House valued Burleson's political skills and his mastery of patronage, but found him too partisan in his approach to politics. (Library of Congress Prints and Photographs Division, Washington, D.C., LC-H25-10795-BC.)

13. Charles A. Culberson. Culberson became Texas attorney general in 1890 and in 1894 succeeded Hogg as governor. House admired Culberson's "fine analytical mind" and became his patron, helping him move to the Senate in 1898 and also helping him stay there for four terms, despite health problems which gradually eroded his effectiveness. (Library of Congress Prints and Photographs Division, Washington, D.C., LC-USZ62-51124.)

14. Sidney Mezes. Mezes was a well-educated, cosmopolitan man who joined the philosophy faculty of the University of Texas in 1894 and became president of the university in 1908. In December 1896 he married Loulie's sister, Annie Hunter. House adored his gentlemanly, reserved brother-in-law, and over the years maneuvered to keep him by his side. In 1914, with House's help, Mezes was appointed president of the College of the City of New York, and in 1917 House chose him, with Wilson's approval, to head the Inquiry, the group of experts who studied the nature of the peace settlement. (Photographed by The Cactus, Prints and Photographs Collection, di_08342, Dolph Briscoe Center for American History, University of Texas at Austin.)

and complained of his "pussy-cat way of slipping about & of purring at the wrong times and in the wrong tones." After House arrived in London on January 6, he excluded Page from most of his meetings with Grey and other British leaders. House knew, however, that the ambassador could not be completely ignored and saw him often during his stay in London. But House found Page increasingly tiresome. "It has become a punishment for me," he recorded in his diary, "to be with him because he is so critical of the President, Lansing, and our people generally."[15]

On January 20 the House party left London on a private railway car and crossed the English Channel via Folkestone to Boulogne on a ship filled with soldiers. Despite strong winds, House stood on the deck with hundreds of troops, watching them put on life preservers as the ship zigzagged to avoid mines. He relished the excitement of the war zone, listening to soldiers "talk and sing" and laughing with them "when the waves broke over the boat and drenched some of the less fortunate." When he arrived at Boulogne he found that "The entire city has the appearance of a huge military camp and arsenal." The next day, on account of the bad weather, he took a train to Paris, reaching the French capital in time for dinner with Ambassador and Mrs. Sharp. But House spent only two nights in Paris— he planned to see French officials on his return from Berlin—and left for Geneva on January 23. As in March 1915, House crossed the Swiss-German border near Bale and arrived in Berlin early on the morning of January 26.[16]

In Berlin, he found that the patriotic outbursts that had greeted the outbreak of war in August 1914 had disappeared.[17] The kaiser was absent from the city and German civilians, especially in the nation's urban areas, had begun to feel the burdens of the war—the mounting casualties, food shortages, and the emergence of a thriving black market. Isolated on the continent of Europe, Germany could not, like the Allies, draw on the resources of its overseas empire.[18]

By the end of 1915, Germany's short-term military position pleased Chief of Staff Falkenhayn, but he was gloomy about its long-term prospects. In January 1916, he told the kaiser that "time [is] against us. Our allies, Austria and Turkey, [cannot] carry on the war beyond autumn of this year." The only way to defeat Great Britain, Germany's "archenemy," was by "knocking its best sword," France, "out of its hands." Thus Falkenhayn planned a massive operation on a narrow front—one directed at the French fortresses at Verdun—designed (though this is a point of considerable debate) to bleed the French army white and bring about its collapse. Determined to break

Britain's will to resist, he also accepted Admiral Tirpitz's clamor for unrestricted U-boat operations, calculating that the United States could not decisively interfere before the war was over.[19]

As the war progressed Bethmann Hollweg realized that the domestic consensus in favor of war, fragile from the start, had begun to fray. The Socialist Party called for domestic reforms and a negotiated peace, while parties on the right wanted a decisive victory and territorial annexations. Much of the nation's political and social elite favored an ambitious program to make Germany the hegemonic power on the continent. Bethmann-Hollweg sympathized with this program but sought to appease forces on both the left and the right and to avoid a bitter debate over war aims. Nor did he like Falkenhayn's preoccupation with the Western Front; the chancellor hoped for a decisive victory on the Eastern Front that would prepare the way for a peace settlement with France and Britain.[20] In January 1916, Bethmann Hollweg also had to resume the struggle with supporters of all-out U-boat warfare. He realized that the public agitation had intensified and that Falkenhayn was moving toward Tirpitz's camp. The chancellor, however, feared war with the United States and argued that "the longer the war lasts, so much clearer does it become that he will win the war who keeps his nerves under best control." Despite these fears, he felt that he had no choice but to move toward a sharpened U-boat campaign.[21]

House had arrived in Berlin in good spirits. "We have all," he reported to his son-in-law, "kept wonderfully well. The weather has been delightful. In Paris and in Switzerland it is like the best Texas winter weather." Once in Berlin, he, Loulie, and Fanny settled in at the American Embassy with Ambassador Gerard and sought to assess the shifting currents of German politics.[22]

The day after his arrival House talked with the Minister for Colonies Wilhelm Self, who warned of the " 'controversy in process between the chancellor, on the one hand, and von Tirpitz and von Falkenhayn on the other regarding underseas warfare.' " While Bethmann-Hollweg held the upper hand, Self was uncertain about the outcome and urged House to warn the chancellor about the "danger of a break between the United States and Germany."

On January 28, at a large dinner at the American Embassy, House finally talked with Chancellor Bethmann Hollweg and with Foreign Secretary Jagow. For an hour and a half, House and Bethmann Hollweg discussed the war while the chancellor "drank copiously of beer" and House matched him with glasses of mineral water. Bethmann Hollweg, House recorded in his diary, "deplored the war and its ghastly consequences and declared the guilt did not [lie] upon his soul." He blamed the Allies who, he claimed, had not responded to his pleas for peace; Germany "would be willing to evacuate both France and Belgium if an indemnity were paid." In turn, House emphasized the reasonableness of Grey, warned that the British "were a stubborn race and felt no concern as to the ultimate result," and pointed out that Germany's peace terms would not be considered by the Allies "for a moment." House eventually grew weary of the conversation, concluding that "the beer did not apparently affect him, for his brain was as befuddled at the beginning as it was at the end. Into such hands are the destinies of the people placed." After finishing with the chancellor, House and the foreign secretary covered much of the same ground. It was nearly midnight when House and Jagow finished their talk. Discouraged by his encounter with Germany's leaders, House noted in his diary, "I went to bed with a feeling that not much had been accomplished by my discussions with the Chancellor and von Jagow."[23]

House found Undersecretary of State Zimmermann more reasonable than the chancellor and foreign secretary. Zimmermann, House declared, was "one of the statesmen who might lead his country into better paths," and House urged him to join idealistic leaders in America, France, and Great Britain to move civilization forward. It was "the most earnest talk" he had made to any German official.[24] He hoped for support not from the powers that were, but from those that might be. On the evening of January 29, House left Berlin by train for Switzerland "after four strenuous and not altogether happy days." He had made no progress in his quest for peace but wrote Auchincloss that he was "having an extraordinarily interesting and valuable visit to Berlin." He knew that "these are fateful days."[25]

Once back in Paris, on February 1, House reported fully to the president both by cable and by letter. He summarized his conversations with German officials, informed Wilson of the "great controversy" over underseas warfare, and warned that Bethmann Hollweg would not be able to control U-boat enthusiasts much longer. The stakes could not be higher. If Germany was victorious, he predicted, "the war lords will reign supreme and democratic governments will be imperiled throughout the world." House's visit to Berlin had increased his sense of urgency; Wilson's peace initiative could not wait until the fall of 1916.[26]

House stayed in Paris for a full week. He was proud of the fact that his staff had expanded and now included, besides Fanny Denton, Lanier Winslow, whom he had borrowed from the Berlin Embassy, and Clifford Carver, who had previously worked for Ambassador Page in London. He needed more help than ever. "The pressure upon me here," he confided to Auchincloss, "is beyond anything. Newspaper men, photographers, Americans, Frenchmen and what not take up every moment of my waking hours."[27] Paris was closer to the front lines than any other capital city; Parisians could hear the heavy artillery fired during the Battle of the Marne, which took place only fifty miles away. After the war of movement on the Western Front had ended, the government returned to Paris, and the city had begun to adjust to the strains of the war. Many shops and most museums closed and more than one-third of the workforce left the city, but food supplies remained adequate and life remained bearable. Authorities in Paris were more successful than their counterparts in Berlin in containing the instabilities brought by the war.[28]

As France settled down to a long struggle, the *union sacrée* began to fracture and discontent grew over the Viviani government's conduct of the conflict. The failed French offensives on the Western Front lowered troop morale and increased tension between the parliament and the army's high command. "What worries me," President Poincaré noted in mid-summer 1915, "is the state of mind revealed by this correspondence: a spreading malaise which, by gnawing away at French powers of patience, can bring disaster." In late October, Poincaré removed Prime Minister Viviani, whom he found "flaccid as a rag," and replaced him with what he hoped would be a new and more vigorous leader, Aristide Briand.[29] And in December 1915, Poincaré expanded the powers of General Joseph Joffre, making him commander-in-chief of French armies. Russian defeats in the east concerned Joffre, who refused to go on the defensive or to surrender the initiative to Germany. Despite French setbacks in 1915, he had not lost faith in the offensive, wanted Great Britain to assume a greater share of the war's burdens, and pressed for a coordinated effort by the Allies on the Western Front in the spring of 1916. The French government was determined to fight the war to a finish and, through a victor's peace, unite the "lost provinces" with France.[30]

House realized that were Wilson to intervene to end the conflict, he must persuade French leaders that America was their true friend. Only if convinced of American goodwill would they be inclined to accept the president's intervention. On February 1, the first day of his stay in Paris, he had a ceremonial meeting with Prime Minister Briand (with Hugh Frazier of the American Embassy acting as his interpreter). The next day he had a far more substantive talk with Jules Cambon, the secretary general of the foreign ministry. Without mentioning his plan for American mediation, House told Cambon that U-boat extremists would gain the upper hand in Germany and force a break with the United States. He also warned that Germany might make a separate peace with Russia and that it was a "terrible gamble" for Great Britain and France to prolong the war. The Allies were unlikely "to have a decisive victory on any of the fronts during the coming spring and summer," and in the autumn they would still face a stalemated war. But America, he reassured Cambon, would draw closer "to France and England when their fortunes were at low ebb."[31]

For the next four days House was curiously inactive. Paris seems to have had that effect on him. Not until February 7, the day before his departure, did he have a long conference at the Quai d'Orsay with Briand (with Jules Cambon acting as interpreter)—"an important—perhaps the most important, conference I have had during this visit to Europe." He and Briand, House recorded, reached "a complete understanding as to the immediate future. *In the event the Allies are successful during the next few months I promised that the President would not intervene. In the event they were losing ground I promised the President would intervene.*" House urged Briand "not to let the fortunes of the Allies recede beyond a point where our intervention could save them," and he and the prime minister then moved on to a discussion of a territorial settlement. France would regain Alsace and Lorraine, while Germany and Russia would be given remnants of the Ottoman Empire. Only at the end of the conversation did House urge French leaders to "use their influence with England" to moderate the blockade.[32]

House assurances of American sympathy and support excited Briand and Cambon, who emphasized his prediction that the United States would enter the war in 1916 on the Allies' side. According to Cambon, House had declared that "the war will be long, that the Allies will win in the end, and that in a year's time America will be with us." Cambon pointed out, however, that the occasion for Wilsonian intervention "had not arrived." And Briand and Cambon neglected to tell House that the French, British, and Russian governments had already agreed to drastic territorial changes that assumed the defeat of Germany, and that French and British officials were engaged in secret discussions about the eventual partition of the Ottoman Empire.[33]

House now believed—mistakenly—that he had won the confidence of French leaders. In reports to the president he predicted that, after severe fighting in the spring and summer, "I am as sure as I ever am of anything that by the end of the summer you can intervene." His friend in the White House would then have a "great opportunity" to lead the belligerents out of the awful cataclysm.[34] House's curious performance in Paris revealed once again his uneven skills as a diplomat. He had exaggerated his own accomplishments, misunderstood French leaders, and conveyed to Wilson an inaccurate assessment of the possibilities for peace.

While House conferred with leaders in London, Berlin, and Paris, a variety of domestic issues absorbed the president's attention. By early 1916, Secretary of War Garrison's plan for a continental army had no chance of passing Congress, where Democratic leaders were unsympathetic. But the secretary of war would not retreat, while Republicans prepared to attack the administration's foreign and defense policies. Finally, on January 18, 1916, Wilson decided to go to the country (a "swing around the circle"), make a plea for reasonable preparedness, and break the impasse. From January 27 to February 4 he traveled throughout the Midwest, calling for increases in the nation's army and navy so that the United States could remain at peace and play its part in "the redemption of the affairs of mankind." The administration regained the initiative on the preparedness issue, but Garrison refused to compromise with congressional leaders and on February 10 resigned. In early March, Wilson chose Newton D. Baker, the former progressive mayor of Cleveland, Ohio, to be his new secretary of war and to find a preparedness program that could move through the Congress.[35]

When the president returned to Washington he found that negotiations over the *Lusitania* had once again become critical. Secretary of State Lansing pushed for a formal break unless the German government finally admitted that the sinking of the *Lusitania* had violated international law. House warned against abrupt action; he and Ambassador Gerard urged the president to accept something less than an outright admission of wrongdoing. Their warnings, along with the public's anti-war mood, convinced Wilson to back away from Lansing's position and avoid a rupture with Berlin. The quarrel between the two governments over the sinking of the *Lusitania* had finally come to an end.[36]

Since the summer of 1915, the president and secretary of state had considered changes in the rules on the treatment of armed merchantmen. By
early January 1916, they had concluded that it was unreasonable to ask
U-boats to surface and warn armed merchantmen when the latter had the
capacity to destroy the submarines. On January 18, with the president's
approval, Lansing sent a note to the belligerent governments, proposing
that armed merchantmen should be treated as auxiliary cruisers. Hoping
for a final settlement of the submarine controversy, the president wrote
Lansing that "this [the modus vivendi] seems to me reasonable and thoroughly worth trying."[37] The American note disturbed Foreign Secretary
Grey; Page reported that "I have only once before seen Sir Edward so
grave and disappointed." Grey did not want a crisis with the United States,
given the dependence of the Allies on American raw materials, munitions,
and credit, but he also realized that domestic pressures made concessions
impossible. In Berlin, Chancellor Bethmann Hollweg found the American
proposal encouraging, since it promised an understanding with the United
States on submarine warfare and perhaps offered a way out of his impasse
with the military. On February 11, the Admiralty sent orders to the High
Seas Fleet to begin, at the end of the month, treating armed merchantmen
as warships.[38]

When House arrived in London on February 9, it seemed as if a crisis in Anglo-American relations was imminent. He soon discovered the
indignation felt by British leaders—that the United States was attempting
to shift the balance of seapower in favor of the Allies' enemies—and on
February 14 warned Lansing to avoid a quarrel with Great Britain. Wilson
and Lansing, finally aware that they had made a serious mistake that might
imperil House's mediation efforts, abandoned their proposal. On February
15, the secretary of state told reporters that the American government
would not insist on changing the rules governing U-boat warfare.[39]

Lansing's announcement set off a storm in the Congress, where many
thought the American government would now defend the rights of its citizens to travel on armed merchantmen. Soon bills were introduced to keep
Americans from traveling on armed ships. Faced with a rebellion in the
Congress, the president realized that if he was defeated, his influence with
both the Allies and the Central Powers would be greatly diminished. At
the end of February, as House traveled across the Atlantic, Wilson moved
to put down the revolt, sending Burleson and McAdoo to Capitol Hill to
twist the arms of Democratic congressmen. In early March the president

prevailed; both resolutions were defeated by substantial margins. But Wilson now knew, as Bryan pointed out, that "the people of the United States are not willing to go to war to vindicate the right of Americans to take these risks."[40]

On February 9, House crossed the Channel on a troop ship. While the weather was clear and the ocean calm, near Dover the convoy stopped and House and his party had to come on deck, put on life belts, and stand by a lifeboat. Nearby, a steamer had been torpedoed by a U-boat. With British planes circling overhead, House's ship ran along the coast at high speeds to Folkestone.[41]

Once in London, the Houses returned to the Ritz Hotel. Soon after his arrival House met with Page, who now made an outright denunciation of his mediation proposal. The ambassador thought House's scheme was morally wrong—trying to trick the belligerents into peace—and also unrealistic. He was certain that British leaders would not dare accept Wilson's intervention and refused to attend a conference House had arranged with Asquith, Grey, and Lloyd George. Page believed that "they are laughing at the 'Empty House' here," dismissed "all the vain and silly talk about 'intervention,'" and vowed that the president's emissary "cannot come again or I go." Page's pessimism frustrated House, of course. "He frets me to such an extent," he recorded in his diary, "that I fear I talked to him rather roughly . . . . The man hinders me in my work because he tries to discourage me, and would totally do so if I were of a different temperament."[42]

The next day House went to 33 Eccleston Square to give Grey a report on his visit to the Continent. After learning about House's talks in Berlin and Paris, Grey speculated that it would be best for the United States to enter the war over the sinking of the *Lusitania*. House argued that the United States should "smooth over the *Lusitania* incident and intervene by demanding a conference of the belligerents for the purpose of discussing peace terms." In "ten minutes," House claimed, he brought the foreign secretary around, and the two men allegedly agreed that the president should call a conference soon after House returned to America. As he telegraphed Wilson, tomorrow he and Grey would bring their understanding before Asquith and Balfour "and if they consent," House wrote with great satisfaction in his diary, "it should mark the beginning of the end of the war."[43] But House saw only what he wanted to see. He had ignored Page's warnings about the mood of British leaders and had ignored Grey's observation that "If the Allies thought Great Britain was preparing to discuss

peace, something like a panic might ensue." Instead, he continued to pursue his illusion of peace.[44]

Two days after his arrival, February 11, House lunched with Asquith,
Balfour, and Grey. The result was, by any measure, inconclusive; all three
British leaders agreed, as Grey put it, that "Great Britain could do nothing
until some one of her allies was ready to discuss peace." No agreement was
reached, House's diary revealed, over either the nature or the timing of
the president's intervention. In his report to Wilson, House admitted that
British leaders were hesitant, and that evening he dined with Lloyd George
and Lord Reading, both of whom warned "that a peace proposal would
be the most unpopular move that could be thought of in England." House
nonetheless ignored their warning, convinced that he had persuaded two
more British leaders that it would be best for the United States to enter the
war as a result of Wilson's mediation.[45]

On the morning of February 14 House met with Grey in preparation for dinner that evening with Asquith, Balfour, Lloyd George, and
Reading. The foreign secretary now thought that "the time has come
for the President to demand a peace conference," but warned that other
members of the cabinet did not share his views and that the British people, if they learned of this peace plan, would "smash his windows." House
seemed undeterred, and later in the day "sat still and quiet looking into
the fire" while Page denounced the president as "simply not a man of
action."

That evening House and British leaders talked from 8:30 to midnight,
discussing British domestic affairs and the conduct of the war. House predicted a major German offensive at Verdun (which began on February
21) that might bring a decisive breakthrough, and tried to convince
Asquith, Grey, Balfour, Lloyd George, and Reading "what a terrible gamble they are taking in not invoking our intervention." Finally, at 10:30 PM
the group focused on the key issue, "that is, when should the United States
demand that the war should cease and a conference be held?" No consensus emerged, however, on the timing of Wilson's intervention, and the
prime minister moved on to the peace conference itself, asking what would
Wilson do if "the Allies proposed a settlement which he considered unjust?"
House replied "that he would probably withdraw from the conference and
leave them to their own devices." What, Asquith then asked, would the
president do if Germany proposed an unjust settlement? House thought
that, under these circumstances, "the President would throw the weight of

the United States on the side of the Allies." Pressed hard by Asquith, House could offer only vague assurances of American support.[46]

In House's mind what was in fact an inconclusive discussion had been transformed into an understanding. In a brief report to Wilson, he expressed optimism, claiming that British leaders had agreed to the president's presiding over a peace conference and that "there is a difference of opinion only as to the time."[47] The next morning, when House saw Grey, the foreign secretary, if House's diary is to be believed, "was visibly pleased with the result of our meeting last night." Grey stated that the British government faced a "momentous" decision and, pacing up and down the room, claimed that, despite the unpopularity of a peace move, he favored "immediate action." Before House left England Grey promised to write a memorandum of their understanding that he would place before the entire cabinet.[48]

Four days later, however, on February 21, Grey was more cautious, warning that the timing of American mediation "depended upon the opinion of the military leaders of the Allies." On the other hand, Howard Whitehouse, a Liberal member of parliament, fed House's hopes by speculating that Wilson's proposal for a peace conference, if accepted by the cabinet, would be sustained both by public opinion and a large majority in parliament.[49]

On February 23, his last day in London, House conferred with Grey for a final time. The foreign secretary gave House an affectionate farewell, hoping that he would one day visit him at Fallodon, his Northumberland estate, and telling him that he "could never know how much my coming into his life has meant." Grey also gave House the official memorandum, initialed only by him, that embodied his understanding with British leaders.[50] It read as follows:

> Colonel House told me that President Wilson was ready, on hearing from France and England that the moment was opportune, to propose that a Conference should be summoned to put an end to the war. Should the Allies accept this proposal and should Germany refuse it, the United States would probably enter the war against Germany. Colonel House expressed the opinion that, if such a Conference met, it would secure peace on terms not unfavourable to the Allies; and, if it failed to secure peace, the United States would leave the Conference as a belligerent on the side of the Allies, if Germany was unreasonable. Colonel House expressed an opinion decidedly favourable to the restoration of Belgium, the transfer of Alsace and Lorraine to France, and the acquisition by Russia of an outlet to the sea, though he thought that the loss of territory incurred by Germany in one place would

have to be compensated by concessions to her in other places outside Europe. If the Allies delayed accepting the offer of President Wilson, and if, later on, the course of the war was so unfavourable to them that the intervention of the United States would not be effective, the United States would probably disinterest themselves in Europe, and look to their own protection in their own way.

I said that I felt the statement, coming from the President of the United States, to be a matter of such importance that I must inform the Prime Minister and my Colleagues; but that I could say nothing until it had received their consideration. The British Government could under no circumstances accept or make any proposal except in consultation and agreement with the Allies. I thought that the Cabinet would probably feel that the present situation would not justify them in approaching their Allies on this subject at the present moment; but, as Colonel House had had an intimate conversation with M. Briand and M. Jules Cambon in Paris, I should think it right to tell M. Briand privately through the French Ambassador in London what Colonel House had said to us, and I should of course, whenever there was an opportunity, be ready to talk the matter over with M. Briand if he desired it.[51]

The day before his final conversation with House, Grey had taken the peace plan to the war committee. During the discussion the foreign secretary stated that mediation, a poor substitute for victory, "would result in the status quo ante," while the prime minister observed that "to the Allies a draw was much the same as a defeat." All the members of the war committee were skeptical of House's plan, regarding it as full of risks and uncertainties. All agreed with Lloyd George that "nothing should be done at present."[52] Asquith and his cabinet, although worried about the Allies' military prospects, preferred to persevere in the war and to win a clear-cut victory over the Central Powers. If this proved impossible, they then preferred a victory gained through American military intervention brought about by German U-boat warfare. Finally, House's plan for American mediation would only seem attractive if the Allies, confronted with a military defeat, could use it as a way in which to avoid a harsh peace.[53]

Grey and other British leaders had been less than candid with Wilson's emissary, but House had also deceived himself, seeing what he wanted to see instead of realistically analyzing Britain's wartime goals. As Austen Chamberlain, the secretary of state for India, had noted in mid-January, "House lacked a very wide or clear grasp of the European situation."[54]

As his departure neared, House concluded that his visit had been "most successful," and told his friend Horace Plunkett that the United States "would be 'in the thick of it' in the near future perhaps thirty days."[55] On February 23, his last day in London, "books, notes, flowers have arrived in numbers, and callers came in so rapidly at one time that I had to use my bedroom to keep them separated." That evening, he, Loulie, and Fanny left on the train—they had a private sleeping car—for Falmouth, and the next day boarded a Dutch liner, the SS *Rotterdam*. During its North Atlantic passage the ship encountered a storm so fierce that it had to "lay to for ten hours," House noted in his diary. When the *Rotterdam* entered New York harbor on March 5, House boarded a revenue cutter manned by Gordon Auchincloss and Dudley Malone. Malone stayed with him the rest of the day, filling his mentor in on political developments during his absence. Eager to meet with the president, House then took the midnight train to Washington.[56]

19

The Failure of Peace

O n the morning of March 6, 1916, House arrived in Washington and at
8:00 AM joined the president and Edith for breakfast. He did not give
Wilson a report on his European trip until after lunch, when the three took
an automobile ride of over two hours. House had to summarize his activities in Europe while squeezed in between Woodrow and Edith in the presidential limousine. The president's new wife, he now realized, was privy to
all important state papers and had a lively interest in foreign policy.[1] In the
early months of 1916, while House traveled in Europe, Woodrow and Edith
had settled into a routine that was, in important ways, vastly different from
the one he had with Ellen. Edith was involved in all aspects of Wilson's life,
whether he was at work or play, sitting with him in his office as he dictated
letters and accompanying him on the golf course or in an automobile. She
had few interests aside from her husband's, serving both as his constant
companion and as an assistant president. The energy that Wilson had once
devoted to his friendships with Grayson, House, Tumulty, and his three
daughters was now focused entirely on his new wife. As one of Edith's
biographers writes, "Their intimacy was foreclosing all others."[2]

On his first day in Washington, House showed Wilson the memorandum that Foreign Secretary Grey had drafted. The president approved the
whole of the agreement, adding only a third "probably,"—one of his key
words—and the next day the two men sent a cable to Grey informing him
that Wilson accepted the memorandum. As House wrote Grey two days
later, "It is now squarely up to you to make the next move and a cable from
you at any time will be sufficient."[3]

The president, who accepted House's belief that leaders in France and
Great Britain were eager for American mediation, effusively praised his
friend's accomplishments. "The President placed his arms around my
shoulders," House recorded in his diary, "and said: 'I cannot adequately

express to you my admiration and gratitude for what you have done.'" House was deeply touched by Wilson's praise, and imagined him "sitting at the head of the counsel table at the Hague."[4] But the two men still had different views of American mediation. House saw it as a way to enter the war on the side of the Allies, while Wilson saw it as a genuine way to end the conflict. As he told Senator William J. Stone, chairman of the Senate Foreign Relations Committee, "You are right in assuming that I shall do everything in my power to keep the United States out of war."[5]

When Grey received House's cable he once again brought up the issue of American mediation at a meeting of the war committee. Once again Britain's leaders revealed little interest in a negotiated peace. Asquith had already dismissed House's scheme as "humbug, and a mere manoeuvre of American politics," while Conservative Party leader Andrew Bonar Law declared that the public would not stand for a status quo ante peace and Balfour dismissed House's proposal as "not worth five minutes thought." All knew that French leaders were contemptuous of the plan (Jules Cambon had "laughed it to scorn") and realized that this was not the time, with their French ally engaged in the great struggle at Verdun, to suggest peace talks.[6] Despite all this, Grey sent House an evasive reply. Rather than frankly summarize the views of his government, he claimed that British leaders "cannot at this moment take the initiative in asking the French to consider a conference." As one British official concluded, "if House could deliver the goods the goods are not good enough . . . . We must win a complete victory and that I think House cannot secure us."[7]

During the winter of 1915–1916, House, absorbed in the Great War, paid little attention to events in Mexico. For a time, after American recognition of Carranza's regime on October 19, 1915, it seemed as if relations were much improved and American arms and loans flowed to the Constitutionalist regime. In late 1915, the first chief's troops inflicted further defeats on Villa's forces in Chihuahua and Sonora provinces and established control of the border. Much diminished, Villa's army retreated into the mountains of northern Mexico. Convinced that the course of events in Mexico had vindicated his policies, the president in his December 7, 1915, annual message to Congress declared that America would "await the rebirth of the troubled Republic . . . . We will aid and befriend Mexico, but we will not coerce her."[8]

Carranza's triumph, however, was incomplete; the first chief controlled little more than half of the country.[9] In early 1916, Villa began to retaliate, creating incidents along the border that would inflame American Mexican relations and reveal Carranza's subservience to the Colossus of the North. On March 9 his troops rode into the American town of Columbus, looting stores and burning houses. Yielding to the widespread outrage among Americans, Wilson felt he had no choice but to send a military expedition into Mexico in pursuit of Villa, and on March 15 a force of 4,000 American troops, under the command of General John J. Pershing, crossed the border. The president did not want war with Mexico; he hoped that an American expeditionary force could defeat Villa and resolve the crisis.[10] As the Punitive Expedition—as it was called—moved deep into northern Mexico in search of Villa's guerrilla bands, tension mounted with Carranza, who had not formally approved the entry of American troops. Throughout Mexico resentment toward the United States grew; Villa became the symbol of national resistance against foreign invaders.[11]

Incidents continued to occur, and finally on June 20 at the village of Carrizal, an over-confident American commander attacked Mexican forces, leaving fourteen of his soldiers dead and twenty-five captured. For a few days Wilson thought that Carranza had decided on war, and on June 26 he began work on a message to Congress. Two days later, however, Carranza released the American prisoners and the crisis began to ease. The fate of Pershing's expedition remained undecided, but the president, impressed with the outpouring of anti-war sentiment, was still determined to avoid a conflict. At the end of the month, at a speech before the New York Press Club, Wilson reaffirmed his devotion to peace with Mexico.[12]

In mid-March, after news of the Columbus raid reached him, House had urged Wilson to take "positive action" and send Pershing into Mexico.[13] As Pershing's forces moved south and as tension mounted, House was impressed with "the hopelessness of that situation [in Mexico]," but also grew impatient with the lack of a solution, advising the president at the end of May to use "a firm hand and firm tone with Mexico." He seemed resigned that all of Wilson's efforts would end in war. But as the crisis over the Carrizal incident eased and as he noticed the strong anti-war sentiment in the nation, House swung the other way, praising Wilson for sensing "the feeling of the country concerning Mexico. The people do not want war with Mexico. They do not want war with anybody, but least of all a country like that." House seemed uncertain how to deal with revolutionary chaos in Mexico; for him it was an unwelcome distraction from the war in Europe.[14]

In the early weeks of March, House was optimistic about the prospects for peace and felt that, with the exception of the Mexican crisis, "everything has quieted down since my return." He "eagerly await[ed] the summons" from British leaders and predicted that "great things will happen during the spring and summer."[15]

Whatever House's fantasies about peace, he knew enough about the political situation in Germany to realize that "delay is dangerous." Chancellor Bethmann Hollweg could not continue to resist the mounting pressure for unrestricted U-boat warfare, and on March 13 the German High Seas Fleet received orders to renew the submarine campaign that had been abandoned in September 1915. While U-boat commanders were to spare passenger ships, months of inaction had made them eager for results and inclined to stretch their orders. As a consequence, on March 24 the SS *Sussex*, a Channel steamer on its regular voyage from Folkestone to Dieppe, was hit by a torpedo. The *Sussex* did not sink and was towed to port, but eighty of its 325 passengers, including four Americans, were killed or injured.[16] As in previous crises, Wilson's initial reaction was cautious. Secretary of State Lansing urged a "decisive step," an ultimatum to Berlin demanding the end of all submarine warfare. But the president was reluctant to act until he learned of the circumstances surrounding the torpedoing of the *Sussex* and until he understood what kind of submarine campaign Germany had launched.[17]

On March 28, House took the morning train to Washington. Although still recuperating from an unspecified "slight operation," he worried that the president would "delay and write further notes when action is what we need." When he arrived at the White House Wilson was playing golf, and the two had only a brief talk before dinner.[18] Not until the third day of his visit did they finally focus on the new clash with Germany. Like Lansing, House urged Wilson to send Ambassador Bernstorff home to Berlin and to break off diplomatic relations. He now seemed to accept American entrance into the war, warning that unless Wilson acted decisively, "he would soon lose the confidence of the American people, and also of the Allies, and would fail to have any influence at the peace conference." Later in the day House returned to New York, not knowing what action the president would take.[19]

The president and Edith spent the weekend of April 1 and 2 cruising on the *Mayflower*, the presidential yacht, and did not return to Washington until Monday, April 3. While the president deliberated, "his immediate entourage. . . ," House recorded, "are having an unhappy time just now." White House physician Cary Grayson, dabbling in politics and diplomacy, visited House in New York to vent his frustrations. Grayson complained that his chief "is a man of unusually narrow prejudices and is intolerant of advice," and claimed that "a great crisis is impending and the President's place in history is at stake." House agreed, noting that Wilson "does not like to meet people and isolates himself as much as anyone I have ever known."[20]

By early April, Wilson had learned that the Sussex had been unarmed and carried no troops. He now prepared for the worst, instructing Lansing to begin work on a note of protest to Berlin. Lansing's draft, calling for a severance of diplomatic relations, impressed House (he had returned to Washington on April 5), who argued that a break with Germany was "inevitable" now that its U-boats were torpedoing ships without warning. But confronted with the prospect of war with Germany, he and the president wondered if it would not be best to invoke the House-Grey Memorandum, "to give the Allies a last chance to accept our offer of intervention."[21]

With House's assistance, Wilson composed a telegram to Grey, urging the foreign secretary to consult with Britain's allies and then ask for American mediation; otherwise, a break with Germany would soon come, forcing the United States to become a belligerent and prolonging the war.[22]

The foreign secretary quickly rejected the president's appeal, informing House that at the recent Allied conference in Paris, French leaders had not raised the subject of mediation; he was certain that they would not consider the idea of a peace conference. As Grey explained more fully in a letter, "I am bound to say that I think feeling here is the same. Everybody feels that there must be more German failure and some Allied success before anything but an inconclusive peace could be obtained." Grey felt that American entry into the war would shorten it rather than prolong it.[23]

When House returned to Washington on April 11, he found that the president had discarded Lansing's draft of the Sussex note and written one of his own. Wilson now sought to force the issue, to make demands on the German government though without eliminating the possibility of a peaceful solution to the crisis. For two hours on the morning of April 11, Edith and House discussed the note with the president, insisting that the last paragraph was weak and should be changed. That evening House went to New York uncertain what the final shape of the document would be.[24]

After undergoing further refinements, on April 18 the president's *Sussex* note was finally dispatched to Berlin. The next day Wilson went before a joint session of the Congress and in a brief address explained his demands on Germany. As "the responsible spokesman of the rights of humanity," the United States insisted that unless the German government abandoned "its present methods of warfare against passenger and freight carrying vessels this Government can have no choice but to sever diplomatic relations with the Government of the German Empire altogether." Only at the end of the address did members of the Congress, after listening to it in silence, burst into applause. Wilson's ultimatum to Berlin met with widespread approval throughout the nation. As House noted, people are now "beginning to realize that we are on the brink of war and what war means."[25]

The severity of the American note shocked German leaders. Nonetheless Chancellor Bethmann Hollweg concluded that Wilson was not bluffing and felt that Germany had no choice but to yield. On April 26 he traveled to Charleville to once again maneuver within the inner circle of advisers surrounding the kaiser and try to avoid war with the United States. General Falkenhayn—whose influence had been reduced by the bloody stalemate at Verdun—pushed for all-out U-boat warfare, but naval leaders were more reasonable and argued that there was "no need to play [Germany's] last man now." The kaiser, eager to avoid a break with the United States, accepted the chancellor's recommendation that Germany conduct its submarine operations according to the rules of visit and search. Germany had again yielded to America's demands.[26]

On May 5, the German reply arrived in Washington. Lansing disliked the note, but House understood "the real concessions that the Germans have made" and advised the president that "I do not see how we can break with Germany on this note." Wilson accepted House's rather than Lansing's reading of the document, and on May 9 his response finally brought the *Sussex* crisis to an end and met with the widespread approval of the American press. Wilson's diplomacy of patience had been vindicated, though he realized that America's neutrality was more fragile than ever. As Bethmann Hollweg warned, if the United States did nothing "to enforce international law against England" the clamor in Germany for unrestricted U-boat warfare would continue.[27] Berthmann Hollweg had reason to hope the United States would pressure the British.

Throughout the spring of 1916 a variety of British practices, such as the seizure of mail from neutral ships, brought protests from the American government. And the brutal suppression of the nationalist rebellion in Dublin (the "Easter Rising") further strained Anglo-American relations and contributed to a hardening of American opinion toward Great Britain. As Ambassador Spring-Rice informed Grey, "our relations are now entering into a difficult and dangerous stage."[28]

Wilson and House realized the precariousness of America's position. They knew that Bethmann Hollweg might lose the next debate over U-boat warfare and feared that the war, if it continued, might set off political and social revolution in Europe. More than ever before Wilson wanted an American peace move, one that would end the conflict, respond to the pleas of progressive internationalists, and commit the Democratic Party to American membership in a postwar league of nations.[29] On May 3, even before the end of the *Sussex* crisis, House urged the president to act to end the war. By late summer, he reasoned, both sides would realize the futility of continuing the struggle. The battle of Verdun—now in its third month— had already displayed the inability of the Germans to break through on the Western Front, and he predicted that an Allied summer offensive would also end in frustration. Both men agreed that they must once again appeal to the British foreign secretary.[30]

In a telegram to Grey on May 10 and in a letter the next day, House informed the foreign secretary that the president, in his desire "to serve humanity in a large way," was now ready to call for a peace conference. He was also ready to commit the United States publicly to join with other powers "in a convention looking to the maintenance of peace after the war." History would, he concluded, "bring a grave indictment against" British leaders if they failed to act quickly.[31] The British foreign secretary, however, was unmoved. The next day, without consulting Prime Minister Asquith or other colleagues, he rejected House's plea. A peace conference now, he argued, was premature, especially if it was proposed without any indication of what the terms of the settlement ought to be. Nor did Grey now seem enthusiastic about a call for the creation of a postwar league of nations.[32]

The response of Grey—in whom he had invested so many hopes—disappointed House. Nor was the president pleased with the British position. The time had come, he informed his adviser, to "get down to hard pan." Now that relations with Germany had eased, the United States could no longer tolerate Britain's "indefensible" violation of American neutral rights. Either the American government must make a "move for peace. . .

or, if she postpones that, must insist to the limit upon her" neutral rights. If the United States moved for peace—a course Wilson obviously pre-ferred—it would not concern itself with territorial settlements among the belligerents. But it would insist upon "a universal alliance to maintain free-dom of the seas and to prevent any war begun either a) contrary to treaty covenants or b) without warning and full inquiry,—a virtual guarantee of territorial integrity and political independence." House was to cable Grey again, "putting the whole thing plainly to him."[33]

House quickly set to work drafting the cable, and on May 19 telegraphed his appeal to Grey, warning that America must either "inaugurate some sort of peace discussions" or assert its rights against the Allies. Eager for England and America "to link shields in this mighty cause," House reminded Grey that Germany seemed unlikely to accept Wilson as a mediator and that the Allies would have time to launch their summer offensive on the Western Front before a peace conference assembled. And in a letter that followed, House warned, "Your seeming lack of desire to cooperate with us will chill the enthusiasm here—never, I am afraid, to come again, at least in our day." The foreign secretary, now at last aware of the seriousness of the American demands, promised to consult with Asquith at once.[34]

Earlier in May, Wilson had agreed to speak before the League to Enforce Peace on the twenty-seventh of the month. As the date for the address neared, he asked House for advice; his counselor responded with a long memorandum, much of which was incorporated into his address. The pres-ident now backed away from his earlier insistence on linking a call for a postwar league of nations with a call for a peace conference.[35] On May 24, when House and Wilson conferred in New York, they agreed that it would be best to modify Wilson's speech and "not to do more than hint at peace." The president would, House concluded, make a speech "to preserve peace in the future rather than to make peace now."[36]

At 7:30 PM on May 27, Wilson spoke to an audience of 2,000 at the New Willard Hotel in Washington. He asserted that Americans were not con-cerned with the war's "causes and its objects," but they had been deeply affected by the war and were "participants, whether we would or not, in the life of the world." The outbreak of the hostilities, which had grown out of "secret counsels," had taken the world by surprise, and it was now clear that the peace "must henceforth depend on a new and more whole-some diplomacy." If the United States, he went on, should one day seek to bring an end to the war, it would not involve itself in territorial settlements

among the belligerents, but would commit itself to "an universal association of nations. . . a virtual guarantee of territorial integrity and political
independence." "God grant," Wilson concluded, "that the dawn of that
day of frank dealing and of settled peace, concord, and cooperation be near
at hand."[37] The president received tumultuous applause at the end of his
talk; most Americans seemed to approve of his declaration committing the
United States to a new international order. "Mr. Wilson," the *New Republic*
claimed, "has broken with the tradition of American isolation in the only
way which offers any hope to men."[38]

The reaction among leaders in Berlin was far less enthusiastic. General
Falkenhayn was now more optimistic about Germany's military prospects
and Bethmann Hollweg rejected the idea of Wilsonian mediation. As
Foreign Secretary Jagow instructed Bernstorff in early June, the German
government had little faith in the president's good offices; a peace based on
the status quo ante bellum was unacceptable to Germany. The ambassador
was to prevent Wilson from approaching the German government with a
peace plan.[39]

Nor were the Allies receptive to Wilson's peace move. The French
government believed, Ambassador Jusserand told House, that "any peace
talk at this time will have a tendency to encourage her enemies and
break the spirit of her people." With German armies occupying much of
Europe, a settlement in the near future was sure to bring a German victory or, at best, a peace based on the status quo ante. As long as there was
a chance of victory, British and French leaders wanted to fight on. By the
early summer of 1916, Allied military prospects seemed reasonably good,
or at least better than a year earlier. The German assault on Verdun had
failed, and Britain's New Armies were preparing for a major offensive
at the Somme. Far better to continue the war than to get entangled in a
risky mediation scheme that would be based on Wilson's vision of a peace
of reconciliation.[40]

On May 29, Grey finally answered House's May 19 plea for peace. The
foreign secretary once again emphasized the extent to which Great Britain
was bound to its Allies and warned that "a premature announcement of
intervention by the President might be dangerous to the cause he and we
have at heart."[41] House's reply to Grey's telegram was somber, pointing out
that the Allies' rejection of Wilsonian intervention meant "another year
will go by leaving the lines much as they are today."[42] As House and Wilson
absorbed the mounting evidence of the intransigence of both the Allies and

the Central Powers, their mood darkened. House believed that the British and French were prolonging the war unnecessarily, while the president, equally discouraged, concluded that "it will be up to us to judge for ourselves when the time has arrived for us to make an imperative suggestion."[43]

The collapse of the fantasies about American mediation that House had promoted for so long came as a severe blow to both the president and his counselor. The Allies had rejected—for reasons House and Wilson only partly understood—their offer to use America's weight to bring about a pro-Allied peace. It now seemed to them that British and French leaders were more interested in victory than in a peace of reconciliation, and that in their pursuit of it they risked bringing about profound upheavals in Europe.[44]

On March 8, after his return from Washington, House resumed his routine in New York. One British journalist found him sitting at his tidy desk, with a telephone connected to the White House, "a neat, grey, mousy, mustached little man with a high stiff collar, gentle, imperturbable, and omniscient." As House reentered the American political scene, he paused to reflect on his life: "The life I am leading transcends in interest and excitement any romance. I cannot begin to outline here [in my diary] what happens from day to day, how information from every quarter pours into this little unobtrusive study. I believe I am the only one who gets a view of the entire picture. Some get one corner and some another, but I seem to have it all." House knew, however, that if he was to retain his unique position, he must resume the struggle for preferment among the president's inner circle of advisers.[45]

House soon discovered that during his absence, some of the president's advisers had declined in influence while others had drawn closer to the center of power. After a long talk with Secretary of the Treasury McAdoo, House learned that "the President evidently does not tell McAdoo much of what is in his mind." Tumulty, too, had suffered a loss of Wilson's confidence, and House found a new ally in his campaign against the president's secretary. During a talk with Edith on April 26, the two decided "that the most helpful things that could be done for the President at this time, would be the elimination of good Josephus Daniels [secretary of the navy] and Joseph Tumulty. She undertakes to eliminate Tumulty if I can manage the Daniels change." There is no evidence that House moved to undermine Daniels in the spring of 1916, but on May 24 he once again sought to undermine the president's longtime secretary. Wilson seemed ready to make a change, but House could not think of a suitable replacement, and the president's faithful Irish secretary continued to cling to his position.[46]

On the surface, House remained friendly with Ambassador Page, exchanging letters and helping, through the generosity of Wilson's friend Cleveland Dodge, to arrange financing for his stay in London. Beneath the surface, however, sharp disagreements separated the two men. Knowing that Lansing was also unhappy with Page, House finally informed the president of the ambassador's many discontents. Wilson was grateful for his counselor's letter, which "lowers my opinion of the man immensely," but seemed uncertain how to proceed. Rather than make the effort to remove his rebellious ambassador, the president let him linger in London.[47]

In June 1915, when Bryan resigned as secretary of state, House had urged Lansing as his replacement, reasoning that he would serve as little more than a clerk. Since his appointment, however, House had come to respect the expertise of the secretary of state and to realize that he and Lansing agreed on most foreign policy issues. Through his protégé Frank Polk, counselor of the State Department, House carefully monitored Lansing's moods, learning when he was in "thoroughly good humor" with House or when he must be careful of his "sensibilities." The president's reluctance to consult with Lansing troubled House, who was eager to cooperate with him and "to play with all the cards on the table." House worried about Lansing's health, urged Wilson to talk with him more often, and reassured the secretary of state that "you are not only a comfort to the President but an asset that the Administration must not lose."[48]

By the time House returned from Europe, Wilson's new secretary of war, Newton D. Baker, had gained some influence in the inner circle around the president. Baker, only forty-four, had served as the "Boy Mayor" of Cleveland from 1911 to 1915, had supported Wilson at the Baltimore convention in 1912, and, a formidable orator, had become widely known as an advocate of progressive causes. Serene, compassionate, and highly intelligent, Baker took charge of the war department and helped guide Wilson's moderate preparedness program through the Congress in the spring of 1916. "To the end of his life. . . ," one historian writes, "Baker haunted the Democratic Party with a promise of leadership never quite fulfilled."[49]

As Baker's reputation grew, House saw a larger role for him, suggesting that he might become the Democratic candidate for vice-president. Neither the president nor House was impressed with the incumbent, Thomas R. Marshall, who Wilson described as "a very small calibre man."

Always concerned about Wilson's health, House argued that "we should put up a man big enough to fill the place of President. It is too great a risk to allow the life of one man [to] imperil such policies as we have planned to carry out." House believed that with the right man in place, a new office could in effect be created, one in which the vice-president would "be a co-worker and co-helper of the President." But Wilson rejected House's advice, arguing that "Baker was too good a man to be sacrificed" and reminding him "that no Vice President had ever succeeded a President by election."[50]

Edith Wilson, however, had brought the most important change in the president's inner circle. During House's absence she had emerged—as he had noted in that car ride after his return—as an assistant president, following affairs of state and criticizing many of her husband's advisers. She was, however, close to Grayson, who on May 24 married her friend Alice Gertrude Gordon, and also seemed to approve of House, urging him to come to Washington to live. She referred to him as "my dear 'partner in crime,'" and informed Wilson's cousin Helen Bones that Grayson and House "were the only two friends the President had who were serving him without a selfish ambition."[51] Edith's love had given Wilson new energy and a new sense of purpose. On May 12, the journalist Ray Stannard Baker talked with him for two hours in the White House. He found a national leader "quick and light of step," "natty" in dress, with a lively face and a quick, incisive mind, a far cry from his stern public image.[52]

The president's transference of affection to his new wife, however, diminished his intimacy with his trusted adviser. The two men remained on cordial terms and collaborated on a wide range of issues, but the intensity of earlier years was dissipating. Edith was now the focus of his emotional life. Occasionally, when House was in Washington, the three would work together, and Woodrow took great pleasure in the fact that Edith and House had, so it seemed, become friends. During House's stay in early May, the president "went into another room, procured a Century Dictionary, and came back with it balanced on his head very much as the Negroes in the South balance pails of water. Mrs. Wilson and I laughed to see him walk in the grotesque way necessary to keep the book balanced." Then the three examined the portrait of Edith painted by Muller-Ury (which House had given them as a wedding present) and the president "stood with one arm around me and one around Mrs. Wilson and thanked me for having thought to give it to him."[53]

As the end of May approached, House planned to escape the heat of the city by retreating to Sunapee, New Hampshire, a more isolated location than the North Shore of Boston. "The weather is growing so warm," he told Wilson, "and I am so beset on all sides that . . . I would soon be incapacitated here." As always, the president was sympathetic with House's fear of heat. "Be sure," he counseled, "not to linger too long in this heat. Much as I hate to see you go further away, you must take no risks." On June 1, House left New York by car for Sunapee, a town nine miles from a railroad and four miles from a post office, where he could "rest and read and think."[54]

20

Presidential Politics

House had of course long been concerned about the president's pros-pects for reelection in November 1916. In 1912, Wilson had won with slightly under 42 percent of the vote because of the split in the Republican Party. It seemed unlikely, however, that the GOP would remain so bit-terly divided four years later. As early as January 1915, House laid out "a comprehensive campaign in regard to getting the progressive forces in line for 1916 . . . . The Democratic Party must change its historic character and become the progressive party in the future."[1]

House and his associates especially feared that the Republicans would reunite under the banner of Theodore Roosevelt. Robert Woolley, a protégé who served as director of the mint, warned that Roosevelt, "the shrewdest politician in this country," would be the Republican nomi-nee and "is going to give us the run of our lives." But Roosevelt, who remained a divisive figure within his own party—having splintered from it four years earlier—was uninterested in the nomination unless, as he put it, "the country has in its mood something of the heroic." By early May, 1916, House sensed that the tide for Roosevelt had receded and that Charles Evans Hughes, a former reform governor of New York and Supreme Court justice, seemed likely to be the nominee.[2]

After his return from Europe on March 6, House's thoughts turned to what was certain to be a difficult campaign. "The political pot is boiling," he noted, as his old zest for domestic politics returned: "It is a delight to watch the political game, to see amateurs step in, get their wings singed, and fall out."[3]

Throughout the spring, House performed a variety of useful politi-cal chores. He worked through the financier Bernard M. Baruch to ease the ill-tempered William McCombs out of the chairmanship of the Democratic National Committee and led the search to find a replacement.

It proved an arduous task. On June 11, Wilson, only three days before the Democratic convention met in St. Louis, asked his counselor if he could "possibly act yourself?" House, comfortably settled at Sunapee, seemed genuinely alarmed by the prospect[4] and soon persuaded Wilson to select Vance McCormick, a Pennsylvania progressive who had been the Democratic candidate for governor in 1914. The president worried that McCormick might be too "high brow" and unable to handle the "rougher elements" in the party, but House assured him that McCormick was the same "high type" as Counselor of the State Department Frank Polk and that he had "poise and good judgment." McCormick's selection guaranteed that House would win his struggle with Tumulty for control of the Democratic National Committee; other protégés, Gordon Auchincloss, Daniel Roper, Hugh Wallace, and Robert Woolley, would also have key positions in the fall campaign.[5] House urged the president to select former governor of New York Martin H. Glynn to give the convention's keynote speech and agreed with Wilson that Senator Ollie M. James of Kentucky, a powerful orator, ought to be the permanent chairman of the convention.[6]

House was both relieved and unsurprised when the Republican convention in Chicago in early June chose Hughes as its presidential nominee. Woolley reported that "in the far west the sentiment for Hughes is nothing like as strong as it was for Roosevelt," while House observed that "I think we can show Hughes up as a thorough conservative who obtained the name of progressive because of his refusal [as governor of New York] to let the bosses dictate to him." The battle cry of the Democratic Party, he predicted, "will probably be that the President has kept us out of war and the great domestic measures which have been enacted during his administration."[7]

On January 28, while House was in Europe, Wilson had nominated Louis D. Brandeis for a vacancy on the Supreme Court. Brandeis, known as "the people's lawyer," had become a controversial figure because of his attacks on big business and his support for social welfare measures. In 1913, Wilson had wanted to appoint Brandeis to his cabinet but had deferred to his critics and had instead leaned heavily on him for advice in crafting New Freedom legislation. The president's nomination of Brandeis, who would be the first Jewish member of the court, stunned conservatives, who quickly rallied against him. In contrast, progressives viewed the nomination as "a landmark in the history of American democracy," and in the late winter and spring of 1916, the battle over his confirmation unfolded.

Administration leaders worked behind the scenes to gather votes, and on May 4 Wilson publicly entered the fight, claiming that "this friend of justice and of men will ornament the high court of which we are also justly proud." Finally, on June 1, the Senate approved Brandeis's appointment by a vote of 47 to 22. The president had won a major victory and had also signaled his intention to reassert his domestic leadership and to build a new progressive coalition.[8]

In 1913, House had, as we've seen, opposed putting Brandeis in the cabinet, and in February 1916, when he learned of the nomination in London, he was upset. But on his return to the United States in early March, House, knowing of Wilson's deep commitment to the nominee, was careful to conceal his views and refused—despite the urging of many friends—to join the anti-Brandeis coalition.[9] House did not explain his coolness toward Brandeis, but he had never been friendly toward Jews, describing one as "a shrewd and able Hebrew" and another as "the most sorrowful little Jew I have met in a long while." And in early July he warned Wilson that there was a danger of "overdoing" the recognition of Jews in his administration.[10]

Brandeis's nomination was the first sign of the leftward shift of the Wilson administration. In the years prior to World War I, many Democrats, inspired by Bryan's leadership, had embraced a reform agenda that included various social justice measures and an effort to curb corporate power. In the first phase of the New Freedom, in 1913 and 1914, only some of these measures had become law; now, in the spring of 1916, Wilson and congressional Democrats moved toward enacting further progressive reforms.[11] The president was deeply involved in drafting the platform of the St. Louis convention. Wilson's draft, approved by the delegates, committed the party to internationalism abroad and bold reform at home, and included a plank on "Americanism," which called on different groups to be "welded into a mighty and splendid Nation." Wilson wanted "Americanism" to be the theme of the convention.[12]

On June 14, the first day of the convention, Governor Glynn, in his keynote address, gave a powerful anti-war speech, while the next day Ollie M. James, expanding on this theme, praised the president's courage, claiming that "without orphaning a single American child, without widowing a single American mother, without firing a single gun, without the shedding of a single drop of blood, he [Wilson] wrung from the most militant spirit that ever brooded above a battlefield an acknowledgment of American rights and an agreement to American demands." In response, the delegates leaped to their feet and demonstrated for twenty-one minutes. Responding to the mood of the delegates, the platform committee now added the phrase that Wilson had "kept us out of war." The Democratic Party entered the campaign united by its passion for peace and progressivism.[13]

House missed the dramatic St. Louis convention, just as he had missed the one in Baltimore in 1912. In 1912, uncertain of the outcome, he had left for Europe the day the convention opened; in 1916, although convinced that the fate of the world depended on Wilson's reelection, he stayed at his retreat near Lake Sunapee, where he had rented a "camp" that was "delightfully situated and equipped."[14]

House had chosen a more remote location than the North Shore of Boston so that he would have fewer interruptions and more time for reflection. As the Wilson years passed he had become concerned about his place in history. He reassured his old Texas friend Frank Andrews, who worried that history would "lose sight" of him because of his lack of an official position, that he was "making careful notes and someday when the history of these times are written, it will all become known." By the spring of 1916, however, House was not so sure, complaining that his diary entries were often inadequate. He also realized that the record of his Texas years was incomplete; when he sold his Austin mansion in 1914 he had thrown out much of his Texas correspondence. House felt keenly the passage of time— he would be fifty-eight on July 26—and resolved to fill in the gaps in the historical record.[15]

Isolated in his New Hampshire sanctuary, House dictated his *Reminiscences,* seeking to tell the story of his life from his birth on July 26, 1858, to September 25, 1912, when he began to keep his diary.[16] This sixty-page document was an impressionistic narrative of the first fifty-four years of his life, one that filled in many of the gaps, although it idealized his role in Texas politics and exaggerated his role in Wilson's nomination and election. It revealed his reverence for his father, and for Governor Hogg, and for other Texans who had "molded a trackless wilderness into a great commonwealth"; they were the "heroes" of his childhood. "Now when I am growing old and have seen many men and many lands, I go back to them and salute them for I find they are my heroes still." House realized that he had led an exceptional life, concluding "that there are not many who have had a more varied or interesting life than mine. It has been full of adventure from start to finish." He might also have added that if only his friend in the White House was reelected in November, he would follow him onto the international political stage.[17]

Wilson spent the hot and tense summer of 1916 in Washington, pushing an ambitious legislative agenda through Congress and seeking to position his party for the fall campaign. He was so pressed for time that he and Edith decided to start their days at 5:00 AM so they could, as Wilson put it, "steal up on them in the dark." In some cases the president took the initiative; in other cases it came from congressional Democrats. Whatever the source, over the course of the summer the New Freedom was expanded, both out of conviction and from political necessity, to chart a broader role for the federal government in the life of the nation. By early September, Congress had passed, and the president had signed, legislation increasing the size of the navy, banning the products of child labor from interstate commerce, creating twelve federal land banks to provide credit to farmers, establishing a federal workingmen's compensation system, and devising a revenue act that increased taxes on the wealthy.[18]

In August, confronted with the possibility of a national railway strike, Wilson met repeatedly with railway presidents and with leaders of the railway brotherhoods. When his personal intervention failed, he traveled to Capitol Hill to consult with party leaders and finally, on September 2, signed the Adamson Act, which decreed an eight-hour day for railway workers. Republicans denounced it as a craven surrender to labor unions, but Wilson had once again made shrewd political adjustments and revealed his gift for political leadership. A *New York Times* reporter described the president as "especially strong and vigorous and quite youthful," while a Democratic campaign official noted that "anyone who believes that the President is not a practical man or an astute politician is making a profound mistake."[19]

House displayed little interest in the expansion of the New Freedom, preferring to focus on the organizational challenges of the campaign.[20] The president seemed pleased with his efforts and with his plan for the campaign. As always, he was solicitous about House's health, hoping that he was "taking real care" of himself, and also curious about his assessment of the political situation. House sent a noncommittal reply to the president's request. Wilson, he predicted, would win if the election "were held today," but key states needed to be organized, "certain lines of attack" agreed upon, and the issues laid out before "the plain people" who would decide the election. "The keeping the country out of war," House wrote Wilson, "and the great measures you have enacted into law, should be our battle cry." "I am getting in great shape here," House reassured the president, "and by the first of September I shall be ready for the fray."[21]

Hughes's acceptance speech on July 31, criticizing Wilson's foreign and domestic policies without offering any constructive alternatives, aroused House's combative instincts. In a long letter he urged Wilson to call in reporters and to respond, asking what the GOP candidate would do if he became president. Wilson's rejection of this suggestion displeased House,[22] but by mid-August he was satisfied with the Democratic effort. Hughes was a "complete failure on the stump" and had made "almost a total failure in his western campaign," while the Democrats had launched a well-organized effort that was "going famously for us so far." The stakes, House thought, could not be higher. "There is much more involved in this election," he reminded Wilson, "than domestic issues and much more involved in the world situation than our people realize. Democracy hangs in the balance and the result of our election may determine its fate not only here but throughout the world."[23]

Throughout the summer, from his New Hampshire retreat, House tried to keep in touch with the president and to track shifts in his inner circle. When Wilson complained that he had "not been very well for the past week or two," and that his digestion was "upset in some way," House was "distressed." Edith worried about her husband's demanding summer schedule and regretted that House was so far away "You don't know," she reassured him, "how much we both miss your little visits, and I was wishing last night he had you to talk over with the situation [a possible railway strike] that now threatens the country."[24]

During a visit to Lake Sunapee, McAdoo complained that his father-in-law did not confide in him and that "the new Mrs. Wilson was antagonistic to him." The Treasury Secretary claimed that he looked forward to a return to private life, but House, who had followed his emotional ups and downs for years, was skeptical. He believed that McAdoo wanted to be president and, looking beyond Wilson's second term, wondered what kind of president he would make. House thought McAdoo was "able, and has great courage," but lacked "discretion." "I am not sure," House concluded, "he would not make a great President because in addition to his other qualities he has imagination."[25]

In the summer of 1916, the tide of the war seemed, for the first time, to shift toward the Allies. On June 4, General A. A. Brusilov, the most talented of the Russian commanders, attacked the Austro-Hungarian army along a twenty-mile front, breaking through in the center and routing Austrian forces. Only the dispatch of German reinforcements prevented Brusilov from seizing the Carpathian passes. On July 1 General Douglas Haig, who had replaced John French as the commander of the British Expeditionary Force, sent nineteen British divisions along with three French divisions against German lines along the Somme River.[26] However, the Somme offensive, which ground on until mid-November, when it came to a halt in the rain and mud, had become, like Verdun, a battle of attrition, inflicting heavy casualties on both sides and in the end moving the front only a few miles. Minnie Paget, House's American friend who lived in London, lamented "the loss of human life too terrible for words, every one in mourning here."[27]

Nonetheless, political leaders in London were encouraged by the fact that the Allies, for the first time in the war, held the strategic initiative. With Romania's entry into the war on their side on August 27, they reached new heights of optimism. Asquith hoped that a victorious peace might come in the near future and directed the foreign office and the war office to begin to study the nature of the postwar settlement. He vowed that the enormous loss of life and hardships brought by the war could not be "allowed to end in some patched-up, precarious, dishonouring com- promise, masquerading under the name of Peace," while French premier Aristide Briand, in an impromptu speech before the Chamber of Deputies, proclaimed that "peace today would be a humiliating and ignoble peace, and there is no Frenchman who could desire such a peace!" And Lloyd George, viewed by many as a future prime minister, told an American reporter that "the fight must be to a finish—to a knock-out." The Allies had no interest in a compromise peace; they were determined to win a decisive victory.[28]

The events of the summer of 1916 unsettled the German high command. The Austro-Hungarian army had been shattered, the German Fifth Army at Verdun and the Second Army at the Somme had been badly damaged, and Romania's entry into the war placed a further strain on the resources of the Central Powers. Some German leaders knew they would lose a long war of attrition, since the Allies, drawing on the resources of American industry and their great empires, could out-produce them in every area. Initially the ruling elites in Berlin and Vienna had not considered the possibility of a protracted war; now they faced a struggle with no end in sight. In Austro-Hungary, food and fuel shortages had become serious, and economic and political chaos had spread. In Germany, too, the strains of the war had become apparent, as the public protested rising prices and the meager, monotonous diet. "Now," one observer noted, "one sees faces like masks, blue with cold and drawn by hunger, with the harassed expression common to all those who are continually speculating as to the possibility of another meal."[29]

The failure at Verdun, combined with disruptions on the homefront, convinced the kaiser that he must find a new chief of staff. On August 29 he replaced Falkenhayn with General Paul von Hindenburg and his aide General Erich Ludendorff. Hindenburg was the most popular man in Germany, the hero of the Eastern Front and idolized by the German people. Hindenburg's fame and Ludendorff's abrasive, imperious manner intimidated the kaiser, who now "vanished," as one biographer notes, "into a world of empty dreams and futile hopes." The field marshal and his general, the kaiser and chancellor would soon realize, did not share their pessimism about the war. They were confident of victory, determined to mobilize the nation and to widen the conflict.[30]

Throughout the summer, despite the distractions of the presidential campaign, House remained focused on the Great War. He continued to wish that the president "would pay more attention to foreign affairs" and complained that "the French and English are prolonging the war unnecessarily. It is stupid to refuse our proffered intervention on the terms I proposed in Paris and London." The president, too, was losing patience with the Allies, who were, he asserted, "in danger of forgetting the rest of the world." Wilson concluded his letter to House, ominously, "that it will be up to us to judge for ourselves when the time has arrived for us to make an imperative suggestion." House seemed to agree that a tougher policy toward the Allies might be necessary.[31]

While House and Wilson waited on events in Europe, Anglo-American tension grew. On July 18 the Allies announced the blacklisting of American firms suspected of trading with the Central Powers, setting off an angry wave of protest in the United States over Britain's continued violation of American neutral rights. House once again denounced the "stupidity" of the British government, while the president admitted that he was "about at the end of my patience with Great Britain and the Allies. This black list business is the last straw." Wilson ordered the State Department to draft a response. On July 26, the secretary of state dispatched a strong note of protest, and in early September Wilson received the authority from Congress to retaliate against the Allies.[32]

House approved of the black list protest and speculated that if by the first of October the war remained stalemated, the Allies would be ready to discuss peace terms. If not, then Wilson "should seriously consider making the proposal without their consent." House had now given up his hopes in the enlightened leaders of the British government ("reactionary forces" had taken over the Asquith cabinet), and he now placed his faith in the allegedly strong peace sentiment among the people of France and Great Britain. If the ruling elites in these nations failed to respond to a peace initiative, then it might be necessary, he informed the president, "to arouse the latent feeling of the people in both England and France in such a way that they will compel their governments to act."[33]

The president and his adviser had long been dissatisfied with Ambassador Page's performance in London. Both would have preferred to recall him—if only a suitable replacement could be found—but instead decided to bring the ambassador back for a visit. Counselor Polk promised "to try to pump a little of the fog out" of Page, while House urged that he be sent out west in order "to get a complete bath of American opinion."[34] On August 16, Page finally arrived in Washington for a two-week stay, his first visit to the United States since he left for London in May 1913. In five meetings, the secretary of state and the ambassador confirmed their dislike of each other. Page found Lansing "a mere routine-clerk, law-book-precedent man, no grasp, no imagination, no constructive tendency or ability—measuring Armageddon, if he tried to measure it at all—with a 6-inch rule," while Lansing now gave up completely on the ambassador, concluding that "it was useless to present protests and complaints through him."[35]

During his stay Page lunched twice at the White House with the president, but on both occasions other guests were present and the two men could not have a private conversation. Page left Washington in a fury, convinced that Wilson's solitary habits, as Page's biographer writes, deprived "him of contact with vigorous people and fresh ideas." Not until September 22—at Wilson's retreat on the New Jersey shore—did Page finally have a long talk with the president. Wilson, however, did most of the talking, lecturing Page on various Allied provocations of America and suggesting that the origins of the war were obscure. "He showed a great degree of toleration for Germany," Page recorded, "and he was, during the whole morning that I talked with him, complaining of England."[36]

House delayed seeing Page for as long as possible, trying to find out his "frame of mind" before having what he knew might be a contentious meeting.[37] When House finally met Page in New York on September 25, he found that the ambassador's visit to America had not altered his "frame of mind." The two men had a testy exchange. Page's friendship with both Wilson and House had ended; at long last the ambassador realized the depth of the bitterness that pervaded Anglo-American relations and the distance separating him from his superiors in Washington.[38]

21

Reelection and the Plea for Peace

On September 11, 1916, House left Lake Sunapee and drove to Manchester, Massachusetts, where he spent four days with his daughter Mona and son-in-law Randolph Tucker. On September 16 he finally arrived in New York. He found his desk "piled high with accumulated mail, foreign and domestic," and changed his telephone number "so that no one can reach me until I am ready." "It is a perfect joy," he informed the president, "to be back and in the thick of it and I am reveling in the work."[1] Wilson was eager to reestablish contact with his old adviser. "Would it not be possible for you," he wrote, "if the weather keeps cool, to come down and spend the week end with me this week? It would be a great joy if you could." On September 23, House drove to Long Branch, New Jersey, where Wilson had rented Shadow Lawn, a large summer house with ample lawns and spacious porches. He would remain there until the end of the campaign.[2]

On September 2, at an elaborate notification ceremony at Shadow Lawn, Wilson had formally accepted the Democratic nomination. On domestic policy, the president asserted that "we have in four years come very near to carrying out the platform of the Progressive Party as well as our own; for we are also progressives." On foreign policy, he claimed that America must save its strength "for the anxious and difficult days of restoration and healing which must follow, when peace will have to build its house anew." The Democratic campaign was now under way. The party's organization was in place and its morale high, though Wilson's advocacy of an eight-hour day for railway workers had galvanized conservative Republicans and slowed down contributions to the Democrats.[3]

As the long, hot summer drew to a close, Wilson felt tired. Cary Grayson warned the president that he must "slow up" and rest or he would not be able to keep going. At Shadow Lawn, despite the constant press of visitors and of campaign events, Wilson devised ways to escape the pressure. Surrounded by family and friends, he avoided political talk over lunch and dinner and found that Edith's presence eased his burdens. She accompanied him everywhere and even blotted his signature of routine government documents. " 'When you are here,' " he remarked, " 'work seems like play.' "[4]

In September, Charles Evans Hughes's campaign seemed to flounder. On domestic policy, Hughes praised the protective tariff, attacked the president for his hostility toward business, and condemned "government by holdup," as well as of course his imposition of that eight-hour work day. On foreign policy, Hughes attacked Wilson's response to the revolution in Mexico and the war in Europe, calling "for an honest and straightforward neutrality" but without explaining how he would change American policy. Hughes's constant attacks, however, along with the vagueness of his own positions and his lackluster campaign style, disappointed many of his supporters. He could not hold together the factions within his party or outline a vision of the future. As one observer noted, "Hughes is dropping icicles from his beard all over the west and will return to New York clean shaven."[5]

On September 23, when House arrived in Long Branch, he was in a critical mood. He felt that the president did not understand the damage Tumulty and Secretary of the Navy Josephus Daniels had done to his political standing, and believed that Wilson overestimated the intelligence of ordinary people and never felt "it necessary to unduly exert himself to make his position clear." But House seemed more eager to discuss foreign affairs than domestic politics, especially the differences between Great Britain and the United States. He reasoned that America's determination to build a great navy, along with the nation's economic expansion, were the underlying causes of Anglo-American friction and that America was "taking the position Germany occupied before the war." Should the Allies win the war, Britain's alliance with France, Italy, Japan, and Russia would make it "a formidable antagonist." Wilson seemed unconcerned with these geopolitical speculations. " 'Let us build,' " he responded, " 'a bigger navy than hers and do what we please.' "[6]

Not until the evening of the second day of House's visit did the two men focus on the "political situation." The mechanics of the campaign pleased House, but he still found Democratic prospects discouraging and "made him [Wilson] feel the necessity of arousing himself to action." The president, so he seemed to suggest, was responsible for the campaign's lack of momentum.[7] Wilson was reluctant to leave Shadow Lawn, but in early October he traveled to Omaha, Nebraska, where he received an enthusiastic reception. As he defended American neutrality and spoke of the need for a league of nations, the power of the peace appeal in the Middle West and Far West became apparent. Democratic campaign managers picked up the peace theme, claiming that the president had kept the nation out of war and suggesting, as a Democratic Party advertisement put it on November 4, that the voters faced a choice of "Wilson and Peace with Honor? or Hughes with Roosevelt and War?"[8]

The farther west the candidates traveled, however, the more they also realized the importance of the progressive legislation of the last four years. Bryan campaigned tirelessly for the Democratic ticket in the trans-Mississippi region, and in some western states large parts of the Progressive Party's organization defected to Wilson. The support of Progressives and Socialists, along with the assistance of organized labor, strengthened the Democratic cause, as did Hughes's reversion to traditional pro-business Republicanism. As House noted in his diary, "it is true we have organized wealth against us, and in such aggregate as never before. On the other hand, we are pitting organized labor against it, and the fight is not an unfair one."[9]

Not since the Bryan-McKinley campaign of 1896 had the choices been so clear, or the emotional intensity of the contest so great. Republican leaders despised Wilson and his administration. Some Republicans conducted a whispering campaign, claiming that Wilson was a womanizer and had had an illicit relationship with Mary Allen Hulbert (the former Mrs. Peck). As early as June, Robert Woolley, on a swing through the Midwest, warned House that Chicago was filled with "scandalous stories about the president." "The back stairs, sewer gossips. . . ," he reported, "are doing deadly work among the women in states where women vote."[10] At House's suggestion Wilson's brother-in-law Stockton Axson wrote an article, published in the *New York Times Magazine,* on "Mr. Wilson as Seen by One of His Family Circle," portraying the president as a devoted family man, while the popular journalists Ray Stannard Baker and Ida Tarbell described him as an open-minded, humorous, and courteous gentleman.[11]

By late October, Wilson was campaigning at a frantic pace, giving as many as four speeches in a single day. The climax of the campaign came in New York on November 2, when he drove down Fifth Avenue to Madison Square Garden, where 25,000 people crowded outside and 15,000 filled the inside of the auditorium to hear him speak. From New York, the president returned to Shadow Lawn. There on November 4 he gave his final speech of the campaign; now he could only wait for the results of what appeared to be the closest presidential race since 1896. As he wrote his brother in mid-October, "I can only conjecture and hope."[12]

After his return to New York on September 25, House plunged into the campaign, checking daily with his protégés at Democratic National Headquarters and attempting to monitor many different phases of the contest. House edited Stockton Axson's article, urged the president to reiterate his charge that "Hughes's election would mean war," and tried to placate a disgruntled McAdoo. As he explained to one American diplomat stationed abroad, "we are in the midst of one of the fiercest campaigns of recent years and I have but little time for anything else but politics."[13]

By mid-October, House concluded that the Democratic campaign was "going well," and throughout the rest of the month he remained optimistic. A report from Daniel C. Roper (who ran Democratic Headquarters in New York) indicated that Wilson was ahead of Hughes, although the margin of victory in all the states the Democrats hoped to win was close. And McAdoo, traveling in the Midwest, reported that the people were interested only in peace and prosperity; he was confident of the president's election even without New York. House informed the American ambassador in Vienna that "the tide has turned so rapidly in our favor during the past few weeks that if no untoward incident occurs the President should be re-elected by a handsome majority."[14]

On October 18, House and Wilson conferred while the latter changed trains in New York. House updated the president on the campaign, advised him on several speeches, and urged Edith to make certain that her husband appeared at train stops in New York and Indiana. Both men, caught up in the demands of the campaign, missed their leisurely visits and talks. Wilson wished "every day that I were near enough to you to talk things over, because many matters of judgment are constantly turning up, and besides it has been a long time since we had a genuine talk."[15]

Despite House's apparent confidence, doubts lingered in his mind. On October 18, when he and Wilson conferred in New York, he decided to suggest to the president that if he was defeated, he should ask both Marshall and Lansing to resign and then appoint Hughes Secretary of State. "He should then resign himself making Hughes President of the United States. Times are too critical to have an interim of four months between the election and inauguration of the next President." The following day House wrote Wilson, outlining his proposal, and told his old friend Attorney General Gregory, who was "startled and was silent for full five minutes" and then approved of the proposal. Later, House explained his plan to Secretary of State Lansing, who "was somewhat staggered at first, but recovered himself and finally expressed approval." The president did not respond to House's letter, but two days before the election he informed the secretary of state of his intention to resign if Hughes prevailed. Only after Wilson's reelection did House learn that his friend had decided to leave office immediately if he lost the election.[16]

As the campaign neared its end, House's days had "become a mad whirl of telephone talks and visitors." He had long conferences with his political associates, schemed to force Tumulty's resignation because anti-Catholic organizations "do not like a Catholic censoring the President's mail," and laid careful plans for the last great rally of the campaign at Madison Square Garden on November 2.[17] On that morning, when the president arrived in New York harbor on the *Mayflower,* House gave him a state-by-state breakdown of the campaign, concluding that Wilson was certain to win twenty-two states for a total of 230 electoral votes. He would need an additional thirty-six electoral votes to win the election. Two days later, taking a "final survey of the field," House concluded that "the fight is won." He praised the performance of McCormick and his associates; "it is the first time," he boasted, "we have ever known in advance with any degree of certainty the final results."[18]

On November 7, Wilson, surrounded by family and friends at Shadow Lawn, played the game of twenty questions—animal, mineral, or vegetable?—while he waited for the returns. As early figures arrived, it looked as if the election was lost. At 10:30 PM the president had a glass of milk and went to bed, telling his companions that "I might stay longer but you are all so blue." It appeared that Hughes, drawing on traditional Republican strength in the East and Midwest, would be the next president.[19]

Early the next morning, as the returns from states west of the Mississippi began to filter in, Tumulty called the president and informed him that the election was now in doubt. By late afternoon of November 8, it was clear that Wilson had carried most of the states beyond the Mississippi and by midnight the electoral count stood at 251 for Wilson and 247 for Hughes. By the evening of the next day, November 9, Wilson's victory was almost certain, and by the morning of November 10 the president, in Williamstown, Massachusetts, for the christening of his granddaughter, received a telegram from Tumulty that he had won reelection. That evening he appeared on the porch of the Sayre house and greeted 5,000 enthusiastic demonstrators who had staged an old-fashioned political rally. "Let us remember," he said in a somber mood, "now that the campaign is over, to get together for the common good of all and not merely for the good of parties."[20]

House received the returns in New York, where for two days he was so busy he could not record events in his diary. On the evening of November 7, when the election seemed lost, House declined to attend a banquet of campaign managers at the Biltmore Hotel, which, he later learned, was a "morgue-like entertainment." Instead, he stayed in his apartment at 115 East 53rd Street trying to assess the situation. "When things were at their worst," House and Gregory took up the question of the president's resignation and "went to the Bar Association to look up the Federal Statutes on the subject." The attorney general then left for his hotel "under the firm impression we were defeated."

But House had not, so he recorded, given up hope, since Wilson was carrying all the states that on November 2 he had listed in the certain column. On the evening of November 7, House went to bed at 11:00 PM and left Gordon and Janet Auchincloss in his study to receive the returns. At 5:00 AM on November 8 he awoke and realized that the favorable results from the Far West guaranteed a close election. With the margin of victory so narrow in so many states, House worried that Democrats "might be robbed of victory" and ordered Democratic Headquarters to telegraph county chairmen in doubtful states, urging them to be on the alert for fraud. These were "strenuous hours" in which "everyone I knew was telegraphing, telephoning or wanting to see me." During the critical two days after November 7, when the result was in doubt, Wilson did not telephone House (although he had White House officials do so); House proudly noted that the president "left everything in our hands." Throughout the ordeal House claimed that he had not "worried a moment. If I had, I could not have stood the strain."[21]

On November 12, when the president passed through New York on his way from Williamstown to Washington, House found Wilson "a happy and contented man." House too was no doubt pleased with the result, but he left no record, either in his diary or in letters to friends, of his elation over the victory. His response was curiously flat, despite the fact that Wilson's reelection had ended four years of anxiety over the president's health and political future and opened up a vista of further accomplishments on the national and international stage.[22]

By any measure the president had achieved a stunning personal triumph. He had received 9,129,606 votes and 277 electoral votes, and he had carried thirty states; Hughes had received 8,538,221 votes and 254 electoral votes, and had carried eighteen states. Wilson had won with 49.3 percent of the vote to 46.1 for Hughes, while the Democrats had retained control of the Senate by twelve votes and by a narrow margin had held onto the House. Wilson had run 2,830,000 votes ahead of his total in 1912 and had drawn 300,000 votes from the Socialist Party's total in that year. He had carried virtually the entire West, along with Ohio, New Hampshire, and the South, achieving a combination Bryan had narrowly missed in 1896. The president's message of peace, prosperity, and progressivism had resonated throughout the nation, and he had laid the foundation for a new Democratic coalition. The poet Witter Bynner caught the mood of many Americans:

> The morning-sun arose, the evening star:
> America renewed her light all day
> And stood serene at evening, and from far
> Freedom was visible with lifted ray. . . .
> Wilson!—humanity once more is true—
> The light that shone on Lincoln shines on you.[23]

Throughout the fall, House had kept in close touch with the situation in Europe. Reports from London and Paris continued to indicate that the Allies had no interest in peace talks, while reports from Berlin described widespread anti-American feeling, food riots in major cities, intense agitation for all-out U-boat warfare, and the ebbing of Chancellor Bethmann Hollweg's strength. "As these people get desperate," Ambassador Gerard wrote, "the submarine question gets deeper and deeper under their skin. I really think that it is only a question of time."[24]

On November 2, when House saw Wilson in New York, prior to the campaign's final rally at Madison Square Garden, he brought up the torpedoing of the armed British steamer *Marina*, with the loss of six American lives. Wilson's reply "astonished" his adviser. "I do not believe," he asserted, "the American people would wish to go to war no matter how many Americans were lost at sea." Worried about the president's growing disenchantment with the Allies and the danger that he might launch an independent peace move, House sought to restrain him, as well as to remind him that the only way to end the war was to implement the House–Grey Memorandum.[25]

Once Wilson's triumph was secure he quickly moved to reestablish contact with his "Dearest Friend." "Would be delighted," he cabled, "if you would come down in time for dinner tomorrow and spend a little while with us." On November 14, House traveled to Washington for a one-night stay. At long last he could discuss many matters the presidential campaign had forced the two men to defer. As soon as House arrived at the White House, the president came to his room and explained that he wanted "to write a note to the belligerents demanding that the war cease." What, he asked, did his counselor think? House argued that the Allies, particularly at a time when they were making progress in the war, would consider such a proposal "an unfriendly act." At a quarter to nine, after Wilson fulfilled a speaking engagement, the two men returned to their discussion. The president suggested that House "go to England and France and upon my arrival he would give out the message." House, more attuned than the president to the feeling in the Allied capitals, remarked that "I should prefer hades for the moment rather than those countries when such a proposal was put up to them."[26] The president and his adviser could not find any common ground. House wanted to "sit tight and await further developments" while Wilson contended "that the submarine situation would not permit of delay and it was worth while to try mediation before breaking off with Germany."

The next morning Wilson arrived late for breakfast, a sign, House noted, that he had had a "bad night." At 9:00 AM, when the two resumed their discussion, they continued to disagree, and Wilson finally decided that he would draft a peace note and then "we could go over it again and discuss it with more intelligence."[27] That same day House discussed Wilson's position with both Polk and Lansing. Polk was "much disturbed," while Lansing warned that it would lead to "a storm of indignation" against him.

All three men agreed "that it would be stupendous folly to wage war against the Allies. If war must come, we thought it should be on their side and not against them."[28]

Wilson and House also talked about possible changes in the cabinet. The president wanted to keep all of its members in place, including, no doubt to his adviser's disappointment, Secretary of the Navy Josephus Daniels. During this discussion Edith, who now sat in on many of her husband's conferences, asked "what about Tumulty?" Wilson now agreed to remove his longtime secretary and give him another appointment; Tumulty's political mistakes, the pressure of anti-Catholic spokesmen, and the arguments of both House and Edith had finally convinced Wilson that his secretary had become a political liability. But House's and Edith's plot against Tumulty would once again end in failure. When the president requested his resignation, Tumulty begged to stay on, writing that "I am heart-sick that the end should be like this." And interventions by Tumulty's friends convinced Wilson to relent and let his secretary remain, although the trust between him and his chief would never be restored.[29]

Despite their disagreements, Wilson and House parted warmly. Wilson urged his friend to return without an invitation and thanked him for his contribution to his campaign. And House had already learned from Helen Bones that her uncle Woodrow "was not concerned about it [the campaign] because I was directing it."[30]

In the autumn of 1916 the momentary advantage that the Allies gained through Romania's entry into the war disappeared. U-boats threatened British shipping lanes, Zeppelins continued to attack London, and on December 5 German troops entered Bucharest, destroying Allied hopes that Romania would strengthen their war effort. The Central Powers were now the conquerors of five capitals, Belgrade, Brussels, Bucharest, Cetinje (Montenegro), and Warsaw. Despite these successes, however, the Great War remained a stalemate, and as the third Christmas of the conflict approached in December 1916, it seemed certain to continue into the next year.[31]

The elevation of Hindenburg and Ludendorff revealed the conviction of the nation's leaders that only a dramatic change of course could rescue the German war effort. Two of Germany's key allies, Austria and Turkey, were faltering, and signs were appearing of cracks in the morale of both Germany's soldiers and civilians. Germany's new commanders, however, made a powerful team. Hindenburg had immense popular prestige, while

Ludendorff had an impressive command of military engineering and technology. Together, in the autumn of 1916 they brought renewed energy and new ideas to the German war effort and soon became the dominant force in German politics. They were determined to mobilize all the resources of German society for total war, the so-called Hindenburg Program. They also sought to harness the economic resources of occupied Europe to the German war effort and, like a large segment of opinion in Germany, adopted an expansive vision of a postwar German *Mitteleuropa*. This huge customs union, with the Austro-Hungarian and German empires at its core, would span the continent and dominate satellites from Belgium to Poland and from the Baltic provinces to the Ottoman Empire. Germany would gain access to enormous markets and resources and finally have a secure base from which to compete with Great Britain and the United States.[32]

Hindenburg and Ludendorff were also eager to intensify the submarine blockade, since they calculated that without American supplies Britain could not sustain its war effort. They dared not act, however, until Romania was defeated; then they could join the demand of naval leaders—supported by much of Germany's political and industrial elite—for unlimited U-boat warfare. As one historian notes, the U-boat had become a "panacea, the wonder weapon," one that promised to humble Great Britain and bring an end to the terrible sacrifices of the war.[33]

By the fall of 1916, Chancellor Bethmann Hollweg found himself on the defensive. He was nearly sixty, tired and lonely, confronted with relentless U-boat agitation and growing hostility to his leadership. As discontent over the war mounted, the chancellor's power ebbed, and by the end of October his hold on the kaiser weakened and his control of the Reichstag had slipped away. He dared not directly confront the supreme command over U-boat warfare, although his vice chancellor, Karl Helfferich, did lay out the arguments against the submarine. He warned: "We must bear in mind: if the card of ruthless U-boat warfare is played, and it doesn't win, then we are lost. Then we are lost for a century."[34]

Only a peace move would allow Bethmann Hollweg to escape from his dilemma. Earlier in 1916 he had discouraged Wilson's mediation efforts; now, as his power weakened and as his sense of desperation grew, the chancellor, through Ambassador Bernstorff, urged the president to act. Finally, as Wilson delayed his call for peace, Bethmann Hollweg decided that he could not wait any longer and on December 12 read the text of Germany's peace offer to the Reichstag. The note stated that the Central Powers had already demonstrated their invincibility on the field of battle but were now willing to meet the Allies at the conference table and to consider how to bring the war to an end. Despite the truculent tone of the message and Bethmann Hollweg's refusal to state terms, negotiations to stop the fighting now seemed at least a remote possibility.[35]

Among British leaders the flicker of optimism about the war soon passed. In the fall of 1916 it seemed as if the position of the Allies had weakened. The Brusilov offensive had reached its limit, the Somme offensive had failed, a renewed U-boat campaign inflicted heavy losses on British shipping, and it became apparent that Germany was mobilizing its resources for another year of war. British policy had been based on the assumption that the Allies, with their greater resources, could wear down the Central Powers and win a war of attrition. But they now faced a shortage of men, money, and ships, while their economic dependence on the United States for war supplies and finances had grown at an alarming rate. Britain had sold off most of its gold and securities and now faced the prospect of financing the Allied war effort through large unsecured public loans in America. British officials could only hope, as Grey pointed out, "that their [United States] weapons against us are too big for them to use."[36]

Asquith's coalition government seemed tired, unable to summon the will to address these problems. The prime minister presided over an unruly and divided coalition; Ambassador Page found him "a spent force, at once nimble and weary." He could not resolve the deep divisions within his government or address the growing anxiety about the war that had spread among Britain's ruling elite. Some wondered how long Britain could continue to fight, while others, led by Lord Lansdowne (a minister without portfolio), wondered if the price of victory was not too high. But no end to the war seemed in sight; in late November Asquith concluded that "the time has not yet come for peace feelers."[37]

More and more Conservative leaders concluded that the prime minister was inadequate as a war leader. Lloyd George, the war minister and a key member of the coalition government, warned that unless Britain and its partners mended their ways "we are going to lose this war." He sought to break through the apparent paralysis of Asquith's coalition regime and reform the machinery of the government, placing the conduct of the war in the hands of a new and smaller committee which he would chair. But

Asquith would not yield and become a nominal prime minister. Unwilling to dissolve his government and call for new elections, and unable to reconstruct his coalition without Lloyd George's cooperation, he resigned on December 4. In three days, Lloyd George put together a new government with Balfour as foreign secretary. The Liberal ministers that House had idealized were now gone.[38]

On November 16, after his brief stay in Washington, House returned to New York, worried about the president's plan to go ahead with a peace note. After a long talk with Polk the two men agreed that "we are in deep and troublous waters," and House urged him "to have Lansing keep in close touch with me until the skies are clear. We must do team-work and keep our wits about us." Convinced that he understood the Great War better than Wilson, House now sought, in collaboration with Polk and Lansing, to restrain his friend in the White House.[39]

Wilson had "a really overwhelming cold" for nearly a week, which delayed his draft of a peace note, but he finally finished it on November 25 and summoned his counselor to Washington. House, worried about what the president might do, arrived at the White House late in the afternoon on November 26; after dinner he and the president retreated to his study for a long talk.[40] Once again the two strongly disagreed over the best way to achieve peace. House objected to Wilson's claim that "the causes and objects of the war are obscure" and opposed any independent American mediation effort. As the standoff continued, House urged Wilson to delay the dispatch of the note until he prepared the way for its reception by Allied governments. "My whole idea," House confided in his diary, "is to delay until the time seems propitious. It is too important a matter to bungle, and if he is not careful, that is what he will do."[41] On November 27, House returned to New York on a midday train. Over his last two visits the two men had disagreed more deeply and persistently than ever before. It is hardly surprising that Wilson had given his counselor a cool farewell.[42]

Despite the opposition of his advisers, Wilson was nonetheless determined to proceed with his peace note and, if necessary, to use American power to force the Allies to the conference table. As the Allies' financial resources neared exhaustion, the question arose of the purchase of short-term British and French treasury notes by American banks. When he learned that the Federal Reserve Board planned to issue a warning to American banks, the president urged the board to make it stronger. When the warning appeared on November 27, it caused deep concern in London. Ambassador Spring-Rice informed his superiors that the president "is fully conscious of his power. And he is prepared to use it."[43]

Prime Minister Asquith's resignation on December 4, however, further delayed the president's note, since he now had to wait until the cabinet crisis was over and Lloyd George formed a new government. House regretted the collapse of Asquith's coalition and predicted that with Lloyd George and his conservative allies in power "there will be no chance for peace until they run their course."[44]

On December 17, Wilson finally completed his note (House did not see the final draft) and the next day Lansing dispatched it to American ambassadors in belligerent capitals. The objections of House and Lansing had softened the original draft. The president no longer called for a peace conference or warned that the future of American foreign policy would depend on the response of the Allies and Central Powers. Now he only asked the warring nations to state the terms on which they would stop the fighting and work for the restoration of peace. Wilson went on to point out that, according to the public statements of government officials, the goals of each side "are virtually the same," and warned that if the war continued too long the injury done to "civilization itself. . . can never be atoned for or repaired." The war must stop if "a new world community," based on a league of nations, was to be created. In launching this independent peace initiative the president had, at long last, rejected the advice of House and Lansing. His appeal for peace was similar to the one that Bryan had urged in the fall of 1914.[45]

In a letter of December 20 to Wilson, House concealed how upset he was over the president's plea for peace. In his diary, however, he complained that the president had once again failed to distinguish between the Allies and the Central Powers and to indicate in his note that he understood what the Allies were fighting for. "The President," House lamented, "has nearly destroyed all the work I have done in Europe." But House failed to mention that his cultivation of British and French leaders—extending all the way back to the early summer of 1914—had yielded few results. British ministers, for all their congenial talk, had never wanted to risk an American mediation effort. If America was to have any chance of restoring the peace and avoiding involvement in the war, Wilson sensed that he must move in a different direction.[46]

22

America Goes to War

The president's peace note, which was published on December 21, received a cool response from official circles in Berlin, London, and Paris. German leaders had no intention of publishing peace terms or of allowing Wilson to preside over a peace conference. Their reply on December 26 discouraged Wilson and called for a direct exchange of views among the warring powers. Nor did Allied leaders wish to be drawn into negotiations with the Central Powers. The official Allied response, however, which did not come until January 10, 1917, seemed conciliatory, stating reasonable terms, although Foreign Secretary Balfour, in a covering letter, warned that the Allies believed that a just settlement could only be achieved through victory. The president's bold note had not, as both Lansing and House feared, brought reconciliation with Germany or a confrontation with Britain and France.[1]

At home, Wilson's peace note was widely praised, although Republican Party interventionists, led by Theodore Roosevelt, denounced it as full of "preposterous absurdities" and "wickedly false" statements. Within the administration, however, the president's key foreign policy advisers sought to undercut his efforts. Secretary of State Lansing maneuvered to promote American intervention, while House reassured British leaders, through talks with his friend Horace Plunkett, that the administration's attitudes toward Britain had not changed. Unlike Lansing, House did not seek to draw America into the war, but he did make it clear, Plunkett recorded, that he was "disgusted at many of his [Wilson's] recent utterances."[2]

On January 3, 1917, House finally traveled to Washington to deal with the thorny issue of peace. He arrived at the White House in time for dinner with Wilson, Edith, and Margaret, and as soon as the meal ended the two men retired "to the upstairs sitting room and were in continuous session until half past ten." The president believed, House discovered, that the end of the war was in sight and "wished to know what I thought of his stating in some way what, in his opinion, the general terms of settlement should be, making the keystone of the settlement arch the future security of the world against wars, and letting territorial adjustments be subordinated to the main purpose." No longer fearful that a peace note would align the United States with the Central Powers, House replied that he was "enthusiastic," convinced that "this war and its consequences have become too great for any ordinary settlement."

That evening the president and his counselor sought to outline the terms of a settlement and to decide where Wilson should deliver his address. They quickly agreed that he should appear before the Senate, and that "the main principle he should lay down was the right of nations to determine under what government they should continue to live." They also agreed that Poland should be free, Belgium and Serbia restored, the Ottoman Empire dissolved, and Russia given a warm water seaport. They were not "quite certain" what to do about Alsace and Lorraine. House encouraged Wilson to do "this great and dramatic thing" and reassured him that "You are now playing with what the poker players term 'the blue chips' and there is no use sitting by and letting great events swamp you. It is better to take matters into your own hands and play the cards yourself."[3]

On December 17, 1916, the day before Wilson had dispatched his peace note to the belligerents, House had met Sir William Wiseman, "the most important caller I have had for sometime." Wiseman, only thirty-two and a baronet, had served on the Western Front, where he was gassed at Ypres and incapacitated for duty in the army. In 1915 he was recruited by British military intelligence and sent to Washington in a position loosely attached to the British Embassy. There Wiseman, with his trim mustache, Oxbridge accent, and political astuteness, made many American friends. When the British naval attaché, Sir Guy Gaunt, returned to London on leave, Ambassador Spring-Rice sent Wiseman to New York to deliver material to House.[4]

House was immediately drawn to the young Englishman. As they saw more of each other and had long talks about Anglo-American relations, he concluded that Great Britain would be better represented by Wiseman than by Spring-Rice. Dissatisfied with the ambassador because of his temperamental defects and intimacy with the Republican opposition, House decided in the early months of 1917 that Wiseman could serve as his special emissary to the leaders of the British government. He and his English friend shared liberal political beliefs, a quiet and unostentatious manner, and, one journalist noted, "the same appraising competent blue eyes." On their faces was "the same stamp of unemotional alertness, though House's had the leanness of advanced middle age and that of Wiseman was round and youthful." Soon Wiseman became a part of House's inner circle, close also to Gordon Auchincloss and Frank Polk, and an important intermediary in Anglo-American relations.[5]

On January 11, six days after House and Loulie had returned from Washington, they once again took the train to the nation's capital. As soon as he arrived at the White House, he and the president went into "executive session" for two hours to discuss Wilson's forthcoming speech. Wilson read his adviser a portion of what would become his "Peace without Victory" address—he had not yet finished writing it—and House declared it "a noble document and one which I think will live." He suggested only minor corrections. The next day, when House read more, he was certain that his friend had done "marvelously well." But the president refused to show the draft to his secretary of state who was, he knew, "not in sympathy with his purpose to keep out of the war."[6]

Three days after his return to New York, on January 15, House talked with Ambassador Bernstorff. The ambassador, exceeding his instructions and badly misjudging the situation in Berlin, informed House that his government was now willing to submit to arbitration, would enter a postwar league of nations, and would allow Wilson to formulate a program for the peace conference. And its territorial terms would be moderate. House concluded that German leaders felt their nation was "tottering, otherwise they would not make such concessions," and that "a change of heart has come over the governing class in Germany." He excitedly wrote the president that peace seemed much nearer than he had thought, since Germany had consented "to almost everything that liberal opinion in democratic countries have demanded."[7]

House now saw all the pieces of the peace puzzle falling into place. France, he was sure, "is also reaching the verge of exhaustion. Russia is an uncertain quantity and Great Britain is the only one of the belligerents that has taken a firm grip and shut her eyes to all outside influence and proposals." Through his new friend Wiseman he sought to convince British leaders that their nation's safety "lay in the freedom of the seas" and that the war was entering its final phase. The British government, he argued, "ought to take advantage of the fact that Germany was willing to make peace upon liberal terms, embracing practically all the democratic world was contending for."[8]

Amid their growing excitement over the prospects for peace, House and Wilson sought to pin down the German ambassador, asking him to confirm that his statements reflected the views of his government.[9] Bernstorff soon revealed that the hopes of the president and his counselor were misplaced. The liberal terms that he had outlined referred to some future deliberations, not to terms on which Germany would agree to end the war. Worse still, the German ambassador, who learned on January 19, 1917, that his government planned to resume unrestricted U-boat warfare on February 1, warned House that "the situation in Berlin is getting out of hand."[10]

As the date for Wilson's Senate speech neared, the president urged House to travel to Washington. "Can't you come down and be present," he pleaded, "staying with us, of course? Do, please." But House, reflecting the distance that had grown up between the two men, resisted, replying lamely that he would delay another trip to Washington until the address "has been digested."[11]

At 1:00 PM on January 22 the president stood before the Senate and began his talk. After outlining the belligerents' response to his note of December 18, Wilson stated that "if the peace presently to be made is to endure, it must be a peace made secure by the organized force of mankind . . . . There must be, not a balance of power, but a community of power; not organized rivalries, but an organized common peace." There must be, in short, "a peace without victory . . . . Only a peace between equals can last." He then went on to outline the terms for a "just settlement"—the equality of nations, that governments "derive all their just powers from the consent of the governed," a united and independent Poland, freedom of the seas, and the limitation of armaments. These, Wilson summed up in his peroration, "are American principles, American policies . . . . They are the principles of mankind and must prevail."[12] When he finished, the president received a great burst of applause; many in the audience realized that they had heard an extraordinary speech, one that offered a new framework for world order and a healing vision to a war-torn world. House quickly caught the popular response. "I am very very happy tonight," he wrote Wilson, although he now realized that he had missed a momentous event. "I feel that I have lost something that I can never recover by not being there, but something told me it was best not to go."[13]

For a few days after the "Peace without Victory" address, House was optimistic about the prospects for peace.[14] Late in the afternoon of January 31, however, he received, amid much excitement in the press, a letter from the ambassador, enclosing a memorandum from Berlin, announcing the inauguration of unrestricted U-boat warfare on February 1 (a note which Bernstorff had delivered to Lansing earlier in the day). House now realized that Germany had long ago determined on U-boat warfare and that its peace proposals were designed for domestic and foreign consumption. Determined to deliver Bernstorff's letter in person to the president, House boarded the midnight train to Washington. He now realized that American peace efforts had failed and that the United States would have to confront a new and more deadly phase of the Great War.[15]

At the beginning of 1917 the Great War continued with no end in sight. Eleven European nations were now at war, along with Japan and the Ottoman Empire and the British dominions. On the Eastern Front the trench line had moved 300 miles, while on the Western Front a broad zone of destruction wound for 400 miles from the North Sea to Switzerland.[16] All of the belligerent governments struggled with the unprecedented costs and challenges of the conflict. In France, the long, bloody contest over Verdun had eroded, President Poincaré noted, the morale of the nation. "The edifice," he wrote, "is slowly falling apart, one can feel it . . . . The unease increases the anarchy everyday." In the Chamber of Deputies, dissatisfaction with the military grew so strong that Poincaré had to relieve General Joffre of the supreme command and replace him with a younger general, Robert Nivelle, who promised a breakthrough on the Western Front. On March 14, Prime Minister Briand resigned, ushering in a period of political instability. Political and social divisions in France were rising to the surface; no one had a plan to bring the war, now two and a half years old, to an end.[17]

In Great Britain Lloyd George maneuvered to consolidate his coalition cabinet and to address urgent issues of the war. Ten years younger than Asquith, he was a political leader of great energy and imagination, one who was determined to get things done.[18] The new prime minister reorganized the machinery of government; replaced Asquith's large, unwieldy cabinet with a war cabinet of only five members; addressed the critical problems of food and shipping; and tried to find a way out of the stalemate on the Western Front. He realized that morale in Britain remained high, but he also knew that the British people were unaccustomed to heavy casualties and if the war continued with no victory in sight, he might face a crisis at home. The conflict, he remarked, was "the grimmest and most perilous struggle in which this country has ever been engaged"; like all the belligerent leaders, one biographer writes, he was like an explorer "in a strange land full of unimaginable dangers."[19]

Russia was the first country to crack under the strain of the Great War. There the conflict had brought not only huge casualties but also, by the winter of 1916–1917, severe inflation, food shortages, and a breakdown of the transportation system. The wartime boom had drawn people into Russia's urban areas, especially St. Petersburg, which, with 2.4 million inhabitants, became the nation's industrial center as well as a center of radicalism and discontent with the war. On March 8, factory workers went on strike and rioters filled the broad boulevards in the center of the city. Authorities declared martial law, but on March 12 the garrison there revolted. As discontent spread throughout the nation, Nicholas II and his entourage left the front and attempted to return to the capital, but their train was blocked, and on March 13, the czar, isolated and fearful of anarchy, abdicated, ending three centuries of Romanov rule.

Politicians in Russia's Duma or parliament quickly put together a Provisional Government that was committed to Western-style representation. But this new regime, which would rule for eight months, was weak, forced to share power with street crowds, military garrisons in St. Petersburg and Moscow, and councils of workers and soldiers or soviets, which were moving toward a socialist revolution. Russian liberals wanted to continue the war and hoped that massive Allied economic aid, along with the resurgence of the Russian military, would turn the tide and bring victory in 1917. But two and a half years of fighting, along with the collapse of the military's chain of command and the spread of Soviet-sponsored committees throughout the army, had left Russia's forces on the Eastern Front in a shambles. The nation had plunged into a tremendous domestic crisis that would take years to resolve.[20]

Within the Central Powers, too, the strains of the war had become severe. The Austro-Hungarian government had made no plans for a lengthy conflict, and by the winter of 1916–1917, inflation, along with fuel and food shortages, led to widespread misery and spreading discontent. One American diplomat found the people "hungry and discouraged." Emperor Franz Josef had died in November 1916, ending a long reign, and his successor, Emperor Karl, knew that time was running out. In March 1917, he sought to scale down German objectives and opened direct negotiations with the French government. These efforts failed, but Vienna warned its ally in Berlin that "the Monarchy is at the end of its endurance."[21]

In Germany, despite economic hardships and the death of over one million men by the end of 1916, the morale of the army and of the people remained resolute. Previously German strategy had focused on breaking through on the Western Front and knocking France out of the war, but Hindenburg and Ludendorff planned to stay on the defensive in 1917 and rely on the navy to bring Great Britain to its knees. They agreed with Admiral Henning von Holtzendorff, who argued that if unrestricted U-boat warfare began on February 1, Britain would be starved into submission by August 1, 1917. Naval leaders were prepared "to accept the risk of a break with America." [22] On January 8, 1917, when Holtzendorff presented his recommendations to the general staff, Hindenburg declared that "It has to be. We expect war with America and have made all preparations [for it]. Things cannot get worse." At an imperial conference the next day, only Vice Chancellor Helfferich challenged the navy's figures, warning that "your plan will lead to ruin." But Bethmann Hollweg now gave way, and, as the conference drew to a close, Ludendorff exclaimed "I don't give a damn about America," while Hindenburg concluded that any future American war effort was certain to be "minimal, in any case not decisive." The kaiser, once again bending before the prevailing wind, declared that no compromise was possible between the two systems of government represented by the Allies and the Central Powers. "One must *win* the other must *perish*."[23]

On January 31, with Bernstorff's U-boat letter in hand, House left on the midnight train for Washington. The next day, after breakfast at the White House, he and the president conferred until two in the afternoon. He found Wilson "sad and depressed" and "deeply disappointed" that his peace efforts, which had seemed on the verge of success, had failed. The president and his counselor, however, found that they had little to discuss. They "sat listlessly" much of the morning, waiting for the secretary of state to arrive, while Wilson "nervously arranged his books and walked up and down the floor." When Lansing arrived the three men quickly agreed that Ambassador Bernstorff should be sent home. While Wilson "spoke of Germany as 'a madman that should be curbed,'" he did not want a break in relations to lead to war. Later in the day House, convinced that the president would be resolute, returned on the train to New York.[24]

The president believed that the conflict was in its final stages and that America's national interests, as well as those of humanity, would best be served by a negotiated peace. But Germany's declaration of unrestricted U-boat warfare was, in violation of previous pledges to the American government, an assault on neutral shipping and forced Wilson to choose between a surrender of America's rights or a break in relations. On February 3, at 2:00 PM he appeared before a joint session of Congress to announce the end of diplomatic ties with Germany. Once again Wilson had shrewdly measured the popular mood, choosing the middle course of a break in diplomatic relations rather than a declaration of war. While some interventionists clamored for more, an outpouring of peace sentiment suggested that most Americans were not ready to see their nation enter the conflict in Europe.[25]

Throughout February, the president and his adviser watched as the two nations edged closer to war. House worried about disturbances by German Americans in New York, warned the Allies against overconfidence, and rejected overtures from the Republican opposition.[26] Like House, Wilson was suspicious of those urging stronger measures against Germany; he had no interest in drawing Republicans "into consultation and have a coalition cabinet at my elbow." The president still had hopes that peace negotiations could be started and realized that, given the divisions over the war among the American people, he had to proceed cautiously. On February 16, he decided to ask Congress for the power to arm American merchant ships—to move, in effect, toward armed neutrality as a middle course between peace and all-out war. Ten days later Wilson addressed Congress, pointing out that although Germany's new U-boat policy had been in force for nearly four weeks, "no overt act" against American rights had occurred. He asked for authority to place defensive arms on American ships, in order to defend not only "the rights of Americans to go and come about their proper business by way of the sea, but also . . . I am thinking of those rights of humanity without which there is no civilization."[27]

On March 1, four days after this message, Secretary of State Lansing released a telegram from German Foreign Secretary Zimmermann to the German minister in Mexico City, offering Carranza's government, in the event of war, an alliance in which Mexico would receive territory it had lost to the United States. Zimmermann's telegram, which had been handed by Foreign Secretary Balfour to Ambassador Page on the evening of February 24 (the British had broken the German diplomatic code), shocked and angered the president, who now lost all faith in the rulers of Germany. House seemed less surprised over this "astounding dispatch," since he had concluded that if war came, Germany had "laid plans to stir up all the trouble they could." But the American public, like the president, was stunned by the news of Germany's machinations; for the first time editorial writers across the nation called for war with Germany.[28]

On March 3, as the Senate debate resumed on the armed ship bill, House and Loulie arrived in Washington to attend the president's inauguration. On March 4, when Wilson delivered his inauguration address on the east front of the Capitol, the sky was overcast and a cold wind blew from the northeast. Loulie accompanied the president and his family to the ceremony, but House stayed behind in the White House. "I never like," he explained, "to be conspicuously in evidence. There is enough jealousy abroad without accentuating it unnecessarily." Or, as he wrote to Fanny, "I cannot see what pleasure one gets in such an affair." After the address, Wilson and his entourage spent the afternoon reviewing the inaugural parade; House joined them later in the day. "We had a quiet dinner," he recorded, "and went upstairs to the oval sitting room to witness the fireworks. The family generally were at the main windows. The President and Mrs. Wilson sat by a side window, curtained off, and asked me to join them. The President was holding Mrs. Wilson's hand and leaning with his face against hers. We talked quietly of the happenings of the day and I spoke of my joy that we three, rather than the Hughes family, were looking at the fire-works from the White House windows." The three of them had begun another long four-year voyage.[29]

In the meantime, while most senators favored the armed ship bill and were ready to assume the risk of a war at sea with Germany, four Midwesterners, fearful of conflict, blocked a motion to limit debate. When he returned from the Capitol after taking the oath of office, Wilson bitterly denounced this small group of senators. Despite his anger, Congress adjourned without acting and on March 9, determined to show America's resolve, he instructed the navy to arm American merchant ships. Germany, Wilson realized, had given no signs of conciliation and had announced on March 2 that the period of grace for neutral ships in the Atlantic had expired. Now U-boats would sink all ships—neutral and belligerent—without warning. War seemed more and more likely.[30]

December 18, 1916, was the wedding anniversary of Wilson and Edith. During the first year of their marriage, Edith, one biographer writes, became accustomed to "monitoring the nation's events in person," working at her husband's side, sitting in on many of his conferences, and accumulating grudges against all of his advisers. And she was concerned about her husband's health. In late November 1916, Wilson had what he described as a "bad cold." The illness, which lasted for twelve days, led the president to lighten his schedule. He no longer went to his office in the morning, instead remaining in his private quarters, with time out for golf. He had, as one historian notes, a "quickening of feelings of mortality."[31]

On the surface, House's relationship with Wilson did not change, but their sharp disagreement over the president's peace note in late 1916 had further loosened the emotional ties between them. On his first visit to the White House in 1917, House asked the president what he intended to do about Ambassador Page. Wilson responded that he planned to accept his resignation. "Mrs. Wilson asked," House recorded, "if I would take his place. She thought I ought to do so during the war. The President also expressed a wish that I accept it." House quickly convinced the two, so he claimed in his diary, that this would not be a wise move, but initially he seemed to miss the significance of the suggestion. For four years Wilson had pressed House to visit him more often and stay longer; now, with Edith at his side, he could contemplate sending him abroad on an ambassadorial appointment.[32] Despite Edith's attempt to exile House in London, however, she continued to share with him her complaints about other members of her husband's inner circle. When House arrived in Washington on January 3, 1917, Cary Grayson met him at Union Station and talked about his appointment to rear admiral, which Secretary of the Navy Daniels seemed to be blocking. The behavior of the ambitious White House physician disappointed House and also troubled Edith, who felt "that Grayson has been pushing his own fortunes in an indelicate and objectionable way." With Grayson's apparent fall from grace, and a rumor that Tumulty might resign, House observed that "the little circle close to the President seems to have dwindled down to the two of us, Mrs. Wilson and myself."[33]

Grayson's fortunes, however, soon improved. Wilson overcame his reluctance to advance his physician over many more experienced naval officers and recommended his promotion. But Grayson's preoccupation with his own career offended House. "Even at such a time," he complained in his diary, "do we think of our own puny interests."[34]

House may have sensed that his own position was also insecure. "If actual war occurs," he wrote the president on February 4, "could I not be of more service to you if you placed me on your Staff, letting me help wherever the pressure was greatest?" Wilson was pleased by his counselor's startling proposal but wondered just what he had in mind. "My thought," House replied, "was that I could form a little bureau to make your burden less heavy in the event of war. It would necessitate our moving to Washington for the time being and I would be at your disposal both day and night." House suggested that they talk about his plan when he was next in Washington, on March 3, but they never did so, and during this visit Edith once again suggested that he replace Page in London.[35] House's extraordinary proposal would have brought profound changes in his life. He had always kept a safe distance from Wilson, preferring to pursue his role as a confidential adviser at a distance and keeping his stays at the White House brief. And he had taken long trips to Europe and retreated to the North Shore during the summers. He had convinced his family and friends that his delicate health required this migratory routine. Wilson must have been perplexed by his counselor's willingness suddenly to change the well-established rhythms of his life.

Other members of the president's inner circle fared less well than House. Page continued to hang on in London, but largely because the president could find no one to take his place. Lansing remained as secretary of state, but Wilson avoided consulting him and viewed him, quite correctly, as disloyal. On the eve of war with Germany, Wilson dismissed Lansing as "the most unsatisfactory Secretary in his Cabinet; that he was good for a second place but unfitted for the first. That he had no imagination, no constructive ability, and but little real ability of any kind."[36]

Nor did Secretary of the Treasury McAdoo escape the displeasure of the president and his wife. McAdoo's belligerence—he wants, House noted, "war to the hilt"—and his intrusions on his father-in-law's privacy, irritated the president, while Edith confided to House that "she disliked McAdoo; that she had always disliked him. She considered him thoroughly selfish in as much as he would let nothing stand in the way of his ambition." House agreed with Edith's assessment of McAdoo's ambition, but took a more balanced view of his personality, noting that "he is an affectionate and generous friend." He also realized that McAdoo, with all his "shortcomings. . . is the great driving force in the Cabinet." He urged his intense friend to concentrate on the treasury department and "to leave the President and the other Departments alone."[37]

House's visits to Washington, and his maneuvering within the president's inner circle, were only a part of his wide-ranging activities. Throughout

December 1916 and the early months of 1917 he remained extraordinarily busy, consulting with visitors seven days a week, cultivating many different journalists, handling, with the help of Fanny, a diary and a large correspondence, and maintaining an active social life of dinner parties and evenings at the theater and opera.[38] Somehow House also found the time to consolidate his hold on the state department, moving William Phillips to first assistant secretary of state (and consulting with him often about diplomatic appointments), and placing a new protégé, Breckinridge Long of Missouri (a wealthy contributor to Wilson's 1916 campaign), as third assistant secretary of state. House and another member of his inner circle, State Department Counselor Frank Polk, talked on the phone several times a day, and with Polk's help he secured for his son-in-law, Gordon Auchincloss, a lucrative position as the representative of the state department in New York "in secret service, financial, and trade matters." At the end of March, a direct, secure telephone line was installed from his apartment in New York to Auchincloss's office and then to the state department. He could now keep in even closer touch with Washington.[39]

As America moved toward war, Wilson pondered what his next step should be. On March 7 he went to bed—with a cold and sore throat—and stayed in his private quarters for nine days. Every day the pressure on the president for a decision grew more intense. Interventionists clamored for war, frustrated with his indecision.[40] On March 12, a German U-boat sank the steamer *Algonquin* without warning, the first attack on an American vessel since the decree of February 1. More sinkings of American ships soon followed. On March 17, the day after Wilson went to his office for the first time since his inauguration, he learned that the czar had been deposed and a new, liberal Provisional Government formed in St. Petersburg. Like most Americans, he was encouraged by what seemed the liberation of the Russian people and further evidence that autocracy everywhere was doomed. House concluded that "now that Russia bids fair to be free, one sees more hope for democracy and human liberty than ever before." He urged immediate recognition of the new Russian government; Wilson agreed, and on March 22 the American government granted formal recognition.[41]

The continued sinking of American ships, and Wilson's inaction, sent a wave of excitement across the country and brought a statement by Teddy Roosevelt insisting that the United States join the Allies. Those close to the president also argued that the time had come for a declaration of war.

On March 20, when Wilson held a cabinet meeting, he found that all the members of his official family felt the nation must enter the conflict. The president listened coolly to the views of his advisers without revealing what action he would take, but he did call a special session of Congress for April 2. Two days later, when Frank Polk visited House in New York, he described "a feeling in governmental circles that if the President did not act promptly, a strike would come about in Cabinet and official circles." He did not know that Wilson had begun to assemble materials for his war message.[42]

House watched with growing impatience as Wilson agonized over his decision for war. Like the president's other advisers, he was eager to see him "take the reins in his own hands and not allow Congress to run with the situation." Finally, on March 26, he decided to go to Washington, convinced that he needed "to talk matters out with the President."[43] In the late afternoon, when House arrived at the White House, he found Wilson, despite a headache, eager to discuss his war message. Since both men now agreed that the nation must go to war with Germany, House sought to bolster the president's spirits and prepare him for the difficulties that lay ahead.[44] The next day, after lunch, Wilson and House again discussed his war message. Since their talk of the previous evening, Wilson had made some changes, all of which his counselor approved. "He will have," House recorded, "a message which could not please me better had I written it myself."[45] The last night of House's visit, he, Wilson, and Edith "dined alone and after dinner we played games until ten o'clock." After a "thoroughly delightful evening" House caught a midnight train to New York; the next day he reassured Wilson that "I had an unusually happy visit with you this time."

House was back in New York only three nights when he learned from Edith that her husband would definitely address Congress on April 2. On April 1 he left on the midnight train, arriving at the White House in time for breakfast. Later in the day the president read his war message to House, who wrote "that no address he has yet made pleases me more than this one, for it contains all that I have been urging upon him since the war began." During the remainder of the afternoon the two did nothing except " 'kill time" until he [the president] was called to the Capitol." House accompanied Edith and family members and noted that the president began speaking at twenty minutes to nine and talked for thirty-two minutes. After the address, Wilson, Edith, Margaret, and House gathered in the oval room of the White House and discussed the occasion.[46] House confided to Fanny that "History may record this the most important day in the life of our country—one of the most important, indeed, in the life of the world. It may mean the turning point in the affairs of men. When the President has spoken tonight we will have definitely abandoned our policy of isolation, and have embarked upon the uncertain seas of world affairs."[47]

In his brief but memorable address the president declared that "the present German submarine warfare against commerce is a warfare against mankind . . . . It is a war against all nations." Dismissing armed neutrality as unfeasible, he asserted that the nation could "not choose the path of submission and suffer the most sacred rights of our nation and our people to be ignored or violated." He next outlined the steps that the United States would need to take to prepare for war, and reminded his audience, and the world, that America's quarrel was with the German government, not the German people. "A steadfast concert for peace," the president continued, "can never be maintained except by a partnership of democratic nations. No autocratic government could be trusted to keep faith within it or observe its covenants. It must be a league of honor." The Russian revolution had, Wilson reasoned, purified the Allied cause and indicated the trend of world affairs.

Finally Wilson reached his great peroration, one that would echo down through the years:

> It is a distressing and oppressive duty, Gentlemen of the Congress, which I have performed in thus addressing you. There are, it may be, many months of fiery trial and sacrifice ahead of us. It is a fearful thing to lead this great peaceful people into war, into the most terrible and disastrous of all wars, civilization itself seeming to be in the balance. But the right is more precious than peace, and we shall fight for the things which we have always carried nearest our hearts,—for democracy, for the right of those who submit to authority to have a voice in their own governments, for the rights and liberties of small nations, for a universal dominion of right by such a concert of free peoples as shall bring peace and safety to all nations and make the world itself free at last. To such a task we can dedicate our lives and our fortunes, everything that we are and everything that we have, with the pride of those who know that the day has come when America is privileged to spend her blood and her might for the principles that gave her birth and happiness and the peace which she has treasured. God helping her, she can do no other.[48]

The president, a trained orator, was the master of the occasion. As he entered the chamber of the House of Representatives, his face was pale and stern and the audience silent. When he finished, there was a brief silence, then thunderous applause. For those who were there, Secretary of State Lansing recalled, the scene was "indelibly impressed on the memory—a vivid picture which can never fade or grow dim."[49]

Wilson's address, a powerful expression of America's sense of mission, seemed to have expressed the thoughts of the American people. Beneath the surface unity, however, there were currents of opposition; members of the Socialist Party opposed American entry into the war and anti-war congressman and senators were deluged with appeals for peace. Nevertheless, on April 4 the Senate approved a war resolution by a vote of 82 to 6, while two days later the House approved it by a vote of 373 to 50. The president had received a powerful mandate to lead the nation into war.[50]

Wilson's decision had been slow and full of anguish, for he sensed the terrible cost of American participation, both at home and abroad. Each of his diplomatic victories, however, since August 1914 had committed the United States more deeply, and he concluded in late March 1917 that only a declaration of war could bind the nation together and protect its position as a great power. He had lost all confidence in the militarists who controlled the German government and had concluded that America's entry into the war would bring an early end to the conflict and effect, under his leadership, a just peace and the transformation of the international community. As one historian remarks, Wilson's dream of peace "finally led him paradoxically to a decision for war." House, who had often disagreed with Wilson during the long period of American neutrality, could stand firm behind his inspired leadership. The two men had been partners in power for slightly over four years; now their sweeping aspirations for America's role in world affairs would test both their friendship and their political and diplomatic skills.[51]

PART IV

America at War, 1917–1918

23

America Prepares for War

In his message on April 2, President Wilson had warned that American belligerency would require "the organization and mobilization of all the material resources of the country"—massive credits to the Allies, taxation at home, the expansion of the navy, and an addition to the army of at least 500,000 men, who should be chosen "upon the principal of universal liability to service." Wilson knew that the war seemed remote to most Americans and that some of these measures would be controversial. He presided over a sprawling, fragmented society, one whose population of 100,000,000 was divided along class, ethnic, and ideological lines. Some were enthusiastic for war, others opposed it, but most Americans had only a hazy notion of their nation's stake in the conflict and were unaccustomed to the assertion of federal authority over their lives.[1]

The nation, in short, was poorly prepared for war. Prior to April 1917, the administration had engaged in little planning for the mobilization of its industrial and scientific resources or moved to create an effective military machine. In 1916 the Congress had, at Wilson's urging, approved a substantial expansion of the navy and had also increased the size of the regular army. But as of April 1, 1917, the army was still a tiny force, with only 5,791 officers and 121,797 regulars, along with 80,446 National Guard officers and men on federal service and another 101,174 National Guard troops under state control. The army's general staff was weak, its bureau chiefs all-powerful, its officer corps unacquainted with modern war, and American industry unprepared to equip even a small force with adequate weapons.[2]

Among European officers there was, the American military attaché in St. Petersburg reported, "a universal belief that our army is not worthy of serious consideration." Even after American entry into the war, British and French military leaders did not expect much from their new ally's army, while in Washington confusion reigned over what the nature of the American military contribution to the Allied war effort would be. Initially it seemed unlikely that the United States would dispatch a large expeditionary force to Europe; rather, it seemed more likely that it would, as House noted in March, "constitute ourselves a huge reservoir to supply the allies," sending food, credits, and munitions across the Atlantic.[3]

In April and May of 1917, Wilson—despite the many uncertainties—moved swiftly to mobilize the nation. Immediately after the declaration of war he sent a conscription bill to Congress, and soon more bills followed—to control espionage and treason, to raise taxes for the war effort, and to allow Secretary of the Treasury McAdoo to raise millions of dollars through the issue of government bonds. Wilson also used his executive powers to set up a Committee on Public Information, led by the progressive journalist George Creel, and to create a Food Administration led by Herbert Hoover, the dynamic director of the Belgium relief effort. Creel's task was to sell the war to the American people; Hoover's to rally the nation's farmers, middlemen, and grocery shoppers behind the conservation of food.[4]

Some of these measures quickly became controversial. The army's plan to draft two million men—with no provision for the volunteers that Teddy Roosevelt hoped to lead—aroused bitter opposition. The Democratic Party leaders in the House deserted Wilson; for a time in mid-April it looked as if the administration might lose its first major war bill. It was only with Republican help that on May 18 the Congress finally passed the Selective Service Act. The measures that gave the president power to suppress dissent and censor publications also encountered opposition in the press and from congressional Republicans, and not until mid-June did Wilson sign compromise legislation. Finally, the question of who should pay for the war provoked fierce debate, as Democratic leaders and progressive Republicans sought to impose higher corporate and personal taxes.[5]

In the spring of 1917, amid all of these debates, partisanship remained strong. In early April, Republicans sought to create a Joint Committee on the Conduct of the War, a move that so alarmed Wilson that he made a special trip to Capitol Hill to suppress it. Republican leaders in Congress made a show of cooperation with the administration, but in fact they sought partisan advantage over the controversies generated by the war and attacked the performance of various executive agencies, particularly the war department. Senator Henry Cabot Lodge complained that "the President has no administrative capacity. He lives in the sunshine. He wants nobody to tell him the truth apparently, and he has a perfect genius for selecting little men for important places." These quarrels in Congress revealed the widespread confusion over the nation's stake in the Great War; since America faced no clear and present danger, the administration would have to find ways to rally the people behind an unprecedented war effort.[6]

The rush to prepare the nation for war increased the pressure on House. "The days are," he noted on April 5, "a continual turmoil now. Telephone calls, telegrams, letters and personal interviews occupy every waking hour." While not closely involved in the legislative battles in Washington, he defended the administration and sought to advance its agenda, cultivating liberal journalists and seeking to placate those opposed to the war. He also reached out to the Republican opposition, dining with the elder statesman Elihu Root at the Plaza Hotel and explaining to him the troubles the administration was having with its conscription bill. Root interested House, who concluded that "he has a steadier mind than Wilson's and a more practical one, but he is not so brilliant and so alert, neither has he the literary and historic background which comes to the President's aid in almost every conversation on public affairs."[7]

The administration's early mobilization efforts pleased House. "Things are going wonderfully well here," he wrote the diplomat Hugh Frazier in Paris; "the Administration is doing all in its power to justify the reputation America has for efficiency."[8] In the spring of 1917, however, foreign affairs preoccupied House far more than domestic affairs. For years he had been intrigued with Russia's size and backwardness, traveling to Moscow in the summer of 1912 as part of a grand tour of Europe and in *Philip Dru*, written in the early months of that year, wondering what the future would bring to "that despotic land."[9] In early April 1917, House, worried about the "Russian situation," advised the president to send a commission of distinguished Americans to St. Petersburg, one that would assess conditions there and urge the Provisional Government to carry on the war. Russian officials must be told, he informed Wilson, that if they wanted American support, they must not make a separate peace. The president agreed. On April 24, Root accepted the chairmanship of the commission and in June the American delegation arrived in St. Petersburg.[10]

News of America's entry into the war encouraged leaders in London and Paris. Foreign Secretary Balfour announced that "It's a great day for the world," while the Ribot government in Paris declared April 22 "United

States Day" and held festivities throughout city. Both governments quickly decided—without coordinating their efforts—to send special missions to Washington to solicit American support.[11]

Lloyd George and his advisers realized that with the Russian Army near collapse and with the decline in French morale, Great Britain carried more of the burden of continuing the fight against Germany. They remained confident of victory but saw little prospect of ending the conflict in the near future; they believed, as Lord Milner, a member of the War Cabinet, observed, that "the entrance of America into the war has introduced a new factor, of great ultimate promise but small immediate value." They needed to make American leaders realize the magnitude of the task that the Allies confronted and to coordinate Anglo-American efforts. On April 13, the British mission, led by Balfour, left for Canada.[12]

The French mission, led by Marshall Joseph Joffre and former prime minister René Viviani, left France two days later. Joffre wanted a powerful American force on the Western Front but he realized that the United States would insist on enlarging its own army and would resist efforts to feed troops directly into French units. As the French delegation crossed the Atlantic, Joffre also learned that General Nivelle's ambitious attack on the German lines on the southern Aisne sector, the Chemin des Dames, launched on April 16, had been a costly failure. "Things are not," he commented, "going very well"; the French desperately needed even a token American force on the Western Front, if only to boost their morale.[13]

On April 5, House learned of the decisions of the British and French governments to send high-powered missions to Washington. Both he and Wilson realized that the United States must welcome these Allied delegations, although the president, determined to pursue a separate diplomatic course, worried about the "manifest dangers" of these missions, that they might make it appear that the American government was no more than an "assistant" to the Allies.[14] House soon learned, from Polk and Wiseman, of the schedule of Balfour and his party. On April 20, the British officials arrived at Halifax, Nova Scotia, and left on a special train to Washington. Two days later, House and Gordon Auchincloss boarded the train at New York and left it at Trenton, New Jersey, so that House and the foreign secretary could talk for over an hour.[15] Without consulting the president, House gave Balfour his version of how the British mission should proceed. Now worried about the lethargy of the American mobilization effort, House urged the foreign secretary to emphasize the difficulties the

Allies confronted and warned that any discussion of peace terms would be premature, since "the problem now was to beat Germany and not discuss peace."[16] Later in the day the British mission arrived at Union Station, where a great, cheering crowd lined the streets through which it drove. But the next day, General Tom Bridges, the senior military officer attached to the mission, found that the city had returned to normal. "There is no hustling," he noted, "but rather the calm of a university town and little conception of the need for haste."[17]

The War Cabinet had instructed Balfour to press upon leaders in Washington urgent British needs. He was to persuade Wilson and his advisers to expand rapidly America's shipping tonnage (the British had lost a record 900,000 tons of shipping to U-boats in April); to ask for the immediate dispatch of a token force of regulars to the Western Front, with more troops to follow; and also to send American recruits—initially 500,000—to complete their training in France and to be amalgamated into British divisions. Finally, he was to emphasize the massive financial needs of the Allies.[18]

On April 25, three days after the British mission arrived in Washington, House boarded the midnight train to the nation's capital. The next morning, when House arrived at the White House, he found that the president was dissatisfied with the first conversation that he and Secretary of State Lansing had had with the foreign secretary. "Lansing," Wilson complained, "had a wooden mind and continually blocked what I was trying to convey. I would like to have a conversation with Balfour, you being present.'" The two men agreed that Wilson would invite Balfour to a family dinner and afterward confer with him. They also agreed that a discussion of peace terms made sense, so long as it was unofficial.[19]

Prior to the informal White House dinner, however, House and Eric Drummond, Balfour's private secretary, agreed that the foreign secretary should see House again before he talked with the president, "so I might know how to guide the conversation and make it effective and harmonious." On April 28, with a large map of Europe and Asia Minor spread out before them, House and Balfour plunged into a discussion of peace terms in the event of a decisive Allied victory. They quickly agreed that Alsace and Lorraine would be returned to France, and that France, Belgium, and Serbia "would be restored." House "warmly advocated a restored and rejuvenated Poland," but Balfour had doubts about the creation of a new Polish state and the two men could not figure out what its boundaries would be or how to provide an outlet to the sea. The Austro-Hungarian Empire would be dissolved, with Serbia regaining Bosnia and Herzegovina and with minor territorial adjustments in the Balkans. They came to no conclusion about Italian claims, although Balfour "referred to Italy as being greedy," and their discussion of Italy led House to ask about treaties among the Allies "as to the division of spoils after the war." Balfour, in a conciliatory mood, regretted these arrangements, "'dividing up the bearskin before the bear was killed,'" and he agreed with House's request that the Allies give copies of their secret treaties to the president.

As the two men discussed the dissolution of the Ottoman Empire and the division of Turkey in Asia into British, French, Italian, and Russian "spheres of influence," House became upset. "It is all bad," he warned Balfour. "They are making it a breeding place for future war." House urged him "not to look upon Germany as a permanent enemy," but the foreign secretary was more concerned about a future "German menace than he was by the possible danger from Russia." House concluded that "a right solution [to these territorial issues] could only come by the British and American Governments taking a stand together for the right."[20]

On April 30, the president, his counselor, and the foreign secretary gathered for dinner at the White House. Over dinner the conversation remained general, with Wilson, House noted, doing "most of the talking." After dinner the three men retreated to the president's study, where Wilson continued to dominate the conversation. With House's discreet guidance, the three men covered the same ground discussed by House and Balfour two days earlier. At the end of a two and a half hour conversation, the foreign secretary, House recorded, "was quite enthusiastic [about his encounter with Wilson] and said he had never had a more interesting interview. He spoke of the President as having a wonderful combination of human philosophy and political sagacity."[21]

The French mission, led by Joffre and Viviani, arrived in Hampton Roads, Virginia, on April 24 and the next day transferred to the *Mayflower* for the voyage to Washington. Joffre, the hero of the Marne, was widely known in America and, as he and the delegation drove down Pennsylvania Avenue, thousands of people crowded into the streets to give these French dignitaries a remarkably enthusiastic demonstration.[22]

On April 29, House drove to the Washington navy yard to board the *Mayflower* and meet the French notables. The next day he lunched at the French Embassy and learned for the first time from one of its members "of how serious conditions were in France and how necessary it was to send our troops at once." House now realized that if the United States had not entered the war, "Germany would have had more than an even chance of success." House was more impressed with the British than the French delegation, for the French had sent envoys who could not speak English, and he also now understood the distrust between the British and French and "the danger of friction between the Allies." He noticed that the "Japanese, Russians and Italians are being left out of English, French, and American calculations," and worried about the future of the Allied coalition.[23]

The day before his departure, House confided to Fanny that "I am well and going strong. The weather has been delightful, else I could not have done it all. From first to last it has been a fateful week, and would make a great story." Once back in New York, he wrote the president that "I do not think I have ever had a pleasanter time in Washington than upon my last visit."[24]

On May 1, when House returned to New York, the rash of callers, both in person and over the telephone, seemed greater than ever. He was especially concerned about the shipping crisis and food shortage, and conferred with General George Washington Goethals, director of the Emergency Fleet Corporation, and with Herbert Hoover, who had just returned from Europe. House believed that the dour Hoover "has the energy and driving force which [Secretary of Agriculture] Houston lacks." He urged Wilson "to give Hoover the authority he desires."[25] House also watched closely as the pressures of mobilization intensified the struggle for preferment in wartime Washington. With his protégé Frank Polk he arranged for Gordon Auchincloss to become his assistant, convinced that "Gordon has won his distinction because of his good sense, his modesty and his great discretion." In late May, Gordon and Janet moved to Washington, where they took an "old fashioned house" in Georgetown with a garden and several acres of land. House's son-in-law was delighted with his new position, which put him, as he neared his thirty-first year, "in the very centre of the big game."[26]

The war seemed to intensify the ambition of Secretary of the Treasury McAdoo. House found his friend "full of his worries," complaining that the president would "not give him all the power he wishes" and demanding sweeping authority over many aspects of the American war effort. McAdoo criticized his father-in-law's wartime leadership, asserting that he underestimated "the seriousness of the situation."[27]

House was also uneasy over the leadership of Wilson, who lacked, so he claimed, "the power of large administration." House ignored the fact, however, that in April and May 1917 Wilson was absorbed in complex legislative battles and was beginning to draw into his administration a group of powerful war managers to whom he delegated sweeping authority: Hoover became the head of the Food Administration, Creel of the Committee on Public Information, and General John J. Pershing the new commander of the American Expeditionary Force.[28] Wilson also admired the convivial Wall Street speculator Bernard Baruch, who was a member of the advisory commission of the Council of National Defense, and made him purchasing agent for the Allies. House sought to block Baruch's ascent, explaining that "I believe Baruch is able and I believe he is honest, but I do not believe the country will take kindly to having a Hebrew, Wall Street speculator given so much power. He is not the type that inspires confidence." But aware of Wilson's fondness for Baruch, he did not take his objections directly to the president.[29]

In the spring of 1917, House also became friendlier with Ignace Jan Paderewski, the renowned Polish composer and pianist. In February 1915, Paderewski had arrived in the United States to begin an extensive speaking and concert tour and to promote the cause of Polish independence. House had first met Paderewski in November 1915 and was immediately attracted to the great artist, with his flamboyance, emotional intensity, and reverence for men of power. "He rumples his hair," one observer noted, "does all bowing and scraping as if he were appearing before a regular set audience, and even sits as if he were at the piano, at the edge of his chair." Flattered by Paderewski's courtship, House became an advocate of a free Poland.[30] Paderewski for his part shrewdly cultivated his powerful friend. On April 10, he and his wife gave a dinner in honor of House and Loulie at Delmonico's restaurant in New York. The table was beautifully set, and after dinner French musicians played on "ancient instruments." "We have never," House recorded, "had hosts kinder or more complimentary . . . . No one was allowed to talk politics or of serious matters, which I appreciated." Nor did Paderewski neglect Loulie, who had, he told House, "the most heavenly face I have ever seen."[31]

By early May, House had lost interest in the French mission, which lingered in the United States until May 22. The British mission, however, was different, since Balfour was a powerful figure in the British political establishment and sure to play, so House thought, a prominent role at the peace conference.[32] On May 13, when Balfour appeared in New York, House entertained him for lunch and the two men went over the "international situation" until four in the afternoon. On April 28 they had focused on the terms of a victorious peace; now House tried to explore the terms of a negotiated settlement. He sought to convince Balfour that it might not be possible to punish those responsible for the war and that the conflict might end with Germany, the Ottoman Empire, and the Austro-Hungarian empires left intact. The foreign secretary, like other Allied leaders, had no interest in a peace without victory, but he avoided any sharp disagreements with the president's counselor.

House also took up, with Eric Drummond, the Allies' demand for a dramatic expansion of American destroyer production. The Wilson administration was reluctant to suspend its battleship program—designed for a postwar conflict with Japan—in order to build anti-submarine craft. Without consulting the president, House now suggested that if the United States shifted its production to destroyers, Great Britain should "agree to give us an option on some of her major ships in the event of trouble with Japan." If Drummond understood correctly, House then went further, proposing a secret "defensive alliance on the sea between [the] United States and ourselves." The prospect of an Anglo-American alliance excited Balfour, but the War Cabinet in London was more skeptical and House's extraordinary proposal fell into abeyance.[33]

As the British mission came to an end (it left for Canada on May 22), House and Wiseman felt that everything was "going well" and arranged a special code with the British Foreign Office to facilitate communications. Balfour and Drummond, House reasoned, now appreciated Wiseman's "integrity and ability," and he looked forward to his young friend's "future career in English politics."[34] The foreign secretary, however, had doubts about relying on such an inexperienced diplomat. The French government had dispatched André Tardieu to Washington as a special High Commissioner, and Balfour urged the War Cabinet to send Sir Edward Grey to coordinate British efforts in America. When Grey declined the offer, Lloyd George proposed sending the powerful and unconventional British press baron Lord Northcliffe, who was widely disliked both in Britain and the United States. Balfour strongly objected, describing Northcliffe as a "vigorous hustler and loud voiced propagandist," and Wilson, House, Wiseman, and Spring-Rice also deplored the appointment. Nevertheless, with the prime minister's support, on June 11 Northcliffe sailed for New York.[35]

On June 2, House left New York for the North Shore. The president was once again "both glad and sorry that you have got off to the Massachusetts shore," while House once again thanked him for his "kindly thoughts" and reminded him that "my only concern is that I cannot do more for you."[36] The British and French missions were gone, and the conversations of Balfour, Joffre, Viviani, and their experts with Wilson and his advisers had brought the war across the Atlantic and impressed American leaders with the plight of the Allied cause. The American government had agreed to extend massive financial and material assistance, to join the British Navy in an all-out war against the U-boat menace, and to dispatch as soon as possible an American division to the Western Front, where it would fight in the French zone and be trained and equipped by the French. But the president had insisted that the United States would be an "Associated Power" rather than a full-fledged member of the Allied coalition, and that it would not become a recruiting ground for the British and French armies. The United States, in short, would mobilize in its own way and at its own pace, and much remained unclear about the scale of American participation in the land war in Europe.[37]

24

The Strains of Coalition Warfare

On June 4, 1917, after a leisurely two-day drive, House arrived in Magnolia, Massachusetts, where he, Loulie, and Fanny settled into a "simple little farm house in the trees." He was pleased with the private, secure telephone line that had been installed, and concluded that "with the help of this private wire I can accomplish as much as if I were in either New York or Washington."[1] House now had more time for reflection and for his family. His granddaughter Louise, who was two and a half, spent the whole summer in Magnolia; Louise, he recorded, "added more joy to the summer than anything else." Mona and Randolph Tucker summered nearby, Janet spent the second half of the summer with her father and mother, and Gordon Auchincloss, who labored in the nation's capital, visited occasionally. House heard "only good reports of Gordon's work from Washington. Janet, too, has had her share of admiration and attention."[2]

While House enjoyed the "cool salt air" of the North Shore, the president stayed in Washington throughout the exceptionally hot and humid summer of 1917. Sometimes he and Edith would escape from "the people and their intolerable excitements and demands" for a few days on the *Mayflower*, although Wilson brought his papers and stenographer with him. America's entrance into the war had accelerated the rush of people and events, and Edith's glamorous image faded as she and the ladies of the cabinet pledged to deny themselves luxuries, to forgo entertaining, and to dress and eat simply. She volunteered for Red Cross work and soon took up sewing clothing for American troops.[3]

Edith continued to guard her husband's health. Along with frequent breaks for golf and automobile rides, she and Woodrow spent quiet evenings in the White House with family and a few old friends. Even so, the uncertainties of the war weighed heavily on the president. "There would come days," Edith remembered, "when he was incapacitated by blinding headaches that no medicine could relieve. He would have to give up everything, and the only cure seemed to be sleep . . . . He would awaken refreshed and able at once to take up work and go on with renewed energy."[4]

As America entered its first summer of war, the president and his advisers worried about the response of the American people. Tumulty, who tried to keep his finger on the popular pulse, warned that the "general mass of people" were indifferent toward the war and urged his chief to speak to the people in a way that would arouse "their righteous wrath." Secretary of War Baker feared that the unprecedented effort to draft millions of Americans would bring widespread resistance, but on June 5, registration day, ten million men registered at more than 135,000 local draft boards. In many parts of the country there were local parades and festivities; few Americans had any real grasp of the nature of the fighting on the Western Front.[5]

House believed that the "liberal movement in Germany is strong" and that Wilson should lead the "war against the Prussian autocracy from within as well as from without." Wilson agreed, and in his Flag Day address on June 14 explained that the United States had been "forced into the war" by the "military masters of Germany," who were fighting as much to maintain their power at home as to maintain their empire in Europe. The United States was not, he continued, the enemy of the German people; they were "themselves in the grip of the same sinister power that has now at last stretched its ugly talons out and drawn blood from us." The war had become a "People's War, a war for freedom and justice and self-government amongst all the nations of the world." Given these enormous stakes, the United States had "but one choice. We have made it. Woe be to the man or group of men," Wilson warned opponents of the war, "that seeks to stand in our way in this day of high resolution when every principle we hold dearest is to be vindicated and made secure for the salvation of nations."[6]

The Flag Day address impressed House, who believed that the president, far better than any Allied leader, had made "a proper indictment of Germany . . . that will stay for generations." He was annoyed, however, that Wilson had not sent him the whole speech for review before it was delivered, complaining in his diary that "he speaks too casually and without sufficient consideration. It has led him into all the errors of speech he has made, and for which he has been so censured."[7]

During the hot summer of 1917, as the nation mobilized for war, social and political tensions broke through to the surface. Booming war industries had drawn southern blacks into northern cities, creating racial tension and a vicious race riot on July 2 in East St. Louis, Illinois. Labor unrest also spread, especially in the Rocky Mountain states, where the Industrial Workers of the World was strong, inciting vigilante violence against striking workers. And the poor wheat crop of 1917, for the second year in a row, brought rising prices and rising discontent, especially in the nation's urban centers.[8]

The president struggled to maintain national unity and to respond to criticism, from the press and the Congress (which stayed in session until October), that the nation's mobilization effort was moving too slowly. He found new leadership for the Shipping Board, transformed the Council of National Defense into the War Industries Board to better coordinate the efforts of the government and private industry, and convinced the Congress, after much controversy, to establish a Fuel Administration and a Food Administration (sanctioning his earlier executive order) and to give him the power to regulate the supply and prices of fuel and food. He also allowed the Committee on Public Information to erect an enormous propaganda apparatus and to lead the drive for wartime unity, sponsoring a campaign for "Americanization" and controlling the information the American people received about the war. Nor did he object when zealous subordinates, especially Postmaster General Burleson and Attorney General Gregory, used the greatly expanded powers of the federal government to suppress dissent, both in newspapers and periodicals and among radical organizations that challenged the nation's war effort.[9]

Comfortable in his sanctuary on the North Shore, House seemed disengaged from much of the domestic tumult brought by American entry into the war. He talked frequently, however, with Frank Polk and Gordon Auchincloss,[10] and he also listened to complaints about Wilson's leadership. He spent the better part of a day with Herbert Hoover, who thought that "matters are getting into a jam at Washington and wonders why the President does not take some action." The food administrator's complaint only confirmed House's earlier judgment about the president's lackluster administrative abilities.[11] On August 7, McAdoo, whose influence in Washington had grown with America's entry into the war, finally spent a day with House in Magnolia. The secretary of the treasury wanted to use the war to further expand his already formidable powers. He criticized the president for not giving him "sufficient authority" and asserted that his father-in-law's "unwillingness to face any sort of friction or trouble . . . has grown of late rather than diminished."[12]

House also carefully monitored the position of Secretary of State Lansing, concerned that Lansing's dismissal could undermine his own unique position. Polk thought the president was unfair to Lansing, as did House, who felt sympathy for the secretary of state. "What he lacks," House observed, ". . . is imagination, the diplomatic touch and a spiritual outlook. He is practical, has a legal mind, and desires to do things largely by precedent." House was relieved that Lansing displayed "no jealousy toward me, although he realizes that I have the full confidence of the President and he has not."[13]

During the summer of 1917, as he reached his fifty-ninth year, House claimed that he was satisfied with his life and "free from personal ambition." In fact, however, House was less satisfied with his position than he claimed, and in conversations with the progressive journalist Lincoln Colcord in the summer of 1917 he revealed his frustration with the tangled, constricted world in which he lived, one in which he had to maneuver among powerful forces and personalities to influence events. For years he had fantasized about a different, more heroic role, imagining himself, one historian notes, "as the tribune of the people, engaged with the representatives of organized imperialism in a battle to the death. He caught glimpses of Armageddon: the old order collapsing, the new democracy arising on its ruins, himself in the center, his possession of the most intimate secrets of corruption of the old regime the key to power in the new."[14]

On June 11, Lord Northcliffe landed in New York with no staff and no idea about how he was to coordinate the sprawling British establishment in America. Confronted with a hostile Ambassador Spring-Rice in Washington, Northcliffe decided to make his headquarters in New York, a city he regarded as the center of America life. From there he would seek to bring together various British missions in America and, through articles in the press and extended speaking tours, sell the war to the American people. He regarded his mission to America as "the most important task in his life."[15]

Both House and Wiseman worried that the great press baron might disrupt their key role in the Anglo-American connection and decided that it would be best to "try to guide" him and to make sure that his mission was a success.[16] House carefully monitored Northcliffe's movements, arranged for him to be properly received in Washington, and also tried to smooth over the tension between the special emissary and the ambassador. House and Wiseman agreed that Spring-Rice should be recalled. If the ambassador was to be replaced, however, House wanted to be certain that any new appointment would be passed "up to the President through me." He decided to dispatch Wiseman to London so that he could explain conditions in America to Lloyd George and establish a better channel of communication. Eager to bolster Wiseman's credentials, House even arranged for his young friend to attend a White House reception and meet the president.[17]

On June 29, House received, through Wiseman, a cable from Foreign Secretary Balfour, warning that "we seem on the verge of a financial disaster which would be worse than defeat in the field . . . . You know I am not an alarmist, but this is really serious." Great Britain and the United States faced the first crisis of their new wartime partnership.[18] Prior to the American entry into the war, the British government had been forced to borrow from American private banks, and on July 1, a $400 million overdraft with J. P. Morgan and Co. would come due. During his stay in Washington, Balfour had gained the impression that the American government would cover the overdraft, but McAdoo, politically ambitious and aware of his extraordinary powers, refused to pay it, and at the end of June the United States Treasury suspended all loans to Great Britain. Without massive American financing, the Allied war effort would soon collapse.[19]

Balfour's "panicky cable" annoyed House, since British leaders, rather than explaining to him their precarious financial situation, had "bluffed it out almost to the end."[20] Nevertheless, he worked "assiduously" to solve the financial crisis, and his efforts helped bridge the impasse between the two governments. The secretary of the treasury, supplied with more information on British financial needs, resumed the extension of credits. But the larger issue, the lack of any coordination among the Allies in their demands for money, shipping, and raw materials, remained unresolved.[21]

In the summer of 1917, the war dragged on. Despite revolution in Russia, mutinies in the French army, and the horrors of trench warfare, all the belligerent governments were determined to continue the struggle. Leaders in the warring capitals realized that both their armies and their homefront consensus had weakened, but none had given up their hopes of winning the conflict or were willing to moderate their war aims in order to achieve a negotiated peace.[22]

In France, the failure of Nivelle's offensive in late April had precipitated a crisis in national morale in the spring and early summer of 1917. In
his memoirs, President Poincaré labeled 1917 *L'année trouble*; after nearly
three years of war the *union sacrée* had begun to fall apart as political and
social divisions emerged. A steep rise in prices, along with strikes in war
industries in May and June, fed doubts about the war and ushered in a
period of political instability that brought down first the Ribot and then
the Painlevé cabinets. At the end of April, one infantry battalion refused
to go back into the line, and soon half the divisions of the French army
were in various states of indiscipline, mutinies in which troops defied
their officers and refused to take up positions at the front. On May 15,
General Philippe Pétain replaced Nivelle as the commander of French
forces and moved to suppress the mutinies and bring about the recovery
of the army. By mid-June, acts of indiscipline decreased and army morale
began to improve, but Pétain knew that his soldiers were no longer capable of launching a major offensive. He decided that "we shall wait for the
Americans and the tanks."[23]

On June 13, General Pershing and his staff arrived in Boulogne and took
a special train to Paris, where they were greeted by what the American
general described as a "wildly enthusiastic reception." When Pershing
and Pétain met a few days later, the French general remarked, "I hope it is
not too late." On June 26, the first contingent of 14,000 American troops
arrived in France, and on July 4, some units marched through Paris as part
of a massive celebration of the Franco-American military alliance. These
American troops, however, were unprepared for combat; they were poorly
trained and lacked the weapons necessary for modern warfare. Pershing
realized that the American Army would not play a major role on the
Western Front until the spring of 1918.[24]

In Russia, conditions were far more desperate than in France. In the
spring of 1917 anti-war sentiment spread, strikes broke out in factories,
and the St. Petersburg Soviet issued a manifesto demanding "a platform
of peace without annexations or indemnities." On the Eastern Front
the Russian Army was still in place, despite a massive number of deser-
tions, but officers no longer had much power over their troops and the
commander-in-chief of Russian forces warned in late April that information from all sides "indicates that the Army is systematically falling apart."
The Provisional Government, however, remained determined to stay in
the war, and in mid-May Minister of War Alexander Kerensky, trying to

halt the drift toward anarchy and peace, convinced himself that Russian soldiers would continue to fight. On July 1, under the leadership of General Brusilov, they attacked Austro-Hungarian lines in Galicia. Soon German and Austro-Hungarian divisions counterattacked, while on the northern front they broke through Russian lines and on September 3 captured Riga, bringing the Central Powers one of the most dramatic and decisive victories of the war. The Provisional Government, now assaulted from both the right and the left, found itself helpless in the face of growing Bolshevik power. On November 7, the Russian revolution entered a new and more radical phase when the Bolsheviks seized control of St. Petersburg.[25]

By the early summer of 1917 British leaders viewed the position of their nation with alarm. Two allies, France and Russia, were faltering, German U-boats threatened Britain's command of the seas, and the nation's manpower and financial resources were nearly exhausted. A series of strikes in May raised questions about labor's willingness to continue its support of the war, and heavy casualties, rising prices, and local food shortages had led to popular weariness. America was, to be sure, now in the conflict, but it was unclear what price Wilson would extract for assistance to the Allied cause. All of these events had undermined the self-confidence of Lloyd George's government; the prime minister feared that if it did not produce a decisive victory, another major offensive would bring more defeatism at home.[26] Therefore, Lloyd George wanted to avoid a massive offensive on the Western Front and to reserve the strength of the British Expeditionary Force until 1918, when the French army would have been revived and the American army would have arrived in strength. But Haig, supported by William Robertson, chief of the Imperial Staff, was determined to launch a great offensive in Flanders, one that he believed would break through enemy lines and force German forces out of Belgium. In June, British leaders debated the Flanders offensive, and Lloyd George in the end would not oppose the wishes of his military commanders. On July 31, the third battle of Ypres, or Passchendaele, began and continued intermittently until November 10. A total of 275,000 men died or were wounded, for only negligible gains.[27]

The strain of the long war also affected the Central Powers. Austria-Hungary and Turkey were on the edge of internal collapse, while hunger and war weariness had also spread across German society. One Berlin official informed the minister of the interior that the public was gripped by a mood of "despondency and fear of the future."[28] During the first two years of the war, opposition to the struggle was scattered and ineffective. Strikes of industrial workers, however, had broken out in May and June of 1916, and as the war continued and hardships spread, more strikes erupted in industrial centers, and in April 1917, 300,000 workers went on strike in Berlin. The stalemated war and the radicalization of the German labor movement brought the collapse of the political truce as the debate over the nature of the peace revealed growing divisions in German society. Political parties on the left demanded a compromise peace and democratic reforms at home, while parties on the right demanded, as a reward for Germany's suffering, massive territorial acquisitions or a "Ludendorff peace." For those groups that had dominated politics and society in Imperial Germany, victory was essential if the prewar order was to endure.[29]

In the summer of 1917, however, the German high command took a somber view of the war. The army's defensive positions on the Western Front had held and German forces had made impressive gains on the Eastern Front. Russia had descended into revolutionary chaos and U-boats had sunk an impressive number of British merchant ships. But Britain did not seem close to collapse, the convoy system was beginning to take hold, and Germany's new enemy, the United States, was mobilizing its massive resources. Germany's short-term prospects were good, but the Allies, with a decisive superiority in men and material, seemed likely to prevail if the conflict continued beyond the spring of 1918.[30]

Hindenberg and Ludendorff sought to shift the blame for the military stalemate to Chancellor Bethmann Hollweg. By the summer of 1917 he was old and tired, aware of the fact that his policies had failed to prevent the growing polarization of German society. "By trying," one historian notes, "to satisfy everyone he had satisfied no one"; his peace policy was confused and contradictory and his endless vacillations had disillusioned those on both the left and the right. In the Reichstag, which reconvened in early July, political parties were increasingly divided and restless. On July 19 a "peace resolution majority," in defiance of Germany's ruling establishment, passed a resolution that called for an end to the war "without annexations or indemnities." The chancellor had lost control of the parliament.[31] Hindenburg and Ludendoff now insisted that they could no longer work with Bethmann Hollweg and the kaiser accepted his chancellor's resignation on July 13. "I have had to dismiss," he sadly remarked, "the very man who towers by heads over all the others." In his place the kaiser appointed Georg Michaelis, an obscure bureaucrat who had no experience in diplomacy or domestic politics. Germany was moving toward a military dictatorship.[32]

By the summer of 1917, House had put together an extensive network of correspondents who reported with regularity about conditions in Europe. A stream of letters flowed into his study in the little farm house in Magnolia, describing the prospects of all the warring powers.[33]

By the end of June he saw "evidences of all the belligerents weakening, and the cracking process being actively at work." While he viewed the immediate prospects for peace as poor, he believed that this "terrible condition cannot go on indefinitely."[34] On August 15, all of the warring governments received an appeal for a moderate peace from Pope Benedict XV. House was eager to respond to the pope's plea to end the carnage, although he realized that he was "running counter" to the views of the secretary of state and the president. He was, however, confident of his own judgment, convinced that he had "a more complete picture of the situation than either the President or Lansing."[35]

Wilson, however, was far less interested in the pope's plea than his counselor. Initially he was not even inclined to reply; he did not regard a return to the status quo ante as an acceptable peace and did not believe that the American government could deal with the "autocratic regime" in Germany, which was "morally bankrupt." House worried that Wilson would "make a colossal blunder if he treats the note lightly and shuts the door abruptly." Now he regretted his isolation in Magnolia. "I wish," he recorded in his diary, "I could be with him. I feel it something of a tragedy to be heat bound at this moment."[36]

Perhaps influenced by his adviser's pleas, Wilson sent him the draft of a reply on August 23. In it the president insisted that his goal was a "stable and enduring peace," not a return to the status quo ante. Such a peace "must be based upon justice and fairness and the rights of mankind," and could not be negotiated with "the present rulers of Germany." Only a government in Germany, Wilson concluded, that represented "the will and purpose of the German people" would be a fit partner in a peace agreement.[37] The enthusiastic response of the American press to the president's note, which was published on August 28, pleased House, who optimistically claimed that "It is having an enormous effect in Germany and I do not believe that Government will be able to stem the tide that will soon set in against them."[38]

As the two men pondered the possibility of an end to the war, their thoughts turned to American preparations for the peace conference. On September 2 Wilson raised the subject with House, suggesting that the American government ought to study the terms of the Allies, so that it could prepare its "case with a full knowledge of the position of all the litigants. What would you think," he asked his counselor, "of quietly gathering about you a group of men to assist you to do this?"[39] Throughout the spring and summer of 1917, concern about preparations for peace had been growing in and outside the Wilson administration. But the president—indifferent to formal lines of authority—wanted House to undertake the assignment. Aware of its extraordinary importance, House quickly agreed "to undertake the work." In private, however, he was concerned about Lansing's "sensibilities" and the magnitude of the task, worried about how he would proceed and how he would find the time to carry the "additional burden."[40]

At seven o'clock on the evening of September 8, House learned that the president and Edith would arrive at Gloucester Harbor in the early afternoon of the next day. The day before, they had boarded the *Mayflower* in New York for a cruise along the New England coast, one that would allow Wilson to escape the heat and political tension in the nation's capital and to consult with his counselor, whom he had last seen on April 30.[41]

At two o'clock on September 9, House and Loulie met the *Mayflower* and then motored with the president and first lady for two hours along the North Shore. Both before and after dinner—which was on the yacht—the two discussed the fate of Secretary of State Lansing. Once again Wilson felt intense dissatisfaction with his secretary of state, but the possibility of Lansing's resignation continued to alarm House. The secretary of state, he realized, had been exceptionally deferential, accepting his role as the president's primary foreign policy adviser and working amicably with Auchincloss and Polk in the state department. House argued against Lansing's dismissal, doubting that Wilson "could do better." Since there was no obvious candidate to replace the secretary of state, House suggested that the president "allow Lansing to remain until he fell ill again" and then offer him the ambassadorship to Great Britain. Lansing might, House suggested, accept the transfer to London if offered "a place on the peace commission," but Wilson disagreed, responding that his secretary of state was not "fit for a peace commissioner."[42]

The next day, after lunch at the Essex Country Club, they resumed their discussion of affairs of state. They pondered how House and the new organization that he headed, which would become known as "the Inquiry," would collect data for the peace conference, and returned to the question of what to do about the secretary of state. House maneuvered to delay a confrontation, suggesting that Wilson first have "a frank talk" with him and promising to have Polk "prime Lansing and get him in a frame of mind to accept the President's rebuke kindly." After they had finished their discussion, Wilson and House posed for photographers and spent the rest of the afternoon, along with Loulie and Edith, motoring and relaxing. Over dinner they continued their "entirely social" conversation, as the Houses tried to keep the president "in as merry a mood as possible."[43]

On September 13, as House prepared to return to New York, he noted that he had had "a delightful and profitable summer." The day before he left Magnolia, Wiseman arrived, full of news from his stay in London. House's protégé, who in early September would move into his apartment building at 115 East 53rd Street, had learned how to flatter his mentor: " 'You have no conception,' " House proudly recorded Wiseman explaining, " 'of the influence you have with the British Government. There are only three nations to be considered in this war, Prussia, Great Britain and the United States, and the strings are all being pulled at Magnolia.' "[44]

When Wiseman had arrived from Great Britain he was accompanied by Lord Reading and a young adviser to the British treasury, John Maynard Keynes. In his discussions in London, Wiseman had urged British leaders "to consider that Washington had become the diplomatic centre of the world" and that they would have to court Wilson and House and find a way to end the squabbling between Ambassador Spring-Rice and Lord Northcliffe.[45] As a result, Lloyd George had decided to dispatch Lord Reading, his close friend and adviser, to the United States as a high commissioner, authorized to resolve the lingering financial crisis and to convince the American government to integrate its war effort more closely with that of the Allies. House had been consulted by Lord Robert Cecil, the acting foreign secretary, about this new arrangement and had approved the dispatch of Reading, who had "both a financial and political outlook." Wiseman believed that this new arrangement would improve the "prospect of sympathetic cooperation between our countries." House, too, was surely relieved that, after a tumultuous summer, he had preserved his vital role in the Anglo-American connection.[46]

25

Envoy to the Allies

On his return to New York on September 16, 1917, House's schedule became far more crowded than it had been on the North Shore. He was clearly pressed for time, complaining about an "exhausting day," the "great nuisance" of the telephone, and recording that he was often "weary" of his diary, which "never gives a true picture of the day." He still, however, occasionally went to the theater in the evening and also kept in touch with his granddaughter, "baby Louise."[1]

As America's involvement in the war deepened, a wide range of issues and people flowed through his modest study. He discussed the tension between China and Japan with Ambassador Roland S. Morris, listened to Socialist leaders complain about the administration's harsh censorship of their newspapers,[2] and sympathized with Ambassador Boris Bakhmeteff as he described the travail of revolutionary Russia. He also followed the shifting currents of the war, concluding that Russia was eager for peace and learning from Hugh Frazier in Paris that "the morale of the army is good . . . . France will hold out through the winter."[3]

On September 12, four days before House returned to New York, Lord Reading arrived in the United States. A highly successful barrister and Liberal member of parliament, Reading had become a confidant of Lloyd George and in 1913 had been appointed lord chief justice. He was a persuasive advocate, a man of charm and tact who knew how to win the confidence of other men and bridge differences among them. He and House had met during Reading's first mission to the United States in the fall of 1915 and had become close friends during House's stay in London in January and February 1916. The two men now took long automobile rides in Central Park, going over every phase of the war and the "political situation in England." House found Reading "a calm, clear-headed statesman with more of the political than the judicial mind" and believed it was easy for them "to open our minds to one another."[4]

In the fall of 1917, while House cultivated Lord Reading, he also moved quickly to put together the organization to collect data for the peace conference.[5] With the secretary of state on the sidelines, House decided that Sidney Mezes and Walter Lippmann would be the two key members of his new enterprise. Mezes would be his "confidential man" and Lippmann his secretary. "The objection to Lippmann," he informed the president, "is that he is a Jew, but unlike other Jews he is a silent one." The objection to Mezes, he continued, might be that "he is Mrs. House's brother-in-law," but Mezes was "one of the ablest men I know, has a broad progressive outlook, is well grounded in both political and economic history, speaks French and German and understands Italian and Spanish." The president had no objection to either man, informing his friend that he could "certainly do the work best with the assistance of men you know and trust."[6]

House's choice of Lippmann to help run the Inquiry was obvious (despite the fact that Lippmann had written a scathing review of *Philip Dru*). The brilliant journalist, only twenty-eight, was eager to work with the president's counselor and, as House realized, was "easy to get along with" and a valuable link to liberals.[7] His choice of Mezes, however, was puzzling. His fifty-four-year-old brother-in-law was a philosopher of religion with a thin knowledge of international relations. Mezes had had a long administrative career, first as a dean and then president of the University of Texas and, after 1914, as president of the City College of New York. He was, one scholar involved with the Inquiry remembered, "a man of mediocre talent," "a quiet-mannered gentleman of the old school." Mezes never took hold of the new organization; in choosing him, House placed loyalty and family ties ahead of competence.[8]

Both British and French leaders were eager for House to travel to Europe and participate in Allied deliberations.[9] Initially Wilson had resisted sending an American representative, but when House arrived in Washington on October 9, he soon changed his mind and informed his counselor that he should attend the Inter-Allied Conference in Paris. "No one in America," he insisted, "or in Europe either knows my mind and I am not willing to trust them to interpret it!" House agreed to go, but only if he could return immediately after the end of the Allied war council. The president "was pleased and said he felt confident that I would keep free from entanglements and antagonisms."[10]

On October 22, House took the train to Washington, where he was met by Gordon and Janet and then stopped to see Louise before continuing on to the White House. There the president and his counselor rushed to complete the preparations for House's trip to Europe. Initially Wilson had naïvely thought that House should go on the mission alone, but now the two men agreed that representatives of the "Army, Navy, Munitions, Food, Finances, Shipping and Embargo" should accompany House so that they could consult with their counterparts in London and Paris. House spent the better part of a day conferring with members of his proposed staff. The president also typed out a "letter of marque," introducing his emissary to the leaders of the Allied governments.[11]

After House returned to New York, Wilson wrote that "I hate to say good-bye. It is an immense comfort to me to have you at hand here for counsel and for friendship. But it is right that you should go." And House reassured Wilson that "I shall think of you and dear Mrs. Wilson constantly while I am away, and I shall put forth the best there is in me to do the things you have intrusted to me . . . . [Y]ou are the one hope left to this torn and distracted world. Without your leadership God alone knows how long we will wander in the wilderness."[12]

Once back in New York, House received a letter from Cary Grayson, who continued to meddle in matters far removed from his duties as White House physician. Grayson had accompanied McAdoo on a nationwide tour to sell the second Liberty Loan and reported that every place the secretary of the treasury went he was "mentioned as the next President." Like House, Grayson was aware of Edith's dislike of her husband's son-in-law (she never forgave him his opposition to their marriage in 1915) and warned that "we have all got to be very careful about mentioning McAdoo's name around the White House for future honors—especially with the female members." He also reported that Tumulty "is an entirely changed man . . . . His attitude toward McAdoo and yourself entirely reversed from the past three years. He is always praising you—and most enthusiastic about McAdoo." Grayson pledged to do his best "in the interest of harmony and loyalty."[13]

On October 29, the House Party, as it came to be called, now with a capital "P," left New York on a special train for Halifax, Nova Scotia. It included representatives of all the departments of the American government that were concerned with the conduct of the war, along with House and his entourage—Loulie, Fanny, and Gordon Auchincloss. Wiseman had left two days before House, so that he could perfect arrangements for his mentor's stay in London, while Hugh Frazier of the American Embassy in Paris planned to meet House in London and act as his diplomatic secretary. Prior to American entry into the war, House had traveled abroad with only Loulie and Fanny; now the scale of the conflict and the complexities of America's participation in it required a far larger mission to Europe.[14]

On October 30, the House Party reached Halifax. House, Loulie, Fanny, and Gordon, along with General Tasker H. Bliss (army chief of staff) and Admiral William S. Benson (chief of naval operations) and Vance McCormick (head of the War Trade Board), boarded the cruiser *Huntington*, while the rest of the officials boarded the cruiser *St. Louis*. House and Loulie occupied the admiral's quarters, which were "commodious and comfortable."[15] House enjoyed the long voyage across the North Atlantic, observing the constant drills of the crew, watching the refueling of escort destroyers, and feeling the tension mount as his flotilla entered the war zone. It now consisted of eight warships, "going at top speed, zig-zagging every ten to twenty minutes," while everyone on the cruiser had to wear "a life belt night and day." Finally, on November 7 the House Party reached Plymouth and took a special train to London, where it arrived at midnight at Paddington Station. At the station, Foreign Secretary Balfour, Ambassador Page, and other dignitaries met the American envoy and his retinue. House and his immediate party were then driven to Chesterfield House, which had been placed at his disposal by the British government, while the rest of the American officials went to Claridges Hotel.[16]

Chesterfield House, the home of the duke of Roxburghe, was one of the most beautiful homes in London, filled with valuable paintings, old china and books, and servants with cockades. Its magnificent library, where House conducted his interviews, had a coved ceiling filled with portraits of the grandest dames of the eighteenth century.[17] The British government had received House like a visiting head of state. The *New York Times* reported that "never in history has any foreigner come to Europe and found greater acceptance or wielded more power."[18]

House arrived at a critical moment for the Allied cause. On October 24, German and Austro-Hungarian divisions attacked Italian lines at Caporetto (a small frontier town on the Isonzo River) and achieved a dramatic breakthrough, routing a large part of the Italian army and advancing more than fifty miles. Three days later German and Austrian troops had left the mountains and were moving across the Veneto Plain toward Venice.

Only with the help of British and French divisions were the remnants of the Italian army able to establish a new line of defense on the Piave River.[19]

On November 7, Bolshevik forces surrounded the ministers of the Provisional Government in the Winter Palace in St. Petersburg and on the morning of November 8 overran it, installing Vladimir Lenin as the new ruler of the Russian capital, while in Moscow, Red Guards occupied the Kremlin. The next day the new Bolshevik regime issued a "Decree on Peace" directed at the peoples of the world, calling for a "just and democratic peace" without annexations or indemnities. On November 20, the Bolsheviks proposed a three-month armistice with Germany; two days later their foreign secretary, Leon Trotsky, began to publish the secret treaties negotiated among the Allies earlier in the war. Russia's repudiation of its previous commitments, along with its decision to leave the war, elicited alarm and indignation from Allied leaders, raising the possibility that German divisions would soon be transferred to the Western Front.[20]

On November 3, four days before House arrived in England, Lloyd George had left for the continent, stopping in Paris for a day and then moving on to an Allied conference at Rapallo, Italy, on November 6 and 7. The prime minister, fearful that heavy losses would exhaust the army and the nation, wanted to preserve British manpower and eventually shift the burden on the Western Front from British and French divisions to the newly formed American Expeditionary Force (AEF). He was determined to gain control of British strategy and, in the aftermath of the disaster at Caporetto, convinced French and Italian leaders to create a Supreme War Council (SWC), a new structure in which Allied prime ministers, assisted by a military staff, would set the strategy for the war.[21]

Prior to Lloyd George's return to London on November 13, House consulted with a wide range of British officials and journalists, while members of the mission collected data and advice.[22] His most extensive conversations, however, were with Foreign Secretary Balfour, who "greeted me with something akin to affection." House and Balfour covered "the entire field" and agreed that Spring-Rice "must come home and soon." House wanted his old friend Viscount Grey, with whom he had a "delightful evening," to be the new ambassador, but Grey reminded him that "he did not possess the confidence of the present Government" and that he had no desire to assume the burdens of an ambassadorship.[23] House and Balfour also discussed the new Supreme War Council. The foreign secretary wanted American representatives to sit on it, but House, wary of entanglements with the Allies, did not think an American political representative would be necessary, although he did agree that General Bliss should serve as a permanent military member of the new organization.[24]

Throughout his stay in London, House was assisted by a large staff, or, as he called it, his "entourage." Auchincloss saw those people his father-in-law did not wish to see, the "overflow," while Wiseman provided essential support. He accompanied House on visits to prominent officials, arranged for press releases, scheduled meetings, and looked after the Houses' personal comfort (especially making certain that Chesterfield House was properly heated). He was also involved in all the pressing issues of the day—manpower, the Russian revolution, the machinery for improved cooperation, and the formulation of war aims.[25]

The remainder of House's stay in London, from November 13 until his departure for Paris on November 22, was dominated by meetings with Lloyd George. On November 13, the day the prime minister returned from the continent, he and House dined alone at 10 Downing Street. Lloyd George, aware that he would have to deal with the American president through his counselor, praised House for his prescience about the war, emphasized the importance of American representation on the newly created Supreme War Council, and touched on many other aspects of the conflict. As in his previous encounters, House found Lloyd George a talented but flawed war leader; "it is strange," he observed, "that so brilliant a man could [on occasion] talk such nonsense."[26]

House discussed British war aims and the situation in Russia with Lloyd George and Balfour. He discovered that British leaders wanted Germany's African colonies, an independent Arabia under British control, a new Zionist state in Palestine under British or American supervision, an independent Armenia, and the internationalization of the Dardanelles Straits. Balfour "pleaded earnestly" for the recognition of General A. M. Kaledin, the leader of anti-Bolshevik Cossack forces in southern Russia, but House was not eager to meddle in the Russian Revolution.[27] He wanted to put off a detailed discussion of postwar territorial divisions, but he did want an "announcement of war aims, and the formation of an international association for the prevention of future wars." But House, Balfour, and Lloyd George could not act alone; they would have to convince French and Italian leaders—soon to gather in Paris—to accept these goals.[28]

Throughout his stay in London, House sent the president regular, if somewhat fragmentary, reports on his deliberations there. He complained about the difficulty of having "any definite program formulated and put through"; warned that the war, which had become "a waiting game," needed to be fought for "some higher purpose"; and emphasized, as his stay lengthened, how much he had been able to accomplish. As with House's previous trips, the president seemed content with the activities of his counselor, willing to wait for a full report on his return to Washington.[29]

Late on the morning of November 22, House and the other members of his party left Charing Cross Station on a special train to Dover and then took a speedy British destroyer across the Channel, which was calm and had been swept for mines. At Calais, they boarded a special train, arriving at the Gare du Nord at eight in the evening. They were met by a large group of dignitaries and driven to the Hôtel de Crillon, where House and his immediate staff occupied a lavish suite of rooms on the first floor. The whole trip, which House found "a delightful rest," took only eight hours and twenty minutes.[30]

By the autumn of 1917, grave doubts had spread throughout French society about the nation's ability to achieve victory. The French Army was still fragile, the sacrifices of the war weighed heavily on the populace, and the withdrawal of Russia from the war and the near-collapse of Italy made the prospects for 1918 appear grim.[31] Faced with bitter squabbling among politicians, President Poincaré turned to seventy-six-year-old Georges Clemenceau who was, he remarked, "our last trump." Clemenceau, drawing on the parties of the center and right, formed a new government on November 16, only six days before House arrived in Paris.[32] Clemenceau, or "the Tiger" as he was called, was a controversial figure in the history of the Third Republic, one who had had a long career as a politician, writer, and speaker. Over the years, he had accumulated many enemies but also a large popular following, and after the outbreak of war had, as a member of the Senate's war and foreign affairs committee, gained an exceptional knowledge of French military operations. Even before he became prime minister he often visited troops at the front. There, in his boots, old felt hat, and worn overcoat, he became a familiar figure and a symbol of France's determination to fight on to victory. In his first speech as prime minister he declared that "my formula is the same in every respect. Domestic policy? I wage war. Foreign policy? I wage war. I always wage war."[33]

Clemenceau was a man of exceptional curiosity and sophistication. He had many contacts in the literary, artistic, and theatrical worlds of Paris and had, for a French politician of his generation, an unusual range of international experiences. As a young man he had lived for four years in New York, where he taught French and learned to speak fluent English. Lloyd George found him an "arresting and compelling personality," while Lord Milner's wife caught his exceptional qualities: "[He] was a vivid, dark man of medium height; he had a heavy moustache and expressive flashing eyes. He was vital to a degree, swifter in thought, wittier in talk, more unexpected in what he said, than anyone I ever knew. He had an immense power of entertaining and of being entertained, and this made him the most enchanting company . . . . No one ever was such fun as he was. We hung upon his every word."[34]

The day after his arrival in Paris, House met Clemenceau for the first time and talked "intimately" with him. House reported to the president that "I like him very much," while Clemenceau was pleased with his new American friend. He found him sensible, cultured, well informed, and a sincere admirer of France. It was the beginning of a lifelong friendship between the two men.[35]

On November 25, House and General Bliss went to the Ministry of War "to talk matters out" with the prime minister and General Pétain. Worried about the slow progress of the American Expeditionary Force and fearful of a major German offensive on the Western Front in 1918, Pétain laid out the condition of the French Army and made clear that the United States must send "soldiers and not merely men" to France at the rate of two divisions [each with 27,000 men] per month until May, when the rate should be increased to three divisions, for a total of thirty divisions by the end of 1918. Pétain also doubted that the Supreme War Council, as conceived by Lloyd George, would be effective, for it did not designate one person as a supreme commander who could carry out the council's decisions. But French leaders, aware of their nation's dependence on Great Britain, were not eager for a quarrel with the prime minister.[36]

When Lloyd George arrived in Paris on the evening of November 27, House tried to convince him to strengthen the Supreme War Council. At first Lloyd George agreed, then changed his mind and angrily denounced Clemenceau as "a stubborn old man." House felt Lloyd George was "acting like a spoiled child"; "he changes his mind," House complained, "within a few minutes after a definite agreement has been reached." But worried about his political vulnerabilities at home, Clemenceau (with House's concurrence) yielded and agreed to a civilian-dominated Supreme War

Council that would "make it impossible to carry out the general desire for complete unity of military action."[37]

On December 1, when the Supreme War Council met in the Trianon Palace Hotel at Versailles to plan military strategy for 1918, House and General Bliss did not speak, since the United States had "no men on the firing line." Once the AEF was deployed in force, however, House was certain "it will be another story." While Bliss proceeded to set up a military staff, the SWC would not have an American political representative until House returned for the armistice negotiations in late October 1918.[38] House doubted the effectiveness of the SWC and also questioned the usefulness of the large Inter-Allied Conference scheduled to convene on November 29. He believed that the gathering of over 120 officials from Allied governments "was of no importance" and his aim was "to get through it without any mishap." Following a brief address by Clemenceau, the conference adjourned in eight minutes and delegated its serious work to various committees.[39]

The day the Inter-Allied Conference met, Lord Lansdowne published a letter in the London *Daily Telegraph* asserting that if the war continued, European civilization would be completely destroyed and that it would be better to seek a compromise peace. During his stay in London, House had talked with the former viceroy of India and foreign secretary, who had denounced "the folly and madness of some of the British leaders." House admired Lansdowne, a "great gentleman" with an "indefinable air," and now he sought to exploit the defection of one of the members of Britain's ruling elite. The day after the publication of this letter House urged Allied statesmen to adopt a resolution asserting that the Allies and the United States were waging war for idealistic purposes. House thought that this attempt to commit the Allies to enlightened war aims was of "vast importance." The president agreed, observing that "our people and Congress will not fight for any selfish aims on the part of any belligerent with the possible exception of Alsace-Lorraine . . . . [I]t would be a fatal mistake to cool the ardor in America."[40]

House calculated that Lloyd George would strengthen his position at home by advocating a moderate peace, but he could not "pin him down to anything definite." In fact, the prime minister, along with his Conservative supporters, dismissed the Lansdowne letter and believed that peace with Germany would not come until the German army was defeated and its control of the German state broken. Nor would Clemenceau or the Italian

Foreign Minister Sidney Sonnino support House's resolution. House concluded that the United States "must rest just where we were now; that is, upon the broad constructive and progressive statements which the President had from time to time made."[41] He found Sonnino "an able man but a reactionary of the worst type. If his advice should carry, the war would never end, for he would never consent to any of the things necessary to make a beginning toward peace." He was more impressed with Clemenceau, concluding that he "is one of the ablest men I have met in Europe, not only on this trip, but on any of the others. He has many faulty characteristics, but there can be no doubt of his great courage and his unusual ability."[42]

Allied intransigence and indecisiveness discouraged House, who now observed that Germany had been able to withstand their armies because it had "superior organization and method. Nothing is buttoned up with the Allies; it is all talk and no concerted action." Still, despite the "wasted effort" and the inadequacy of the SWC, House believed that much progress had been made in the "coordinating of Allied resources" and that the conferences in Paris were "the turning point in the war even though the fortunes of the Allies have seemed never so low as now."[43]

The day after the adjournment of the Inter-Allied Conference House and other American officials took a special train to the American sector of the front, where they visited General Pershing's headquarters at Chaumont.[44] As 1917 drew to a close, British and French leaders were increasingly impatient with the slow progress of the AEF (which had only 175,000 troops in France) and, as German divisions began moving from east to west, fearful of what lay ahead on the Western Front in 1918. Frustrated by Pershing's insistence on building up an autonomous American Army, they proposed an alternate plan—the amalgamation of small American units into British and French forces. On December 6, General Pétain complained about the intransigence of Pershing and his subordinates, declaring that "Pershing was a good man but narrow, that he did not take a broad view of the situation, and that his chief of staff, General Harbord, was even worse."[45] House listened carefully to French complaints but had no solution to their quarrel with Pershing.

Earlier in his stay in Paris, House had met with Bliss and Pershing to discuss military matters. He had also begun to size up these American generals but had "not come to a definite conclusion as yet." Pershing did not record his impressions of House, but James G. Harbord, his chief of staff, was critical of the president's counselor. Harbord found House's eyes impressive, but noted that "he is one of the few men with practically no chin, whom I have ever met, who were considered forceful."[46] During his last day in Paris, House conveyed to Pershing some of the French complaints, but the general defended his insistence on building a separate American force, noting that "if the American troops went in [Allied units], very few of them would ever come out." Pershing urged House to return to Paris to sit on the Supreme War Council and take over the diplomatic aspects of his work. House had sympathy for Pershing and his dilemmas. No one, he thought, could satisfy both the British and the French and, at the same time, build a great army in "an alien land where the habits, thoughts and point of view are so different."[47]

After dinner on December 6, the House Party took a special train to Brest, where its members boarded the cruiser SS *Mount Vernon* for the return journey to America. House was ready to head home, but confided to Wiseman, "I hated to leave you last night in Paris. I have come to feel that your place is by my side."[48]

During the voyage home, blessed with smooth seas and mild temperatures, House concluded that his mission had been a great success. He realized that the conferences in London and Paris had not resulted in any major decisions—aside from the commitment to send twenty-four American divisions to France by June 30—and that the United States and the Allies had not brought about a unification of overall policy or agreed on war aims or on the treatment of Russia. Nevertheless, he and his associates had gained firsthand impressions of British, French, and Italian leaders and now understood that the Allies would be defeated unless the United States made a larger and quicker military contribution. "The one all-absorbing necessity now," General Bliss wrote, "is soldiers with which to beat the enemy in the field, and ships to carry them."[49]

As he reflected on his stay in Europe, House remained disappointed in Lloyd George, who "makes an appealing speech, states his case well, has a charming personality, and there, as far as I can see, his usefulness ends." Worse still, he believed that the world suffered from political leaders such as the British prime minister, that "the governments of the world are largely controlled by brilliant and eloquent speakers and writers." "What is lacking," he noted in his diary, "is some great executive mind at the head to bring together those elements of strength and make them as great a force against the Germans as is necessary to win the war." The Inter-Allied

Conference in Paris was an example of this lack of a "directing mind." It had no fixed program or clear purpose, and to the extent that it was a success, House claimed the credit for himself and his associates. His experience in summit diplomacy had bolstered his confidence; he was moving toward the conclusion that he, more than the man in the White House whom he advised, possessed the qualities necessary for success both on the field of battle and at the peace table.[50]

During the first phase of the voyage, the cruiser *San Diego* and six destroyers escorted the *Mount Vernon*; once out of the danger zone the *San Diego* and *Mount Vernon* proceeded on their own. Crossing the Atlantic in wartime fascinated House; for the first few nights the ship proceeded without lights, dinner was eaten before dark, and then passengers "lounged about and slept with our clothes on." House did not, however, mind the discomfort of the voyage; "when sitting in the dark it reminded me of the old days in Texas and the camp life I enjoyed so much."[51]

The House Party arrived in New York on the afternoon of December 15; two days later House was on the train to Washington, where he was met at Union Station by Gordon, Janet, and Louise, and by Frank Polk and Cary Grayson. At the White House he found the president waiting for him, and for two hours he reported to both Woodrow and Edith on his mission to Europe.[52]

They agreed that General Bliss should return to Paris as the American military representative on the SWC and that the weaknesses of that body could not be corrected until more American troops were on "the firing line." Cables from Lloyd George and Wiseman emphasized the precariousness of the situation on the Western Front; the prime minister urged the amalgamation of American troops into British units. Wilson and House, however, decided that there would be no change in American policy and that Pershing could continue to build up an autonomous American force.[53] The president was determined to create an independent American Army and to use the economic and military strength of the United States to force his political objectives on the Allies. He had no interest, he informed William Howard Taft, in drawing the United States and Britain closer together and warned that the United States "must not be put in a position of seeming, in any way, involved in British policy." There would, in short, be no special Anglo-American connection.[54]

Since the Allies, at the Inter-Allied Conference, had rejected a moderate declaration of war aims, the president decided, after talking with his counselor for only ten or fifteen minutes, to speak out himself and asked Mezes for a memorandum on the various issues the peace conference would confront. House was pleased that Wilson would now formulate "a broad declaration of war aims that would unite the world against Germany" but "never knew a man who did things so casually."[55]

House realized that his long stay in London and Paris had left him out of touch with important domestic issues. In his absence, the president, confronted with a breakdown of the nation's transportation system, had decided to take over the railroads and put McAdoo in charge. Many details remained to be settled, but House hoped that his friend "would do for the railroads what he had done for the banks."[56]

After a brief trip back to New York, the Houses once again took the train to Washington to spend Christmas with Gordon, Janet, and Louis at 1827 Nineteenth Street. House saw Wilson briefly at the White House, but spent Christmas Eve at Gordon's office in the State Department, consulting with Lansing, Polk, Phillips, and members of his mission. That evening, while he and his family decorated their Christmas tree, the president called unannounced and stayed for half an hour. Christmas day was cold and wet and House did not venture outdoors, but a number of officials sought him out, including Secretary of the Treasury McAdoo, who "showed an almost childish delight in assuming this new and great responsibility [over the railroads]." House worried about his long-time protégé, convinced that he had "ability, vision and an enormous amount of energy," but failed to delegate authority and was "a poor judge of men."

For two days after Christmas, House lingered in Washington, meeting with friends and dining with Wilson and Edith at the White House. He worried about "signs of weariness" that he found in the president and promised to return in a week to help him prepare two important addresses—the first on the railroad question, the second on war aims.[57]

26

Crises at Home and Abroad

A t mid-day on January 4, 1918, House took the train to Washington, eager to consult with the president about his war aims address. He carried with him so many maps and documents that a member of the Inquiry had to accompany him on the train. Arriving at Union Station three hours late, House did not reach the White House until 9:00 PM, when he went into "an immediate conference with the President." He and Wilson conferred until 11:30, and then House and Edith insisted that they not begin before 10:00 AM the following day so that Wilson could "have a good night's rest." The next morning, January 5, when House returned from the state department, he found the president waiting, and they "got down to work at half past ten and finished remaking the map of the world. . . at half past twelve o-clock."[1]

Wilson and House worked quickly, finishing a draft on January 5 and reading it over three or four times. Both had given the question of war aims considerable thought and quickly resolved minor differences. The president, however, worried that Lloyd George might anticipate his forthcoming address with one of his own, and when he learned that the prime minister had, in fact, outlined moderate terms for a settlement on January 5, he was "depressed," concerned that his own address was no longer necessary. But House remained optimistic, predicting that once the president spoke, Lloyd George's speech would soon be forgotten and that Wilson "would once more become the spokesman for the Entente, and, indeed, the spokesmen for the liberals of the world." Reassured, Wilson "set to work again with renewed zest."[2]

On January 6, a Sunday, Wilson finished the conclusion of the message and read it to House, who congratulated him on his "declaration of human liberty" and observed that "it was the most important document that he had ever penned." Once again the president's boldness as a political leader impressed his counselor. "The more I see of him," House noted in his diary, "the more firmly am I convinced that there is not a statesman in the world who is his equal. He is the only one who measures up to the requirements of the day when the world is in such agony."

On Monday afternoon, January 7, the president called in Secretary of State Lansing, the only member of the cabinet informed about the address. House wanted him to consult with his cabinet and to give "notice to the world" in Tuesday morning's papers that he would speak to the Congress on war aims at 12:30 PM. But Wilson, wishing to avoid speculation about the contents of his message, wanted his oratorical effort, a biographer writes, to be "delivered out of silence." When he stepped before both houses of Congress on January 8 to deliver his Fourteen Points Address, much of the diplomatic corps, along with four members of his own cabinet, were absent.[3]

The president and his counselor had crafted a remarkable document, one designed to answer the Bolsheviks' plea for peace, encourage the political opposition within the Central Powers, rally various groups both at home and in the Allied nations behind a liberal peace settlement, and outline a compelling vision of a new world order that would summon people around the world to support their peacemaking efforts. For the president, as one historian notes, the war was "as much a conflict of ideals and worldviews as a clash of arms or interests."[4]

The first five points, and number fourteen, dealt with general principles that were familiar to all progressive internationalists, both at home and abroad. In them Wilson called for open diplomacy, freedom of the seas, the removal of economic barriers, a reduction of armaments, a fair-minded "adjustment of all colonial claims," and the creation of a "general association of nations."

Points six through thirteen laid out in detail, for the first time, the American position on territorial claims so crucial to the belligerents. Point six outlined a liberal policy toward revolutionary Russia, point seven called for the evacuation and restoration of Belgium, point eight the return of Alsace-Lorraine to France, and point nine the "readjustment of the frontiers of Italy. . . along clearly recognizable lines of nationality," in effect postponing the issue of Italian territorial claims. In point ten, Wilson rejected the division of Austria-Hungary into a series of independent states, instead asking for internal autonomy for various nationalist groups within the empire. In point eleven, which dealt with the Balkans, Wilson insisted on the evacuation of Romania, Serbia, and Montenegro, but avoided making specific territorial recommendations. Point twelve guaranteed the sovereignty of Turkey, granted autonomy to the subject peoples of the Ottoman Empire, and provided "international guarantees" for the passage of ships through the Dardanelles. The final point dealing with territorial claims, thirteen, proposed the establishment of an "independent Polish state" with "free and secure access to the sea."

Beneath all of these bold proposals, Wilson concluded, lay "the principle of justice to all peoples and nationalities, and their right to live on equal terms of liberty and safety with one another, whether they be strong or weak." The people of the United States were "ready to devote their lives, their honor, and everything that they possess" to the vindication of this principle. "The moral climax," Wilson prophesized, "of this the culminating and final war for human liberty has come."[5]

In the United States the Fourteen Points Address received warm approval across the political spectrum. The *New York Herald* described it as "one of the great documents in American History," while the *New York Times* ran a headline, "The President's Triumph," above its main editorial. The leaders of the British and French governments, however, were circumspect in their responses, but left-of-center groups in Britain and France were enthusiastic, as was some of the press. Wilson's words also resonated around the world, making him, as he and House had long desired, the only statesman who seemed to possess both the stature and vision to bring about a new international order.[6]

The winter of 1917–1918 brought growing discontent with what seemed the leisurely pace of the American war effort. Republicans, led by Theodore Roosevelt, bitterly attacked the alleged failures of the administration and the apparent confusion and inefficiency of the nation's preparations for war.[7] Some congressional Democrats shared the Republican critique, and after the 65th Congress convened on December 4, five major investigations of the administration's conduct of the war were soon under way. The chairman of the senate's military affairs committee, George E. Chamberlain (Democrat, Oregon), brought Secretary of War Baker before his committee and grilled him for three days. On January 19, Chamberlain's committee reported a bill to establish a war cabinet, in effect taking the direction of the war effort out of the president's hands. The next day, in a sensational public speech, Chamberlain charged that "the military establishment of America has fallen down; there is no use to be optimistic about a thing that does not exist; it has almost stopped functioning." The president, revealing his zest for political combat, defended his secretary of war and challenged Chamberlain's accusations, declaring them "an astonishing and absolutely unjustifiable distortion of the truth."[8]

Extreme weather added to the nation's discontent. On December 28, the worst blizzard in forty-one years swept through the area east of the Rocky Mountains, followed by a wave of sub-zero temperatures. On January 16, Harry A. Garfield, the head of the Fuel Administration, issued an order restricting the use of coal by all factories and businesses east of the Mississippi. Garfield's sudden order brought a violent reaction and only further emboldened critics of the administration.

The president moved quickly to rally his forces in Congress and improve the administration's war effort. In early February, Democratic leaders introduced the Overman Bill, which gave him sweeping powers to reorganize government agencies. After much hesitation, he appointed Bernard Baruch the head of a strengthened war industries board, while Baker appointed a new chief of staff, General Peyton T. March, who began the reform of the war department. Wilson also assembled a war cabinet or council, consisting of Baker, Daniels, McAdoo, and the heads of key war agencies that met every week. By the middle of March, much of the confusion and anxiety over the nation's mobilization for war seemed to have passed. Public opinion had not crystallized against the administration; on the contrary, letters from constituents urged congressmen to stand by the president during a time of national crisis. Wilson's leadership seemed more secure than ever.[9]

House had long been critical of the president's reluctance to provide strong, centralized direction to the nation's war machine. During his early January stay in Washington he once again wondered why his friend "is so obstinate when it comes to administrative affairs." The navy, he reasoned, was in good shape, but House found widespread criticism of Baker's management of the War Department. The secretary of war, he observed, "seems to be getting deeper into the mire, and the President cannot see it. Baker's mind is so sympathetic with that of the President's that the President does not realize that he is no more of an administrator than he is himself."[10]

On the evening of January 8, before leaving Washington, House dined with McAdoo and his wife Eleanor. Once again the two friends discussed the secretary of the treasury's presidential ambitions. "He does not conceal from me," House recorded, "his keen desire to be President, although he declares he does not exhibit this feeling to anyone else. I cautioned him against it." McAdoo, suddenly imagining what his administration would look like, offered House the position of secretary of state. House declined the honor but did reassure his protégé that he would "help him as I had helped Wilson." House was already pondering how he might continue in his role as a confidential adviser after Wilson left the presidency.[11]

Once back in New York, House remained concerned about the organization of the administration's war effort. When Harry Garfield issued his coal order on the evening of January 16, House was deluged with reporters who "made my life miserable."[12] His frustration over his diminished role in domestic affairs now spilled over. Even strong supporters of the administration, he noted, condemned its management of the war and, much to his discomfort, expected him to influence the president. But the president did not seek his counselor's advice on most domestic issues. House was, however, determined to "give a helping hand whether he asks for it or not."[13]

Late on the morning of January 26, House caught the train to Washington and went directly to Gordon and Janet's home, where he spent a "delightful evening." The next day he did not go to the White House until dinnertime, since Wilson had a severe cold. When House tried to bring up the attacks on the administration's management of the war, the president brushed the issue aside. After dinner, when the two retreated to the president's study, together with Edith, their talk turned immediately to foreign affairs. Wilson, who was concerned about a letter from William Jennings Bryan assuming that he would be on the American peace commission, wanted his counselor's advice, and the two men canvassed the possibilities.

House's experience at the Inter-Allied Conference in Paris had convinced him that the American peace commission should consist of more people than the president and himself. Edith was disappointed, noting that " 'I thought you and Woodrow would go alone.' " They discussed whether five, or seven, commissioners would be best, but whatever the number, Wilson asserted that he would not appoint more than two Republicans. Much to House's surprise, he conceded that " 'I suppose Lansing would have to go,' " and, with at least two more places open, Edith mentioned two Republican elder statesmen, Elihu Root and William Howard Taft. Once again the president did not object, but House advised that Taft would be better than Root, since he "would be more flexible and tractable, for he is good natured and easily led." Other names, such as Senator William J. Stone (Democrat, Missouri), chairman of the foreign relations committee; Senator Henry Cabot Lodge; and A. Lawrence Lowell, president of

Harvard University, were quickly dismissed.[14] Despite the fact that the American war effort was lagging and that a great German offensive on the Western Front was imminent, the president, his wife, and his counselor seemed curiously detached from the realities of the conflict, assuming that the United States and the Allies would win the war and organize the peace conference.

By the late afternoon of January 29, the fourth day of his stay, House had completed all his business in the nation's capital and boarded the train for New York. The president hoped that he "would soon come back" and the next day wrote that "it was a delight to have you here and have one or two real talks." Clearly Wilson still valued his friendship with House and his foreign-policy expertise. In a long interview with Wiseman he praised his counselor's accomplishments during his recent mission to London and Paris, asserting that he "has a wonderful gift for getting a detached view-point and fixing on the really important issues." "His last words," Wiseman reported to his mentor, "were 'Give my love to House, and tell him we have had a *bully talk.'*"[15]

After his return to New York, House remained exceptionally busy, often going home after dinner parties rather than attending the theater or the opera, to deal with the documents that had accumulated in his study. All of the important cables that flowed into the State Department were now sent to House or read to him over the phone by Polk or Auchincloss. He noted his son-in-law's growing influence and observed that he was, next to Lansing and Polk, the most important person in the department. He also continued to expand his network of informants, dispatching Felix Frankfurter, a young lawyer working in the War Department, to Paris, to report on opinion in "liberal and labor circles," and a popular journalist and ardent progressive, Ray Stannard Baker, to Great Britain to serve a similar purpose. And he pondered Wiseman's future, informing him that he ought to succeed Reading as British ambassador. House was pleased with his success in promoting Wiseman, praising his "ability, loyalty and trustworthiness."[16]

On January 24, Germany's Chancellor, Count Georg von Hertling, and Austria-Hungary's Foreign Minister, Count Ottokar Czernin, replied to Wilson's Fourteen Points Address. Hertling's response was vague and evasive, but Czernin's was more reasonable and initiated secret negotiations between American and Austro-Hungarian diplomats looking toward a separate peace. The president wanted to continue the peace dialogue with the leaders of the Central Powers, possibly driving a wedge between Berlin and Vienna and increasing the tension between liberals and militarists in Germany. House agreed, observing on January 31 that "things were at last beginning to crack." He worried, however, about the response of the Allies, since "the reactionaries are in control of almost all the belligerent governments."[17]

At ten o'clock on the morning of February 8, House learned from Auchincloss that the president was eager to see him. An hour later, he left on the train to Washington and, before dinner with him and Edith at the White House, Wilson read to him the address that he had prepared and which he was "holding for my critique." After dinner, the three went into "executive session" and worked on the president's speech until bedtime. As was his custom, House initially praised the draft, then began to suggest changes—far more than in any previous address—and over the next two days they returned to the draft until finally, on February 10, House concluded that he "approve[d] the message as it now stands."[18]

The next day he accompanied Edith, Sallie Bolling (her mother), Margaret Wilson, and Janet Auchincloss to the Capitol to hear the president deliver his address to a joint session of Congress. Wilson praised Czernin's reply, offered an extensive critique of Hertling's, denounced the "military and annexationist party in Germany," and warned that the United States was mobilizing its resources for this "war of emancipation." The nation, he concluded, was dedicated to a new international order and would "in no circumstance consent to live in a world governed by intrigue and force."[19]

On February 25, House returned to Washington, since the president was eager to discuss a peace note sent to him by Emperor Karl of Austria-Hungary through the king of Spain. Over the next few days the two men consulted widely and decided on a noncommittal response, one that asked for further information about the Austrian position. But the Dual Monarchy would not, in fact, break with Germany and make a separate peace with the Allies.[20]

The first day of his stay, a Sunday, House reluctantly agreed to accompany the president and Edith to a service at the unfinished Washington National Cathedral, and as the day progressed the three companions covered a wide range of topics and motored more than fifty miles into Maryland. House discovered that Edith, for all her surface cordiality, remained suspicious of his role as presidential adviser. When he noted that Melville Stone of the Associated Press was "offended" because the president had refused to see him, Wilson replied: "You may tell Stone I never expect to receive him, for I do not believe in him, and want nothing to do with him." Suddenly Edith intervened, asking House, "Are you going to tell him that?," to which House replied, "You know well enough I am not going to tell him any such thing." Edith pressed further, asking what he would tell him. House replied sharply "That I will decide later, but it will not be the message the President has sent." Woodrow found this exchange amusing and "smiled broadly" as it ended.[21]

House also worried about the president's safety, fearful "that some day someone will try to assassinate him," and continued to monitor his health closely. He thought that Wilson looked "better than upon my last visit, [but] I can see indications of fatigue. He does not remember names as well and he does not think to do the things we decide upon." Grayson admitted to House that "while he gave the impression to everyone that the President worked day and night, he and I knew that eight hours work a day was about all he was equal to." His friend's limited energy, however, did not concern House. "I believe the President," he recorded in his diary, "can do more in eight hours than any man I know. He wastes no time in talking or useless arguments or energy of any sort. McAdoo has more energy and staying power, and works perhaps twice as many hours as the President, but he does not accomplish as much because he wastes so much energy in talking."[22]

One night at dinner the three companions, when talk of affairs of state ebbed, discussed "how ubiquitous Jews were; one stumbled over them at every move and they were so persistent that it was impossible to avoid them." House thought their ubiquity was surprising "in view of the fact that there were so few in the world." They each guessed at the actual number—House thought fifteen million, Wilson one hundred, Edith fifty—and to the president's astonishment, the *World's Almanac* revealed that there were fewer than thirteen and one half million.[23]

The president did not want his counselor to leave and "wondered if it would not be better for me to come oftener and remain longer rather to come infrequently and cause a sensation." Despite the presence of Gordon, Janet, and Louise in Washington, House had no intention of changing his long-established routine of shuttling and of not spending long periods in the nation's capital.[24]

In January 1918, the middle of the fourth winter of the war, the struggle continued, with no end in sight. Despite widespread shortages and war weariness in all of the belligerent nations, the diplomatic impasse remained;

none of the ruling elites, given the vast human and material sacrifices of the conflict, dared contemplate a compromise peace. An American expatriate living in London wrote House, "Oh I am so weary of it all. Shall we have anything left to love?"[25]

The strains of the war were evident in the Central Powers. In Austria-Hungary, severe food and fuel shortages, along with a breakdown of the transportation system, led to strikes and mutinies. The public was desperate for peace, the army close to disintegration. "This Monarchy," the German ambassador noted, "is lurching on the edge of the abyss." In Germany, hunger, cold, and disillusionment with the war led to waves of strikes that spread across the nation, with 350,000 workers leaving their jobs in Berlin alone. Moreover, politics in Germany had become highly polarized, as bitter debates erupted among political parties over reform at home and peace abroad. The conservative forces in control of the German government, however, had no intention of abandoning their privileges or of accepting a moderate peace. Neither Chancellor Hertling nor Foreign Secretary Richard von Kuhlmann (appointed in August 1917) could stand up to Hindenburg and Ludendorff, who made it clear that they "bore the responsibility before the German people for the conduct of the war and its end result." By early 1918, few restraints were left on the authority of the supreme command's "silent dictatorship."[26]

Despite precarious conditions at home, the Central Powers' prospects for victory in 1918 seemed bright. Allied offensives on the Western Front in 1917 had failed, Romania had collapsed, the Italian army had been routed, and Russia had left the war. Negotiations between the Bolsheviks and the Central Powers had resumed at the end of January but broke down on February 10. Germany responded by renewing operations on the Eastern Front and on February 24 the Bolsheviks capitulated, signing the Treaty of Brest Litovsk on March 3.[27] Hindenburg and Ludendorff imposed a victor's peace on Russia, one that created a vast arc of client regimes stretching from the Baltic to the Black Sea, depriving Russia of one-third of its population and much of its coal production and heavy industry. Germany's great victory on the Eastern Front, embodied in the Treaty of Brest Litovsk, improved domestic morale and reduced political discord. It seemed that the Supreme Command's leadership and vision of how the war should end had been vindicated. As Ludendorff told the Austrian Foreign Minister Czernin, "If Germany makes peace without profit, then Germany has lost the war."[28]

With Russia out of the war, Hindenburg and Ludendorff could now concentrate on the Western Front, which they knew remained the decisive theater. They realized that the U-boat gamble of 1917 had failed either to stop American troops from crossing the Atlantic or to force Great Britain out of the war. By transferring troops from the Eastern to the Western Front, Ludendorff hoped to "deliver an annihilating blow to the British before American aid can become effective."[29] During the winter of 1917–1918 German forces flowed westward, until by March 1918 the German Western army numbered 136,618 officers, 3,438,288 men, and 710,827 horses; its 191 divisions now faced 178 Allied divisions. Germany had a numerical superiority for the first time since the summer of 1914. Finally, on the morning of March 21, after an intense, accurate artillery barrage, German storm troopers moved through the dense fog against the British Third and Fifth Armies on the old Somme battlefield in Central France. It was the beginning of Operation Michael, Germany's "last card."[30]

If 1917 was the best year of the war for the Central Powers, it was the worst year of the war for the Allies. British and French forces were on the defensive, and Allied leaders had to deal with signs of strain and uncertainty among their people. In France, Clemenceau continued his tours of the front and purged defeatist elements; in Great Britain, Lloyd George worried about morale at home and realized that the Bolshevik Revolution had emboldened advocates of a negotiated peace. His January 5 speech had reflected a widespread consensus that the government had to make a fresh declaration of war aims, and that the Allies might not win a decisive victory.[31]

Lloyd George remained, as one historian notes, "a Prime Minister without a Party." Most Liberals remained loyal to Asquith, Labor offered no support, and only Conservatives kept him in power. Nor had his quarrels with generals Haig and Robertson been resolved. He had no confidence in either, commenting that "I don't trust Haig with men." On February 18, only after much maneuvering was he able to push Robertson out and appoint Sir Henry Wilson chief of the imperial general staff. In the early months of 1918, Lloyd George was confident that the Allies had enough manpower on the Western Front to withstand a German attack. Haig agreed, observing that if the Germans gambled for victory and failed, their position "would become critical" by August, when far more American troops would be on the Western Front. The prime minister and his supporters, in short, sought to limit Britain's commitment in France and, concerned about German and Turkish imperial ambitions, to divert more of the nation's military resources to the protection of its empire.[32]

The withdrawal of Russia from the war and the possibility of a great German offensive on the Western Front caused British and French leaders to look to America for help. They renewed their pressure on the president for the amalgamation of American troops into their armies and began a frenzied search for a way to relieve the pressure in the West by renewing the war in the East. Only Japan and the United States had the troops available for such a massive effort.[33] Throughout the early months of 1918, Lloyd George and Clemenceau urged the president to act. They hoped to slow down the transfer of German divisions to the Western Front and find a way to safeguard the vast depots of war supplies that had accumulated at Vladivostok and at the north Russian ports of Archangel and Murmansk. From the start, however, House opposed any Allied intervention in the Russian civil war. He was in touch with liberals and radicals such as William Bullitt, Raymond Robins, and Lincoln Steffens, who were sympathetic to the Bolshevik revolution; in helping the president prepare his Fourteen Points Address, he had been eager to insert a passage expressing sympathy for Russia. House found that "our minds ran parallel" and believed that what Wilson wrote on Russia was "in some respects, the most eloquent part of the message."[34]

The president and his counselor doubted the effectiveness of any military intervention in Siberia, had little confidence in Japan, and worried that such an enterprise would draw resources away from the Western Front and drive the Russian people into the hands of Germany. They hoped for the emergence of democracy in Russia and wanted the Russian people to work out their own destiny.[35] Rather than sanction Japanese intervention, House suggested that Wilson send a "reassuring message" to the people of Russia through the Congress of Soviets. The president quickly complied, declaring in his note that "the whole heart of the people of the United States is with the people of Russia in the attempt to free themselves forever from autocratic government and become the masters of their own life." The president and his counselor had no intention of recognizing the Soviet government, but they seemed to assume some kind of community of aims between Americans and those who held political power in Russia.[36]

The British Fifth Army, understrength and battle weary, was unprepared for the German onslaught on March 21, in which seventy-six elite German divisions fell on twenty-six British divisions. Soon German troops were only a few miles from the vital transportation hub of Amiens and threatened to separate British and French forces and drive the British Expeditionary Force (BEF) toward the northwest and the Channel ports. Ludendorff's armies, however, could not sustain their momentum. They had to move across the wasteland of the old Somme battlefield and found that logistical limitations made it impossible to supply lead divisions as they moved miles beyond their railheads. The German army was inferior to the Allies in the machines of war—airplanes, tanks, and trucks—and had existed for years on meager rations. On April 5, Ludendorff called off Operation Michael. Both sides had suffered heavy losses, but many German divisions were now exhausted and demoralized and many soldiers understood, as one officer noted, "that the hope [for victory] has been dashed."[37]

The last days of March were a time of high anxiety for the Allies. The collapse of the Fifth Army was the BEF's worst defeat of the war; Lloyd George quickly realized that the crisis on the Western Front had ended his plan for conserving British manpower. "We are all here," he wrote, "full of anxiety about this terrible battle." Confronted with the possibility of defeat, Lloyd George and Clemenceau agreed to appoint General Ferdinand Foch as the supreme commander of Allied forces, with the power to coordinate the operations of the British and French armies on the Western Front. With no American units involved in combat, they were determined to press Wilson even harder on the brigading of American troops with British and French divisions.[38]

As the crisis on the Western Front mounted, the president wanted his counselor at his side, writing that he was eager "for one of our clearing talks, which I stand in much need of." On March 28, House boarded the late morning train to Washington. After dinner the two men went into "executive session and cleared up our budgets." They primarily worked on the speech the president planned to give on April 6, the anniversary of America's entrance into the war and the opening of the third Liberty Loan drive, and found that they "were practically of one mind" on the contents of the address.[39] On the third day of his visit, House felt a return of the flu he had caught earlier in Washington and hoped to go to Gordon's and Janet's home to recuperate. The president and Grayson, however, insisted that he remain in the White House, and for the next eight days he had a fever, "nausea and everything disagreeable that could happen to me." Wilson repeatedly sat by his counselor's bedside and, in order to be close to his friend, did not go to the theater the entire time that he was ill. He, Edith, and Grayson wanted House to stay in the White House another week, but he was determined to go home, and on April 9, after an eleven-day stay in Washington, he returned at last to New York.[40]

The massive German offensive had surprised and shocked the president, who had hoped for peace, not an intensification of the war. Wilson now devoted more time to military affairs, meeting with his war cabinet weekly, with Secretary of War Baker nearly every day, and drawing on the expertise of several military advisers. House reminded the president of the political consequences of a German breakthrough on the Western Front and urged him to act decisively. But he also seemed confident that America and the Allies would ultimately prevail, confiding to Pershing that "if we can send a sufficient American force to make good the Allies' losses during the Spring and Summer, I believe Germany will see the end of her ambitions."[41]

Further German offensives increased the pressure on the president. On April 9, Ludendorff launched a second attack, Operation Georgette, against British forces farther to the north, in Flanders, designed to drive all the way to the coast; and after a long pause, Germany's Supreme Command launched a third offensive against French positions in Champagne. On May 27, German storm troopers assaulted poorly prepared French divisions, breaking into open country and five days later reaching the Marne River, only fifty-six miles from Paris. As in September 1914, Paris seemed in danger, and a million people fled the city.[42]

However, German forces, weakened by heavy losses and now ninety miles from their railheads, could not sustain their offensives. On June 2, Foch counterattacked with twenty-five French and two American divisions at Chateau Thierry and Belleau Wood. American troops in large numbers were finally in the battle. While one German commander remarked that the soldiers of his army "are all utterly exhausted and burned out," a French officer, observing American troops arrive at the front, remembered that "we all had the impression that we were about to see a wonderful transfusion of blood. Life was coming in floods to reanimate the dying body of France."[43]

These formidable German attacks increased the frustration of British and French leaders over General Pershing's resistance to brigading. On May 1, at a meeting of the Supreme War Council at Abbeville, near the Channel coast, Clemenceau, Lloyd George, Orlando, and Foch pressed for the release of more American infantrymen. But Pershing was adamant.

After bitter debates the two sides reached a compromise, agreeing that 130,000 American infantrymen and machine gunners would cross the Atlantic in May in British ships, with a further 150,000 in June, all of whom would be sent to the Allies' front lines. Nonetheless, Pershing continued to build up a separate force, and by the end of May, 650,000 American troops were in Europe, most of whom would join the fighting only as part of the American Army.[44]

Despite the anger in London and Paris over Pershing's intransigence, Wilson and Secretary of War Baker were reluctant to overrule their commander in the field, to whom they had delegated so much authority. Pershing was, by any measure, a formidable figure. When appointed commander of the American Expeditionary Force in May 1917 he was fifty-seven years old, a robust, ramrod straight, meticulously groomed career soldier. After his graduation in 1886 from West Point, Pershing had fought in the Indian wars, led troops in the Spanish-American War (where he had acquired the nickname "Black Jack"), and served three tours in the Philippines. Through his friendship with Theodore Roosevelt, in 1906 he had been promoted over many other officers and had become the youngest brigadier general in the American Army. When Wilson decided to send that army after Pancho Villa in March 1916, he chose Pershing to lead the Punitive Expedition; at the time of America's entrance into World War I, he was the only officer in the army who had, since the Spanish-American War, led a large body of troops in the field.[45]

Pershing was distrustful of Lloyd George and impervious to his charm. He dismissed Allied strategy as tired and timid and was determined to build an independent army that would eventually engage in a massive confrontation with German forces on the Western Front. While he allowed some American soldiers to be fed directly into British and French units, he gambled that during the crisis in the spring of 1918 the Allies could hold off the Germans and that he would have the time to win the war with American forces.[46] Even after the compromise reached at Abbeville, Allied leaders remained critical of Pershing. Haig thought Pershing was "very obstinate and stupid," while Lloyd George, frustrated in his conversations with Pershing, sought to go over his head by appealing to his superiors in Washington. On May 20, House learned that the prime minister wanted the president to send him to Europe for the next meeting of the Supreme War Council, where he could "supersede General Pershing and. . . dominate our military action over there." But House had no desire to travel to

Europe and overrule the commander of the AEF. Wilson agreed, although he noted, House carefully recorded, "that if he sent anyone he would send me, for I was the only one who knew his mind and whom he would be willing to have speak for him."[47]

Pershing's conduct, however, worried House. When Wiseman returned from Europe on May 25, he reported that Pershing was "getting 'the big head,'" and urged his mentor to "go to Europe and assume authority over everything except purely military work." House seemed ambivalent about undertaking such an ambitious mission, and finally on June 3 sent his conclusions to the president. He criticized Allied commanders, praised Foch's appointment as supreme commander, and urged that Wilson, Clemenceau, and Lloyd George "insist that commanders in the field subordinate themselves to Foch." Pershing, House continued, should be "relieved from all responsibility except the training and fighting of our troops" and two men, Edward Stettinius and Vance McCormick, should be sent to Europe to take charge of all non-military matters. Once again House urged the president to confront organizational weaknesses in the American war effort.[48]

In the late winter and spring of 1918, as the crisis on the Western Front deepened, House pondered his place in history. During the Wilson years he had been remarkably disciplined, dictating diary entries to Fanny Denton at the end of each day's work. And in June 1916 he had written his *Reminiscences*, which provided an account of his youth and of his years in Texas politics. Suddenly, on January 21, 1918, Arthur D. Howden Smith, a reporter for the *New York Evening Post*, gave House the opportunity to tell the story of his whole life.[49] House faced a dilemma. He worried about the impact of this sort of publicity on his friendship with the president, but also yearned for public recognition of his role in the administration. Despite his ambivalence, he decided to cooperate with Howden Smith, answering his questions about his life and career. In mid-February House read some of what the journalist had written, noting that "he writes in the most complimentary way—too complimentary for my safety . . . . I shall endeavor to have him tone down his praise for I am fearful lest it will lead to trouble."[50]

In early April, when House was sick in Washington, he showed the president some of the "lurid advertisements" carried by newspapers for the syndicated version of the forthcoming book, *The Real Colonel House*, which first appeared in twenty-six installments in the *New York Evening Post* from April 8 to May 7, and complained that he was being advertised "like a brand of soap." He wrote Edith that the articles had driven him "near to drink," but both Wilson and Edith seemed amused by their friend's discomfort. The president, who had read many of the articles, consoled his counselor that "we just have to grin and bear it when these things happen," while Edith "had to laugh over your agony of being in print" and revealed that she found the articles "all interesting and nothing to object to."[51]

Howden Smith's biography, which relied heavily on interviews with House, sought to remove the mystery surrounding the president's counselor and portrayed him as a disciplined, idealistic, selfless adviser who lifted many burden's from Wilson's shoulders. House was, so the author claimed, a "political genius," "one of the most remarkable characters in American history" and, after Wilson, "no man in public life exerts so dominant an influence upon international affairs as this slim, quiet gentleman." If Smith was lavish in his praise of House, the latter provided a whole chapter full of glowing estimates of Wilson, claiming that he was a "fascinating man" who combined "the capabilities of the dreamer, the seer, and the man of action." House believed that one day Americans would realize that their president was "the greatest living statesman in the world, the foremost exponent of progress of this generation, a ruler who will be linked in American history with Washington and Lincoln."[52]

As summer neared, Edith and her husband were eager to see House before he left for Boston's North Shore. "Why don't you," Edith suggested, "come down here for another little visit before the hot weather [comes]," while the president feared that "if this hot weather keeps up, you will be driven away northward. I am praying for some interval when you can come down and see us." House did not travel to Washington in May, but on the seventeenth of the month, Edith and Wilson arrived in New York for a three-night stay.[53]

After a short conference at the Waldorf Astoria, the Houses and Wilsons drove for two hours along Riverside Drive and in Central Park, touching on many topics. Before going to the theater, Wilson and his counselor turned to the bitter quarrel between McAdoo and Harry A. Garfield, head of the Fuel Administration, over the price of coal for the nation's railroads.[54] Earlier in May, House had spent the whole morning with the secretary of the treasury and director general of the railroads and had learned that McAdoo was threatening to resign, exasperated by the way in which the president was "constantly hampering his management" of the railroads. Rather than write the president, House waited until the evening of May 17 to warn him that on his return to Washington, he would have a "stormy interview" with his son-in-law. Obviously irritated by McAdoo's behavior, the president complained that he "had gotten so arbitrary that he presumed that, sooner or later it would have to come to a crisis between them . . . . He said 'son-in-law or no son-in-law, if he wants to resign he can do so.'"

The next day, May 18, Wilson marched two miles down Fifth Avenue at the head of a large parade in honor of the Red Cross, and in the evening the president, Edith, Cary Grayson, and Joe Tumulty dined with the Houses. After dinner they all drove to the Metropolitan Opera House, where the president delivered an address praising the Red Cross and its accomplishments. House was pleased with Wilson's reception, which he regarded as a "great triumph."[55]

The third day of the visit, Woodrow, Edith, Edward, and Loulie drove to Cleveland Dodge's home in Riverdale, where they "sat on the open veranda overlooking the Hudson enjoying the beauties of the Spring." On the drive, Wilson and House "sat together on the small front seats and discussed many pending questions of interest." They now wondered how to reorganize the cabinet if McAdoo did, in fact, resign, and agreed that McAdoo's resignation would destroy his political prospects. Wilson wondered if McAdoo could earn a living out of office and worried about the impact of their strained relationship on his daughter Eleanor.[56]

On May 26, House left New York, driving to Chestnut Hill, Massachusetts, where he spent a week resting with Mona and Randolph Tucker. By June 5 he was back in Magnolia, insulated from the heat and political strife of the nation's capital. But his mediation of the dispute between the president and his son-in-law continued through the mail. McAdoo, who was "run down" and suffering from tonsillitis, retreated to White Sulphur Springs, West Virginia, where he hoped to escape from "business cares and responsibilities for a time."[57] Distance from Washington improved the mood of the secretary of the treasury; in mid-June he reported that he was getting better and heading west, "away from people and into the woods, for four weeks and expect to come back full of energy and I hope equal to my task." He planned to return to Washington on July 15 and then decide what to do. House had, at least for the moment, maintained the peace within the president's inner circle of advisers and retained his position as counselor to both the president and his son-in-law.[58]

27

The Turning Point

In early June, as he neared his sixtieth birthday, House settled into a "little farm cottage" for another summer on the North Shore. Mona and Randolph summered nearby, and Janet and Louise (now four and a half) spent the entire three months with Loulie and her "little Popsie." House kept in touch with affairs of state through long telephone conversations with Auchincloss and Wiseman, and through a special messenger who delivered letters and cables from the State Department twice a week. And a steady stream of visitors made their way to Magnolia to consult with the president's counselor, who nearly every day had company for lunch and dinner. "Someone said recently," he carefully recorded, " 'Magnolia is the first port of call for foreigners coming over, and the last port before returning home.' " Even the president, House observed, knew little about the scope of his activities: "He does not realize that there is but little of importance that goes to him, either directly or indirectly, that I have not either passed upon beforehand or at least know about. It may be well that this should be so." Worried about the security of his papers and conversations, House had the secret service post a watchman at his cottage and check the security of his telephone line every other day.[1]

In June, fierce fighting continued on the Western Front, as Ludendorff's storm troopers pushed for an elusive breakthrough and as Foch ordered a series of Allied counterthrusts. Pershing believed that "the tide will soon turn" and predicted that the war could be won in 1919. House shared the confidence of the commander of the American Expeditionary Force, reassuring the president that "if their [England, France, and Italy] morale can be kept up until Autumn in my opinion, our fight against Germany will be largely won."[2]

House's confidence was not shared by leaders in London, who feared that a French collapse would put the Central Powers in control of the continent and in a position to expand against the British Empire in Asia and Africa. They were aware of the Allies' increasing dependence on American power, but they worried about American intentions and a peace settlement that Wilson, with his idealistic worldview, would dominate. "Is not the time approaching," Lord Milner asked the prime minister, "when we should try to find out, what she [the United States] *will* do in case of a collapse of the Continental campaign against Germany?"[3] The crisis in the west intensi-fied Allied demands for intervention in Russia and the recreation of the Eastern Front. In early June Wilson agreed to send a small American force to Murmansk and Archangel so long as Foch agreed to the diversion of men and ships. But the pleas of the Allies for a Siberian expedition, which they now seemed to regard as crucial to their survival, continued, as influen-tial visitors descended on Washington and Magnolia to make the case for intervention. In early July, Secretary of War Baker remarked that "We have been literally beset, with the Russian question in its various forms."[4]

As Allied pressure mounted, House concluded, along with Secretary of State Lansing, that something must be done. On June 12, Auchincloss sug-gested that Herbert Hoover head a "Russian Relief Commission," one that would capitalize on Hoover's fame and experience to bring massive aid to the Russian people. House and Lansing liked the plan and somehow con-vinced themselves that it would satisfy both the Allies and the president. If Wilson approved, Hoover would take a large staff to Vladivostok, where he and his aides would help the Russians organize their resources and coor-dinate the efforts of existing relief organizations. A sizable military force would accompany Hoover to protect him and the members of his com-mission.[5] Despite the murkiness of this project, Hoover was enthusiastic over the proposal and on June 17 arrived at Magnolia for lunch. Once again House complained that "I have never known a man with a less sympathetic personality. If I were running Hoover for President I would keep him at home, and let him talk to the people entirely through the press."[6] House pressed his commission idea on the president, but also realized—though he did not so inform Wilson—that "the Russian situation is so confused that it is hard to come to a satisfying conclusion."[7]

On July 3, after receiving a strong appeal for intervention from the Supreme War Council, Wilson realized that he must act. Three days later he assembled Baker, Daniels, Lansing, Chief of Staff March, and Chief of Naval Operations Benson to make a decision. The president and his advisers continued to reject the reasoning behind the Allied appeal, dismissing the possibility of establishing an Eastern Front through Siberia and declaring their opposition to any interference in the "internal affairs of Russia." But Wilson did want to help the Russians overcome chaos and radicalism and had been touched by the plight of the Czech Legion (former Austro-Hungarian deserters and prisoners of war who had fought with the Russian Army), which he believed was eager to leave Russia. He and his advisers agreed that "on sentimental grounds" the United States and its Allies should help the gallant Czechs. The American government would agree, therefore, to supply arms and ammunition to the Czech troops at Vladivostok and to dispatch 7,000 troops to guard the Trans-Siberian Railway as their comrades moved toward Vladivostok.[8]

Wilson did not consult House about his decision; nor did he display any interest in discussing differences with the British and French governments and perhaps reaching a compromise solution. Not until July 17 did he release a memorandum explaining his decision to the public and to the Allies. British leaders were upset, viewing Wilson's declaration as still another example of American unilateralism. But Wiseman warned his superiors in London that the president still rejected their arguments for intervention and that "we are up against a new conception of foreign policy which no amount of argument will reconcile with. . . traditional British policy."[9]

Wilson's decision only added to the confusion in eastern Siberia, where Bolshevik, Chinese, Czech, Japanese, and White Russian forces struggled for power. The British and French also proceeded unilaterally, sending small military forces of their own, while the Japanese refused to set a limit on their own expedition and eventually sent 70,000 troops. But the president, despite his failure to reach an agreement with the Japanese government, could not now abandon the Czech Legion, and on August 3 he finally gave the order to dispatch American soldiers to Vladivostok.[10]

House realized that he was on the sidelines of Russian policy, especially after the president moved away from his proposal for a relief commission. He did not approve of the way Wilson treated the British and French governments and had mixed feelings about his explanation of American policy. On July 23, Assistant Secretary of State William Phillips found him "discouraged over the Siberian situation."[11]

On July 15 the German High Command launched its last offensive of the war, an attempt finally to break through to Paris. But Ludendorff's army was now a tired and depleted force and made little headway against the elaborate "elastic defense" devised by Foch. The Allied Supreme

Commander, who had anticipated the German attack, soon launched a counteroffensive in what became known as the Second Battle of the Marne. Early on the morning of July 18 massive Allied formations emerged through the mist and fog, moving behind 750 tanks and a creeping artillery barrage, while British planes strafed retreating German soldiers. German troops withdrew with skill, but they now faced an Allied force that was not only superior in numbers but was also more mechanized and had learned by the summer of 1918 how to employ infantry, armor, artillery, and aircraft in a combined assault. Limited mobility had finally returned to the Western Front.[12]

Foch, Haig, and Petain all understood that the time had come to "pass to the offensive" and that they must apply unrelenting pressure on retreating German forces, not allowing Ludendorff's armies time to recover and reorganize. On August 8, Australian, British, and Canadian troops, along with 450 tanks, attacked at Amiens, breaking through German lines and inflicting at the end of the day the worst defeat on the German Army since the beginning of the war. Ludendorff announced that "it was the black day of the German army," while the kaiser concluded that "we are at the end of our capabilities. The war must be ended." Hindenburg and Ludendorff, however, had no fallback plan after the failure of their spring and summer offensive. Germany's allies—Austria-Hungary, the Ottoman Empire, and Bulgaria—were at the brink of collapse, and American troops were arriving at the rate of 30,000 a day, until by early August over a million were in France. While the outlook for Germany seemed bleak, the kaiser and his advisers deferred any appeal for peace, concluding that future German successes on the battlefield might lead to a more favorable settlement.[13]

American troops were heavily involved in the Second Battle of the Marne. They were high-spirited and eager to close with the enemy, but most were poorly trained and not ready for combat on the Western Front. In four days of fighting the 1st Division lost 50 percent of its infantry and 60 percent of its officers. American troops had advanced, with poor artillery and tank support, in steady, dense lines across open wheat fields. One American journalist witnessed the result: "Everywhere I looked, the trampled wheat was dotted with recumbent figures. There was one field, two or three acres, on which it seemed you could not have stood ten feet from some one of those figures . . . . There lay the best of America, not dead nor sleeping, but alive so long as we will them to live." The war had finally come home to America.[14]

By the early summer of 1918 House felt, along with Secretary of War Baker and Chief of Staff March, that Pershing was attempting to do too much. He urged the president to make important changes in the structure of his command and wanted to transform the Supreme War Council into an Allied General Staff.[15] Nothing came, however, of these ambitious proposals. Under Pershing's leadership the AEF had virtually acquired an identity of its own; the president and secretary of war were unwilling, at such a critical stage of the war, to challenge their commander in the field. By August 17, House realized that, with the war going so well, no changes would be made, and learned from the president "that nothing would be done contrary to Pershing's wishes."[16]

Wilson's Fourteen Points Address, delivered on January 8, had focused the attention of the world on the nature of the postwar settlement and had especially encouraged groups in Britain and America that were agitating for a league of nations. In Great Britain, the League of Nations Society had widespread support and, within the war cabinet, Lord Cecil had emerged as the most influential advocate of an association of nations. Cecil hoped for an Anglo-American partnership in building a new postwar world and in early January 1918 convinced Foreign Secretary Balfour to appoint a special committee, under the leadership of Sir Walter Phillimore, to draft a constitution for the new organization. In its report on March 20 the Phillimore Committee proposed a peacekeeping system that was only a modest departure from current diplomatic practice and that left many questions unanswered.[17]

In the United States, the League to Enforce Peace (LEP), under the leadership of William Howard Taft, had grown into an impressive organization by the early months of 1918, with many state chapters, a substantial budget, and a roster of prestigious members. The LEP had won public acceptance of the league idea and by the spring of 1918 had begun to press Wilson for leadership of the movement. House, who closely followed developments in America and Great Britain, suggested on March 8 the formation of a committee, with Wilson's tacit approval, to devise a plan that could be used at the peace conference. "Further than this," he advised, "I do not think it would be wise to go, and yet public opinion is driving so hard in this direction, that I doubt if it would be wise to do less."[18]

The president, however, had no interest in working with advocates of a league of nations either in Great Britain or the United States. He had not given much thought to the nature of a new organization and wished to proceed slowly, to establish general principles and to avoid specifics. He warned House of "the folly of these League to Enforce Peace butters-in" and explained to his counselor on March 22 that "my own conviction. . . is that the administrative *constitution* of the League must *grow* and not be made; that we must *begin* with solemn covenants, covering mutual guarantees of political independence and territorial integrity . . . . Why begin at the impossible end when. . . it is feasible to plant a system which will slowly but surely ripen into fruition?"[19] On March 28, Wilson shared his thoughts with Taft and Harvard President A. Lawrence Lowell, but he did not share them with the Congress or with the American people. During the war Wilson held no press conferences, made few public addresses except before Congress, and did not travel widely. As one biographer notes, his image as a popular leader had begun to fade; "his presence flashed intermittently across the public consciousness."[20]

House tried to mediate between the president and those on both sides of the Atlantic who advocated more aggressive leadership. He faced a delicate task—to hold off pressure from league advocates while encouraging Wilson to assume leadership of the movement.[21] On June 25, House wrote Cecil, outlining his tentative thoughts on the peace settlement and a postwar league. On the same day, he wrote the president, warning him that he must step forward and guide the movement; "It is one of the things with which your name should be linked during the ages."[22]

As the summer progressed the pressure on the president grew. In early July, after receiving a copy of the Phillimore Report, he concluded that the time had come to devise a more detailed plan for a postwar league. On July 8 he asked his counselor to undertake this task, in effect to rewrite the Phillimore Report along the lines of his letter to Cecil. Wiseman reported that Wilson told him "quite frankly that he was not able to give much thought to the matter now."[23] On July 13, when David Hunter Miller, the Inquiry's (the group of experts led by House to study the nature of the peace settlement) specialist on international law, arrived from Washington, House set to work. For the next two days the two men worked on a draft for what they termed the "covenant" of the League of Nations. On July 15, House rewrote some sections of the draft and wrote a letter to the president explaining each part of the document. Anticipating his approval, he urged him "to take some means of giving it to the world and as quickly as possible in order to let thought crystallize around your plan instead of some other." House also explained that this was to be a league of great powers; "if the smaller nations are taken in the question of equal voting power is an almost insurmountable obstacle."[24]

Drawing heavily on the Phillimore Report, House's and Miller's draft consisted of a preamble, which set standards for international conduct, and twenty-three articles which outlined the essence of the league of nations. Asserting that "any war or threat of war is a matter of concern" to the members, the covenant called for the creation of an international court, the arbitration of disputes, and diplomatic and economic sanctions against offending nations. It guaranteed the "territorial integrity and political independence" of the contracting powers, but also provided for future "territorial modifications. . . pursuant to the principle of self-determination." And it contained a strong article on disarmament and banned the manufacture of munitions and the "implements of war" by private enterprise. House was clearly pleased with the elaborate document that he mailed to the president. He now waited impatiently for Wilson's response.[25]

On the morning of August 14 House learned that the president, Edith, and Admiral Grayson would arrive in Magnolia the next morning on a special train. Both Wilsons were eager for a break from the heat and stress of the nation's capital, where they had been confined for the whole of the summer, and both were also eager for a reunion with their counselor. Or as Edith put it, "we miss you dreadfully, and will welcome our first reunion and an oldtime conference."[26] House had arranged for the presidential party to stay at the mansion of Mrs. Thomas Jefferson Coolidge Jr.—the "Marble Palace" which stood on a point between the beaches of Manchester and Magnolia. Protected by the secret service and a company of Marines on shore and destroyers offshore, they could embark on five days of work and relaxation. Most mornings, Wilson, Edith, and Grayson could play golf, then join House, Loulie, and a variety of guests for lunch. After lunch, Wilson and House would confer on affairs of state and would then end the day over dinner at the Coolidge home. They would also stroll on the beach, take several long drives, and in general enjoy the crisp, clear weather and cool ocean breezes.[27]

On August 15, as soon as Wilson and House arrived at the Marble Palace, they went to "the beautiful loggia overlooking the sea and. . . at once plunged into a discussion of the League of Nations." The president was not satisfied with the Magnolia Draft of the covenant and proceeded to read to his counselor the rewritten document. He had revised the preamble, reduced the number of articles from twenty-three to thirteen, and had made four important changes. Wilson's covenant dropped the international court, gave equal representation to small nations, and strengthened the sections on disarmament and arbitration and the commitment of the league members to maintain international order. House regarded most of the changes as minor, but the two friends disagreed about the need for a world court and Wilson "dissented quite warmly" from House's view that an organization based on the equality of small and large states was an "idealistic dream." House eventually gave way, convinced that at the peace conference the "great nations" would insist on dominating the new organization.[28]

Nor was the president willing to assume the leadership of the League of Nations movement. If the covenant was published prior to the peace conference, Wilson reasoned, it would lead to criticism both "by Senators of the Lodge type" and also by some pro-league Americans and "would increase the difficulty of getting a proper measure through at the Peace Conference." House did not argue the point, but observed that if only Wilson "had taken the lead earlier and had pushed the matter vigorously, he could have rallied the world around his own conception of what a league of nations should be."[29]

The two once again discussed the composition of the American delegation to the peace conference, but the president seemed more rigid than in late January. When House suggested that he should place a prominent Republican on the peace commission, "either Roosevelt, Taft, or Root," Wilson "at once dismissed Taft and Roosevelt as impossible and argued against Root." House disagreed, convinced that "Root, at the moment, was the best in sight." The president also wanted to include Secretary of War Baker, but House thought that the secretary of state should be the only cabinet member taken.[30]

The second day of the visit House "sounded" the president on the question of a third term. Wilson thought that he did not want one, but House saw "evidence of his being a candidate." Given the magnitude of the challenges that lay ahead, House concluded that "there is no one but the President who has the proper background and outlook. The Republican Party is devoid of suitable material; nor is there anyone in the Democratic Party who could fill the President's place in such work." Curiously, over the course of the five-day visit the two of them did not discuss the forthcoming congressional elections. Various correspondents had warned House that the Democrats might lose control of the Congress, but absorbed in questions of war and peace, he seemed unable to focus on domestic politics.[31]

The question of a third term was closely connected with Wilson's health. On the fourth day of the visit House had a long talk with Grayson, who was optimistic about the president's condition, claiming that his patient "might go on for another ten years if nothing untoward happened."[32] House had no reason to question the admiral's judgment, since the president, despite occasional complaints of tiredness, seemed to be in good spirits and good health during the spring and summer of 1918, maintaining his careful regime of work and relaxation. But Wiseman, who saw a great deal of Wilson during his Magnolia vacation, observed that despite his affection and admiration for the president, "he is a most difficult person to deal with as head of the government. His attitude lately has tended to become more arbitrary, and aloof, and there are times when he seems to treat foreign governments hardly seriously." The president had, in fact, become less resilient than in earlier years, consulting fewer advisers and, in the case of the covenant of the league, refusing to discuss his ideas with either congressional or foreign leaders.

The last day of the visit, Wilson and House conferred nearly the whole afternoon, spending part of the time "on the lawn in the sun with Mrs. Coolidge and Sir William Wiseman." As the visit neared its end, House concluded that "the President looks a different man from what he did when he arrived. He feels rested and looks it." But Wilson complained that "his mind was becoming 'leaky'" and explained that he now asked officials who had conferred with him to write memoranda of what they had agreed upon. House spoke to Edith about her husband's "over-burdened mind" and urged him to delegate more work to others. Edith, however, was unsympathetic, responding that when he "delegated it [work] to others he found it was not well done."[33]

At 8:00 PM on August 19, the presidential party left on its special train. Gordon, Janet, House, and Loulie went to Magnolia Station to see Woodrow, Edith, and Grayson off. The president had had a good time, writing his daughter Jessie that "our little stay on 'the north shore' refreshed us very much indeed and it was quite long enough . . . . We were beautifully taken care of and have fallen back into the old routine with a new zest and freshness."[34]

As the summer drew to a close, the tide of battle on the Western Front shifted decisively toward the Allies. After the British Expeditionary Force's rout of the Germans at the battle of Amiens, General Foch was determined to "give the enemy no respite," and in early September ordered American, British, and French forces to attack all along the Western Front. Both Foch and Haig now sensed that the war might end in the autumn of 1918. On September 12, the American First Army (established on August 10), along with some French forces, attacked the St. Mihiel Salient, which had been under German occupation for four years. By nightfall of the next day it was cleared; the Americans had recovered more than 200 square miles of French territory.[35]

House also realized that Allied successes might bring an end to the war before the spring and summer of 1919, before Pershing's vision of a fully independent American Army could be fulfilled. On September 3 he wrote the president a long, prophetic letter, warning that American power might be greater in the autumn of 1918 than at a peace conference in 1919 and asking Wilson if the time had not come "to try to commit the Allies to some of the things for which we are fighting?" House predicted that since the war was going so well, the leadership of the Allied governments was unlikely to change and that Wilson "should count upon having to reckon with Lloyd George, Clemenceau, and Sonnino and their kind." The president had, to be sure, widespread if somewhat diminished support along liberal and labor groups in Britain and France, but it would not, House predicted, "be steadfast or powerful enough to compel the reactionaries in authority to yield at the Peace Conference to American aims." If they "come to the [peace] congress flushed with victory, no appeal that you can make over their heads will be successful. In each country there will be men of vision and loftiness of purpose who will rally to your support, but they will be in the minority and their voices will be heard faintly by the great exultant throng intoxicated not alone by victory but by the thought of freedom from war."

In short, House wanted Wilson to engage in diplomacy, in give-and-take with Allies leaders, and to focus on securing the agreement of the British, French, Italian, and Japanese governments to the covenant of the League of Nations. If such a document could be agreed upon and made public, House believed that the opposition to a league in the United States would be swept away. If Wilson took a western trip in September, he urged him to give speeches that would "clear the way for further action."[36]

While House awaited Wilson's reply, he learned on September 7 that McAdoo would arrive on a special train that evening and spend the night. In order that he and the secretary of the treasury could talk without interruption, Loulie "took her dinner upstairs so that we might be alone for dinner and until bed time." Like House, McAdoo had noticed "signs" that his father-in-law would be a candidate for a third term. House agreed, and urged his protégé to carry on his duties and "leave his fate in the hands of Providence."[37] House revealed to McAdoo the difficulties of his position, complaining about the president's unreasonable expectations.[38] But he did not mention that whatever his complaints, his friendship with Wilson had brought him power and fame. Walter Lippmann, writing to Sidney Mezes from Paris, noted the four Americans who had entered the "consciousness" of the people of Europe. The president had become "a figure of mystical proportions, of really incredible power but altogether out of reach of direct contact"; House had become "the Human Intercessor, the Comforter, the Virgin Mary"; Hoover "incarnates all that is at once effective and idealistic in the picture of America"; and finally Pershing, "about whom there is heartfelt enthusiasm among the troops and a very deep respect everywhere."[39]

On September 11, House and Wiseman left the North Shore and drove to Chestnut Hill, Massachusetts, where they had expected to relax for a few days with Mona and Randolph Tucker. But they found House's son-in-law ill with influenza and motored on to New York, arriving on September 13. Looking back over the summer, House concluded that "it has been a busy and strenuous summer but successful from many points of view."[40]

28

The End of the War

On the morning of September 21, House received a call from the White House, asking him to leave for Washington that very night. The weather had turned cooler and the president was eager to consult with his counselor. When Edward arrived the next morning, he sat with the Wilsons as they ate their breakfast and learned that the president had no interest, as House had suggested, in negotiating with the Allies, but had written a speech outlining American war aims. After lunch he read it to House, who suggested only a few changes, and the two men agreed that Wilson would deliver the address at a Liberty Loan rally in New York on September 27.[1]

While House focused on international politics, the president and many of his advisers worried about the precarious position of the Democratic Party and its prospects in the congressional elections in early November. Some Senate and House Democrats, elected from normally Republican states or districts in 1916, were now vulnerable, and pressing sectional issues—such as the administration's decision to impose price controls on wheat but not on cotton—imperiled Democratic congressmen in the Midwest. As Allied prospects on the Western Front improved, Republican leaders, aware of the high stakes of the election, focused less on Wilson's management of the war and more on his terms for ending it. Or as Senator Henry Cabot Lodge declared, "It cannot be a peace of bargain. The only peace for us is one that rests on. . . unconditional surrender . . . . [We] must go to Berlin and there dictate peace." The rising tide of partisanship was engulfing leaders in both parties.[2]

During House's two-day stay at the White House the president sought his advice on several pressing political questions. Prohibition advocates had attached a "bone-dry" rider to an appropriation bill, and Postmaster General Burleson and Tumulty—both ardent anti-prohibitionists—urged

Wilson to veto it. House thought it best to leave the bill alone but was unfamiliar with the issue and "did not press" his point of view. Nor did House seem interested in the congressional campaign. On May 27, Wilson had declared that "politics is adjourned" for the duration of the war, but now, pressed by his advisers and by Democratic candidates, he told House that "he intended making a speech or writing a letter about two weeks before the elections, asking the people to return a democratic House." Two years earlier House had been deeply involved in Wilson's presidential campaign; now he "did not express any opinion as to the wisdom of this [a presidential appeal]."[3]

On September 27, three days after House's return to New York, he and Loulie met the presidential party in the early afternoon at Pennsylvania Station. After stopping briefly at the Waldorf Astoria Hotel, Wilson's motorcade drove up Fifth Avenue to House's apartment at 115 East 53rd Street. Once in the apartment—where the telephone had been cut off to ensure privacy—the president and his counselor considered the appeal of the Bulgarian government for an armistice. After House read the draft of Wilson's response, he convinced him to ignore Lansing's advice and not to specify any terms. Both men condemned the clumsy diplomacy of the secretary of state. Wilson concluded that "Lansing was so stupid that he was constantly afraid he would commit some serious blunder," while House "could not but confess that he was stupid. He seems less alert than when he first became Secretary of State, and I wonder whether his health has not made this difference."[4]

In the evening, Wilson, Edith, Margaret Wilson, Cary Grayson, Thomas Watt Gregory, and Jessie Jones (a Houston businessman), joined House and Loulie for dinner at their apartment. Then the entire party drove to the Metropolitan Opera House, which was crowded with dignitaries and "beautifully decorated" for what was an "historic occasion."[5]

In this address the president declared that the conflict had become "a peoples' war" and that "all agreed that there can be no peace obtained by any kind of bargain or compromise with the governments of the Central Empires." The key to a "*secure* and *lasting* peace" would be a League of Nations, which would be the "most essential part of the peace settlement itself." Beyond these general goals, Wilson listed more specific "particulars" of a peace settlement—"impartial justice" for all, no concessions to special leagues or alliances, no "selfish economic combinations," and no secret "international agreements and treaties." The peoples of the world, he concluded, did not want the terms of a settlement; they wanted "the final triumph of justice and fair dealing."[6]

After the address, Wilson asked House to ride with him back to the Waldorf, where he was "flushed with excitement and altogether pleased with the day's effort." But House seemed unenthusiastic about the speech, noting that Wilson "read his address," and speculating that "most of it seemed somewhat over the heads of his audience." He wondered how the press would receive it.[7] In fact, much of the American press praised the president's speech, but the Republican opposition was circumspect. And no leaders of the Allied governments endorsed the president's exalted pronouncements. Wilson had pushed the idea of a League of Nations to the center of the nation's political stage, but he had provided few details about how it would operate or rallied Democrats and moderate Republicans to his cause. In fact, he still seemed convinced, despite the draft covenant that he and House had written, that the procedures of the new organization would slowly evolve—"organically"—and "gradually become the law of the world."[8]

Throughout September, Germany's military situation continued to deteriorate. The German army, demoralized and confronting a shortage of men, weapons, and munitions, faced a crisis of effectiveness; in contrast, Allied and American armies had become over the course of the summer even more formidable. American troops provided a crucial edge in manpower, while British and French forces, relying on new technology and new tactics, had at last achieved a decisive advantage over their enemy.

By the end of September, Germany's situation was desperate. On September 29, Bulgaria surrendered, and leaders in Berlin realized that both the Austro-Hungarian and Ottoman Empires were on the verge of collapse. Powerful Allied and American armies had begun a coordinated offensive all along the Western Front, overrunning the Hindenburg Line and inflicting heavy casualties on German defenders. Ludendorff now panicked, informing the general staff on October 1 that the war could not be won. The Allies, he warned, could soon gain "a *great* victory, a *breakthrough in grand style*." The High Command wanted a quick end to the war and the formation of a new government, one representing the majority parties in the Reichstag, that would sue for peace. On the evening of October 3, Prince Max von Baden, a moderate Bavarian aristocrat, became chancellor, and two days later the German government sent a note to Wilson, asking for peace negotiations based on the Fourteen Points. Germany's ruling elite hoped for either a moderate peace—in which their nation could keep many of its territorial gains—or a breathing space in which the army, if necessary, could regroup and fight on.⁹

On October 6, Germany's peace note arrived in Washington. House sensed the excitement in the air, noting that "these are momentous days." He quickly wrote the president, warning that the armistice terms proposed by the Germans were unacceptable; even so, House realized the importance of the German note, explaining that "With Foch hammering on the west and with you driving the diplomatic wedge deeper, it is within the range of possibilities that the war may be over by the end of the year."¹⁰

The next day, October 7, House learned through Auchincloss that the president wanted him to come to Washington "immediately." An hour after receiving this summons House boarded the train at Pennsylvania Station and arrived at the White House at 9:00 PM, where he and Wilson waited for Secretary of State Lansing. All three men agreed that Germany's appeal should not be rejected, but the president's first draft, House believed, was too conciliatory. He warned the president that the American people would not accept what he had written. The president and his counselor— Lansing took little part in the discussion—worked on a new draft until 1:00 in the morning, when they decided to go to bed. House realized that Wilson was entering dangerous, uncharted terrain.¹¹

The next morning, as Wilson and House gathered in the president's study after breakfast, Wilson read an account of the Senate debate over the German request for an armistice. Every senator who spoke, he must have noticed, demanded unconditional surrender. House now found that Wilson had "come around" to his own point of view. After finishing a final draft, Wilson and House decided to try it out on Tumulty, who had urged an unqualified rejection of the German note. The president's secretary, while not enthusiastic about the proposed reply, felt that it would be accepted by the American people.¹²

The American response, dispatched to Berlin on October 8, adopted the delaying tactics that House had recommended. Rather than accepting or rejecting the German note, it asked the German government three questions: First, was it, in fact, accepting without any reservations the Fourteen Points and Wilson's subsequent pronouncements as a basis for negotiations? Second, would it demonstrate its good faith by withdrawing its forces from all invaded territories? Finally, was the chancellor "speaking merely for the constituted authorities of the Empire who have so far conducted the war?" Wilson and House had put German authorities on the defensive.[13]

Three days after Edward returned to New York, on October 11, Wilson and Edith arrived to march in the Liberty Loan campaign and to attend a benefit concert at the Metropolitan Opera House. The next day the Houses and Wilsons dined at the Waldorf Astoria, along with Jessie and Frank Sayre, Helen Bones, and Cary Grayson. Just before dinner was served, Tumulty came in with the news that the German government had accepted the president's terms. After dinner, the presidential party went to the concert, but House was "so stirred by the news that had come from Berlin that I could not listen to the program." Shortly after 10:00 PM he returned home, where he thought about the momentous event that was now beginning to unfold. "I did not try to sleep for a long while," he recorded, "for it seemed to me that the war was finished, certainly finished if the Allied statesmen have the judgment to garner victory." On October 13, the president and his counselor returned to Washington, where they had to digest the second German note and craft a suitable reply.[14]

When Wilson's note of October 8 had arrived in Berlin, Ludendorff was less gloomy over his army's condition and convinced that if America's terms were too harsh Germany could continue the war into 1919. Some on the right wanted to break off negotiations and continue to resist through a *levee en masse*, but Prince Max and his ministers, aware of the widespread longing for peace among the German people, had lost confidence in Ludendorff and the High Command. On October 12 they dispatched a reply to Washington that answered some, but not all, of the president's questions. That same day a U-boat sank the British steamer SS *Leinster* in the Irish Sea, with the loss of nearly 200 American and English passengers.[15]

Immediately after breakfast on October 14, Wilson and House began working on a reply to the German note. This time the president and his counselor, fearful of alienating the American people and the Allied governments, realized that they must harden the American response. The second American note, dispatched to Berlin on October 14, took a harder line, insisting that the United States would only accept an armistice that was approved by Allied and American military leaders and that guaranteed the military supremacy of American, British, and French forces. Wilson also insisted that Germany must discontinue its "illegal and inhumane practices" on land and on sea and that the current German government constituted the kind of arbitrary power which the United States had opposed during the war. "It is indispensable," he concluded, "that the governments associated against Germany should know beyond a peradventure with whom they are dealing."[16]

Throughout October, as notes passed back and forth between Washington and Berlin, anxiety grew among Allied leaders, who resented Wilson's unilateral conduct of peace negotiations. On the night of October 12, when the German response to Wilson's inquiries reached London, Lloyd George's private secretary recorded that "There is awful language going on upstairs. I can tell you! He thinks that the Allies are now in a devil of a mess. Wilson has promised them an armistice." Whatever their feelings about the American president, Lloyd George and Clemenceau also realized that rejecting an armistice and prolonging the war into 1919 would only put the United States in a more commanding position. When Allied leaders gathered in Paris from October 6 to 9 to consider ceasefire conditions, they learned that Marshal Foch wanted Allied forces to occupy all the territory, including the east bank of the Rhine River, that they would wish to control in the final peace treaty. While they reached no agreement on the military terms for an armistice, it was clear that the British and French governments had no intention of allowing Wilson to dictate the terms on which the war would end.[17]

As Wilson and House had completed the drafting of the second American note to Germany, the president realized that the time had come to dispatch his counselor to Europe to negotiate with the Allies on the terms of the armistice. House, he confided to Wiseman, "knows my mind entirely; but you must ask them [British leaders] to realize though how hard it is for me to spare him. On many problems he is the only person I can consult." After dinner on October 14, Wilson wrote a letter of credentials, designating House his "personal representative" at the meetings of the Supreme War Council. Their last evening together in the White House the two friends, worn out by their labors during the day, avoided serious matters, although they agreed on a secret code. As House left to catch the midnight train to New York, Wilson remarked that " 'I have not given you any instructions because I feel you will know what to do.' " House could not help but wonder "at the strange situation our relations have brought about. I am going on one of the most important missions anyone ever undertook, and yet there is no word of direction, advice or discussion between us."[18]

After returning to New York, House wrote Wilson that "I am leaving with a deep sense of gratitude for the opportunity to serve which you are giving me," while Edith wrote her "dear 'Comrade'" thanking him for her birthday card and violets and reassuring him that "We miss you dreadfully and I can't bear to think you are going so far away, but—"Tell *em* We are coming too"! and do take good care of yourself."[19]

The day before House left for Europe he arranged for Wiseman to lunch with the president and to give him a report on their conversation. Armed with this more detailed account of the president's views, House boarded the U.S.S. *Northern Pacific* on a foggy evening on October 17. House's entourage included Loulie and Fanny, of course, as well as Gordon Auchincloss, Joseph Grew (a career diplomat), Admiral Benson, Frank Cobb (an editorial writer for the *New York World*), a naval surgeon, and five or six clerks and stenographers. Through the first three days of the long, eight-day voyage, the *Northern Pacific* encountered rough seas that left many members of the House party sick.[20]

While House crossed the Atlantic, the president continued his exchange of notes with the German government. His second note of October 14, laying down strict conditions for an armistice, caused consternation along leaders in Berlin, who now realized that they must accept American terms or break off peace negotiations. After receiving further German concessions, Wilson agreed on October 23 to convey Germany's request for an armistice to the Allies, but he imposed still further conditions on the German government.[21] Wilson's final note, like those that preceded it, turned out to be a triumph for American diplomacy. He had drawn the German government into peace negotiations, induced sweeping constitutional changes in Germany, and brought about an end to the war sooner than most observers had thought possible.[22]

Two days after leaving New York, House learned of the President's appeal for a Democratic Congress. Pressed by his political advisers and dismayed by fierce Republican attacks on his administration, Wilson had, on October 19, asked the American people to avoid a "repudiation of my leadership" and to return a Democratic majority to the House and Senate on November 5. If the president, House noted, had asked the American people to reelect members of Congress who had supported "American war aims, regardless of party, he would be in a safe position." But his partisan appeal was a "needless venture"; House now regretted that during his last visit to Washington he had not spoken out against it.[23]

On October 25, the *Northern Pacific* arrived at Brest, where the dense fog made landing difficult. Once in Paris, House spent a few days at the Hôtel

de Crillon, and then moved his party to a "spacious and comfortable residence" on the Left Bank at 78 Rue de l'Université.[24]

House now confronted the most difficult diplomatic challenge of his
career. The president wanted him to impose American war aims, embodied in the Fourteen Points, on the Allies. But Clemenceau, Lloyd George,
and Orlando were wily and experienced leaders who realized that these
pre-armistice negotiations were the first step in achieving their national
aspirations. Wilson's views could not be ignored, but neither was the
United States in a position to impose its will on the Allies. The American
government had, to be sure, contributed huge quantities of men, money,
and materiel to the Allied war effort, but the strength of the American
Expeditionary Force would not peak until the spring of 1919, when it
would have been the dominant force on the Western Front. During the
final hundred days of the war, however, the British and French armies had
led the way in the battle against Germany while Pershing's First Army
bogged down on the Meuse-Argonne battlefield.[25]

For over four years Britain and France (Italy entered on May 20, 1915) had
fought in a conflict that had brought the mobilization of their entire nations
and unprecedented death and destruction. Of the 4,822,000 Allied war
dead, Britain and its Dominions had lost 921,000, France 1,398,000, Italy
578,000, and Russia 1,811,000. The United States, which had fought for a
little over a year and a half, had lost 114,000 killed in action. Given the scale
of Allied sacrifices,[26] it seemed unlikely that Allied leaders would allow the
distant American president or his representative in Paris to dominate the
armistice negotiations.

On October 26, after a short night's sleep, House plunged into a series of
meetings with important Americans and foreigners. "I do not know how,"
he recorded, "I have lived through the day." For the next three days these
meetings continued as he sought to discover the attitude of Allied leaders
toward a peace based on the Fourteen Points. House learned that Bliss,
Haig, and Milner favored moderate armistice terms, while Clemenceau,
who "received me with open arms," gave him far harsher terms drawn
up by Foch. The prime minister and his general were convinced that
"Germany was so thoroughly beaten she would accept any terms offered."[27]

Despite the crucial importance of the Fourteen Points, which Wilson
had declared on January 8, 1918, neither the president nor his counselor had
bothered to explain them in more detail. Not until October 28, the day
before he began negotiations with Allied leaders, did House direct Walter

Lippmann, who had joined his staff, to prepare an elaboration for his meeting the next morning. Lippmann had no documents with him, but with the help of Frank Cobb, he finally finished at 3:00 AM.[28]

On October 29, House settled into a pattern of meetings that would last for the next seven days. In the mornings he generally held informal conversations with the prime ministers and foreign ministers and some of their aides—Lloyd George and Balfour, Clemenceau and Pichon, Orlando and Sonnino (and Maurice Hankey, secretary of the British War Cabinet)—which were sometimes held at the Quai d'Orsay, sometimes at the War Office, and sometimes at House's residence at 78 Rue de l'Université. The actual decisions were made at these gatherings, which served as a steering committee, while the much larger meetings of the Supreme War Council, which began on October 31, reviewed and then confirmed them.[29]

On October 29, House discovered the true magnitude of his task; Auchincloss noted that "The Colonel is up against an awful stiff proposition, and if he pulls through he will indeed be a wonder." Clemenceau and Lloyd George pointed out that their governments had never been consulted about Wilson's proposed peace terms, and Lloyd George objected to the second of the Fourteen Points guaranteeing freedom of the seas. Confronted with British, French, and Italian reservations to the Fourteen Points, House warned that Allied resistance to Wilson's program might lead to a separate peace between the United States and Germany. He believed that this vague threat had "a very exciting effect upon those present," but Lloyd George seemed unfazed, responding that "we should deeply regret it, but, nevertheless, should be prepared to go on fighting." With the discussion at an impasse, all the participants agreed that the British, French, and Italian governments should put together a memorandum listing their exceptions to the Fourteen Points. As the meeting drew to a close, Lloyd George made the crucial observation—which House did not refute—that, aside from clause two dealing with freedom of the seas, "the others of the Fourteen Points appear to him sufficiently elastic to enable us to put our own interpretation upon them." The British prime minister had dominated the meetings of the first day; he was, one of his associates noted, "very amusing on the way in which he and Clemenceau had pushed poor House about over 14 points. He. . . had made it quite clear that we would sooner carry on the war single-handed than agree to the 'freedom of the seas.' "[30]

House conveyed the substance of the discussions, along with French and Italian objections to a League of Nations, to the president, who instructed his counselor that he could not accept a settlement that did not include a commitment to freedom of the seas and the League of Nations. Early in the morning of October 30, House, awakened by messengers on motorcycles, decided that he would now threaten a public break with the Allies, warning the three prime ministers that unless they accepted the Fourteen Points as the basis for the peace, the president would go before Congress and ask if the United States should make peace with Germany or continue fighting in order to achieve Allied war aims. "Unless," he cabled Washington, "we deal with these people with a firm hand everything we have been fighting for will be lost." As he prepared for the day's meetings, he "had a feeling of great satisfaction. . . knowing I had found a solution of a very troublesome problem." The Allies would "not dare take the responsibility of continuing the war without us."[31]

House believed that on the second day of meetings, everything had "changed for the better." Meeting in the morning with Clemenceau and Lloyd George, he found the British prime minister in a more conciliatory mood. Lloyd George handed him a draft note in which the Allied governments agreed to make peace with Germany on the basis of the Fourteen Points and Wilson's subsequent addresses, with two reservations: First, they pointed out that the clause on the freedom of the seas "is open to various interpretations, some of which they could not accept. They must therefore reserve to themselves complete freedom on this subject when they enter the peace conference." Second, they insisted that Wilson's declaration that invaded territories must be evacuated and restored meant that Germany must pay compensation "for all damage done to the civilian population of the Allies, and their property by land, by sea, and from the air." House, worried that Clemenceau and Sonnino would submit reservations of their own, now employed his threat of a public break. "Clemenceau and Lloyd George," he recorded, "looked at each other significantly," and the French prime minister quickly accepted the British draft note.[32]

Clemenceau's conciliatory attitude was no doubt linked to House's acceptance of the harsh armistice terms devised by Marshal Foch, especially his insistence on the occupation of the Rhineland. Despite Lloyd George's objections, House sympathized with the French demands, accepting Clemenceau's "word of honor that France would withdraw after the peace conditions had been fulfilled." House had, in effect, ignored Wilson's instructions. While the president wanted an armistice that would prevent a renewal of hostilities by Germany, he also wanted one that would be "moderate and reasonable within that condition." He had especially questioned Allied occupation of the east bank of the Rhine, which was "practically an invasion of German soil under armistice."[33]

On October 31, the third day of deliberations, House was optimistic, giving the president the sweeping reassurance that "nothing will be done to embarrass you or to compromise any of your peace principles." Wilson seemed willing to accept his counselor's assessment, cabling him that "I am proud of the way you are handling the situation." He was dissatisfied, however, with the Allied position on the freedom of the seas and rejected Lloyd George's suggestion that the United States and the Allies should get together "before the peace conference and thresh out their differences." Wilson had no intention of reducing the peace conference to a "mere form."[34]

On the morning of November 1, House and Allied leaders went over the naval and military terms of the armistice. Lloyd George and Haig worried that Foch's insistence on bridgeheads on the east bank of the Rhine was too extreme, leaving Allied forces only two miles from Frankfurt. But Foch was adamant, and House, while he did not play a major part in the discussions, was inclined "to leave the matter in Marshal Foch's hands." Abandoned by Pershing, who wanted to keep fighting, he chose to appease Clemenceau and Foch rather than support the more moderate British position.[35] The following day House remained preoccupied with resolving his "difficulties with the Prime Minister" over the freedom of the seas and avoiding "a violent controversy with George just now."[36]

Finally, on November 3, in what he described as "a red letter day," House concluded that he had "brought Lloyd George to terms concerning the 'freedom of the seas,'" and that he had "won a distinct victory." First in a morning meeting, and again in the afternoon, House pressed the British prime minister to accept the principle of the freedom of the seas. Lloyd George refused to do so, but finally agreed to write House a letter in which he confirmed his modest assertion that "we were quite willing to discuss [at the peace conference] the freedom of the seas in the light of the new conditions which have arisen in the course of the present war."[37] Wiseman concluded that his mentor had won "one of the greatest diplomatic triumphs in history," while Auchincloss recorded in his diary that "Before we get through with these fellows over here we will teach them how to do things and to do them quickly." House agreed with his sycophantic protégés, recording that "the diplomatic battle of the past few days has resulted in a complete victory . . . . I have had to persuade; I have had to threaten, but the result is worth all my endeavors."[38]

After pondering his alleged success for two days, House cabled the president that "we have won a great diplomatic victory . . . . I doubt whether any of the heads of the Governments with whom we have been dealing quite realize how far they are now committed to the American peace program."[39] Lloyd George, however, presented a different version of events to the Imperial War Cabinet in London. He was convinced that he had refused to accept the American position on the freedom of the seas and that the vagueness of the Fourteen Points did not threaten British interests. Where disagreements existed, the British government had clearly stated its dissent, and it appeared that the president had no objections to the territorial objectives of Britain and its Dominions. In short, the prime minister envisaged a peace settlement that would be as much British as American.[40]

Despite his extravagant claims, House's success in these pre-armistice negotiations was more apparent than real. He had faced a daunting set of circumstances: the war had ended too soon, before American power had become overwhelming; the Allies had been emboldened by victory; and he had been handicapped by Wilson's unrealistic expectations and his own weaknesses as a negotiator. The pre-armistice agreement, as events would prove, did not commit the Allies to all that much. The issue of freedom of the seas, on which House had expended so much effort, was never even discussed at the peace conference, while on the key issue of reparations, on which Wilson had provided no instructions, House had made major concessions. While House stumbled as a negotiator, Clemenceau quickly gave up his opposition to the Fourteen Points and focused on the real issues for France: reparations and security against any future German attack. He knew what House did not see clearly—that the military terms of the armistice, once in place, would be difficult to reverse at the peace conference.[41]

On November 6, House learned that the Republicans had won the congressional elections, gaining a majority of forty-five seats in the House and two in the Senate, and placing the bitter opponent of Wilson's peace program, Henry Cabot Lodge, as chairman of the Senate Foreign Relations Committee in the new Congress. The Wilson coalition of 1916 had weakened. While the voters had primarily been concerned with domestic issues, not with Wilson's peace program, the president realized that the results "made his difficulties enormously greater." His counselor agreed, noting that "I am afraid it will make our work harder at the Peace Conference and, heavens knows, it will be hard enough."[42]

While House and Allied prime ministers deliberated in Paris, events had moved rapidly in Germany. Wilson's third note, which arrived in Berlin on October 23, made it clear that peace would depend on the kaiser's abdication and on the army's renunciation of power to a new civilian government. On October 28 the German constitution was revised, making the chancellor responsible to the Reichstag and giving that body control over foreign and military affairs. The next day, Ludendorff resigned and a naval rebellion broke out at Kiel, quickly spreading to other parts of the country. As revolutionary agitation grew, some parts of Germany seemed on the verge of civil war. Finally, on November 9 the kaiser, learning that he had lost the support of the army, fled to Holland. That same day Prince Max announced his abdication and handed the government over to Friedrich Ebert, the leader of the Social Democratic Party, and a new German Republic was proclaimed. Germany was finally ready to make peace.[43]

On the morning of November 8, German delegates crossed the front lines under a flag of truce and made their way to Foch's railway car on a siding in the dense woods of Compiègne. There Foch gave them the terms of the armistice which were not, Wilson and House must have realized, in the spirit of the Fourteen Points. They included the evacuation of Belgium, France (including Alsace and Lorraine), and Luxemburg; the Allied occupation of the western bank of the Rhine River and the creation of three bridgeheads across the Rhine at Coblenz, Mainz, and Cologne; the surrender of enormous quantities of military and railroad equipment; the withdrawal of all German troops in the east behind Germany's 1914 frontiers; the surrender and internment of the German battle fleet; and the requirement that Germany "make reparation for damages done" in Belgium and northern France.[44]

The stunned German delegates conveyed the terms to the government in Berlin, which accepted them on November 10. The next morning the armistice was finally signed; 1,597 days had passed since the Archduke Franz Ferdinand had entered Sarajevo on a state visit and had been assassinated, precipitating what the historian and diplomat George Kennan describes as "*the* great seminal catastrophe of this [the twentieth] century." The war had transformed Europe, devastating its infrastructure, decimating a generation of young men, sweeping away old dynasties, and bringing new ideologies and revolutionary movements to power. Nor, despite the unprecedented destruction of the conflict, did it seem likely to bring peace to a troubled continent.[45]

In Paris, House watched intently as the war drew to a close. On November 10 he stayed up until midnight, keeping in touch with Clemenceau and the negotiations between Foch and the German delegates. At 5:30 AM on November 11, fifteen minutes after the actual signing took place, he received word that the war had ended, and telegraphed the president: "Autocracy is dead—Long live democracy and its immortal leader— In this great hour my heart goes out to you in pride, admiration and love."[46]

In Washington, Wilson learned of the signing at 3:00 AM, and he and Edith, she remembered, "stood mute—unable to grasp the full significance of the words." At 12:30 PM Wilson left for the Capitol, where half an hour later, before a joint session of Congress, he declared that the war had attained its objectives and that the victorious nations had now united "to set up such a peace as will satisfy the longing of the whole world for disinterested justice." In the evening, the president and Edith drove through the crowded streets of Washington, watching the celebrations, and, when they returned to the White House, sat on a couch in Edith's room and talked until the early hours of the morning. Then Wilson read a chapter of the Bible and went to bed. He surely realized, as the liberal journalist Ray Stannard Baker wrote a few days before the armistice, that he "has yet to prove his greatness. The fate of a drama lies in its last act, and Wilson is now coming to that."[47]

PART V

Peacemaking, 1919–1920

29

Waiting for the Peace Conference

By the end of the war, four great empires—the Austro-Hungarian, German, Ottoman, and Russian—had collapsed, bringing the breakdown of the prewar order in Central and Eastern Europe. In the aftermath of war, starvation spread across large parts of Europe, the great influenza epidemic killed millions of civilians on both sides of the Atlantic, and Bolshevism threatened to move beyond Russia into other parts of the Continent. The leaders of the victorious powers, having fought a war of unprecedented violence and destruction, now faced the perplexing task of constructing a new postwar order, one that would justify the enormous sacrifices of the conflict. "At Paris," Walter Lippmann wrote, "men looked out upon two continents in revolt, upon conflicts and aspirations more intricate and more obscure than any they had ever been called to resolve."[1]

The end of the war brought more immediate questions for the president and his advisers. Where would the peace conference be held, who would lead the American delegation, and who would Wilson select to negotiate with the Allies? On October 28, three days after arriving in France, House raised the issue of the location of the conference with Allied leaders. Clemenceau preferred Versailles, while House and Lloyd George thought it best to hold the conference in a neutral city such as Geneva or Lausanne, Switzerland.[2] Initially the president agreed, but then changed his mind, informing House on November 8 that "Versailles may be the best place for the Peace Conference." The president's decision did not please House, who wanted to avoid the poisoned atmosphere of a belligerent capital. While Lloyd George and Orlando had still to agree, it now seemed almost certain that the French capital would be the site of the gathering.[3]

In mid-August, nearly three months before the end of the war, House had concluded that were the president to attend the peace conference it would be best if he did not sit on the American delegation and instead continued his role as an outside observer. The armistice negotiations confirmed House's belief, if he ever had any doubts, that he possessed superior diplomatic skills. He had gone to Europe on special missions every year of the war, beginning in the summer of 1914, and by the end of the conflict had met leaders in Berlin, London, and Paris and become especially familiar with Britain's ruling elite. House fervently hoped that Wilson, whatever the length of his stay in Europe, would make him the head of the American peace commission.[4]

He was, however, badly out of touch with the president's convictions. The peace conference represented the culmination of Wilson's career, an opportunity for him to convince Allied leaders to conclude a peace of justice that would embody his vision of a new international order. In the realm of foreign affairs he had not groomed, with the possible exception of House, what one historian describes as "strong, trustworthy lieutenants"; instead he had held the strands of policy mostly in his own hands. And while Wilson regarded House as a valuable emissary, he had always viewed him as a counselor, not as a statesman, and during the armistice negotiations may have developed some doubts about House's ability as a diplomat.[5] Despite widespread misgivings among American officials in Washington, Wilson told his cabinet on November 12 that he would attend the peace conference. "It is now my duty," he later explained to Congress, "to play my full part in making good what they [American soldiers] offered their life's blood to obtain. I can think of no call to service which can transcend this."[6]

On November 14, House, unaware of the president's decision, cabled Wilson that "Americans here whose opinions are of value are practically unanimous in the belief that it would be unwise for you to sit in the Peace Conference." House's advice surprised and upset the president, who was clearly eager to impose his will on Allied leaders. Your telegram, he quickly responded, "upsets every plan we have made . . . . It is universally expected and generally desired here that I should attend the Conference, but I believe that no one would wish me to sit by and try to steer from the outside." On November 18, Wilson announced to the public that he would sail for France on December 3 and take part in the discussions leading to a settlement.[7]

House did not contest Wilson's decision, concluding that "he should come over and decide for himself" whether or not to attend the formal deliberations. He may have hoped that he could persuade the president, once he had arrived in Paris and consulted with Clemenceau, Lloyd George, and Orlando, to return to the United States and to place the leadership of the American delegation in his hands. On December 3, House wistfully concluded that "I wish in my soul the President had appointed me as Chairman of the Peace Delegation with McAdoo and Hoover as my associates. I could have attended to the political end, McAdoo to the financial, and Hoover to the economic end . . . . If I could have had these two men as associates and only these, I would have been willing to guarantee results."[8]

For many months House had pondered the selection of the American delegates to the peace conference. In mid-August, when Wilson had visited him at Magnolia, he had urged the president to save a place for a prominent Republican, either Elihu Root, Theodore Roosevelt, or William Howard Taft (House preferred Root). Once back in New York, he focused on another prominent Republican, Governor Samuel Walker McCall of Massachusetts, and over lunch on October 13 "put [him] through his paces." Wilson tentatively accepted McCall, who, he and his counselor agreed, would join the president, House, Lansing, and Secretary of War Newton Baker to complete the five-man delegation.[9]

Once in Europe, House lost track of the selection process. The president decided against the appointment of Governor McCall and learned from Baker that, given McAdoo's resignation from the cabinet (on November 14, 1918), he, Baker, ought to stay in Washington to look after national affairs. At Baker's suggestion, Wilson turned to General Bliss, the American representative on the Supreme War Council, as his replacement. As the fifth member of the delegation he chose Henry White, an elderly diplomat and Republican who had served as American ambassador to France and who was close to Lodge and Roosevelt. On November 29, the White House announced the appointment of the five peace commissioners. His friend's selections disappointed House. He thought highly of Bliss, but observed in his diary that "Lansing and White are weak and will be of little help. As a matter of fact, the President should have appointed a Republican of the standing of Root. He has made again one of his common mistakes."[10]

Some of the president's selections met with derision from the Republican opposition. Lansing and Bliss appeared to be acceptable delegates, but

House and White were regarded as weak appointments and Republican critics complained that Wilson had chosen no senator or prominent Republican or, aside from the president himself, any figure of national stature. But the president had, in fact, faced a virtually insoluble dilemma. Had he selected any senator he would have had to choose Lodge, soon to be chairman of the Foreign Relations Committee; nor did he feel he could work with Root, Roosevelt, or Taft, given their ideological differences and the bitter residue of the 1918 campaign. As a keen student of American politics, Wilson knew, of course, that he would need help in guiding the peace treaty through the Senate, but he was no longer capable of reaching out to the Republican opposition. As he approached the great gathering in Paris, he was determined to keep a free hand and to pursue a solitary course.[11]

The period from the signing of the Armistice on November 11 to the president's arrival in France on December 13 was a busy one for House. He was especially concerned about disorder in many parts of Europe and the urgent need for food relief to stem the tide of revolutionary unrest. House proposed a plan, which Wilson quickly accepted,[12] for the creation of an international relief organization under the leadership of Herbert Hoover, and he worked closely with Hoover, after his arrival in Europe on November 26, to convince the Allies to accept the American proposal. Despite Allied resistance, in mid-December Hoover began to set up a relief organization in eighteen countries and in 1919 would become the dominant figure in the economic reconstruction of Europe.[13]

In the decade and a half before the outbreak of World War I, Hoover had traveled the world as an international mining engineer, reorganizing mines with such skill that he became a millionaire by the age of forty. In the summer of 1914, he was in London, yearning for a larger role in world affairs, and with the outbreak of war in August he organized aid for the thousands of American tourists who were stranded in Europe and eager to return home. Hoover then became chairman of the Commission for Relief in Belgium and, after America's entry into the war, the head of the Food Administration and in 1918 a member of Wilson's war cabinet. His administrative achievements brought him fame and great prestige, both at home and abroad; his energy, determination, and youthful appearance, as well as his dedication, idealism, and boundless capacity for work fascinated Americans; he seemed a rising star in American public life and inevitably, as the war progressed, speculation grew about his presidential ambitions.[14]

In February 1915, when House first met Hoover in London, he found him a "resourceful fellow." He quickly recognized Hoover's exceptional organizational skills and became his patron, drawing on his knowledge of European affairs and promoting him for various administrative positions. Hoover's dour, gloomy personality intrigued House, who, as we've seen, often commented on his protégé's pessimism and his lack of affability and charm. Despite these weaknesses, as 1918 drew to a close, House regarded Hoover as a formidable talent and believed that he, McAdoo, and Pershing would be the next presidential candidates. Hoover denied any presidential ambitions, but House concluded that "he is mistaken in believing he would not like to be president." Even as he prepared for the peace conference House looked ahead to 1920 and what would surely be a new political landscape.[15]

In the fall of 1918, House, stimulated by his wartime missions to Europe and by his contact with Allied leaders, had given considerable thought to the organization of the American peace commission and to the ways in which large international meetings worked. Before leaving for Europe on October 17 he had developed elaborate plans for the American commission, but the president seemed uncertain how to proceed. Wilson did not anticipate the stresses of what would later be called summit diplomacy. After House left for Europe, Wilson accepted a far more modest plan devised by Lansing, one that gave the State Department the dominant role in the American delegation's staff. He did so without consulting his counselor.[16]

By the middle of November, the exhilaration House and his aides felt at the end of the war had passed. Fanny was ready to return to the United States, although she realized that the peace conference would run into the spring. "I feel rather 'let down,'" she wrote her mother, "and tired of it all. I have been on a strain for five years and am ready to rest awhile. I believe Mr. House shares this feeling." Illness also affected the mood of House and his staff. Auchincloss complained that "all day long we live in an atmosphere of coughing" and wrote that "this is the most depressing atmosphere I have ever been in." On the morning of November 21, House awoke with a temperature of 101 degrees, and not until eight days later did he feel strong enough to leave his bed and go for a short drive. House concluded that "it has been a dark, dreary, sickly season in Paris."[17]

On December 3, the president, along with 113 staff members, left New York harbor on the SS *George Washington* for the ten-day voyage across the Atlantic. Six days later House realized that his mission to Europe, begun on October 26, had come to an end, since the president was in European waters and could easily be reached by wireless.[18] Initially he had planned to travel to Brest to greet the president when the *George Washington* arrived on December 13. Not only was it a historic occasion, but Janet Auchincloss and Nancy and Sidney Mezes were also on board. But at 3:00 PM when the *George Washington* swung into its anchorage outside the breakwater and Wilson and his party boarded a tender to reach the main dock, House was not there to greet Wilson and to witness the tumultuous welcome he received from the people of Brest as he drove to the railway station. Instead of going himself, House sent Auchincloss, who handed Wilson a letter from his father-in-law explaining that he "had not come down to Brest by reason of the Doctor's orders." The president, Auchincloss recorded, "readily understood and said he would much rather have the Colonel well than making trips around the country." But as House revealed in his own diary, he yielded to his doctor's advice because he had not wanted to witness the president's triumphal entry into France."[19]

At Brest the president and his party boarded a special overnight train to Paris, arriving at the Bois de Boulogne Station at 10:00 in the morning, where they were met by President Poincaré and Prime Minister Clémenceau. They then rode in eight carriages over a four-mile route lined by troops and massive crowds to the Murat Palace. Edith was overwhelmed, writing that "here the *world* seemed to be waiting to welcome and acclaim my wonderful husband."[20]

Later in the morning, House and Wilson finally met at the Murat Palace. House gave the president "a brief summary of the situation," reassuring him that relations with Great Britain and France were growing "steadily better" and making the astonishing claim that "our relations with Italy have always been good." House quickly discovered, no doubt to his relief, that Wilson disliked the men Lansing had chosen to head the state department's peace organization and that he would instead rely on the organization that House had built up.[21] At midday, House attended an elaborate luncheon for the president at the Elysée Palace, where Poincaré spoke without notes while Wilson read his remarks. House thought Wilson was "visibly nervous. I suppose it was on account of acting a new role and on a new stage and he was not sure of himself." After lunch the president and his counselor resumed their deliberations for two hours, going "over all matters of importance." House told Wilson of the arrangements he had made and urged him to make the League of Nations the center of his program. "Once that is a *fait accompli*," he optimistically reassured the president, "nearly all the very serious difficulties will disappear." Despite the urgings of both Wilson and Edith, he declined to stay for dinner.[22]

The next day, December 15, House greeted Wiseman, who had traveled to Paris from London. "When he is with me," House observed, "I often wonder how I got along while he was away." According to Wiseman's memorandum, House was pleased with his reunion with the president and relieved that Wilson had turned to him for advice and had "asked him to arrange his Secretariat and map out his program of work." Most important, House had allegedly persuaded the president to abandon his idea of sitting at the peace table as the head of the American delegation and instead to stay in the background and presumably designate House as the chief American negotiator. For House this would be the ideal arrangement, one that would allow him to remain in the limelight and use the president, as he had done during the pre-armistice negotiations, as a distant, somewhat menacing authority.[23]

Late in the afternoon, House brought Clemenceau and Wilson together for an hour, coaching each beforehand about what it would be appropriate to say in their initial encounter. Both men followed House's instructions and avoided controversial topics, but the prime minister surprised House by noting that he had changed his mind and now thought it would be a "good idea" if Wilson sat at the peace conference. Clemenceau had reopened an issue that House thought he had closed.[24]

House also sought to solidify his relationship with members of the Inquiry and the other three peace commissioners. He spent half an hour talking to Mezes and his specialists, and reached out to Henry White, Lansing, and Bliss. White impressed him as "a well meaning, accomplished old gentleman. . . [who] may be of some service later on," but he found the secretary of state "completely ignorant of most of the things with which he should be cognizant." "Lansing," he concluded, "is a man that one cannot grow enthusiastic over." House thought Bliss was a "scholarly, statesman-like soldier," but would be "of no value whatever from a political standpoint" and regretted that Wilson had not appointed "someone who would have been a political asset." He expected little from these three commissioners, noting that "the President and I are doing everything."[25]

Wilson wanted a more "serious conversation" with Clemenceau, so House arranged for a second meeting on December 19. For an hour and a half the prime minister mostly listened as Wilson explained his ideas about a peace settlement. Clemenceau seemed unimpressed with the president, telling Lord Derby (the British ambassador in Paris) that Wilson "was very amiable but shockingly ignorant of the European situation. They [Clemenceau and Poincaré] however thought on the whole he will not give much trouble."[26] House realized that Clemenceau had little faith in a League of Nations and concluded that "he believes in war. He has something of the Roosevelt idea that war ennobles." Despite these profound differences, he was drawn to the prime minister and sought to deepen his friendship with him, telling him "something of my career" and confiding that he would retire from politics after the end of Wilson's second term. Their "intimate talk" pleased House, who recorded, with obvious satisfaction, that "I have never had Clemenceau seize my hand with so much warmth and express so much feeling for me as he did after this talk."[27]

A day after his conversation with Clemenceau, the president had a contentious meeting with Prime Minister Orlando and Foreign Minister Sonnino. Wilson, who had studied the Treaty of London carefully while on the *George Washington*, urged the Italian leaders, without success, to reduce their territorial demands. In fact, they were expanding those demands, since the collapse of the Austro-Hungarian Empire had created a new situation in the Adriatic and on the Dalmatian Coast which Italian expansionists were eager to exploit.[28]

Even before Wilson's arrival, House complained of his "strenuous routine" and noted that "the days are filled from rising until bedtime." After December 13, he found that his workload increased even more. "The president," he observed, "cheerfully unloads matters upon me," and House worried that he would have to curtail his diary since "I am so busy up to bedtime that it is not possible for me to dictate [to Fanny] the happenings of the day." Despite the mounting pressure, House enjoyed his prominence and felt that "everything so far goes well." He was pleased when, at a dinner at the Italian embassy to meet the king of Italy, Victor Emanuel III paused and "expressed pleasure" as he moved down the reception line "at meeting me and said a few other complimentary words."[29]

Since the peace conference had been delayed until mid-January 1919,[30] House wanted the president to exploit his phenomenal popularity among the people of Europe, who, he believed, found in him "an exponent of their hopes for a better world and for a lasting peace." He also concluded that Wilson should visit England, where he would receive such an enthusiastic reception that "Lloyd George and his colleagues would not dare oppose his policies at the Peace Conference." The president quickly agreed, as did the British government, and he prepared to leave for London on December 26, return on December 31, and then leave for a brief visit to Italy on the evening of January 1, 1919.[31]

No doubt Wilson assumed that House would join him on this important visit, but on December 24, two days before his departure, House decided not to go and instead dispatched Auchincloss to London to assist the president. When Wilson realized that House would not accompany him, he was upset. Shortly before 11:00 in the evening on December 24 he telephoned his counselor and told him, House recorded, that "he was surprised and seemed disappointed that I was not going to England with him. He said he needed me to guide and counsel him."[32] Once he reached London, Auchincloss was surprised that his father-in-law would not soon join the president and his party, and warned him that "you will be making a grave mistake [if you do not come]." But House would not relent. Auchincloss concluded that "I am afraid the Colonel won't come to London because he doesn't want to and not because he has a cold." House had, after all, visited England five times since the summer of 1914 and had grown accustomed to having a free hand in his discussions with British leaders. He had no desire to travel to London and subordinate himself to the president.[33]

On December 26, Wilson received an enthusiastic welcome in London, where he and Edith were guests of the king and queen at Buckingham Palace. During the president's stay in England he delivered five major addresses and had a nearly three-hour talk with Lloyd George and Balfour, one that covered all of the major issues before the peacemakers and that revealed to British leaders that Wilson would be more reasonable than they had expected. If House had been primarily concerned with keeping in touch with the president's thoughts, he would have been a part of this conversation.[34]

On December 28, after he finished his speech at the Guildhall, Wilson learned the results of the British election that had taken place on December 14. When the campaign began, Lloyd George and his supporters emphasized problems of domestic reconstruction and called for a peace of moderation and justice; but as the campaign progressed and as they sensed the nationalistic mood of the electorate, they focused more and more on demands for a harsh peace with Germany and the alleged sympathy of the Labour Party with Bolshevism. The result was a triumph for the prime minister's coalition, especially for the Conservative Party members who dominated it, and a disaster for Asquith and the remnants of his Liberal Party. Lloyd George was now unchallenged in the British political arena, hailed as "the man who won the war."[35]

Auchincloss accompanied the president throughout his visit to England, briefing him before his meeting with Lloyd George and Balfour and conveying advice from House (with whom he talked over the phone). But Auchincloss lacked his father-in-law's accommodating personality and soon quarreled with members of the president's staff, complaining that "they have all got awful swell heads and make me perfectly sick." Wilson's assistants, in turn, found Auchincloss brash and officious and made sure the president knew of their feelings. House's attempt to use his son-in-law as a surrogate had not been a success.[36]

Late in the evening of December 29, two days before the president returned to Paris, Clemenceau responded to the attacks of Socialist leaders on his peace policy in a passionate and uncompromising speech in the chamber of deputies. It was easy, he proclaimed, for a distant America to express lofty thoughts, but France was the country nearest Germany and had been bled white and devastated by the war. It must therefore think in practical terms of "solid frontiers" and a "system of alliances" to safeguard its territory. A league of nations could only serve as a "supplementary guarantee." Clemenceau's challenge to Wilson's vision of the peace settlement, reflecting his intense preoccupation with France's security, won a lopsided vote of confidence in the chamber. Like Lloyd George, he would now enter the peace negotiations with overwhelming support at home.[37]

The prime minister's uncompromising address disturbed House. "It is about as bad," he concluded, "an augury for the success of progressive principles at the Peace Conference as we could have . . . . Coming on the heels of the English elections, and taking into consideration the result of recent elections in the United States, the situation strategically could not be worse." He now informed the president that "we would have to work with England rather than France if we hoped to get the things for which we were striving through."[38]

On January 1, 1919, the president left for Rome. Wilson's tour of Italy—which he did not ask his counselor to join—first took him to Rome, then northward to the industrial cities of Milan and Turin. Despite the fact that Orlando had won an overwhelming vote of confidence in parliament on November 20, the president made no attempt to engage Italian leaders over their extensive territorial claims. He dismissed Italian statesmen as "quite incapable of taking a wide view of things," thought Orlando and Sonnino were "obsessed" with the Eastern Adriatic, and concluded from his frenzied popular reception that he had overwhelming support for his peace program from the Italian masses.[39]

While Wilson traveled in Italy, House busied himself with preparations for the peace conference. He now realized that financial and economic questions would be crucial and worried about the "growing demand of the Allies" that the United States should cancel "the sums which they owe us" and even help them pay their own debts. He also worried that with the Austro-Hungarian, German, and Russian armies gone, France had become the "dominant Continental Power" and had developed "imperialistic tendencies." House was more convinced than ever that in order to achieve a peace of justice, the United States would "have to link up closely with England."[40]

By January 8, 1919, House was prepared for the beginning of the peace conference. He approved of Wilson's new draft of the League of Nations covenant, one that drew heavily on a memorandum of South Africa's foreign minister Jan Smuts and that House found a much-improved version of his Magnolia draft. His staff was in place on the third floor of the Crillon and a private wire had been strung between Wilson's study in the Murat Palace and House's suite at the Crillon (connected to a telephone at his bedside). Even so, the magnitude of the task that lay ahead worried him. "I do not know," he confided to his diary, "how I am to go through the many weeks ahead if matters are crowded upon me as they have been during the past few days. The other Commissioners are willing to help, but...the President seems to have no intention of using them effectively. It is the story of Washington over again. We settle matters between the two of us and he seems to consider that sufficient without even notifying the others. I feel embarrassed every day when I am with them [Bliss, Lansing, and White]." House could not help but wonder whether the peculiar system that he and Wilson had devised would meet the challenges of summit diplomacy.[41]

30

The Peace Conference, I

On January 12, nearly a month after Wilson had arrived in France, he and Allied leaders had their first meeting at the Quai d'Orsay in Paris. The meeting began as a session of the Supreme War Council and then, after the military advisers left, continued as a session of what became known as the Council of Ten. The political heads of the chief Western powers, along with their foreign ministers (Clemenceau and Pichon, Lloyd George and Balfour, Wilson and Lansing, Orlando and Sonnino, and Prince Saionji Kimmochi and Baron Nobuaki Makino of Japan), generally met five days a week, along with secretaries and interpreters, in the private office of the French foreign minister, an overheated, elegant room, with its high domed ceiling, heavy chandelier, and mirrors and tapestries. The Council of Ten, chaired by Clemenceau, would serve as an executive committee for the peace conference until it was replaced by a smaller body, the Council of Four, later in March. Not until January 18 did the conference hold its first plenary session (there would only be six of these), filled with delegates from over thirty nations, that met in a larger and more elaborate conference room in the Quai d'Orsay.[1]

For six months, while the peacemakers deliberated, Paris was the center of the world. "Old nations—Poland, Lithuania, Estonia, Latvia—," one historian writes, "came out of history to live again, and new nations—Yugoslavia and Czechoslovakia—struggled to be born," at a moment when all sensed that the world was in the middle of a vast transformation. A vivid cast of characters, ambitious men and women from many nations, gathered in Paris to participate in this grand event. For those with no official duties, Paris seemed an exhilarating place. "Every day," one socialite remembered, "was like a sparkling holiday." Paris was, to be sure, still a city with elegant women and wonderful restaurants, but evidence of the war was everywhere: in the captured German cannon in the Place de la Concorde and

Champs-Elysées, in the piles of rubble and boarded up windows, or in the demobilized, limbless soldiers, begging for change. The city reminded all who worked and played there that it was the capital of a nation that had suffered severely in the Great War.[2]

On January 11, the day before the peace conference got under way, House "fell ill with a painful attack of kidney trouble." The next morning, after a restless night, he had a temperature of 101. Wiseman found him "lying in bed unshaven, weak in voice, looking bad, but very cheerful and as usual perfectly delightful."[3] From January 11 until January 21, when he resumed entries in his diary, House was out of touch with the conference. After the first few days of his illness his fever lifted and he managed nearly every day to consult with the president. But House was slow to regain his strength, noting on January 23 that he found a two and a quarter hour conference with Wilson—his first since his illness—"fatiguing." While he longed to go south, he would not, in fact, have any rest during the peace conference. He was no longer an unofficial adviser who could come and go more or less as he pleased, but now had a formal position as a member of the American peace commission.[4]

Allied and American statesmen had not worked out any procedures in advance, and during the first few weeks of the peace conference they spent long hours discussing its organization and listening to the long-winded territorial claims of representatives from the smaller powers. While restless over the slow pace of the proceedings, Wilson, a skilled debater, seemed to enjoy the give-and-take with other leaders. Cary Grayson, after listening to one session of the Council of Ten, expressed his admiration for the president who "towers above the others. . . [and who] are not in the same class with our great man . . . . He is a marvel and all realize it—and are afraid of him."[5]

By January 21, when House had recovered some of his strength and had begun once again to keep his diary, he realized that the conference was floundering. Worse still, House felt that he was on the sidelines, since Secretary of State Lansing sat with the president on the Council of Ten. He now began to realize that, given the many pressures on the peacemakers, it would be more difficult to maintain his relationship with the president.[6] Still, Wilson and he concurred that all major issues should be put off until an agreement was reached on the covenant of the League of Nations. Lloyd George and Clemenceau deferred to Wilson's wishes, and on January 22 the British prime minister introduced a resolution, approved by the Council of

Ten, calling for the creation of a league and its inclusion "as an integral part of the general treaty of peace." Three days later the second plenary session of the peace conference set up a League of Nations Commission, chaired by Wilson, to draft the covenant of the new organization. The president had, so it seemed, won a major victory.[7]

Lloyd George hoped that by cooperating with Wilson on the League issue, he would gain American support for other British objectives. Britain and its Dominions entered the peace conference in a relatively strong position, having gained possession of most of the German fleet and occupied much of the German empire. The German naval and imperial threat had disappeared, but British leaders realized the closeness of the margin of victory and also realized the enormous cost that Britain's intervention in the war had imposed on the nation and its empire. Lloyd George, while he was skeptical of many of Wilson's aspirations, knew that the prewar order had to be reformed and hoped for a new partnership with the United States, one in which it would share the burden of maintaining stability in postwar Europe.[8]

The prime minister could not, however, allow Wilson to dominate the peace conference. He faced unsettled conditions at home—labor unrest, discontent in Ireland, unrealistic public expectations of the peace—and led a coalition government dominated by the Conservative Party. If he was to survive politically, he must use his formidable skills and abundant energy to achieve a pro-British peace. Younger and more resilient than either Clemenceau or Wilson, he thrived on the challenges of the peace conference. Lord Cecil remembered that "Whatever was going on at the Conference. . . Mr. Lloyd George was certain to be at the top of his form— full of chaff intermingled with shrewd though never ill-natured comments on those with whom he was working."[9]

Nor could Lloyd George ignore the demands of the Dominions, who had made substantial sacrifices during the war (the British Empire lost 198,000 men, while the United States lost 114,000). Despite the call in the Fourteen Points for a "free, open-minded, and absolutely impartial adjustment of all colonial claims," on January 24 the prime ministers of Australia, Canada, New Zealand, and South Africa made their demands before the Council of Ten. For the next few days Wilson resisted, insisting that captured enemy territory be held in trusteeships through mandatory nations appointed by the new League. For a time it looked as if no agreement could be reached, until Lloyd George and Jan Smuts of South Africa worked out a compromise proposal in which the great powers accepted Wilson's general principle while devising a system of different categories of mandates which would, in effect, give Britain and its Dominions the control they wanted. The president was reluctant to accept even this concession; in the end, however, Wilson had little choice but to give way, since he had no support within the Council of Ten from the prime ministers of France, Italy, or Japan, all of whose nations also had claims on captured enemy territory. It was a sharp reminder, early in the peace conference, of the limits of the American negotiating position.[10]

On January 29, House's protégé Hugh Frasier urged the president somehow to find a way to include his counselor in the meetings of the Council of Ten. Since only prime ministers and foreign secretaries were supposed to be there, Wilson could think of no way to draw House into these deliberations. He did, however, ask House to join him as one of the two American representatives on the League of Nations Commission. House was now in a position to collaborate closely with the president and to advance his principal objective at the peace conference.[11] On February 3, the League of Nations Commission held its first meeting in House's suite on the third floor of the Hôtel de Crillon, seated around a large table, with the president as its chairman. It would meet almost daily—usually in the evening—until Wilson read the final draft of the covenant before the Council of Ten on February 14.[12]

Prior to its first meeting, House had worked closely with Cecil, Lloyd George's primary adviser on the league, to resolve differences between British and American drafts of the covenant and to present to the commission a joint Anglo-American proposal. On the evening of January 31, Wilson, House, Cecil, and Smuts discussed their "difficulties regarding the League and brought them," House concluded, "nearly to a vanishing point." They agreed that David Hunter Miller and C. J. B. Hurst, the chief legal advisers of the American and British delegations, should work on a new draft of the covenant. This Anglo-American understanding pleased House, who now advised Wilson that before his departure for the United States on February 15, he should concentrate on the League, since it was the key to the creation of a new world order. As House would soon discover, however, no lasting peace could be achieved without resolving difficult issues such as the boundaries of Germany and the scale of its reparations burden.[13]

Over the next eleven days, House sat as a member of the commission, where he said little and worked behind the scenes to gain acceptance of the president's version of the covenant. In the commission meetings, Wilson used his chairmanship skillfully to win support from the smaller powers for his more advanced version of the League. His performance impressed House, who noted that he "excels in such work. He seems to like it and his short talks in explanation of his views are admirable. I have never known anyone to do such work so well."[14]

The president and his counselor, however, had underestimated the degree to which French leaders feared a revival of German power. France had paid a terrible price for its victory over Germany, and Clemenceau, who dominated the French government, believed that his nation's security in the postwar period depended on the support of its allies along with military, economic, and territorial restrictions that would keep Germany, with its larger economy and population, in check. He understood France's dependence on the United States but distrusted Wilson and his vague schemes for world betterment. "God himself," he scoffed, "was content with ten commandments. Wilson modestly inflicted fourteen points on us. . . the fourteen commandments of the most empty theory." While Clemenceau, a flexible and tenacious negotiator, dared not block Wilson's scheme for a League of Nations, he had little faith in it and wanted a punitive peace that would permanently reduce German power.[15] On February 11, three days before the League of Nations Commission planned to complete its draft of the covenant, French representatives introduced a series of amendments that would transform the League into an alliance of the victorious powers, one that would include a general staff and an international army. Wilson responded that no nation would consent to this kind of international organization and that it would be unwise to try to specify in advance how the mutual guarantee of territorial integrity would be carried out. Cecil told the French negotiators that their demands were unacceptable, and if they persisted, they would destroy the league and "would be left without an ally in the world."[16]

House also worried about the French obsession with military security and warned its leaders that if the victorious powers imposed unjust conditions on Germany, "it will simply mean the breeding of another war . . . . Our only chance for peace, I thought, was to create a league of nations, treat Germany fairly and see that she did not have an opportunity to again equip an army that would be formidable." At the last meeting of the commission, the French amendments were voted down.[17]

On February 14, Wilson read the draft covenant to a plenary session of the peace conference, occasionally stopping to offer some explanation of the text. The covenant, he declared, was "not a straightjacket, but a vehicle of life. A living thing is born." Despite all of the "terrible things that have come out of this war," the creation of the League of Nations had swept away the "miasma of distrust, of intrigue . . . . Men are looking eye to eye and saying: 'We are brothers and have a common purpose.'" Wilson's hope, as Walter Lippmann phrased it, was that the League would become a "temporary shelter from the storm" and help release "some of the more generous forces of mankind." House believed that the president's address was a great triumph, and after he finished speaking slipped him a piece of paper that read: "Your speech was as great as the occasion. I am very happy." The president replied: "Bless your heart. Thank you from the bottom of my heart."[18]

The draft covenant that Wilson presented was a much more forceful document than the Hurst–Miller draft with which the commission had begun its deliberations. The covenant created an organization with a permanent secretariat, a body of delegates, and an executive council consisting of the five great powers (France, Great Britain, Italy, Japan, and the United States, and four other countries selected on a rotating basis), the decisions of which had to be unanimous. It guaranteed "as against external aggression the independence and territorial integrity" of its member states, declared that the league could concern itself with "war or [the] threat of war" anywhere in the world, and laid down procedures for the settling of disputes. Any member state that did not follow them could be subjected to economic and financial boycotts and eventually to naval and military force. The document also called for disarmament, set up a system of mandates for former enemy territories, and expressed its concern for labor conditions throughout the world. Wilson's bold leadership had created a league that was primarily political in its nature, an organization that could, as one historian notes, bring a "radical departure" in international affairs.[19]

The morning of February 14—Wilson did not address the plenary session of the conference until 3:30 PM—the president and his counselor talked for twenty minutes about how to proceed during his absence (the president, who planned to be gone about a month, had chosen House as his replacement on the Council of Ten). Reflecting the widespread desire to speed up the conference, House explained that "I thought we could button up everything during the next four weeks." Wilson, however, "seemed startled and even alarmed at this statement. I therefore explained that my plan was not to actually bring these matters to a final conclusion but to have them ready for him to do so when he returned. This pleased him." House then noted that a preliminary peace treaty must deal with German armaments, frontiers, reparations, and postwar economic relations. Wilson accepted this agenda and later in the morning called in the three other commissioners, Bliss, Lansing, and White, and talked for about an hour in general terms. But he gave them no instructions and observed that decisions could wait until his return.[20]

House also advised his friend on how to handle the political difficulties he would face at home. "I asked him to bear in mind," House recorded in his diary, "while he was gone it was sometimes necessary to compromise in order to get things through. Not a compromise of principle, but a compromise of detail, and I called his attention to the fact that he had made many since he had been here." He urged Wilson to land in Boston rather than in New York, since Boston's Democratic mayor would arrange a warm reception that would "make a good impression in Europe." He also convinced a reluctant president to instruct Tumulty to invite all the members of the Foreign Relations committees in both the Senate and House to a dinner at the White House, where he could discuss with them the draft covenant of the league.[21]

After dinner on February 14, House accompanied Wilson and Edith to the Bois de Boulogne Station to say goodbye. Despite the drizzling rain, the atmosphere was festive, and the station was crowded with foreign ambassadors and delegates and with many French officials, including both Poincaré and Clemenceau. As the president boarded the train he "bade me," House recorded, "a fervent goodbye, clasping my hand and placing his arm around me . . . . He looked happy, as well indeed he should." And the next day, on board the *George Washington*, Edith wrote that "It was fine to see you last night, and I am going away without our long talk, when I had so many things I wanted to know about. Please take good care of your dear self and let us know if we can do any thing for you . . . . Love from us both."[22]

Wilson left Paris in a confident mood, ready to confront his political enemies in the United States. He had dominated, so it appeared, the first phase of the peace conference, insisting on the priority of the League of Nations and gaining the conference's approval of a draft covenant that created a stronger league than many members of the Anglo-American political elite desired. But in concentrating on the covenant, he had encouraged the peace conference, which was, on the day of his departure, over a month old, to put off critical issues, such as the fate of Germany, reparations, and the problem of French security.[23]

On February 15 the president and his party left Brest for the eight-day crossing of the Atlantic. Wilson, who had been abroad for slightly more than two months, would now spend ten days at home to catch up with the large accumulation of official business. On the evening of February 23, the *George Washington* reached Boston, where the president received an enthusiastic welcome, and early on the morning of February 25 he finally arrived in Washington. Wilson immediately launched into a hectic schedule, meeting with his cabinet, with Democratic leaders in the Senate, and on the evening of February 26 entertaining thirty-four senators and representatives for dinner at the White House. After dinner he talked about the covenant of the League and answered questions until midnight. As House had advised, he had reached out to key members of the Congress.[24]

The president returned to a complicated political scene. He was convinced "that the people are absolutely with the purposes and plan of the thing [the League]," and certainly the initial reception of the covenant had been favorable. Despite the widespread approval of newspaper editorials and the support of the League to Enforce Peace, however, few people had a solid understanding of Wilson's vision of a new international order, and his Republican opponents in the Senate were already raising doubts about the covenant. They were skeptical of the League, eager to impose a harsh peace on Germany, and worried about the administration's plans for postwar domestic reconstruction. On the evening of March 3, Henry Cabot Lodge, soon of course to be chairman of the Foreign Relations Committee, introduced a resolution on the Senate floor declaring that the League of Nations in its present form was unacceptable. This Round Robin, as it came to be called, was signed by thirty-seven Republican senators (with two more soon to add their names to the list). Thirty-nine Republicans in the Senate, along with one Democrat (out of a total of ninety-six), were now on record as opposing Wilson's League. Republicans were clearly in a position to force amendments to the covenant.[25] Wilson badly needed to speak out, to launch a campaign that would rally a broad range of conservatives and progressives behind his version of a league. On March 4, a gray and drawn president took the stage at the Metropolitan Opera House in New York to strike out at his opponents and to defend the covenant, declaring that "the critics of this Covenant have not observed. . . the temper of the world." The next day the *George Washington* sailed for France.[26]

The president's absence left House as the dominant American at the peace conference. Since the early days of the Wilson administration House had been carefully observed, but his prominence at the peace conference led to even greater intense scrutiny. One day in Paris, Ray Stannard Baker, the press officer of the American delegation, encountered him on a sofa, with a dressing gown over his knees, "a little, light, deft, bright-eyed man with a soft voice and winning manners." One member of the Inquiry found him "much like a very kindly, mature and gentle old scholar," while another concluded that House "had a gift for personal negotiations, a gift to the point of genius, shrewd in his judgments of men and naïf about the possibilities of international organization."[27]

European diplomats and politicians, by and large, liked the president's counselor. Lloyd George, however, had reservations. House, he remembered, was "intelligent, tactful, understanding and sympathetic," but "intellectually he was nowhere near the same plane as Wilson." Others were more generous in their estimates. A young British diplomat at the peace conference, Harold Nicolson, had the most profound respect for House, "considering him to be the best diplomatic brain that America has produced," while Balfour wrote that "I saw him under the most varying and often the most trying circumstances and found him always resourceful, and always with unruffled temper." Lord Cecil, who early in the peace conference worked closely with both Wilson and House on the League of Nations Commission, quickly decided that he did not like the president. "I do not know quite," he confided in his diary, "what it is that repels me: a certain hardness, coupled with vanity and an eye for effect." But he remained fond of House, whom he found "a delightful person to work with."[28] Clemenceau preferred dealing with House rather than Wilson and told an American journalist that "your man House is really first-class . . . . I really have a great affection for him. We are almost like brothers, brothers who disagree on everything . . . . He doesn't always see eye to eye with the Great Mogul, Wilson, but he is intensely loyal." Or as he told one of House's friends: "Colonel House is practical, I can understand him, but when I talk to President Wilson, I feel as if I were talking to Jesus Christ."[29]

House also, however, had detractors who observed him more closely at the peace conference, and whose numbers would grow as the conference progressed. George Creel, head of the Committee on Public Information, dismissed House as a "middle age wisp of a man, oozing deprecation at every pore and remarkable only for a pair of steadfast blue eyes that mirrored an invincible belief in fairies," while Bernard Baruch, one of the economic experts attached to the American delegation, concluded that House, "despite his calm and quiet exterior and his loyalty to Wilson, gradually became intoxicated by power" and convinced that "he alone could save Wilson from his ideals." As long as House retained the president's trust, however, his critics would have to bide their time.[30]

In mid-January, when the peace conference opened, the United States and its Allies were still more or less at war with the Bolshevik government in Russia. Remaining there were 180,000 troops, and several White Russian armies continued to receive British and French money and arms. The president wanted to pull American troops out of north Russia and eventually to withdraw American forces from Siberia as well. Point six of the Fourteen Points, after all, had stated that "the treatment accorded Russia by her sister nations in the months to come will be the acid test of their goodwill." Wilson hoped to find a way to end the Russian civil war and to fit Russia into his new world order.[31] Differences among the Allies, however, ran deep. Lloyd George was eager to end Britain's military intervention, but others in the War Cabinet favored a greater military effort. On the other hand, Clemenceau wanted to destroy Bolshevism, or at the least find a way to contain it by creating strong states on Russia's borders. The prospect for a unified American and Allied response to the chaos in Russia remained remote.[32]

Early in the peace conference Lloyd George, with Wilson's support, took the initiative, proposing in the Council of Ten that all the warring factions in Russia cease their hostilities and send representatives to Paris. Clemenceau violently objected to allowing Bolsheviks to attend the conference but did agree to a meeting on the island of Prinkipo, off the coast of Constantinople in the Sea of Marmora. While American and Allied observers would also be present, the various factions apparently would be left to sort things out by themselves. White Russian groups, however, rejected the Prinkipo overture, while the Bolsheviks sent an evasive reply. By February 12 it was clear to all that the first effort of the peace conference to deal with the Russian civil war had failed.[33] House seemed unenthusiastic about the Prinkipo proposal, but he worried about the "interminable Russian problem" and sought to prevent a policy that would drive Germany and

Russia together. He wanted to keep in touch with the Bolsheviks, gradually bringing them to terms and eventually restoring American and Allied influence in Russia. Like the president, he strongly opposed any further military intervention. Both men agreed, as Wilson put it, that "it would be fatal to be led further into the Russian chaos."[34]

Late in the afternoon of February 14, Winston Churchill, Lloyd George's war minister, arrived in Paris, determined to push the Council of Ten into a military crusade against the Bolsheviks. The president had left Paris that evening and House, who took his place on the Council of Ten, opposed Churchill's plan in what became an "acrimonious debate." "It was," he boasted in his diary, "Balfour and myself against Churchill, the French and the Italians." House and Balfour managed to block the war minister's interventionist scheme, but with the failure of the Prinkipo conference and the rejection of Churchill's plan, the Council of Ten was left with no policy toward the Russian revolution.[35]

Earlier in the peace conference House had discussed the possibility of a mission to Russia with William Bullitt, an energetic young protégé who in December 1917 he had placed in the State Department. Bullitt believed that the Bolshevik leaders were ready to come to terms with America and the Allies, and on the day of his tense exchange with Churchill, House decided—with the support of Balfour—to dispatch Bullitt and Lincoln Steffans, a radical journalist, to Moscow to negotiate with the Bolsheviks. Apparently Wilson approved of the mission, although he did not realize that House had given his emissary terms to propose to Soviet officials. Bullitt and Steffans left Paris on February 22, arrived in St. Petersburg on March 8, and two days later left for Moscow to meet with Lenin.[36]

Even before Wilson left Paris on February 15, impatience was growing throughout Europe over the slowness of the deliberations, and a fear was also growing, as House put it, "that Bolshevism is steadily creeping westward." The conference had already considered a wide range of issues, special committees were hard at work, and it seemed to many delegates, as one historian notes, "that the outlines of a settlement were beginning to emerge." Convinced of his superior negotiating skills, House concluded that the time had come for decisive action.[37] He now worked, in close cooperation with Balfour (who led the British delegation during Lloyd George's absence in London) to speed up the conference. On February 22, the Council of Ten passed a resolution, drafted by Balfour, that called for the completion of a preliminary peace treaty with Germany. Various special commissions were to finish their reports by March 8, six days before Wilson's return.[38] House cabled the president that "I am doing everything possible to hasten the work of the [conference] so that upon your return the terms of the preliminary peace will be ready for your consideration." But Wilson, aware that Foch wanted to impose a harsh peace on the German government, warned his counselor to be cautious: "The determination of the geographical boundaries of Germany involves the fortunes and interests of many other peoples and we should not risk being hurried into a solution arrived at solely from the French official viewpoint." Wilson clearly did not want House to reach any agreements on sensitive issues such as the fate of the west bank of the Rhine.[39]

On February 22, House traveled to Clemenceau's "humble" apartment for a conference with the French prime minister, who had been shot three days earlier during an assassination attempt by an eighteen-year-old anarchist and since then was unable to "leave his chair." Clemenceau now sensed, given the mounting pressure for quick decisions and Wilson's absence from Paris, that the time had come to press French demands. First he spoke of House as his "'dear friend,' and declared that he opened his heart to me," and then explained that he realized "the danger of delay" and was eager to make an early peace with Germany. Clemenceau insisted that Poland should acquire Danzig (giving it access to the Baltic), that Germany and Austria should be prohibited from joining together, and most important, that a separate Rhenish Republic, consisting of about four million Germans, should be created.[40] The next day André Tardieu, Clemenceau's most trusted adviser, gave House more details about the French proposal for a Rhenish Republic. He suggested that this new state would be "set up only for a limited period of years," at the end of which there would be a referendum on its future. Thus France would secure a breathing space on its eastern frontier until it had recovered from the war and Wilson's principle of self-determination would eventually be observed. House made no objection to this proposal in his report to the president.[41]

By February 27, House was "delighted with the way things are going." When Maurice Hankey asked when Lloyd George should return to Paris, he "urged him to keep him away until the 8th so we might finish up the important work we are doing and have things ready for a preliminary peace with Germany." He felt that the presence of the prime minister and the president would only interfere with his agenda. As Auchincloss wrote Frank Polk, reflecting his father-in-law's point of view, "Some day I will tell you about the stupid waste of time between the middle of January and the middle of February. Things are going fast now and the Colonel's genius for getting things done without a lot of talk is beginning to bear fruit." House optimistically cabled Wilson that if he could arrive in Paris on March 13 or 14, it might be possible to settle the peace terms with Germany by the twenty-third.[42]

On March 2, House and Tardieu had a conference in the office of Vance McCormick, one of the American economic advisers. In his diary House only wrote that "I had a long talk with Tardieu, and we got nearer together on the question of the Rhenish Republic and Luxembourg." McCormick, however, left a fuller account. Tardieu and House, he recorded, "agreed on plan for Rhenish Republic and discussed method for getting [Lloyd] George's approval, also on Saar Coal Basin [France would be permitted to annex the coal-rich Saar Valley]. Agreed Poland should have Danzig and Belgium Luxembourg, all of this, of course, with proper reservations. Agreed to push to conclusion work of committees so that reports would be ready for President on his arrival on [March] 14, and Tardieu said Foch very anxious to get the Germans at conference, Versailles, [March] 26. Colonel agreed and they both hope it can be wound up May 1." Despite the president's explicit instructions, House had now clearly exceeded his authority and had agreed to substantial parts of the French program. He made no report to Wilson on his conversation with Tardieu.[43]

The next day House's optimism about the outcome of the peace conference suddenly collapsed, as if a veil had dropped, and he finally let go of earlier illusions and realized that it would be a hard peace. No doubt he was concerned about revolutionary conditions in Germany and Austria, about evidence of growing Republican opposition to a Wilsonian peace, and about the weakness of the American negotiating position. "It is now evident," he began a long and gloomy entry in his diary, "that the peace will not be such a peace as I had hoped, or one which this terrible upheaval should have brought about . . . . I dislike to sit and have forced upon us such a peace as we are facing. We will get something out of it in the way of a League of Nations, but even that is an imperfect instrument from my point of view."[44] On March 4, the day after his lament, House had a meeting with Balfour and Clemenceau and his mood brightened. Both men, he noted, "promised to drive ahead at full speed so that everything might be ready by the 14th [of March, the date of Wilson's arrival], and I undertook to get decisions from the President upon every subject relating to a preliminary peace with Germany by the 20th [of March]." House still assumed that the current deliberations were a preliminary conference between the United States and its Allies and that once they agreed on terms, a general peace conference would be held in which the terms would be presented to Germany. According to House's fanciful timetable, the German delegation would arrive at Versailles immediately after March 20 and be given the treaty. As House telegraphed Wilson, "Everything has been speeded up and I feel confident that by the time of your arrival all questions will be ready for your approval."[45]

On March 6, Lloyd George returned, now ready to focus on issues vital to Britain and its empire. He was especially concerned about reparations, asking House to "help him out" in the forthcoming negotiations. House made no commitments, observing that he knew that the prime minister had made extravagant promises to the British people. Even so, House was willing to work with him because "with all his faults, he is by birth, instinct and upbringing, a Liberal."[46] Lloyd George and House also agreed to urge Orlando to return from Rome so that the three prime ministers and House could "thresh out everything before the President came and arrive at decisions." House was proud of his decisiveness, boasting in his diary that "when the President is away I never hesitate to act and to take as much responsibility as either of the others [as if, in fact, he too was a head of state]. We decided many other things that I did not put in my cable to the President because too much explanation would have been needed."[47]

In his March 7 report to the president House mentioned that Clemenceau insisted on a Rhenish Republic permanently detached from Germany, while Tardieu took a more moderate position. House's failure to indicate his own opposition to these French schemes unsettled Wilson, who telegraphed from the *George Washington* that I "am made a little uneasy by what you say of the left bank of the Rhine. I hope you will not even provisionally consent to the separation of the Rhenish Provinces from Germany under any arrangement but will reserve the whole matter until my arrival." The day House received Wilson's telegram he, Clemenceau, and Lloyd George set up a secret committee consisting of Philip Kerr (Lloyd George's private secretary), Mezes, and Tardieu to determine the western boundaries of Germany. Initially Mezes, on House's instructions, was inclined to accept a buffer state, but on March 12 he asked that the decision on Germany's western frontier be postponed until the president's arrival. Wilson's peremptory instructions had forced his counselor to proceed more cautiously.[48]

As the president's arrival neared, Clemenceau, Lloyd George, and House hastened to settle a wide range of issues. They appointed, along with the committee to delineate Germany's western boundaries, another secret committee to consider the reparations question and report back to them. House was "amused" by the cynicism of the two prime ministers, who both "hoped a large sum would be agreed upon because of the political situations in France and England." The three men also discussed Italian claims, the fate of German ships interned at Scapa Flow in Scotland, and the Anglo-French quarrel over the division of Syria. And they agreed to an important procedural change—that "the three Prime Ministers and the President should continue the meetings we have held in the President's absence." In short, they planned, in order to speed up their deliberations, to reduce the Council of Ten to a Council of Four.[49]

The day before Wilson arrived at Brest, House seemed worried about the next phase of the peace conference. He did not know that the president, on board the *George Washington*, had picked up press reports from Paris indicating that the peace treaty would provide for the creation of a buffer state on the west bank of the Rhine. Wilson declared "that this could not be," that such a blatant violation of the principle of self-determination would create the conditions for another war. House surely realized that the president would face a diplomatic situation far different from the one he had left on February 14, and that, once again, his own role at the peace conference would change. Auchincloss caught his father-in-law's anxieties: "I have a terrible idea that now that the President is back he will want to go along leisurely with his conferences and will never get anything pinned down and buttoned up. He needs the Colonel by him all the time to clean up business in a systematic way."[50]

31

The Peace Conference, II

On the evening of March 12, House boarded the special train that was to meet the president and his party at Brest. The next day, when the *George Washington* arrived, House waited for Wilson on the pier, hoping for a long talk on the train ride back to Paris. But it was not until the next morning, before the train arrived at the Gare des Invalides at noon, that House had time to "go over the entire situation with him and to get from him his story of his visit to the United States." He found the president in a critical mood, complaining to his counselor, "Your dinner to the Senate Foreign Relations Committee was a failure as far as getting together was concerned" and speaking with "considerable bitterness" about the way in which some of the senators had treated him. House concluded that Wilson had come back "very militant and determined to put the League of Nations into the Peace Treaty."[1]

House's description of his encounter with the president, however, was curiously incomplete. Grayson left a fuller account: "Leaving Brest the President and Colonel House went into conference and Colonel House told the President of the various developments, including the apparent desire on the part of the French authorities to have the League of Nations covenant side-tracked and a preliminary peace treaty signed which would include the complete disarmament of Germany, the creation of a Rhenish Republic, and would in effect do what the President had declared on a number of occasions he would not countenance—absolutely denude Germany of everything she had and allow Bolshevism to spread throughout that country."[2]

Writing nearly twenty years later in her memoir, Edith delivered a more dramatic version. Late on the evening of March 13, after Wilson left House and returned to his stateroom, Edith was shocked by her husband's appearance; "He seemed," she remembered, "to have aged ten years, and his jaw was set in that way it had when he was making a superhuman effort to control himself. Silently he held out his hand, which I grasped, crying: "What is the matter? What has happened?" He smiled bitterly. "House has given away everything I had won before we left Paris. He has compromised on every side, and so I have to start all over again and this time it will be harder, as he has given the impression that my delegates are not in sympathy with me."[3]

Whatever the exact exchange between the two men, there is no doubt that Wilson realized that, in his absence, things had not gone well and that House had made tentative but damaging compromises on key issues—the left bank of the Rhine, the Saar, and the inclusion of the covenant in the peace treaty. Wilson did not reprimand House, but the trust he had placed in him for so many years now disappeared. The change in their relationship, however, took place slowly. As one historian writes, "They needed each other too much—House for his own self-esteem, Wilson for a thousand practical services—to have their bond cut at one stroke."[4]

The president quickly sought to reestablish the American position. On his first day back in Paris he met with his commissioners, including House, and chided them for their concessions to the French during his absence. In private talks with Clemenceau and Lloyd George, and in a public statement, he insisted on a single treaty that would include the covenant of the League. But Wilson realized that critical issues remained unresolved and that the peace conference, in fact, was stalemated.[5]

During the first half of the conference Clemenceau had allowed Lloyd George and Wilson to advance their claims; now he decided that it was France's turn to secure economic, military, and territorial safeguards against a revival of German power. Under pressure from Foch and others on the right, he made the case for a Rhenish Republic, sought sovereignty over the Saar Valley, argued for a strong Poland, and demanded economic terms that would place a heavy burden on Germany.[6] Both Lloyd George and Wilson worried about the extremism of French demands, and during the last two weeks of March maneuvered to moderate them. If the French would give up their plan for a separate Rhenish state, they offered a British and American military guarantee in the event of a German attack. The offer pleased Clemenceau, but he and his advisers, after pondering it, demanded further concessions. Wilson complained that talking to the French was like handling a rubber ball: "You tried to make an impression but as soon as you moved your finger the ball was as round as ever."[7]

In the Fontainebleau Memorandum of March 25, the British delegation argued that were Germany treated too harshly it might "throw her lot with Bolshevism and place her resources, her brains, her vast organizing power, at the disposal of revolutionary fanatics," while Wilson observed that "at this moment there is a veritable race between peace and anarchy." In Central and Eastern Europe Czechoslovak, Hungarian, Polish, Romanian, and Russian armies were fighting over disputed borders, and Southern Germany appeared to be moving toward revolution. On March 21, the communist Bela Kun overthrew the Hungarian government and the next day established a Soviet Republic.[8]

On March 24, Clemenceau, Lloyd George, Orlando, and Wilson, eager to speed up their deliberations, began to meet as the Council of Four (often as the Council of Three, given Orlando's frequent absences). They met twice a day, mostly in Wilson's study at his new home at 11 Place des États-Unis, in what became tense, contentious sessions, marked by especially sharp exchanges between Clemenceau and Wilson. In early April, Ray Stannard Baker found his chief discouraged, "growing grayer & grimmer all the time."[9]

By March 22, House was also "discouraged at the outlook." He believed that the peacemakers were on the verge of a major crisis and worried that Wilson was "taking terrible chances by frittering away his time and opportunity."[10] Two days later House decided to act. Feeling isolated and insecure, he sought out Wilson at his residence and tried to reestablish his connection with the president. Rather than urge the president to compromise, House now presented himself as a tough negotiator who was ready for a "showdown" with the Allies. The covenant of the League, he asserted, must be placed in the peace treaty, and Wilson should insist that he and the prime ministers meet in "continuous session" to resolve other issues: reparations, French security, and the boundary between what was once Austria-Hungary and Italy. As House surely anticipated he would, Wilson agreed with his advice.[11]

The League of Nations was the one issue where the two men continued a close collaboration. By March 21, Wilson had accepted Taft's suggestions of changes to the covenant that would satisfy Senate critics. He had agreed to three main amendments: the right of withdrawal from the League; the exemption of domestic issues from the League's jurisdiction; and the inviolability of the Monroe Doctrine. During long evening sessions of the League of Nations Commission, and behind the scenes in discussions with

Cecil, House worked to gain acceptance of these changes. But obstacles raised by British and French negotiators delayed their approval until April 11.[12]

Despite his attempt to draw close to the president, House still pursued, to some extent, a separate course. At six o'clock every afternoon he continued to "talk freely" with American correspondents, although he knew Wilson disapproved. But if the president objected, he vowed that "then we will have it out together." He also boasted about the size of his staff and the number of meetings held in his rooms at the Hôtel de Crillon. "I now have," he carefully noted in his diary, "the entire tier on the third floor front and one tier back. I have twice as many rooms as all the other Commissioners put together." House seemed oblivious to the growing resentment among many members of the American delegation over the size and independence of his organization.[13]

On March 25, as the peace conference moved toward a crisis, William Bullitt returned from Russia, full of enthusiasm over the deal he had struck with Lenin to end hostilities between the Allies and the Bolsheviks. Initially House seemed attracted to Bullitt's solution for the "vexatious" Russian problem,[14] but he soon discovered that the president would not see his young emissary and that none of the peacemakers, given all the pressing issues they confronted, wished to take up the tangled Russian question. Wilson was uncertain how to deal with the Bolsheviks; Lloyd George confronted a deeply divided cabinet and strong anti-Bolshevik feelings among Conservatives in his coalition; and Clemenceau, while he opposed Foch's grand schemes for military intervention, wanted to wait on events, to "let the Russians stew in their own juice." Moreover, House found that two of his key subordinates, Gordon Auchincloss and David Hunter Miller, disliked Bullitt and were strongly opposed to his schemes.[15]

House quickly realized that "no one [at Paris] wanted to deal with such as Lenin and Trotsky," and that Wilson was drawn to a plan proposed by Hoover to use food relief to undermine the Bolshevik regime. Hoover, who wanted no recognition of "Bolshevik murders," urged that the effort should be led by a neutral figure, the Norwegian explorer Fridtjof Nansen. On April 3, Nansen formally proposed a relief commission to the Council of Four, and Wilson and Allied leaders in their reply welcomed his proposal, stipulating that food relief would be offered only if the Bolsheviks agreed to a ceasefire and agreed that the relief commission would control the distribution and transportation of food supplies within Russia. Lenin could not, however, accept what would have been a new form of Allied and American intervention in the Russian civil war, and on May 13 his rejection of the project arrived in Paris. The president and Allied leaders had, once again, failed to devise a policy toward the Russian Revolution. Wilson was at a loss what to do; as one historian remarks, the high hopes he had once had for the treatment of Russia now "lay in the dust." "The only way," he ruefully observed, "to act against Bolshevism is to make its causes disappear. This is, however, a formidable enterprise; we do not know exactly what its causes are."[16]

By the first of April, the sluggish performance of the Council of Four continued to trouble House. He dismissed Lloyd George as "a mischief maker who changes his mind like a weather-vane. He has no profound knowledge of any of the questions with which he is dealing." On the other hand, Orlando was "level-headed, but he is handicapped by not speaking English" and had little interest in non-Italian issues. His friend Clemenceau was "of the old regime . . . . He is the ablest reactionary in the Conference, but it is almost hopeless to try to deal with him except in ways that the world will no longer consider, and which we hope to make forever obsolete." Even Wilson, in House's judgment, left much to be desired. "The President," he observed, "is becoming stubborn and angry, and he never was a good negotiator . . . . I think the President is becoming unreasonable, which does not make for solutions."[17]

By early April, key members of House's staff—Auchincloss, Frazier, and Wiseman—complained that he was not "pushing the President" as hard as he ought to and that he "was letting matters drift." Rather than reveal his own anxiety about his growing distance from Wilson, House replied with bravado that "when the President really needed me, he would not hesitate to call." On the evening of April 2, Wilson did so and the two men talked for three quarters of an hour on the phone. House and Wilson "went over the situation from start to finish." Wilson complained about Clemenceau's stubbornness, wondered if Lloyd George was sincere, and asked House to discuss Italian claims with Orlando and to explain forcefully to Tardieu the American position on the Saar. House now proposed to give the French an ultimatum,[18] and the next day, April 3, he carried out the president's instructions, meeting with both Tardieu and Orlando and reporting back by phone to Wilson. That evening a telephone call from Edith brought disturbing news—that her husband "was sick with a cold and had gone to bed." She asked if he should remain in bed or try to meet with the Council of Four the next day. House advised that he stay in bed. The next morning Wilson asked him to take his place in the Council of Four.[19]

Late on the afternoon of April 3, Wilson had become, as Grayson put it, "violently sick . . . seized with violent paroxysms of coughing, which were so severe and frequent that it interfered with his breathing." He had a temperature of 103 degrees, "profuse diarrhea," and intense pain in his back, stomach, and head. Over the next four and a half days he was confined to his bed,[20] and House once again moved to the center of the negotiations, although his health, too, had been strained by the incessant demands of the conference. Auchincloss worried about his father-in-law's condition, noting that "he has had one cold after another and at the present time can hardly talk."[21]

On the afternoon of April 8, Wilson returned to the deliberations of the Council of Four with a new sense of urgency. Shaken by the severity of his illness and by the stalemate in the negotiations, he concluded that the time for decisive action had arrived. Prior to resuming his place on the Council of Four, Wilson had instructed Grayson to summon the *George Washington* to Brest, so that the ship would be in port if he wished to leave the peace conference. The president's order, soon leaked to the press, sent a shock wave through the conference and showed, he surely hoped, that he had returned to the bargaining table with a new resolve.[22] Wilson now moved swiftly to break the impasse, realizing that if peace was to be concluded, he would have to compromise on major issues. He quickly worked out an agreement on the fate of the Saar and the left bank of the Rhine. On the Saar, the Big Four agreed that the coal mines should be put under French ownership, but that the area would be administered by a League of Nations' commission, with a plebiscite to be held in fifteen years to determine the fate of the territory. On the Rhine, Wilson and Lloyd George rejected French demands for a Rhenish state but agreed to the demilitarization of the Rhineland and Allied occupation of the left bank and key bridgeheads to the right bank for a period of fifteen years. In return, the United States and Great Britain, as Wilson and Lloyd George had earlier agreed, promised to come to France's assistance in response to renewed German aggression.[23]

The president, however, was less successful on the issue of reparations. Earlier in the conference Wilson had resisted what he regarded as the unrealistic British and French demands. The Allies wanted far more than payment for the damages inflicted by Germany on France and Belgium; they argued for reparations that would cover the entire costs of the war (which

guaranteed Britain a larger share of the total) and resisted naming a definite sum. The president and his economic experts fought for a fixed sum
to be paid over a period of thirty years, but after returning to the Council
of Four, Wilson yielded on the crucial issue of the inclusion of pensions.
Rejecting the advice of his experts, an angry and exhausted president
exclaimed: "Logic! Logic! I don't give a damn for logic. I am going to
include pensions." He also agreed to abandon a fixed sum and to postpone
the issue of how much Germany should pay by creating a reparations commission that would not report until May 1921.[24]

By the middle of April, after days of intense negotiations, most of the
major French demands had been met, and the Council of Four invited
German delegates to Paris later in the month to receive the terms of the
treaty.[25]

During this critical period, House played a useful, if minor, role in the
negotiations. Wilson's retreat on the reparations issue pleased him, and
he remained in touch with the president, who used him as a go-between
with French officials. House consulted with Tardieu about the Saar controversy and continued to have warm relations with Clemenceau. When
he told the prime minister of Wilson's concessions on the Rhineland, the
old warrior "grasped both my hands and then embraced me, saying I was
his good friend and that he would never forget how much I had done for
France."[26]

As the peace conference stalemated and especially after Wilson fell ill on
April 3, the discontent and frustration of the president's intimates focused
on House. In late March, Ray Stannard Baker, who saw Wilson nearly
every day, had portrayed House favorably, as an indispensable "universal conciliator, smoother-over, connector!" But on the evening of April
3, after learning of Wilson's illness, Baker had a long talk with House,
"who was sitting in his long lounge with a figured blanket over his chilly
legs—quite serenely dictating his diary to Miss Denton. More & more
he impresses me as the dilettante—the lover of the game—the eager secretary without profound responsibility. He stands in the midst of great
events, to lose nothing. He gains experiences to put in his diary, makes
great acquaintances, plays at getting important men together for the sheer
joy in making them agree. He is a matchless conciliator but with the faults
of his victim for he conciliates over the border of minor disagreements
into the solid flesh of principle . . . . This bright, lively little man, optimistic in the presence of tragic events!"

Baker's devastating dismissal of House contrasted with his portrayal of Wilson. While House placated adversaries, the president was "the great serious man of the conference—gray, grim, lonely there on the hill—fight[ing] a losing battle against heavy odds. He can escape no responsibility & must go to his punishment not only for his own mistakes and weaknesses of temperament but for the greed & selfishness of the world. I do not love him—but beyond any other man I admire & respect him. *He is real.* He is the only great man here."[27]

During his illness Wilson brooded about many matters, including his relationship with his counselor. On the morning of April 7 he asked his physician: "Do you see any change in House; I don't mean a physical change; he does not show the same free and easy spirit; he seems to act distant with me as if he has something on his conscience." Grayson, reluctant to reveal his true feelings—which was that he had "made a mess of things" in Paris, and been too influenced by Clemenceau—blamed Auchincloss, who had "the air and attitude as if he and Colonel House were the prime movers in the Peace Commission."[28]

It was Edith, however, who forced a confrontation. Her first impression of House, formed in the summer of 1915, had been that he was a "weak vessel," but over the years she had, on the surface at least, built an affectionate relationship with him and even, on occasion, made common cause against Tumulty. On April 7, H. Wickham Steed, the editor of the *London Times*, who was close to House, published a news report praising his role at the peace conference. Steed's article was reprinted in the *Philadelphia Public Ledger*, which Edith apparently read on April 21. On the very day that she read the article, House appeared, as he often did, to discuss events at the conference. As Edith recalled, she picked up the paper and said: " 'Colonel, have you been reading these awful attacks on Woodrow, or have you been too busy? Just listen to this, which I know you will resent.' I read several paragraphs aloud. The Colonel's face turned crimson. 'Has the Governor [Wilson] seen that article?' he asked. 'No, it has just come,' I replied. He sprang up, and taking his coat in one hand he held out the other saying: 'Please let me have that to read. After all, I will not wait for the Governor.' 'Why,' I said, 'I thought you said you wanted to see him!' By this time he had reached the door, through which he fled as though pursued."[29]

Edith's conversation with House was to be their last face-to-face encounter. When he later came to 11 Place des États-Unis for business meetings,

Edith did not see him, and when he sent her flowers while she was recovering from an infected foot, she sent him a note. She never spoke to him again.[30]

The peace conference had brought changes in the names and roles of those within the president's inner circle of advisers. After resigning from his cabinet position, McAdoo opened a law office in New York, while Tumulty had remained in Washington to look after a multitude of domestic tasks. Edith and Grayson had, of course, traveled with the president to Paris, but during the conference their duties had expanded. Given the intense pressure on Wilson and his limited energy, they acquired more responsibility, advising him on a wide range of political as well as personal matters. Grayson in particular now became far more than the president's personal physician; he became virtually a member of the Wilson family, eating frequently with Edith and Woodrow, listening carefully to Wilson's description of each day's deliberations, and undertaking a variety of political chores for the president.[31]

During the peace conference two new people entered the small circle of presidential intimates, Ray Stannard Baker and Bernard Baruch. Both became important figures in the president's life and would remain so until his death in 1924. Baker, a forty-nine-year-old midwesterner, had become, in the years after the turn of the century, a highly successful journalist who focused on human interest themes and who explored the darker aspects of American life. He wrote for popular magazines, published influential books, and, through his "David Grayson" novels, in which he created an alter ego in the form of a farmer-philosopher, reached over two million readers. A passionate reformer and muckraker, Baker supported Wilson's New Freedom reforms as well as his wartime policies. In 1918, he became, with House's encouragement, a special agent of the State Department reporting on domestic currents in France, Great Britain, and Italy. Wilson liked the quiet, soft-spoken journalist and asked him to direct the American delegation's press bureau. In this position, he had daily contact with the president and the opportunity to view the peacemaking process through his eyes and to record in his diary vivid portraits of men and events. While Baker opposed some of Wilson's concessions, he believed in the president's greatness, defended the peace settlement, and eventually, in the 1920s, would become his leading biographer.[32]

Baruch was born in Camden, South Carolina, on August 19, 1870, and at the age of eleven moved to New York City, where his father was a

prominent physician and leader in public health. After graduation from the
City College of New York, he launched a career as a Wall Street speculator. Working as a "lone wolf" operator and "maverick investor," Baruch
met with great success, becoming a multi-millionaire by the early years of
the twentieth century. By any measure Baruch was a dazzling figure—tall,
handsome, charming, and physically fit, with just the trace of a southern
accent. Although he was married and the father of three children, women
found him irresistible, and he was skillful in manipulating his image and
accumulating a wide range of friends, whom he entertained lavishly in
private railway cars and on his estate in South Carolina. In 1912, Baruch
supported Wilson and became one of his principal financial backers, but he
did not emerge as an important figure in the administration until, in 1916,
the president began to think seriously about preparedness. Baruch became
a member of the Advisory Commission of the Council of National Defense
and, pushed by his friend McAdoo, joined the War Industries Board in
April 1917, assuming its chairmanship in the summer of that year. As the
"czar" of American industry, Baruch won much public acclaim and became
a key member of the war cabinet, always sitting on the president's left at its
weekly meetings.[33]

The president enjoyed Baruch's style and wit, appreciated his intellectual
boldness, and liked to have him nearby. Baruch joined Wilson at the peace
conference, where he served as a loyal supporter, an economic adviser, and
a bon vivant.[34] As the peace conference progressed, Baruch and Grayson,
who were close friends, spent more and more time together, especially
enjoying outings at the racetrack. Grayson and Edith, aware of Wilson's
need for relaxation and male companionship, encouraged the deepening
of the president's friendship with Baruch. Especially after Wilson's return
from America, and the end of his intimacy with House, the president drew
on Baruch for advice and friendship. Sometimes on Sundays, Wilson and
Edith drove to St. Cloud, where they would enjoy lunch in the garden of
Baruch's villa and talk in a relaxed way. Baruch, Grayson noted, "is making
a great hit over here with the President, Miss E & every one except Colonel
House."[35]

House had mixed feelings about Baruch. He appreciated the financier's
value to Wilson and his administration, but wished to keep Baruch at arm's
length, dismissing him as a "Hebrew Wall Street speculator" who should
not be given too much power. "He is," House wrote in September 1917,
"a curious mixture of patriotism and egotism. He wishes to serve, and

is willing to serve under any condition, but his admiration for Bernard Baruch and his methods are wonderful to contemplate." Nor was House impressed by Baruch's performance at the peace conference, convinced that he had played only a minor role.[36]

During the first half of the peace conference, Prime Minister Orlando and Foreign Minister Sonnino had displayed little interest in most issues, waiting patiently for the opportunity to present Italian claims. The war had brought tremendous economic, social, and political dislocations in Italy, where some nationalists now referred to a "mutilated victory" and where many concluded that territorial acquisitions were the only possible compensation for the costs of the conflict. While the Treaty of London promised substantial gains along the old border with the Austro-Hungarian Empire and in the northern Adriatic, Orlando and Sonnino, under intense domestic pressure, now demanded more, a larger portion of the Dalmatian Coast and the port city of Fuime (which Italian forces had occupied in mid-November 1918). They were determined to transform the Adriatic into an Italian sphere and launched a campaign against the new state of Yugoslavia, whose leaders opposed Italian claims to sections of the Dalmatian Coast that were mostly Slavic.[37]

Orlando and Sonnino, however, badly overreached. Clemenceau and Lloyd George, while they felt bound by the terms of the Treaty of London, viewed Italy as a "greedy beggar," the "least of the great powers," and viewed the behavior of its leaders with contempt. They were not willing to make concessions beyond the Treaty of London. Nor was Wilson. He had long been suspicious of Italian leaders and now, with the emergence of new democratic states in Eastern and Central Europe, opposed any compromises that would undermine the governments of these areas. Wilson felt strongly about Fuime, whose acquisition by Italy would be a blatant violation of his principle of self-determination and deprive Yugoslavia of a decent port on the Adriatic.

On April 19, Orlando and Sonnino presented Italy's case to the Council of Four. They were determined to acquire Fuime, which had become a symbol of Italy's national honor, and the efforts of Clemenceau and Lloyd George to find a compromise between the American and Italian positions soon failed. Finally, on April 24, in an effort to break the impasse, Wilson issued his appeal to the Italian people, asking them to join him in his efforts to build a new world order. A few days later Orlando and Sonnino returned to Rome, where huge crowds there and throughout Italy supported their demands. The Italian question had become another major crisis of the peace conference.

While the absence of Italy's leaders upset Clemenceau, Lloyd George, and Wilson, they were prepared to conclude a peace without them. The president, in particular, was reluctant to continue further negotiations. "It is curious," he remarked, "how utterly incapable these Italians are of taking any position on principle and sticking to it." On May 9, Orlando and Sonnino returned to Paris, but the deadlock continued, and on June 19 Orlando's coalition dissolved and he and Sonnino left office.[38]

During the war, House had viewed Italy as of minor importance and had never traveled to Rome to confer with its leaders. At the peace conference, however, he listened sympathetically to Orlando and was flattered by the fact that the prime minister viewed him as Italy's "next friend." On April 3, Orlando, rebuffed at a meeting of the Council of Four, spent much of the afternoon with "my dear friend Colonel House," who outlined, on Wilson's instructions, a proposed settlement that excluded Fuime. Orlando's rejection of the compromise puzzled House. "Why," he recorded, "they have set their hearts on a little town of 50,000 people, with little more than half of them Italians, is a mystery to me."[39] Even so, House believed that a settlement could be reached, but his efforts to find one bothered Grayson, for one, who concluded that he "had been telling the Italians that in the last analysis they would find that the President would compromise and that he [House] would be able to persuade him to do so."[40]

After Wilson issued his appeal to the Italian people, House focused on the Italian crisis which, he noted, "has absorbed. . . my every thought." On May 13, he launched, with Wilson's reluctant acquiescence, a concerted effort to break the deadlock with Italy. Although he was convinced that "the difference between them [the Italians and Yugoslavs] is now very slight," no agreement was reached, and on May 17 he spent an hour and a half working on the "Adriatic problem" without success. Wilson seemed uninterested in his efforts and remained "inflexible in his determination to yield nothing." House concluded that "a great mistake is being made in the way they [the Italians] are treated, for it will surely throw them into the arms of Germany."[41] Whatever the validity of House's position, he had badly misjudged the determination of both Italian leaders and the president. His efforts to resolve the crisis with Italy had increased, rather than lessened, the suspicions of Wilson and his close advisers.

On April 22, just as the crisis with Italy reached a climax, Baron Makino addressed the Council of Four, insisting that if Japan did not receive recognition of its rights in China, it would not sign the peace treaty. Japan had entered the war on August 23, 1914, intent on using the global crisis to advance its own expansionist agenda in Asia. The Japanese government had sent troops into Russian Siberia, seized German concessions in the Shantung Peninsula, and occupied a string of small German-held islands in the North Pacific. Both in secret treaties with the Allies and in agreements with a weak and unstable Chinese government, Japan had won recognition of these gains. Throughout the first half of the peace conference Makino and Chinda had waited patiently; now they had chosen an opportune time to advance Japan's claims.

For years Wilson had been preoccupied with the fate of China and convinced that the American people must be the "champions of the sovereign rights of China." He now had the opportunity to stand up for China and to challenge Japan's attempt to perpetuate the old, imperialistic diplomacy in East Asia.[42] Of all his major advisers, only House urged a conciliatory approach. On April 26, four days after Makino addressed the Council of Four and precipitated a crisis over Shantung, Wilson met with the American commissioners to seek their advice. House claimed that his sympathies were "evenly divided" between China and Japan, but worried about Japan's withdrawal from the conference and "argued the matter at some length with the President." He did not think there would be "much difficulty in reaching a settlement with Japan." As Wilson pondered what to do, Balfour and Makino reached a compromise—that Japan would not push for the adoption of a racial-equality clause if the great powers would accept its claims to Shantung. The Japanese agreed that while taking over Germany's economic concessions, in the near future they would withdraw their occupation force and return political sovereignty to China.[43]

The president accepted what he knew was an unsavory compromise. Confronted with the possibility that Japan along with Italy would leave the conference and refuse to join the League, Wilson relented. It was, he said, "the best that could be accomplished out of a 'dirty past.'" House agreed, convinced that concessions were essential and that Japan's expansion in Asia might somehow be contained within Wilson's new world order. Or as he wrote the president: "My feeling is that while it is all bad, it is no worse than the things we are doing in many of the settlements in which the Western Powers are interested. I feel, too, that we best clean up a lot of old rubbish with the least friction, and let the League of Nations and the new era do the rest."[44]

On May 4 the peace treaty with Germany went to the printers, and at a hotel in Versailles a large German delegation, which had left Berlin on April 28, waited anxiously to receive it. The leader of the delegation, Foreign Minister Count Ulrich Brockdorff-Rantzau, a haughty aristocrat, assumed, as did most Germans, that Wilson would prevail and that the terms of the peace would be moderate.

On May 7, Brockdorff-Rantzau and his aides were summoned to the Trianon Palace Hôtel to receive the peace terms. After Clemenceau opened the ceremony in a packed, tension-filled room, the German foreign minister spoke. He remained seated, and in a harsh, rasping voice delivered a long response, one in which he claimed that Germany was not solely responsible for the war and that the terms of the treaty violated the Fourteen Points. Clemenceau and Lloyd George reacted angrily to the count's speech, as did Wilson, who remarked, wrote House in his diary, that "this is the most tactless speech I have ever heard. The Germans are really a stupid people. They always do the wrong thing."[45]

The presentation of the preliminary terms of the peace treaty to Germany marked the beginning of the end of the peace conference. Much, of course, remained to be done; the peace treaty with Austria had to be completed and the dissolution of the Ottoman Empire dealt with, along with negotiations with German leaders over the final terms of the treaty. For the next two months the Council of Four continued to meet twice a day to resolve these and other pressing issues. Even so, with the end of their deliberations in sight, the peacemakers felt a lessening of pressure.[46]

Certainly House felt that his workload had "slackened." He found time to sit for a portrait by Sir William Orpen, went to the theater for the first time since he had arrived in Paris seven months earlier, and made several excursions into the countryside.[47] Aside from his involvement in the crises with Italy and Japan, he continued his work on the formation of the League of Nations. On April 28, after a plenary session of the peace conference approved a final draft of the covenant, House noted that the committee on the organization of the League was now in his hands. This committee, under House's leadership, decided that the new organization should be located in Geneva and approved the appointment of Eric Drummond as the first secretary general of the League. As his role in the peace conference declined, House focused more on the future role of the League of Nations. He planned to spend the summer in England setting up the League and arranging for its first meeting, which he hoped would take place in Washington on October 1.[48]

During the second half of the peace conference the president and his counselor still met often or talked on their private telephone line, but their relationship was now decidedly more formal. Finally, on May 30, House admitted in his diary what had been true for several months—that "I seldom or never have a chance to talk with him seriously and, for the moment, he is practically out from under my influence." House now moved toward a major reassessment of Wilson's leadership: "I am quite sincere in believing that the President will rank with the great orators of all time. In truth, I believe that it is as an orator that he excels rather than as a statesman. The feeling has become fairly general that the President's actions do not square with his speeches. There is a *bon mot* going the round in Paris and London, 'Wilson talks like Jesus Christ but acts like Lloyd George.' "[49]

On May 30, the Council of Four received the formal German response to the peace treaty, a lengthy document that challenged many of its terms. German leaders had been shocked by the treaty, and after May 7, when members of the American, British, and French delegations saw the document as a whole, there was a growing sense of unease, a feeling that Germany had made a persuasive case against the Allies. Lloyd George in particular had second thoughts, concluding that the British public would not support such a harsh settlement and that it was not in Britain's interests to leave, in the aftermath of the war, an unstable Germany in the heart of Europe. The British Empire delegation agreed that serious modifications must be made, and on June 2, at a meeting of the Council of Four, Lloyd George revealed his doubts to Clemenceau and Wilson.[50]

Both the prime minister and the president were alarmed at the thought of redoing the treaty at such a late date. They were exhausted by the peace conference and looking forward to its conclusion; now they were confronted with the prospect of reopening issues that had been resolved only with great difficulty. Although many members of the American delegation were disappointed with the terms of the treaty, most agreed with Wilson that it was too late to revise it in any substantial way, and that only those portions shown to be "unjust" should be corrected. Nevertheless, for the next few weeks Lloyd George dominated the meetings of the Council of Four, clashing with Clemenceau and on occasion with Wilson himself. In the end he received few concessions, and Germany was told it must accept the treaty by June 23.[51]

House also had no desire to revise the treaty, convinced that he had tried his best to "get a just peace" and had failed. He sympathized with Clemenceau, who "was for a bad peace in the beginning and he is for a bad peace now. The more I see of Clemenceau, the more I like and admire him, little as I sympathise with his views." He watched the acrimonious discussions in the Council of Four at a distance, occasionally consulting with the president and prime minister and sharing their dislike of Lloyd George, whose "constant shifting is a source of irritation to all who have to do with him."[52]

On June 10, House went to view Orpen's portrait of the president. Viewing Orpen's painting led House to reflect on his friend's personality, as if he sensed that their long relationship, if not coming to an end, would be much diminished in the future. "He is," House concluded,

> so contradictory that it is hard to pass judgment upon him. He has but few friends and the reason is apparent to me. He seems to do his best to offend rather than to please, and yet when one gets access to him, there is no more charming man in all the world than Woodrow Wilson. I have never seen anyone who did not leave his presence impressed. He could use this charm to enormous personal and public advantage if he would, but in that, he is hopeless. Everything that does not square with good sense seems to him not worth while when, as a matter of fact, all of us have to yield to the prejudice, weakness and whims of our fellow men . . . . We must work collectively in order to work effectively. The President understands this intellectually, for he is always saying what he does not practice. He speaks constantly of "teamwork" but seldom practices it.[53]

House did not intend to remain in Paris with the other three American commissioners after the treaty with Germany had been signed. He realized that there was little left for him to accomplish in Paris. On June 12, House drove to Boulogne, and the next morning crossed the Channel to Folkestone. He then drove to Sussex to spend a week relaxing with Gordon, Janet, and his granddaughter Louise at Greenwood Gate, Withyham, Sussex, at a large house rented for the summer by his friend Frank Trumbull. He found the weather "glorious," "the air as dry as Western Texas and [the] grass in places looked more like August than June." He slept, played with Louise, and on June 18 he, Gordon, and Edward Andrews (the son of an old Texas friend) drove to Folkestone, crossed the Channel, and reached Paris on the night of June 19, ready for the final phase of the peace conference.[54]

As the deadline for German acceptance of the treaty neared, speculation grew about whether the German government would sign the document and how the United States and its Allies would respond if it refused to do so. In Germany, the political situation was chaotic; the coalition government was divided over what to do and finally, on June 20, the deadlocked cabinet resigned. Two days later, President Friedrich Ebert put together a new government. After a long debate in the National Assembly and a stern ultimatum from the Council of Four, a resolution to accept the treaty passed, and late on the afternoon of June 23 news reached Paris that German officials would take their place in the Hall of Mirrors at the Palace of Versailles on June 28, the fifth anniversary of the assassination of Archduke Franz Ferdinand and his wife at Sarajevo. Clemenceau, Lloyd George, and Wilson could finally relax—there would be no invasion of Germany. As Grayson noted, "every where pandemonium broke loose— crowds gathered and cheered that the war was won."[55]

For House, June 23 was "a red letter day." After learning that Germany would sign the treaty, he went to the Ministry of War "to embrace Clemenceau and to be embraced in turn." House wanted the treaty signed as quickly as possible, since he worried—especially after the sinking of the interned German fleet at Scapa Flow on June 21—about the "temper and unreliability" of the new German government.[56]

On June 28, "the great day" finally arrived. House did little in the morning, and reached his seat in the Hall of Mirrors about ten minutes before the German delegates arrived. Amid elaborate pageantry, at 3:00 PM the two German officials entered the hall, and in three-quarters of an hour the meeting was over and the celebrations in Paris began. House disliked ceremonies of this sort and "had a feeling of sympathy for the Germans who sat there quite stoically."[57] After the signing, he, Loulie, and Gordon, along with Wilson and the three prime ministers, went out on the terrace, where the fountains were "playing for the first time since the war began." It was, House observed, "a brilliant and momentous scene," as planes filled the air, cannon fired, and thousands cheered and crowded around the peacemakers. But as House and his son-in-law walked across the terrace, as Auchincloss recalled in his diary, they "suddenly met four horribly mutilated French soldiers-men who had had their faces shot away and had had new and shapeless masses put in place of their faces. They seemed to be cheerful enough but they were ghastly reminders of the horrible war which had just finished."[58]

In the evening, House went to the Gare des Invalides to see the president and his party off as they boarded the train for Brest. He had a final conversation with Wilson, one that "was not reassuring." He urged the president "to meet the Senate in a conciliatory spirit. I was certain that if he treated them with the same consideration he had used with his foreign colleagues here, all would be well." His optimism, however, left Wilson unmoved: "'House, I have found one can never get anything in this life that is worth while without fighting for it.' I combated this, and reminded him that Anglo-Saxon Civilization was built on compromise. I said that a fight was the last thing to be brought about, and then only when it could not be avoided." The two men would never see each other again.[59]

On June 29, the day House left Paris, he felt mixed emotions on leaving. Now that the conference had ended and he could reflect on its accomplishments, he doubted that a better peace could have been achieved, since "the greater part of civilization had been shattered and history could guide us but little in the making of this peace." He still believed that "Wilson might have had the power and influence if he had remained in Washington and kept clear of the Conference," failing to note that the president's skill and persistence as a negotiator had resulted in a more moderate peace and the inclusion of the League of Nations as its centerpiece. And House forgot to mention that on many key issues of the peace settlement—the Saar, the Rhineland, Italian claims, Shantung—Wilson had resisted, and he had favored, concessions that would have led to a harsher peace. In the supreme moment of his career, House had failed his chief, succumbing to Clemenceau's flattery and his own conviction that he was the master of the negotiating process.[60]

House's assessment of the peace settlement, however, was close to the mark. On May 16 Wilson had asserted that "the treaty is undoubtedly very severe indeed," but it was not "on the whole unjust. . . [given] the very great offence against civilization which the German state committed."[61] Germany had, to be sure, lost 13 percent of its territory, 10 percent of its population, and all of its colonies, but the nation was not crushed by a vindictive peace and would, in the postwar years, return to its great power status. The treaty, the historian Zara Steiner notes, "failed to solve the problem of both punishing and conciliating" Germany, although it is hard to imagine how it could have done so. And as Henry Kissinger writes, "having considered the prewar world too confining, Germany was not likely to be satisfied with *any* terms available after defeat."[62]

None of the peacemakers was satisfied with the final document, since it was the result of complex compromises and postponed solutions. It was a mixture of realism and idealism, one that contained some traditional elements for securing the peace and that also contained the outlines of a new international order, embodied in the League of Nations. What the future would bring was uncertain, for much would depend on the will of France, Great Britain, and the United States to enforce the terms of the treaty. House's friend Clemenceau succinctly summoned up the settlement: "In the end, it is what it is; above all else it is the work of human beings and, as a result, it is not perfect. We all did what we could to work fast and well."[63]

32

The Fight for the League

On the afternoon of June 29 House motored to Boulogne, spent the night there, and the next day crossed the Channel. He and his entourage returned to Frank Trumbull's home at Greenwood Gate in Sussex for a long stay. "It was almost comical," House reported to Mezes, "to see the endeavors of everyone to leave [Paris]. It was like the proverbial rats from a sinking ship." Or as Auchincloss noted, his father-in-law "was so sick of the Paris game before he left that it almost hurt."[1]

House quickly settled into a familiar routine, making Greenwood Gate his base but traveling often to London, mingling with the nation's social and political elite. He "took tea" with the novelist H. G. Wells; enjoyed dinner at the Reform Club, where he met "the editors and writers of liberal opinion in England"; and especially treasured a visit to Grey's "fishing lodge" near Winchester, "a primitive place, nothing more than a 'shack' but covered with roses and surrounded by beautiful lime trees." There House and the former foreign secretary "had many long and intimate talks." He hoped to return to the United States around the middle of September.[2]

As House approached his sixty-first birthday, he thought of a trip to Texas, which he had last visited in January 1914. A letter from Thomas Watt Gregory, who had just returned from a visit there, reminded him of the passage of time. Gregory visited House's brother T. W. in Houston, drove by his old family home there, and experienced a flood of "happy memories and I wondered if we should ever meet in the old town again." He was convinced that House would receive a warm welcome, for "everywhere I went in the state people inquired about you and took great pride in your accomplishments."[3]

Soon after arriving in England, House went to London and visited Sunderland House, the temporary home of the League of Nations. There Eric Drummond, the first secretary general, labored to define a structure for the new secretariat, the world's first international civil service. He also sought, with no instructions and a small budget, to prepare for the first meeting of the League's council and assembly, which he thought would take place early in the New Year. Drummond proceeded with caution, aware that the "great experiment," as Cecil termed it, was viewed with skepticism by the leaders of France and Great Britain. Clemenceau and Lloyd George preferred to deal with European affairs through meetings of the heads of state; they considered the new Geneva system an adjunct to, not a substitute for, traditional great power politics.[4]

On July 8, House took his place on the League's Commission on Mandates, which throughout the summer worked on drafts of class A, B, and C mandates to be submitted to the council of the League for its approval. He reported frequently to the president on the progress of the commission, and also conferred with Cecil and Drummond about the best way to set up the League. House wanted its first meeting to be held in Washington in October or November 1919, convinced that the leaders of the world must be shown that the League was a functioning organization.[5]

At the end of July, House sent the president a tour of the international horizon, arguing that the war had greatly expanded the power of Great Britain and the United States. House now worried about an emerging Anglo-American antagonism. He was eager for Grey to go to Washington as the new British ambassador (after the peace conference, Reading had not returned to his post), and to take up three critical issues—naval rivalry, the Irish question, and the future of the League of Nations. He warned Wilson that "the world is in a belligerent mood, and the next ten years will be the most dangerous to its peace. If we can get over this period safely and get the League in satisfactory operation, war may conceivably become almost obsolete . . . . At present, the world is a long way from being safe, and another upheaval now may completely wreck civilization."[6]

The prospect of Grey residing in Washington excited House. He soon discovered, however, that his English friend would only go as a special envoy, not as the regular ambassador, and in late July and August the two had long discussions about the terms of the mission. House felt that Grey's "Washington adventure" was essential for the resolution of Anglo-American tensions, and once again, as during the wartime years, fell under Grey's spell. "It is a great pleasure," he wrote, "to come in touch again with a man of Grey's high character. He is. . . in many ways the most splendid figure that has come out of this war."[7]

Throughout July and August, House kept the president informed of his activities in England. Wilson approved of the decisions of the mandates commission, looked forward to Grey's arrival in Washington, and wrote his counselor a cordial letter, urging him and his family to "keep well."[8] Neither man wished to acknowledge, either in their letters or in public statements, that their relationship had changed. In late August, when a dispatch from New York to the *London Times* reported a "falling out" between the two men, House denied the reports and wrote Wilson that "our annual falling out seems to *have* occurred." But a report from Paris in the *New York Sun* on August 27 entitled "Wilson-House Break Is Near," noted accurately that "No open break has occurred in the relations between Col. E. M. House and President Wilson, but the two men for the first time in their long acquaintance no longer are *en rapport*. The Colonel virtually has ceased to function as the President's unofficial diplomatic agent in Europe." Soon the story was picked up by London papers and became, House noted, "a new sensation for London." This time he wisely refused to comment, while Wilson cabled "Am deeply distressed by malicious story about break between us and thank you for the whole message about it. The best way to treat it is with silent contempt."[9]

The president did not, however, want his counselor back in the nation's capital. Clearly Wilson, along with Grayson and Tumulty, worried that House, if he returned before the ratification of the treaty, would be forced to testify before a hostile Senate Foreign Relations Committee.[10] House had, however, looked forward to returning to America with Grey on the SS *Mauretania*, and was "greatly upset over the change in my plans." He had no choice, however, but to yield to the president's wishes and return to Paris. He now planned to sail for the United States on October 10, when the treaty would, so he assumed, be "out of the way."[11]

House reluctantly pulled up stakes in England. He said goodbye to Janet and Louise, who sailed on the SS *Aquitania* to join Gordon in New York, and then motored with Loulie and Fanny from Greenwood Gate to London, where he stayed at the Ritz and had a farewell dinner with Grey to prepare him for his mission to America. His summer in England had been memorable, "one of those happy adventures which seldom come in a lifetime."[12]

On July 8 the SS *George Washington* had reached New York, where the president received an enthusiastic welcome and spoke briefly at Carnegie Hall. Two days later Wilson presented the peace treaty to the Senate. In his thirty-seven-minute address, however, he was not at his best, stumbling several times and speaking in generalities instead of addressing specific criticisms of the treaty.[13] Exhausted from the peace conference and in declining health, Wilson faced a complicated domestic situation. Popular interest in the peace treaty had fallen off, many liberals and intellectuals, such as his former ally Walter Lippmann and the *New Republic*, had turned against the peace treaty, and the leader of the Republican opposition, Senator Henry Cabot Lodge, had maneuvered to unite Senate Republicans and the party behind a series of reservations that would, in fact, be part of the instrument of ratification and severely restrict American membership in the League. Were Wilson to succeed, he would need the votes of Senate Democrats and around twenty Republican mild reservationists to forge a two-thirds majority.[14]

The American people, as McAdoo wrote House, were "more concerned in domestic questions than in the League Covenant." The administration, however, had not devised any program for postwar reconstruction, and throughout 1919 the nation experienced strikes, inflation, unemployment, a growing fear of radicals, and racial violence in Washington and other northern cities. Federal troops had to be called out to put down riots only a few blocks from the White House.[15]

The president, no longer the vibrant leader of earlier years, took few initiatives to address the wide range of pressing domestic issues. Instead, he focused his waning energies on the League fight. On July 18, Wilson began to meet with moderate Republican senators, all of whom told him that reservations were essential if the treaty was to be ratified by the Senate. Prominent Republicans such as Taft and Charles Evans Hughes agreed, and both Tumulty and McAdoo urged their chief to take the lead and devise his own modifications of the treaty. But the president failed to do so. When Wilson met with the Senate Foreign Relations Committee on August 19 for three and a half hours, he asked for swift action and rejected reservations of the sort that Lodge was preparing.[16]

Frustrated and angry over the stalemate in Washington, the president announced on August 27 that he would make a "swing around the circle," taking the League issue to the people. He rejected the advice of Edith and Grayson, both of whom feared that his fragile health could not withstand the rigors of such a trip. Wilson had always enjoyed campaigning and drawing strength from his contact with the people; now he felt that he was on a sacred mission to win American acceptance of the treaty, whatever personal sacrifices might be involved, and he may also have calculated that a successful tour would strengthen his hand when he returned to Washington to negotiate with opponents of the League. House, who had not been consulted, learned of the tour from London newspapers.[17]

On the evening of September 3, the special presidential train left Union Station for a twenty-one-day trip that would carry Wilson, Edith, Grayson, Tumulty, a small staff, and a large group of reporters all the way to the West Coast. In forty speeches the president made the case for the League, defending and explaining the covenant and warning that if this experiment failed the next war "would be the destruction of mankind." His extraordinary effort marked, as one biographer notes, the "closing lines of one of the greatest speaking careers in American History—a final burst of eloquence from a dying star."[18]

On the surface the tour seemed a success, but Grayson and Edith worried about the stress of the trip, the endless speeches, receptions, and parades, and especially the heat. As Grayson noted, "the steel cars of the special train hold the heat like ovens." They knew that Wilson was plagued by severe headaches, asthmatic attacks, double vision, and extreme fatigue. Finally, on the afternoon of September 25, twenty miles outside of Pueblo, Colorado, the special train stopped; the president was in such extreme discomfort that Grayson decided that a walk in the open might help. Early the next morning Wilson became so sick that Grayson convinced him to cancel the remainder of the tour and head back to Washington.[19] The president's train reached Union Station on September 28, and three days later, on the morning of October 2, the long years of hypertension finally took their toll. Wilson suffered a stroke that paralyzed the left side of his body and, for several days in mid-October, he was near death because of an infection in his prostate gland. Grayson's frequent bulletins described the president as a "very sick man" but obscured the nature of his illness.[20] For nearly a month Wilson was so ill that he was unable to carry out any of the functions of his office. Edith, once she realized the severity of his condition, made a series of critical decisions. She discouraged her husband from admitting that he was incapacitated and resigning from office, insisted on concealing the severity of his illness from the public, and assumed a major role in the workings of the government. Edith decided what issues would be brought to his attention and what visitors he would see. She dominated a triumvirate—including Grayson and Tumulty—that managed the affairs of state. Documents and letters that flowed to the president would often be returned with Edith's handwritten notes on them, filled with spelling and grammatical errors, prefaced with the message that "The President says." At the most important moment of his public life, Wilson lay incapacitated while three members of his much-diminished inner circle struggled to carry out his wishes and to keep the government functioning.[21]

While the president's train headed west, on September 14 House crossed the Channel, motored from Boulogne to Paris, and once again prepared to take up the affairs of the peace conference. He quickly discovered, however, that "there is nothing for me to do [in Paris]." Once the Allies finished peace treaties with Bulgaria and Hungary, he urged the president to close down the conference. House had lost interest in the final details of the settlement; for seven days he made no entries in his diary. He was eager to return home, help Wilson in his fight, and, if necessary, testify before the Senate Foreign Relations Committee.[22] House's thoughts turned to the remarkable drama unfolding in America. "I am watching with great interest," he recorded in his diary, "the President's speaking tour in the West . . . . What a gamble it all is, and how easily he might have made it a certainty rather than a gamble . . . . He is not a good pilot."[23]

On September 29, when House first learned of Wilson's breakdown, he wired his friend that "We are greatly distressed to hear of your illness. Our love and good wishes are always with you." For years he had worried about Wilson's health; now, as further reports of the president's illness appeared in the Paris press, House speculated that he had "broken himself down," and returned to earlier themes about Wilson's lack of organization. "He has all the facilities," House complained, "and all the power to get the most efficient help to be had in the United States. It is a wonder that the President has been able to keep going as long as he has, and I fear the mainspring has snapped at last."[24]

In early October, House prepared to leave Paris. In their last talk, Clemenceau declared that "I love you—you know that," and on October 5 the premier came to the railway station, along with many other dignitaries, to see House off on his special train to Brest. It was a gathering more appropriate for a head of state than for a private citizen.[25] When House left Paris he "was sick with fever. . . and it was a trying ordeal to stand up under." Once the train pulled out, he went to bed, and the next day at Brest had to be helped onto the SS *Northern Pacific*. He had had "an attack of renal colic" which continued for the entire seven-day voyage to America. When the *Northern Pacific* docked in New York, House went directly to his apartment at 115 East 53rd Street, where he stayed in bed for almost a week. Not until October 21 did he begin to see callers again.[26]

House returned to what was, from his perspective, a depressing domestic situation. The president was gravely ill, isolated in bed, while Grayson issued misleading reports about his "nervous exhaustion." The majority of Senate Democrats wished to reach a compromise with Republicans, but, deprived of leadership from the White House, they did not take any initiative on their own. While Democrats dithered, Senate Republicans coalesced behind Lodge's leadership and on October 24 the Foreign Relations Committee reported fourteen reservations to the Senate floor. The most important of these, on Article X of the covenant, restricted America's obligation to act and, in general, these reservations embodied a negative, suspicious view of the peace treaty and the covenant that contrasted with Wilson's more hopeful vision of a new international order.[27]

On November 7, when the Senate Minority leader, Albert Hitchcock (Democrat, Nebraska), finally saw the president, he found "an emaciated old man with a thin white beard which he had permitted to grow," one who was uninterested in compromise. Ten days later, when Hitchcock again visited the White House, Wilson was more assertive and still firmly against any concessions. The president, whose emotional balance and judgment had been undermined by his stroke, regarded the Lodge reservations as a virtual nullification of the treaty and the League and claimed that it was the reservation to Article X in particular "that cuts the very heart out of the Treaty." With each side holding firm, the Senate on November 19, after an exciting and tense ten-hour debate, finally came to a decision. When it voted on the peace treaty with the Lodge reservations attached, the treaty was rejected by a vote of 39 for and 55 against. When it voted on the treaty without any reservations, it was also rejected by a vote of 38 for and 53 against. Although the majority of the Senate members favored American membership in the League with some sort of reservations, Wilson's and Lodge's rigidity had doomed any efforts at compromise and left all sides stunned by the results of the debate and wondering whether the fight over American membership in the League had ended.[28]

After her return to New York on October 12, Loulie had written Edith (her letter is lost), and five days later Edith replied, revealing that she had "not yet told him [Woodrow] of the Col's illness or that he has left Paris— for I knew how anxious he was that he remain there for the time." House quickly tried to clarify the record, explaining to Edith why he had felt compelled to leave Paris. In response, Edith now admitted that she had no idea whether House's letters and cables had "ever reached the President," given the fast pace of the western tour, and given the fact that, once they had returned to Washington, Grayson "forbid his looking at the vast accumulation here." She still had not told Woodrow of his counselor's return, since "not knowing anything of your coming home can do him no harm." And Edith had no need for House's services in Washington. House did not realize how far his stock had fallen with Edith and Wilson, or the depth of Edith's determination to keep him away from Washington.[29]

On October 21, after House was "up and about," he tried to pick up "the thread of affairs." He was relieved to learn that Lodge would not ask him to testify before the Senate Foreign Relations Committee, and from Burleson, Lansing, and other visitors he began to piece together the situation in Washington, hearing of disagreements within the cabinet over how to proceed and of the discussion over whether Wilson had suffered a stroke. He concluded that his breakdown was "one of the great tragedies of the times."[30] House now sensed that the Wilson era might be drawing to a close. He had not quite, however, given up on the president and assumed he might be called to Washington to direct affairs of state. On November 17, House sent Edith another letter, enclosing a brief note to the president and a cable from Wiseman. This time Edith read both to her sick husband, who asked her to tell House "how sorry he is to know that you have been ill." Woodrow said—" 'oh! poor fellow I am so sorry' " But since he did not ask where House wrote from, Edith admitted that "I fancy he still thinks you are in Paris."[31]

Late in November, Ray Stannard Baker, a perceptive observer and gifted diarist, had a long talk with House in New York. House was in a philosophical mood, explaining that the chief asset of the politician was not money but "the ability to play upon men's vanity . . . . Roosevelt had this gift but Wilson has it not. He never plays on the vanity of anyone." While Baker listened to House expound his philosophy of politics with his quiet voice and expressive hands, he thought of his "own reaction toward the Colonel."

> I like him very much: he interests & attracts me. I see him playing also on *my* vanity, and remark it to myself . . . . For there is beneath it a basis of real sincerity: he does like people, he does enjoy winning them . . . . This genius for appealing to men's vanity is never wholly artifice. No flatterer who was all flatterer ever succeeded . . . . So with the Colonel—who was absolutely

ingenuous to-day in revealing his secret of political success. Smooth people along: keep contacts: lay on vanities—No doubt the President has kept ·
House close to him because he recognized that he possessed the arts in which
he himself was wanting.[32]

In early November, the news from Washington continued to be bleak.
House's journalist friend Stephen Bonsal reported that "the outlook
here is dark indeed. So many Senators have dug themselves in so deeply
that dynamite, much less waves of intelligent thought, can hardly reach
them." House had "never seen conditions [in America] in such an unsatisfactory condition."[33] The day after the Senate vote, House commiserated
with Grey, who had been unable to see the president and whose mission
to Washington had been a failure. He wished Wilson had turned the
presidency over to Vice-President Thomas Marshall during the period of
his disability. With Marshall in command the treaty would "have gone
through with such mild reservations as leave no question of its acceptance
by the other powers." Whatever the administration's blunders, however,
he deplored the actions of the Republican majority in the Senate. "I
would never have thought it possible," House lamented, "that personal
hatred and partisanship could have gone so far."[34]

For two weeks after the Senate vote Wilson said nothing about the fate
of the treaty. On December 5, when the president saw Senator Albert
Fall (Republican, New Mexico) and Gilbert Hitchcock (what he termed
a "smelling committee" to assess his health), he displayed no interest in
a compromise. A few days later, when the minority leader saw Wilson
by himself, the president, whose health had improved, was defiant. "Let
Lodge compromise," he said, and on December 14 he issued a public statement declaring that rumors that he would make any effort to break the
deadlock were "entirely without foundation." Wilson seemed more interested in pinning the blame for the treaty's defeat on Senate Republicans
than on finding a resolution to the impasse.[35]

Despite the president's attitude, many national leaders wanted the
Senate to reconsider its vote and find a way to approve the peace treaty.
Responding to the intense pressure, on November 24 House reluctantly
wrote Edith that "it seems to me vital that the Treaty should pass in some
form. His place in history is in the balance. If the Treaty goes through with
objectionable reservations it can later be rectified. The essential thing is
to have the President's great work in Paris live." In an enclosed letter to
Wilson, House, in effect, urged the president to withdraw from the debate,

return the treaty to the Senate, and let "Senator Hitchcock know that you expect it to be ratified in some form."[36]

House learned through Gregory that Edith did not like his proposal, which she feared would "much disappoint" the president. He worried that Edith would not "even allow the President to have my letters," and found it "astonishing that Mrs. Wilson is willing to assume responsibility of action in this matter . . . . The small entourage of the President evidently feel that he should be kept in office at all costs. In doing so they are crucifying his reputation."[37]

House also lamented the power of Baruch and Grayson. He had been told by many friends that "the drive being made against me from Washington is engineered by Baruch, Grayson and Tumulty." But he was puzzled by the duplicity of his opponents. While Grayson and Baruch sought to end his influence on Wilson, they also continued to declare their friendship. Grayson sent House a Virginia ham for Christmas, while Baruch visited House and telephoned often to reassure him of his friendship. It was as if they had studied House's own behavior and imitated the way in which he, for years, had manipulated those close to the president.[38]

Edith was less subtle. Possessive and opinionated, with a shaky grasp of public affairs, she could now exclude certain advisers from the president's inner circle. Over the years she had tolerated House, but his behavior at the peace conference had confirmed her earlier doubts and now she cut him off from contact with her beloved husband, never answering his most recent letter. She only put up with Tumulty because she realized that he was indispensable for the functioning of the Wilson White House. At the very time when Wilson needed House's conciliatory advice and his personal connections, Edith ignored the overtures of the man who had once been his most trusted adviser and closest friend.[39]

On December 11, the New York World, an administration newspaper, carried an article entitled "Colonel House and President Wilson?" This report of a break, House recorded, caused a "great sensation." Deluged with requests for a response, House issued a statement in which he made no comment "further than to say that my admiration and affection for the President are unchanged." House still would not admit that the friendship had ended. While he realized that Edith's feelings toward him had "cooled," he was "uncertain as to the President."[40] On December 30, Gregory once again talked with Edith, who "failed. . . to throw light on the mysterious silence of the White House toward me." Constant rumors of a break upset House, as did the "fatuous" belief of "his [Wilson's] immediate entourage. . . that in some way it is hurting me and helping the President." But, denied access to the White House, he could only "feel deeply for the President for I have never known a man more crucified from day to day."⁴¹

The New Year brought more bad news. House learned that Edith was "white-hot with indignation" toward Secretary of State Lansing and wanted him to resign, while Tumulty admitted that rumors of a break with House were harming his chief but that he was "helpless" to stop them. Worse still, the president on January 8, 1920, sent a strident letter to the Democrats' Jackson Day dinner declaring that the next election should be a "great and solemn referendum" on the issues dividing him and Senate Republicans. With the state of affairs in Washington more "terrible" than ever, House was relieved late on the afternoon of January 12 to begin his much-anticipated visit to Texas. He chose to head west to St. Louis rather than south to Washington, determined to avoid being drawn into the confusion and controversy in the nation's capital.⁴²

Edward and Loulie stopped first in Houston, staying at the home of his brother, T. W., renewing their friendship with their four nieces and two nephews. After a few days in Houston they moved on to Austin, staying at the home of a friend, Lewis Hancock. Since House's last visit to Texas in January 1914, his fame had grown, and he was overwhelmed by the warmth and intensity of his reception. The *Austin American* declared him the "Greatest U.S. Diplomat," and Governor William P. Hobby gave a "brilliant" reception in the governor's mansion. The mansion was decorated "with palms, ferns, Texas bamboo and cut flowers," and Loulie dressed for the occasion in a "white satin Parisian gown with crystal garniture." Early in his visit House wrote that "there had been one continuous demand upon me since we arrived, and I am all in today . . . . I cannot keep up the pace." Carried away by the evidence of affection and by memories of his earlier life in Texas, House declared "Austin is the only place in the world I call my home and I am coming back here to live."⁴³

On January 26, 1920, they returned to New York. During their absence a bipartisan conference of Democratic and Republican senators had tried to resolve the stalemate, but by the end of the month their efforts had failed and it was clear that only an acceptance of the Lodge reservations would bring Senate consent to the peace treaty. Both Tumulty and Edith now wanted the president to accept a compromise, but he was obdurate, suffering from mood swings and depression and from another attack of influenza. Wilson was out of touch with political reality.[44]

By early February, Wilson's health had improved and he became more assertive and obstructive. On February 7 he precipitated a confrontation with Lansing, rebuking him for calling the cabinet together during his illness. In a sharp exchange of letters, the secretary of state offered his resignation, which Wilson accepted on February 13. In choosing Lansing's successor, he bypassed Frank Polk, House's friend and the second-ranking official in the State Department, and instead chose Bainbridge Colby, a fervent supporter and a member of the Shipping Board with no experience in foreign policy. By the end of February, doubts were growing about his ability to govern. The president's behavior in office now became a major political issue.[45]

On February 9, the Senate once again took up the consideration of the peace treaty. Democratic defections made it likely that the treaty, with the Lodge reservations attached, would gain a two-thirds majority. The president, however, was unmoved. While Democratic leaders in the Senate were eager for a compromise, he stood firm, and on March 8 gave a defiant statement to Hitchcock, observing that "I hear of reservationists and mild reservationists, but I cannot understand the difference between a nullifier and a mild nullifier." On March 19, when the roll call was taken, the treaty with the Lodge reservations passed by a vote of 49 to 35, seven short of a two-thirds majority. The president seemed reconciled to the outcome, telling Grayson that "It is evident[ly] too soon for the country to accept the League—not ready for it. May have to break the heart of the world and the pocketbook of the world before the League will be accepted and appreciated."[46]

From his vantage point in New York, House watched the final chapter of the League debate with a sense of foreboding. All of his efforts to reach his old friend the president had failed, and he remained uncertain about their relationship. "There is so much mystery," he observed, "surrounding the President and his condition that I am wholly at a loss to form an opinion as to the truth." He noted that Edith had made no attempt, either in private or in public, to deny the frequent stories about a break between the two men. "As it is," House complained, "I am helpless and the only thing I can do is to remain aloof until I receive some direct word from the President."[47]

He realized, however, that he was no longer near the center of power in Washington, noting that "I see many people but after my work in Europe most things seem trivial." He fretted over the failure of Grey's mission and his discourteous treatment by the White House, and watched the bitter public exchange between Wilson and Lansing, uncertain "who has the right of the situation." House believed that if only he had "a moment with the President," he could convince him to turn the government over to Vice-President Marshall and to issue a public statement explaining that "he had fallen ill before his work was finished." If Wilson left office in a dignified way, he was certain that "he would have become a world martyr . . . . The Treaty would have been ratified at once and the work for which he was responsible would have lived." House blamed "the short-sighted coterie around him" for the president's stubbornness, claiming that "they have done their best to wreck one of the most splendid careers the world has known." He failed to understand the devastating impact of Wilson's stroke on his emotional balance, and to realize that the president himself, far more than Edith or Grayson, was the instigator of his own self-destructive behavior.[48]

On March 11, House sent a letter to Edith, enclosing a conciliatory note to her husband. Wilson's prompt response, cordial but unrevealing, disappointed House, who had hoped that his friend would use the occasion to reach out to him. "It is more," House noted, "what he refrains from saying than what he says that strikes me . . . . I shall accept the letter as the end of our relations or, at least, the end of our official relations."[49]

By the end of March, House felt a sense of despair over "the low state of the President's health and the frightful condition into which public affairs have fallen." He condemned those around him who persuaded Wilson to continue in office and for the way in which they had misled the public about his health. House felt a "deep sorrow over the President's unhappy condition. He deserved a better fate than to have been stricken so sorely, and to be surrounded by a lot of incompetents who are day by day wrecking his reputation and influence." His own influence over the president was long gone, and the peace treaty was dead, along with the ambitious vision they had shared of American leadership in a new world order. It was time to move on.[50]

PART
VI

Elder Statesman,
1921–1938

33

The End of the Wilson Era

For many months, prior to the peace treaty's final defeat on March 19, 1920, House had followed the presidential aspirations of various Democratic and Republican candidates. He talked with General Pershing, who hoped for the Republican nomination, consulted with McAdoo, the leading contender on the Democratic side, and had long conversations with Herbert Hoover, who clearly had presidential ambitions. As he wrote in his diary, House appreciated Hoover's great talent, noting that he "is the kind of man I like to help push to the front. He cannot fail to have much influence upon our public life. He has sense and a spirit of fairness that appeals to me."[1]

House wanted Hoover to run on the Democratic ticket, claiming that he could dominate the Democratic Party and that even if he lost in 1920, he could run again in 1924 and win. But Hoover, who planned to run as a Republican, argued that "the President had made it impossible for anyone to win on the democratic ticket."[2] House agreed, and by May 11 concluded that "everything is going from bad to worse." Wilson continued to reject any reservations to the peace treaty and seemed determined to make its ratification the leading issue of the campaign. House was discouraged. The president was intensely unpopular, his administration was in disarray, but he would listen "to no one." House wondered "how I influenced him so many years and yet retained his friendship and affection."[3]

House could not imagine that the president was seriously thinking of running again, but that is exactly what Wilson, as the spring unfolded, seemed intent on doing. He believed that were the Democratic convention deadlocked the delegates might turn to him as "someone to lead them out of the wilderness."[4] As the convention neared, Wilson, as one biographer notes, "held with such tenacity to the shreds of power," convinced that a third term would vindicate his policies. McAdoo, who had been the most

visible and successful member of his cabinet, was the obvious heir and carrier of the Wilsonian legacy, but the president would not stand aside for his
son-in-law. Neither Edith nor Grayson would tell him that his candidacy
was a delusion.[5]

When the Democratic convention opened in San Francisco on June
28, the delegates cheered the president as a large American flag was lifted,
revealing a portrait of their fallen leader. But most of the delegates realized
that he was unfit to run. McAdoo and James M. Cox, the three-term governor of Ohio, were the leading contenders, and on July 6, on the forty-fourth
ballot, Cox finally prevailed. He chose Assistant Secretary of the Navy
Franklin D. Roosevelt as his running mate. When Cox and Roosevelt visited the White House on July 18, they found the president seated in his
special chair, so feeble that in a low, weak voice he said: "Thank you for
coming. I am very glad you came."[6]

Cox and Roosevelt faced an uphill struggle. Their party was divided and
disorganized, while the Republicans, who had met in Chicago in June, had
nominated Warren G. Harding, an amiable and experienced Ohio politician. Harding, who had served in the Senate since 1914, was viewed by
many as a shallow candidate, but he and the party leaders ran a disciplined,
shrewd campaign, claiming that Wilson and the Democrats were responsible for all the nation's troubles. They promised a return to "normalcy," or,
as Harding put it, "not heroics, but healing; not nostrums, but normalcy;
not revolution, but restoration;. . . not surgery, but serenity." Republican
leaders sensed that the American people were tired of years of reform at
home and entanglement abroad.[7]

On June 12, while the Republicans were deliberating in Chicago,
House, Loulie, and Fanny sailed on the SS *Lapland* for England. Initially
House had planned to spend the summer on the North Shore, but an offer
from Cyrus H. K. Curtis, publisher of the *Philadelphia Public Ledger* convinced him to change his plans. Curtis proposed to send House to Europe
in an advisory capacity, one in which he would not write dispatches in
his own name but offer guidance to the paper's foreign correspondents. In
return, he was to be paid a handsome sum, $2,500 a month, a $10,000 letter
of credit, and passage to and from Europe.[8] Shortly before leaving, House
sent Wilson a sympathetic letter, claiming that "future generations will
read with amazement and shame the story of the warfare waged upon you."
The president promptly replied. He was pleased that his onetime counselor
would "have the refreshment of a trip across the water" and reported that

"I am improving in health. It is an uphill work and the hill is very steep, but with patience and persistence I think I can breast it."[9]

House quickly settled into a comfortable routine, pleased by the cool English summer and by the fact that he was deluged with more invitations than he could accept. He dined with a series of notable figures—Balfour, Cecil, Grey, Lloyd George, Paderewski—and was surprisingly frank with his British friends about his relationship with the president, explaining that "I am not in touch with him although we have never quarreled; that I have ceased to act in an advisory capacity and have not seen him since he left Paris."[10]

House relished the "mad rush" of his days in England. "The strenuous life," he wrote Auchincloss, "is still going on with us." He and Loulie had dinner with the reformers Sidney and Beatrice Webb, but House agreed with only some of their socialist doctrines and found that he liked Beatrice more than her husband (while she dismissed Loulie as a "typical American society woman, eager to be in the centre of the picture, with an ugly voice and fussy egotistical intelligence"). He listened to the playwright George Bernard Shaw talk brilliantly over lunch, dined with Liberal editors at the Reform Club, and attended a garden party at Buckingham Palace, where George V reminded him of their many wartime conversations. House "was surprised at the number [of people] I knew," and felt that he was "on the inside of everything that is going on."[11]

On July 6, House learned that Cox had won the Democratic nomination. He did not know the governor well but believed that he would "make a strong candidate" and now thought that the chances for the Democrats were far better than first appeared. Like many Democrats, House underestimated Harding, concluding that "if we cannot beat Harding we cannot beat anybody." In a letter of congratulation to Cox, House promised to return to the United States by mid-September in order to help the Democratic ticket.[12]

As the summer progressed House began to write weekly articles for the *Public Ledger* that reflected his deep concern over the situation in Europe.[13] Throughout the Continent all governments, whether they had won or lost the war, faced massive financial problems, political instability, and public disillusionment with the outcome of the struggle. The war had dramatically reshaped the map of Europe, bringing a collapse of four empires, the emergence of many new or restored states, and a reshaping of the boundaries of others. All of these changes led to what seemed an endless series of internal disputes and small wars. The largest of these conflicts, between Russia and Poland, reached a critical stage in the summer of 1920, when the Red Army approached Warsaw and threatened the new Polish state. Only a desperate Polish counterattack saved the capital and in early October brought an armistice. In Germany a dispute raged over how to fulfill the terms of the peace treaty, and France and Britain, whose differences extended around the globe, disagreed on how to treat their old foe. House agreed with Paul Mantoux, a high-ranking League official, who in June 1920 saw "threats of war from all sides. . . if these are fulfilled, catastrophe is inevitable."[14]

As House's stay in England drew to a close, he reflected on the warm reception he had received. "My opinion" he wrote Mezes, "is constantly asked and even about the most intimate affairs. I see no difference from former visits." His break with the president had apparently not affected his British friends and he was now full of optimism about his life. When his Texas boyhood friend Paul Cruger lamented the passage of time, House (now sixty-two) replied that "you lay too much stress on your age. There is no reason why you should not be able to do your work with pleasure for many years to come. I feel no difference myself and am able to do more now than when I was much younger. It is largely a condition of mind."[15]

On August 29, after brief stays in the Hague, Brussels, and Paris, House returned to London and nine days later left for New York on the SS *Olympic*. His visit to Europe, he reflected, had been the "most delightful" that he had ever had. "Cool weather, interesting work, pleasant surroundings and every courtesy that could possibly be shown us, and someone else paying the freight." His voyage across the North Atlantic, on the other hand, was "an unhappy one," since the ocean was rough and foggy and the passenger list uninteresting.[16]

When House returned to New York—and a spacious new apartment at 112 East 74th Street—he found letters from friends giving a pessimistic assessment of Cox's campaign. "The Democratic campaign," Auchincloss asserted, "is in the mess that we expected it to be in." Robert Woolley, an experienced party organizer, believed that the tide had set in against Cox and warned House against visiting national headquarters—"your stomach can not stand the jolt. It is a snug harbor for incompetents and a clearing house of gloom." "Never," Woolley concluded, "has there been a more pathetic performance on the part of a great political party."[17] Nevertheless, House tried to influence the course of the campaign. He urged Cox to attack Harding for his "absurd proposal to substitute a new plan of world organization [for Wilson's League]" and, in a long letter to Newton Baker, pointed out that it was a mistake for the secretary of war and other Democratic orators to lay so much stress on a defense of Article X—which did not "touch the day to day life of the League"—and to ignore the many ways in which the League was promoting international cooperation. The League, in short, had "become a living organism . . . [that] is over the top and that within the next year. . . will enter fully into its own."[18]

By early October, House concluded that Cox's prospects were "hopeless," that he had no more "than a gambler's chance." The campaign was being mismanaged and lacked funding, but even the most efficient campaign organization, in House's judgment, could not overcome the "unreasonable and unreasoning desire for change" and the refusal to give the president and his administration any credit for what they had accomplished. Harding, who "seems to have no mind of his own upon any subject," was almost certain to be the next president.[19]

At the end of October, House reached out to the president, reassuring him "how often I think of you and wish for the triumph of the great cause which you have sponsored and have advocated with such eloquence and force." Wilson replied with a brief, nondescript note, the last letter that House would ever receive from him. House was ready for the bad news that came on election day, concluding that "Another Samson has pulled a temple down upon himself."[20] The outcome of the election had really never been in doubt. Cox, who appealed to conservative, business-oriented Democrats, ran a confused, under-funded campaign, while Harding combined a front-porch campaign—he mostly stayed in Marion, Ohio—with a sophisticated, well-funded organization. He took few clear positions on domestic issues and straddled the issue of American membership in the League, although in October he made it clear that he did not want to join Wilson's League. The result was a Republican triumph, greater than most observers had expected, a massive repudiation of Wilson's presidency. Harding won by a margin of 60 to 34 percent (Eugene Debs also ran as the Socialist candidate), sweeping the East, Midwest, and West, carrying Democratic strongholds such as Boston and New York City, and winning ample margins in the House and Senate. As Tumulty remarked, "it wasn't a landslide, it was an earthquake."[21]

At the end of November, Edith invited Ray Stannard Baker to the White House for lunch. Baker arrived early to watch moving pictures. While he waited in the parlor he saw the president—"a broken, ruined old man, shuffling along, his left arm inert, the fingers drawn up like a claw, the left side of his face sagging frightfully." Edith, Baker, Grayson, and a few other guests then watched films of Wilson's triumphant tour of Europe and were transported into another world. Soon the films ended, and "all that glory had faded away with a click and a sputter." Wilson "turned slowly, and shuffled out of the doorway, without looking aside and without speaking." While he would remain in office until March 4, 1921, his presidency was, in fact, over.[22]

After the election, House received a note from Edith. In cleaning out the White House, she had found two suits of clothes belonging to House, which had hung in a closet for several years. She had mailed them to Edward. And "My own dear One," she informed the Colonel somewhat cryptically, "is slowly climbing the long hill which [he] seemed never to begin to ascend." In November and December various friends stopped by to share gossip from Washington, but House was now trying to put his break with Wilson behind him and had no interest in trying to secure an invitation to the White House. A meeting with the president would now only embarrass both men. "I thought the matter had gone too far," he reflected in his diary, "to be rectified and no good could come of it. The opportunity to serve has now passed and matters are best left where he has chosen to leave them during the past year."[23]

Throughout the winter of 1920–1921 House remained busy, seeing a wide variety of people. He and Loulie went out to dinner nearly every night, often attending a performance at the Metropolitan Opera afterward, and occasionally entertained lavishly—for example, giving a dinner for sixty-four people at the Colony Club honoring Paderewski and his wife. He maintained his arrangement with the *Public Ledger*, writing a weekly column on current affairs, and put together, with the help of a young Yale historian, Charles Seymour (who had been one of the Inquiry's experts at Paris), a series of fifteen lectures at the Academy of Music in Philadelphia by major American participants in the peace conference. These weekly talks, which began on December 10, 1920, were then published in a book in 1921, edited by House and Seymour, entitled *What Really Happened at Paris: The Story of the Peace Conference, 1918–1919*. House contributed a foreword and a final, bland essay on "The Versailles Peace in Retrospect," one in which he was careful not to criticize Wilson's leadership.[24]

House also tried to evaluate the new administration that was taking shape. Richard Washburn Child, one of Harding's speechwriters, told him that the new president "was an indolent man but there was nothing of the fakir about him," and that while he was "ignorant of most of the big questions that would confront him. . . he was not opinionated and would take advice." Early in 1921 House met the new vice-president, Calvin Coolidge, and was not impressed. "He may have ability, doubtless has," House commented, "but there was nothing in his conversation to indicate it and he is totally without charm." Hoover "shone in comparison."[25]

House made no mention, either in his diary or in his letters, of the inauguration in Washington on March 4. On a cold, clear day Wilson rode in an open car with Harding to the Capitol, where he performed the final duties of his presidency. Unable because of the steep stairs to attend the inaugural ceremony, Wilson, Edith, Grayson, and Tumulty then drove to his new home at 2340 S. Street. His presidency had finally ended. The grim scene in Washington seemed far away to House, who by March 6 was in Camden, South Carolina, enjoying the "soft and warm" air and the fact that "there are real negroes about and they are of the old time and live in the old way. I feel as if I had gone back some fifty years and was looking upon familiar boyhood scenes."[26]

During the winter of 1920–1921, Ray Stannard Baker visited the White House often, and on February 12 had a talk with House in New York. He had long been fascinated by the relationship between the president and his counselor, and now, as the Wilson era drew to a close, reflected on the friendship between the two men. He found House "as busy as ever seeing people of all kinds." His description merits quoting in full:

> I never met the Colonel without a new sense of personal liking such as I have never at any time felt for the President. He is a human soul: he is generous: he is kindly: he wants good in the world: and he has a kind of common-sense (not wisdom) which grows out of his knowledge of what human beings are. His intellectual equipment is small: he has no real mind of his own: his instincts & feelings keep him generally upon the liberal & and democratic side, but when confronted with real events & and hard-set personalities—as often at Paris—he compromises everything away in order to preserve "harmony" & keep people liking one another. He has no *inner structure*: no bony framework: and yet a lovable man. Such men, with the best intent in the world, often do as much harm as good . . . . I think the Colonel understood the President better than most men: & wanted to serve him well: but got too little *explanation*, too little human sympathy and encouragement . . . . The President always hated to bother with human arrangements . . . . The President had vast labor to do, great legislative plans to work out, many

speeches to make: and he was always at the edge of his physical capacity, always having to conserve his energy—and he let cultivation of these ordinary human relationships. . . slip by . . . . He never seemed to realize what an intensely human world this is! . . . It was perhaps because these two men were at opposite poles of temperament: one cold & negative, the other warm & positive, that they so flew together, each recognizing in the other what he lacked. Both had a kind of sincerity & disinterestedness—a greatness!—in his quality. People love House. . . and he loves his friends: and is to-day, as he was at Paris, cheery, optimistic-yes, happy! He lives always in a kind of warm haze of good-feeling. What a contrast with the grim, bitter, tragic, lonely old man there in S. street!

Baker concluded with an assessment of their respective legacies that would have deeply upset House, who had planned so carefully, through his voluminous diary, to shape posterity's view of him: "And yet twenty years from now he [House] will be utterly forgotten. . . except as he was a friend, a helper, of the President: an incident in the President's career & one of the men who reflected for a moment the light from that great figure and then suffered his displeasure."[27]

34
New Beginnings

On May 3, 1921, House, Loulie, and Fanny left New York on the SS *Aquitania*. It was, House noted, "a delightful voyage—pleasant weather and good company." House was particularly interested in the new ambassador to the Court of St. James, George B. Harvey, a prominent editor and publisher, with whom he had long conversations. The ambassador's "frankness" astonished House, who urged him to participate in the deliberations of the European powers and to work "to bring about an American-British-Japanese understanding in the Pacific." Clearly House hoped to have some influence with the new administration. On the morning of May 10, the *Aquitania* docked at Cherbourg, France, and the next day House reached Paris, where he took elegant rooms at the Ritz Hotel looking out over a large garden. There he found more invitations to luncheons and dinners than he could accept.[1]

From May until the end of August, House traveled in Europe, visiting Berlin, Prague, Vienna, and London, conferring with political leaders, and especially trying to understand the shifting currents of British politics. By August 25, when he left Liverpool on the SS *Empress of France*, he was "sick and tired" of his busy social life in London, although Loulie, he noted, "is flourishing like a bay tree."[2] On August 31, he, Loulie, and Fanny arrived in Quebec, where Janet and Gordon met them at the dock. They spent three days motoring from Quebec to the North Shore, visited Mona and Randolph for two weeks, and by the end of September were back in New York.[3]

In the fall of 1921, House returned to his familiar routines. Although sixty-three years old, he remained full of energy, walking for half an hour twice a day, usually with a companion, with whom he would carry on a vigorous conversation. Hamilton Fish Armstrong, the editor of *Foreign Affairs* (the publication of the newly created Council on Foreign Relations), saw House often in the 1920s and found the famous elder statesman always "kind and courteous," someone who "paid less attention to things in print than to what came in by the ear." Occasionally "he would lay his hand on yours, if you were beside him, and you knew he was going to open his mind, beginning either with 'This is between you and me and the angels,' or, more solemnly still, 'This is graveyard.'" Armstrong also observed Loulie, who was a year younger than her husband. He felt that she "must have been very beautiful as a girl, and her lovely complexion, white hair and sweet smile made her charming still." By the early 1920s, however, she had a poor memory, and often misused words, referring to anyone who was dead or in trouble as "pore dear." They had been married forty years.[4]

On October 7, House's learned that his publisher friend, Cyrus Curtis, planned to take his yacht to Washington and to entertain President Harding for lunch. He asked House to join him. On October 13, House boarded the yacht, along with Harding, his wife, Vice-President Coolidge, and various members of the administration. House recorded no impression of Harding, but enjoyed talking to his wife, Florence, who he found "is a handsome woman, well dressed and a good type of the Middle West." The behavior of the "staid and solemn Vice President" amused him. He was "gotten up *a la rigueur* with silk hat and its accompaniments" and insisted on a rigid proto-col on boarding the launch that would take guests to the yacht.[5]

While in Washington, House stopped at 2340 S Street to leave his call-ing card for Edith and Wilson, who were out for their daily automobile ride. House remained curious about the reasons for the break, and had a long talk with Irving Hoover, chief usher at the White House. Hoover explained that the president's "change of feeling toward me [House] began at Paris, just after his return from the United States in March," and that it was Wilson himself, jealous of his counselor's behavior, who initiated the break. Those around him, especially Edith and Grayson, "fanned the flame," and for months they controlled all the decisions that the enfeebled president made.

House enjoyed his trip to Washington but no longer liked "the atmo-sphere of the place."[6] During his stay, he met with several foreign lead-ers who had arrived to attend the Washington Naval Conference. Called together at the invitation of Secretary of State Charles Evans Hughes, leaders from Britain, France, Italy, Japan, China, and several other nations began deliberations on November 12, 1921, on naval disarmament and on ways to achieve security in the Pacific. House was skeptical of the conference, which he thought the administration had called "largely for the purpose of killing the League," but he was eager to meet foreign dignitaries as they arrived in the United States. In New York he had long discussions with Admiral David Beatty about Anglo-American naval rivalry, while in Washington he talked with Balfour, Briand, Foch, and members of the Chinese delegation. With all the delegates he asserted that while the Harding administration opposed the League, a Democratic administration would be for it. He insisted that "the League [should be kept] as the main rock upon which disarmament and future peace must finally rest."[7]

Toward the close of 1921, as books on the Wilson years appeared, House contemplated his own place in history. On November 19, and again on December 6, he had long talks with Charles Seymour about "my papers and what was best to do with them," and both he and Sidney Mezes, who were impressed with Seymour's *Woodrow Wilson and the World War*, decided to ask the young Yale historian to edit them. Later in December, House and Fanny began "going over" his papers.[8] As he read through his diary, he decided that December 31, 1921, would be the last "regular entry." He felt a sense of relief that he was "done with it for it has been an irksome task, both for me and Miss Denton my secretary. Day by day and oftentimes hour by hour we have striven to record events as they occurred. Always pressed for time, they were set down hastily but accurately as best I knew." House only hoped that his large collection of letters and memoranda would place in context many of the events and conversations recorded in his diary.[9]

On February 6, 1922, the Washington Conference came to an end. The results were a triumph for American diplomacy and a confirmation of America's new role in world affairs. Secretary of State Hughes's skillful diplomacy had brought about a naval limitation agreement, a non-aggression pact in the Pacific, and an accord protecting American rights in China. House congratulated Balfour, the head of the British delegation, on the way in which his diplomacy had helped bring about an Anglo-American rapprochement. But he disliked the fact that the administration's independent initiative had overshadowed the League and he urged Democratic senators, when presented with the conference's three treaties for ratification, to point out "their faults" and to compare "the treaties with what might have been accomplished by the League of Nations."[10]

Throughout the late winter and spring House remained busy with interviews with a variety of people and with a crowded social life. He devoted much of his energy, however, to a series of conversations with

Charles Seymour. In these talks, two of which were held in December 1921, and ten from January through May 1922, House covered the politics, diplomacy, and personalities of the Wilson era, taking positions that would have been familiar to any reader of his diary. As he came to know Seymour better, he realized that he had found in the young academic (he was only thirty-seven) the perfect biographer. Seymour, who came from an old and distinguished family, had graduated from Yale and had also studied at Cambridge University, the University of Freiburg, and the Sorbonne. He had risen rapidly through the ranks, becoming a full professor at the age of thirty-two and the Sterling Professor of History at Yale five years later.

By the winter of 1921–1922, House was concerned about his own reputation and charges that he had been disloyal to Wilson. He wished to commission a chronicle of his life, based on his diary and letters, one that would explain his point of view and defend the positions he had taken. Seymour met all of his requirements. He admired Wilson, had impressive academic credentials, and, best of all, had an uncritical admiration of House. In effect, House's memoirs would be published under Seymour's name, giving them more legitimacy in what was sure to be a struggle over the historical reputation of the president and his advisers.[11]

On May 30, 1922, the House Party left New York on the SS *Resolute* for what had become their annual visit to Europe. The *Resolute* reached Boulogne on the night of June 7, and the next day they reached Paris. House had "come to Paris this year," he informed Loulie, "to rest and to see and not to talk and eat."[12] House lingered in Paris, where he saw Clemenceau often, spent July at Cabourg, Calvados (a fashionable resort on the Northeast Coast), and in mid-August ended up in London, where he conferred with Asquith, Cecil, and Grey. In the summer of 1922 the "general situation" in Europe worried House, who thought it "worse, much worse, than it was last year." The problem of French security had not been resolved, and while the inter-allied reparations commission in early 1921 had set a figure for German payments to the Allies, the British and German governments felt the figure was too high, while the French government felt it was too low. House worried that Raymond Poincaré, who had returned to power in January 1922, would take unilateral action to collect reparations and occupy Germany's Ruhr valley. In an hour and a half breakfast with Lloyd George, the two men discussed the looming crisis in Europe and ways in which to protect France and finally resolve the reparations tangle. But the wily prime minister, who was also preoccupied with his own political future, made no commitments to specific policies.[13]

During House's stay in London, he read some of the serialization in the *New York Times* of Ray Stannard Baker's forthcoming *Woodrow Wilson and the World Settlement*. What he found outraged House. He responded vigorously to Baker's criticism of his role at the peace conference and to his version of the break with the president, dispatching a fourteen-page letter to Balfour. The acting foreign secretary also objected to "misrepresentations" of the historical record and directed Maurice Hankey to write an elaborate refutation. As the battle over the Wilson presidency intensified, House learned that Seymour was "keen as mustard" about their project, had outlined proposed chapters, and would have several completed when he returned to America at the end of the summer.[14] On September 6, the House Party left Liverpool on the SS *Tyrrhenia*.

During his summer in Europe, House had closely followed American presidential politics. He was convinced that the Harding administration was a "failure," that the Republicans were "helplessly floundering about," and that the Democrats, if they displayed any political wisdom, could sweep them out of power. Unless Wilson became a candidate for a third term—which seemed an extremely remote prospect—he reassured McAdoo that his nomination seemed certain.

House had kept in touch with McAdoo who, after completing a speaking tour of ten states west of the Mississippi, assured his old friend that "there is a general feeling that Harding, although a nice, amiable gentleman, is hopelessly weak and incompetent, and directly controlled by Wall Street and big business." He believed that the Democrats would "gain substantial victories" in the forthcoming congressional elections.[15] McAdoo read the popular pulse correctly. Low farm prices in the Midwest, combined with Republican factionalism and an aggressive campaign by the American Federation of Labor and the railroad brotherhoods, narrowed the gap between the two parties in the House and Senate. While Republicans still held nominal majorities in both houses of Congress, in fact they lost control because of the alienation from the administration of many Republican insurgents. House was "never more certain of party success than I am now in 1924."[16]

By the end of 1922, Franco-German relations had grown more tense. German leaders, unwilling to accept the consequences of defeat, pursued a campaign to undermine the Versailles settlement and to reduce reparations payments to France, while Poincaré, aware of the mood in the Chamber of Deputies, considered independent action. Finally, on January 11, 1923, French and Belgian troops entered the industrial heartland of Germany, the Ruhr Valley, to escort engineers and technicians who would now begin to exploit the area's rich industrial resources. The German government responded by suspending reparations payments and by ordering German miners and railway workers to withhold their cooperation, a policy of passive resistance. The standoff in the Ruhr led to chaotic conditions in Germany and to a realization among all the great powers that for the sake of the economic and political stability of Europe, some sort of comprehensive reparations compromise was essential.[17]

The Franco-German deadlock alarmed House, who on February 20, 1923, urged the Belgian financier, D. N. Heineman, to pursue a plan that included German concessions on reparations, a guarantee of French security, and foreign loans that would bring about the stabilization of the German currency. But as the crisis lengthened, House realized that if he were to play a role in its resolution he would have to talk directly with political leaders in London and Paris.[18]

On May 26, 1923, the House trio left New York on the SS *Homeric,* arriving in London on June 4. They would remain there for nearly two months. House quickly settled into a busy routine, complaining that "the hospitality of our friends here is very wearing. Last week we had two meals at our hotel, other than breakfast, and the coming week is as bad." Soon after his arrival in London, House dined with Lloyd George, who was now out of power. Despite his formidable political skills, dissent among Conservatives in his coalition government had grown and on October 23, 1922, he had resigned from office.[19] After Lloyd George's resignation, Andrew Bonar Law, the Conservative Party leader, had formed a new government, and on November 15, 1922, the Conservatives had won a decisive victory in the general elections. But on May 20, 1923, Bonar Law, ill with cancer, resigned, and Stanley Baldwin, whom one historian describes as an "agreeable, tolerant, broad-minded man of business," became the new prime minister. Over the next ten years, Baldwin was to play a major role in British politics.[20]

On June 13 House met with Baldwin. Convinced that it was a fear of Germany that was shaping French policy, House wanted to tie a reparations settlement to German assurances "for the security of France." After an inconclusive hour-long discussion, House decided that Baldwin was "as much at sea as what to do as everyone else." He thought the new prime minister was "an intelligent, honest and courageous man without marked ability."[21] Throughout the remainder of his stay in England House promoted an Anglo-French-German settlement, but by July 26, when House left London for Paris, French troops remained in the Ruhr, the German policy of passive resistance continued, and Franco-German relations were, in House's judgment, more "critical" than at any time since the Armistice.

On July 31, after House arrived in Paris, he tried to assess the French point of view. But because of Poincaré's stubbornness and his support from the French people, House could see no way out of the impasse.[22] Rather than reach out to members of the French government, he left Paris on August 11 for an eight-day trip through the northwestern provinces of France, the Vendée, and the Loire Valley. He visited Clemenceau's home at St. Vincent-sur-Jard in the Vendée, where his old friend, immaculately dressed, greeted him at his "unpretentious little house on the sand dunes of that wind swept coast and seems entirely happy." House relished his leisurely trip, noting that "it is the first time for years I have gotten completely out of touch with things."[23] On August 18, when House returned to Paris, he found a cable announcing that his brother T. W. had died at the age of seventy-seven. Although House knew that he was in failing health, his death was, he wrote his nephew, "a great shock to me although I have been fearful all summer. It is hard for me to realize that he has gone and the thought of it saddens me greatly." Of the eight House children, only Edward and his sister Mary were still alive. After news of T. W.'s death arrived, House canceled all of his engagements, including a trip to Switzerland, and a few days later left Paris for London. On September 6 he sailed for Boston on the SS *Scythia,* and after his arrival on September 13 lingered on the North Shore. By the end of September he was back in New York.[24]

Throughout the summer of 1923 House had observed the shifting American political scene. Democratic gains in the November 1922 congressional elections, as well as Harding's weakness as a leader, led many Democrats to conclude, as Bernard Baruch put it, that "we have the next election in the hollow of our hand." Before sailing for Europe, House had found McAdoo "cheerful and confident," although he realized that the "Crown Prince" might be unable, given the deep divisions within the Democratic Party, to win a two-thirds vote at the national convention in the summer of 1924.[25]

Harding's sudden death from a heart attack on August 2, 1923, changed the political landscape. Both House and his friends believed that Vice-President Coolidge was a "much shrewder politician than Harding" and would be a much stronger presidential candidate in 1924.[26] House still placed his hopes in McAdoo, conferring with him when he visited New York, working on planks for his platform, and seeking to promote his candidacy with a variety of politicians. It looked as if McAdoo, with his progressive credentials, national prominence, and support from organized labor and prohibitionists, would be a formidable candidate. He might be able to carry the South and West and recreate the Wilson coalition of 1916.[27]

At the time of Harding's death a variety of financial and kickback scandals—which came to be known as the Teapot Dome—had begun to emerge. In the fall of 1923, Senate investigators began to explore the underside of the Harding administration, and in January 1924, as disclosures mounted, it became apparent that McAdoo's behavior as a lawyer, while it did not directly involve him in the Teapot Dome, raised questions about both his character and his electability. Democrats had hoped to use Republican corruption as a major theme in their 1924 campaign; now the scandal had tainted their leading candidate for the nomination.[28] Many of McAdoo's most important backers, such as Bernard Baruch and Daniel Roper, thought he had no chance to win the nomination and should withdraw. House agreed, concluding that if his old friend made a graceful withdrawal he might still be chosen as the nominee by a deadlocked convention. But McAdoo refused to leave the race and House continued to support him, although he feared that he "will be beaten and humiliated, for the democrats will hardly take a candidate for whom they must explain throughout the campaign."[29] Just as House was pondering McAdoo's fate, word came from Washington that Wilson was seriously ill, and late on the morning of February 3, 1924, House learned that the president had died. Edith arranged two funeral services on February 6. The first, a small one, was held at 2340 S. Street; the second, a public one for 400 people, was held in Bethlehem Chapel of the unfinished Washington National Cathedral. Initially House planned to travel to Washington and attend the funeral, but Tumulty called and said that he had not been invited. Finally, House made what must have been a humiliating phone call to Baruch, asking if he could find out from Grayson whether he would be admitted to the ceremonies. Baruch claimed he could not get in touch with Grayson, and House concluded that "this was an evasion and that he had made the request and had been told that I was not expected." House was understandably cautious, since he knew that Edith was determined to keep him away from her husband. It seemed in character that she would not even include his longtime counselor in these final ceremonies.[30]

Instead of traveling to Washington, House attended a memorial service at Madison Square Garden, where he sat on the platform while 10,000 people crowded into the great hall. "I have never," he recorded, "attended a more impressive and touching service." Four days later he published in the *New York Times* an effusive tribute to his old friend, concluding that "no man of his time touched so deeply the conscience and aspirations of mankind."[31]

In the late winter and spring of 1924, as he recovered from Wilson's death, House remained busy. "Every hour of the day," he recorded, "is filled one way or another," and his evenings, too, were overflowing with social events, although he complained that "Loulie likes to go and I hate to deprive her of the pleasure although it is a constant strain upon me." He had a long talk with Tumulty about Cary Grayson's (the "slimy one") responsibility for the break, and worked out final arrangements with Charles Seymour for the completion of the four-volume edition of his papers. House agreed to give the bulk of his papers to Yale University, with the understanding that the young scholar would have sole use of them until the volumes were completed. Seymour was grateful for the arrangement, expressing his "appreciation of the new factors you have brought into my life, not merely historical and intellectual in value, but personal and philosophical,—especially in that I have been allowed to see how a life ought to be lived."[32]

As the Democratic convention approached, a stream of presidential candidates found their way to House's modest study. Convinced that McAdoo would not win the nomination, House cast about for another candidate, settling on John W. Davis, a native of West Virginia who had had an extraordinary career as a successful Wall Street lawyer, Wilson's solicitor general, and his last ambassador to Great Britain.[33] Whatever House's doubts, however, McAdoo was relentless in his pursuit of the nomination. He had no intention of becoming a "quitter" and informed House that "If I go down at all, my face will be toward the enemy but I am not going down." In the spring Democratic primaries, and especially the Texas primary at the end of May, McAdoo won big majorities over his chief rival, Governor Alfred E. Smith of New York. In late May, House found his friend "militant and confident of getting the nomination. The man has great charm, unlimited courage and fine imagination."[34]

On May 17, 1924, the House trio left New York, arriving in London on the morning of May 26 and settling in at the Connaught Hotel. Initially House had planned to sail directly to France, but the new Labour prime minister, James Ramsay MacDonald (who had formed a government with Liberal support in January), had asked him to come to London first. The afternoon of his arrival he received an invitation to spend the night at Chequers, the official country estate of the prime minister.[35] On June 1, House arrived at Chequers at six o'clock. The prime minister greeted him and gave him a tour of the mansion, which House found full of "beauty and charm." The two men then began "an intimate talk which lasted with interruptions until twelve o'clock the next day." MacDonald was eager to reach out to the American elder statesman, but their discussion focused primarily on the League of Nations and House's plan for American membership in the League as an associate member. House and MacDonald did not discuss in any detail "the composure of the European situation."[36]

By June 1924 the crisis in Europe had greatly eased. In August of the previous year, Gustav Streseman had become chancellor of Germany, and his new government had ended the policy of passive resistance in the Ruhr, resumed reparation deliveries, and moved toward Franco-German economic cooperation. In November, Poincaré had accepted an Anglo-American recommendation to appoint a reparations commission of experts led by a prominent American financier, Charles G. Dawes. The Dawes Commission, which in January 1924 began meetings in Paris, produced a report on April 9, one that proposed a French withdrawal from the Ruhr, a reduction of Germany's debt, and a loan by American banks to Germany. Since the Dawes Plan involved changes in the Versailles Treaty, an international conference opened in London on July 16 to resolve differences among the powers. House was optimistic about the outcome.[37]

While in London, House received detailed reports on the deliberations of the Democratic national convention, which on June 24 opened in New York's Madison Square Garden. The convention, which lasted for sixteen days—an unusually long time—in oppressive heat, revealed the deep divisions that ran through the party. More conservative eastern and midwestern Democrats, led by New York Governor Al Smith, disliked McAdoo's progressivism and his ties to the Wilson administration and were determined to block his nomination. Bitter disputes over the Ku Klux

Klan, the League of Nations, and many economic questions disrupted the convention. It was not until the 99th ballot that McAdoo finally released his delegates and not until the 103rd ballot that they chose John W. Davis as a compromise candidate.

Davis's nomination was a victory for conservative forces within the Democratic Party. He was, his biographer observes, "an instinctive conservative," one who wanted to return the party to its nineteenth-century tradition of limited government and laissez-faire liberalism.[38] House found the nomination of the dignified, graceful former ambassador "a most satisfactory outcome." House's identification with Davis revealed, once again, his interest in people rather than ideas, and how years of preoccupation with foreign affairs had weakened his progressivism.[39]

House hoped to play a major role in the Davis campaign. Soon after the convention, he wrote the nominee several long letters, recommending three political operators—Homer Cummings, Daniel Roper, and Robert Woolley—to organize his campaign, and offering suggestions for his acceptance speech. House wanted Davis to get "out of the shadow of Wall Street" and make Chicago his headquarters. He was also eager for Gordon Auchincloss, an enthusiastic Davis supporter, to work his way into the "inner councils" of the campaign. House realized, however, that "Davis' chances are not good at best," and worried about a report that the former ambassador wore spats. The candidate, he cautioned Auchincloss, should "wear rough and tumble clothes from now until November 4th, and knickerbockers, spats, English butlers, the Prince of Wales, etc. etc. should be put in moth balls until after the election."[40]

On August 3, after a "stormy crossing" of the Channel, the House trio settled in at the Ritz Hotel in Paris. The main purpose of House's visit was to encourage the French government to accept the settlement finally reached in mid-August at the London Conference. The French premier, Edouard Herriott (who had formed a government on June 13 after Poincaré resigned), in effect accepted American and British terms, agreeing to the Dawes Plan and the evacuation of the Ruhr by August 1925. France could no longer act unilaterally to enforce the Treaty of Versailles. After conferring with French officials, House left Paris on August 30, arriving in London in the evening. Six days later he left on the SS *Scythia* for Boston.[41]

House returned to a discouraging political landscape and quickly discovered that in supporting Davis, he had made a monumental misjudgment. He tried, without success, "to stir him to action and to make his speeches more forceful and more pertinent to the trend of the times," but Davis could not change the habits of a lifetime. Nor did he show any "aptitude for organization or judgment of men." "The result," House concluded, was "about the worst managed and most confused campaign that I have ever had any knowledge of, and this is saying much for it was thought that our campaign in 1920 reached the high water mark of incompetency." Early in October House lunched with the forlorn candidate and, over the course of a three-hour meeting, "tried to get him to rise to what I considered the necessary heights in his campaign." But as he sadly concluded, he was no longer dealing with Woodrow Wilson.[42]

From the start of his campaign, Davis's prospects for success were bleak. Senator Robert La Follette of Wisconsin, running on a third party ticket, promised to win much of the progressive vote, while President Coolidge benefited from the return of prosperity as well as from the resolution of the European crisis. He stood for rectitude, stability, and prosperity. Coolidge ran a front-porch campaign, using newsreels and radio effectively and projecting a personality that appealed to many Americans. As one reformer remarked, people felt that Coolidge "is just what the country needs, a quiet, simple, unobtrusive man, with no isms and no desire for any reform."[43]

Confronted with a popular incumbent, Davis's campaign never hit its stride. He presided over a bitterly divided party, failed to develop an effective organization, and pursued a strategy—against House's advice—that was oriented toward the Northeast and that emphasized tax reduction, government economy, and opposition to Prohibition. Davis had no interest in attacking concentrations of economic and financial power or of trying to unite the South and West behind his candidacy. Nor did Davis, whose precise, unemotional style had been developed over the years in the courtroom, know how to appeal to a diverse electorate. The results on November 4 were another resounding Democratic defeat. Coolidge swept the North and West, winning 48.9 percent of the vote, while Davis won 36.1 percent and La Follette 15.0. Davis carried no eastern state, and the Democratic presidential ticket ran behind candidates for the House and Senate throughout the country. It looked as if the Democrats would remain in the wilderness for many more years, while the nation, House concluded, would be led by a man who "does not understand what it is all about and [who]. . . is fitted merely for the business routine of the great office which he occupies."[44]

On election night, Daisy Harriman, Gordon, and Janet dined with House and Loulie, and then they all went to the *New York Times* office to receive the returns. Defeat, House knew, "was a foregone conclusion," but he was "surprised. . . by the magnitude of Coolidge's victory." "If the Democrats," he gloomily concluded, "could not win after four such years as Harding and Coolidge have given us then success would seem to be hopeless." House worried that the "religious war started in the Democratic Party" by McAdoo and the Catholic Al Smith could last another four years. Forgetting that his candidate, Davis, was nearly as conservative as Coolidge, he wondered "just how long the people of the country will permit organized wealth to direct our destiny."[45]

35
Marking Time

As 1924 drew to a close, House pondered the "rehabilitation of the Democratic Party" and also worried "that it may yet take another catastrophe like the Great War to bring the world wholly to the right view regarding the League and the necessity for settling disputes without recourse to war." Early in the New Year, however, he was encouraged by the news that Frank D. Kellogg would replace Charles Evans Hughes as secretary of state. House did not share the widespread admiration of Hughes and his accomplishments, concluding that "the best thing Coolidge has done so far was to get rid of Hughes." While he thought Kellogg would be an improvement, he was in general critical of Republican foreign policy, convinced that "today the United States is the greatest obstacle to world peace."[1]

House was eager to return to Europe, and on May 23, 1925, House, Loulie, and Fanny headed off. After a "delightful trip" they landed at Cherbourg on May 31, and later in the day reached Paris for a stay that would last more than two weeks. They would not return to the United States until late September.[2]

House arrived in Paris preoccupied with the question of French security. He made little effort, however, to see Foreign Minister Aristide Briand who, along with Foreign Minister Gustav Stresemann in Berlin and Foreign Secretary Austen Chamberlain in London, would dominate European diplomacy in the second half of the decade. But he did discuss French affairs with Minister of Labour Louis Loucheur, and remained convinced that the anxieties of French leaders over their nation's security must be addressed.[3]

After a brief stay in Brussels, on June 20 House arrived in London. The next day he met with Prime Minister Stanley Baldwin, who had returned to power on October 29, 1924, and with Foreign Secretary Chamberlain.

Finding the prime minister a "better listener" and "much more alert" than the foreign secretary, House emphasized the danger of a French invasion of Germany if there was failure of the negotiations then under way for a pact guaranteeing France's border with Germany. He also revealed that he "had tried. . . to touch President Coolidge's conscience and by impressing the Puritan streak in him stir him to action."[4]

After his conversation with Baldwin and Chamberlain, House wrote Henry White (his go-between with President Coolidge), giving his analysis of the situation in Europe. In a letter clearly intended for the president, he urged Coolidge not to "push" France on its indebtedness to the United States and explained that "France's diminishing power" was a danger for all of Europe. France, House speculated, would "soon be faced with two alternatives, a radical reduction of armaments or, as a last throw of the dice, the invasion of Germany in order to render her impotent for a great number of years. If she does not do this and reduces her army and air fleet without any security pact, she will at once become a second class power and will be at the mercy of Germany in the future." Clearly House wanted Coolidge to use his influence to bring the negotiations between Great Britain, France, and Germany to a successful conclusion.[5]

"I am seeing," House reported to Auchincloss, "lots of people here." He lunched with Balfour ("in his old time good form"), Lloyd George and his wife (who invited him to Wales), and with other notables such as Herbert and Margo Asquith, Winston Churchill, and George Bernard Shaw. House and the great playwright "got along very well together." And he especially enjoyed a visit with Grey at Fallodon.[6]

On August 2 the House trio left London for Paris, traveling, as they always tried to do, with a group of family and friends. In London they had been joined by Sidney and Nancy Mezes and Mona and Randolph Tucker, and Gordon and Janet and Louise Auchincloss planned to cross the Atlantic later in the summer. They remained in Paris for a week,[7] and then traveled to Evian-les-Bains, a fashionable spa town in southeastern France on the shores of Lake Geneva, where Loulie took a cure. On August 26 House motored to Geneva, conferred with League officials, and visited Paderewski at his home at Morges, the Villa Rond Bosson. He then moved on to Italy, stopping at Genoa, Milan, and Venice, and on September 16 boarded the SS *Duilio,* which reached New York six days later. After a long absence abroad, House found that "our home coming was unusually pleasant the weather being delightful and many friends to greet us."[8]

Once back in New York, House picked up the threads of his busy life there. He was "delighted beyond measure" at the signature of the Locarno treaties on October 16, 1925. In this settlement Belgium, France, and Germany pledged never to attack one another, to respect the western boundaries of Germany, and to maintain the demilitarization of the Rhineland. Great Britain and Italy signed as guarantors of these agreements. The American government, while it played no part in the negotiations, did make it clear that loans from American bankers were contingent on the signature of the security pact. While the Locarno treaties did not completely satisfy French or German leaders, they marked a milestone in the reintegration of Germany into the concert of Europe and brought what many observers thought was a new dawn in the rebuilding of the European state system. "There was no sense," one historian writes, "that this was a transient gleam of sunlight in the darkness of the twentieth century."[9]

Early in November McAdoo came to House's apartment for lunch, and the two friends had one of their "old time, intimate talks." House missed McAdoo, "who had so much charm, so much courage, so much vigor that it is always a pleasure to be with him," and regretted that he would never become president because "he would give this country a shaking up which it needs." House disliked the materialism and new consumer culture of the 1920s as well as the shortsighted policies of Republican administrations in Washington. He believed that "hard times would come sooner or later and that we had lifted the scale of living among our working people to such a level that they would be loathe to adjust themselves to anything lower. When depression came trouble would follow."[10]

In May, House had put off a visit to the White House, but on December 18, after another invitation from the president arrived, he boarded the train at Pennsylvania Station for the familiar journey to Washington.[11] After his arrival, Coolidge and House talked for an hour in the president's study, and then were joined by Grace Coolidge for dinner. After dinner the two men returned to the study and conversed until 10:15 in the evening. While House had met the president before, this was the first time he had had the opportunity to "make an estimate" of him. He quickly concluded that "he has more ability than I had given him credit for, but he has little imagination and no initiative. He will make a safe President and I predict that he will not do anything foolish. On the other hand, it will be nearly impossible to induce him to do anything brilliant or spectacular." As the two men covered a wide range of international issues, House "found the President singularly ill-informed regarding foreign affairs . . . . He has no background and no personal knowledge of either men or conditions outside the United States." Despite these limitations, House tried to impress on Coolidge "the necessity of our taking a position in world councils commensurate with our importance [as a nation]." The United States could no longer live "an isolated life."[12] House found the president "not at all reticent," although there was "but little small chatter," and he especially liked Grace Coolidge, "who ranks in dignity, in presence, in manner and in charm with any of her predecessors in the White House."[13]

In November, prior to House's journey to Washington, the first two volumes of his *Intimate Papers* had been put out for syndication bids (House accepted the *New York Herald Tribune*'s offer). This version of the manuscript had included Wilson's letters to House. House and Seymour had not counted, however, on Edith's determination to collect all of the information related to Wilson's life. She had chosen Ray Stannard Baker as his authorized biographer and had established her legal right to control the publication of her husband's manuscripts. When Baker set to work, he quickly discovered that most of Wilson's letters to House—which he had generally typed himself—were missing, but that they were all carefully preserved in House's files. "I tremble," Baker wrote Edith, "until I get the letters; they are simply invaluable." Initially Seymour and House had expected a reciprocal arrangement—that they would provide copies of the president's letters to House with the understanding that Seymour could publish these letters in his forthcoming volumes. But Edith had no intention of agreeing to such an equitable arrangement and refused to give Seymour the necessary permission. Edith's high-handed behavior angered House, who asked Baker "how they had the face to refuse when they had used letters of mine to the President in *Woodrow Wilson and the World Settlement* without referring them to me or asking my permission." He and Seymour realized that without Wilson's letters, the first two volumes of *The Intimate Papers* would be weakened, since the evidence for the closeness between the two men would rely too heavily on letters and diary entries written by House.[14]

With the coming of the New Year, after a stay of only four months in New York, House resumed his travels. After visits to Pass Christian, Mississippi, and Houston, Texas, on February 17, 1926, Edward, Loulie, and Fanny boarded the SS *Mauretania* for an ambitious cruise of the Mediterranean, with stops at Madeira, Gibraltar, Algiers, Villefranche,

15. Wilson and House, enjoying the adulation of a crowd. Date unknown. (Manuscript and Archives, Yale University.)

16. Wilson and House at Cornish, New Hampshire, September 1914. In late August, stricken with grief after the death of his wife Ellen, Wilson traveled to Cornish to escape the heat of Washington. House joined him for two days. The president now relied more than ever on his counselor's support. (Library of Congress Prints and Photographs Division, Washington, D.C., LC-B2-3527-3.)

17. Ellen Axson Wilson. A widely read, reflective woman, she was completely devoted to her husband's career. She respected House's political skills and welcomed him into the Wilson family, once thanking him for "being so good to us all." (Manuscript and Archives, Yale University.)

18. Left to right: Cary Grayson, Joe Tumulty, and Bernard Baruch in 1919. They all were part of the president's inner circle of advisers. From the start House had mixed feelings about Baruch, but initially he was close to Grayson and Tumulty. Eventually he broke with all three. (Library of Congress Prints and Photographs Division, Washington, D.C., LC-USZ62-138651.)

19. William Gibbs McAdoo. McAdoo was an early Wilson supporter and one of the driving forces of his presidential campaign. Wilson appointed him secretary of the treasury, and he became the most forceful member of the president's cabinet. In May 1914 he married Eleanor Wilson and also became the president's son-in-law. House admired McAdoo's energy and idealism and encouraged his ambition, convinced that he had great talent and that he might one day succeed Wilson. (Library of Congress Prints and Photographs Division, Washington, D.C. LC–USZ6-1532.)

20. Wilson and Edith, shortly after their marriage in December 1915. House supported Wilson's remarriage, but did not anticipate the extent to which Edith's love for her husband would change his own relationship with the president. (Library of Congress Prints and Photographs Division Washington, D.C., LC–USZ62-65032.)

21. House seated in the study of his New York apartment. House spent long hours seven days a week in this small study, interviewing a wide range of people. (Manuscript and Archives, Yale University.)

22. Wilson, Edith, and House, date unknown. House soon discovered that Edith was a different kind of person from Ellen. Edith was lively and stylish, but poorly educated, intolerant of the president's closest advisers, and curious about affairs of state. (Corbis.)

23. Left to right: Janet, Mona, House, his granddaughter Louise, on the North Shore, around 1920. (Author's collection.)

24. H. H. Asquith. Prime minister since 1908, Asquith had led the Liberal Party in a remarkable period of domestic reform. He gave his foreign secretary, Edward Grey, a free rein in the conduct of diplomacy. House admired Asquith's intellectual gifts, but as the war progressed grew dissatisfied with his disorganized leadership. (Library of Congress Prints and Photographs Division Washington, D.C., LC-B2-4064-14.)

25. Sir Edward Grey. Foreign secretary since the Liberals assumed power in December 1905, Grey was a tall, melancholy country squire whose love of nature seemed greater than his love of politics. As his stay in office lengthened he acquired great prestige at home and abroad. House found Grey a reassuring figure and was convinced that he was one of the great statesmen of his era. (Library of Congress Prints and Photographs Division, Washington, D.C., LC-H261- 4395.)

26. Arthur Balfour. A former prime minister and leader of the Conservative opposition in parliament, Balfour was charming, rich, and highly intelligent. In December 1916, when Asquith's coalition government collapsed, he replaced Grey as foreign secretary. Balfour's intellectual qualities and physical presence appealed to House, who felt that he possessed many of the same qualities as Wilson. (University of Glasgow.)

27. David Lloyd George. He was the rising star of the Liberal Party, a supremely gifted politician who served as Asquith's chancellor of the exchequer and who became in May 1915 minister of munitions. Dissatisfied with Asquith's wartime leadership, Lloyd George replaced him in a new coalition government in December 1916. House appreciated Lloyd George's forcefulness and accomplishments, but as the war progressed was put off by what he viewed as his opportunism and lack of principle. (Library of Congress Prints and Photographs Division, Washington, D.C., LC-USZ62-8054.)

28. House, Clemenceau, and Loulie, August 1923, taken during a visit to Clemenceau's home at St. Vincent-sur-Jard in the Vendée. (Manuscript and Archives, Yale University.)

29. House confers with the rising star of the Democratic Party, Franklin Roosevelt. Probably taken in June 1931. (Corbis.)

30. The elder statesman, circa 1934, a portrait by Charles Hopkinson. Edward
H. Auchincloss Collection. Photo by Adam Reich.

Naples, Athens, Haifa, and Alexandria.[15] For four weeks they cruised the Mediterranean. On March 17 the party left the *Mauretania* at Naples, stopped briefly in Rome, and by March 21 arrived at Cannes, where they settled in at the Hotel des Anglais. There House enjoyed the excellent food, moderate rates, and a "beautiful suite consisting of a salon and three bedrooms and bath," with separate rooms for Fanny and Loulie's maid.[16]

House lingered at the Hotel des Anglais, which was "about the best place we ever struck." There, as was true everywhere he traveled, he made new friends and met old ones. He visited with Arthur Balfour, Albert Bigelow Paine, Brand Whitlock, and one day he and Loulie lunched with Rudyard Kipling. Kipling, who sat next to Loulie, was put off by her clumsy efforts to make conversation and concluded that "she was more completely full of self and national esteem than anyone I had met in a long time. Edward was opposite to me but he was singularly quiet."[17]

House had left early for Europe in part because he anticipated the "sensation" that the publication of the first two volumes of *The Intimate Papers* would create in America and Europe. These volumes, which totaled 979 pages, were an impressive achievement, two handsomely designed books with a soft red binding, high-quality photographs, and an elegant design of type and page. Seymour's narrative linked together sometimes lengthy quotations from House's letters and diaries, and the text also included material from letters sent to House and from interviews with some of his closest associates. But he could not include Wilson's letters to House and admitted that with their absence "something of the personal attractiveness of Mr. Wilson has thus been lost."[18]

Seymour was a skilled diplomatic historian, and his re-creation of the international atmosphere in which House and Wilson operated was, especially considering how recently the Great War had ended, a model of clarity and conciseness. His talents as a biographer, however, were far less evident. In writing about the years before House met Wilson he relied entirely on House's *Reminiscences,* written in the summer of 1916, and accepted myths that House had created about his delicate health and his progressive record in Texas politics. And Seymour's unreserved admiration for House—"the pure gold of his nature, his rare humour, and supreme thoughtfulness as well as his political capacity"—influenced his narrative. In Seymour's version of events House moved shrewdly and quietly through the corridors of power in both America and Europe, rarely making a misstep in either domestic politics or international diplomacy. With his "genius for quiet persuasion," he was more radical than the president on domestic affairs and more informed about events in Europe.[19]

The Intimate Papers left the reader with no doubts about Wilson's greatness as a political leader. In his preface House wrote that "Happy the nation fortunate enough to have a Woodrow Wilson to lead it through dark and tempestuous days!" and at the end of the second volume House praised the president's s ability "to voice prophetically the subconscious hopes of the common people, a faculty which formed the basis of Wilson's title to political greatness." But the president's shortcomings were also a prominent theme that ran through the narrative. In various diary passages House noted Wilson's alleged defects—his strong prejudices, his one-track mind, and his slowness to appreciate the importance of world affairs. The result was a reversal of the roles of the two men, one that made House the dominant partner in their extraordinary collaboration and one that reduced Wilson to a subordinate position. Seymour's version of Wilson's presidency was bound to be controversial.[20]

During his travels in Europe House closely followed the reaction to *The Intimate Papers*. Most of the English reviews, he noted, with the exception of some Conservative journals, were "exceedingly complimentary," but in America the reviews were mixed, and it seemed as if *The Intimate Papers* had "stirred up the snakes." Albert Shaw wrote a sympathetic assessment in the *Review of Reviews*, Walter Lippmann a mixed one in *Foreign Affairs*, while Oswald Garrison Villard published a critique in *The Nation* entitled "The Nakedness of Colonel House." In a lead editorial, the *New York Times* gave the two volumes the "worst roast" of all, noting that they "might give the impression that the errand-boy considered himself of more consequence than the employer."[21]

One longtime friend and political associate, Breckinridge Long, was relieved that House was not in Washington "because I know that your sensitive nature would have been hurt by some of the antagonism manifested." He thought that Seymour had displayed an "incapacity to deal with living men and with living issues." Wiseman agreed, complaining that "his treatment is heavy-handed and utterly misses the true spirit and value of your work."[22] House nonetheless felt that "Seymour has done a wonderful piece of work." He blamed the poor quality of the syndication in the *New York Herald Tribune* for the impression many had received that *The Intimate Papers* were critical of Wilson, and vowed that the next two volumes would "contain less of me and more of Wilson and will put him in yet a better light." But House found all the controversy surrounding *The Intimate Papers* distasteful. "It has been a great trial," he confided to Long, "and has taken all my philosophy to meet it with equanimity."[23]

On May 19 House traveled from Paris to London, and on June 18 left Liverpool for Halifax, Canada. House regretted that he and Mezes had not been together in the summer of 1926, reminding his devoted brother-in-law that "we are getting too old for these long separations."[24]

House stayed in Bar Harbor, Maine, where he rented a house, for over two months, enjoying the "superlatively beautiful place" and the many friends he had there. Mona visited for one week, Janet and Louise for another. By August 12 House finished reading through the manuscript that Seymour had prepared for the third volume of *The Intimate Papers*. He was convinced that this volume was "an improvement on the first two in as much as he is heeding criticism . . . . What little he has left in editorial praise of me will be cut out ultimately . . . . He has also left out my smart sayings about people." But both he and Seymour were undecided whether to publish only a third volume, which would end with the Armistice, or a fourth which would include the peace conference.[25]

On September 8 House left Bar Harbor, slowly drifted southward, and ten days later was back in his apartment in New York.[26] Throughout the fall he worked on *The Intimate Papers*. He, Seymour, and Ferris Greenslet (their editor at Houghton Mifflin) agreed that two additional volumes should include the peace conference, and House insisted that Seymour "leave out every word of complimentary editorial comment of me." By the end of the year, however, after showing the manuscript to several friends, he was still dissatisfied, convinced that Seymour "makes the case out for me as against Wilson." Guiding the young historian had turned out to be an arduous task.[27]

By early November, House, who had been back in New York for less than two months, was already planning another Mediterranean cruise, one that would hopefully include Sidney and Nancy Mezes. House had tired of his life in New York and thought of finding a place in the country or of going "further afield." He disliked the mood in America. "Our people," he complained, "seem to have merely a local outlook and hardly give the rest of the world a thought. Sometime we will get a terrible jolt which will awaken us to the fact that there are people other than ourselves to be considered."[28]

It seemed unlikely, however, that the era of Republican ascendancy would soon end. House worried that in 1928 "McAdoo and Smith would have another head-on collision with the result that the party will meet with as great disaster in '28 as in '24." In 1924, Smith had blocked McAdoo's nomination; now it looked as if the New York governor, who was gaining strength, would be blocked by his old rival. House remained committed to McAdoo, his "steadfast friend through thick and thin," but thought he would never become president. He believed that "either McAdoo or Smith would make a great President" and regretted the fact that they had appeared on the "national stage" at the same time.[29]

As 1926 drew to a close, House, who was sixty-eight, was in a reflective mood. In mid-December he received a letter from a boyhood friend, T. C. Dunn, who had driven by the "old House homestead" on lower Capitol Street in Houston and described all of the children and adults who had once lived there. "You and I, Ed," Dunn reminisced, "are the only persons now living, who knew all of these people." Dunn's letter brought back a flood of boyhood memories for House, reminding him of the passage of time and of the fact that he had outlived all of his siblings except his sister Mary.[30]

On January 1, 1927, House left instructions that he wished "to die and be buried with as little ceremony and ostentation as is possible." He believed that his "soul after death will retain its conscious entity" and that he would be "on a journey of adventure in an unknown land where, sooner or later, we shall meet again."[31]

On March 5, 1927, the House trio left New York for another lengthy Mediterranean cruise. House wished "to be quiet," while "Loulie needs rest more than anyone as she has gone constantly all winter." On March 21 they disembarked at Naples, then moved on to Rome, and reached Paris in time to witness Charles A. Lindbergh's arrival on May 21. The young aviator's daring transatlantic flight had transfixed the world, and, as House noted, the people of Paris have "gone wild over Lindbergh."[32]

On June 12, House left Paris for London. There he settled into a new hotel, the Green Park on Piccadilly Circus, which was, he had learned, "about the smartest in London." On July 2 he traveled to Wilsford Manor, the country home of Grey's wife. Over the weekend the two friends "wandered through the field and woods along the banks of the Avon and talked of many things." The high point of the visit, however, was a talk with the prominent psychical researcher, Oliver Lodge, who rented a cottage on the grounds of Wilsford Manor. Lodge informed House that he had no doubts about a "conscious hereafter" and, while he had not seen anyone "distinctly" from the "other side," "he had seen forms but could not distinguish the features." Lodge thought that "the mind was indestructible and quite separate from the body" and believed that "telepathy was beyond dispute."[33] House found what he said fascinating.

On July 15, the House trio left London for Rotterdam, where they boarded the SS *Volendam* for the trip across the Atlantic. They disembarked at Halifax, and then drove to Wenham for a leisurely month's visit with Mona and Randolph. Life at the Tucker estate in Wenham appealed to him. He and Loulie stayed at a farmhouse a quarter of a mile away from the main house, while Fanny stayed in Manchester and worked with House every morning on his correspondence. In the afternoon he read, saw visitors, and walked around the 130 acres of meadow and woodland. Even here, however, he and Loulie went out often for lunch and dinner. House disliked so much social activity but realized that "It is the price one has to pay for any success in life."[34]

In Wenham, House learned that Seymour had been operated on for a ruptured appendix and was in a serious condition at a hospital in New Bedford, Massachusetts. He had also been offered, and had accepted, the position of provost of Yale. House had been in no hurry to publish the final two volumes of *The Intimate Papers*, but he now realized that Seymour's illness, along with his new administrative responsibilities, would delay publication until the autumn of 1928.

On September 20, House left Wenham, stopped at New Bedford to visit Seymour, and arrived in New York on September 22. He had been gone for over six and a half months.[35]

House returned to a changed and changing political scene. On August 2, 1927, President Coolidge, despite his widespread popularity, announced that "I do not choose to run for president in 1928." Coolidge had never relished the power of the presidency, had no unfinished agenda, and disliked the thought of serving what would, in effect, have been a third term. His most likely successor was Secretary of Commerce Herbert Hoover, who had gained further national attention when he directed the federal government's response to devastating Mississippi River floods in the spring of 1927.[36]

Coolidge's apparent departure did not change the dismal prospects of the Democratic Party. Although Democrats had made modest gains in the 1926 congressional elections, party leaders had not recovered from John

W. Davis's overwhelming defeat in 1924. Since then McAdoo's star had waned, and on September 17, 1927, he announced that he would not seek the nomination in 1928. House now realized that Al Smith's road to the nomination was clear, although he thought the governor's chances of success against the Republican nominee were "slender." The nation, he observed, "is republican by a safe majority, and that party has enough money to bring out their support." Only a major schism in Republican ranks, as in 1912, would make a Democratic victory possible. The mood of the nation discouraged House. "Americans today," he lamented, "are absorbed in money making and but few are interested in politics or anything else excepting the increase in their bank accounts. Not even during the days of the McKinley Administration was there such a sordid outlook."[37]

Although House deplored the rampant materialism of the 1920s, he was pressed for money and continued to speculate in Houston real estate and to profit from the stock market boom. All of the leading financiers, he noted in early 1928, were optimistic, and he studied carefully the contrasting approaches of his two sons-in-law. Gordon (Auchincloss) tended to be a "plunger," making money from short-term investments, while Ran (Tucker) "is the only pessimist I know. He is sitting close to shore nursing his bonds while Gordon has ventured forth and reaped a fortune."[38]

In early 1928, House consulted with Franklin D. Roosevelt about the prospects of the Democratic Party. He approved the decision of Democratic leaders to meet in Houston—since he had "great affection" for the city of his birth—and concluded that Smith's nomination was virtually inevitable. Smith was the only Democratic candidate, House calculated, who had a chance of success in November, but that was not the primary reason that he supported his candidacy. "I want the religious question," House explained, "taken out of our politics . . . . If he is nominated and defeated he will not be like Bryan and [Theodore] Roosevelt, constantly agitating for re-nomination. He will go into business and disappear from the picture and the question will be settled. If he is elected, he will do for the nation what he has done for the State of New York and the question will disappear even in a better way."[39]

House's attention, however, was focused more on his travel plans than on national politics. He missed the companionship of Sidney and Nancy Mezes, who were now spending most of the year in Italy, and he planned during his forthcoming trip to Europe to "link up" with them. But finding a suitable time and place was not easy, for House's brother-in-law had to have "heat and altitude, neither of which I can stand."[40] He and his trio left for Europe and didn't return until August.

By the end of June, both party conventions had met. At Kansas City, Republicans nominated Herbert Hoover on the first ballot. Aside from Coolidge, Hoover was the best-known Republican in Washington, with a powerful reputation as an engineer and humanitarian administrator. Later in the month the Democrats, meeting in Houston, nominated Al Smith on the first ballot. It was, considering the two-thirds rule and the turmoil of the 1924 convention, a remarkable victory, but party leaders, who doubted that any Democrat could win in 1928, were primarily concerned with unity and with preparing the way for 1932.[41] House was encouraged over Democratic prospects but seemed uninvolved in the campaign, sending Smith a lackluster letter on the need for organization. His political associates in the United States gave him differing estimates of Smith's prospects, and House concluded that while "Hoover has much the better chance, I am sure that Smith will make such a virile and popular campaign that he will scare the life out of him."[42]

By the time of House's return to New York in September Hoover's campaign had gathered momentum. The Republican candidate had enormous prestige, stood for many progressive measures, and seemed to embody both the new technology and self-sufficient individualism of the moment. Those who looked closely noted his lack of personal magnetism, but in a time of Republican ascendancy, he would be difficult to defeat.[43]

In contrast, Al Smith was a problematic presidential candidate, one who represented an urban, ethnic America. While Smith, as a four-term governor of New York, had supported social welfare measures, he had a limited view of the role of the federal government in American life and rejected most of the progressive vision of Bryan and Wilson. His conservative views, and those of the northeastern Democrats who supported him, were embodied in the Houston platform. "The Houston Convention," Newton Baker complained, "was a great disappointment to me. McKinley could have run on our tariff plank and Lodge on our plank on international relations." Smith and his strategists hoped to unite the industrial Northeast with the solid South, but his opposition to Prohibition, his Catholicism, and his personal style alienated many southern Democrats. He had little chance of carrying the Northeast, which had voted by wide margins for Harding and Coolidge. Smith remained, in many ways, a provincial politician unable to transform himself into a national figure.[44]

While House gave Smith only a one-in-four chance of victory, he thought the "Happy Warrior"—as Smith was universally known—was conducting an "able campaign," and House was contemptuous of Hoover's refusal to commit himself on various issues. In early October, however, he remained convinced that Catholicism was Smith's "heaviest handicap" and that in the West and South a "wet, Tammany candidate is hard to put over."[45] Later in the month, as the campaign neared its end, House detected a surge for Smith and thought it was possible that he might win. But the results of the election were a bitter disappointment. Smith's northeastern strategy failed, and in the South he lost Florida, North Carolina, Virginia, Tennessee, and, worst of all, Texas. Hoover won with 21,392,000 votes to Smith's 15,016,000, while Republicans increased their majorities in the House and Senate. Peace and prosperity had triumphed.[46]

"What a blow the election was," House noted. "Ignorance, greed and bigotry won the day in America," and he regretted the fact that in the Houston Platform, the Democratic Party had "cut loose from all its moorings." Franklin D. Roosevelt's election as governor of New York, on the other hand, brought "some consolation and a great hope" that he would be the party's candidate in 1932. House reasoned the country might "be ripe for a change. . . and that Roosevelt easily may succeed Hoover."[47]

36

Victory at Last

A few weeks before Herbert Hoover's election, volumes three and four of *The Intimate Papers* finally appeared, covering the period from the American entry into the war until the end of the peace conference. In these volumes Seymour curbed his praise of House, excluded diary entries critical of others, and paraphrased many of Wilson's letters to his counselor (even quoting a few in defiance of Edith's ban). The result was a narrative less centered on House and one that provided more context for his relationship with the president. Nor did Seymour admit that a sharp break had occurred in the friendship between Wilson and House. Rather, he argued that the "friendship lapsed. It was not broken." At the conclusion of volume four Seymour quoted from a letter House had written him on April 20, 1928. "My separation from Woodrow Wilson," House claimed, "was and is to me a tragic mystery, a mystery that now can never be dispelled, for its explanation lies buried with him."[1]

House followed the reviews in American and British newspapers and journals closely, noting that even "papers formerly antagonistic" gave the volumes "good notices." With the exception of Oswald Garrison Villard's critique in *The Nation*, he found all the American reviews favorable. The "paean of praise" for volumes three and four pleased him, but he worried that Ray Stannard Baker would have "a whack at us" in the next volumes of his Wilson biography.[2]

House spent Christmas 1928 in New York, confiding to an old Texas friend that "Christmas is not like it was when all the family and friends foregathered under our roof" in Austin during the late 1880s and 1890s. He missed Sidney and Nancy Mezes and wrote his brother-in-law, "It saddened me to feel you were both so far away." The death of T. C. Dunn, a boyhood friend, heightened House's sense of the passage of time. "I cannot tell you," he wrote Dunn's son, "how grieved I am. His death comes near to severing the link which has bound me to my childhood."[3]

In the early months of 1929 House remained concerned about his precarious finances, distressed that the holder of the lease on his Houston Ship Channel property could only pay interest on his note. He continued to follow the stock market closely, and, after a brief slump, informed Mezes that the "business of the country seems in better condition than it has ever been and there is no reason for alarm unless something unforeseen happens."[4]

At the end of March, House suddenly developed a "violent nosebleed," then a "hemorrhage of the bladder." His condition was critical, and on April 2 he underwent two major operations, one for the removal of a tumor (which turned out to be benign) from his bladder, the second for the removal of his prostate gland. It was the first serious illness of his life.[5] "Because of my age [he was seventy-one] and the nature of the operations," House carefully recorded, "my chances of recovery were not great, yet, loving life as I do, I had no fear . . . . Thinking the matter over I feel sure that my calmness was the result of innumerable years of mental preparation." At Harbor Hospital in New York, receiving only a spinal anesthesia, he was conscious throughout the surgery and could therefore "talk to the surgeons & attending physicians from start to finish." His observations gave a striking glimpse into the state of surgical procedures in 1929. He was surrounded by seven doctors, three of whom actually conducted the operation, while one stood ready to give him gas if needed, another to administer a blood transfusion, a sixth to monitor his pulse, and a seventh to keep track of his blood pressure.

When news of his illness spread, House was touched by all of the "cables, telegrams, letters, books and flowers" that arrived at his apartment. House recovered slowly; he was, Fanny wrote, "down among the shadows during the past few days." For a time he was too ill to read, and not until May 7 did he leave Harbor Hospital. But a "small leak in. . . [his] wound about the size of a pinhead" refused to heal, and he only gradually regained his strength. As the summer's heat closed in on New York, House yearned for the cool ocean breezes of Magnolia. "I would rather," he confided to a friend, "take my chances with the undertaker than to stay around New York much longer." By June 9 he was back on the North Shore.[6]

House's trip to Magnolia had been uneventful, but soon after his arrival "things broke loose again" and he experienced two "of the worst days

I have had in a long while." He soon improved, spending most of his days outdoors in a hammock on the veranda of his cottage overlooking the ocean. By June 10, his wound finally closed, but he remained weak, following a cautious routine and reporting frequently to his doctor in New York.[7]

House endured a fairly isolated period on the North Shore. He and Loulie seldom went out, although as the summer progressed they began to entertain for lunch and dinner in their cottage. "You cannot know," he confided to Mezes, "how I miss Europe. I like the diversion over there and I like the weather and I enjoy seeing my innumerable friends. I feel marooned here." And sometimes even on the North Shore he suffered from extreme heat. He hoped, somewhat wistfully, that he would be strong enough to travel to Europe late in the summer.[8]

House had long been worried over his failure to keep a diary during his years in Texas politics. By the spring of 1929, prior to his April 2 operation, he had begun to dictate another memoir, like *Reminiscences*, which he had dictated in 1916. His surgery and long recuperation interrupted this effort, but later in the summer he completed his *Memories*, a sixty-three-page document in which House sought to "leave some record, covering the period from the cradle to the grave, for my grand-children to ponder over." *Memories*, a more fragmented document than *Reminiscences*, filled in some of the gaps of his earlier recollections. House concluded that these two memoirs, along with his diary and large manuscript collection, would allow his grandchildren as well as a future biographer to understand the whole sweep of his life.[9]

On September 23, House left the North Shore for New York. Once back in the city he felt reasonably well and resumed his daily walks but did not feel as strong as before his operation. As he aged, family affairs absorbed more and more of his attention. The financial success of both of his sons-in-law pleased him. Randolph was worth a million and a quarter, Gordon more than a million and a half, while House calculated his worth at about as much as their combined fortunes, although he complained that "my income is next to nothing."[10]

From early 1927, the stock market had undergone what President Hoover described as an "orgy of mass speculation"; money poured in as investors marveled at the magical increase in their wealth. In September 1929 stock prices broke, then quickly recovered, but on October 23 mass liquidations began and on the next day, October 24 or "Black Thursday," mass sell orders continued as anxiety spread over Wall Street. During the next few weeks prices continued to fall until by mid-November 1929, stocks had lost one-third of their September value. Many observers had warned against speculative excesses and now regarded the stock market crash as a healthy cleansing of the economic system. No major banks or companies had failed and, since only about three million Americans owned stocks, the decline of the market had not affected most of the population. On October 25, President Hoover offered what seemed reasonable reassurances when he claimed that the "fundamental business of the country, that is, production and distribution of commodities, is on a sound and prosperous basis."[11]

Initially House seemed unconcerned about the collapse of the stock market. He had shifted Loulie's, Nancy's, and Sidney Mezes's money from stocks to bonds and, while he had not shifted his own investments, he had never bought stocks on margin and believed that eventually their value would return. And he took comfort in the fact that "I have a million or more in good Texas real estate sitting placidly on the Bayou and else-where."[12] He soon realized, however, that the stock market collapse was unlike anything he had ever seen. He was "anxious for the future," con-vinced that "hard times" would come but also convinced that the country was in "sound condition" and that the economy would slowly recover.[13]

By early 1930, House was more worried about his own finances. He loaned his old protégé, Dudley Field Malone, $3,000 (he had asked for $5,000), but warned that he was running "close to the wind." His regular income was about $12,000 a year; he confided to his nephew in Houston, T. W. House Jr., that "we cannot begin to live on that in the way we do with the obligations we have." Worse still, he no longer felt able to supple-ment his income by writing for popular journals and had borrowed money to pay his medical expenses, which totaled $13,000. He pressed his nephew to make an "extra effort" to sell some of his Houston real estate.[14]

In February 1930, a long article appeared in the *New York Times Magazine* in which House contrasted the Paris Peace Conference and the naval disar-mament conference that opened in London in January 1930. The *New York Times* reporter interviewed the elder statesman in the library of his apart-ment at 104 East 68th Street (he had moved from East 74th Street), a room filled with blue-painted bookcases, photographs of Wilson and Mark Twain, engravings of Lincoln and Jackson, and early English furniture. House believed that the Washington Conference, the Kellogg-Briand Pact, and the current meeting in London were all foreshadowed by Wilson's efforts to create the League of Nations in 1919. He was more optimistic about the prospects for world peace in 1930 than he had been in 1919, in part because of the spread of democracy, in part because of the memory of the suffering of the Great War, and in part because of inventions, such as the radio, which had brought the people of the world much closer together. "It would be hard to conceive," he concluded, "of any two or more Ministers today declaring war on some other country, because their people would not be back of them." House saw no signs of the breakdown of the world order that had been created at Versailles.[15]

House was eager to leave for Europe, and on March 7 he, Loulie, and Fanny sailed on the SS *Vulcania* directly to Cannes. They settled in at the Hotel des Anglais, enjoying the warm, sunny weather and the many English and American friends who had gathered there. In early April they motored from Cannes to Paris, where they stayed at the Ritz Hotel. "So far," he reassured Mona, "we have had a glorious time."[16] By May 1, however, House was once again in bed, attended by several doctors and two nurses, suffering from severe pain in the muscles and nerves around his heart. Not until May 7 did he feel strong enough to make the trip from Paris to London. In London he cut back on his social activities, initially seeing only a few close friends who came to the house he had rented (with a cook and several servants) in order to reduce his expenses. In fact, the leaders in London and Paris with whom House had worked so closely were now either dead or out of office. Asquith had died in February 1928, Clemenceau in November 1929, Balfour in March 1930, while Lloyd George and a small group of Liberals had little hope of returning to power. In both Britain and France, House now found himself out of touch with a younger generation of political leaders. All in all, as Fanny observed, the visit to England was "not as pleasant as usual," since the weather was wet and cold and House was "not up to much yet."[17]

On May 31, 1930, the Houses sailed for Boston. On the first day out he caught a cold and had a "miserable crossing," confined to his bed for the whole trip. Once on the North Shore, he quickly recovered, but by the end of June again developed severe pain in his back and chest. Throughout the summer he struggled to regain his health and by early September, while he was much better, he was still in considerable discomfort.[18] Poor health forced House to curtail his activities, but Loulie, he noted, "is having the time of her life lunching with the old ladies up and down the Shore. She has been out every day this week." House took great pleasure in two small, shaggy Scottish terriers that Will Hogg had given him in Paris. He took them walking in the woods and on the beach twice a day, and let one, Rob Boy, sleep in his room every night.[19]

During the summer of 1930, House followed the decline of President Hoover's political fortunes. After taking office in March 1929, Hoover had gotten off to a fast start, convening a number of commissions and conferences to study national problems and meeting with Prime Minister MacDonald to pursue naval disarmament. In October, when attending a World Series game in Philadelphia, Hoover received a standing ovation from the crowd. But the president, who had spent most of his adult life abroad, had few political skills—he had trouble getting along with Republicans in Congress, alienated the press, and failed to convince most Americans, as the depression deepened, that he cared about their plight. His suspicion of federal power and his belief in the tradition of private giving and local governmental responsibilities constrained his response to the economic crisis. By the summer of 1930, as unemployment and bread lines grew and as a drought spread throughout the Midwest, disappointment with his leadership increased. As one historian remarks, "he had no sense of how to reach out to a desperate nation."[20] House relished the president's growing unpopularity. "Hoover," he observed, "is being tanned from one end of the country to another and mostly by Republicans." He expected Democratic gains in the November 1930 elections, and still thought Franklin Delano Roosevelt (FDR), if he was reelected as governor in November, would be the "best bet" for his party.[21]

By September 22 House was back in New York, looking forward to the November congressional elections. "I feel it in my bones," he confided to Woolley, "that we are going to give the republicans the surprise of their lives in November." As House anticipated, Democrats made dramatic gains in both the Senate and House. In the Senate, Republicans lost eight seats, clinging to a slender one-vote majority, while in the House they lost fifty-two seats. When the new Congress met in December 1931 the Democratic Party would organize the House for the first time in twelve years. The outcome delighted House, who was especially pleased with Roosevelt's overwhelming victory for governor of New York. For the first time in many years he took a keen interest in national politics, especially in FDR's campaign for the presidency. "Between us and the angels," he wrote a friend, "I am playing with him . . . . Prohibition and the tariff should be winning issues in '32 even if the depression lifts by then which it shows no signs of doing now."[22]

Toward the end of 1930, the nation's banking system began to collapse, and on December 11 the Bank of the United States in New York went out of business, destroying the savings of 400,000 depositors. It was the largest failure of a commercial bank in the nation's history. House appreciated the depth of the crisis and its effect on national politics. He had never experienced a "financial crisis so acute" or "seen the American people in such an unhappy and pessimistic state of mind." Nor had he ever "known a President of the United States so excoriated both by his own party and the opposition."[23]

In early 1931, as he surveyed the political landscape, FDR remained, in his judgment, the leading Democratic contender for the presidency, certain to be nominated "provided he does not let his foot slip in the meantime." In letters written to influential people throughout the country House dismissed other potential candidates—Newton Baker, Al Smith, Owen D. Young (chairman of General Electric), Albert C. Ritchie (governor of Maryland)—and argued that Roosevelt was the most available, logical candidate. To his old friend Thomas Watt Gregory, he claimed that "Roosevelt has grown tremendously since you knew him. He is a different man from the Washington Roosevelt. Responsibility, the struggle against an impossible physical disability and experience has made him the best of the bunch."[24]

Both FDR and his longtime political adviser, Louis Howe, viewed House as a key figure in their efforts to win the support of old Wilsonians, and in the early months of 1931 FDR courted the elder statesman, dispatching Howe to House's apartment to seek his advice on a variety of issues. Howe found House out of touch, but left him with the impression that he could once again be a kingmaker in presidential politics. House quickly succumbed to Howe's flattery, convinced that if FDR would follow his advice he would win the nomination. On March 23, after consulting with Howe about the draft of a letter he was to send to prominent Democrats, House congratulated FDR on "having such a loyal and efficient lieutenant." "It is a joy to cooperate with him," he concluded, "for the reason that he is so able and yet so yielding to suggestion."[25]

By the end of April, House informed his protégé Woolley that "I never saw things coming our way so fast." He believed that most Americans felt that Hoover was a "colossal failure," and that Republican leaders feared FDR would be the Democratic nominee. House was eager for two of the original member of "our crowd" in Texas, Frank Andrews and Gregory, to organize the Roosevelt forces in his home state, since he wanted Texas to send an instructed delegation to the Democratic convention and, by supporting FDR early and vigorously, win an influential position for Texas Democrats in the new administration. House seemed unaware, however, that for years he had been detached from Texas politics and ignored Gregory's warning that "the old machine of 1912 no longer exists, that a world of younger men are largely in the saddle and that Roosevelt would not have that gripping pull on a large body of Texans which the name Wilson carried."[26]

Not all of those who had supported Wilson shared House's enthusiasm for FDR. McAdoo, who had not given up his own presidential ambitions, informed House that none of the contenders for the Democratic nomination "had a very strong hold on the masses." McAdoo argued that the party should select a candidate who was "militant and progressive," "free from boss or machine taint," and "sound on prohibition." In short, he believed that Democrats, recognizing their mistake in 1924, should turn to him for leadership.[27]

House also had some reservations about FDR, viewing him as the most "logical," not necessarily the best, candidate, and sometimes describing the younger man (who was forty-nine) in condescending terms. He informed Mezes that "his mentality is more like Sayers, steady and dependable. He has as much charm as the best of them. He is not lacking in political sense and I believe will have sufficient courage. 4 U's [Woodrow Wilson, playing on his initials] liked humanity as a whole and disliked people individually. This one is genuinely fond of people and shows it."[28]

On June 1, 1931, House and Loulie, along with their two Scottish terriers, left New York for the North Shore. Soon after arriving, House announced to reporters that he had reentered national politics and backed Roosevelt for the nomination. On June 13 he gave a carefully planned luncheon for FDR, Massachusetts Democratic leaders, and some independent Republicans. Prior to the luncheon, House had a long conference with Roosevelt, and at its end offered a toast to the governor as a "man upon whom the eyes of the nation are fastened." He thought his luncheon would convince Smith and his followers that even in Massachusetts, supposedly their strongest state, they could not count on the support of its delegates at the 1932 convention. He boasted about the "splash" his luncheon made, about the fact that it was covered by seventy-five to one hundred reporters, photographers, and movie men.[29]

House overestimated his ability to manipulate Democratic politicians in Massachusetts. Roosevelt had, to be sure, won the support of Boston's mayor James M. Curley, but he represented a minority faction within the state's Democratic Party; its leaders, Senator David I. Walsh and Governor Joseph B. Ely, had no intention of supporting FDR if Smith wanted the nomination.[30]

Throughout the summer, House continued to write Democratic leaders across the country promoting FDR's candidacy. His own inner circle of political operators—Robert M. Field, Daniel C. Roper, and Robert W. Woolley—collected an endless stream of political information from all sections of the nation. They were, like House, optimistic about the New York governor's prospects. When doubts arose about FDR's candidacy, House rushed to his defense. "You will find the Governor," he reassured Frank Andrews, "as physically fit from the hips up as any man you know . . . . Franklin Roosevelt can stand more work than any President I have known excepting Theodore Roosevelt and Hoover. He is much tougher than Wilson, Harding or Coolidge." When another correspondent raised questions about FDR's ties to city machines, House claimed that "Governor Roosevelt is in no sense a city man. He lives in the country, he is of the country and his support is almost wholly from the open spaces. The machines in the cities do not love him."[31]

House sought to draw closer to Louis Howe, who, he realized, was FDR's closest political adviser. Howe, a "gnome-like looking little man," had run FDR's campaign for reelection to the New York State Senate in 1912, served as his chief of staff in Washington when he was assistant secretary of the navy, and had become determined to make him president. He had unpleasant personal habits, chain-smoking cigarettes and dropping the ashes over his rumpled suits, and an irreverent sense of humor, combined with impatience with pomposity and pretense. It is hard to imagine that House, with his ordered life and meticulous grooming, really liked FDR's devoted lieutenant.[32]

House was less enthusiastic about James A. Farley, the other key member of FDR's inner circle. Farley, chairman of the New York State Democratic Committee, was a tall, affable Irishman who had a passion for politics and a rare ability to make friends with a wide range of people. His task was to travel from coast to coast, selling FDR to local Democratic leaders. Acting on Woolley's advice, House sought to restrict Farley's role, but Howe praised the results of his June 1931 western tour and urged House to meet him when he returned to New York.[33]

During the summer of 1931, President Hoover's political fortunes continued to decline. With the collapse of the European financial system, Hoover claimed that the major sources of the depression were in Europe, and on June 20, 1931, he proposed a bold one-year moratorium on German reparation payments and on the war debts of the European powers. He was now, however, on the defensive, no longer the aggressive and self-confident leader of earlier years and faced a rising tide of popular anger over his inability to lead the nation out of what had become the Great Depression. At the end of the summer, House told a Canadian friend that "he [Hoover] is the worst that we have ever had in my memory and the most unpopular. If we cannot defeat him in the next election you may place me down as a false prophet."[34]

Aside from the excitement of the Roosevelt campaign, House found that "things are very quiet on the North Shore this summer. Almost everyone is broke, or nearly so, and one can see it in the way expenses are curtailed." On July 28 he quietly celebrated his seventy-third birthday, and on August 4 his fiftieth wedding anniversary. House wanted to visit Mezes (who was now in Altadena, California), but he confessed that "I am not up to much in the way of traveling and must be careful." Even had he made the effort, he would have arrived too late to see his beloved brother-in-law. Mezes died on September 10, 1931, only a few days short of his sixty-eighth birthday. House felt that "something had gone out of my life that can never be replaced."[35]

On September 19, House and Loulie closed up their cottage at Manchester and went to Mona and Randolph's for a week. Edward wanted to avoid returning to New York until the heat was gone, while Loulie wanted everything in their apartment properly arranged (which was one of Fanny's many tasks) so she would not arrive there "before the servants can prepare her soup." By the end of September they were back in New York.[36]

From his base in New York, House continued to monitor FDR's presidential campaign. By early October he informed Woolley that "our friend has many hurdles to jump before he lands and no one knows this better than you and I." Woolley fretted about many aspects of the Roosevelt campaign[37] and also realized that the movement among some state Democratic leaders to pledge their delegates to a favorite son was "loaded with dynamite for *our* man." By the end of November it looked as if Texas Democrats, who

House had earlier predicted would rally behind FDR, would instruct the party's delegates to vote for congressman John Nance Garner. House still remained confident but confided to a friend that "Between you and me and the angels I am not taking much part in the Roosevelt campaign." He was reluctant to travel to Albany and upset by the slow response of the governor to the many letters he forwarded to him.[38]

By the fall of 1931 House could no longer ignore the mounting evidence of the growth of nationalism in Europe and the rise, in Germany, Italy, and Japan, of revisionist regimes. Germany pushed for equality of status, French anxieties over security remained acute, while Japanese expansion in Manchuria challenged the authority of the League of Nations and further eroded confidence in the international system created at Versailles. By the end of the year House had become pessimistic, writing Grey that "I am afraid the Hitlerites will capture Germany before long, and I also fear that there may be dictatorships elsewhere. The whole world seems ripe for political revolution, and some of the best American observers believe that unless we are careful and fortunate we may have one here."[39]

House had not heard from Ray Stannard Baker for several years and was understandably worried about how Baker would treat him in volumes three and four of Baker's massive biography (which covered Wilson's governorship and presidency through 1914). In late November, as House read the serialization of Baker's forthcoming volumes, he concluded that Wilson's biographer "is belittling me in every way he thinks he can safely do so." While Baker recognized House's value as a "political reporter and adjuster," he claimed that in his diary House exaggerated his influence on Wilson, whose friendship was "the crowning achievement of his life." "There was in House," Baker continued, "something of the quality that Wilson admired in fine women: something intimate, sympathetic, unarguing." As Seymour pointed out in a critical review in the *American Historical Review*, Baker portrayed House "in good-humoured but rather patronizing phrases as a simple-minded individual who failed to understand Wilson, for whom the President had warm personal affection but for whose advice he had small respect."[40]

Christmas 1931 was not a good holiday for House. He had no money to pay taxes on his Texas real estate, and Loulie, Janet, and Mona had all agreed not to give each other Christmas presents. House gloomily concluded that "I have never been up against just such a situation and practically every friend we have here is in the same condition."[41]

On January 22, 1932, Roosevelt formally announced his candidacy for the presidency. He did not, however, expand his campaign organization, choosing to rely on Howe, Farley, and a small group of New Yorkers, and he pursued a cautious preconvention strategy, seeking to maneuver among the various factions in the Democratic Party and to avoid drifting too far either to the left or the right. FDR had said little on foreign policy, but on February 2, pressed by the newspaper magnate William Randolph Hearst, he repudiated his earlier support of the League of Nations. "But the League of Nations today," FDR declared, "is not the League conceived by Woodrow Wilson." The absence of the United States had allowed it to evolve into an instrument for the advancement of the narrow interests of the European powers. He was against American participation.[42]

The night before Roosevelt gave his League of Nations speech, he had the text telephoned to Howe in New York, so that House could read it and make suggestions. The hurried consultation upset House, who disapproved of what FDR said about the League and worried that he would now fail to support American membership in the World Court. He warned FDR that his speech had strained the loyalty of many of his supporters or, as he put it to Farley, FDR's repudiation of the League had "created something akin to panic among the devoted Wilson followers." Roosevelt, House concluded, "is doing things of which I do not approve and with which I do not care to be credited."[43] As during the Wilson years, however, House was more interested in power than policy. "I want," he confided to Woolley, "to help Roosevelt, and I want our crowd to dominate for I am foolish enough to believe that it will be for his good and for the good of the country." But FDR, as House would soon realize, had no intention of letting "our crowd" take over his campaign. He kept House and his associates on the margins.[44]

In mid-April House had urged Roosevelt to "strike a conservative note" in a speech that he planned to give in St. Paul, Minnesota, but during the spring FDR moved in a different direction, giving some speeches that fore-shadowed the New Deal. He spoke of the "forgotten man at the bottom of the economic pyramid" and declared that America, "in the midst of an emergency at least equal of that of war," needed "bold, persistent experi-mentation." Clearly House, like many observers of the political scene, had little understanding of where FDR, once in office, might lead the nation.[45]

During the spring of 1932, Roosevelt's delegate count steadily grew; a few weeks before the Chicago convention in June he had a commanding lead, although he lacked the two-thirds necessary for the nomination. While the Roosevelt forces had mixed success in the East, they had captured most of the South (with the exception of Texas and Virginia, which supported favorite sons) and the West (with the exception of California, where Garner won the primary). If Garner, with his group of delegates from California and Texas, would join the Roosevelt ranks, victory would be assured.[46]

Despite the success of FDR's campaign, the late winter and spring of 1932 were a gloomy time for House. He had to cash in his life insurance policies to pay off debts and lacked the funds to travel to Europe. The future seemed bleak. Nor was his health good enough to allow him to write and supplement his income, as he had done during the 1920s. He suffered from "rheumatism, neuralgia or whatever it is, in my chest, back and side. I can just get about and that is all."[47] It had also been, House complained, "a terrible winter for me in the loss and sickness of friends." In March 1932, Pat Fitzhugh, an old Texas friend; Edward Sammons, his accountant in Austin; and Horace Plunkett, the Anglo-Irish statesman, had "all crossed the river," while Frank Andrews lay seriously ill in Houston. As old friends died off, House grew even closer to his family, congratulating a grandniece on her marriage, "a great adventure," and urging his nephew in Houston, T. W. House Jr., to "keep a stiff upper lip" until the turn comes, and reassuring him that "you cannot know how much I love you."[48]

On May 27, House left New York for Beverly Farms, where he relaxed in a large cottage with spacious grounds and a "superb" view of the ocean. He found the mood on the North Shore somber.[49] As the Democratic convention approached—it opened in Chicago on June 27—House closely followed Roosevelt's campaign. Before leaving for the North Shore, he had met with FDR in New York and discussed "every detail of the political situation." House seemed to have reconciled himself to playing a secondary role in Roosevelt's organization. When the governor met on June 5 with his advisers at Hyde Park, House knew that he should be there, but the trip, he lamented, was "too much for me." He was, after all, nearing his seventy-fourth birthday and no longer had the energy he had displayed during the Wilson years. He now advised Woolley that many things will happen in FDR's campaign that "you and I do not approve of," but nevertheless urged him to work with Farley: "Do not let us quit the game but play it to a finish . . . . We will win out."[50]

When the Chicago convention opened, the Roosevelt forces were still one hundred votes short of a two-thirds majority. Various candidates favored by conservatives within the party—Al Smith, Newton Baker, Harry Bird, and Albert Ritchie—totaled only two hundred fourteen votes, and on the fourth ballot one of the favorite son candidates, John Nance Garner, unwilling to deadlock the convention, threw his support to FDR, giving him the nomination. In a dramatic break with tradition, the party's nominee decided to fly to Chicago—a move House supported—to deliver his acceptance speech before the cheering delegates. It was a confident, optimistic speech in which the governor pledged a "new deal for the American people." Conservative Democrats were upset, but House thought FDR gave a "great" acceptance speech and was pleased with the results of the convention. "Things have come out," he wrote, "as I wished and planned."[51]

In mid-June, Republicans, also meeting in Chicago, renominated Herbert Hoover, but few observers thought he had any chance of winning the election. During the third winter of the depression, Hoover had, in fact, realized that more aggressive federal action was necessary and had won congressional approval for several innovative programs. By early 1932, however, 20 percent of the nation's labor force was out of work, and in some industrial cities, such as Chicago and Detroit, the figure was nearly 50 percent. Unemployment, along with mass destitution, was now pervasive, and the needs of the poor and unemployed overwhelmed state and local governments and private relief agencies. But Hoover, concerned about the effects of relief on the federal budget and the moral fiber of the nation, vetoed a federal relief bill; many Americans were now convinced that he was a "Great Scrooge," out of touch with the suffering of the nation.[52]

After the convention, House found himself more involved in the campaign than he had anticipated, deluged with visitors and a correspondence of "alarming proportions." By the end of July he confidently predicted that if the election was held next week, FDR "would sweep the country . . . . He is in good physical condition, in good spirits and confident of success."[53] House dreaded, however, "getting down to New York where I shall be in the thick of it." He had enjoyed the summer in his North Shore sanctuary. Guests—friends and family—filled his roomy cottage all summer, and he had a "happy time" at a "fancy dress party" given by Mona, where young people "played old fashioned games," reminding him of lazy summers when his own children were young.[54]

Roosevelt's advisers, including House, wanted him to stay in Albany and Hyde Park, where he could avoid making mistakes and escape the strains and risks of cross-country travel. FDR rejected their advice, leaving in early September on a campaign trip that would carry him all the way to the West Coast. In a series of speeches he argued that the American capitalist system had broken down and that the federal government would have to play a larger role in planning and managing the economy. While the specifics of his plans remained undefined, it was clear that the Democratic candidate had an expansive vision of the role of the federal government in American life and a receptivity to change and experimentation.[55]

His campaign message, however, was often confusing. While advocating a "new deal," he also attacked Hoover for excessive spending and for his mismanagement of the federal budget. Sometimes he called for social planning, sometimes he criticized Hoover for excessive centralization in Washington. The president took FDR's attacks personally, claiming that he was a "chameleon in plaid" who advocated class warfare and "the same philosophy of government which has poisoned all Europe." Hoover's campaign, however, was dispirited, and as he toured the country he encountered widespread hostility.

In mid-September, when House returned to New York, he was quickly drawn into the details of the campaign. Reports from the field indicated a Roosevelt landslide. One of House's agents, traveling with FDR in California, reported that "people everywhere, in cars, trucks, even wagons, are driving miles and miles to hear him or even see him." Woolley, a veteran campaigner, could hardly believe "the good news which comes to us here from all parts of the country." On November 1 House learned that a soon-to-be published *Literary Digest* poll indicated that Hoover would only carry Maine and Vermont.[56]

House seemed more concerned with the politics than with the substance of the campaign. He showed little interest in the meaning of Roosevelt's new domestic programs and, even in the case of foreign policy, agreed that FDR "has very properly and wisely kept foreign affairs out of the campaign." Early in the summer House's thoughts had turned to patronage; he encouraged protégés such as William Bullitt, Breckinridge Long, and Daniel Roper to hope for appointments in the new administration. He informed Roper, his prime candidate, that he had had a "comforting" talk with FDR who "will justify the faith we have in him . . . . Keep in touch with me and let us play ball together."[57]

On November 8, election night, Hoover and the Republican Party suffered a crushing defeat. Roosevelt won forty-two of forty-eight states, twenty-three million to sixteen million votes, and the landslide created a Democratic majority of 60 to 35 in the Senate and 310 to 117 in the House. A new day had dawned in Washington.[58]

The night of the election, FDR telephoned House from New York headquarters "to felicitate with me over the results." House left, however, no thoughts on the significance of Roosevelt's remarkable victory. At the age of seventy-four, in uncertain health, and with a cordial but somewhat distant relationship with the new president, he felt none of the excitement that had swept over him twenty years before, when his new friend Woodrow Wilson had won the presidency.[59]

37

The Crisis of the 1930s

Throughout the winter of 1932–1933 America, as one historian remarks, "lay tense and still, a wasteland of economic devastation," waiting for the new administration to take office on March 4. The president-elect faced intense pressure from many different sources. But FDR, unlike Hoover, emphasized the domestic sources of the economic collapse and planned to pursue a highly nationalistic program of recovery. Affable, gregarious, and full of vitality, he listened to a wide range of advice. His so-called Brain Trust, a group of academic advisers, wanted powerful public controls over the economy, while Democratic leaders in the Congress, largely from the South, had few ideas about how to attack the Depression—beyond government frugality and a balanced budget—and resented the professors who had gathered around the president-elect. Prior to March 4, however, it was unclear what policies FDR would pursue.[1]

The day after the election, House lunched with FDR, Raymond Moley (a Columbia University professor and key member of the Brain Trust), and James Farley, but during the winter he saw more of Sara Roosevelt, the president-elect's seventy-nine-year-old mother, than he saw of her son. Office seekers now sought out House, who confided to Mona that "the public assumes that I have an influence with the President-elect that is not warranted, for I seldom see him and what advice he gets is not from me." House hoped to place several friends in the cabinet and to influence ambassadorial appointments in Western Europe, but knew that he could not rush FDR, that he would have "to wait until he is ready to discuss such matters, if at all."[2]

While he waited, House sought to promote his own role as a presidential adviser. In January 1933, Arthur D. Howden Smith, a journalist with close ties to House, published an article in *Scribner's Magazine* on "Roosevelt's Pilots—Colonel House and Colonel Howe," one that was clearly inspired by House. "Where House," Howden Smith wrote, "is suave, cordial, a fluent talker, Howe is shy, brusque, diffident, stiff in manner." It was House who had formed the basic strategy of FDR's campaign while Howe and Farley "had done the drudgery." "A practical idealist," House hoped to move the new administration toward a "positive role in international affairs" so that the United States would "assume her just share of the burden of maintaining civilization." When House denied that he would accept any office, Howden Smith replied: " 'You would be glad to lead our first delegation to Geneva.' His eyes lit up. 'I guess you're right,' he admitted."[3]

Howden Smith missed the fact that FDR, having grown up in an upper-class Anglo-American social world, was familiar with foreign policy issues and eager to talk with overseas visitors and American diplomats. FDR had not lost all of his Wilsonian ideals, and in foreign affairs he was committed, as one historian remarks, "to a kind of abstract, prospective internationalism." He faced, however, a profound domestic crisis, and knew that the mood of the country, and of important Republican progressives in the Senate, was deeply isolationist. He had no intention of launching foreign policy initiatives that would disrupt his domestic coalition.[4]

In January and February 1933, House watched at a distance as the new administration took shape. With his help, William Phillips returned to the State Department as undersecretary, and three friends, Homer Cummings, Cordell Hull, and Daniel Roper, were included in FDR's cabinet. Hull, a long-term congressman from Tennessee and, since 1930, a senator from that state, had supported American membership in the League and was an ardent advocate of reciprocal trade agreements, while Cummings and Roper had worked with House during the Wilson years and would, he hoped, give him access to the inner circle around the president. By inauguration day, however, House realized that FDR was not the same kind of leader as Woodrow Wilson. Wilson was a solitary figure, one who had relied on House to deal with a wide range of people; FDR's "methods," House observed, "are different from those of Wilson. He has many advisers but no one is very close to him." House realized that "my health is not equal to my trying to do for him [FDR] what I did for Wilson."[5]

During the winter months, as House adjusted to a different style of presidential leadership, he felt confined in New York—"about the most depressing place in the world." He wanted to travel, possibly to Winter Park, Florida, and especially to Britain, but lacked the money to take either trip. "Unhappily," he complained to one nephew, "we are just about at the bottom of the barrel financially and have no money to go anywhere."[6] Thomas Watt Gregory's death at the age of seventy-one also reminded House that the ranks of his old Texas friends were "thinning out constantly." Gregory, he wrote his widow, "was like a brother to me, and I shall always feel that something has gone out of my life that cannot be replaced."[7]

On March 4, 1933, inauguration day, FDR declared that "the only thing we have to fear is fear itself," and emphasized the primacy of domestic over international affairs. The next day he called Congress into special session on March 9, and over the next Hundred Days gave an extraordinary display of presidential leadership, moving a wide variety of programs through the Congress. The New Deal, as it was now officially being called, reflecting Roosevelt's desire for action and experimentation, brought far-reaching changes in the nation's economy and transformed the role of the federal government. Moreover, as one historian notes, the president "had touched the hearts and imaginations of his countrymen like no predecessor in memory." Those who knew FDR before 1932 were amazed at his emergence as a powerful national leader. As a Democratic elder statesman told Raymond B. Fosdick, who had worked with Roosevelt in the Wilson administration, "Ray, that fellow in there is not the fellow we used to know. There's been a miracle here."[8]

House seemed uncertain what to make of the flood of legislation passed during the Hundred Days. "There are many things," he wrote a friend, "he [FDR] is doing with which I do not agree but I hope he is right." He was, however, impressed with Roosevelt's qualities of leadership. House liked the fact that the new president did not "show any strain and was optimistic over the future." Even so, in a *Redbook Magazine* article entitled "Looking at Tomorrow," House hoped that the new administration would avoid impulsive action at home or abroad. "If we are wise," he urged, "we will move slowly and cautiously."[9]

On May 19, House left New York for Beverly Farms, Massachusetts. Initially he did not feel well, but soon his health improved and he fell into a familiar routine. Old friends, such as William Wiseman, made their way to his summer cottage, as did his granddaughter Louise and his grandson Eddie. On the night of his seventy-fifth birthday, July 26, Mona and Randolph gave him a "fancy dress birthday party." At Edward's request, they invited only young people, and later in the evening "played old fashioned games." It was a happy evening that took House "back into the long ago."[10]

Throughout the spring and summer of 1933, House had received alarming reports from friends in Europe. Hitler's rise to power (he became chancellor on January 30, 1933), his rapid transformation of Germany into a totalitarian state, and his persecution of Jews, had alarmed some observers of European affairs. Lord Lothian, a prominent Liberal, predicted that "events in Germany are going to transform the whole world situation" and unless the United States came forward in the next year or two, there would be a "further triumph of reaction: a further war, with the liberal nations of 1919 not triumphant but confronted with a more formidable combination than that which they had to meet in 1914."[11] In an April 5 issue of *The Nation*, its editor, Oswald Garrison Villard, who had opposed American entry into World War I, wrote "An Open Letter to Colonel House," in which Villard asked him if he had read the news from Germany and reminded him that Wilson's decision to lead the nation into war had not brought the creation of a new world order. America's sacrifices, Villard argued, had been in vain, and the United States now faced "a world so confused, so bewildered, so oppressed, that the most optimistic are now ready to suggest that civilization is in jeopardy." House did not respond to Villard's attack, either in public or in private letters to friends; he would not consider the possibility that his wartime policies had failed.[12]

Indeed, House seemed unconcerned about the German threat to the postwar international system. Early in the summer he believed that "the world situation" had improved and that the American people were beginning to realize the need for stability in Europe. He approved of FDR's decision, on July 3, to reject international economic cooperation and to undercut the World Economic Conference meeting in London, and over the course of the summer House focused on building a network among American ambassadors in Europe. House had been instrumental in the appointment of four of these men: Robert W. Bingham, owner of the Louisville, Kentucky, *Courier-Journal*, went to London; John Cudahy, a Wisconsin businessman, to Warsaw; William E. Dodd, a Wilson admirer and University of Chicago history professor, to Berlin; and Breckenridge Long, a wealthy Missouri Democrat who had served as assistant secretary of state under Wilson, to Rome.[13] House established close ties with each ambassador, entertaining Cudahy and Dodd at Beverly Farms before their departure for Europe. He also meddled in internal affairs of the State Department, supporting Hull's insistence, after the debacle at the London Economic Conference, that Moley leave the department. House realized, however, that he was on the margins of the new administration and felt that only one member of the cabinet, Daniel Roper, cooperated with him. On June 21, when FDR's yacht, the *Amberjack II*, docked at Gloucester harbor, House boarded it for an hour-long conversation with the president. He found Roosevelt in "high spirits," insisting that "he plans to see more of me in the future." But he knew that his relationship with the president was unlikely to change.[14]

On September 20, 1933, House left the North Shore for New York, where he resumed his old routine. The president's qualities as a leader continued to impress him. On the morning of October 17, he and Loulie left New York for a one-night stay at the White House. Loulie was eager to go, and House knew that it was best for him to go if he was to maintain a cordial relationship with the president. But he was not feeling well and did not relish making the familiar journey from Pennsylvania Station to Union Station, with all the memories that it would evoke.[15]

Once there, however, House enjoyed his stay. After dinner he and FDR talked until after midnight, going "into all phases of the foreign situation particularly the debts, the stabilization of the dollar, etc." They agreed on the importance of Anglo-American understanding, but also agreed that nothing could be done until the British government changed its attitude toward payment of its debts. House had a long talk with Secretary of State Hull, lunched with the British and Italian ambassadors, and met for the first time Secretary of the Interior Harold Ickes. Back in New York he carefully reported the details of his visit to the American ambassadors in Berlin, London, Rome, and Warsaw, reminding them of his connection to FDR.[16]

By the fall of 1933, conservative Democrats felt a growing discontent with the president's financial advisers. House shared some of this unease but would not join the party's conservative leaders in an open rebellion against the president's policies. He was, he insisted, "a friend of the President and all the advice I had to give would be given him privately"; early in the New Year he wrote FDR that "I am following all that you do with appreciation, admiration and affection."[17] House realized that the nation's monetary problems were unprecedented and that "we are all groping in the dark." He also realized that the administration had no settled foreign policy, "that they were so absorbed, at the moment, with pressing domestic affairs that they were not thinking a great deal about Europe." He seemed, in the winter of 1933–1934, complacent about events there, convinced that "the people want peace" and that "there is practically no possibility of the different governments starting a war with one another."[18] The previous summer, before Dodd left for Germany, he had visited House at Beverly Farms. At some point the two men's conversation turned to Hitler's persecution of Jews, which had grown severe during the first half of 1933. House hoped that the new ambassador could exercise a moderating influence on Hitler and "ameliorate Jewish sufferings," but he also felt that "Jews should not be allowed to dominate economic or intellectual life in Berlin as they have done for a long time." Like many Americans, House believed that Germany's Jews were in part responsible for their own plight. In late March 1934, when Dodd returned to the United States on leave, he and House discussed Jewish propaganda in America and the division among American Jews about how to deal with Germany. House hoped that Hitler would modify "his drastic policy against the Jews" and that a compromise might be found. But he thought a Jewish problem existed in America as well as in Europe and did not want FDR or any member of his cabinet to "appoint another Jew," since "the feeling against Jews in this country is growing so rapidly that unless it is checked, some such prejudice against them will be as strong as it is now in Germany."[19]

The winter of 1933–1934 was a gloomy time for House, who was bothered by the extreme cold and who lacked the money to head south or to look forward to a spring or summer excursion to Europe. Taxes on his properties in Texas consumed most of his income, and he continued to live off his principal. Mona was sick much of the winter, as was Fanny, who suffered from pleurisy and could not join the Houses when they left, no doubt with great relief, for the North Shore on June 4.[20]

After House arrived at Beverly Farms he missed Fanny's presence. "We are crazy," he wrote his longtime secretary, "to have you here, but want you to be prudent." He took much comfort, however, in his two Scottish terriers, Twinkle and Rob Boy. "They eat well, sleep well," he reported to Fanny, "and seem to enjoy every moment of the day. They never leave me—upstairs, downstairs, at the table and out of doors they are at my feet. Bless their hearts. How I do love them."[21]

When House opened the July 14 issue of the *Saturday Evening Post*, he discovered an article written by the longtime head usher at the White House, Irwin H. Hoover, entitled, "The Case of Colonel House." Hoover's article, and the book that followed, *Forty-Two Years in the White House*, portrayed House in a sympathetic fashion, emphasizing Wilson's heavy reliance on his counselor. According to Hoover, had it not been for the president's illness at the peace conference, no break would have occurred between the two men.[22] Hoover's explanation of the break pleased House, since it did not require him to reflect on his own behavior. He had bitter feelings, however, toward those who had intrigued against him, claiming melodramatically that after Wilson's breakdown, "every decision reached was made by Mrs. Wilson and her advisers. The result of their ignorant efforts literally wrecked the world, and almost civilization itself." Later in the month, in an interview with the *New York Times* on his seventy-sixth birthday, he reaffirmed his version of the break, explaining that after the peace conference Wilson was a sick man, "a man in the hands of a bedroom circle." While he would not criticize Edith directly, he explained that "the situation between myself and Mrs. Wilson remains precisely what it always was: We never were close friends; we are not now. We never have been enemies; we are not now."[23]

Throughout his life House had had a penchant for grand, vague schemes of international betterment in which he moved nations effortlessly across a geopolitical chessboard. In early August 1934, viewing the growing tension in Europe, he contemplated an Anglo-American agreement on restoring the "world balance, both economic and political," one that would be joined by France and Italy and that would "straighten out Germany." House assumed that FDR, if presented with a plan for a world settlement, would be sympathetic. But he gave no hint of the specifics of his plan, or how he would overcome the weakness of Prime Minister Ramsay MacDonald's National Government.[24]

House enjoyed the summer of 1934 on the North Shore. He had felt "unusually well," had done "much work," and had had a steady stream of visitors, including prominent foreign leaders such as Prince Konoye Fumimaro and Vittorio Orlando. As he wrote an old Cornell classmate, he led a "happy contented life."[25]

On September 17, House left the North Shore for New York, and soon after his arrival he and Loulie traveled to Hyde Park to join the president and his family in a celebration of Sara Roosevelt's eightieth birthday. Despite the presence of seventy-five family members at lunch, House found FDR "as cordial and confidential as ever . . . . I had ample time before and after to discuss the matters I had in mind. I saw no indication whatever of an exaggerated ego. He was simple, unaffected and direct." House discussed with FDR a plan that he and Secretary of Commerce Roper were working on "to bring about a reconciliation between business and the President," one that would have included, after the congressional elections in early November, a conciliatory statement by FDR. House expected Democrats to "win handsomely throughout the country." "There is," he noted, "no Republican Party left and no Republican leaders of any standing."[26]

House's prediction proved correct. Republicans lost more seats in the House and Senate, giving Democrats a two-thirds majority in each chamber. The elections also revealed a broadening of the base of the Democratic Party, as new groups in northern and western cities—blacks, Catholics, Jews—joined Democratic ranks. The triumph of the Democratic Party gave FDR the opportunity to advance further his reform agenda. As one close adviser, Harry Hopkins, remarked, "Boys—this is our hour. We've got to get everything we want—a works program, social security, wages and hours, everything—now or never." FDR was unlikely to heed House's counsels of moderation.[27]

Throughout the fall of 1934, House made no progress on his plan for an understanding with Great Britain. He learned from Lord Lothian that British leaders were pessimistic about the prospects for Anglo-American cooperation, convinced that the United States was "fundamentally isolationist." They wanted FDR to "take the leadership of the world for peace" and for the United States to "throw its whole weight behind the collective principle."[28] The president, House knew, was unlikely to go this far. Roosevelt was, in fact, worried about the situation in Europe and on January 16, 1935, asked the Senate to approve American membership in the World Court, the judicial arm of the League of Nations. The membership of the United States, he reasoned, would send a signal that the nation was still concerned about events abroad. But FDR underestimated the deepening isolationism of Congress and the American people; on January 29 the treaty failed to get a two-thirds vote in the Senate. He was stunned, as was House, who complained that FDR's support for the measure had been "lukewarm," and that the defeat had damaged his prestige and strengthened the opposition.[29]

During the early months of 1935, tension continued to grow in Europe. On January 13, 1935, the Saar plebiscite brought that region's return to Germany; Hitler had now survived a period of vulnerability and began to move more boldly to challenge the status quo. On March 8, he revealed that Germany had a new air force and a week later announced that Germany was expanding its army and would no longer abide by the military clauses of the Treaty of Versailles. Few observers had expected such dramatic moves, and

British and French leaders, while they feared a rearmed Germany, could not agree on any common policy. Ambassador Bingham warned of the inevitability of war, while House concluded that "There is a feeling that unless Germany changes her policy, it would be better to have it out now." House was especially puzzled by "the madness of Hitler in going to such extremes."[30]

What FDR described as the "dangerous situation" at home also concerned House. At the beginning of 1935, the New Deal, entering its third year, seemed a spent political force. More than 20 percent of the workforce remained unemployed, and on both the right and left of the political spectrum disillusionment with the president and his administration grew. Conservatives joined the American Liberty League and began a more systematic critique of the New Deal, while demagogues on the left, such as Senator Huey Long (Democrat, Louisiana) and the radio priest Father Charles Coughlin, called for radical solutions to the nation's problems. FDR and his advisers knew that they needed to find a way to channel the discontent into another round of reforms. By early 1935 the president was ready to proceed with a new phase of the New Deal. On January 17 he proposed the Social Security Act, and in the months that followed asked for legislation that provided for work relief, unemployment insurance, and tax reform. As the summer drew to a close, the legislative record of the New Deal was complete; many wealthy Americans now denounced FDR as "a traitor to his class."[31]

In mid-March, Secretary of Commerce Roper had sent a memorandum to FDR, urging him to end uncertainty among businessmen and to declare that his reform program had ended. House believed that the president could "still right the situation" but worried that he might "swing violently to the left," and before leaving for the North Shore in mid-June House traveled to Hyde Park for a talk with FDR. "I urged him," House reported to Bingham, "to keep to the middle of the road and not try to please either extreme . . . . I told him furthermore that he would never swing far enough to the left to satisfy Huey Long, La Follette and Father Coughlin and their like. The President said he knew it and did not want to please them." Despite the radical changes that House had once called for in *Philip Dru*, he was, in fact, a cautious reformer, out of touch with the waves of discontent sweeping across the nation.[32]

In the summer of 1935, House had to reduce his scale of living on the North Shore. He could no longer afford a spacious cottage with an ocean view, and instead rented a smaller one farther back from the beach.[33] House seemed unimpressed with the bold reform measures that marked the new phase of the New Deal. When Gordon Auchincloss denounced the president and the "intellectual fanatics who are around" him, House agreed that FDR was "badly advised" and "does not get at the real facts and conditions." But he planned to "stick to F. R. through thick and thin" and had "no doubt that he will be nominated and elected."[34]

Throughout the summer House continued to follow closely the situation in Europe. His reports from Germany were encouraging, and, despite mounting evidence of Mussolini's imperial ambitions in Africa, House declared on September 14, just before leaving Manchester, that he was "confident the Ethiopian situation would be settled without bloodshed." On the same day, House's article, "Wanted—A New Deal among Nations," appeared in *Liberty* magazine. Ignoring Hitler's territorial ambitions in Central and Eastern Europe, as well as the revolutionary nature of his regime, House warned that without some appeasement of these revisionist powers, "chaos and catastrophe will be upon us."[35]

On October 3, 1935, Italian troops moved from Somalia into Ethiopia, and seven days later the League Council voted to take collective action against Italy; a colonial war had now become a major European crisis and a challenge to the League of Nations. On the evening of October 15, House addressed the crisis in a radio address over the National Broadcasting Company network. He urged America to join the League, praised the stand of the League against Italy as "a forward step that will be historic," and declared that if the League was successful in stopping the war, "civilization will have advanced beyond the limits of the dreams of philosophers and saints." He remained sympathetic, however, toward the aspirations of Germany, Japan, and Italy, and suggested once again that "a potent League" could bring about a "readjustment of territory and induce those nations having a surplus to share with those who lack it."[36]

House's vision of a potent League, however, was not to become a reality. While the member states were in theory committed to sanctions against Italy, the British and French governments, fearful of alienating Mussolini, would not take the decisive step of imposing an oil embargo, while FDR would not agree to more than a moral embargo of oil shipments to Italy. In December, the foreign secretaries of Britain, Samuel Hoare, and France, Pierre Laval, reached an agreement that handed most of Ethiopia to Italy. While a public outcry forced a repudiation of the Hoare-Laval plan, the League had failed in a crucial test. Its weakness was now apparent to all.[37]

Throughout the winter of 1935–1936, House's energy seemed to be fading. He and Fanny suffered from the flu for several weeks in February, and he lacked the energy, or the desire, to travel to Hyde Park to visit the president. He was annoyed by FDR's choice of advisers, complaining that "it always astonishes me that the President sees and advises with the men that he does," and toward the end of 1935 House thought FDR's hold on the American people was "slipping." By the spring of 1936, however, House concluded that FDR's "political situation" had improved and that "even the most ardent Republicans admit that he is practically certain of re-election." After his reelection House planned to "make a drive" on FDR to get him to take a stand on American membership in the League.[38]

On March 7, 1936, Hitler dispatched 22,000 German troops into the Rhineland, a surprise move that struck at the heart of the Versailles settlement and the Locarno treaties. The reaction of the British and French governments was muted; British leaders feared provoking a war, while French leaders had already reconciled themselves to a German reoccupation of this vital area. Hitler had gambled and won, delivering a blow to the French and further undermining confidence in the Geneva system. By the spring of 1936, there was, as one historian notes, "a darkening of the general mood." Ambassador Cudahy warned House that "barring a miracle, we shall have war on this continent—it is only a question of time."[39] House recognized the mounting tension in Europe and lamented the fact that the American people "are singularly unaware of the threatened danger." He seemed uncertain what to make of Hitler. One diplomat warned him that the German people "are crouched like some tiger, hungry and bloody, ready to spring," but another adviser reassured him that Hitler desired a "long peace."[40]

By the middle of June, 1936, House was back in Manchester for what he soon realized would be a "dull summer."[41] From his North Shore sanctuary House watched the unfolding of the 1936 presidential campaign. Republicans, much as they disliked the New Deal, realized that some of its reforms were popular, and at their Cleveland convention they nominated Governor Alfred M. Landon. Landon promised to wage an aggressive campaign and claimed that he could accomplish many of the objectives of the New Deal in a more efficient manner.[42] On June 27, when FDR accepted the Democratic nomination at Franklin Field in Philadelphia, he issued a stirring call for economic equality, ending his address with a memorable peroration: "There is a mysterious cycle in human events. To some generations much is given. Of other generations much is expected. This generation of Americans has a rendezvous with destiny."[43]

House realized that FDR had "made a wonderful hit in his acceptance speech," while Woolley, who was actually at the convention, reported that not even Wilson could have surpassed FDR's performance. "Much as I admire the President," House's astute protégé continued, "I didn't really know he had that masterpiece in him." Both House and Woolley realized, however, that they would be even more on the margins in 1936 than they had been in 1932.[44] As FDR traveled across the country, he reminded Americans of their plight when he took office. The president campaigned against "greed" and "autocracy," and explained to voters how the many programs of the New Deal had transformed the lives of most Americans. On October 31, addressing a Democratic rally in Madison Square Garden, he denounced the enemies of the people who sought to discredit his administration and regain their power: "They are unanimous in their hatred for me, and I welcome their hatred."[45] The results of the election justified the confidence of Roosevelt and his advisers and the shrewdness of their strategy. They had laid the basis for a durable political coalition, winning huge majorities in the nation's great industrial cities. FDR received 28 million votes, or nearly 61 percent of the total, carried forty-six states, and increased Democratic majorities in the House and Senate. He had won an enormous mandate.[46]

At the end of the summer, House had received a "most affectionate communication" from FDR and, after he returned to New York in mid-September, concluded that he would be reelected. He soon found himself "up to my neck in campaign work" and in October had a "pleasant and satisfactory" visit with the president at Hyde Park. The extent of Roosevelt's victory, however, surprised House, and he presciently noted that "I am not certain that it would not have been better to win by a smaller majority."[47] Woolley, however, understood the reasons for FDR's extraordinary victory better than his aging mentor. "Roosevelt was re-elected," he wrote House, "because he has touched the heart string, has stirred the very soul of the common man." House, now in his seventy-eighth year, had lived to witness a Democratic president receive the largest portion of the vote in American history.[48]

During the winter of 1936–1937, House seemed more reconciled to remaining in New York. He was in good health and was "never busier with public affairs and am enjoying it." He and Loulie continued to go out often. In early February, 1937 Loulie had a "bad spell" when her maid "found her in the bathtub where she had been nearly for an hour unable to get up." But her doctor found nothing wrong, and she soon resumed her active social life.[49]

Many observers found the situation in Europe threatening. The Spanish Civil War raged on. Britain and France pursued a policy of non-intervention while Germany and Italy aided the fascist forces of General Francisco Franco. The conflict in Spain drew Hitler and Mussolini closer together. Mussolini's victory in Ethiopia had fed his ambitions for Italy to become the dominant power in the Mediterranean; Hitler, sensing the weakness of Britain and France, set 1939 as the year that Germany should be ready to go to war and begin the process of finding *lebensraum*—living space—in the East. Most European leaders understood that Hitler had expansionist goals, but his more specific intentions were unclear and British leaders in particular hoped that he could be drawn into a general European settlement.[50] At the end of 1936, Ambassador Cudahy informed House that Hitler would not stop his military program and warned that "one has a presentiment of impending momentous events." House doubted the imminence of war, although he admitted that "as in 1914, it may come over night." He also believed that American-Japanese relations had improved, and that if the Japanese "are left alone they will let other people alone."[51]

House did not attend FDR's second inaugural, held for the first time on January 20, 1937. The president spoke of the work still to be done to improve American society; he saw "one-third of a nation ill-housed, ill-clad, ill-nourished." At the beginning of his second term he was determined to act boldly. To prepare the way for further reform, he believed that the threat of judicial nullification by the Supreme Court must be removed. On February 5, 1937, in a special message to Congress, he asked for the appointment of additional justices to the court (for every justice over the age of seventy), what his opponents soon labeled his "Court-packing" scheme. The president, however, had badly underestimated both popular reverence for the Supreme Court and the degree of discontent among some congressional Democrats with many aspects of the New Deal. The battle over the expansion of the Supreme Court, which FDR had lost by the middle of May, revealed deep divisions within the Democratic Party and hastened the formation of a conservative coalition in Congress, an alliance of Democrats and Republicans determined to stop any further reform legislation. By the middle of 1937, the New Deal had lost its political momentum.[52]

House seemed disengaged from the political turmoil in Washington. He admired FDR's achievements and initially thought the battle over the Supreme Court would "simmer down." As it continued, however, he complained that Roosevelt had failed to consult the very people—Hull, Roper, and Woolley—who could be of great help to him. But he made no effort to visit the president at Hyde Park before he left New York on June 10 for the North Shore.[53]

On June 11, 1937, when House arrived in Manchester for his fortieth summer on the North Shore, reporters asked him whether there would soon be war in Europe and whether FDR would run for an unprecedented third term. House replied that the American people, along with those in Britain and France, were determined to maintain peace, and that the "Italian and German people are also vehemently opposed to war." Apparently thinking that he was not to be quoted, he also asserted that the president would "not be a candidate for a third term" and would "probably do some writing after he retires." House did not, in fact, want FDR to run again, but he realized that he had misspoken and quickly explained to the president that the journalists had made his remarks "into a sensation."[54]

By early July 1937, House found himself in bed, attended by a doctor and a trained nurse. The pain in his chest and rib cage, along with a fever, left him in a weakened condition for most of the summer. He also suffered from rheumatism in his hand and foot, and at the end of the summer complained that his eyes had weakened considerably. The flow of letters that he had dictated to Fanny for so many years now became a trickle of short notes in which he described the progress of his illness.[55] By the third week in September he was back in New York, hoping that the cool weather would improve his health. He now got up around 11 in the morning, took a drive, along with a second one in the afternoon, and then went back to bed around 5:30 or 6:00. He realized that "it might be a long while before" he got better, and was grateful to three women friends who "read to me and make life endurable." His male friends were "not much comfort at such times."[56]

House no longer had the energy to follow national or international affairs. Woolley wrote about the political turmoil in Washington and concluded that "the renomination of our esteemed Chief is out of the picture."

House also heard from FDR, who was sorry he lacked the strength to visit Hyde Park and wondered if he liked his October 5 "Quarantine Speech," in which he spoke vaguely of an effort to contain "an epidemic of world lawlessness." But House was too sick to respond to what would have been, in his better days, issues that deeply concerned him.[57] By early December, he felt better, however, and was, he reported to Mona, "leading a more normal life." The death of Albert Burleson (at the age of seventy-four), the last of his old Texas friends, saddened him, and he worried about Loulie, who was in good health but had become very deaf, "which is distressing as she loves to go out socially." At the end of the month he and Loulie gave a dinner party for seventeen people. It was the last time they would entertain their friends.[58]

Epilogue

Crossing the River

On January 5, 1938, Charles Seymour, now president of Yale, lunched with House at his New York apartment. When Seymour arrived he found the elder statesman "dressed and lying on the sofa in the little front sitting room . . . . He looked like a wax effigy, motionless except for the hand he raised to greet me, the face that of an eastern philosopher who had discovered the answer to the riddle of life, no emotional disturbance at any time touching his voice or the lines around his eyes and mouth."

> He began at once: . . . "I don't expect to stay here long. The doctors tell me that there is nothing wrong with me organically . . . . I can live for ten years, they say, if I adjust my manner of life to a certain level. It means no exertion . . . . I decided to live over Christmas and the New Year. I wanted to see the grandchildren and I had work I wanted to finish. But now that is done and I don't think I will stay. I think I will go out sometime in the late spring. It's not worth while living in the way I have to . . . . I can't read. I'm too weak. I get tired of the radio. I get tired having the women fuss over me. Miss Fanny ought to have the chance to travel and she can't do it while I am here. I have had an interesting life. I have fulfilled my aspirations. I did just what I wanted to do in the Wilson period, although our plans were spoiled by the catastrophe that followed the Peace Conference. During these last fifteen years I have been close to the center of things . . . . No important foreigner has come to America without talking to me. I was close to the movement that nominated Roosevelt. He has been very nice to me, although it was not worth my while advising him . . . . All the ambassadors have reported to me frequently. My hand has been on things. But now I am too weak to go on with this. And it's not worth while living as a vegetable. So I think I will cross the river shortly."

"This was said," Seymour continued, "in a low, even tone, without emphasis . . . . As he talked his eyes lit up and his ironic amusement expressed itself in the characteristic high-pitched cackle. Because of weakness his voice was husky and enunciation thick, but his alert sense of humor and his memory of details were keen."

For all his acceptance of the fact that his life was coming to an end, House was still obsessed with his break with Wilson. Once again the old man placed much of the blame on Edith, claiming that the "rift" began right after the Armistice, when House's alleged diplomatic triumph had received "extravagant praise." Both Wilson and Edith had been offended by Edward's advice that the president not attend the peace conference, and once there, the two men "were separated by half of Paris and did not see each other so constantly as had been our custom." After Wilson's return in March there was a further change, since "unfriendly persons had carried to Mrs. Wilson the story. . . that during the President's absence I had yielded to unwise suggestions of compromise . . . . As the Peace Conference closed there was no coolness between us; merely a slackening in intimacy." House reviewed his relations with the president after his stroke, concluding that Wilson had no reason for "hard feelings against me . . . . But he didn't have the force to break through the ring [of House's enemies] and resume relations." And so, House concluded, "my separation from Wilson was not a break. It was caused by the illness of each of us, that drove a wedge between us. When the rift was opened it was kept open by those who did not wish us to come together . . . . My love and admiration for Woodrow Wilson have never faltered or lessened."[1] Even at the end of his life House refused to reflect deeply on his behavior during the Wilson years, or to accept any blame for what had happened.

In January and February 1938, House felt "much better" and had "regained considerable strength." But by the end of February his brief surge of energy faded, and Fanny reported that he "has been very ill for the past week and the doctor thinks the end is not far off. He is so weak and takes no notice of anyone or anything." Early on the morning of March 28, House's nurse summoned members of his family to his bedroom, and Loulie, Janet, Gordon, and Fanny were there when he died in his sleep. "The dear Wise Man," as Sara Roosevelt called him, was gone.[2]

House had asked for a private funeral, with only members of his family present. On March 29, Loulie, Gordon and Janet, Fanny, and Louise Robbins left for Houston, where they would be joined by Mona and Randolph (who were spending the winter in California). The governor of Texas offered a place for House at the state cemetery in Austin, but Loulie decided that he should be buried as he had lived, as a private citizen. He was buried on March 31 at Glenwood Cemetery in Houston, in a modest

grave in the House family plot, close to his mother, father, and six brothers. At the grave were many floral tributes, filled with springtime flowers,
the most impressive of which was a huge Texas star made of bluebonnets.
An Episcopal minister read the twenty-third Psalm, and also Alfred Lord
Tennyson's *Crossing the Bar*, a poem selected by House:

> Sunset and evening star,
>   And one clear call for me!
> And may there be no moaning of the bar,
>   When I put out to sea,
>
> But such a tide as moving seems asleep,
>   Too full for sound and foam,
> When that which drew from out the boundless deep
>   Turns again home.
>
> Twilight and evening bell,
>   And after that the dark!
> And may there be no sadness of farewell,
>   When I embark;
>
> For tho' from out our bourne of Time and Place
>   The flood may bear me far,
> I hope to see my Pilot face to face
>   When I have crossed the bar.[3]

Tributes poured in from leaders in America and abroad. President
Roosevelt praised House as a "great and unique figure," while Lloyd George
said that "this struck very close to me . . . . He was a genius for diplomacy."
Those who sought to evaluate the meaning of House's life found it difficult
to measure his elusive career. Walter Lippmann wrote that "the career of
Colonel House was like that of an actor or of a singer in that there is no record
left by which posterity can form an independent estimate of his worth." The
New York Times, in its lead editorial, noted that House was an "idealist and
dreamer," as well as a master of the practical art of politics, and that his

> life was full of paradoxes. There was a puzzling combination of shrewdness
> with what often seemed the naivete of the inexperienced. It was this, how-
> ever, which made him so distinctly American. He instinctively felt the qual-
> ity of mind of those with whom he talked, judging them generously because
> he understood their foibles and their unexpressed desires. Perhaps, after all,
> this was his greatest quality, a spirit that was akin to noble aspiration and
> could at the same time appreciate the fumbling and the ineptitude of those
> who dimly sought their own uncharted way in this mysterious world.[4]

House had led a remarkable life, dreaming of fame as a youth when he roamed the Gulf Coastal Plain near Houston, searching for a career in the aftermath of his father's death, and eventually moving to Austin and mastering the art of Texas politics. After the turn of the century he left Texas, joining an Anglo-American cosmopolitan elite and then waiting for the "man and the opportunity" that would carry him to the pinnacle of American politics. House's friendship with Woodrow Wilson—for it was really nothing less—catapulted him into national and international fame. For over seven years the two men remained close, thanks in part to House's unusual insight into his friend's needs and aspirations and to his clever and sometimes cynical maneuvering within the president's inner circle of advisers. In domestic affairs House was content to help implement Wilson's vision of reform; in foreign affairs he was the most cosmopolitan of Wilson's advisers, having traveled extensively in Western Europe in the years before the outbreak of the war. House followed great power politics closely, and during his wartime trips to Europe he tried to assess the complex currents of the struggle. He understood, earlier than most Americans, that the United States could not stand apart from events in Europe, that it must find a way to end the war and to rebuild the international community.

Many people were drawn to this small, imperturbable man, who seemed to have mastered the vicissitudes of life. He was the center of a warm, devoted family and collected over the course of his life a wide circle of friends, some of whom made eloquent testimonials to his thoughtfulness and generosity. House was a keen student of human behavior, who seemed to lack the fierce ambition of many of his contemporaries. He preferred to stay out of the official limelight, turning down offices and appointments that were offered over the years, and enjoying the power conferred by concealment. But as his fame and power grew, a few observers noted the emergence of a streak of vanity, of an exaggerated sense of his own importance. Bernard Baruch remembered that during the war, when leaving House's apartment, the Colonel turned to him and said: "Isn't it a thrilling thing to deal with the forces that affect the destiny of the world!"[5]

As House accumulated experiences in the capitals of Europe—where he was treated virtually as a head of state—he found it increasingly difficult to accept his role as counselor and came to feel that his diplomatic skills were superior to those of the president he had befriended but also served, that he was the only person in the American government to see the whole picture. Wilson was, in fact, partly responsible for House's inflated estimate of himself, sending him abroad with only vague instructions and carelessly monitoring his negotiations in the capitals of Europe, and leaving a void for self-importance to fill.

The Paris Peace Conference challenged the peculiar system that the two men had devised. House, who had grown accustomed to a large degree of autonomy, now had to subordinate himself to the president, who was no longer a distant figure in Washington but the head of the American delegation in Paris. Worse still, both Wilson and House brought to the conference grandiose expectations about the nature of the settlement. As their efforts to build a new world order faltered, and as Wilson's health collapsed, their friendship faltered as well. Wilson's withdrawal of confidence was the great failure of House's life, and during the fourteen years that he lived after Wilson's death he sought to advance his own version of events while defending his friend's legacy.

After her husband's death, Loulie stayed in New York until her death at the age of eighty-one on December 26, 1940. In the last few years she became, Fanny Denton's niece remembered, "terribly senile." Fanny, who had taken care of Loulie, moved to Chestertown, Maryland, where she prospered, learning how to drive, forming many friendships, and helping to send her nieces and nephews through college. She died on February 25, 1948. All the members of the president's inner circle of friends and advisers, with the exception of Ellen Wilson, survived House. Cary Grayson continued to look after Wilson after the president had moved to S Street. He retired from the Navy in 1928, chaired the American Red Cross for three years, and bred horses on Blue Ridge Farm in Virginia. He died prematurely in 1938. William Gibbs McAdoo moved to Los Angeles in 1922, where he set up a law practice and pursued a variety of often risky business ventures. In 1932 he won a Senate seat and, back in Washington for the next six years, became a strong supporter of the New Deal. He died in 1941. In 1921, Joseph Tumulty began what became a thriving law practice in Washington. He remained fascinated with Democratic Party politics, and though he disliked much of the New Deal, stayed loyal to Roosevelt and his party. He died in 1954.

After her husband's death, Edith Wilson retained a key interest in presidential politics, appearing at the Democratic convention in Houston in 1928 and, over the years, attending many White House functions. She became the fiercely protective guardian of Wilson's legacy, promoting his memory in many different ways. In January 1961, the year of her death, she stood on the reviewing stand at John F. Kennedy's inauguration. Bernard Baruch served as Edith's adviser and patron, continued his involvement in the affairs of the Democratic Party, and became an *eminence grise*, speaking out often on public affairs until his death in 1965.

Over the years, all of these friends of the president remained devoted to Wilson, convinced that he was a great man and that the years of his presidency were the high point of their lives. All agreed with McAdoo, who wrote that Wilson "looked over the heads of other men, above the confusion of contemporary events, to distant horizons." Edward House believed the same. He also knew, as Lippmann noted, that "almost all that he did is indistinguishably fused with Woodrow Wilson's career." House's historical reputation, like that of his great collaborator, would ebb and flow over the years, but House went to his death convinced that he and Wilson were right, that the ideas for which they stood would continue, in the words of George F. Kennan, to have a "great and commanding relevance" in the life of the nation.[6]

Acknowledgments

On May 3, 1966, the late Arthur S. Link warned me that a biography of Colonel House was "an enormous project. . . one that will involve you in at least six or eight years of research."[1] How I wish he had been right! When I began this project in the late 1960s, I badly underestimated both its scale and the many demands of academic life. House lived a long and exceptionally full life, and as I proceeded, I realized that his biography, if properly done, required a large canvas. And as the years passed I also discovered, as Leon Edel wrote in the preface of one of his Henry James volumes, "that a biographer has his own life to lead as well as the life of his subject."[2]

I began this project in Houston, Texas, where I taught at Rice University. I am grateful to that institution for its generous support and to friends in Houston who encouraged me in one way or another: the late S. I. and Susie Morris, Elizabeth Phillips, Louisa Sarofim, and John and Dominique de Menil, who were especially kind to a sometimes awkward young scholar. My onetime neighbor, Larry McMurtry, deepened my interest in Texas and its history through his friendship and brilliant novels and social commentary. At Brown University, where I moved in 1970, Provost Maurice Glicksman offered encouragement at a critical moment, Chancellor Artemis Joukowsky and Vice-President Ronald Margolin taught me much, during my six years as chair of the history department, about how the university worked, and President E. Gordon Ghee offered an example of inspired leadership. At the University of Miami, where I moved in 2003, I received a warm welcome from my colleagues in the history department. Over the years I was fortunate to receive fellowships from the American Council of Learned Societies, the National Endowment for the Humanities, the Howard Foundation, the Guggenheim Foundation, and the Woodrow Wilson International Center for Scholars. My two stays at the Wilson Center, as a Guest Scholar in the summer of 1988, and as a Public Policy Scholar in the fall of 2007, were productive and stimulating. I am especially grateful to Lee Hamilton, Michael Van Dusen, and Sam and Sherry Wells for making my second stay a memorable one. I cannot begin to thank all the archivists and librarians who have helped me in one phase or another of this book. At Yale University, where I spent a year and a half working through the House Papers and other manuscript collections, Judith Schiff was always ready to assist, while the late Herman Kahn offered his friendship and encouragement, as did Gaddis Smith and the late Robin Winks. And my thanks to Eric Vettel, Heide Hackford, and Arthur Link III at the Woodrow Wilson Presidential Library for guiding me through collections there.

I began this book at a time when many people who remembered the Colonel were still alive and who were willing to share their memories with me. Mona and Randolph Tucker were generous with their time, as was Fanny Denton's niece, Frances Denton Miller. I am especially indebted to Ed and Steena Auchincloss, who offered all kinds of support over the years and who must have wondered when, if ever, this book would be finished. My agent Gerry McCauley has been extraordinarily helpful and patient, and at various phases of this book, four research assistants have eased my labors: Julie Roy Jeffrey organized stacks of House correspondence, Betty Hartman tried to identify the House mansion in Galveston, Susan Burneson pursued obscure periodical articles and newspaper reports, and Dan Larsen explored the Kathleen Scott Papers. Finally, Michael Williams drew on his computer wizardry to supplement my modest skills at word processing.

The completion of this book has given me the opportunity to reflect on what has become a long academic career. At Northwestern University, where I majored in English and History, a number of gifted teachers— Bergen Evans, Jean Hagstrum, Richard W. Leopold, Arthur S. Link, Peter Seng, and Eliseo Vivas—offered a small-town Iowa boy a glimpse into a world of learning and scholarship. At Harvard University, where I received my Ph.D., I learned from a remarkable group of historians: Bernard Bailyn, Giles Constable, Frank Freidel, Oscar Handlin, Ernest R. May, Arthur Schlesinger Jr., and William L. Langer. Over my years in the profession I benefited from many conversations with Sadao Asada, Andrew Davidson, Bob Brigham, Louis Galambos, David Hall, the late Stephen Kurtz, David Mayers, and Randall Woods. John Lewis Gaddis offered generous and timely advice. I especially benefited from the friendship of Arthur and Margaret Link, who welcomed me into the community of Wilson scholars and who set an example of dedication to a life of scholarship which I could not hope to emulate. As Wilson once remarked, "We are carried forward, gentlemen, by our association with men of deeper and wider experience than ourselves."[3]

At Oxford University Press I have been fortunate to work with an outstanding group of professionals. Sheldon Meyer recognized the significance of a life of Colonel House and over the years offered advice and encouragement; I regret that he did not live to see the completion of this biography. Susan Ferber read early chapters with care, and I am especially grateful to Niko Pfund for the interest he took in this manuscript and for putting me in touch with Timothy Bent. Tim offered perceptive and sometimes painful advice, and showed me how to improve the flow of the narrative and how to put the Colonel's life in a broader perspective. It has been a pleasure to work with such a gifted editor. Keely Latcham, his assistant, carried out all sorts of chores and was especially efficient in tracking down obscure photographs. Patterson Lamb suggested further improvements through her thorough copyediting, and Mary Jo Rhodes guided the manuscript through the production process with skill and patience.

My old friend Larry McMurtry read the manuscript as only he can, while Samuel R. Williamson, Jr. drew on his mastery of the literature on World War I to sharpen my analysis of that conflict. My daughter Hilary helped guide me through a medical crisis, and my brother Art always seemed confident that one day he would be able to read this book. My wife Sabina, with her vitality of mind and spirit, kept me going as the stack of chapters grew bigger and bigger, and also kept me focused on the need to write for the general reader as well as the specialist. Her love helped carry this book to its completion.

C.E.N.

Notes

PROLOGUE

1. *Reminiscences* (House Papers, Yale University), 51.
2. House to Wilson, May 28, 1914, House Papers.
3. Edith Galt to Wilson, Aug. 26, 1915, in Arthur S. Link, ed., *The Papers of Woodrow Wilson [PWW]*, 68 vols. (Princeton, N.J., 1966-93), XXXIV, 336–39.
4. Robert E. Sherwood, *Roosevelt and Hopkins: An Intimate History* (New York, 1950), 4; David L. Roll, *The Hopkins Touch: Harry Hopkins and the Forging of the Alliance to Defeat Hitler* (New York, 2013), 3–8.
5. David Lloyd George, *The Truth about the Peace Treaties* (London, Eng., 1938), I, 245–46; a detailed analysis of House's diary is in Inga Floto, *Colonel House in Paris: A Study of American Policy at the Paris Peace Conference 1919* (Princeton, N.J., 1980), 18–19.
6. House Diary, June 24, 1915.

CHAPTER I

1. John Q. Anderson, ed., *Tales of Frontier Texas, 1830–1860 (Dallas, Tex., 1966)*, 7–8, 13–25; Roy Bedichek, *Karankaway County* (Garden City, N.Y., 1950), 2, 23, 105.
2. Mark E. Nackman, *A Nation within a Nation: The Rise of Texas Nationalism* (Port Washington, N.Y., 1975), 3–6, 39–44, 64.
3. *Reminiscences*, 6; The family came from Holland, where its name was Huis; Edward House left two memoirs, *Reminiscences*, written in 1916, and *Memories*, written in 1929. Both are in the House Papers at the Yale University Library. Subsequent references to *Reminiscences* or *Memories* refer to these memoirs.
4. W. Eugene Hollon, *The Southwest: Old and New* (New York, 1961), 131; David G. McComb, *Houston: A History* (Austin, Tex., 1981), 10–32.
5. Frederick Law Olmsted, *A Journey through Texas; or a Saddle-Trip on the Southwestern Frontier* (New York, 1857), 361–64; Kenneth W. Wheeler, *To Wear a City's Crown: The Beginnings of Urban Growth in Texas, 1836–1865* (Cambridge, Mass., 1968), 21, 51–54; McComb, *Houston*, 44–48.
6. Henry Cushing Grover, "The Dissolution of T. W. House and Company" (M. A. Thesis, University of Houston, 1962), 1–8; McComb, *Houston*, 22–26.

7. Earl Wesley Fornell, *The Galveston Era: The Texas Crescent on the Eve of Secession* (Austin, Tex., 1961), 4–10; David G. McComb, *Galveston: A History* (Austin, Tex., 1986), 42–72. Wheeler, *To Wear a City's Crown*, 90–103, 130–32, 163–65; Randolph B. Campbell and Richard G. Lowe, *Wealth and Power in Antebellum Texas* (College Station, Tex., 1977), 91.

8. Wheeler, *To Wear a City's Crown*, 150–54; *Reminiscences*, 1–3; James L. Haley, *Passionate Nation: The Epic History of Texas* (New York, 2006), 303–14.

9. *Reminiscences*, 1–4, 6; Jesse A. Ziegler, *Wave of the Gulf: Ziegler's Scrapbook of the Texas Gulf Coast Country* (San Antonio, Tex., 1938), 275–76, 300–303; *Memories*, 1.

10. McComb, *Houston*, 52–55; *Reminiscences*, 4; *Memories*, 1–2.

11. Fornell, *The Galveston Era*, 13; Grover, "The Dissolution of T. W. House and Company," 27–29.

12. *Memories*, 3–5; Ziegler, *Wave of the Gulf*, 115, 187.

13. Richard Maxwell Brown, *Strain of Violence: Historical Studies of American Violence and Vigilantism* (New York, 1975), 237–38, 262–65; Wheeler, *To Wear a City's Crown*, 54–55.

14. *Reminiscences*, 4–5, 37.

15. *Memories*, 4, 8–9; George R. House to Edward M. House, May 13, 1976, House Papers.

16. *Memories*, 8.

17. *Reminiscences*, 5; *Memories*, 9; interview with Mrs. George Shelley, June 22, 1970.

18. *Reminiscences*, 11–12; *Memories*, 9–10.

19. *Reminiscences*, 7; Mary Ann McDowall, "A Little Journey through Memory's Halls," 117, San Jacinto Museum of History.

20. *Memories*, 5, 8–9.

21. *Reminiscences*, 7–8; *Memories*, 9–13; Theodore R. Sizer, ed., *The Age of the Academies* (New York, 1964), 27–29, 40.

22. *Reminiscences*, 7–8; *Memories*, 11–13; Rupert Norval Richardson, *Colonel Edward M. House: The Texas Years, 1958–1912* (Abilene, Tex., 1964), 15.

23. *Reminiscences*, 8; *Memories*, 13–14.

24. Thomas B. Davis, Jr., *Chronicles of Hopkins Grammar School, 1660–1935* (New Haven, Conn., 1938), 406–38; John M. Ferren, "Edward Mandell House: The Preparation" (Honors Essay, Harvard College, 1959), 10–12; Most students who went through Hopkins in the 1870s retained vivid memories of the rector, but Edward recalled only his peers and his life outside of the classroom. He remembered Walter Camp, who became the father of American football; Robert Tuttle Morris, who became a noted surgeon; Oliver T. Morton, who became one of his closest boyhood friends; and a scholarly student from Alabama, Adrian Sebastian Van de Graaff, *Reminiscences*, 8–9; *Memories*, 14–15; Robert T. Morris, *Fifty Years a Surgeon* (New York, 1935), 17.

25. William Dudley Foulke, *The Life of Oliver P. Morton* (Indianapolis, Ind., 1899), II, 489, 507–33; "Oliver Perry Morton," in John A. Garraty and Mark C. Carns, eds., *American National Biography* (New York, 1999), XV, 956–58.

26. Keith Ian Polakoff, *The Politics of Inertia: The Election of 1876 and the End of Reconstruction* (Baton Rouge, La., 1973), 202–314; Michael F. Holt, *By One Vote: The Disputed Presidential Election of 1876* (Lawrence, Kans., 2008), 175–243; Morton Keller, *Affairs of State: Public Life in Late Nineteenth Century America* (Cambridge, Mass., 1977), 245–46, 258–64.

27. Keller, *Affairs of State*, 242; *Reminiscences*, 9–10; *Memories*, 14–16.

28. *Reminiscences*, 9–11; *Memories*, 2, 15–16.

29. *Reminiscences*, 8–9; *Memories*, 17; House to Robert T. Morris, Feb. 8, 1936, House Papers.

30. Brooks Mather Kelley, *Yale: A History* (New Haven, Conn., 1974), 239–54; Morris Bishop, *A History of Cornell* (Ithaca, N.Y., 1962), 73–90; Frederick Rudolph, *The American College and University: A History* (New York, 1962), 266–68.

31. Bishop, *A History of Cornell*, 201; Kermit Carlyle Parsons, *The Cornell Campus: A History of Its Planning and Development* (Ithaca, N.Y., 1968), 24–33, 37–90.

32. *Reminiscences*, 10; *Memories*, 20–22; Ferren, "Edward Mandell House," 14–17.

33. Anderson, ed., *Tales of Frontier Texas*, 275; *Memories*, 6–8; Alexander L. and Juliette L. George, *Woodrow Wilson and Colonel House: A Personality Study* (New York, 1956), 80–81; *Memories*, 18–21.

34. *Memories*, 18–21.

35. *Reminiscences*, 39; *Memories*, 22; House to Edward H. Andrews, June 30, 1927, House Papers.

CHAPTER 2

1. *Memories*, 8, 23; *Reminiscences*, 1, 3, 39–41; House to T. W. House Jr., Oct. 20, 1935, House Papers.

2. Mark E. Nackman, *A Nation within a Nation: The Rise of Texas Nationalism* (Port Washington, N.Y., 1975), 9–12, 56–58, 70–71; *Reminiscences*, 4.

3. *Memories*, 33.

4. *Memories*, 23–28.

5. *Memories*, 29.

6. *Memories*, 29–33; *Reminiscences*, 35–38; Rupert Norval Richardson, *Colonel Edward M. House: The Texas Years, 1958–1912* (Abilene, Tex., 1964), 36–38; William D. Carrigan, *The Making of a Lynching Culture: Violence and Vigilantism in Central Texas, 1836–1916* (Urbana, Ill., 2004), 1–15, 132–87.

7. Richardson, *Colonel House*, 30–31; interview with Ima Hogg, Oct. 13, 1967, and Mr. and Mrs. Randolph F. Tucker, Oct. 15, 1966; Sketch of Col. House by Col. John Tilghman Dickinson, Nov. 1918, House Papers.

8. *Reminiscences*, 12; Mona House (later Mrs. Randolph F. Tucker) wrote Rupert Richardson on Jan. 29, 1959, that she was born in Naples (Richardson, *Colonel House*, 31), but she told the author on two separate occasions, Aug. 25 and Oct. 15, 1966, that she was born in Florence. House's "Vital Statistics" record at Cornell, which he filled out, indicates that Mona was born on April 26, 1882, in Florence. (Deceased Alumni Records, Cornell University Archives); the photographs are in the San Jacinto Museum of History.

9. *Reminiscences*, 12.

10. Henry Cushing Grover, "The Dissolution of T. W. House and Company" (M.A. Thesis, University of Houston, 1962), 16–17, 31–41; Loulie H. House Scrapbook, House Papers.

11. Grover, "The Dissolution of T. W. House and Company," 11–12, 16; *Houston Post*, Aug. 19, 1923 and Aug. 12, 1934, in the Edith R. House Scrapbook, San Jacinto Museum of History.

12. Richardson, *Colonel House*, 31–32; David G. McComb, *Houston: A History* (Austin, Tex., 1981), 63–64, 70.

13. *Reminiscences*, 12; *Memories*, 36.

14. William O. Douglas, *Farewell to Texas: A Vanishing Wilderness* (New York, 1967), 201–3; Mary Starr Barkley, *History of Travis County and Austin, 1839–1899* (Waco, Tex., 1963), 22–30, 123–36; "Austin," and "Capitol," in Ron Tyler, ed., *The New Handbook of Texas* (Austin, Tex., 1996), I, 298–301, 966; Katherine Hart, et al., *Austin and Travis County: A Pictorial History, 1839–1939* (Austin, Tex., 1975), 93; *Austin, Texas, Illustrated: The Famous City of the Lone Star State*, undated pamphlet, in the Austin History Collection, Austin Public Library.

15. Richardson, *Colonel House*, 317; Richardson gives House's height as five feet nine inches, but his 1915 passport indicates that he was an inch and a half shorter. From 1893 to 1937, House kept a series of small black address books containing notes on his weight and health and on other personal matters. They are in the House Papers.

16. Frances Taylor Love, *My Home Is Austin Texas* (Lafayette, La., 1958), 70; *Austin Statesman*, Feb. 1, 1888, and other undated newspaper clippings, in the Loulie House Scrapbook, House Papers.

17. Loulie House Scrapbooks, House Papers; *Leslie's Weekly*, Nov. 21, 1895; interviews with Ima Hogg, Oct. 13, 1967 and with Mrs. Milton Gutsch, June 22, 1970.

18. *Reminiscences*, 41; interview with Frances Denton Miller, Oct. 8–9, 1977; interview with Ima Hogg, Oct. 13, 1967.

19. House to Frances B. Denton, Sept. 8, 11, 1893, House Papers; interview with Mona and Randolph Tucker, Aug. 25, 1966.

20. John M. Ferren, " 'Edward Mandell House: The Preparation" (Honors Essay, Harvard College, 1959), 18–19; *Memories*, 35.

21. Richardson, *Colonel House,* 34–41; John Stricklin Spratt, *The Road to Spindletop: Economic Change in Texas, 1875–1901* (Dallas, Tex., 1955), 41; House

to Holmes and Bierschwale, Jan. 4, 1888. The correspondence between House and this land agent in Mason is in the possession of Mrs. Charles E. Coombes.

22. House to Frank Freeman, Jan. 10, 1901, House Papers; House's letter to posterity, dated April 25, 1891, describes the ceremony. This letter, along with the other contents of the cornerstone, are in the Austin History Collection, Austin Public Library. After years of neglect, in 1966 the house was badly damaged by fire, and in 1967 it was demolished.

23. *Austin Statesman*, July 4, 1892; *Reminiscences*, 43; Richard W. Bond, "The Residence of E. M. House: Texas Historical Architecture," *Texas Architect*, 18 (June 1968), 12–17.

24. Bond, "Residence of E. M. House," 15–16; Roxanne Kuter Williamson, *Austin, Texas: An American Architectural History* (San Antonio, Tex., 1973), 116–17; *Austin Statesman*, Nov. 20, 1964. Contemporaries estimated the cost of the house at $50,000, but Bond regards this figure as very low considering the lavish use of imported materials. Including the furnishings from Marshall Field's in Chicago, he thinks the total cost may have been close to $100,000. Bond, "The Residence of E. M. House," 16. House recalled spending $75,000. House to David Harrell, Ap. 20, 1909, Harrell Papers.

25. Undated newspaper clippings, Loulie House Scrapbook, House Papers; Richard O'Connor, *O. Henry: The Legendary Life of William S. Porter* (Garden City, N.Y., 1970), 24–25; *Reminiscences*, 34–35, 41–42; Albert Bigelow Paine, *Captain Bill McDonald, Texas Ranger: A Story of Frontier Reform* (New York, 1909), 13–15; Harold J. Weiss Jr., *Yours to Command: The Life and Legend of Texas Ranger Captain Bill McDonald* (Denton, Tex., 2009), 11–22; Robert M. Utley, *Lone Star Justice: The First Century of the Texas Rangers* (New York, 2002), 256–63.

26. *Memories*, 36; Richardson, *Colonel House*, 40.

27. Alwyn Barr, *Reconstruction to Reform: Texas Politics, 1876–1906* (Austin, Tex., 1971), 117–18; Robert C. Cotner, *James Stephen Hogg: A Biography* (Austin, Tex., 1959), 130; Lewis L. Gould, *Progressives and Prohibitionists: Texas Democrats in the Wilson Era* (Austin, Tex., 1973), 6; "James Stephen Hogg," in Ron Tyler, ed., *The New Handbook of Texas* (Austin, Tex., 1996), III, 652–53.

28. J. Morgan Kousser, *The Shaping of Southern Politics: Suffrage Restriction and the Establishment of the One-Party South, 1880–1910* (New Haven, Conn., 1974), 196–98.

29. Barr, *Reconstruction to Reform*, 93–110; Michael Perman, *Pursuit of Unity: A Political History of the American South* (Chapel Hill, N.C., 2009), 156–69.

30. Lawrence Goodwyn, *Democratic Promise: The Populist Movement in America* (New York, 1976), 25–50, 77–90, 126–27, 220–23, 240–42; Charles Postel, *The Populist Vision* (New York, 2007), 3–22, 121–26, 188–95; Donna A. Barnes, *Farmers in Rebellion: The Rise and Fall of the Southern Farmers Alliance and People's Party in Texas* (Austin, Tex., 1984), 50–135.

31. C. Vann Woodward, *Origins of the New South, 1877–1913* (Baton Rouge, La., 1951), 238–39; Barr, *Reconstruction to Reform*, 117–31.

32. *Reminiscences*, 12; Richardson, *Colonel House*, 42.

33. Gould, *Progressives and Prohibitionists*, 6–7; Richardson, *Colonel House*, 44–50, 71–72.

34. Cotner, *Hogg*, 295–302; Evan Anders, *Boss Rule in South Texas: The Progressive Era* (Austin, Tex., 1982), 3–25.

35. Barnes, *Farmers in Rebellion,* 136–45; "People's Party," in Ron Tyler, ed., *The New Handbook of Texas* (Austin, Tex., 1996), V, 145–47; Culberson to W. F. Ramsey, Sept. 28, 1892, Culberson Papers.

36. Richardson, *Colonel House*, 61–63, 223; in Greek mythology, Pythias was nearly executed while serving as a voluntary hostage for his condemned friend Damon; Governor Hogg sent with the commission a fancy dress uniform which House gave to his black coachman, Allen Carthen. According to Arthur Howden Smith, "House detested the honorary title of Colonel, which he never earned and never sought . . . . He regarded it—and endured it good–humoredly—as a political nickname. Those of his friends who used it did so in that sense. All who knew him familiarly addressed him formally, as did the members of his family, as plain 'Mr. House.'" Whatever form of address House preferred, it is unlikely he found the title of Colonel as offensive as he later told Smith. Three successive governors repeated the honor, and he did nothing to discourage friends from using it. Howden Smith, *Mr. House of Texas,* 1, 27; interview with Allen Carthen, Oct. 19, 1937, part of W. P. A. Slave Narratives in the Austin History Collection, Austin Public Library; interview with Elizabeth Baker Blaine, April 20, 1977.

37. Richardson, *Colonel House*, 43–44; interview with Ima Hogg, Oct. 13, 1967.

38. *Reminiscences*, 11, 13, 18; A critique of Hogg's progressivism is in Gould, *Progressives and Prohibitionists*, 8–11.

39. Spratt, *Road to Spindletop*, 135–46; Barr, *Reconstruction to Reform*, 147–56; Gould, *Progressives and Prohibitionists*, 13; "Charles Allen Culberson," in Ron Tyler, ed., *The New Handbook of Texas* (Austin, Tex., 1996), II, 435–36.

40. *Reminiscences*, 13, 18; Cotner, *Hogg*, 399–405; Ben H. Procter, *Not without Honor: The Life of John H. Reagan* (Austin, Tex., 1962), 293–96.

41. *Reminiscences*, 16; Richardson, *Colonel House*, 70–76; House to A. R. Starr, May 14, 1894, Culberson Papers.

42. "Frank Andrews" and "Thomas Watt Gregory," in Ron Tyler, ed., *The New Handbook of Texas* (Austin, Tex., 1996), I, III, 173–74, 331.

43. Richardson, *Colonel House*, 77–79; Culberson to House, May 24, 1894, House Papers; House to J. L. Willson, July 3, 1894, Culberson Papers; Andrews to Culberson, July 5, 1894, Culberson Papers; circular letter by House, July 2, 1894, House Scrapbooks, House Papers.

44. Richardson, *Colonel House*, 85–91; *Reminiscences*, 15; Cotner, Hogg, 413–18.

45. Barr, *Reconstruction to Reform*, 157–60; Culberson to Hogg, Oct. 22, 1894, Culberson Papers; Goodwyn, *Democratic Promise*, 331–32; Randolph B. Campbell, *Gone to Texas: A History of the Lone Star State* (New York, 2003), 333–34; Barnes, *Farmers in Rebellion*.

46. *Dallas Morning News*, Aug. 17, 1894, in House Scrapbooks, House Papers; Culberson to House, Aug. 17, 1894, House Papers; Morton Keller, *Affairs of State: Public Life in Late Nineteenth Century America* (Cambridge, Mass., 1977), 540.

CHAPTER 3

1. Rupert Norval Richardson, *Colonel Edward M. House: The Texas Years, 1858–1912* (Abilene, Tex., 1964), 93–97; *Reminiscences*, 17; *Memories*, 31, 44, 47.

2. Culberson to House, Feb. 1, 1895, July 26, 1897, House Papers.

3. Culberson to House, Sept. 13, 1896, Feb. 4, no year, House Papers; "Charles Allen Culberson," in John A. Garraty and Mark C. Carns, eds., *American National Biography* (New York, 1999), V, 833–34; "Charles Allen Culberson," in Ron Tyler, ed., *The New Handbook of Texas* (Austin, Tex., 1996), II, 434–35; A critique of Culberson and his career is in Lewis L. Gould, *Progressives and Prohibitionists: Texas Democrats in the Wilson Era* (Austin, Tex., 1973), 13–14.

4. *Reminiscences*, 17; *Memories*, 44; House to Andrews, Aug. 5, 1989, House Papers; "Frank Andrews" and "Thomas Watt Gregory," in Ron Tyler, ed., *The New Handbook of Texas* (Austin, Tex., 1996), I, 173–74, III, 331; "Thomas Watt Gregory," in Garraty and Carns, eds., *American National Biography*, IX, 568–70.

5. Evan Anders, *Boss Rule in South Texas: The Progressive Era* (Austin, Tex., 1982), 3–25, 70–72; "James B. Wells" and "Albert Sidney Burleson," in Ron Tyler, ed., *The New Handbook of Texas* (Austin, Tex., 1996), I, 836, VI, 876–77; "Albert Sidney Burleson," in Garraty and Carns, eds., *American National Biography*, III, 962–64; Richardson, *Colonel House*, 306–7; Wells to House, April 10, 1923, House Papers.

6. Wells to House, July 18, 1898, Jameson to House, Aug. 16, 1898, Andrews to House, Oct. 1, 1898, House Papers.

7. Burleson to House, July 17, 1900, House Papers; interview with Judge James W. McClendon, Sept. 7, 1966; Richardson, *Colonel House*, 226–29.

8. For various assessments of House's political career in Texas, see Richardson, *Colonel House*, 304–12; Gould, *Progressives and Prohibitionists*, 11–12, 15–16; Alwyn Barr, *Reconstruction to Reform: Texas Politics, 1876–1906* (Austin, Tex., 1971), xii–xiii, 220–21, 228. *Reminiscences*, 16; House to Jameson, summer of 1898, House Papers.

9. House to Burleson, June 12, 1900, Burleson Papers; House to Jameson, summer of 1898, House Papers.

10. Richardson, *Colonel House,* 93–94; House to Jameson, summer 1989, House Papers; George F. Burgess to House, July 23, Aug. 8, 1989, House to Burgess, late July, 1898, House Papers.

11. Barr, *Reconstruction to Reform,* 162–63; Hogg to W. A. Shaw, March 25, 1896, Hogg Papers.

12. Barr, *Reconstruction to Reform,* 163–68; Charles Postel, *The Populist Vision* (New York, 2007), 269–75; Donna Barnes, *Farmers in Rebellion: The Rise and Fall of the Southern Farmers Alliance and People's Party in Texas* (Austin, Tex., 1985), 161–88.

13. Arthur C. Wakeley to House, July 20, 1896, House Papers; Richardson, *Colonel House,* 110–11.

14. Allison Mayfield to House, Sept. 18, 1896, House Papers; Culberson to House, Sept. 18, 1896, House Papers; Randolph B. Campbell, *Gone to Texas: A History of the Lone Star State* (New York, 2003), 335–36.

15. C. A. Rogers to House, Oct. 19, 1896, House Papers; Culberson to House, Oct. 12, 1896, House Papers; Blake to House, Oct. 8, 1896, House Papers; Richardson, *Colonel House,* 113–15; Barr, *Reconstruction to Reform,* 169–70.

16. *Reminiscences,* 22; Jameson to House, Oct. 31, 1896, House Papers; W. M. Giles to House, Oct. 23, 1896, House Papers; A. W. McIver to House, Oct. 27, 31, House Papers; Wells to House, Oct. 30, 1896, House Papers.

17. Barr, *Reconstruction to Reform,* 174; Lawrence Goodwyn, *Democratic Promise: The Populist Movement in America* (New York, 1976), 533; Amory Starr to House, Nov. 11, 1896, House Papers.

18. House to Robert W. Washburn, June 4, 1931, House Papers; Joseph E. Garland, *Boston's North Shore: Being an Account of Life among the Noteworthy, Fashionable, Wealthy, Eccentric and Ordinary, 1823–1890* (Boston, Mass., 1978), xi–xiv.

19. Newspaper clippings in the Edith R. House Scrapbook, in the possession of Mrs. George Shelley; Loulie House to Mrs. John Orr, undated, Orr Family Papers.

20. Interviews with Edward H. Auchincloss, Dec. 29, 1966, Mrs. Allston Boyer, April 25, 1969, Mrs. Milton Gutsch, June 22, 1970, Judge James W. McClendon, Sept. 7, 1966, Frances Denton Miller, Oct. 8–9, 1977, and Jane Prendergast, Jan. 4, 1979; Hogg to House, May 27, 1899, Hogg Papers.

21. Barr, *Reconstruction to Reform,* 172, 208–10, 221; Gould, *Progressives and Prohibitionists,* 16–23; Anders, *Boss Rule in South Texas,* 69–70; Barnes, *Farmers in Rebellion,* 189–98; "Joseph Weldon Bailey," in Garraty and Carns, eds., *American National Biography* (New York, 1999), I, 888–90.

22. Culberson to House, Sept. 26, 1897, House Papers; *Reminiscences,* 17; Richardson, *Colonel House,* 124–27.

23. Sayers to House, June 7, 19, 1897, House Papers; *Reminiscences,* 19, 25; Colonel Richardson, *House,* 128–31; "Martin M. Crane" and "Joseph D. Sayers," in Ron Tyler, ed., *The New Handbook of Texas* (Austin, Tex., 1996), II, 389, V, 906–07.

24. Barr, *Reconstruction to Reform*, 211–14; *Reminiscences*, 19–20; Hogg to House, May 16, 1898, House Papers.

25. Sayers to House, Nov. 10, 1896, House Papers; Richardson, *Colonel House*, 131–35; *Reminiscences*, 21.

26. Sayers to House, Jan. 25, April 21, 1898, House Papers; Jameson to House, June 28, 1898, House Papers.

27. Richardson, *Colonel House*, 137–40; Sayers's Central Campaign Club Circular, June 13, 1898, House Scrapbooks, House Papers; newspaper clipping, Dec. 23, 1897, House Scrapbooks, House Papers.

28. *Galveston News*, May 12, 1898, House Papers.

29. *Reminiscences*, 21; Sayers to House, May 17, 1898, House Papers.

30. L. L. Foster to House, May 28, 1898, House Papers; Sayers's Central Campaign Club Circular, June 20, 1898, House Papers; Sayers to House, June 15, 1898, House Papers.

31. Robert Cotner, *James Stephen Hogg: A Biography* (Austin, Tex., 1959), 478; House to Sayers, July 1898, House Papers; Hogg to House, July 6, 1898, House Papers; Richardson, *Colonel House*, 152.

32. Burleson to House, Aug. 11, 1898, House Papers.

33. *Reminiscences*, 22; Culberson to House, Sept. 15, 1898, House Papers.

34. Newspaper clippings, Nov. 11, 1898, House Scrapbooks, House Papers; *Reminiscences,* 23.

35. House to Andrews, Aug. 29, 1899, Aug. 2, 1901, in James A. Tinsley, ed., *Letters from the Colonel: Edward M. House to Frank Andrews* (Houston, Tex., Dec. 1960), 6–7, 10; House to David Harrell, Harrell Papers.

36. House to Sayers, Aug. 21, 1898, House Papers; Andrews to House, Oct. 17, 1898, House Papers; Richardson, *Colonel House*, 154–55; Jameson to Sayers, July 7, 1898, House Papers.

37. Sayers to House, Dec. 13, 1898, House Papers; *Reminiscences*, 23–24; Richardson, *Colonel House*, 157–58.

38. Richardson, *Colonel House*, 159–64, 170–71; House to Sayers, Dec. 9, 1898, House Papers; Sayers to House, Sept. 1, 1899, House Papers; *Reminiscences*, 24–25; House to R. W. Hudson, March 19, 1900, Hudson Papers; Campbell, *Gone to Texas*, 337; Burleson to House, July 27, 1900, House Papers; House to Burleson, Aug. 29, 1900, House Papers.

39. Newspaper clipping, Nov. 18, 1894, House Scrapbooks, House Papers; Andrews to House, Feb. 12, 1895, P. A. Fitzhugh to House, Dec. 25, 1896, Wells to House, July 8, 1898, House Papers; Sayers to House, Aug. 16, 1898, House Papers; House to Sayers, Aug. 21, 1898, House Papers.

40. Burleson to House, July 17, 1900, House Papers; House to Burleson, July 22, 1900, Burleson Papers.

41. Burleson to House, July 27, 1900, House Papers; House to Burleson, Aug. 29, 1900, Burleson Papers; *Memories*, 48.

CHAPTER 4

1. *Reminiscences*, 27, 31.

2. Robert C. Cotner, *James Stephen Hogg: A Biography* (Austin, Tex., 1959), 474–75, 477, 483–84; Rupert Norval Richardson, *Colonel Edward M. House: The Texas Years, 1858–1912* (Abilene, Tex., 1964), 231–33; Louis W. Koenig, *Bryan: A Political Biography* (New York, 1971), 165–67, 202, 222.

3. *Reminiscences*, 28–29; Arthur D. Howden Smith, *Mr. House of Texas*, (N. Y., 1940), Culberson to House, Feb. 2, June 23, Dec. 21, 1900, Hogg to House, Jan. 25, Feb. 10, 1900, House Papers; Hogg to House, July 11, 1900, to James K. Jones, Aug. 28, 1900, Hogg Papers; Michael Kazin, *A Godly Hero: The Life of William Jennings Bryan* (New York, 2006), 80–108.

4. J. Morgan Kousser, *The Shaping of Southern Politics: Suffrage Restrictions and the Establishment of the One-Party South, 1880–1910* (New Haven, Conn., 1974), 204–5.

5. The phrase "our crowd" was used in a letter from House to David Harrell, Aug. 7, 1899, and often thereafter; House to Burleson, Aug. 29, 1900, Burleson Papers; House to Andrews, June 11, 18, Aug. 2, 18, Sept. 4, 8, 1901, in James A. Tinsley, ed., *Letters from the Colonel: Edward M. House to Frank Andrews* (Houston, Tex., 1960), 7–14; "Samuel Willis Tucker Lanham," in Ron Tyler, ed., *The New Handbook of Texas* (Austin, Tex., 1996), IV, 69–70; Evan Anders, *Boss Rule in South Texas: The Progressive Era* (Austin, Tex., 1982), 73–77.

6. House to Andrews, Oct. 13, 1901, in Tinsley, *Letters from the Colonel*, 17.

7. Richardson, *Colonel House*, 181–83; House to Andrews, Jan. 16, 26, 1902, in Tinsley, *Letters from the Colonel*, 17–20; House to Burleson, Feb.7, April 19, 1902, Burleson Papers; Burleson to House, Feb. 1, 10, 1902, House Papers.

8. House to Burleson, Jan. 26, April 12, 1902, Burleson Papers; Burleson to House, Feb. 1, 1902, House Papers; House to Lanham, June 9, 1902, Burleson Papers; *Reminiscences*. 26.

9. Burleson to House, May 21, 1902, House Papers; House to Burleson, May 15, June 16, 21, 1902, Burleson Papers; Anders, *Boss Rule in South* Texas, 79–80; Richardson, *Colonel House*, 185–86, 191–92; Alwyn Barr, *Reconstruction to Reform: Texas Politics, 1876–1906* (Austin, Tex., 1971), 220–22.

10. On the lure of New York, see Lewis Mumford, "The Metropolitan Milieu," in Waldo Frank, et al., eds., *America and Alfred Stieglitz: A Collective Portrait* (Garden City, N.Y., 1934), 38–45; *Reminiscences*, 27.

11. House to Andrews, Aug. 2, 1901, in Tinsley, *Letters from the Colonel*, 10.

12. Henry Cushing Grover, "The Dissolution of T. W. House and Company" (M. A. Thesis, University of Houston, 1962), 13–14; Richardson, *Colonel House*, 210–17.

13. Richardson, *Colonel House*, 199–200, 209–10; House to James H. Hyde, Oct. 30, 1902, Hyde Papers.

14. James A. Clark and Michel T. Halbouty, *Spindletop* (New York, 1952), 55–88; House to Andrews, Feb. 10, 1902, in Tinsley, *Letters from the Colonel,* 20; "Spindletop Oil Field," in Ron Tyler, ed., *The New Handbook of Texas* (Austin, Tex., 1996), VI, 29–30.

15. Coolidge to House, Feb. 14, April 30, 1902, Coolidge Papers; House to Andrews, Feb. 10, 1902, in Tinsley, *Letters from the Colonel,* 20.

16. J. L. Allhands, *Boll Weevil: Recollections of the Trinity & Brazos Valley Railway* (Houston, Tex., 1946), 1–9; S. G. Reed, *A History of the Texas Railroads* (Houston, Tex., 1941), 402–3; "Robert H. Baker," and "Trinity and Brazos Valley Railway," in Ron Tyler, ed., *The New Handbook of Texas* (Austin, Tex., 1996), I, 351, VI, 565.

17. House to Coolidge, June 14, 1904, Coolidge to House, Nov. 5, 1904, House Papers.

18. Richardson, *Colonel House,* 192–93; Lanham to House, Dec. 4, 1902, Burleson to House, Dec. 22, 1902, House Papers; *Reminiscences,* 26.

19. House to Lanham, May 20, 1904, to Burleson, June 4, 1904, House Papers; Lanham to House, May 12, 1904, House Papers.

20. Richardson, *Colonel House,* 197; House to Culberson, May 14, 1904, to Sam de Cordova, May 14, 1904, House Papers.

21. Culberson to House, Feb. 2, 1900, May 4, Feb. 4, 1901, Feb. 3, 11, 1904, House Papers.

22. House to Culberson, June 7, 9, 1904, House Papers; Culberson to House, Feb. 3, May 29, 1904, House Papers.

23. Culberson to House, Oct. 31, no year, May 23, 1900, Jan. 20, 1904, March 6, 1905, House Papers.

24. John J. Broesamle, "The Democrats from Bryan to Wilson," in Lewis L. Gould, ed., *The Progressive Era* (Syracuse, N.Y., 1974), 84–85; Lewis L. Gould, *Grand Old Party: A History of the Republicans* (New York, 2003), 146–52; David Nasaw, *The Chief: The Life of William Randolph Hearst* (New York, 2000), 177–85; House to Culberson, June 9, 1904, House Papers.

25. *Reminiscences,* 29–30; House to August Belmont, late May, 1904, to Culberson, June 1, 1904, to Burleson, June 4, 1904, House Papers.

26. House to Paul B. Cruger, June 9, 1904, to Culberson, June 14, 1904, House Papers.

27. Richardson, *Colonel House,* 238; House to Hogg, Nov. 9, 1904, Hogg Papers.

28. House to Cruger, June 9, 1904, House Papers; Coolidge to House, April 14, 1904, Coolidge Papers.

29. Nancy Mezes to Fanny Denton, June 24, 1904, Janet House to Fanny Denton, Aug. 6, 1904, House Papers.

30. Hogg to House, Dec. 28, 1904, House Papers; House to Fanny Denton, Jan. 4, 18, 1905, House Papers.

31. *Boston Sunday Herald,* Aug. 31, 1902, House Scrapbooks; Joseph E. Garland, *Boston's Gold Coast: The North Shore, 1890–1929* (Boston, Mass., 1981), 43–51.

32. House to Miss Spence, Dec. 30, 1903, Janet House to Fanny Denton, March 5, 1904, House to Fanny Denton, Jan. 18, 1905, House Papers; interview with Ima Hogg, Oct. 13, 1967.

33. *Boston Herald,* Aug. 10, 1905, House Scrapbooks; newspaper clippings in House biography file, Austin Public Library, and in House Scrapbooks; interview with Mona and Randolph Tucker, Aug. 25, 1966.

34. Culberson to House, Jan. 14, 1906, House Papers; interview with Mona and Randolph Tucker, Aug. 25, 1966.

35. *Reminiscences,* 42; House to Hogg, Feb. 26, 1906, Hogg Papers.

36. House to Fanny Denton, Aug. 26, 1905, House Papers.

37. *Reminiscences,* 26–27; Barr, *Reconstruction to Reform,* 237–40; Anders, *Boss Rule in South Texas,* 81–88.

38. Newspaper clippings, House Scrapbooks; Culberson to House, Oct. 3, 1906, House Papers; "Progressive Era," in Tyler, ed., *The New Handbook of Texas,* V, 347–55.

39. Barr, *Reconstruction to Reform,* 225, 231–42; Lewis L. Gould, *Progressives and Prohibitionists: Texas Democrats in the Wilson Era* (Austin, Tex., 1973), 24–27; Randolph B. Campbell, *Gone to Texas: A History of the Lone Star State* (New York, 2003), 337–38, 341–42; Michael Perman, *Struggle for Mastery: Disfranchisement in the South, 1888–1908* (Chapel Hill, N.C., 2001), 270–81.

40. Grover, "The Dissolution of T. W. House and Company," 15, 114; Coolidge to House, May 5, Nov. 15, 1906, Coolidge Papers; House to Barkley, Aug. 10, 27, 1906, House-Barkley Correspondence, Austin Public Library.

41. Richardson, *Colonel House,* 214–15; House to Barkley, Feb. 3, 9, 1906, House-Barkley Correspondence.

42. Grover, "The Dissolution of T. W. House and Company," 26, 53–85.

43. *Memories,* 39; Grover, "The Dissolution of T. W. House and Company," 103–115.

44. Richardson, *Colonel House,* 219–22; Margaret C. Berry, *The University of Texas: A Pictorial Account of Its First Century* (Austin, Tex., 1980), 33–38; interview with Jane Prendergast, Jan. 4, 1979; *Reminiscences,* 44–46; "Sidney Edward Mezes," in Tyler, ed., *The New Handbook of Texas,* IV, 701–02.

45. House to Harrell, July 25, Nov. 3, 1907, April 22, 1908, July 4, Sept. 8, no year, Harrell Papers; interview with Mona and Randolph Tucker and Janet Auchincloss, Sept. 5, 1967; John Malcolm Brinnin, *The Sway of the Grand Saloon: A Social History of the North Atlantic* (New York, 1971), 336–44; Christopher Endy, "Travel and World Power: Americans in Europe, 1890–1917," *Diplomatic History,* 22 (Fall 1998), 565–94.

46. *Reminiscences,* 30; Lewis L. Gould, *Reform and Regulation: American Politics from Roosevelt to Wilson* (Prospect Heights, Ill., 1996), 100–109); Kazin, *A Godly Hero,* 145–68; Gould, *Grand Old Party,* 167–70.

47. *Reminiscences,* 44; House to Harrell, April 22, Oct. 12, 29, 1908, Harrell Papers; House to Allison Mayfield, Oct. 29, 1908, M. R. Gutsch Papers;

David Sarasohn, *The Party of Reform: Democrats in the Progressive Era* (Jackson, Miss., 1989), 35–58.

48. R. Laurence Moore, *In Search of White Crows: Spiritualism, Parapsychology, and American Culture* (New York, 1977), 46–68, 230–32.

49. "Sir Oliver Joseph Lodge," in H. C. C. Matthew and Brian Harrison, eds., *Oxford Dictionary of National Biography* (Oxford, Eng., 2004), XXXIV, 79–82; Deborah Blum, *Ghost Hunters: William James and the Search for Scientific Proof of Life after Death* (New York, 2006), 161–67; Sir Oliver Lodge, "Psychical Research," *Harper's Monthly Magazine*, 117 (Aug. 1908), 373–82; House to Fanny Denton, Aug. 17, 1908, House Papers.

CHAPTER 5

1. House used the phrase "the man and the opportunity" in a letter to Mezes Nov. 25, 1911, House Papers; House to Harrell, July 4, Aug. 1, Sept. 8, 1909, Harrell Papers.

2. House to Harrell, Sept. 19, Nov. 5, 1909, Sept. 7, 1910, Harrell Papers; House to Barkley, Feb. 3, 1908, House–Barkley Correspondence.

3. House to Barkley, Nov. 12, Dec. 17, 1908, Feb. 11, Nov. 18, 1909, March 6, 1911, House–Barkley Correspondence.

4. House to Harrell, April 20, 1909, Harrell Papers.

5. Lewis L. Gould, *Progressives and Prohibitionists: Texas Democrats in the Wilson Era* (Austin, Tex., 1973), 39–45; Campbell to House, June 21, 1909, Culberson to House, June 27, 1909, House Papers; Randolph B. Campbell, *Gone to Texas: A History of the Lone Star State* (New York, 2003), 343–46.

6. Gould, *Progressives and Prohibitionists*, 174–75; Culberson to House, Jan. 25, Feb. 8, 21, July 31, 1910, House Papers; "Charles Allen Culberson," in Ron Tyler, ed., *The New Handbook of Texas* (Austin, Tex., 1996), II, 435–36.

7. Robert E. Cowart to Thomas B. Henderson, Nov. 30, 1910, Henderson Papers.

8. House to Harrell, Oct. 15, 1909, Harrell Papers; Thomas Lately, *The Mayor Who Mastered New York: The Life and Opinions of William J. Gaynor* (New York, 1969), 157–63, 277–79, 288–338; *Reminiscences,* 46–48; Arthur D. Howden Smith, *Mr. House of Texas* (New York, 1940), 33–35; Gaynor to House, Jan. 30, 1911, Creelman to House, Feb. 14, 1911, House Papers.

9. Arthur S. Link, *Wilson: The Road to the White House* (Princeton, N.J., 1947), 309–30; John Milton Cooper Jr., *Woodrow Wilson: A Biography* (New York, 2009), 140–48.

10. *Reminiscences*, 48; Harvey to Wilson, March 1, 1911, in Arthur S. Link, ed., *The Papers of Woodrow Wilson* [subsequent references are to *PWW*] 68 vols. (Princeton, N.J., 1966-93), XXII, 466; Martin to House, March 27, 1911, House Papers.

11. Gould, *Progressives and Prohibitionists*, 58–64; "Thomas Bell Love," in Ron Tyler, ed., *The New Handbook of Texas* (Austin, Tex., 1996), IV, 306.

12. *Reminiscences*, 49; Gregory to Wilson, Sept. 4, 1911, House Papers; House to Gregory, Aug. 28, 1911, to Wilson, Aug. 29, 1911, to Martin, Aug. 30, 1911, House Papers.

13. Gould, *Progressives and Prohibitionists*, 66–68.

14. Interview with Mona and Randolph Tucker, Aug. 25, 1966; House to Mezes, Sept. 13, 1911, House Papers.

15. William G. McAdoo, *Crowded Years: The Reminiscences of William G. McAdoo* (Boston, Mass., 1931), 127; William F. McCombs, *Making Woodrow Wilson President* (New York, 1931), 75–76; McCombs to House, Oct. 19, 1911, Culberson to House, Oct. 13, 1911, House Papers; House to Culberson, Oct. 10, 20, 1911, Nov. 2, 1911, to Gregory, Oct. 22, 30, 1911, to Bryan, Oct. 25, 1911, House Papers.

16. House to Gregory, Oct. 30, Nov. 10, 1911, House Papers; Gregory to House, Nov. 4, 1911, House Papers.

17. House to Gregory, Oct. 22, 1911, to Houston, Oct. 27, 1911, House Papers.

18. House to McCombs, Nov. 14, 18, 1911, House Papers; Paolo E. Coletta, *William Jennings Bryan: Progressive Politician and Moral Statesman, 1909–1915* (Lincoln, Neb., 1969), 25–38; Michael Kazin, *A Godly Hero: The Life of William Jennings Bryan* (New York, 2006), 180–83.

19. House to Gregory, Nov. 19, 1911, to Houston, Nov. 15, 1911, House Papers.

20. Howden Smith, *Mr. House of Texas*, 41–42; House to Mezes, Nov. 25, 1911, to Culberson, Nov. 27, 1911, to George W. Watt, May 14, 1932, House Papers.

21. Howden Smith, *Mr. House of Texas*, 42–43.

22. *Reminiscences*, 51; Edwin A. Weinstein, *Woodrow Wilson: A Medical and Psychological Biography* (Princeton, N.J., 1981), 264–71.

23. House to Houston, Nov. 27, 1911, House Papers; Houston to Mezes, Dec. 11, 1911, House Papers; *Reminiscences*, 51–52.

24. House to Wilson, Dec. 15, 1911, to Brown, Dec. 2, 7, 14, 1911, House Papers; Wilson to House, Dec. 22, 26, 1911, House Papers; Link, *Wilson: The Road to the White House*, 342–43.

25. *Reminiscences*, 52–53; House to Bryan, Dec. 6, 1911, House Papers; Bryan to House, Dec. 17, 1911, House Papers.

26. House to Gregory, Nov. 26, 1911, to Barkley, Nov. 29, 1911, House Papers.

27. House to Burleson, Nov. 26, 1911, House Papers; Link, *Wilson: The Road to the White House*, 337–38; Cooper, *Wilson*, 145.

28. House to Barkley, Nov. 29, 1911, House Papers; McCombs to House, Dec. 22, 1911, House Papers; *Reminiscences*, 53.

29. *Reminiscences*, 52; House to Culberson, Jan. 7, 1912, to Wilson, Feb. 2, 1912, House Papers.

30. House to Wilson, Dec. 26, 1911, Feb. 2, 1912, House Papers; Wilson to House, Jan. 2, 27, 1912, House Papers.

31. Link, *Wilson: The Road to the White House*, 347–402; Evans C. Johnson, *Oscar W. Underwood: A Political Biography* (Baton Rouge, La., 1980), 170–180; David

Nasaw, *The Chief: The Life of William Randolph Hearst* (New York, 2000), 227–28; Cooper, *Wilson*, 146–51.

32. House to Martin, Jan. 18, 1912, to McCombs, Jan. 20, Feb. 10, 1912, to Culberson, Feb. 15, March 19, 1912, House Papers; Culberson to House, March 6, 1912, House Papers.

33. Gould, *Progressives and Prohibitionists*, 71–75; *Reminiscences*, 49–50.

34. House to McCombs, March 4, 1912, to Thomas H. Ball, March 4, 1912, to Sells, March 6, 18, 1912, to Burleson, March 6, 1912, to Culberson, March 19, 1912, House Papers; Gregory to Sells, March 18, 1912, Sells to House, March 25, 1912, House Papers.

35. House to Gregory, April 6, 10, 1912, to Culberson, April 16, 1912, House Papers; Link, *Wilson: The Road to the White House*, 403–19; Cooper, *Wilson*, 151–53.

36. House to Gregory, April 23, 1912, to Culberson, April 19, 23, 1912, House Papers.

37. *Reminiscences*, 54–55; House to Mezes, April 15, 1912, to Barkley, April 17, 1912, to Culberson, April 28, 1912, House Papers.

38. Gregory to House, April 19, 1912, House Papers; House to Culberson, April 23, 28, 1912, House Papers.

39. House to Burleson, May 6, 1912, Burleson Papers; Burleson to House, May 8, 1912, House Papers; House to Gregory, May 7, 13, 1912, to Love, May 7, 1912, to Thaddeus A. Thomson, May 9, 29, 1912, to Wilson, May 10, 1912, House Papers; Gregory to House, May 30, 1912, House Papers; House also sought to pledge Wilson to a one-term presidency so that Bryan could be assured the succession. "I am urging him now," he informed Gregory, "to declare that he will not accept more than one term provided he is elected. I think it will have a good effect not only upon the country at large but upon Bryan and some of the other candidates that would hesitate to support a man upon whom they would have to wait eight years to fill his place." House to Gregory, May 13, 1912, House Papers.

40. Link, *Wilson: The Road to the White House*, 420–30; Cooper, *Wilson*, 152–54; House to Thomson, May 9, 20, 1912, House Papers.

41. House to Wilson, May 29, June 7, 1912, House Papers.

42. House to McCombs, June 12, 1912, to Wilson, June 23, 1912, House Papers; *Reminiscences*, 56.

43. House to Wilson, June 20, 1912, House Papers; Wilson to House, June 24, 1912, House Papers.

44. Culberson to House, June 18, 20, 1912, House Papers.

45. House to Bryan, June 22, 1912, House Papers.

46. House to Mezes, April 26, 1912, House Papers.

47. John Milton Cooper Jr., *The Warrior and the Priest: Woodrow Wilson and Theodore Roosevelt* (Cambridge, Mass., 1983), 157–63; Lewis L. Gould, *Four Hats in the Ring: The 1912 Election and the Birth of Modern American Politics* (Lawrence, Kans., 2008), 45–75.

48. David Sarasohn, *The Party of Reform: Democrats in the Progressive Era* (Jackson, Miss., 1989), 119–43; Cooper, *Wilson*, 155–58; Gould, *Four Hats in the Ring*, 76–102.

49. *Reminiscences*, 56–57; House to Wilson, June 20, 1912, House Papers.

50. Wilson to House, July 17, 1912, House Papers; House to Wilson, July 31, 1912, *PWW*, XXIV, 576–77.

51. House to McCombs, Aug. 18, 1912, to Wilson, Aug. 21, 1912, House Papers.

52. Auchincloss Diary, Dec. 1, 5, 13, 1914; House to Culberson, Nov. 28, 1911, House Papers; *New York Times*, Sept. 15, 1912; Fanny Denton's niece remembered Auchincloss as a "pompous bore. He was kind of an intrusion in a quiet family. He was a big man with a red face who always spoke very loudly." Interview with Frances Denton Miller, Oct. 8–9, 1977.

53. Link, *Wilson: The Road to the White House*, 472–75; Cooper, *Wilson*, 159–62.

54. Link, *Wilson: The Road to the White House*, 480–87.

55. Sarasohn, *The Party of Reform*, 143–54; Cooper, *Wilson*, 159–67; Melvin I. Urofsky, *Louis D. Brandeis: A Life* (New York, 2009), 340–47.

56. Cooper, *Wilson*, 167–74; Gould, *Four Hats in the Ring*, 151–74.

57. *Reminiscences*, 58–59; House to McCombs, Aug. 20, 27, 1912, House to Culberson, Aug. 24, 1912, to Houston, Sept. 13, 1912, House Papers.

58. Howden Smith, *Mr. House of Texas*, 53–55; Link, *Wilson: The Road to the White House*, 480–86; House Diary, Sept. 26, Oct. 8, 13, 16, 17, 21, 22, 24, 28, 1912. House began his diary on Sept. 25, 1912.

59. Burleson to House, Aug. 21, 1912, Wilson to House, Aug. 22, 1912, House Papers; House to Andrews, Sept. 27, 1912, House Papers; House Diary, Oct. 12, 20, 24, 30, 1912.

60. Robert F. Wesser, *A Response to Progressivism: The Democratic Party and New York Politics, 1902–1918* (New York, 1986), 88–98; Cooper, *The Warrior and the Priest*, 203; Cooper, *Wilson*, 169–70; House Diary, Sept. 25, 28, Oct. 12, 15, 16, 20, 26, Nov. 1, 2, 1912; House to Mezes, Oct. 21, 1912, House Papers.

61. House Diary, Nov. 5, 1912; Cooper, *Wilson*, 172–81; Gould, *Four Hats in the Ring*, 174–87.

62. House to Mezes, Nov. 4, 1912, to Culberson, Nov. 5, 1912, House Papers.

CHAPTER 6

1. House to Houston, Dec. 6, 1910, to Charles W. Eliott, April 6, 1911, House Papers; Arthur S. Link and Richard L. McCormick, *Progressivism* (Arlington Heights, Ill., 1983), 1–25; Walter Nugent, *Progressivism: A Very Short Introduction* (New York, 2010), 1–5, 35–90.

2. Daniel T. Rodgers, *Atlantic Crossings: Social Politics in a Progressive Era* (Cambridge, Mass., 1998), 52–60; House to Houston, Dec. 6, 1910, to Martin, June 14, 1911, House Papers; Robert Rhodes James, *The British Revolution, 1880–1939* (New York, 1977), 231–57; Hugh Purcell, *Lloyd George* (London, Eng., 2006), 20–34.

3. House to Martin, June 14, 1911, House Papers.

4. John A. Garraty, *Right-Hand Man: The Life of George W. Perkins* (New York, 1960), 247–51; House to Culberson, July 26, Aug. 3, 1911, House Papers.

5. House to Eliott, April 6, 1911, House Papers; Houston to House, Aug. 4, Oct. 24, 1911, House Papers.

6. *Reminiscences*, 53; Houston to Mezes, Dec. 11, 1911, House Papers.

7. House to Houston, Jan. 30, March 11, 12, 1912, House Papers; John Milton Cooper Jr. claims that *Philip Dru* was "largely ghostwritten." The House Papers, however, contain the original draft of the novel, in House's handwriting, on small sheets of yellow paper. By Feb. 28, 1912, this longhand draft was transformed into a typed draft, one that contains many corrections. Cooper, *Woodrow Wilson: A Biography* (New York, 2009), 193. *Reminiscences*, 54.

8. House to Mezes, April 3, 1912, House Papers; Houston to House, April 16, 1912, House Papers.

9. House to Mezes, April 5, 1912, House to Steger, May 1, June 25, 1912, House Papers; *Reminiscences*, 57.

10. Steger to House, July 19, Aug. 23, 1912, G. P. Putnam and Sons to House, summer 1912, House Papers.

11. Martin to House, Aug. 22, 1912, House Papers; House to Houston, Sept. 13, 1912, House Papers.

12. House Diary, Sept. 26, Oct. 27, 1912.

13. Joseph Blotner, *The Modern American Political Novel, 1900–1960* (Austin, Tex., 1966), 12–27, 56–62, 139–45, 165–73.

14. Neil Harris, "Utopian Fiction and Its Discontents," in Richard L. Bushman, Neil Harris, David Rothman, Barbara Miller Soloman, and Stephen Thernstrom, eds., *Uprooted Americans: Essays in Honor of Oscar Handlin* (Boston, Mass., 1979), 211–37; Billie Barnes Jenson, "Philip Dru: The Blueprint of a Presidential Adviser," *American Studies*, 12 (Spring, 1971), 49–58; David M. Esposito, "Imagined Power: The Secret Life of Colonel House," *The Historian*, 60 (Summer, 1998), 741–55.

15. *Philip Dru: Administrator, A Story of Tomorrow, 1920–1935* (New York, 1912), *passim*.

16. Ibid., 3–5, 8, 14, 106, 166.

17. House Diary, Oct. 9, 10, 11, 1912; House to Barkley, Nov. 21, 1912, House-Barkley Correspondence.

18. Advertisements and press releases in *Philip Dru Scrapbook*, House Papers.

19. *Philip Dru*, 30, 73–74, 83, 234.

20. *The North American*, Dec. 7, 1912, *San Francisco Chronicle*, Jan. 5, 1913, *Book News Monthly*, Feb. 1913, *New York Times*, Dec. 8, 1912, *Philip Dru Scrapbook*, House Papers; Christopher Lasch, *The New Radicalism in America: 1889–1963* (New York, 1965), 230–34.

21. Mezes to House, Nov. 8, 1912, House Papers; Gregory to House, Dec. 2, 1912, Roberts to House, Nov. 27, 1912, Mary Bryan to House, Dec. 1, 1912, *Philip Dru Scrapbook,* House Papers.

22. *Reminiscences*, 58; Roberts to House, Nov. 27, 1912, *Philip Dru Scrapbook*, House Papers; House Diary, Nov. 20, 1912.

23. House Diary, Nov. 16, 1912.

CHAPTER 7

1. Gregory to House, Aug. 26, Sept. 9, 1912, House Papers; House to Burleson, Sept. 27, 1912, House Papers; House Diary, Oct. 15, 16, 28, Nov. 2, 7, 1912.

2. Andrews to House, Sept. 20, 1912, House Papers; House to Andrews, Sept. 27, 1912, House Papers.

3. House Diary, Sept. 25, Oct. 20, 30, Nov. 2, 1912.

4. House to Burleson, Nov. 12, 1912, House Papers.

5. House Diary, Nov. 16, 1912; Arthur S. Link, *Wilson: The New Freedom* (Princeton, N.J., 1956), 7–8.

6. Link, *Wilson: The New Freedom*. 4; House Diary, Nov. 21, 1912.

7. House Diary, Nov. 25, 1912; House to Wilson, Nov. 25, 28, Dec. 6, 1912, Wilson to House, Nov. 30, 1912, House Papers.

8. Link, *Wilson: The New Freedom*, 8–9; House Diary, Dec. 18, 19, 22, 1912; Michael Kazin, *A Godly Hero: The Life of William Jennings Bryan* (New York, 2006), 216; The controversy over Brandeis's appointment, and House's role in it, is analyzed in Melvin I. Urofsky, *Louis D. Brandeis: A Life* (New York, 2009), 372–77.

9. House to Culberson, Nov. 5, 1912, to Mezes, Dec. 22, 1912, House Papers; T. W. House to House, Dec. 2, 1912, House Papers.

10. William Gibbs McAdoo, *Crowded Years* (Boston, Mass.,1931), 70–93; John J. Broesamle, *William Gibbs McAdoo: A Passion for Change, 1863–1917* (Port Washington, N.Y., 1973), 12–75; Jordan A. Schwarz, *The New Dealers: Power Politics in the Age of Roosevelt* (New York, 1993), 3–10; Douglas B. Craig, *Progressives at War: William G. McAdoo and Newton D. Baker, 1863–1941* (Baltimore, Md., 2013), 11–50.

11. House Diary, Oct. 9, 10, 11, 20, Nov. 2, 20, 1912; Broesamle, *McAdoo*, 34.

12. Broesamle, *McAdoo*, 76–77; House Diary, Nov. 2, 8, 11, Dec. 11, 18, 1912.

13. House Diary, Dec. 19, 21, 23, 1912.

14. John M. Blum, *Joe Tumulty and the Wilson Era* (Boston, Mass., 1951), 3–52; Phyllis Lee Levin, *Edith and Woodrow: The Wilson White House* (New York, 2001), 169–73.

15. House Diary, Oct. 20, Dec. 15, 18, 1912.

16. House Diary, Dec. 14, 15, 19, 21, 28, 29, 1912, Jan. 5, 8, 10, 11, 15, 19, 1913; Tumulty to House, Jan. 30, 1913, House Papers.

17. Lewis L. Gould, *Progressives and Prohibitionists: Texas Democrats in the Wilson Era* (Austin, Tex., 1973), 80–84, 98.

18. McAdoo, *Crowded Years*, 180; Gould, *Progressives and Prohibitionists*, 98–101; "Albert Sydney Burleson," in Ron Tyler, ed., *The New Handbook of Texas*

(Austin, Tex., 1996), I, 836; House to Burleson, Oct. 15, 1912, House Papers; Burleson to House, Nov. 9, 1912, Burleson Papers; Burleson to House, Jan. 14, 1913, House Papers; House Diary, Oct. 17, Nov. 25, Dec. 3, 24, 1912, Jan. 6, 12, 27, Feb. 12, 23, 24, 1913.

19. House Diary, Nov. 16, 1912, Jan. 6, 15, 1913; the animosity between House and Daniels continued throughout the Wilson administration. Daniels dismissed House as a "yes–yes man." Lee A. Craig, *Josephus Daniels: His Life and Times* (Chapel Hill, N.C., 2013), 221, 357.

20. House Diary, Jan. 8, 17, 24, 25, 26, Feb. 13, 14, 23, 24, 1913; House to Mezes, Jan. 13, 1913, to Gregory, Jan. 25, 1913, House Papers; Gould, *Progressives and Prohibitionists*, 99–101.

21. House Diary, Oct. 16, Nov. 16, 20, 21, Dec. 10, 11, 18, 21, 1912, Jan. 6, 7, 17, 20, 22, 23, 24, 25, 26, Feb. 11, 13, 14, 15, 16, 28, 1913; John Milton Cooper Jr., *Woodrow Wilson: A Biography* (New York, 2009), 182–85.

22. House Diary, Nov. 7, 1912, Jan. 7, 18, Feb. 22, 23, March 7, 25, April 13, 25, 1913; House to Mezes, Nov. 10, 1912, to Gregory, Feb. 3, 1913, House Papers; Gregory to House, Jan. 28, Feb. 21, March 27, 1913, House Papers.

23. House Diary, Dec. 6, 14, 18, 23, 31, 1912, Jan. 10, 15, 17, 19, Feb. 19, 21, 22, 24, 25, March 31, April 1, 4, 19, May 1, 1913.

24. House Diary, Jan. 8, 1913.

25. House Diary, Jan. 8, 1913; House to Wilson, Jan. 9, 1913, House Papers.

26. House Diary, Jan. 8, 15, 17, 18, 1913.

27. House Diary, Jan. 24, 25, 1913.

28. House to Wilson, Jan. 29, 30, 1913, House Papers; House Diary, Jan. 27–Feb. 11, 1913; Paolo E. Coletta, *William Jennings Bryan: Progressive Politician and Moral Statesman, 1909–1915* (Lincoln, Neb., 1969), 89–91; Kazin, *A Godly Hero*, 243–44.

29. House Diary, Jan. 29, 30, Feb. 1, 1913.

30. Wilson to House, Feb. 7, 1913, House Papers; House Diary, Feb. 13, 14, 18–22, 24, 28, March 1, 1913.

31. Cooper, *Wilson*, 89–92; Auchincloss Diary, Dec. 27, 1914; Alan Dawley, *Changing the World: American Progressives in War and Revolution* (Princeton, N.J., 2003), 24; House Diary, March 4, 8, 1913. The code was Bryan, Primus; Burleson, Demosthenes; Daniels, Neptune; Garrison, Mars; Houston, Mansion; Lane, Alley; McAdoo, Pythias; McReynolds, Coke; Redfield, Bluefields; Wilson, Vulcan.

32. Gould, *Progressives and Prohibitionists*, 102; Keith W. Olson, *Biography of a Progressive: Franklin K. Lane, 1864–1921* (Westport, Conn., 1979), 49; House to Mezes, Jan. 24, 1913, House Papers; House Diary, March 3–8, 16, 19, 20, 24, 25, 31, April 1, 10–18, May 1–2, 11–12, 1913.

33. House Diary, April 14, 16, 18, 1913.

34. Edmund W. Starling, *Starling of the White House* (New York, 1946), 37; Raymond Fosdick, *Chronicle of a Generation: An Autobiography* (New York, 1958), 44–47, 195–97.

35. Fosdick, *Chronicle of a Generation*, 45; Link, *Wilson: The New Freedom*, 61–70; John Milton Cooper Jr., *The Warrior and the Priest: Woodrow Wilson and Theodore Roosevelt* (Cambridge, Mass., 1983), 206–47.

36. Edwin A. Weinstein, *Woodrow Wilson: A Medical and Psychological Biography* (Princeton, N.J., 1981), 107–244; Bert Edward Park, *The Impact of Illness on World Leaders* (Philadelphia, Penn., 1986), 3–7, 331–42; Cooper, *Wilson*, 89, 95, 109.

37. Weinstein, *Wilson*, 79–81, 111–16, 243–44; Erik H. Erikson, *Young Man Luther: A Study in Psychoanalysis and History* (New York, 1958), 67.

38. Weinstein, *Wilson*, 75–81, 113–17; Frances Wright Saunders, *Ellen Axson Wilson: First Lady between Two Worlds* (Chapel Hill, N.C., 1985), xiii, 58, 79, 87–92, 124, 145, 162–64, 213, 221–32.

39. Saunders, *Ellen Axson Wilson*, 246, 248; Weinstein, *Wilson*, 248; House Diary, Jan. 8, March 20, 25, 1913; House's favorite meals were breakfast, oranges, eggs with bacon, toast, and coffee; lunch (his main meal), raw oysters, roast chicken, sweet potatoes, green peas, plain lettuce salad with egg dressing, deep peach pie with cream, black coffee; dinner, cereal, milk, and fruit. House to Mrs. A. C. Sharon, April 1, 1935, House Papers.

40. Cooper, *The Warrior and the Priest*, 241–43; Cooper, *Wilson*, 206–7; W. Barksdale Maynard, *Woodrow Wilson: Princeton to the Presidency* (New Haven, Conn., 2008), 164–65, 170–72.

41. Cooper, *The Warrior and the Priest*, 243–45; Weinstein, *Wilson*, 265–78; A more critical view of House's role is in Cooper, *Wilson*, 192–94.

42. House Diary, Jan. 17, 22, Feb. 13, 14, 26, 1913.

43. House Diary, Dec. 15, 1912, Jan. 1–5, March 20, April 15, 1913.

44. House to Wilson, April 23, 1913, House to Mezes, April 24, May 8, 1913, mid-May, 1913, to T. A. Thomson, May 13, 1913, House Papers; House Diary, May 7, 1913; Peter Clark MacFarlene, "The President's Silent Partner," *Collier's Magazine*, April 30, 1913; "Silent Power in Politics," *Boston Daily Globe,* March 30, 1913.

45. House Diary, May 11, 1913; Wilson to House, May 17, 20, 1913, House to Wilson, May 20, 193, House Papers.

CHAPTER 8

1. House Diary, Jan. 22, 1913, House Papers.

2. John Milton Cooper Jr., "'An Irony of Fate,' Woodrow Wilson's Pre–World War I Diplomacy," *Diplomatic History*, 3 (Fall 1979), 425; Cooper, *Woodrow Wilson: A Biography* (New York, 2009), 210–11; Kendrick A. Clements, *The Presidency of Woodrow Wilson* (Lawrence, Kans., 1992), xiii.

3. August Heckscher, *Woodrow Wilson* (New York, 1991), 293; Alan Dawley, *Changing the World: American Progressives in War and Revolution* (Princeton, N.J., 2003), 75–83; Christopher McKnight Nichols, *Promise and Peril: America at the Dawn of a Global Age* (Cambridge, Mass., 2011), 1–21.

4. Heckscher, *Wilson*, 294.

5. Robert H. Wiebe, *The Search for Order, 1877–1920* (New York, 1967), 254–55; Patrick Devlin, *Too Proud to Fight: Woodrow Wilson's Neutrality* (New York, 1975), 468–69. "'The President,' Devlin remarks, 'might almost have been running a parish with the help of his wife and a curate and a portable typewriter'"; Charles E. Neu, "Woodrow Wilson and His Foreign Policy Advisers," in William N. Tilchin and Charles E. Neu, eds., *Artists of Power: Theodore Roosevelt, Woodrow Wilson, and Their Enduring Impact on U.S. Foreign Policy* (Westport, Conn., 2006), 77–94.

6. Rachel West, O.S.F., *The Department of State on the Eve of the First World War* (Athens, Ga., 1978), 4–23, 56–76.

7. House Diary, Jan. 17, 1913, House Papers.

8. Arthur S. Link, *Wilson: The New Freedom* (Princeton, N.J.), 97–98; West, *The Department of State*, 52–54.

9. House Diary, Jan. 17, 1913; Link, *Wilson: The New Freedom*, 97–110; Heckscher, *Wilson*, 287–89.

10. House Diary, Nov. 16, 1912, Feb. 22, 1913; West, *The Department of State*, 93–97.

11. John Milton Cooper Jr., *Walter Hines Page: The Southerner as American, 1855–1918* (Chapel Hill, N.C., 1977), 235–50; Link, *Wilson: The New Freedom*, 99.

12. West, *The Department of State*, 51–55; House Diary, March 8, 1913.

13. Link, *Wilson: The New Freedom*, 7–9, 95–97; Michael Kazin, *A Godly Hero: The Life of William Jennings Bryan* (New York, 2006), 216–17; A vigorous defense of Bryan, and denunciation of House, is in Robert M. Cruden, *Ministers of Reform: The Progressive Achievement in American Civilization, 1889–1920* (New York, 1982), 225–30.

14. West, *The Department of State*, 27–31; House Diary, April 18, 1913, House Papers.

15. John Milton Cooper Jr., *The Warrior and the Priest: Woodrow Wilson and Theodore Roosevelt* (Boston, Mass., 1983), 266–68.

16. Link, *Wilson: The New Freedom*, 280–83.

17. Kazin, *A Godly Hero*, 219–22.

18. Warren I. Cohen, *America's Response to China: A History of Sino–American Relations* (New York, 1990), 69–72.

19. Heckscher, *Wilson*, 296.

20. Charles E. Neu, *The Troubled Encounter: The United States and Japan* (New York, 1975), 80–82.

21. House Diary, March 20, 27, May 2, 18, 1913.

22. Link, *Wilson: The New Freedom*, 304–7; House Diary, Jan. 24, 1913, House Papers.

23. John Mason Hart, *Revolutionary Mexico: The Coming and Process of the Mexican Revolution* (Berkeley, Calif., 1987), 1–12, 237–45, 261–62; Kenneth J. Grieb, *The United States and Huerta* (Lincoln, Neb., 1969), 51–56.

24. Hart, *Revolutionary Mexico,* 262–66; John Womack Jr., *Zapata and the Mexican Revolution* (New York, 1969), 159–77.

25. Link, *Wilson: The New Freedom,* 347–50; Cooper, *Wilson,* 237–39.

26. Link, *Wilson: The New Freedom,* 350–54; House to Wilson, May 6, 1913, in Arthur S. Link, ed., *The Papers of Woodrow Wilson* [*PWW*], 68 vols. (Princeton, N.J., 1966–93), XXVII, 404–5; Mark T. Gilderhus, *The Second Century: U.S. Latin American Relations since 1889* (Wilmington, Del., 2000), 40–42; over the years House invested in Mexican land, silver mines, and oil fields, but in 1914 he denied having any "large interests" in Mexico. House never visited Mexico; Hart, *Revolutionary Mexico,* 112–56; Hart, *Empire and Revolution: The Americans in Mexico since the Civil War* (Berkeley, Calif., 2002), 25, 92, 161, 306; House Diary, May 11, 1913, April 25, 1914, Jan. 14, 1918.

27. House Diary, Nov. 10, 19, 1912, Jan. 8, March 27, April 1, May 2, 3, 1913; William A. Tucker to House, April 17, 1913, E. N. Brown to House, April 23, 1913, House Papers; House Diary, March 27, April 1, May 2, 3, 1913.

28. House Diary, May 21–27, 1913.

29. House Diary, Feb. 23, May 11, 1913.

30. House Diary, May 21–27, June 12, 1913; House to Wilson, June 14, 1913, House Papers.

31. House Diary, June 19, 1913, House Papers; Cooper, *Page,* 256–58.

32. House Diary, June 19, 1913.

33. House Diary, June 20, 22, 23, 25, 26, 27, 29, 30, July 2, 3, 1913.

34. Burton J. Hendrick, *The Life and Letters of Walter Hines Page,* 3 vols. (New York, 1924–26), I, 245.

35. Joyce Grigsby Williams, *Colonel House and Sir Edward Grey: A Study in Anglo–American Diplomacy* (New York, 1984), 6–9; Bradford Perkins, *The Great Rapprochement: England and the United States, 1895–1914* (New York, 1968), 274–76; Robert K. Massie, *Dreadnought: Britain, Germany, and the Coming of the Great War* (New York, 1991), 580–93; Zara S. Steiner and Keith Neilson, *Britain and the Origins of the First World War* (New York, 2003), 38–43.

36. David Reynolds, *Britannia Overruled: British Policy and World Power in the Twentieth Century* (London, 2000), 62–80.

37. George M. Trevelyan, *Grey of Fallodon* (London, Eng., 1937), 102; Perkins, *The Great Rapprochement,* 289–91.

38. House Diary, July 3, 1913.

39. House Diary, July 8–16, 1913; House to Wilson, June 8, 14, July 15, 1913, House Papers; John Milton Cooper Jr., writes of House retreating to his "seaside estate." Over the years House rented a variety of cottages on the North Shore, some larger than others, but none were elaborate enough to be termed an "estate." Cooper, *Wilson,* 207.

40. When McAdoo visited House at Beverly, Mass., House "told him of my conversation with Sir Edward Grey, and I asked him to impart it to the President." House Diary, July 20, 1913.

CHAPTER 9

1. Alan Dawley, *Changing the World: American Progressives in War and Revolution* (Princeton, N.J., 2003), 41–68; Arthur S. Link and Richard L. McCormick, *Progressivism* (Arlington Heights, Ill., 1983), 1–47.

2. Arthur S. Link, ed., *The Papers of Woodrow Wilson* [*PWW*], 68 vols. (Princeton, N.J., 1966–93), XXVII, 149–50; Trygve Throntveit, " 'Common Counsel': Woodrow Wilson's Pragmatic Progressivism, 1885–1913," in John Milton Cooper Jr., ed., *Reconsidering Woodrow Wilson: Progressivism, Internationalism, War, and Peace* (Washington, D.C., 2008), 25–56.

3. Arthur S. Link, *Wilson: The New Freedom* (Princeton, N. J., 1956), 243–52; John Milton Cooper Jr., *Woodrow Wilson: A Biography* (New York, 2009), 170–71, 204–6; House Diary, Oct. 29, 1913; *Philip Dru: Administrator, A Story of Tomorrow, 1920–1935* (New York, 1912), 284; David W. Southern, *The Progressive Era and Race: Reaction and Reform, 1900–1917* (Wheeling, Ill., 2005), 122–30; Eric S. Yellin, *Racism in the Nation's Service: Government Workers and the Color Line in Woodrow Wilson's America* (Chapel Hill, N.C., 2013), 1–8, 81–172.

4. John Milton Cooper Jr., *The Warrior and the Priest: Woodrow Wilson and Theodore Roosevelt* (Cambridge, Mass., 1983), 229–32; Lewis L. Gould, *The Modern American Presidency* (Lawrence, Kans., 2003), 47–48; David Sarasohn, *The Party of Reform: Democrats in the Progressive Era* (Jackson, Miss., 1989), vii–xvii.

5. Sarasohn, *The Party of Reform*, 155–68; *PWW*, XXVIII, 311.

6. *PWW*, XXVII, 271; Link, *Wilson: The New Freedom*, 177–97; Cooper, *Wilson*, 213–19; Elizabeth Sanders, *Roots of Reform: Farmers, Workers, and the American State, 1877–1917* (Chicago, Ill., 1999), 226–30.

7. Morton Keller, *Regulating a New Economy: Public Policy and Economic Change in America, 1900–1933* (Cambridge, Mass., 1990), 200–03.

8. August Heckscher, *Woodrow Wilson* (New York, 1991), 317–18.

9. Link, *Wilson: The New Freedom*, 199–214; Michael Kazin, *A Godly Hero: The Life of William Jennings Bryan* (New York, 2006), 222–26; Melvin I. Urofsky, *Louis D. Brandeis: A Life* (New York, 2009), 379–84, *PWW*, XXVII, 570–73; Sanders, *Roots of Reform*, 232–59.

10. House Diary, April 1, 3, 18, 1913.

11. House Diary, Sept. 25, Nov. 22, 24, 25, Dec. 3, 1912; House to T. C. Dunn, Nov. 29, 1912, House Papers.

12. House to William Garrott Brown, Dec. 8, 1912, House Papers; House Diary, Dec. 19, 26, 1912, Jan. 6, 8, 14, 15, 22, 23, Feb. 20, 24, 26, 27, March 9, 1913.

13. House Diary, Feb. 26, March 20, 22–26, 28, 30, 31, April 5, 11, 14, 17, 21, May 3, 8, 11, 1913; House to Wilson, May 15, 1913, to McAdoo, May 20, 1913.

14. Link, *Wilson: The New Freedom*, 213–27.

15. House to Wilson, May 26, 1913, to McAdoo, June 28, July 24, 25, 29, 1913, House Papers; House Diary, June 20, July 23, 25, Aug. 18, 1913.

16. Link, *Wilson: The New Freedom*, 228–34.

17. House to E. S. Martin, Sept. 2, 1913, to Thomas C. Dunn, Sept. 23, 1913, House Papers; House Diary, Oct. 15, 16, 27, 1913, House Papers.

18. Link, *Wilson: The New Freedom*, 234–38; Cooper, *Wilson*, 219–26; House to Wilson, Dec. 20, 1913, *PWW*, XXIX, 49.

19. House to C. A. Culberson, Oct. 4, 1913, House Papers.

20. Heckscher, *Wilson*, 308–10; Wilson to Mary Allen Hulbert, June 29, 1913, *PWW*, XXVIII, 12–14.

21. Cooper, *Wilson*, 208; Rear Admiral Cary T. Grayson, *Woodrow Wilson: An Intimate Memoir* (New York, 1960), ix–xi.

22. Edwin A. Weinstein, *Woodrow Wilson: A Medical and Psychological Biography* (Princeton, N.J., 1981), 249–52.

23. Heckscher, *Wilson*, 275–84; Cooper, *Wilson*, 200–201; Link, *The New Freedom*, 70–73.

24. Link, *Wilson: The New Freedom*, 94–144; Kazin, *A Godly Hero*, 222–27; Heckscher, *Wilson*, 322–23.

25. House Diary, May 21, July 8, 16, Sept. 19, 21, Oct. 14, 1913, House Papers.

26. Hugh C. Wallace to House, July 10, 1913, House Papers; House Diary, Aug. 7, 16, 19, Sept. 3, 1913.

27. Wilson to House, July 17, 18, Sept. 4, 18, 1913, House to Wilson, Sept. 10, 1913, House Papers.

28. Wilson to House, Sept. 26, 1913, House to Wilson, Sept. 27, 1913, House Papers; House Diary, Oct. 14–16, 1913.

29. House Diary, Oct. 29, 30, Nov. 11–13, 24–26, 28–29, Dec. 10–12, 21–23.

30. House Diary, Dec. 12, 22, 1913.

31. House Diary, March 8, April 18, Aug. 3, 10, Sept. 6, Dec. 22, 1913; Link, *Wilson: The New Freedom*, 94–95.

32. House Diary, Oct. 29, 30, Nov. 11, 12, 23–25, Dec. 3, 10, 12, 22, 1913.

33. House Diary, May 14, 18, 1913; John J. Broesamle, *William Gibbs McAdoo: A Passion for Change, 1863–1917* (Port Washington, N.Y., 1973), 138.

34. House Diary, July 20, Aug. 18, Nov. 26, 1913.

35. House Diary, Dec. 15, 18, 1912, Jan. 15, March 7, 1913; John M. Blum, *Joe Tumulty and the Wilson Era* (Boston, Mass., 1951), 51–52.

36. House Diary, July 20, Sept. 12, 26, Nov. 29, 30, Dec. 11, 12, 1913.

37. House Diary, Dec. 18–20, 1913, Jan. 22, 1914; Blum, *Tumulty*, 115–16.

38. Kenneth J. Grieb, *The United States and Huerta* (Lincoln, Neb., 1969), 85–104, 104–12, 124–41; Mark T. Gilderhus, "Revolution, War, and Expansion: Woodrow Wilson in Latin America," in John Milton Cooper Jr., ed., *Reconsidering Woodrow Wilson: Progressivism, Internationalism, War, and Peace* (Washington, D.C., 2008), 165–88; Mark T. Gilderhus, *The Second Century: U.S.–Latin American Relations since 1889* (Wilmington, Del., 2000), 40–44. House Diary, Aug. 10, Sept. 5, 22, Oct. 2, 14, 21, 24, 27, Oct. 30, Nov. 4, 11, 12, 13, 26, 1913; Link, *Wilson: The New Freedom*, 369–77; Friedrich Katz, *The Secret War in Mexico: Europe, the United States, and the Mexican Revolution* (Chicago, Ill., 1981), 170–83.

39. Link, *Wilson: The New Freedom*, 388–91; Cooper, *Wilson*, 236–42; House Diary, Jan. 16, 21, 1914.

40. House Diary, Jan. 15, 16, 21, 22, 1914.

41. Wilson to House, Jan. 28, 1914, House to Wilson, Jan. 29, 1914.

CHAPTER 10

1. Randolph B. Campbell, *Gone to Texas: A History of the Lone Star State* (New York, 2003), 347; Lewis L. Gould, *Progressives and Prohibitionists: Texas Democrats in the Wilson Era* (Austin, Tex., 1973), 98–119.

2. House Diary, Feb. 10, 1914, House Papers; David G. McComb, *Houston: A History* (Austin, Tex., 1981), 65–100; *Houston Daily Post*, Feb. 3, 1914; "Houston, Texas," in Ron Tyler, ed., *The New Handbook of Texas* (Austin, Tex., 1996), III, 721–23.

3. *Austin Statesman*, Feb. 9–11, 1914; House to T. W. Gregory, March 6, 1914, House Papers.

4. Richard W. Bond, "The Residence of E. M. House: Texas Historical Architecture," *Texas Architect*, 18 (June 1986), 12–17; House Diary, Feb. 10, 1914, House Papers; *Austin Statesman*, March 19, 1914.

5. House Diary, Feb. 10, 1914, House Papers; House to Hugh C. Wallace, Feb. 22, 1914, House Papers.

6. House to Walter Hines Page, Feb. 26, 1914, House Papers; House Diary, May 16, 1913, House Papers; House to Page, Jan. 4, 1914, House Papers; Rupert Norval Richardson, *Colonel Edward M. House: The Texas Years, 1858–1912* (Abilene, Tex., 1964), 215–19.

7. House Diary, March 23, 24, 25, House Papers; Wilson to House, March 30, 1914, House Papers.

8. Edwin A. Weinstein, *Woodrow Wilson: A Medical and Psychological Biography* (Princeton, N.J., 1981), 254–55; House Diary, March 25, 1914, House Papers; Weinstein, *Wilson*, 164–67, 296. Wilson's stroke occurred in 1906.

9. Arthur S. Link, *Wilson: The New Freedom* (Princeton, N.J., 1956), 417–44; W. Elliot Brownlee, "Wilson's Reform of Economic Structure: Progressive Liberalism and the Corporation," in John Milton Cooper Jr., *Reconsidering Woodrow Wilson: Progressivism, Internationalism, War, and Peace* (Washington, D.C., 2008), 56–89. Thomas K. McCraw, *Prophets of Regulation: Charles Francis Adams, Lewis D. Brandeis, James M. Landis, Alfred E. Kahn* (Cambridge, Mass., 1984), 81–142; John Milton Cooper Jr., *Woodrow Wilson: A Biography* (New York, 2009), 226–36.

10. Link, *Wilson: The New Freedom*, 445–60; John Milton Cooper Jr., *Pivotal Decades: The United States, 1900–1920* (New York, 1990), 201–11.

11. House Diary, Jan. 16, 1914, House Papers; House to Page, April 2, 1914, House Papers.

12. House Diary, April 2, 5, 27, May 7, 1914, House Papers.

13. Link, *Wilson: The New Freedom*, 445–57; House Diary, Jan. 21, 1914, House Papers.

14. Wilson to House, Feb. 16, 25, March 7, 30, 1914, House to Wilson, Feb. 13, 21, March 3, 11, 31, April 3, 7, May 1, 12, 15, 1914, House Papers; House Diary, April 15, 28, 1914, House Papers.

15. Link, *Wilson: The New Freedom,* 307–14; Cooper, *Wilson,* 249–50.

16. Link, *Wilson: The New Freedom,* 392–94.

17. Friedrich Katz, *The Secret War in Mexico: Europe, the United States, and the Mexican Revolution* (Chicago, Ill., 1981), 183–96; "An Annual Message to Congress," Dec. 2, 1913, in Arthur S. Link, ed., *The Papers of Woodrow Wilson* [*PWW*], 68 vols. (Princeton, N.J., 1966-93), XXIX, 4-5.

18. Link, *Wilson: The New Freedom,* 395–402; "An Address to Congress on the Mexican Crisis," April 20, 1914, *PWW,* XXIX, 472; Robert E. Quirk, *An Affair of Honor: Woodrow Wilson and the Occupation of Vera Cruz* (Lexington, Ky., 1962), 78–120; Cooper, *Wilson,* 241–46.

19. Link, *Wilson: The New Freedom,* 402–7; Katz, *The Secret War in Mexico,* 197–200.

20. Grayson to House, April 26, 1914, House Papers; House Diary, April 14, 15, 22, 26, 27, 28, May 8, 9, 1914, House Papers.

21. House Diary, April 15, 17, 1914, House Papers.

22. House Diary, April 16, 27, 28, House Papers.

23. House to Eleanor Wilson, March 10, 1914, House Papers; Ellen Wilson to House, May 14, 1914, House Papers; House Diary, April 2, 15, 1914, House Papers.

24. House Diary, May 10, 11, 1914, House Papers.

25. Wallace to House, Feb. 17, 18, House Papers; House Diary, May 7, 11, 1914, House Papers; John M. Blum, *Joe Tumulty and the Wilson Era* (Boston, Mass., 1951), 78–80.

26. House Diary, Dec. 12, 14, 1913, Jan. 16, 20, 21, 26, 27, March 25, April 15, House Papers; Rachael West, *The Department of State on the Eve of the First World War* (Athens, Ga., 1978), 67–69; Michael Kazin, *A Godly Hero: The Life of William Jennings Bryan* (New York, 2006), 219–22.

27. McAdoo to House, Feb. 22, March 3, 1914, House Papers.

28. House Diary, March 27, April 14, 15, May 7, 1914, House Papers; Frances Wright Saunders, *Ellen Axson Wilson: First Lady between Two Worlds* (Chapel Hill, N.C., 1985), 268–72; William G. McAdoo, *Crowded Years: The Reminiscences of William G. McAdoo* (Boston, Mass., 1931), 272–77; Cooper, *Wilson,* 258–60.

29. House Diary, May 9, July 31, Aug. 28, Sept. 1, 1913, Jan. 24, April 16, May 7, 1914, House Papers; House to Gerard, Jan. 1, Feb. 26, April 21, 1914, House Papers.

30. House Diary, Nov. 13, Dec. 23, 1913, Jan. 21, 1914; House to Page, Sept. 10, Nov. 14, Dec. 13, 1913, Jan. 4, 10, 19, Feb. 26, April 2, 6, 19, 20, May 12, 1914, House Papers.

31. John Milton Cooper Jr., *Walter Hines Page: The Southerner as American, 1855–1918* (Chapel Hill, N.C., 1977), 266–70; Page to House, Aug. 28, Nov. 23, Dec. 20, 1913, Jan. 2, April 27, 1914, House Papers.

32. Christopher Clark, *The Sleepwalkers: How Europe Went to War in 1914* (New York, 2012), 242.

33. House Diary, Dec. 2, 1913, Jan. 1, 1914; House to Page, Jan. 4, 1914, House Papers.

34. House Diary, Dec. 12, 1913, April 18, 1914, House Papers.

35. House Diary, May 11, 1914, House Papers; Wilson to House, May 15, 1914, House Papers.

CHAPTER II

1. House Diary, May 16, 1914, House Papers; David Fromkin, *Europe's Last Summer: Who Started the Great War in 1914?* (New York, 2004), 104; House to Fanny Denton, May 22, 1914, House Papers.

2. House to Mrs. Clarence J. Shearn, May 20, 1914, to Wilson, May 28, 1914, to Fanny Denton, May 24, 1914, House Papers; House Diary, May 23–June 1, 1914; Thomas Friedrich, *Berlin between the Wars* (New York, 1991), 22–24; Giles MacDonogh, *The Last Kaiser: The Life of Wilhelm II* (New York, 2000), 252–54.

3. House to Fanny Denton, May 25, 26, 27, 1914, House Papers; Bernstorff had written the German Foreign Office, urging that House be treated in a "friendly fashion." Bernstorff to Count von Montgelas, May 4, 1914, in E. T. S. Dugdale, *German Diplomatic Documents, 1871–1914* (New York, 1969), IV, 347–49.

4. House to Fanny Denton, May 27, 1914, to Wilson, May 28, 1914, House Papers; Robert K. Massie, *Dreadnought: Britain, Germany, and the Coming of the Great War* (New York, 1991), 164–85, 841–42; Gordon A. Craig, *Germany, 1866–1945* (New York, 1978), 303–10.

5. House Diary, May 26, 1914.

6. House to Wilson, May 28, 1914, to Fanny Denton, May 27, 1914, House Papers; House Diary, May 26, 1914.

7. Ibid.

8. House to Wilson, May 28, 1914, House Papers. In the original letter which he sent to the president, House changed the word "militarism" to "jingoism," without changing the letter-press copy. Arthur S. Link, *Wilson: The New Freedom* (Princeton, N.J., 1956), 315; House to Fanny Denton, May 31, 1914, House Papers.

9. MacDonogh, *The Last Kaiser*, 349–50; House Diary, June 1, 1914.

10. House Diary, June 1, 1914.

11. Ibid.

12. House Diary, June 1, 1914; House to Page, June 3, 1914, House Papers.

13. House to Wilson, June 3, 1914, to Edward S. Martin, June 4, 1914, House Papers.

14. Massie, *Dreadnought*, 104–6; Lamar Cecil, *Wilhelm II*, Vol. 2: *Emperor and Exile, 1900–1914* (Chapel Hill, N.C., 1996), 1–73; Gerhard Masur, *Imperial Berlin* (New York, 1970), 89–93.

15. Craig, *Germany*, 229–30, 286–301; Ernest R. May, *The World War and American Isolation* (Cambridge, Mass., 1959), 90–97; Christopher M. Clark, *Kaiser Wilhelm II* (London, Eng., 2000), 123–59, 186–224.

16. V. R. Berghahn, *Germany and the Approach of War in 1914* (New York, 1993), 9–30, 156–74.

17. House to Fanny Denton, May 29, 1914, to Albert Bigelow Paine, June 7, 1914, House Papers; House Diary, June 8, 1914; Patrice Higonnet, *Paris: Capital of the World* (Cambridge, Mass., 2002), 230–31, 319–33; House to McAdoo, June 12, 1914, House Papers.

18. Leonard V. Smith, Stephane Audoin-Rouzeau, and Annette Becker, *France and the Great War, 1914–1918* (New York, 2003), 20–26; on June 17 House assured the president that "In France I did not find the war spirit dominant. Their statesmen dream no longer of revenge and the recovery of Alsace and Lorraine. The people do, but those that govern and know, hope only that France may continue as now . . . . It is this new spirit in France which fills me with hope . . . . France, I am sure, will welcome our efforts for peace." House to Wilson, June 17, 1914, House Papers. It is difficult to know how House reached this conclusion, since he did not talk to any French leaders. In fact, leaders of the Third Republic were determined to regain the "lost territories" and reestablish France as a great power. Smith, Audoin-Rouzeau, and Becker, *France and the Great War,* 11–15.

19. House to Gordon Auchincloss, June 3, 1914, Auchincloss Papers; *New York Times,* June 6, 1914.

20. Michael S. Neiberg, *Dance of the Furies: Europe and the Outbreak of World War I* (Cambridge, Mass., 2011), 10–35; House to Bryan, June 13, 1914, House Papers.

21. House Diary, July 2, 1914; Michael Leapman, ed., *The Book of London: The Evolution of a Great City* (New York, 1989), 8, 34–35; Roy Porter, *London: A Social History* (Cambridge, Mass., 1994), 280.

22. House Diary, June 8, 14, 17, 20, 23, July 1, 8, 9, 1914; House to Gordon Auchincloss, July 2, 1914, Auchincloss Papers.

23. House to Page, May 28, June 3, 1914, House Papers; House Diary, June 12, 14, 1914; John Milton Cooper Jr., *Walter Hines Page: The Southerner as American, 1855–1918* (Chapel Hill, N.C., 1977), 270–73.

24. House Diary, June 12, 19, 28, 30, July 7, 1914.

25. Robert Rhodes James, *The British Revolution, 1880–1939* (New York, 1977), 281; Joyce Grigsby Williams, *Colonel House and Sir Edward Grey: A Study in Anglo–American Diplomacy* (Lanham, Md., 1984), 42–43; House to Wilson, June 17, 1914, House Papers.

26. House Diary, June 17, 1914.

27. Ibid.

28. House Diary, June 17, 21, 1914; House to Gordon Auchincloss, June 17, 1914, Auchincloss Papers; Grey did not tell House that, concerned about the

resurgence of Russian power, he planned later in the summer to send Tyrrell on a secret mission to confer with Jagow. The outbreak of war aborted the mission. T. G. Otte, "Détente 1914: Sir William Tyrrell's Secret Mission to Germany," *Historical Journal*, 56, 1 (2013), 175–204.

29. House Diary, June 24, 1914.

30. House to Wilson, June 26, 1914, to Mezes, June 27, 1914, House Papers.

31. House Diary, July 3, 1914.

32. House Diary, June 21, 26, 1914; James, *The British Revolution*, 323–25; House to Wilson, June 26, 1914, House Papers.

33. Roy Jenkins, *Asquith: Portrait of a Man and an Era* (New York, 1964), 93–95, 256–58, 279; Massie, *Dreadnought,* 576–80.

34. House Diary, July 2, 1914; House to Wilson, July 3, 1914, to Martin, June 23, 1914, House Papers.

35. House Diary, June 24, 1914; House to Wilson, July 4, 1914, to Mezes, July 3, 1914, House Papers.

36. House Diary, July 3, 8, 1914.

37. Mrs. J. Borden Harriman, *From Pinafores to Politics* (New York, 1923), 150.

38. Holger H. Herwig, *The First World War: Germany and Austria-Hungary, 1914–1918* (New York, 1997), 8–18; Martin Gilbert, *The First World War: A Complete History* (New York, 1994), 19; Fritz Fellner, "Austria-Hungary," in Keith Wilson, ed., *Decisions for War, 1914* (New York, 1995), 9–25; Holger Herwig, *The Marne, 1914: The Opening of World War I and the Battle that Changed the World* (New York, 2009), 3–29.

39. Herwig, *The First World War*, 18–23; John C. G. Rohl, "Germany," in Wilson, ed., *Decisions for War, 1914*, 27–54; Christopher Clark, *The Sleepwalkers: How Europe Went to War in 1914* (New York, 2013), 112–30, 515–27.

40. Craig, *Germany*, 324; Herwig, *The First World* War, 11–23.

41. Keith Neilson, "Russia," in Wilson, ed., *Decisions for War, 1914*, 97–120; Sean McMeekin, *The Russian Origins of the First World War* (Cambridge, Mass., 2011), 6–97; David Stevenson, *Cataclysm: The First World War as Political Tragedy* (New York, 2004), 21–24; Clark, *The Sleepwalkers,* 480–87.

42. Smith, Audoin-Rouzeau, and Becker, *France and the Great War,* 9–30; John F. V. Keiger, "France," in Keith Wilson, ed., *Decisions for War, 1914* (New York, 1995), 121–49; Hew Strachan, *The First World War*, Vol 1: *To Arms* (Oxford, Eng., 2001), 91; Clark, *The Sleepwalkers,* 294–313.

43. Smith, Audoin-Rouzeau, and Becker, *France and the Great War,* 27–8; Clark, *The Sleepwalkers,* 294–313.

44. House Diary, July 11, 20, 1914.

45. Keith Wilson, "Britain," in Wilson, ed., *Decisions for War, 1914*, 182–83; Gilbert, *The First World War,* 20.

46. Gilbert, *The First World War,* 22–23; Jenkins, *Asquith,* 324; Zara S. Steiner and Keith Neilson, *Britain and the Origins of the First World War* (New York, 2003), 227–48; Clark, *The Sleepwalkers,* 488–98.

47. Niall Ferguson, *The Pity of War* (New York, 1998), 56–81.

48. House to Edward S. Martin, July 12, 1914; House Papers; House Diary, July 20, 21, 29, 1914.

49. Page to Wilson, July 5, 1914, in Arthur S. Link., ed., *The Papers of Woodrow Wilson* [*PWW*], 68 vols. (Princeton, N.J., 1966-93), XXX, 258; Wilson to House, June 16, 22, 26, July 9, 1914, House Papers; House to Wilson, July 1, 1914, House Papers; Williams, *House and Grey*, 47–48.

50. House to Mona Tucker, June 28, 1914, House Papers; House to Wilson, July 31, 1914, House Papers.

CHAPTER 12

1. Martin Gilbert, *The First World War: A Complete History* (New York, 1994), 25–32; Holger H. Herwig, *The First World War: Germany and Austria–Hungary, 1914–1918* (New York, 1997), 28.

2. Zara S. Steiner and Keith Neilson, *Britain and the Origins of the First World War* (New York, 2003), 246–57; Niall Ferguson, *The Pity of War* (New York, 1998), 163; Christopher Clark, *The Sleepwalkers; How Europe Went to War in 1914* (New York, 2013), 539–47.

3. John Keegan, *The First World War* (New York, 1999), 73–77; Mrs. J. Borden Harriman, *From Pinafores to Politics* (New York, 1923), 157.

4. "The United States and Anglo–German Rivalry," *National Review*, 60 (Jan. 1913), 736–50; Rachael West, *The Department of State on the Eve of the First World War* (Athens, Ga., 1978), 125–27; Michael Kazin, *A Godly Hero: The Life of William Jennings Bryan* (New York, 2006), 215–18.

5. West, *The Department of State*, 128–34; James W. Gerard to House, July 7, 1914, House Papers.

6. Wilson to Mary Allen Hulbert, Aug. 2, 1914, in Arthur S. Link, ed., *The Papers of Woodrow Wilson* [*PWW*], 68 vols. (Princeton, N.J., 1966-93), XXX, 327–28; House to Wilson, Aug. 1, 1914, House Papers.

7. "Remarks at a Press Conference," Aug. 3, 1914, and "A Press Release," Aug. 4, 1914, in *PWW*, XXX, 331–32, 342; House to Wilson, Aug. 4, 1914, House Papers; Wilson to House, Aug. 5, 1914, House Papers.

8. House Diary, Aug. 5, 1914, House Papers; House to Gerard, Aug. 11, 1914, House Papers.

9. House Diary, Aug. 6, 1914; House to Walter Hines Page, to Gerard, Aug. 17, 1914, House Papers.

10. Arthur S. Link, *Wilson: The New Freedom* (Princeton, N.J., 1956), 460–65; Wilson to Hulbert, Aug. 7, 1914, *PWW*, XXX, 357; John Milton Cooper Jr., *Woodrow Wilson: A Biography* (New York, 2009), 260–61.

11. House Diary, Aug. 6, 1914; House to Wilson, Aug. 7, 1914, House Papers.

12. Wilson to House, Aug. 18, 1914, House Papers; House Diary, Aug. 29, 30, 1914.

13. House Diary, Aug. 30, 1914.

14. House Diary, Aug. 30, 1914.

15. McAdoo to House, June 28, 1914, Wallace to House, July 2, 1914, Auchincloss to House, July 2, 1914, House Papers.

16. August Heckscher, *Woodrow Wilson* (New York, 1991), 278; House to Grayson, Aug. 6, 1914, to Culberson, Aug. 12, 1914, House Papers.

17. Grayson to House, Aug. 11, 1914, House to Grayson, Aug. 12, 1914, Grayson to House, Aug. 20, 1914, House Papers.

18. Edwin A. Weinstein, *Woodrow Wilson: A Medical and Psychological Biography* (Princeton, N.J., 1981), 256; Grayson to House, Aug. 20, 1914, House Papers.

19. House Diary, Aug. 30, 1914.

20. House Diary, Aug. 17, 22, Sept. 5, 18, 24, 28, Oct. 1, 3, 9, 13, 17 and 23, 1914; House was determined to find the "right man" as ambassador to Mexico and now regretted earlier ambassadorial appointments. "It makes me shiver," he wrote Wilson, "when I think of some of the men we now have abroad and what may happen under the stress of circumstances." But he was still tempted to dispatch the troublesome McCombs to Mexico City. The president, however, rejected McCombs, pointing out that "he does not speak Spanish or have any knowledge of the Spanish people." House to Wilson, Aug. 25, 1915, House Papers; House Diary, Aug. 30, 1914.

21. Link, *Wilson: The New Freedom*, 421–22: House Diary, July 13, 1914; House to Wilson, July 15, 1914, to Horace Chilton, Aug. 9, 1914, House Papers; Gregory to House, early Aug. 1914, House Papers; "Thomas Watt Gregory," in Ron Tyler, ed., *The New Handbook of Texas* (Austin, Tex., 1996), III, 331.

22. House to Gregory, Aug. 3, 20, 1914, House Papers; Gregory to House, Aug. 22, 1914, House Papers; House Diary, Aug. 10, 1914.

23. Link, *Wilson: The New Freedom*, 409–16.

24. House to Wilson, June 26, July 3, 16, 17, 1914, House Papers; Arthur S. Link, *Wilson: The Struggle for Neutrality, 1915–1915* (Princeton, N.J., 1960), 232–58; Friedrich Katz, *The Secret War in Mexico: Europe, the United States and the Mexican Revolution* (Chicago, Ill., 1981), 253–68; Friedrich Katz, *The Life and Times of Pancho Villa* (Stanford, Calif., 2008), 309–73. House Diary, Aug. 19, 30; Thaddeus A. Thomson to House, Oct. 2, 1914, House Papers.

25. Herwig, *The First World War*, 81–87.

26. Ibid., 96–101; Lamar Cecil, *Wilhelm I*, Vol. 2: *Emperor and Exile, 1900–1941* (Chapel Hill, N.C., 1996), 214.

27. Herwig, *The First World War*, 99–116; Holger H. Herwig, *The Marne, 1914: The Opening of World War I and the Battle that Changed the World* (New York, 2009), 266–319; Sean McMeekin, *The Russian Origins of the First World War* (Cambridge, Mass., 2011), 76–97.

28. Gilbert, *The First World War*, 112–116; Keegan, *The First World War*, 136–137.

29. Link, *Wilson: The Struggle for Neutrality*, 17–91; "An Appeal to the American People," Aug. 18, 1917, *PWW*, XXX, 393–94; John J. Broesamle, *William*

Gibbs McAdoo: A Passion for Change, 1863–1917 (Port Washington, N.Y., 1973), 189–99.

30. Link, *Wilson: The Struggle for Neutrality,* 57–73: Ernest R. May, *The World War and American Isolation, 1914–1917* (Cambridge, Mass., 1959), 34–53; Cooper, *Wilson,* 262–67.

31. House to Wilson, Aug. 1, Sept. 5, 1914, to Gerard, Aug. 17, 1914, House Papers; House Diary, Aug. 30, Sept. 5, 1914; Link, *Wilson: The Struggle for Neutrality,* 44–45, 196–200; Paolo E. Coletta, *William Jennings Bryan, II, Progressive Politician and Moral Statesman, 1909–1915* (Lincoln, Neb., 1969), 252–55; Kazin, *A Godly Hero,* 234–35. Robert J. Young, *An American by Degrees: The Extraordinary Lives of French Ambassador Jules Jusserand* (Montreal, Canada, 2009), 79–80.

32. House Diary, Sept. 9, 16, 1914; House to Wilson, Sept. 9, 1914, House Papers; Wilson to House, Sept. 16, 1914, House Papers; Link, *Wilson: The Struggle for Neutrality,* 200–203.

33. Reinhard R. Doerries, *Imperial Challenge: Ambassador Count Bernstorff and German-American Relations, 1908–1917* (Chapel Hill, N.C., 1989), 14–25, 39–40, 77–86; Sir Arthur Willert, *The Road to Safety: A Study in Anglo-American Relations* (New York, 1953), 57.

34. David H. Burton, *Cecil Spring Rice: A Diplomat's Life* (Cranbury, N.J., 1990), 54–61, 146–55; Sir Arthur Willert, *Washington and Other Memories* (Boston, Mass., 1972), 53.

35. Spring-Rice to House, Sept. 12, 1914, House Papers; House Diary, Sept. 18, 19, 20, 21, 26, 1914; House to Wilson, Sept. 18, 20, 22, 1914, House Papers; Spring-Rice to Grey, Sept. 22, 1914, in Stephen Gwynn, ed., *The Letters and Friendships of Sir Cecil Spring Rice: A Record* (Boston, Mass., 1929), II, 224–27; Doerries, *Imperial Challenge,* 87–92.

36. House Diary, Sept. 27, 1914; Link, *Wilson: The Struggle for Neutrality,* 105–110.

37. House Diary, Sept. 27, 1914; Cooper, *Wilson,* 265–66.

38. House Diary, Sept. 28, 1914; Link, *Wilson: The Struggle for Neutrality,* 111–129.

39. House Diary, Sept. 28, 1914; House soon reconciled himself "to do nothing at present." House to Wilson, Oct. 8, 1914, to Page, Oct. 3, 1914, House Papers.

40. House Diary, Sept. 26, 1914.

41. House Diary, Sept. 28, 1914; Weinstein, *Woodrow Wilson,* 259–60.

42. House Diary, Sept. 29, 30, 1914.

43. House Diary, Oct. 20, 27, 29, 30, 1914.

44. House Diary, Nov. 4, 1914.

45. House Diary, Oct. 3, 22, 27, 1914.

46. Link, *Wilson: The New Freedom,* 465–71; Wilson to Oscar W. Underwood, Oct. 17, 1914, in *PWW,* XXXI, 168–74; Lewis L. Gould, *Reform and Regulation: American Politics from Roosevelt to Wilson* (Prospect Heights, Ill., 1996), 174–77; John Milton Cooper Jr., *Pivotal Decades: The United States, 1900–1920* (New York, 1990), 212–13.

47. House Diary, Nov. 3, 4, 1914; House to Gerard, Nov. 11, 1914, House Papers.

CHAPTER 13

1. Martin Gilbert, *The First World War: A Complete History* (New York, 1994), 84; House Diary, Nov. 10, 1914.

2. Roy Jenkins, *Asquith: Portrait of a Man and an Era* (New York, 1964), 332–48.

3. Robert Rhodes James, *The British Revolution, 1880–1939* (New York, 1997), 294–309; Nicholas A. Lambert, *Planning Armageddon: British Economic Warfare and the First World War* (Cambridge, Mass., 2012), 303–22.

4. Keith Robbins, *Sir Edward Grey: A Biography of Lord Grey of Fallodon* (London, 1971), 298–304; Ernest R. May, *The World War and American Isolation, 1914–1917* (Cambridge, Mass., 1959), 7–33; Viscount Grey of Fallodon, *Twenty-Five Years, 1892–1916* (New York, 1925), II, 103.

5. May, *The World War and American Isolation*, 81–84; David Stevenson, *Cataclysm: The First World War as Political Tragedy* (New York, 2004), 110–22.

6. Gordon A. Craig, *Germany, 1866–1945* (New York, 1978), 339–58.

7. Ibid., 358–67.

8. Holger H. Herwig, *The First World War: Germany and Austria-Hungary, 1914–1918* (New York, 1997), 114–18; Christopher Clark, *Kaiser Wilhelm II* (London, Eng., 2000), 226–29; Konrad H. Jarausch, *The Enigmatic Chancellor: Bethmann Hollweg and the Hubris of Imperial Germany* (New Haven, Conn., 1973), 185–200; Stevenson, *Cataclysm*, 104–11.

9. Craig, *Germany*, 367–68; Lamar Cecil, *Wilhelm II*, Vol. 2: *Emperor and Exile, 1900–1941* (Chapel Hill, N.C., 1996), 210–20.

10. May, *The World War and American Isolation*, 106–9.

11. House Diary, Nov. 4, 5, 6, 1914.

12. House Diary, Nov. 7, 1914.

13. House Diary, Nov. 7, 8, 1914; House to Fanny Denton, Nov. 5, 1914, to Wilson, Nov. 9, 1914, House Papers.

14. House Diary, Nov. 14, 1914.

15. House Diary, Nov. 14, 1914.

16. House Diary, Nov. 15, 25, 1914.

17. House Diary, Dec. 16, 1914.

18. House to Fanny Denton, Dec. 17, 18, 1914, House Papers; House Diary, Dec. 20, 1914; John Milton Cooper Jr., *Woodrow Wilson: A Biography* (New York, 2009), 266–68.

19. John Whiteclay Chambers II, *To Raise an Army: The Draft Comes to Modern America* (New York, 1987), 73–81; Jack McCallum, *Leonard Wood: Rough Rider, Surgeon, Architect of American Imperialism* (New York, 2006), 262.

20. House Diary, Nov. 3, 4, 8, 1914.

21. House Diary, Nov. 25, 1914; House also saw the need for "greater artillery plants and more artillery"; "An Annual Message to Congress," Dec. 8, 1914, in Arthur S. Link, ed., *The Papers of Woodrow Wilson* [*PWW*], 68 vols. (Princeton, N.J., 1966-93), XXXI, 414–24; Arthur S. Link, *Wilson: The*

Struggle for Neutrality, 1914–1915 (Princeton, N. J., 1960), 136–43; Cooper, *Wilson*, 267–68.

22. House to Page, Nov. 13, 1914, House Papers; House Diary, Nov. 8, 11, 25, Dec. 3, 14, 1914.

23. House to Wilson, Nov. 30, 1914, House Papers; House Diary, Dec. 3, 1914, House Papers; Michael Kazin, *A Godly Hero: The Life of William Jennings Bryan* (New York, 2006), 234–35.

24. House Diary, Dec. 16, 1914.

25. House Diary, Nov. 25, Dec. 16, 1914; Arthur S. Link, *Wilson: The New Freedom* (Princeton, N.J., 1956), 324–25; Thomas J. Knock, *To End All Wars: Woodrow Wilson and the Quest for a New World Order* (New York, 1992), 39–40.

26. House Diary, Dec. 16, 17, 20, 1914; Mark T. Gilderhus, *The Second Century: U.S.-Latin American Relations since 1889* (Wilmington, Del., 2000), 46–47.

27. Knock, *To End All Wars*, 39–40; "Memorandum of Interview with the President," Dec. 14, 1914, in *PWW*, XXXI, 458–60; Link, *The Struggle for Neutrality*, 52–53.

28. House Diary, Dec. 19, 20, 27, 1914; Link, *The New Freedom*, 325–27; Knock, *To End All Wars*, 40–41.

29. House Diary, Dec. 17, 1914; Bernstorff did not, in fact, represent the views of his government. Reinhard R. Doerries, *Imperial Challenge: Ambassador Count Bernstorff and German-American Relations, 1908–1917* (Chapel Hill, N.C., 1989), 90–92.

30. House Diary, Dec. 18, 20, 1914; Link, *The Struggle for Neutrality*, 211–12.

31. House Diary, Dec. 23, 27, 29, 30, 1914; Gerard to House, Nov., 1914, Zimmerman to House, Dec. 3, 1914, House Papers; House to Wilson, Dec. 26, 27, 1914, House Papers.

32. Gilbert, *The First World War*, 117–19.

33. August Heckscher, *Woodrow Wilson* (New York, 1991), 343; House Diary, Dec. 25, 1914; House promoted Mezes for the presidency of the City College of New York. House Diary, Oct. 17, 30, Nov. 3, 1914; House to Wallace, Nov. 21, 1914, House Papers; Jordan A. Schwarz, *The Speculator: Bernard M. Baruch in Washington, 1917–1965* (Chapel Hill, N.C., 1981), 43–44.

34. House to Ruth House, summer 1914, Edith House Scrapbook; House to Mrs. J. C. Lamkin, Oct. 27, 1914, House Papers.

35. Wilson to House, Dec. 25, 1914, House to Wilson, Dec. 25, 1914, House Papers.

36. "A Talk with the President," by Samuel G. Blythe, in *PWW*, XXXI, 390–403.

CHAPTER 14

1. Arthur S. Link, *Wilson: The Struggle for Neutrality, 1914–1915* (Princeton, N.J., 1960), 212–13; George Macaulay Trevelyan, *Grey of Fallodon: The Life and Letters of Sir Edward Grey, afterwards Viscount Grey of Fallodon* (Boston, Mass., 1937), 357–58.

2. Spring-Rice to House, Jan. 8, 1915, House to Wilson, Jan. 8, 1915, House Papers; House Diary, Jan. 11, 1915.

3. House Diary, Jan. 12, 1915.

4. House Diary, Jan. 13, 1915.

5. House Diary, Jan. 13, 1915, House Papers; Edwin A. Weinstein, *Woodrow Wilson: A Medical and Psychological Biography* (Princeton, N.J., 1981), 260–64.

6. House Diary, Jan. 24, 1915, House Papers.

7. House Diary, Jan. 24, 25, 1915; House to Auchincloss, June 24, 1914, House Papers; Auchincloss Diary, Jan. 14, 16, 27, 30, Feb. 10, 1915.

8. House Diary, Jan. 30, 1915; Diana Preston, *Lusitania: An Epic Tragedy* (New York, 2002), 45–49.

9. House Diary, Feb. 5, 6, 1915; House to Auchincloss, Feb. 11, 1915, House Papers.

10. Martin Gilbert, *The First World War: A Complete History* (New York, 1994), 124–25; David Stevenson, *Cataclysm: The First World War as Political Tragedy* (New York, 2004), 81–84.

11. Stevenson, *Cataclysm*, 127–28; Leonard V. Smith, Stephane Audoin–Rouzeau, and Annette Becker, *France and the Great War, 1914–1918* (New York, 2003), 77–80; Robert Doughty, *Pyrrhic Victory: French Strategy and Operations in the Great War* (Cambridge, Mass., 2005), 107–52.

12. Stevenson, *Cataclysm*, 126–28; George H. Cassar, *Kitchener's War: British Strategy From 1914 to 1916* (Washington, D.C., 2004), 119–29; Robert Rhodes James, *The British Revolution, 1880–1939* (New York, 1977), 312–13; Nicholas A. Lambert, *Planning Armageddon: British Economic Warfare and the First World War* (Cambridge, Mass., 2012), 319–38.

13. Stevenson, *Cataclysm*, 123–26; Holger H. Herwig, *The First World War: Germany and Austria-Hungary, 1914–1918* (New York, 1997), 130–34.

14. Link, *The Struggle for Neutrality*, 309–20; Ernest R. May, *The World War and American Isolation, 1914–1917* (Cambridge, Mass., 1959), 113–28.

15. Roy Jenkins, *Asquith: Portrait of a Man and an Era* (New York, 1964), 241; Keith Robbins, *Sir Edward Grey: A Biography of Lord Grey of Fallodon* (London, Eng., 1971), 285, 303, 319, 321.

16. House Diary, Feb. 7, 11, 1915; House to Wilson, Feb. 9, 1915, to Auchincloss, Feb. 11, 1915, House Papers; Grey invited House to drop by his home between seven and eight in the evening whenever he wanted to talk. Viscount Grey of Fallodon, *Twenty-Five Years, 1892–1916* (New York, 1925), II, 124.

17. House Diary, Feb. 10, 1915; Page to Wilson, Feb. 10, 1915, in Arthur S. Link, ed., *The Papers of Woodrow Wilson* [*PWW*], 68 vols. (Princeton, N.J., 1966–93), XXXII, 211–15; House to Wilson, Feb. 9, 1915, to Auchincloss, Feb. 15, 1915, House Papers.

18. House Diary, Feb. 10, 11, 1915.

19. Grey of Fallodon, *Twenty–Five Years,* II, 124–25.

20. Zimmerman to House, Feb. 4, 1915, House Papers; House to McAdoo, Feb. 12, 1915, House Papers; House Diary, Feb. 13, 1915.

21. House Diary, Feb. 17, 1915; House to Zimmerman, Feb. 17, 1915, to Wilson, Feb. 17, 1915, House Papers; Zimmerman to House, March 2, 1915, House Papers.

22. Gerard to House, Feb. 15, 1915, Wilson to House, Feb. 15, 1915, House Papers.

23. House Diary, Feb. 18, 1915; House to Wilson, Feb. 18, 1915, to Gerard, Feb. 19, 1915, House Papers; Wilson to House, Feb. 20, 1915, House Papers.

24. House to Wilson, Feb. 18, 20, 21, 23, 1915, House Papers.

25. Wilson to House, Feb. 25, 1915, House Papers; House to Auchincloss, Feb. 22, 1915, House Papers.

26. House to Wilson, Feb. 27, 1915, House Papers.

27. House Diary, March 7, 1915; House to Auchincloss, March 2, 1915, to McAdoo, March 8, 1915, House Papers; Walter Hines Page Diary, March 11, 1915; soon after House arrived, Asquith complained that he had come to England with "a lot of chimerical ideas, one is that of a Union of all nations." Asquith to Venetia Stanley, Feb. 15, 1915, in Michael and Eleanor Brock, eds., *Letters of H. H. Asquith to Venetia Stanley* (New York, 1982), 435.

28. House to Auchincloss, March 2, 5, 1915, House Papers; House Diary, March 1, 9, 1915.

29. Robert K. Massie, *Dreadnought: Britain, Germany, and the Coming of the Great War* (New York, 1991), 312–24; Jason Tomes, *Balfour and Foreign Policy: The International Thought of a Conservative Statesman* (New York, 1997), 185–87; House Diary, March 4, 1915; E. H. H. Green, *Balfour* (London, Eng., 2006), 9, 28–9.

30. House Diary, March 4, 1915; House to Auchincloss, March 5, 1915, House Papers; Patrick Devlin, *Too Proud to Fight: Woodrow Wilson's Neutrality* (New York, 1975), 376.

31. House Diary, Feb. 12, 16, 18, 24, 1915.

32. Wilson to Mary Allen Hulbert, April 4, 1915, in *PWW*, XXXII, 475–77; John Milton Cooper Jr., *Woodrow Wilson: A Biography* (New York, 2009), 274–76.

33. Samuel Huston Thompson Jr. to House, Jan. 27, 1915, Grayson to House, Feb. 2, 1915, House Papers; House to Grayson, March 1, 1915, House Papers.

34. House to Mezes, March 1, 1915, House Papers; Wilson to House, March 8, 1915, House Papers.

35. Link, *Struggle for Neutrality*, 320–24; Bryan to Gerard, Feb. 19, 1915, in *PWW*, XXXII, 207–10; May, *World War and American Isolation*, 145–46; Cooper, *Wilson*, 276–77.

36. Link, *Struggle for Neutrality*, 331–48; House Diary, Feb. 22, 24, 27, 1915, House Papers; Wilson to Mary Allen Hulbert, Feb. 14, 1915, *PWW*, XXXII, 232–33.

37. House to E. Sammons, Feb. 24, 1915, to Auchincloss, Feb. 24, 1915, House Papers; House Diary, March 11, 1915, House Papers; House to Auchincloss, March 12, 1915, House Papers.

38. House to Auchincloss, March 12, 1915, House Papers; Gordon Wright, *France in Modern Times: From the Enlightenment to the Present* (New York, 1995), 302–3; Stevenson, *Cataclysm*, 114–16.

39. House Diary, March 12, 13, 14, 15, 1915; House to Wilson, March 14, 1915, House Papers; House and British Ambassador Sir Francis Bertie did not hit it off. House thought Bertie was an indiscreet lightweight; the ambassador was unimpressed with House and his peace mission. House Diary, March 17, 1915, House Papers; Lady Algernon G. Lennox, ed., *The Diary of Lord Bertie of Thame, 1914–1918*, 2 vols. (London, Eng., 1924), I, 130.

40. House to Wilson, March 14, 15, 1915, House Papers; Wilson to House, March 18, 1915, House Papers.

41. House Diary, March 17, 19, 1915; House to Auchincloss, March 20, 1915, House Papers.

42. May, *World War and American Isolation*, 122–28.

43. House Diary, March 19, 1915; House to Page, March 20, 1915, to Auchincloss, March 20, 1915, to McAdoo, March 24, 1915, House Papers.

44. House to Wilson, March 20, 1915, House Papers.

45. Massie, *Dreadnought*, 702–5; Konrad H. Jarausch, *The Enigmatic Chancellor: Bethmann Hollweg and the Hubris of Imperial Germany* (New Haven, Conn., 1973), 66–68, 149–52.

46. Gordon A. Craig, *Germany, 1866–1945* (New York, 1978), 287–88; May, *World War and American Isolation*, 91–93.

47. House Diary, March 27, 1915; House to Auchincloss, April 1, 1915, House Papers.

48. House Diary, March 19–27, 1915.

49. Link labels Gerard "an authentic international catastrophe," incapable of distinguishing "between gossip and truth." Link, *Struggle for Neutrality*, 311, 331.

50. House Diary, March 25, 1915; James W. Gerard, *My Four Years in Germany* (New York, 1917), 68, 221; Joseph C. Grew, *Turbulent Era: A Diplomatic Record of Forty Years, 1904–1945*, 2 vols. (Boston, Mass., 1952), I, 185–86.

51. House Diary, March 28, 1915, House Papers; House to Auchincloss, March 24, 1915, House Papers.

52. House to Wilson, March 20, 26, 27, April 11, 1915, House Papers; Wilson to House, April 1, 1915, House Papers.

53. House to Wilson, March 20, 1915, House Papers; House to Auchincloss, April 1, 1915, House Papers; House Diary, March 25, March 28–April 10, 1915; House to Martin, April 8, 1915, House Papers; Thomas Nelson Page to House, April 15, 1915, House Papers.

54. House to Mezes, April 18, 1915, to Gregory, April 14, 1915, to Auchincloss, April 12, 1915, House Papers.

55. House to Martin, April 19, 1915, to Spring-Rice, April 15, 1915, to Wilson, April 18, 1915, House Papers.

56. House Diary, April 13, 1915; House to Wilson, April 14, 1915, House Papers; House did not convey to the president these statements about the delay of peace negotiations.

57. House Diary, April 16, 1915; House to Wilson, April 16, 17, 1915, House Papers; *The Memoirs of Raymond Poincaré*, translated and adapted by Sir George Arthur (New York, 1975), 12.

58. House Diary, April 22, 26, 28, 1915; Page Diary, April 30, 1915; House to Grey, April 12, 1915, to Wilson, April 12, 1915, to Mezes, April 18, 1915, House Papers; Wilson to House, April, 19, 1915, House Papers.

CHAPTER 15

1. House Diary, April 28, 29, 1915; House to Auchincloss, April 30, 1915, House Papers.

2. House to Grey, April 21, 1915, Grey to House, April 16, 24, 1915, House Papers.

3. Grey to House, April 16, 1915, House Papers; David French, *British Strategy and War Aims: 1914–1916* (London, 1986), 59–63.

4. House to Auchincloss, April 30, 1915, House Papers; House Diary, April 30, 1915; House to Wilson, April 30, 1915, House Papers.

5. House Diary, May 3, 5, 6, 1915; House to Wilson, May 3, 1915, House Papers.

6. House Diary, May 7, 1915.

7. House to Wilson, May 5, 1915, House Papers; House Diary, May 7, 1915.

8. Arthur S. Link, *Wilson: The Struggle for Neutrality, 1914–1915* (Princeton, N.J., 1960), 370–72; Diana Preston, *Lusitania: An Epic Tragedy* (New York, 2002), 175–217, 303.

9. House to Auchincloss, May 7, 1915, House Papers; Burton J. Hendrick, *The Life and Letters of Walter H. Page* (New York, 1923), II, 1–2; John Milton Cooper Jr., *Walter Hines Page: The Southerner as American, 1855–1918* (Chapel Hill, N.C., 1977), 307; House Diary, May 7, 8, 1915.

10. House to Wilson, May 9, 11, 1915, House Papers.

11. Link, *Struggle for Neutrality*, 372–77.

12. Ibid., 379–89; "An Address in Philadelphia to Newly Naturalized Citizens," May 10, 1915, in Arthur S. Link, ed., *The Papers of Woodrow Wilson* [*PWW*], 68 vols. (Princeton, N.J., 1966–93), XXXIII, 147–50; "A Draft of the First *Lusitania* Note," May 11, 1915, in *PWW*, XXXIII, 155–58; John Milton Cooper Jr., *Woodrow Wilson: A Biography* (New York, 2009), 285–92.

13. House Diary, May 11, 1915; House to Wilson, May 13, 1915, House Papers; Michael Kazin: *A Godly Hero: The Life of William Jennings Bryan* (New York, 2006), 235–37.

14. House to Joseph E. Willard, May 10, 1915, to Edward S. Martin, May 13, 1915, House Papers; "Horatio Herbert Kitchener," in H. C. Matthews and Brian

Harrison, eds., *Oxford Dictionary of National Biography* (Oxford, Eng., 2004), XXXI, 828–36.

15. Robert Rhodes James, *The British Revolution, 1880–1939* (New York, 1977), 296–98; George H. Cassar, *Kitchener's War: British Strategy from 1914 to 1916* (Washington, D.C., 2004), 162–82.

16. House Diary, May 12, 1915; House to Wilson, May 13, 1915, House Papers.

17. House Diary, May 13, 14, 1915; House to Wilson, May 14, 1915, House Papers.

18. Link, *Struggle for Neutrality*, 456–76.

19. House Diary, May 11, 17, 1915; House to Thomas Nelson Page, March 27, 1915, House Papers; House Diary, June 1, 3, 1915.

20. Martin Gilbert, *The First World War: A Complete History* (New York, 1994), 154–75; David Stevenson, *Cataclysm: The First World War as Political Tragedy* (New York, 2004), 126–28.

21. George H. Cassar, *Asquith as War Leader* (London, Eng., 1994), 91–110; Ernest R. May, *The World War and American Isolation, 1914–1917* (Cambridge, Mass., 1959), 305–10.

22. House Diary, June 1, 1915; "David Lloyd George," in *Dictionary of National Biography*, XXI, 890–912.

23. James, *The British Revolution*, 323–26; John Grigg, *Lloyd George: From Peace to War, 1912–1916* (Berkeley, Calif., 1985), 223–55.

24. House Diary, June 2, 1915; Michael G. Fry, *Lloyd George and Foreign Policy: The Education of a Statesman, 1890–1916* (Montreal, Canada, 1977), 217–18; Hugh Purcell, *Lloyd George* (London, Eng., 2006), 37–42.

25. Link, *Struggle for Neutrality*, 389–92; Wilson to House, May 5, 18, 23, 26, 1915, House to Wilson, May 7, 25, 27, House Papers. In response to Bryan's insistence that he publicly call on the belligerents to end the war, Wilson revealed the extent to which he accepted House's advice. "To intrude now," he wrote his secretary of state, "would be futile and would probably be offensive. We would lose such influence as we have for peace." Wilson to Bryan, April 28, 1915, in *PWW*, XXXIII, 85.

26. House to Sidney E. Mezes, May 2, 1915, to Edward S. Martin, May 4, 1915, to Paul B. Cruger, May 11, 1915, House Papers; House Diary, May 28, 29, 30, 1915.

27. House to Wilson, May 25, 1915, to Martin, May 26, 31, 1915, House Papers; House Diary, May 30, 1915; House to Grey, June 1, 1915, House Papers.

28. House to Wilson, May 31, 1915, Wilson to House, June 1, 1915, House Papers; House to Auchincloss, May 25, 1915, House Papers.

29. House to Auchincloss, May 18, 25, 27, 1915, House Papers; Auchincloss Diary, April–late August, 1915, Auchincloss Papers; Janet Auchincloss to "Popsie," May 26, 1915, House Papers; House to Auchincloss, June 1, 1915, House Papers.

30. Gerard to House, June 1, 1915, House Papers; House Diary, June 2, 3, 4, 1915.

31. House Diary, June 3, 1915; Grey to House, June 2, 6, 1915, House Papers.

32. House Diary, March 4, 5, May 6, 9, 25, 30, June 3, 1915; Page Diary, May 3, 1915; Cooper, *Page*, 304–9.

33. House Diary, June 5, 6, 7, 13, 1915; Auchincloss Diary, April–late August, 1915; Page Diary, June 4, 1915.

CHAPTER 16

1. House Diary, June 13, 24, 1915; Michael Kazin, *A Godly Hero: The Life of William Jennings Bryan* (New York, 2006), 235–41; John Milton Cooper Jr., *Woodrow Wilson: A Biography* (New York, 2009), 290–94.

2. Arthur S. Link, *Wilson: The Struggle for Neutrality, 1914–1915* (Princeton, N.J., 1960), 425–27.

3. House Diary, June 13, 16, 19; House to Walter Hines Page, June 17, 1915, House Papers.

4. House Diary, June 14, 1915; David F. Houston, *Eight Years with Wilson's Cabinet, 1913 to 1920* (New York, 1926), I, 141.

5. House Diary, June 14, 20, 1915; House to Wilson, June 16, 1915, House Papers; Link, *Struggle for Neutrality*, 428; Cooper, *Wilson*, 294–95; House to Page, June 17, 1915, 25, House Papers; John Milton Cooper Jr., *Walter Hines Page: The Southerner as American, 1855–1918* (Chapel Hill, N.C., 1977), 309; Edward S. Martin to House, April 6, 1915, House Papers; summary of events from April to late Aug. 1915, Auchincloss Diary; Frank Andrews to House, June 17, 1915, House Papers; House to Burleson, June 20, 1915, House Papers.

6. Wilson to House, June 20, 1915, House Papers; House Diary, June 24, 1915.

7. House to Wilson, June 16, 1915, House Papers; House Diary, June 24, 1915.

8. House Diary, June 24, 1915.

9. Ibid.

10. August Heckscher, *Woodrow Wilson* (New York, 1991), 347–52; Phyllis Lee Levin, *Edith and Woodrow: The Wilson White House* (New York, 2001), 51–73; Edith Bolling Wilson, *My Memoir* (New York, 1938), 56–74; Cooper, *Wilson*, 280–84; Wilson to Edith Bolling Galt, May 5, 1915, in Arthur S. Link, ed., *The Papers of Woodrow Wilson* [*PWW*], 68 vols. (Princeton, N.J., 1966–93), XXXIII, 111–12.

11. House Diary, June 24, 1915; Grayson to House, June 21, 1915, House Papers.

12. House Diary, June 24, 1915; Wilson to House, July 3, 1915, House Papers.

13. Link, *Struggle for Neutrality*, 438–40; House to Grey, June 17, 1915, House Papers; Thomas B. Love to House, June 16, 1915, House Papers.

14. Gerard to House, June 16, 22, 25, 1915, Arthur Hugh Frazier to House, July 9, 1915, Page to House, June 30, 1915, House Papers.

15. Lord Loreburn to House, June 26, 1915, Grey to House, July 14, 1915, House Papers.

16. Ernest R. May, *The World War and American Isolation, 1914–1917* (Cambridge, Mass., 1959), 197–210; Konrad H. Jarausch, *The Enigmatic Chancellor: Bethmann*

Hollweg and the Hubris of Imperial Germany (New Haven., Conn., 1973), 275–78.

17. Ibid., 210–14; Link, *Struggle for Neutrality*, 431–38; Reinhard R. Dorries, *Imperial Challenge: Ambassador Count Bernstorff and German–American Relations, 1908–1917* (Chapel Hill, N.C., 1989), 101–10.

18. House Diary, July 10, 1915; House to Wilson, July 10, 1915, House Papers.

19. Wilson to House, July 12, 14, 1915, House to Wilson, July 15, 1915, House Papers; Link, *Struggle for Neutrality*, 441–55.

20. House to Page, July 15, 1915, to Mezes, July 25, 1915, House Papers.

21. Thomas H. Hartig, *Robert Lansing: An Interpretive Biography* (New York, 1982), 9–79; Cooper, *Wilson*, 295.

22. Harting, *Robert Lansing*, 123–35; George F. Kennan, *Russia Leaves the War* (Princeton, N.J., 1956), 30–31.

23. Link, *Struggle for Neutrality*, 45–46; Hartig, *Robert Lansing*, 152–56, 215–23.

24. House Diary, July 24, 1915; House to Auchincloss, July 26, 1915, to Wilson, July 25, 1915, House Papers.

25. House Diary, April 7, 1913, June 24, July 4, Sept. 12, 1915; House to Wilson, July 25, Aug. 26, 1915, to Polk, July 24, 1915, House Papers; Lansing to House, Aug. 12, 16, 1915, House Papers; "Frank Lyon Polk," in Warren F. Kuehl, ed., *Biographical Dictionary of Internationalists* (Westport, Conn., 1983), 582–83.

26. House Diary, Aug. 4, 1915; interview with Ima Hogg, Oct. 13, 1967, with Frances Denton Miller, Oct. 8–9, 1977; House to Loulie House, Sept. 16, 1915, House Papers; Loulie kept a large stomach pump in her bathroom which she used every day. Interview with Jane Prendergast, January 4, 1979.

27. Wilson to House, July 21, 1915, House to Wilson, July 22, 1915, House Papers.

28. House Diary, July 30, 31, 1915.

29. Heckscher, *Wilson*, 353; Wilson to Edith Galt, July 20, 1915, in *PWW,* XXXIII, 539: Edith Galt to Wilson, Aug. 3, 1915, in *PWW,* XXXIV, 77–78.

30. Edwin A. Weinstein, *Woodrow Wilson: A Medical and Psychological Biography* (Princeton, N.J., 1981), 279; House Diary, Jan. 22, 1914.

31. Edith Galt to Wilson, June 18, 1915, in *PWW,* XXXIII, 421; Wilson to Edith Galt, Aug. 15, 1915, in *PWW,* XXXIV, 207–10; Edith Galt to Wilson, in *PWW,* XXXIV, 130–31; Levin, *Edith and Woodrow*, 98–101; Kristie Miller, *Ellen and Edith: Woodrow Wilson's First Ladies* (Lawrence, Kans., 2010), 115–19.

32. Wilson to Edith Galt, Aug. 13, 1915, in *PWW,* XXXIV, 190–93.

33. Edith Galt to Wilson, Aug. 25, 26, 1915, in *PWW,* XXXIV, 326–29, 336–39; Cooper, *Wilson*, 295–96, 298–99.

34. Wilson to Edith Galt, Aug. 28, 1915, in *PWW,* XXXIV, 350–55.

35. Edith Galt to Wilson, Aug. 28, 1915, in *PWW,* XXXIV, 355–58.

36. Friedrich Katz, *The Secret War in Mexico: Europe, the United States, and the Mexican Revolution* (Chicago, Ill., 1981), 268–70.

37. Link, *Struggle for Neutrality*, 467–94: Wilson to Lansing, Aug. 11, 1915, in *PWW,* XXXIV, 164; Link, *Struggle for Neutrality*, 632.

38. Link, *Struggle for Neutrality*, 633–44.
39. House Diary, June 24, July 15, Sept. 15, 1915; Lincoln Steffans to House, July 30, 31, Aug. 5, 7, Sept. 13, 1915, House Papers; House to Gerard, July 8, 1915, to John Lind, Aug. 2, 1915, House Papers.
40. Link, *Struggle for Neutrality*, 594–99; House to Page, July 18, 1915, House Papers.
41. Wilson to House, July 27, 1915, House to Wilson, July 22, 1915, House Papers.
42. Link, *Struggle for Neutrality*, 599–615; House to Wilson, Aug. 2, 1915, House Papers; House was deeply involved in the resolution of the cotton crisis. House to McAdoo, July 12, 1915, to Lansing, July 29, 1915, to Wilson, July 28, 29, Aug. 2, 6, 14, 1915, House Papers; Nicholas A. Lambert, *Planning Armageddon: British Economic Warfare and the First World War* (Cambridge, Mass., 2012), 442–54.
43. Cooper, *Walter Hines Page,* 311–13; Page to House, Aug. 4, 1915, Sept. 2, 8, 1915; House to Page, Aug. 4, 1915, House Papers.
44. House to Wilson, Aug. 4, 1915, Wilson to House, Aug. 21, 1915, House Papers; Wilson also felt that House had been out of touch with American opinion. "It *is very* interesting," he wrote Edith, "to find how House is getting re-Americanized and now sees how Walter Page also needs repatriation." Wilson to Edith Galt, Aug. 9, 1915, in *PWW*, XXXIV, 150–52.
45. Link, *Struggle for Neutrality*, 554–64; Reinhard R. Dorries, "From Neutrality to War: Woodrow Wilson and the German Challenge," in William N. Tilchin and Charles E. Neu, eds. *Artists of Power: Theodore Roosevelt, Woodrow Wilson, and Their Enduring Impact on U.S. Foreign Policy* (Westport, Conn., 2006), 126–30; House Diary, Aug. 5, 10, 1915; Wilson to House, Aug. 4, 1915, House to Wilson, Aug. 10, 1915, House Papers.
46. Link, *Struggle for Neutrality*, 565–70; May, *World War and American Isolation*, 162; House Diary, Aug. 19, 21, 22, 1915; Wilson to House, Aug. 21, 1915, House to Wilson, Aug. 22, 23, 1915, House Papers.
47. Link, *Struggle for Neutrality*, 570–87; Dorries, *Imperial Challenge*, 112–17; Cooper, *Wilson*, 300–301.
48. House to Wilson, Aug. 31, 1915, House Papers.
49. Link, *Struggle for Neutrality*, 645–53; Wilson to House, Sept. 7, 1915, House to Wilson, Sept. 20, 1915, House Papers. On September 6 the American government learned of still more Austrian and German plots to disrupt the nation's economic life, and Wilson demanded the recall of Austrian Ambassador Dumba; Jarausch, *The Enigmatic Chancellor*, 278–80; Link, *Struggle for Neutrality*, 653–71; House Diary, Sept. 16, 1915.
50. Link, *Struggle for Neutrality*, 588–93; Wilson to Oswald Garrison Villard, Sept. 7, 1915, in *PWW*, XXXIV, 528; Cooper, *Wilson*, 297–98.
51. House Diary, July 10, Aug. 7, 1915; House to Wilson, Aug. 8, 23, 26, 1915, Wilson to House, Aug. 25, 1915, House Papers.
52. Wilson to House, Aug. 21, 31, Sept. 7, 1915, House to Wilson, Sept. 3, 1915, House Papers; House Diary, Sept. 8, 9, 10, 1915.

53. House to Loulie House, Sept. 16, 1915, to Wilson, Sept. 17, 1915, Wilson to House, Sept. 20, 1915, House Papers; Grayson to House, Sept. 10, 1915, House Papers; House Diary, Sept. 22, 1915.

CHAPTER 17

1. House Diary, Sept. 22, 1915.
2. Arthur S. Link, *Wilson: Confusions and Crises, 1915–1916* (Princeton, N.J., 1964), 3–7; John M. Blum, *Joe Tumulty and the Wilson Era* (Boston, Mass., 1951), 116–17; Edwin A. Weinstein, *Woodrow Wilson: A Medical and Psychological Biography* (Princeton, N.J., 1981), 183–94; in *My Memoir* (Indianapolis, Ind., 1939),75–78, Edith Bolling Wilson claims that House later admitted collaborating with McAdoo. It is unlikely that House encouraged McAdoo's clumsy approach to the president. He believed Wilson's early marriage was essential for his physical and emotional well-being. Tom Shachtman in *Edith & Woodrow: A Presidential Romance* (New York, 1981), also dismisses Edith Wilson's account.
3. Edith Galt to Wilson, Sept. 20, 1915, Wilson to Edith Galt, Sept. 21, 1915, in Arthur S. Link, ed., *The Papers of Woodrow Wilson* [*PWW*], 68 vols. (Princeton, N.J., 1966-93), XXXIV, 495–501; John Milton Cooper Jr., *Woodrow Wilson: A Biography* (New York, 2009), 301–3; Phyllis Lee Levin, *Edith and Woodrow: The Wilson White House* (New York, 2001), 108–21.
4. House Diary, Sept. 22, 1915.
5. Ibid., Sept. 24, 1915.
6. Wilson to Edith Galt, Sept. 23, 1915, in *PWW*, XXXIV, 510–11.
7. House Diary, Sept. 23, 24, 1915.
8. Edith Galt to Wilson, Sept. 24, 1915, Wilson to Edith Galt, Sept. 25, 1915, in *PWW*, XXXIV, 518–20; Kristie Miller, *Ellen and Edith: Woodrow Wilson's First Ladies* (Lawrence, Kans, 2010), 117–32. House Diary, Sept. 24, 1915.
9. House Diary, Sept. 22, 23, 24, 1915.
10. House Diary, Oct. 21, 31, Nov. 27, Dec. 15, 1915.
11. House to Fanny Denton, Sept. 23, to Loulie House, Sept. 26, to Wilson, Sept. 26, 1915, House Papers.
12. Holger H. Herwig, *The First World War: Germany and Austria-Hungary, 1914–1918* (New York, 1997), 141–54; Martin Gilbert, *The First World War: A Complete History* (New York, 1994), 196–201.
13. Gilbert, *The First World War*, 207–13; Sean McMeekin, *The Russian Origins of the First World War* (Cambridge, Mass., 2011), 115–40.
14. Gilbert, *The First World War*, 204–5.
15. Ibid., 219–23; John Keegan, *The First World War* (New York, 1999), 256.
16. Wilson to House, Sept. 29, 1915, House to Wilson, Oct. 1, 1915, House Papers; "An Announcement," Oct. 6, 1915, in *PWW*, XXXV, 32; Wilson to Edith Galt, Oct. 7, 1915, *PWW*, XXXV, 40.

17. Wilson to House, Oct. 4, 1915, House to Wilson, Oct. 1, 5, 1915, House Papers; House Diary, Oct. 8, 1915; House to Wilson, Oct. 5, 1915, House Papers.

18. House Diary, Oct. 8, 9, 1915; "First Lady to Be Has Ovation Here," *New York Times*, Oct. 9, 1916.

19. House Diary, Oct. 13, 1915.

20. House Diary, Oct. 15, 1915; Grey to House, Sept. 22, 1915, House Papers; on Sept. 3 House had written Grey asking if "the President could make peace proposals to the belligerents at this time upon the broad basis of the elimination of militarism and navalism and a return, as nearly as possible, to the status quo?" House to Grey, Sept. 3, 1915, House Papers.

21. House Diary, Oct. 15, 17, 1915; House to Wilson, Oct. 17, 1915, to Grey, Oct. 17, 1915, House Papers.

22. Wilson to House, Oct. 18, 1915, House Papers; House Diary, Oct. 19, 1915.

23. Link, *Wilson: Confusions and Crises*, 107; Thomas J. Knock, *To End All Wars: Woodrow Wilson and the Quest for a New World Order* (New York, 1992), 50–55; House Diary, July 19, Aug. 6, Nov. 21, 1915; House also met with Henry Ford, the automobile manufacturer and pacifist who chartered a peace ship to carry delegates from the Woman's Peace Party to Europe. On December 4 it sailed from New York. House dismissed Ford's views on peace as "crude and unimportant." Ford, he concluded, "is a mechanical genius without education and without much general ability. He seems to be a man who may become a prey to all sorts of faddists who desire his money." House Diary, Nov. 21, 1915.

24. Knock, *To End All Wars*, 55–58: John Milton Cooper Jr., *Breaking the Heart of the World: Woodrow Wilson and the Fight for the League of Nations* (New York, 2001), 12–15.

25. David French, *British Strategy and War Aims, 1914–1916* (London, Eng., 1986), 100–31.

26. Ibid., 136–73; David Stevenson, *Cataclysm: The First World War as Political Tragedy* (New York, 2004), 219–21.

27. Roy Jenkins, *Asquith: Portrait of a Man and an Era* (New York, 1964), 370–86: John Grigg, *Lloyd George: From Peace to War, 1912–1916* (Berkeley, Calif., 1985), 331.

28. Ernest R. May, *The World War and American Isolation, 1914–1917* (Cambridge, Mass., 1959), 314–16; Page to House, Dec. 7, 1915, House Papers; Keith Robbins, *Sir Edward Grey: A Biography of Lord Grey of Fallodon* (London, Eng., 1971), 321–36.

29. Grey to House, Nov. 11, 1915, House Papers; in late November James Bryce sent House a less diplomatic letter, asserting that Germany "would not listen to any [peace] terms we could propose." Bryce to House, Nov. 26, 1915, House Papers.

30. Link, *Wilson: The Struggle for Neutrality, 1914–1915* (Princeton, N.J., 1960), 682–93; Grey to House, Nov. 11, 1915, House Papers.

31. House Diary, Nov. 25, 28, 1915.

32. House Diary, Oct. 26, Nov. 28, 1915; House to Wilson, Oct. 30, 1915, Dec. 1, 1915, to T. W. House, Dec. 2, 1915, House Papers.

33. Link, *Wilson: Confusions and Crises*, 17–22; "An Address on Preparedness to the Manhattan Club," Nov. 4, 1915, in *PWW*, XXXV, 167–73; Cooper, *Wilson*, 304–5.

34. Knock, *To End All Wars*, 61–63; Link, *Wilson: Confusions and Crises*, 23–37; Paolo E. Coletta, *William Jennings Bryan: Political Puritan, 1915–1925* (Lincoln, Neb., 1969), 5–15.

35. "An Annual Message on the State of the Union," Dec. 7, 1915, in *PWW*, XXXV, 293–310.

36. House Diary, Oct. 31, Nov. 4, 14, 15, Dec. 5, 1915; House to Wilson, Sept. 29, 1915, to Page, Oct. 6, 1915, House Papers; Wilson to House, Oct. 4, 1915, Thomas B. Love to House, Dec. 13, 21, 1915, House Papers.

37. House Diary, Dec. 14, 15, 1915.

38. House Diary, Nov. 28, Dec. 15, 1915; Wilson to House, Dec. 24, 1915, House Papers; John Milton Cooper Jr., *Walter Hines Page: The Southerner as American, 1855–1918* (Chapel Hill, N.C., 1977), 313–16.

39. Wilson to Edith Galt, Sept. 2, 10, 11, 1915, in *PWW*, XXXIV, 405, 441, 453. House shared many but not all of Wilson's judgments. He agreed that Spring-Rice was unfit for his position and realized that Page saw "but one side of a question." But he liked Bernstorff and felt that he deserved "great credit" for avoiding war with Germany. He realized that Gerard's abilities were limited, but defended him against Wilson's harsh criticisms and wanted to keep him in Berlin. House Diary, Oct. 14, 30, Nov. 5, 11, 24, Dec. 12, 15, 17, 1915; House to Gerard, Oct. 6, Dec. 12, 1915, House Papers.

40. Link, *Wilson: Confusions and Crises*, 111–13; House Diary, Nov. 28, Dec. 18, 1915.

41. Wilson to House, Dec. 17, 24, House Papers; House to Wilson, Dec. 22, 1915, House Papers; throughout the fall Wilson, House, and Lansing had continued to work on the Pan American Pact, on October 15 redrafting its articles. Clearly they regarded it as a model for the postwar settlement in Europe. House Diary, Oct. 13, 14, 15; House to Lansing, Oct. 12, 30, Nov. 20, 1915, House Papers.

42. Wilson to House, Dec. 24, 1915, House to Wilson, Dec. 26, 1915, House Papers.

43. Edith Galt to House, Oct. 18, 1915, to Mr. and Mrs. House, Nov. 7, 1915, House Papers; House Diary, Nov. 4, 5, 22, 1915; Robert S. Lovett to House, Nov. 1, 1915, House Papers.

44. Weinstein, *Wilson*, 294–95; House Diary, Nov. 22, 1915.

45. House Diary, Nov. 30, 1915; Edith Galt to Wilson, Nov. 30, 1915, in *PWW*, XXXV, 275–76.

46. House Diary, Dec. 15, 1915; Levin misinterprets Edith's remark, claiming that she was apologizing for not inviting House to the wedding. Phyllis Lee Levin,

Edith and Woodrow: The Wilson White House (New York, 2001), 146; both Miller and Cooper claim that House was not invited to the wedding. Miller, *Ellen and Edith*, 130; Cooper, *Wilson*, 306.

47. Shachtman, *Edith & Woodrow*, 122–24; House Diary, Dec. 15, 1915.

48. House Diary, Dec. 25, 1915; House to Wilson, Dec. 26, 1915, Wilson to House, Dec, 27, 1915, House Papers.

CHAPTER 18

1. House Diary, Dec. 28, 1915; Auchincloss to House, Dec. 30, 1915, House Papers; Auchincloss Diary, Dec. 28, 1915; House to Auchincloss, Dec. 29, 1915, House Papers.

2. House Diary, Jan. 5, 1916; House to Edward S. Martin, Jan. 4, 1916, to Auchincloss, Jan. 11, 1916, House Papers.

3. Francis Sheppard, *London: A History* (New York, 1998), 321; Page to Wilson, Dec. 31, 1915, in Arthur S. Link, ed., *The Papers of Woodrow Wilson* [*PWW*], 68 vols. (Princeton, N.J., 1966-93), XXXV, 412–17.

4. John Keegan, *The First World War* (New York, 1999), 274–77; George H. Cassar, *Asquith as War Leader* (London, Eng., 1994), 171–72.

5. David French, *British Strategy and War Aims, 1914–1916* (London, Eng., 1986), 173–75.

6. House Diary, Jan. 6, 1916; House to Wilson, Jan. 7, 1916 (telegram), Jan. 7, 1916 (letter), House Papers. In his letter to Wilson reporting on this conversation, House claimed that he had spoken about America's "shipping troubles" with Grey. The next day he also took up the issue with Grey's private secretary, Eric Drummond, when he objected to Britain's "high-handed policy upon the seas." House Diary, Jan. 8, 1916.

7. House Diary, Jan. 10, 1916; Jason Tomes, *Balfour and Foreign Policy: The International Thought of a Conservative Statesman* (Cambridge, Eng., 1997), 148–50.

8. House Diary, Jan. 6, 10, 1916; House to Wilson, Jan. 10, 1916 (telegram), to Wilson, Jan. 11, 1916, House Papers. On January 7 House cabled Wilson asking for "some assurance of your willingness to cooperate in a policy seeking to bring about and maintain permanent peace." Wilson responded that when the opportunity came he would "cooperate in a policy seeking to bring about and maintain permanent peace among civilized nations." House to Wilson, Jan. 7, 1916 (telegram), Wilson to House, Jan. 9, 1916 (telegram), House Papers.

9. Wilson to House, Jan. 12, 1916 (telegram), House Papers; House Diary, Jan. 12, 1916, House to Wilson, Jan. 13, 1913, House Papers.

10. House Diary, Jan. 14, 1916; House to Wilson, Jan. 15, 1916, House Papers; John Grigg, *Lloyd George: From Peace to War, 1912–1916* (Berkeley, Calif., 1985), 420.

11. House Diary, Jan. 14, 1916; House to Wilson, Jan. 15, 1916, House Papers. On January 13 House had first discussed peace terms with Lord Bryce, House Diary, Jan. 13, 1916.

12. House Diary, Jan. 15, 1916; House to Wilson, Jan. 16, 1916, House Papers.

13. House Diary, Jan. 18, 19, 1916.

14. House Diary, Jan. 19, 1916.

15. John Milton Cooper Jr., *Walter Hines Page: The Southerner as American, 1855–1918* (Chapel Hill, N.C., 1977), 310–24; House Diary, Jan. 7, 9, 12, 15, 18, 19, 1916.

16. House Diary, Jan. 20, 21, 23, 24, 25, 26, 1916; House to Auchincloss, Jan. 25, 1916, to Wilson, Jan. 25, 1916, House Papers.

17. Thomas Friedrich, *Berlin between the Wars* (New York, 1991), 27–28; Holger H. Herwig, *The First World War: Germany and Austria–Hungary, 1914–1918* (New York, 1997), 229.

18. Roger Chickering, *Imperial Germany and the Great War, 1914–1918*, 2nd. ed. (Cambridge, Eng., 2004), 32–50; Gerard to House, Jan. 3, 1916, House Papers.

19. Herwig, *The First World War*, 179–183; Robert T. Foley, *German Strategy and the Path to Verdun: Erich von Falkenhayn and the Development of Attrition, 1870–1916* (Cambridge, Eng., 2005), 181–193.

20. Chickering, *Imperial Germany and the Great War*, 60–64.

21. Ernest R. May, *The World War and American Isolation, 1914–1917* (Cambridge, Mass., 1959), 232–48.

22. House to Auchincloss, Jan. 25, 1916, House Papers; House Diary, Jan. 26, 1916.

23. House Diary, Jan. 27, 28, 1916; The chancellor's version of the conversation is in *PWW*, XXXVI, 123–24, while the kaiser's summary of it is in Walter Gorlitz, ed., *The Kaiser and His Court* (New York, 1961), 132; Reinhard R. Doerries, *Imperial Challenge: Ambassador Count Bernstorff and German–American Relations, 1908–1917* (Chapel Hill, N.C., 1989), 133–34.

24. House Diary, Jan. 28, 1916.

25. House Diary, Jan. 29, 1916; House to Auchincloss, Jan. 28, 1916, House Papers.

26. House to Wilson, Jan. 30, 1916 (telegram), Feb. 3, 1916, House Papers.

27. House Diary, Feb. 1, 1916; House to Auchincloss, Feb. 4, 1916, House Papers.

28. Colin Jones, *Paris: Biography of a City* (New York, 2004), 377–79; Jay Winter and Jean-Louis Robert, eds., *Capital Cities at War: Paris, London, Berlin, 1914–1919* (Cambridge, Eng., 1997), 531.

29. J. F. V. Keiger, *Raymond Poincaré* (Cambridge, Eng., 1997), 204–25.

30. Robert A. Doughty, *Pyrrhic Victory: French Strategy and Operations in the Great War* (Cambridge, Mass., 2005), 228–39.

31. House Diary, Feb. 1, 2, 1916; in Cambon's version of the conversation, House assured him that so long as the actions of the Allies were guided by military necessity, "inevitably America will enter the war, *before the end of the year*, and will align herself on the side of the Allies. However, for that to happen, it would be necessary for an incident to occur that would cause the American people to rally behind the President." Cambon recorded that "this statement from Colonel House astonished me. I had him repeat it and, after having noted it in English, I had him read it. He said to me: 'exactly.'" "Conversation

du Colonel House avec M. Jules Cambon, Feb. 2, 1916," in *PWW*, XXXVI, 126.

32. Lady Algernon G. Lennox, ed., *The Diary of Lord Bertie of Thame, 1914–1918* (New York, 1924), I, 297; House Diary, Feb. 4, 5, 6, 7, 1916.

33. Arthur S. Link, *Wilson: Confusions and Crises, 1915–1916* (Princeton, N.J., 1964), 126; Lennox, ed., *The Diary of Lord Bertie of Thame*, I, 301; J. Cambon, "Deuxieme Entrevue du Colonel House," Feb. 7, 1916, in *PWW*, XXXVI, 148–50; David Stevenson, *Cataclysm: The First World War as Political Tragedy* (New York, 2004), 114–16.

34. House to Wilson, Feb. 3, 7, 9, 1916, House Papers.

35. Link, *Confusions and Crises*, 42–54; "An Address on Preparedness in Kansas City," Feb. 2, 1916, in *PWW*, XXXVI, 100–110; John Whiteclay Chambers II, *To Raise an Army: The Draft Comes to Modern America* (New York, 1987), 106–14; John Milton Cooper Jr., *Woodrow Wilson: A Biography* (New York, 2009), 308–12.

36. Link, *Confusions and Crises*, 76–100; Lansing to House, Jan. 26, 1916, House Papers; House to Wilson, Jan. 15, 1916 (letter), Jan. 15, 1916 (telegram), Jan. 30, 1916 (telegram), Feb. 3, 1916, Feb. 7, 1916 (telegram), to Lansing, Feb. 14, 1916, House Papers.

37. Link, *Confusions and Crises*, 142–44; Wilson to Lansing, Jan. 10, 1916, in *PWW*, XXXV, 457.

38. Link, *Confusions and Crises*, 146–59.

39. Link, *Confusions and Crises*, 162–66; House Diary, Feb. 11, 12, 1916; Lansing to House, Feb. 3, 1916, House to Lansing, Feb. 14, 1916 (telegram), House Papers.

40. Link, *Confusions and Crises*, 167–94; Cooper, *Wilson*, 312–15.

41. House Diary, Feb. 8, 9, 1916; House to Wilson, Feb. 9, 1916, House Papers.

42. Page Diary, Feb. 9, 13, 15, 24, 1916, Walter Hines Page Papers; House Diary, Feb. 9, 1916; House to Wilson, Feb. 10, 1916, House Papers.

43. House Diary, Feb. 10, 1916; House to Wilson, Feb. 10, 1916 (letter), Feb. 10, 1916 (telegram), House Papers.

44. House Diary, Feb. 10, 1916.

45. House to Wilson, Feb. 11, 1916 (letter), Feb. 11, 1916 (telegram), to Auchincloss, Feb. 11, 1916, House Papers; House Diary, Feb. 11, 1916.

46. House Diary, Feb. 14, 1916; Link, *Confusions and Crises*, 131–34; Grigg, *Lloyd George*, 419–21; David Lloyd George, *War Memoirs of David Lloyd George, 1915–1916* (Boston, Mass., 1937), II, 137–38.

47. House Diary, Feb. 14, 1916; House to Wilson, Feb. 15, 1916, House Papers.

48. House Diary, Feb. 15, 16, 17, 1916; Balfour to House, March 2, 1916, House Papers.

49. House Diary, Feb. 21, 22, 1916.

50. House Diary, Feb. 23, 1916; Viscount Grey of Fallodon, *Twenty-Five Years, 1892–1916* (New York, 1925), II, 127–36; a perceptive discussion of the

House-Grey Memorandum is in Cooper, *Wilson*, 315–19; see also John Milton Cooper Jr., "The British Response to the House-Grey Memorandum: New Evidence and New Questions," *Journal of American History*, 59 (Mar. 1973), 958–71.

51. "Memorandum," Feb. 22, 1916, House Papers.

52. Cassar, *Asquith as War Leader*, 175; Fry, *Lloyd George and Foreign Policy*, 227–29.

53. Fry, *Lloyd George and Foreign Policy*, 222–24; Joyce Grigsby Williams, *Colonel House and Sir Edward Grey: A Study in Anglo-American Diplomacy* (Boston, Mass., 1984), 84–85; Lloyd George, *War Memoirs*, II, 139–43; Daniel Larsen argues that by early 1916, most British civilian leaders were pessimistic about Allied military prospects and "prepared to accept. . . an American mediated compromise peace." He gives House high marks as a diplomat. Daniel Larsen, "War Pessimism in Britain and an American Peace in Early 1916," *International History Review*, 34, 4 (2012), 795–817.

54. French, *British Strategy and War Aims*, 192–93; British codebreakers, working out of Room 40 in the Admiralty Old Building, had little trouble breaking the codes and ciphers used by the state department and by House and Wilson. As Christopher Andrew remarks, Americans were still in a "state of cryptographic innocence." By 1916, however, House had become more security conscious and sent important information in letters placed in the American diplomatic pouch. *Her Majesty's Secret Service: The Making of the British Intelligence Community* (New York, 1986), 108; Patrick Beesly, *Room 40: British Naval Intelligence, 1914–18* (New York, 1982), 213; Daniel Larsen, "British Intelligence and the 1916 Mediation Mission of Colonel Edward M. House, "*Intelligence and National Security*, 25 (Oct. 2010), 682–704.

55. House Diary, Feb. 10, 14, 16–18, 21, 22, 1916; House to Wallace, Feb. 16, 18,1916, House Papers; Link, *Confusions and Crises*, 137.

56. House Diary, Feb. 23, 24, March 4, 5, 1916; House to Wilson, Feb. 25, 1916 (telegram), Wilson to House, March 3, 1916 (telegram), House Papers.

CHAPTER 19

1. House Diary, May 6, 1916; Edith was "crazy to hear all he ['dear Col. House'] has to tell us." Edith Wilson to Alice Gordon Grayson, March 6, 1916, Grayson Papers.

2. Edith Bolling Wilson, *My Memoir* (Indianapolis, Ind., 1939), 89–93; Tom Shachtman, *Edith & Woodrow: A Presidential Romance* (New York, 1981), 125–33; Kristie Miller, *Ellen and Edith: Woodrow Wilson's First Ladies* (Lawrence, Kans., 2010), 133–37.

3. House Diary, March 6, 7, 1916; House to Grey, March 8, 1916 (telegram), March 10, 1916, House Papers; the phrase now read: "and, if it failed to secure peace, the United States would probably leave the conference as a belligerent on the side of the Allies, if Germany was unreasonable."

4. House Diary, March 6, 1916; Wilson to House, March 9, 1916, House to Wilson, March 10, 12, 1916, House Papers.

5. Robert W. Tucker, *Woodrow Wilson and the Great War: Reconsidering America's Neutrality, 1914–1917* (Charlottesville, Va., 2007), 144–73; John Milton Cooper Jr., *Woodrow Wilson: A Biography* (New York, 2009), 318–19; Wilson to William J. Stone, Feb. 24, 1916, in Arthur S. Link, ed., *The Papers of Woodrow Wilson [PWW]*, 68 vols. (Princeton, N.J., 1966-93), XXXVI, 213–14.

6. John Turner, *British Politics and the Great War: Coalition and Conflict, 1915–18* (New Haven, Conn., 1992), 98–99; Michael G. Fry, *Lloyd George and Foreign Policy,* Vol. I: *The Education of a Statesman, 1890–1916* (Montreal, Canada, 1977), 228–30; Lady Algernon G. Lennox, ed., *The Diary of Lord Bertie of Thame* (London, Eng., 1924), I, 311.

7. Grey to House, March 24, 1916, Plunkett to House, March 29, 1916, House Papers; Arthur S. Link, *Wilson: Confusions and Crises, 1915–1916* (Princeton, N.J., 1964), 140.

8. Link, *Confusions and Crises*, 193–200; John Mason Hart, *Revolutionary Mexico: The Coming and Process of the Mexican Revolution* (Berkeley, Calif., 1987), 310–12; "An Annual Message on the State of the Union," Dec. 7, 1915, in *PWW,* XXXV, 293–310.

9. Hart, *Revolutionary Mexico*, 312–18; Friedrich Katz, *The Secret War in Mexico: Europe, the United States, and the Mexican Revolution* (Chicago, Ill., 1981), 294–97.

10. Katz, *The Secret War in Mexico*, 302–14; Link, *Confusions and Crises*, 201–15; Joseph P. Tumulty, *Woodrow Wilson as I Know Him* (New York, 1921), 157–60.

11. Katz, *The Secret War in Mexico*, 308–14; Link, *Confusions and Crises*, 216–21.

12. Friedrich Katz, *The Life and Times of Pancho Villa* (Stanford, Calif., 1998), 545–82; Link, *Confusions and Crises*, 280–318; Wilson to Jane Addams, June 28, 1916, in *PWW,* XXXVII, 316.

13. House Diary, March 15, 17, 29, 1916; House to Wilson, March 10, 1916, to Page, March 15, 1916, House Papers.

14. House Diary, May 24, 31, 1916; House to Hugh Wallace, March 24, 1916, to Wilson, April 7, June 19, 25, July 1, 1916, House Papers; Wilson to House, June 22, 1916, House Papers; Cooper, *Wilson*, 319–23.

15. House to Plunkett, March 15, 1916, House Papers; Balfour to House, March 2, 1916, House Papers; House to Wilson, March 12, 1916, to Balfour, March 24, 1916, to Gerard, March 24, 1916, House Papers; House Diary, March 12, 19, 29, 1916.

16. Ernest R. May, *The World War and American Isolation, 1914–1917* (Cambridge, Mass., 1959), 248–52.

17. Link, *Confusions and Crises*, 229–30; Cooper, *Wilson*, 323–26.

18. House Diary, March 20, 27, 28, 29, 1916.

19. House Diary, March 30, 1916; House also told Ambassador Jusserand that "in perhaps the not too distant future, [the United States] would take an active

part in the war." Jusserand to Briand, March 31, 1916, in *PWW*, XXXVI, 389–91.

20. Link, *Confusions and Crises*, 232–33; House Diary, April 2, 1916.

21. Auchincloss Diary, April 5, 6, 1916; Link, *Confusions and Crises*, 236–37; House to Wilson, April 3, 1916, House Papers; House Diary, April 5, 6, 1916.

22. House Diary, April 6, 1916; House to Grey, April 6, 1916 (telegram), April 7, 1916, House Papers.

23. Grey to House, April 8, 1916 (telegram), April 7, 1916, House Papers; House to Wilson, April 8, 1916, House Papers; Plunkett to House, April 19, 1916, House Papers.

24. Link, *Confusions and Crises,* 242–45; House Diary, April 11, 1916.

25. "An Address to a Joint Session of Congress," April 19, 1916, in *PWW*, XXXVI, 506–10; Link, *Confusions and Crises*, 252–55; House Diary, April 19, 21, 22, 25, 1916; House to Wilson, April 8, 19, 1916, House Papers.

26. Link, *Confusions and Crises*, 256–72; Konrad H. Jarausch, *The Enigmatic Chancellor: Bethmann Hollweg and the Hubris of Imperial Germany* (New Haven, Conn., 1973), 287–90.

27. House Diary, May 2, 1916; Link, *Confusions and Crises*, 273–79; Wilson to House, May 5, 1916, House to Wilson, May 5, 1916, House Papers; Bernstorff to House, June 16, 1916, House Papers.

28. Arthur S. Link, *Wilson: Campaigns for Progressivism and Peace, 1916–1917* (Princeton, N.J., 1965), 10–16; Spring-Rice to Grey, May 10, 1916, in Stephen Gwynn, ed., *The Letters and Friendships of Sir Cecil Spring Rice: A Record* (Boston, Mass., 1929), II, 331–33.

29. Gerard to House, May 31, 1916, House Papers; Link, *Wilson: Campaigns for Progressivism and Peace*, 16–17; Thomas J. Knock, *To End All Wars: Woodrow Wilson and the Quest for a New World Order* (New York, 1992), 65–76.

30. House Diary, May 3, 9, 10, 1916; House to Wilson, May 7, 1916, Wilson to House, May 8, 9, 1916, House Papers.

31. House to Grey, May 10, 1916 (telegram), May 11, 1916, House Papers.

32. Grey to House, May 12, 1916, House Papers.

33. House Diary, May 13, 1916; House to Wilson, May 14, 1916, Wilson to House, May 16, 1916, House Papers.

34. House Diary, May 17, 18, 1916; House to Wilson, May 17, 1916, Wilson to House, May 18, 1916, House Papers; House to Grey, May 19, 1916 (telegram), May 23, 27 1916, House Papers; Grey to House, May 23, 25, 1916 (telegram), House Papers.

35. Knock, *To End All Wars*, 75–81; Wilson to House, May 18, 1916, House to Wilson, May 19, 21, 1916 (with memorandum on suggestions for Wilson's speech), House Papers; House Diary, May 22, 26, 1916; Polk to House, May 22, 1916, House Papers.

36. Wilson to House, May 22, 1916, House to Wilson, May 24, 26, 1916, House Papers; House Diary, May 26, 1916; Cooper, *Wilson*, 326–28.

37. "An Address in Washington to the League to Enforce Peace," May 27, 1916, in *PWW*, XXXVII, 113–16; Throughout the late winter and spring of 1916, House and Wilson had continued to pursue the Pan American Pact, which they saw as a model for a league of nations. House sought to gain Britain's adherence to the pact, and by June it seemed as if all the obstacles had been cleared away and that the pact would soon be signed by Argentina, Brazil, Chile, and the United States. The Punitive Expedition, however, aroused anti-American feeling throughout Latin America and confirmed the opposition of the Chilean government to the agreement. The Pan American Pact could never be revived. Knock, *To End All Wars*, 72–84; House Diary, Feb. 20, 21, March 28, 29, 31, April 5, 6, 11, 26, May 3, 26; House to Wilson, June 16, 18, 1916, House Papers; Henry P. Fletcher to House, April 12, 18, May 4, June 15, 24, July 10, 1916, House to Fletcher, June 16, 19, 1916, House Papers.

38. House Diary, May 29, 1916; House to Wilson, May 28, 29, 1916, House Papers; Wilson to House, May 29, 1916, House Papers; Link, *Wilson: Campaigns for Progressivism and Peace*, 26.

39. Link, *Wilson: Campaigns for Progressivism and Peace*, 29–32; Gerard to House, June 7, 1916, House Papers; Reinhard R. Doerries, *Imperial Challenge: Ambassador Count Bernstorff and German–American Relations, 1908–1917* (Chapel Hill, N.C., 1989), 138–40.

40. Knock, *To End All Wars*, 79–81; Link, *Wilson: Campaigns for Progressivism and Peace*, 32–35; David French, *British Strategy and War Aims, 1914–1916* (London, Eng., 1986); House Diary, May 31, 1916; House to Wilson, June 1, 1916, House Papers; Polk to House, June 6, 1916, House Papers.

41. Grey to House, May 29, 1916 (telegram), House Papers; James Bryce to House, May 31, June 8, 12, 1916, House Papers.

42. House Diary, May 30, 1916; House to Page, June 15, 1916, to Bernstorff, June 17, 1916, to Grey, June 1, 1916 (telegram), June 8, 1916, House Papers.

43. House Diary, June 23, 1916; Wilson to House, June 22, 1916, House Papers.

44. Link, *Wilson: Campaigns for Progressivism and Peace*, 36–38.

45. Sir Arthur Willert, *Washington and Other Memories* (Boston, Mass., 1972), 90; House Diary, March 10, 1916; Grayson to Alice Gordon Grayson, March 8, 1916, Grayson Papers.

46. House Diary, March 6, 7, 11, April 6, May 24, 31, 1916; Grayson to House, March 13, 1916, House Papers; John M. Blum, *Joe Tumulty and the Wilson Era* (Boston, Mass., 1951), 117–19; Shachtman, *Edith and Woodrow*, 130–31; Miller, *Ellen and Edith*, 138.

47. House to Page, March 10, April 18, 1916, House Papers; House Diary, May 4, 5, 10, 17, 18, 1916; House to Wilson, May 10, 18, 1916, Wilson to House, May 27, 1916, House Papers; John Milton Cooper Jr., *Walter Hines Page: The Southerner as American, 1855–1918* (Chapel Hill, N.C., 1977), 334–36.

48. House Diary, March 28, 29, 30, April 5, 9, 18, 21, May 3, 15, 17, 29, 1916; House to Lansing, May 30, 1916, Lansing to House, May 31, 1916, House Papers.

49. "Newton D. Baker," in John A. Garraty and Mark C. Carnes, eds., *American National Biography*, 24 vols. (New York, 1999), II, 27–28; August Heckscher, *Woodrow Wilson* (New York, 1991), 380; Douglas B. Craig, *Progressives at War: William G. McAdoo and Newton D. Baker, 1863–1941* (Baltimore, Md., 2013), 11–50.

50. House Diary, March 29, April 6, May 18, 24, 1916; House to Thomas Nelson Page, March 10, 1916, House Papers; "Thomas R. Marshall," in *American National Biography*, XIV, 576–78.

51. Phyllis Lee Levin, *Edith and Woodrow: The Wilson White House* (New York, 2001), 154–60; Edith Galt to House, April 26, 1916, House Papers; House Diary, March 30, April 11, 1916.

52. "A Memorandum by Ray Stannard Baker of a Conversation at the White House," May 12, 1916, in *PWW*, XXXVII, 31–38.

53. Edwin A. Weinstein, *Woodrow Wilson: A Medical and Psychological Biography* (Princeton, N.J., 1981), 294–95; House Diary, April 11, May 3, 1916, House Papers.

54. House to Wilson, May 28, 1916, Wilson to House, May 29, June 22, 1916, House Papers; House Diary, June 1, 1916.

CHAPTER 20

1. Franklin K. Lane to House, Nov. 20, 1914, House to Lane, Nov. 23, 1914, House Papers; House Diary, Jan. 28, 1915.

2. Kathleen Dalton, *Theodore Roosevelt: A Strenuous Life* (New York, 2002), 463–66; Woolley to House, April 1, 1916, House to Gerard, May 11, 1916, House Papers.

3. House to Gerard, March 24, 1916, House Papers; House Diary, May 12, 1916.

4. House Diary, March 29, April 13, 18, 21, May 3, 15, 19, 28, 29, June 17, 22, 1916; House to Wilson, April 20, 21, 23, May 30, June 12, 1916, and memo for Wilson June 16, 1916, House Papers; Wilson to House, June 6, 11, 1916, House Papers.

5. Wilson to House, May 22, 1916, House to Wilson, May 19, 1916, House Papers; House to Gerard, July 8, 1916, House Papers; John M. Blum, *Joe Tumulty and the Wilson Era* (Boston, Mass., 1951), 118–19.

6. House Diary, March 29, April 19, May 3, 30, June 1, 1916; House to Wilson, May 15, 29, 30, 1916, and Wilson to House, May 29, 1916, House Papers. House met with Glynn to outline his speech and to read drafts of it.

7. Woolley to House, June 10, 1916, House to Wilson, June 10, 1916, to Gerard, July 8, 1916, House Papers; John Milton Cooper Jr., *Woodrow Wilson: A Biography* (New York, 2009), 334–41.

8. Arthur S. Link, *Wilson: Confusions and Crises: 1915–1916* (Princeton, N.J., 1964), 323–27, 356–62; Maureen A. Flanagan, *America Reformed: Progressives and Progressivism, 1890s–1920s* (New York, 2007), 214–15; Melvin I. Urofsky, *Louis D. Brandeis: A Life* (New York, 2009), 430–59.

9. House Diary, Nov. 16, Dec. 18, 1912, Jan. 23, Feb. 13, 1913, March 31, April 28, 1916; Chandler P. Anderson Diary, Feb. 10, 1916.

10. House Diary, March 4, 5, 24, 1915; House to Wilson, July 3, 1916; David Traxel, *Crusader Nation: The United States in Peace and the Great War, 1898–1920* (New York, 2006), 241.

11. Michael Kazin, *A Godly Hero: The Life of William Jennings Bryan* (New York, 2006), 203–6; David Sarasohn, *The Party of Reform: Democrats in the Progressive Era* (Jackson, Miss., 1989), 183–91.

12. Arthur S. Link, *Wilson: Campaigns for Progressivism and Peace, 1916–1917* (Princeton, N.J., 1965), 40–42.

13. Ibid., 43–48.

14. House to Polk, June 8, 1916, to Page, June 15, 1916, House Papers.

15. House sought to shape his legacy by guiding friendly journalists in their assessment of his career. On June 9, 1916, the *New York Times* magazine section carried an article by Charles Willis Thompson which claimed that House "is a statesman, a politician, a policy-maker, and a Warwick" who had made Woodrow Wilson president. House, Thompson concluded, "is not an errand boy or a phonograph. He is a natural statesman who has done large things and is capable of doing more. It would be worth a good deal to know how much of the history of the Wilson Administration is ascribable to him." Andrews to House, Oct. 28, 1915, House to Andrews, June 22, 1915, House Papers; House Diary, March 8, 19, April 22, June 17, July 9, Aug. 9, Sept. 16, 1916.

16. House Diary, July 9, 1916.

17. *Reminiscences*, 41, 51, 60.

18. Edith Bolling Wilson, *My Memoir* (Indianapolis, Ind., 1939), 102; Sarasohn, *The Party of Reform*, 183–91; Cooper, *Wilson*, 332–33, 341–49; Elizabeth Sanders, *Roots of Reform: Farmers, Workers, and the American State, 1877–1917* (Chicago, Ill., 1999), 367–86.

19. Link, *Wilson: Campaigns for Progressivism and Peace*, 83–92; August Heckscher, *Woodrow Wilson* (New York, 1991), 410; "A Memorandum by Homer S. Cummings," Aug. 7, 1916, in Arthur S. Link, ed., *The Papers of Woodrow Wilson* [*PWW*], 68 vols. (Princeton, N.J., 1966-93), XXXVIII, 5–8.

20. House to Wilson, June 15, 18, 1916, House Papers; House Diary, June 21, 22, 1916; memorandum on campaign organization, June 20, 1916, House Papers. House had outlined a similar scheme in *Philip Dru*, 93–94.

21. Wilson to House, June 22, July 5, 1916, House to Wilson, July 5, 1916, House Papers; House tried to influence Wilson's choice of a second justice for the Supreme Court, urging him "not to appoint a man of too advanced ideas. It will frighten the business element." House to Wilson, June 19, July 5, 13, 1916, House Papers; Gregory to House, July 10, 1916, House Papers; Wilson to House, July 23, 1916, House Papers; House Diary, June 17, 19, 1916.

22. Link, *Wilson: Campaigns for Progressivism and Peace*, 50; House to Wilson, Aug. 3, 1916, House Papers; House Diary, Aug. 15, 1916.

23. House to Wilson, Aug. 3, 1916, to Gerard, Aug. 18, 1916, to Frederick C. Penfield, Aug. 28, 1916, to Lord Loreburn, Aug. 29, 1916, House Papers.

24. Wilson to House, July 23, 1916, House to Wilson, July 25, 1916, House Papers; Edith Wilson to House, Aug. 29, 1916, House Papers.

25. McAdoo to House, July 17, Aug. 30, 1916, House Papers; House Diary, Aug. 27, 1916.

26. Holger H. Herwig, *The First World War: Germany and Austria-Hungary, 1914–1918* (London, Eng., 1997), 199–213; John Keegan, *The First World War* (New York, 1999), 286–99.

27. Minnie Paget to House, summer 1916, House Papers.

28. David French, *British Strategy and War Aims, 1914–1916* (London, Eng., 1986), 204–16; George H. Cassar, *Asquith as War Leader* (London, Eng., 1994), 191–95; John Grigg, *Lloyd George: From Peace to War, 1912–1916* (Berkeley, Calif., 1985), 422–28.

29. Roger Chickering, *Imperial Germany and the Great War, 1914–1918,* 2nd ed. (Cambridge, Eng., 2004), 52, 65–71; Herwig, *The First World War,* 228–96.

30. Chickering, *Imperial Germany,* 71–76; Lamar Cecil, *Wilhelm II: Emperor and Exile, 1900–1941* (Chapel Hill, N.C., 1996), 237–39.

31. House Diary, June 23, 29, Aug. 27, 1916; House to Wilson, June 18, 25, 27, 1916, Wilson to House, June 22, July 2, 1916, House Papers; Page to House, June 16, 1916, Grey to House, June 28, 1916, House Papers.

32. Link, *Wilson: Campaigns for Progressivism and Peace,* 65–71; House to Frazier, July 27, 1916, Wilson to House, July 23, 1916, House Papers.

33. House to Wilson, July 30, 1916, House Papers; House Diary, Sept. 3, 1916.

34. Wilson to House, July 2, 23, House to Wilson, July 5, 1916, House Papers; Polk to House, Aug. 12, 1916, House to Polk, July 25, 1916, House Papers.

35. Link, *Wilson: Campaigns for Progressivism and Peace,* 71–72; Page Diary, Aug. 30, 1916; Robert Lansing, *War Memoirs* (Indianapolis, Ind., 1935), 170.

36. John Milton Cooper Jr., *Walter Hines Page: The Southerner as American, 1855–1918* (Chapel Hill, N.C., 1977), 337–49; Link, Wilson: Campaigns for Progressivism and Peace, 72–73.

37. House to Polk, Aug. 13, 1916, Polk to House, Aug. 18, 1916, House Papers; Page to House, Aug. 26, 1916, House to Page, Aug. 30, 1916, House Papers.

38. Page, "Notes Toward an Explanation of British Feeling toward the United States," Sept. 15, 1916, House Papers; House Diary, Sept. 19, 23, 25, 30, 1916.

CHAPTER 21

1. House Diary, Sept. 16, 1916; House to Wilson, Sept. 21, 1916, House Papers.

2. House Diary, Sept. 18, 23, 1916; House to Wilson, Sept. 19, 1916, Wilson to House, Sept. 20, 1916, House Papers.

3. "A Speech in Long Branch, New Jersey, Accepting the Presidential Nomination," Sept. 2, 1916, in Arthur S. Link, ed., *The Papers of Woodrow*

Wilson [*PWW*], 68 vols (Princeton, N.J., 1966-93), XXXVIII, 126–39; Arthur S. Link, *Wilson: Campaigns for Progressivism and Peace, 1916–1917* (Princeton, N.J., 1965), 93–100; McCormick to House, Sept. 11, 1916, House Papers.

4. Wilson to Cleveland H. Dodge, Sept. 7, 1916, in *PWW*, XXXVIII, 157–58; Edith Bolling Wilson, *My Memoir* (Indianapolis, Ind., 1939), 103–8.

5. Link, *Wilson: Campaigns for Progressivism and Peace*, 100–103, 124–28; David Sarasohn, *The Party of Reform: Democrats in the Progressive Era* (Jackson, Miss., 1989), 199–204; Lewis L. Gould, *Reform and Regulation: American Politics from Roosevelt to Wilson* (Prospect Heights, Ill., 1986), 185–86.

6. House Diary, Sept. 23, 24, 1916.

7. House Diary, Sept. 24, 1916.

8. John Milton Cooper Jr., *Woodrow Wilson: A Biography* (New York, 2009), 347–49; Link, *Wilson: Campaigns for Progressivism and Peace*, 108–11; Thomas J. Knock, *To End All Wars: Woodrow Wilson and the Quest for a New World Order* (New York, 1992), 95–98.

9. Sarasohn, *The Party of Reform*, 213–18; House Diary, Nov. 2, 1916.

10. Link, *Wilson: Campaigns for Progressivism and Peace*, 141–45; Woolley to House, June 1, 10, 1916, House Papers.

11. House to Axson, Aug. 19, 1916, House Papers; House Diary, Sept. 30, 1916; August Heckscher, *Woodrow Wilson* (New York, 1991), 413–14.

12. Link, *Wilson: Campaigns for Progressivism and Peace*, 148–53; "The Final Campaign Address," in *PWW*, XXXVIII, 608–15; Wilson to Joseph R. Wilson, Oct. 10, 1916, in *PWW*, XXXVIII, 451–52; Cooper, *Wilson*, 349–55.

13. House Diary, Oct. 2, 3, 4, 5, 7, 8, 9, 11, 14; House to Wilson, Oct. 5, 1916, to Arthur Hugh Frazier, Oct. 6, 1916, House Papers. House had a second encounter with Henry Ford, who supported Wilson. House was unimpressed with the great entrepreneur, finding him "crude, ignorant, and with very little general information. I cannot discuss foreign affairs because he knows so little about them. He knows even less about politics and the only safe ground was practical mechanics and farming. I think he is a genius along these lines and is an idealist and has many fine qualities. Just how he succeeded in amassing so large a fortune is something of a mystery to me. He is wiry and nervous and has so little composure that one sympathizes with him." House Diary, Oct. 2, 1916; *PWW*, XXXVIII, 187.

14. House Diary, Oct. 16, 1916; House to Wilson, Oct. 20, 23, 1916, to McAdoo, Oct. 24, 1916, to Frederick C. Penfield, Oct. 25, 1916, House Papers; House to Wilson, Sept. 30, Oct. 20, 23, 1916, House Papers.

15. House Diary, Oct. 18, 1916; Wilson to House, Oct. 24, 1916, House Papers.

16. House Diary, Oct. 19, 20, 27, Nov. 3, 19, 1916; House to Wilson, Oct. 20, 1916, House Papers; Link, *Wilson: Campaigns for Progressivism and Peace*, 153–56; Cooper, *Wilson*, 356–57; Gregory's account of the episode is in Gregory to House, June 15, 1931, House Papers.

17. House Diary, Oct. 22, 23, 25, 26, 27, 31, Nov. 1, 1916.

18. House Diary, Nov. 2, 1916; "Estimate Given Woodrow Wilson," Nov. 2, 1916, House Papers; House to Wilson, Nov. 4, 1916, House Papers. House remained loyal to his old Texas protégé, Senator Charles Allen Culberson. Culberson, who had moved from the governorship to the Senate in 1898, suffered from Bright's disease, depression, and alcoholism. Nevertheless, he decided to run for reelection, publicly admitting "that I am not strong enough to campaign in the state." In mid-summer Culberson won a place in the runoff and, with the support of Burleson, Gregory, and other members of "our crowd," won a decisive victory in the Democratic primary in late August. House supported his friend's campaign, reassuring him that "the best work that is being done in the world today is being done by semi-invalids." Lewis L. Gould, *Progressives and Prohibitionists: Texas Democrats in the Wilson Era* (Austin, Tex., 1973), 174–83; House to Culberson, May 11, 1916, House Papers.

19. Edith Bolling Wilson, *My Memoir*, 114–16.

20. Link, *Wilson: Campaigns for Progressivism and Peace,* 156–58; Daniel D. Stid, *The President as Statesman: Woodrow Wilson and the Constitution* (Lawrence, Kans., 1998), 105–17; "President Glad the Fight Is Over," Nov. 10, 1916, in *PWW*, XXXVIII, 625–29.

21. House Diary, Nov. 9, 1916.

22. House Diary, Nov. 12, 1916.

23. Gould, *Reform and Regulation,* 190–91; Sarasohn, *The Party of Reform*, 218–38; Link, *Wilson: Campaigns for Progressivism and Peace,* 160–64; Cooper, *Wilson*, 357–61.

24. Brooks to House, Sept. 15, 1916, Frazier to House, Sept. 29, 1916, Penfield to House, Sept. 20, 1916, Grey to Phillips, Oct. 3, 1916, Gerard to House, Sept. 6, 1916, House Papers.

25. Bernstorff to House, Oct. 18, 1916, with memo from Berlin, House Papers; House Diary, Oct. 3, 8, 11, Nov. 2, 1916; House to Wilson, Oct. 20, 27, Nov. 6, 1916, to Grey, Oct. 24, 1916, House Papers; Wilson to House, Oct. 10, 1916, House Papers.

26. Wilson to House, Nov. 13, 1916 (telegram), House Papers; House Diary, Nov. 14, 15, 1916.

27. House Diary, Nov. 15, 1916.

28. House Diary, Nov. 15, 1916; throughout the fall, House worked closely with Lansing, but was concerned about the "brusqueness" of his diplomatic notes and about his poor health. He recorded that "I feel sorry for Lansing. He is doing his work conscientiously but it is clear that his health is not equal to the strain. When he was here the other day at lunch he looked drawn and I noticed he drank three large cups of coffee. A man cannot keep up on stimulants. I never try to stimulate myself no matter how hard my work or what pressure I am under. I go as far as my strength will allow and then I rest by lying on my back as inertly as possible. The results are better than if stimulants are taken." House Diary, Oct. 13, 1916.

29. House Diary, Nov. 15, 19, 1916; John M. Blum, *Joe Tumulty and the Wilson Era* (Boston, Mass., 1951), 120–22; Phyllis Lee Levin, *Edith and Woodrow: The Wilson White House* (New York, 2001), 169–74; Kristie Miller, *Ellen and Edith: Woodrow Wilson's First Ladies* (Lawrence, Kans., 2010), 144; twice in the fall House conferred with Assistant Secretary of State "Billy" Phillips about diplomatic appointments, sending the president detailed recommendations. He was also instrumental in bringing Ambassador Gerard back to the United States and in arranging for a warm reception. House realized Gerard's weaknesses as a diplomat—his loquacity and "brusqueness of manner"—but resisted the German government's efforts to have him replaced. He valued the ambassador's loyalty to the administration and made sure that "our friend Jimmie" returned to Berlin. House Diary, Oct. 1, 10, 20, Nov. 20, Dec. 2, 14, 1916; House to Polk, Sept. 25, 1916, to Wilson, Oct. 1, Dec. 5, 1916, House Papers.

30. House Diary, Nov. 15, 1916.

31. Martin Gilbert, *The First World War: A Complete History* (New York, 1994), 282–302.

32. Robert B. Asprey, *The German High Command at War: Hindenburg and Ludendorff Conduct World War I* (New York, 1991), 255–62, 286; Holger H. Herwig, *The First World War: Germany and Austria–Hungary, 1914–1918* (London, Eng., 1997), 255–96; Roger Chickering, *Imperial Germany and the Great War, 1914–1918*, 2nd ed. (Cambridge, Eng., 2004), 71–87.

33. Chickering, *Imperial Germany and the Great War*, 87–91; Ernest R. May, *The World War and American Isolation, 1914–1917* (Cambridge, Mass., 1959), 294.

34. May, *World War and American Isolation*, 290–301; Konrad H. Jarausch, *The Enigmatic Chancellor: Bethmann Hollweg and the Hubris of Imperial Germany* (New Haven, Conn., 1973), 294–98.

35. May, *World War and American Isolation*, 387–403; Link, *Wilson: Campaigns for Progressivism and Peace,* 165–75, 184–214; Reinhard R. Dorries, *Imperial Challenge: Ambassador Count Bernstorff and German-American Relations, 1980–1917* (Chapel Hill, N.C., 1989), 198–204.

36. David French, *British Strategy and War Aims, 1914–1916* (London, 1986), 220–30; Robert H. Zieger, *America's Great War: World War I and the American Experience* (Lanham, Md., 2000), 29–33; Link, *Wilson: Campaigns for Progressivism and Peace, 178–84.*

37. "About a talk with the Prime Minister at luncheon at his house on August 1, 1916," in *PWW*, XXXVIII, 255–57; French, *British Strategy and War Aims, 210;* George H. Cassar, *Asquith as War Leader* (London, 1994), 196–210.

38. French, *British Strategy and War Aims,* 232–38; John Grigg, *Lloyd George: From Peace to War, 1912–1916* (Berkeley, Calif., 1984), 435–74.

39. House Diary, Nov. 17, 1916.

40. Wilson to House, Nov. 24, 25, 1916, House Papers; House Diary, Nov. 25, 1916.

41. "A Draft of a Peace Note," c. Nov. 25, 1916, in *PWW*, XXXX, 70–74; Link, *Wilson: Campaigns for Progressivism and Peace,* 197–200; House Diary, Nov. 27, 1916; Robert M. Lansing, *War Memoirs* (Indianapolis, Ind., 1935), 174–84.
42. House Diary, Nov. 27, 1916; House to Wilson, Nov. 30, 1916, House Papers.
43. Link, *Wilson: Campaigns for Progressivism and Peace,* 200–206; House Diary, Dec. 2, 1916; Spring-Rice to Grey, Dec. 15, 1916, in Stephen Gwynn, ed., *The Letters and Friendships of Sir Cecil Spring Rice* (London, 1929), II, 360–61.
44. House Diary, Dec. 7, 14, 1916; House to Lloyd George, Dec. 7, 1916 (draft), to Wilson, Dec. 3, 7, 9, 1916, House Papers; Wilson to House, Dec. 8, 1916, House Papers.
45. House Diary, Dec. 14, 1916 (composite entry covering Dec. 12–13, 1916); Wilson to House, Dec. 18, 19, 1916; Cooper, Wilson, 362–66; Link, *Wilson: Campaigns for Progressivism and Peace,* 214–19; "An Appeal for a Statement of War Aims," Dec. 18, 1916, in *PWW*, XXXX, 273–76.
46. House to Wilson, Dec. 20, 1916, House Papers; House Diary, Dec. 20, 1916.

CHAPTER 22

1. Arthur S. Link, *Wilson: Campaigns for Progressivism and Peace, 1916–1917* (Princeton, N.J., 1965), 227–39; Ernest R. May, *The World War and American Isolation, 1914–1917* (Cambridge, Mass., 1959), 367–69.
2. Link, *Wilson: Campaigns for Progressivism and Peace,* 220–27; editor's note in Arthur S. Link, ed., *The Papers of Woodrow Wilson* [*PWW*], 68 vols. (Princeton, N.J., 1966-93), XXXX, 308–11; note by Fanny Denton, Dec. 27, 1916, House Papers.
3. House to Wilson, Dec. 31, 1916, Jan. 5, 1917, Wilson to House, Jan. 1, 1917, House Papers; House Diary, Dec. 23, 1916, Jan. 2, 3, 4, 12, 1917.
4. House Diary, Dec. 17, 1916; W. B. Fowler, *British-American Relations, 1917–1918: The Role of Sir William Wiseman* (Princeton, N.J., 1969), 12–24; Patrick Devlin, *Too Proud to Fight: Woodrow Wilson's Neutrality* (New York, 1975), 609–13.
5. House to Wilson, Jan. 16, 1917, House Papers; House Diary, Jan. 15, 18, Feb. 2, 9, 23, 1917; Arthur Willert, *The Road to Safety: A Study in Anglo-American Relations* (London, Eng., 1952), 64.
6. House Diary, Jan. 11, 12, 1917; Edith Bolling Wilson, *My Memoir* (Indianapolis, Ind., 1939), 126; during his stay in Washington, House told Wilson that some-time in January he expected to travel to Texas. He had not visited his home state since February 1914; one old Texas friend wrote that "we look for you every Winter, but some people very quietly and privately are beginning to class you with Culberson, so far as coming to Texas is concerned—coming every Thanksgiving and Christmas, and never getting there." During the same visit, House saw his old friend Senator Culberson and was shocked by his physical decline. "I have never seen," he wrote, "such a change in the physical

condition of a man. I could hardly look at him without emotion. Culberson is one of the finest characters I have ever met in political life, and was formerly a perfect specimen of physical manhood, and to see him in this sad plight, filled me with sorrow." House Diary, Jan. 11, 12, 1917; Allison Mayfield to House, Jan. 11, 1917, House Papers.

7. House Diary, Jan. 15, 1917; House to Wilson, Jan. 15, 16, 1917, House Papers; Reinhard R. Doerries, *Imperial Challenge: Ambassador Count Bernstorff and German-American Relations, 1908–1917* (Chapel Hill, N.C., 1989), 210–11.

8. House Diary, Jan. 15, 1917; House to Frederic Penfield Jr., Jan. 17, 1917, House Papers.

9. Link, *Wilson: Campaigns for Progressivism and Peace*, 257–60; Wilson to House, Jan. 16, 17, 1917, House to Wilson, Jan. 17, 18, 1917, House Papers; House to Bernstorff, Jan. 17, 19, 1917, to Bryce, Jan. 17, 1917, House Papers; House Diary, Jan. 19, 1917.

10. Bernstorff to House, Jan. 18, 20, 1917, House Papers.

11. House to Wilson, Jan. 19, 20, 1917, Wilson to House, Jan. 19, 1917, House Papers.

12. "An Address to the Senate," Jan. 22, 1917, in *PWW*, XXXX, 533–39.

13. Link, *Wilson: Campaigns for Progressivism and Peace*, 268–69; House to Wilson, Jan. 22, 23, 1917, Wilson to House, Jan. 24, 1917, House Papers; Tony Smith, *America's Mission: The United States and the Worldwide Struggle for Democracy in the Twentieth Century* (Princeton, N.J., 1994), 84–85.

14. House to Wilson, Jan. 23, 25, 26, 1917, House Papers; editor's note, in *PWW*, XXXXI, 26–27; House Diary, Jan. 26, 1917.

15. House Diary, Jan. 31, 1917; Bernstorff to House, Jan. 31, 1917, with two memoranda, House to Bernstorff, Feb. 2, 1917, House Papers.

16. John Keegan, *The First World War* (New York, 1999), 309–11; Martin Gilbert, *The First World War: A Complete History* (New York, 1994), 303–9; Michael S. Neiberg, *Fighting the Great War: A Global History* (Cambridge, Mass., 2005), 202.

17. J. F. V. Keiger, *Raymond Poincaré* (Cambridge, Eng., 1997), 226–30; Robert A. Doughty, *Pyrrhic Victory, French Strategy and Operations in the Great War* (Cambridge, Mass., 2005), 319–37; Norman Hapgood to House, Dec. 30, 1916, Arthur Frazier to House, Feb. 16, 1917, House Papers.

18. John Grigg, *Lloyd George: From Peace to War, 1912–1916* (Berkeley, Calif., 1985), 470–74; Robert Rhodes James, *The British Revolution, 1880–1939* (New York, 1977), 362–65; Page to Wilson, Dec. 30, 1916, in *PWW*, XXXX, 366–68; Page to Wilson, Feb. 6, 22, 1917, in *PWW*, XXXXI, 136–37, 270–73.

19. Grigg, *Lloyd George: From Peace to War*, 475–503; Grigg, *Lloyd George: War Leader, 1916–1918* (London, Eng., 2002), 1–44.

20. George F. Kennan, *Russia and the West under Lenin and Stalin* (Boston, Mass., 1960), 3–17; David Stevenson, *Cataclysm: The First World War as Political Tragedy* (New York, 2004), 247–54; Norman E. Saul, *War and Revolution: The United States and Russia, 1914–1921* (Lawrence, Kans., 2001), 59–86.

21. Holger H. Herwig, *The First World War: Germany and Austria-Hungary, 1914–1918* (London, Eng., 1997), 272–83, 317; Stevenson, *Cataclysm*, 280–83,

22. Robert B. Asprey, *The German High Command at War: Hindenburg and Ludendorff Conduct World War I* (New York, 1991), 314–21; Herwig, *The First World War*, 311–14; Roger Chickering, *Imperial Germany and the Great War, 1914–1918*, 2nd ed. (Cambridge, Eng., 2004), 88–93.

23. Herwig, *The First World War*, 314–17; Stevenson, *Cataclysm*, 212–14; Konrad H. Jarausch, *The Enigmatic Chancellor: Bethmann Hollweg and the Hubris of Imperial Germany* (New Haven, Conn., 1973), 299–304.

24. House Diary, Jan. 31, Feb. 1, 1917; "A Memorandum by Robert Lansing," Feb. 4, 1917, in *PWW*, XXXXI, 118–25; Link, *Wilson: Campaigns for Progressivism and Peace*, 293–95; House Diary, Feb. 3, 1917; House to Wilson, Feb. 4, 1917, House Papers; Ida Tarbell to House, Feb. 8, 1917, House Papers.

25. Link, *Wilson: Campaigns for Progressivism and Peace*, 298–308; John Milton Cooper Jr., *Woodrow Wilson: A Biography* (New York, 2009), 374–76; "An Address to a Joint Session of Congress," Feb. 3, 1917, in *PWW*, XXXXI, 108–12.

26. House Diary, Feb. 5, 6, 8, 12, 15, 16, March 2, 1917; House to Wilson, March 30, 1917, House Papers; Joseph Allen Baker to Arthur James Balfour, April 2, 1917, in *PWW*, XXXXI, 532–36.

27. House to Wilson, Feb. 11, 1917, Wilson to House, Feb. 12, 1917, House Papers; Link, *Wilson: Campaigns for Progressivism and Peace*, 313–25, 340–49; "An Address to a Joint Session of Congress," Feb. 26, 1917, in *PWW*, XXXXI, 283–87.

28. Link, *Wilson: Campaigns for Progressivism and Peace*, 342–46; Cooper, *Wilson*, 378; Friedrich Katz, *The Secret War in Mexico: Europe, the United States, and the Mexican Revolution* (Chicago, Ill., 1981), 327–83; Wilson to House, Feb. 26, 1917, House to Wilson, Feb. 27, 1917, House Papers; on January 15, 1917, the Joint High Commission adjourned, and on the 28th, Pershing was ordered to withdraw his troops from Mexico. Determined to avoid further crises, Wilson also decided to restore full diplomatic relations with Carranza's government. On March 3, the new American ambassador, Henry P. Fletcher, presented his credentials in Mexico City. House tried to avoid involvement in Wilson's Mexican policy. He did not, he told one visitor, "want to add the Mexican problem to my burdens." Like Wilson, he realized that "it is no time to break with Mexico." Link, *Wilson: Campaigns for Progressivism and Peace*, 335–39; House Diary, Jan. 7, Feb. 11, 1917.

29. House Diary, March 4, 5, 6, 1917; House to Fanny Denton, March 5, 1917, House Papers; "From the Diary of Thomas W. Brahany," March 7, 1917, in *PWW*, XXXXI, 357–60; Kristie Miller, *Ellen and Edith: Woodrow Wilson's First Ladies* (Lawrence, Kans., 2010), 147.

30. House Diary, March 3, 4, 1917; Link, *Wilson: Campaigns for Progressivism and Peace*, 359–65, 372–77; Cooper, *Wilson*, 369–73; "A Statement," March 4, 1917, in *PWW*, XXXXI, 318–20.

31. Phyllis Lee Levin, *Edith and Woodrow: The Wilson White House* (New York, 2001), 166–75; Edwin A. Weinstein, *Woodrow Wilson: A Medical and Psychological Biography* (Princeton, N.J., 1981), 308.

32. House Diary, Jan. 3, 1917; Weinstein, *Wilson*, 310; Wilson to House, Jan. 19, 24, House Papers; Wilson asked Cleveland Dodge to replace Page, but when his old Princeton friend declined, he seemed to lose interest in finding a new ambassador. On March 28 he finally informed House that " 'in a misguided moment,' he had told Page he could continue and he supposed 'we would be compelled to have a British-American representing the United States at the Court of St. James.' " House seemed content with this arrangement since the lack of an effective ambassador in either London or Washington increased his own influence. John Milton Cooper Jr., *Walter Hines Page: The Southerner as American, 1855–1918* (Chapel Hill, N.C., 1977), 354–56; House Diary, Jan. 12, Feb. 22, March 28, 1917.

33. House Diary, Jan. 3, 12, 1917; John M. Blum, *Joe Tumulty and the Wilson Era* (Boston, Mass., 1951), 122–29; Miller, *Ellen and Edith*, 145.

34. Link, *Wilson: Campaigns for Progressivism and Peace*, 252; House Diary, Jan. 17, Feb. 1, 1917.

35. House to Wilson, Feb. 4, 7, 1917, Wilson to House, Feb. 6, 1917, House Papers; House Diary, March 5, 1917.

36. House Diary, Feb. 22, March 28, 1917; Charles E. Neu, "Woodrow Wilson and His Foreign Policy Advisers," in Charles E. Neu and William N. Tilchin, *Artists of Power: Theodore Roosevelt, Woodrow Wilson, and Their Enduring Impact on U.S. Foreign Policy* (Westport, Conn., 2006), 77–94, explores the reasons for Wilson's refusal to replace key foreign policy advisers.

37. House Diary, Jan. 12, Feb. 4, March 3, 28, 1917; "From the Diary of Thomas W. Brahany," March 26, 1917, in *PWW*, XXXXI, 473–75; "He said," House recorded, "his appetite for it [war] was so strong that he would like to quit the Cabinet, raise a regiment and go to the front. All three of his sons had enlisted." House Diary, March 28, 1917.

38. House developed friendships with a number of progressive journalists— including Lincoln Colcord and William C. Bullitt of the *Philadelphia Public Ledger*, David Lawrence of the *New York Evening Post*, and Walter Lippmann of the *New Republic*—and sought to give them "the right steer" about the policies of the Wilson administration. House Diary, Dec. 21, 28, 1916, Feb. 5, 15, March 9, 11, 17, 23, 26, 1917, Feb. 1, 1918; Christopher Lasch, *The New Radicalism in America, 1889–1963: The Intellectual as a Social Type* (New York, 1965), 234–36; Ronald Steel, *Walter Lippmann and the American Century* (Boston, Mass., 1980), 107–15.

39. House Diary, Dec. 20, 1916, Jan. 2, 4, 12, March 10, 12, 13, Feb. 4, 7, March 22, 29, April 12, 1917; Auchincloss Diary, March 9–23, 29, 30, 1917.

40. Weinstein, *Wilson*, 313; Link, *Wilson: Campaigns for Progressivism and Peace*, 373, 390–92; Page Diary, April 1, 1917.

41. Link, *Wilson: Campaigns for Progressivism and Peace*, 391–96; "From the Diary of Thomas W. Brahany," in *PWW*, XXXXI, 424–25; House Diary, March 17, 1917; House to Wilson, March 17, 1917, House Papers.

42. Link, *Wilson: Campaigns for Progressivism and Peace*, 396–419; Lansing to House, March 19, 1917, House Papers; "A Memorandum by Robert Lansing," March 20, 1917, in *PWW*, XXXXI, 436–44; House Diary, March 22, 1917.

43. House Diary, March 24, 26, 1917; House to Wilson, March 25, 1917, Wilson to House, March 26, 1917, House Papers.

44. House Diary, March 27, 1917.

45. House Diary, March 23, 27, 28, 1917; House to Wilson, Feb. 14, March 14, 19, 1917, to James Bryce, March 21, 1917, to Fanny Denton, March 28, 1917, House Papers; Herbert Hoover to House, Feb. 13, 1917, House Papers.

46. House Diary, March 28, April 2, 1917; House to Wilson, March 29, April 4, 1917, House Papers; House's timing of the president's message was different from what was written in the *New York Times*. According to its reporter, Wilson spoke for thirty-six minutes. *New York Times*, April 3, 1917.

47. House to Fanny Denton, April 2, 1917, House Papers.

48. "An Address to a Joint Session of Congress," April 2, 1917, in *PWW*, XXXXI, 519–27; A superb analysis of Wilson's address is in Cooper, *Wilson*, 383–89.

49. Link, *Wilson: Campaigns for Progressivism and Peace,* 426; Robert M. Lansing, *War Memoirs of Robert Lansing* (Indianapolis, Ind., 1935), 239–43; Edmund W. Starling, *Starling of the White House* (New York, 1946), 87; Gregory to House, April 5, 1917, House Papers.

50. Link, Wilson: Campaigns for Progressivism and Peace, 427–31; Thomas J. Knock, *To End All Wars: Woodrow Wilson and the Quest for a New World Order* (New York, 1992), 121–22.

51. May, *World War and American Isolation*, 416–37; Robert H. Zieger, *America's Great War: World War I and the American Experience* (Oxford, Eng., 2000), 50–56; Robert W. Tucker, *Woodrow Wilson and the Great War: Reconsidering America's Neutrality, 1914–1917* (Charlottesville, Va., 2007), 189–214.

CHAPTER 23

1. "An Address to a Joint Session of Congress," April 2, 1917, in Arthur S. Link, ed., *The Papers of Woodrow Wilson* [*PWW*],68 vols. (Princeton, N.J., 1966-93), XXXXI, 519–27; David Kennedy, *Over Here: The First World War and American Society* (New York, 1980), v–vii; Robert H. Zieger, *America's Great War: World War I and the American Experience* (Lanham, Md., 2000), 60.

2. Zieger, *America's Great War*, 64–69; Edward M. Coffman, *The War to End All Wars: The American Military Experience in World War I* (New York, 1968), 8–52, 86–98.

3. Edward M. Coffman, *The Regulars: The American Army, 1898–1941* (Cambridge, Mass., 2004), 203–4; Coffman, *The War to End All Wars*, 50; House to Wilson, March 19, 1917, House Papers.

4. Kennedy, *Over Here*, 13–118.

5. Meirion and Susie Harries, *The Last Days of Innocence: America at War, 1917–1918* (New York, 1997), 91–92; Seward W. Livermore, *Politics Is Adjourned: Woodrow Wilson and the War Congress, 1916–1918* (Middletown, Conn., 1966), 15–37; Zieger, *America's Great War,* 74–75; John Milton Cooper Jr., *Woodrow Wilson: A Biography* (New York, 2009), 390–97.

6. Livermore, *Politics Is Adjourned,* 15–16, 37–39; John A. Garraty, *Henry Cabot Lodge: A Biography* (New York, 1953), 337; Robert H. Ferrell, *Woodrow Wilson and World War I, 1917–1921* (New York, 1985), 103.

7. House Diary, April 5, 6, 11, 13, 16, 17, 1917.

8. House to Arthur Hugh Frazier, April 13, 1917, House Papers; House Diary, April 8, 1917.

9. *Philip Dru: Administrator, a Story of Tomorrow, 1920–1935* (New York, 1912), 276.

10. House Diary, Aug. 6, 1914, April 19, 1917; House to Wilson, Jan. 11, 1916, April 10, 13, 1917, House Papers; Oscar Straus to House, April 5, 1917, House Papers; Wilson to Lansing, April 12, 1917, *PWW,* XXXXII, 45; Norman E. Saul, *War and Revolution: The United States and Russia, 1914–1921* (Lawrence, Kans., 2001), 105–10.

11. Jason Tomes, *Balfour and Foreign Policy: The International Thought of a Conservative Statesman* (Cambridge, Eng., 1997), 173–74; Robert B. Bruce, *A Fraternity of Arms: America and France in the Great War* (Lawrence, Kans., 2003), 32–33.

12. David R. Woodward, *Trial by Friendship: Anglo-American Relations, 1917–1918* (Lexington, Ky., 1993), 44–49, 68.

13. Bruce, *A Fraternity of Arms,* 37–40; John Keegan, *The First World War* (New York, 1999), 322–29.

14. House Diary, April 6, 1917; Eric Drummond to House, April 5, 1917, House to Drummond, April 9, 1917, to Wilson, April 5, 6, 1917, Wilson to House, April 6, 1917, House Papers.

15. House Diary, April, 7, 14, 15, 18, 21, 22, 1917; Blanche E. C. Dugdale, *Arthur James Balfour, 1906–1930* (New York, 1937), 144.

16. House Diary, April 22, 1917; House gave Wilson an abbreviated version of this conversation. In his diary he noted that his letter to the president "tells much of the conversation though not all." House to Wilson, April 22, 1917, House Papers; House Diary, April 22, 1917.

17. "From the Diary of Thomas W. Brahany," April 22, 1917, in *PWW,* XXXXII, 121; Woodward, *Trial by Friendship,* 52.

18. Woodward, *Trial by Friendship,* 52–53; Ferrell, *Wilson and World War I,* 35–36.

19. House Diary, April 25, 26, 1917; House to Wilson, April 25, 1917, House Papers; Balfour to Lloyd George, April 26, 1917, in *PWW,* XXXXII, 140–41.

20. House Diary, April 26, 28, 1917; Charles Seymour, *The Intimate Papers of Colonel House: Into the World War, April 1917–June 1918* (Boston, Mass., 1928), III, 46–51, 61–63, has an excellent discussion of Wilson and the secret treaties.

On May 13, Balfour sent Wilson the texts of the secret treaties, with the exception of the treaty with Japan. Balfour to Wilson, May 13, 1917, in *PWW*, XXXXII, 327.

21. House Diary, April 30, 1917. House told Wilson of Balfour's comments; Cooper, *Wilson*, 395–96.

22. "From the Diary of Thomas W. Brahany," April 25, 1917, in *PWW*, XXXXII, 132–33.

23. House Diary, April 29, 30, 1917; Seymour, *Intimate Papers*, III, 4–8; Frazier to House, April 13, 1917, Hapgood to House, April 5, 1917, House Papers.

24. House to Fanny Denton, April 29, 1917, to Wilson, May 2, 1917, House Papers.

25. House Diary, May 1, 2, 3, 1917; House to Wilson, May 4, 6, 7, 8, 1917, Wilson to House, May 7, 1917, House Papers; David Burner, *Herbert Hoover: A Public Life* (New York, 1979), 96–97.

26. House Diary, May 12, 1917; Auchincloss Diary, May 12, 14, 18, and May 29–July 22, 1917, Auchincloss Papers.

27. House Diary, April 14, May 3, 1917.

28. House Diary, May 19, 30, 31, 1917; John Milton Cooper Jr., *Pivotal Decades: The United States, 1900–1920* (New York, 1990), 296–97.

29. Mark Sullivan to House, April 7, 1917, Thomas F. Logan to House, May 23, 1917, House Papers; House Diary, May 27, 28, 31, 1917; Jordan A. Schwarz, *The Speculator: Bernard M. Baruch in Washington, 1917–1965* (Chapel Hill, N.C., 1981), 53–60; instead, House instructed Vance McCormick to take up Baruch's appointment with Wilson. House Diary, May 28, 30, 1917.

30. Charles J. Phillips, *Paderewski: The Story of a Modern Immortal* (New York, 1934), 311–58; Anita Prazmowska, *Ignacy Paderewski* (London, Eng., 2009), 46–56; House Diary, Nov. 12, 18, 1915, Jan. 17, 1917; Irwin H. Hoover, *Forty-two Years in the White House* (Boston, Mass., 1934), 83–84.

31. House Diary, April 10, May 10, 14, 1917; "Metropolitan Throng Swept by Enthusiasm," *New York Times,* May 11, 1917.

32. House Diary, May 9, 1917.

33. House Diary, May 13, 19, 1917; Drummond to House, May 14, 1917, House to Drummond, May 16, 1917, House Papers; Balfour to Lloyd George, May 14, 1917, in *PWW*, XXXXII, 296; David F. Trask, *Captains & Cabinets: Anglo–American Naval Relations, 1917–1918* (Columbia, Mo., 1972), 102–25. On July 5, Balfour proposed to House a four-power agreement between France, Great Britain, Japan, and the United States. House thought this was "not quite what we had in mind" and wanted to pursue the original proposal, but Wilson insisted that the United States play a "lone hand" and rejected a naval agreement with the Allies. Balfour to House, July 5, 1917; House Diary, July 7, Sept. 9, 1917; House to Wilson, July 8, 17, 1917, House Papers; Wiseman memorandum, July 13, 1917, House Papers.

34. House Diary, May 19, 23, 1917.

35. W. B. Fowler, *British-American Relations: 1917–1918, the Role of Sir William Wiseman* (Princeton, N.J., 1969), 30–32; House Diary, April 25, May 25, 1917; House to Wilson, May 31, June 7, 1917, Wilson to House, June 1, 1917, House Papers; Balfour to Cecil, June 3, 1917, *PWW,* XXXXII, 445.

36. Wilson to House, June 1, 1917, House to Wilson, June 5, 1917, House Papers.

37. Arthur Willert, *The Road to Safety: A Study in Anglo-American Relations* (New York, 1953), 77–81; Woodward, *Trial by Friendship,* 65; Bruce, *A Fraternity of Arms,* 57–59.

CHAPTER 24

1. House Diary, June 9, 10, 1917; Breckinridge Long Diary, July 8, 1917.

2. House Diary, July 28, Sept. 14, 1917; Auchincloss Diary, July 26, 28, Aug. 15, 1917.

3. House to Richard Washburn Child, July 10, 1917, House Papers; Wilson to Jessie Sayre, July 21, 1917, in Arthur S. Link, ed., *The Papers of Woodrow Wilson [PWW],* 68 vols. (Princeton, N.J., 1966-93), XXXIII, 240–42; Edith Bolling Wilson, *My Memoir* (Indianapolis, Ind., 1939), 132; Phyllis Lee Levin, *Edith and Woodrow: The Wilson White House* (New York, 2001), 176–86.

4. John Milton Cooper Jr., *Woodrow Wilson: A Biography* (New York, 2009), 415; Edith Bolling Wilson, *My Memoir,* 134–41; Kristie Miller, *Ellen and Edith: Woodrow Wilson's First Ladies* (Lawrence, Kans., 2010), 149–51.

5. John M. Blum, *Joe Tumulty and the Wilson Era* (Boston, Mass., 1951), 138; Robert H. Zieger, *America's Great War: World War I and the American Experience* (New York, 2000), 60–61.

6. House to Wilson, May 30, June 5, 1917, to James Bryce, June 10, 1917, House Papers; Wilson to House, June 1, 1917, House Papers; "A Flag Day Address," June 14, 1917, in *PWW,* XXXXII, 498–504.

7. House to Wilson, June 14, 15, 1917, House Papers; Wilson to House, June 15, 1917, House Papers; House Diary, June 13, 14, 1917.

8. Meirion and Susie Harries, *The Last Days of Innocence: America at War, 1917–1918* (New York, 1997), 104–110, 178–89; Seward W. Livermore, *Politics Is Adjourned: Woodrow Wilson and the War Congress, 1916–1918* (Middletown, Conn., 1966), 48–49.

9. Livermore, *Politics Is Adjourned,* 48–61; David M. Kennedy, *Over Here: The First World War and American Society* (New York, 1980), 59–92; Cooper, *Wilson,* 397–415.

10. House Diary, July 6–ll, 1917; House to Wilson, June 17, 21, July 2, 13, 24, 1917, House Papers.

11. Hoover to House, June 25, 1917, House Papers.

12. S. R. Bertron to House, Aug. 24, 1917, House Papers; McAdoo to House, June 28, July 14, 1917, House Papers; House Diary, Aug. 7, 1917.

13. House Diary, Aug. 15, 23, 1917.

14. House Diary, June 25, Aug. 31, 1917; Christopher Lasch, *The New Radicalism in America: 1889–1963, the Intellectual as a Social Type* (New York, 1965), 241.

15. Arthur Willert, *The Road to Safety: A Study in Anglo-American Relations* (New York, 1953), 95–119; Patrick Devlin, *Too Proud to Fight: Woodrow Wilson's Neutrality* (New York, 1975), 348; John Grigg, *Lloyd George: War Leader, 1916–1918* (London, Eng., 2002), 122–28; J. Lee Thompson, *Politicians, the Press, and Propaganda: Lord Northcliffe and the Great War, 1914–1919* (Kent, Ohio, 1999), 148–69.

16. House Diary, June 9, 1917.

17. House Diary, June 11, 13, 15, 19, 22, 23, 27, 28, 1917; House to Wilson, June 7, 12, 27, House Papers; Willert, *The Road to Safety*, 61–63.

18. Balfour to Wiseman, June 28, 1917, House Papers; House Diary, June 29, 1917.

19. Kennedy, *Over Here*, 319–22; W. B. Fowler, *British-American Relations: 1917–1918, The Role of Sir William Wiseman* (Princeton, N.J., 1919), 36–47.

20. House Diary, June 29, 30, 1917; House to Balfour, June 29, 1917, to Wilson, June 29, 1917, House Papers.

21. House Diary, July 2, 6, 7, 8, 11, 15, 16, 20, 21, 1917; House to McAdoo, July 1, 17, 1917, to Wilson, June 29, July 11, to Lord Stamfordham, July 15, 1917, to Lloyd George, July 15, 1917, to Balfour, July 15, 1917, House Papers.17, 20, 1917, House Papers; Fowler, *British-American Relations*, 48–50.

22. David Stevenson, *Cataclysm: The First World War as Political Tragedy* (New York, 2004), 263; Martin Gilbert, *The First World War: A Complete History* (New York, 1994), 338.

23. J. F. V. Keiger, *Raymond Poincaré* (Cambridge, Eng., 1997), 228–32; Robert B. Bruce, *A Fraternity of Arms: America and France in the Great War* (Lawrence, Kans., 2003), 95; Leonard V. Smith, Stephane Audoin–Rouzeau, Annette Becker, *France and the Great War: 1914–1918* (Cambridge, Eng., 2003), 113–27.

24. Bruce, *A Fraternity of Arms*, 68–96; Edward M. Coffman, *The War to End All Wars: The American Military Experience in World War I* (New York, 1968), 122–31.

25. Gilbert, *The First World War*, 326–32; Michael S. Neiberg, *Fighting the Great War: A Global History* (Cambridge, Mass., 2005), 216–23.

26. David French, *The Strategy of the Lloyd George Coalition: 1916–1918*, (Oxford, Eng., 1995), 62–92; John Turner, *British Politics and the Great War: Coalition and Conflict, 1915–1918* (New Haven, Conn., 1992), 194–226.

27. Grigg, *Lloyd George*, 155–73; French, *The Strategy of the Lloyd George Coalition*, 94–123; Neiberg, *Fighting the Great War*, 257–69.

28. Roger Chickering, *Imperial Germany and the Great War: 1914–1918*, 2nd ed. (Cambridge, Eng., 2004), 138–44; Holger H. Herwig, *The First World War: German and Austria-Hungary, 1914–1918* (New York, 1997), 376.

29. Chickering, *Imperial Germany and the Great War*, 148–59.

30. Robert B. Asprey, *The German High Command at War: Hindenburg and Ludendorff Conduct World War I* (New York, 1991), 324–25.

31. Asprey, *The German High Command at War,* 326–31; Herwig, *The First World War,* 373–75.

32. Lamar Cecil, *Wilhelm II: Emperor and Exile, 1900–1941* (Chapel Hill, N.C., 1996), 249–51.

33. Examples include Arthur Hugh Frazier to House, June 1, 30, July 11, 27, 1917, S. R. Bertron to House, June 18, Aug. 1, 1917, Lincoln Steffans to House, June 20, 1917, Sidney Brooks to House, June 25, 1917; House Papers; House Diary, July 6, 1917.

34. House Diary, June 30, 1917; House to W. H. Buckler, June 10, July 1, 1917, to Bryce, June 10, 1917, to Lansing, June 27, 1917, House Papers; memo on peace terms, July 19 or 20, 1917, House Papers.

35. "To the Rulers of the Belligerent People," enclosed in Page to Lansing, Aug. 15, 1917, in *PWW,* XXXXIII, 482–85; Wiseman to House, Aug. 11, 1917, House Papers; House to Wilson, July 23, Aug. 9, 15, 19, 1917, House Papers; House Diary, July 22, Aug. 15, 18, 19, 31, Sept. 4, 16, 1917.

36. Wilson to House, Aug. 16, 1917, House Papers; House Diary, Aug. 18, 1917.

37. House Diary, Aug. 19, 1917; House to Wilson, Aug. 17, 19, Wilson to House, Aug. 23, 1917, House Papers; *PWW,* XXXXIV, 33–36, 57–59.

38. House to Wilson, Aug. 24, 25, 29, Sept. 4, 1917, to Edward S. Martin, Aug. 30, 1917, House Papers; Wilson to House, Aug. 23, Sept. 2, 1917, House Papers; House Diary, July 14, Aug. 23, 25, 29, 1917.

39. Wilson to House, Sept. 2, 1917, House Papers.

40. Lawrence E. Gelfand, *The Inquiry: American Preparations for Peace, 1917–1919* (New Haven, Conn., 1963), 14–31; Buckler to House, April 27, 1917, Phillips to House, May 19, 1917, House Papers; House to Buckler, Aug. 21, 1917, to Wilson, Sept. 4, 1917, House Papers; House Diary, Sept. 4, 8, 1917.

41. House Diary, Sept. 9, 1917; Edith Bolling Wilson, *My Memoir,* 141–43; Earlier in the summer House had learned from Auchincloss (who overheard Wilson praise House at a White House dinner party) that "the president said I was wholly detached in my viewpoint and kept it entirely untangled from personal ambition, and, as he expressed it, 'I could see things as through a vacuum.'" House Diary, July 14, 1917.

42. House Diary, Sept. 5, 9, 1917.

43. House Diary, Sept. 10, 12, 13, 1917; Auchincloss Diary, Sept. 10–13, 24, 1917.

44. House Diary, Sept. 13, 16,1917; Fowler, *British-American Relations,* 75; Lloyd George to House, Sept. 4, 1917, House Papers; Lloyd George to Wilson, Sept. 3, 1917, in *PWW,* XXXXIV, 125–30; David R. Woodward, *Trial by Friendship: Anglo-American Relations, 1917–1918* (Lexington, Ky., 1993), 77–80, 90–92.

45. House Diary, Sept. 16, 1917; House to Wilson, Sept. 18, 1917, House Papers; Fowler, *British-American Relations,* 56–67; Wiseman to House, Aug. 24, 1917, House Papers.

46. Cecil to House, Aug. 25, Sept. 3, 1917, House Papers; House to Cecil, Aug. 26, 1917, House Papers; Wiseman to House, Sept. 2, 1917, House Papers.

CHAPTER 25

1. House Diary, Sept. 22, 23, 25, 30, Oct. 1, 2, 5, 1917.

2. Throughout the summer and fall of 1917, American-Japanese relations continued to concern House. He observed that China was in a "deplorable condition" and was "a menace to civilization." After talking to Ambassador Morris, House warned the president that "We cannot meet Japan in her desires as to land and immigration, and unless we make some concessions in regard to her sphere of influence in the East, trouble is sure, sooner or later to come. Japan is barred from all the undeveloped places of the earth, and if her influence in the East is not recognized as in some degree superior to that of the Western powers, there will be a reckoning." Like Lansing, he believed that Japan must have a special position in China and approved of the concessions made in the Lansing-Ishii Agreement, initialed on November 2, 1917. House Diary, July 5, 7, Aug. 20, 30, September 8, 18, 1917; House to Wilson, Sept. 6, 18, 1917; Charles E. Neu, *The Troubled Encounter: The United States and Japan* (New York, 1975), 91–94; On October 17, 1917, Lippmann, upset over the post office's "campaign against seditious newspapers," warned House that "radical and liberal groups are in a sullen mood over the government's attitude toward the socialist press." House forwarded Lippmann's letter to the president, observing that "no matter how much we deplore the attitude of the socialists as to the war, yet, more harm may easily be done by repression. Between the two courses, it is better to err on the side of leniency. I have seen for sometime that trouble was brewing and I spoke to Burleson when in Washington. I believe you will have to take the matter largely into your own hands for he could never have a proper understanding of it." Wilson did not, however, restrain his postmaster general. House Diary, Sept. 26, 29, Oct. 17, 1917; Lippmann to House, Oct. 17, 1917, House to Wilson, Oct. 17, 1917, House Papers; Ronald Steel, *Walter Lippmann and the American Century* (Boston, Mass., 1980), 124–26; Thomas J. Knock, *To End All Wars: Woodrow Wilson and the Quest for a New World Order* (New York, 1992), 132–37; John Milton Cooper Jr., *Woodrow Wilson: A Biography* (New York, 2009), 397–401.

3. House Diary, Sept. 22, 29, Oct. 4, 1917; Frazier to House, Sept. 21, 1917, House Papers.

4. H. Montgomery Hyde, *Lord Reading: The Life of Rufus Isaacs, First Marquess of Reading* (New York, 1967), 176–200; Arthur Willert, *The Road to Safety: A Study in Anglo-American Relations* (New York, 1953), 120–23; House to Lloyd George, Sept. 24, 1917, House Papers; House Diary, Sept. 20, 22, 30, Oct. 1, 2, 3, 1917.

5. House Diary, Sept. 20, 22, 23, 25, 30, Oct. 1, 2, 5, 6, 8, 17, 18, 1917; Wilson to House, Sept. 19, 1917, House Papers.

6. House to Wilson, Sept. 20, 25, Oct. 3, 1917, Wilson to House, Sept. 24, 1917, House Papers; House to Lansing, Sept. 20, 1917, to A. Lawrence Lowell, Oct. 4, 1917, House Papers; Cooper, *Wilson*, 419.

7. Lippmann to House, Sept. 24, 1917, House to Isaiah Bowmann, Oct. 27, 1917, House Papers; Steel, *Lippmann,* 127–31.

8. Lawrence E. Gelfand, *The Inquiry: American Preparations for Peace, 1917–1919* (New Haven, Conn., 1963), 49–50; James T. Shotwell, *Autobiography* (Indianapolis, Ind., 1961), 77; James T. Shotwell, *Reminiscences,* 78–84, Columbia University Oral History Collection.

9. House Diary, Oct. 9, 1917; Wiseman to House, Sept. 25, Oct. 10, 1917, to Drummond, Oct. 13, 1917, House Papers; Frazier to House, Oct. 12, 1917, House Papers.

10. House Diary, Oct. 13, 1917; Phillips Diary, Oct. 11, 1917.

11. House Diary, Oct. 23, 24, 1917; Wilson to prime ministers of Great Britain, France, and Italy, Oct. 24, 1917, House Papers.

12. House Diary, Oct. 24, 1917; Wilson to House, Oct. 26, 1917, House to Wilson, Oct. 27, 1917, House Papers.

13. Grayson to House, Oct. 28, 1917, House Papers.

14. House Diary, Oct. 29, 1917; W. B. Fowler, *British-American Relations: 1917–1918, The Role of Sir William Wiseman* (Princeton, N.J., 1969), 89–91; the House Party included Tasker H. Bliss, Army Chief of Staff, William S. Benson, Chief of Naval Operations, Oscar Crosby, assistant to the secretary of the treasury, Vance McCormick, head of the War Trade Board, Bainbridge Colby of the Shipping Board, Alonzo Taylor of the Food Administration, Nelson Perkins of the War Industries Board, and various aides, secretaries, and stenographers; Gordon Auchincloss agonized over leaving Janet behind: "I hate like anything to leave [Janet] but down in my heart I believe I ought to go for if I don't I'll regret it all the rest of my life. The trouble is Mrs. House insists on going and that leaves no one to look after Janet. I am thoroughly miserable about the whole thing." Auchincloss Diary, Oct. 20, 21, 22, 1917.

15. House Diary, Oct. 30, 1917; McCormick Diary, Oct. 20, 1917.

16. House Diary, Nov. 3, 4, 5, 6, 7, 8, 1917; Auchincloss Diary, Nov. 7, 1917.

17. House Diary, Nov. 8, 1917; Charles Seymour, *The Intimate Papers of Colonel House* (Boston, Mass., 1928), III, 226.

18. Fanny Denton to Marion Weeks, Nov. 16, 1917, House Papers; "British Look to US for Plan to Push the War," *New York Times,* Nov. 18, 1917.

19. David Stevenson, *Cataclysm: The First World War as Political Tragedy* (New York, 2004), 303–11; Michael S. Neiberg, *Fighting the Great War: A Global History* (Cambridge, Mass., 2005), 270–79.

20. George F. Kennan, *Russia Leaves the War* (Princeton, N.J., 1956), 71–94; Martin Gilbert, *The First World War: A Complete History* (New York, 1994), 373–74, 384–87.

21. John Grigg, *Lloyd George: War Leader, 1916–1918* (New York, 2002), 268–74; David R. Woodward, *Trial by Friendship: Anglo-American Relations, 1917–1918* (Lexington, Ky., 1993), 104–11.

22. House Diary, Nov. 8–12, 1917; House to Balfour, Oct. 15, 1917, House Papers.

23. House Diary, Nov. 8, 10, 12, 1917; Grey to House, Nov. 15, 1917, House Papers.

24. House Diary, Nov. 10, 1917.

25. House Diary, Nov. 9, 10, 1917; Auchincloss to Polk, Nov. 9, 1917, Auchincloss Papers; Fowler, *Wiseman,* 97; G. R. Conyne, *Woodrow Wilson: British Perspectives, 1912–21* (New York, 1992), 115.

26. House Diary, Nov. 13, 15, 16, 1917; Woodward, *Trial by Friendship,* 112–16; Fowler, *Wiseman,* 98–101; Lloyd George to House, Nov. 13, 1917, House Papers.

27. House Diary, Nov. 20, 21, 1917; Phillips Diary, Dec. 24, 25, 26, 1917; House to Lansing, Dec. 1, 1917, House Papers; Richard H. Ullman, *Intervention and the War* (Princeton, N.J., 1961), 40–45; Kennan, *Russia Leaves the War,* 160–80; Both Lloyd George and Balfour supported the creation of a Jewish homeland in Palestine, and on November 2, 1917, with the war cabinet's approval, the foreign secretary issued his famous declaration, committing the British government to the "establishment in Palestine of a national home for the Jewish race." In the fall of 1917, the president, when pressed by British leaders, had expressed his sympathy for Zionist aspirations, although he did not publicly endorse the Balfour Declaration until the summer of 1918. House occasionally consulted with Zionist leaders but did not want Wilson to issue any public statement and complained that the president "was willing to go farther than I thought advisable." R. J. Q. Adams, *Balfour: The Last Grandee* (London, Eng., 2007), 330–35; Fowler, *Wiseman,* 93–94; Cecil to House, Sept. 3, 1917, Balfour to House, Oct. 6, 1917, House Papers; Wilson to House, Oct. 13, 1917, House to Wilson, Oct. 16, 1917, House Papers; House Diary, Sept. 23, 1917.

28. House Diary, Nov. 21, 1917.

29. House to Wilson, Nov. 11, 14, 15, 16, 18, 20, 21, 1917, Wilson to House, Nov. 16, 19, 1917, House Papers.

30. House Diary, Nov. 22, 1917.

31. McCormick Diary, Nov. 25, 1917; Robert A. Doughty, *Pyrrhic Victory: French Strategy and Operations in the Great War* (Cambridge, Mass., 2005), 383–404; Rod Kedward, *France and the French: A Modern History* (New York, 2006), 78–85.

32. J. F. V. Keiger, *Raymond Poincaré* (Cambridge, Eng., 1997), 231–33.

33. Robert B. Bruce, *A Fraternity of Arms: America and France in the Great War* (Lawrence, Kans., 2003), 38; David Robin Watson, *Georges Clemenceau* (London, Eng., 2008), 20–42.

34. Grigg, *Lloyd George,* 290–97; Violet Milner, *My Picture Gallery, 1886–1901* (London, Eng., 1951), 62–63.

35. House Diary, Nov. 23, 1917; House to Wilson, Nov. 23, 25, 1917, House Papers; General J. J. H. Mordacq, *Le Ministere Clemenceau* (Paris, France, 1930–31), I, 93–95; Georges Clemenceau, *Grandeur and Misery of Victory* (New York, 1930), 148.

36. House Diary, Nov. 25, 1917; House to Wilson, Nov. 25, 1917, House Papers; "Memorandum of Conversation of Colonel House and General Bliss with M. Clemenceau and General Pétain," in Seymour, *Intimate Papers*, III, 257–60.

37. House Diary, Nov. 27, 28, 1917.

38. House Diary, Dec. 1, 1917; House to Lansing, Dec. 1, 1917; Grigg, *Lloyd George,* 322–25.

39. House Diary, Nov. 28, 29, 1917; House to Wilson, Nov. 28, 1917, House Papers; Grigg, *Lloyd George,* 321.

40. Grigg, *Lloyd George,* 326–34; House Diary, Nov. 14, Dec. 1, 1917; House to Wilson, Nov. 30, 1917, Wilson to House, Dec. 1, 1917, House Papers; Adam Hochschild, *To End All Wars: A Story of Loyalty and Rebellion, 1914–1918* (Boston, Mass., 2011), 301–03.

41. House Diary, Dec. 1, 1917; Grigg, *Lloyd George*, 326–34

42. House Diary, Nov. 29, 30, 1917.

43. House Diary, Nov. 24, Dec. 1, 2, 3, 1917.

44. House Diary, Dec. 4, 1917.

45. Bruce, *A Fraternity of Arms,* 144–49; House Diary, Dec. 6, 1917; Clemenceau to House, Dec. 6, 1917, House Papers.

46. House Diary, Nov. 23, Dec. 4, 1917; James G. Harbord, *Leaves from a War Diary* (New York, 1925), 196–97; Frank E. Vandiver, *Black Jack: The Life and Times of John J. Pershing* (College Station, Tex., 1977), II, 833–34.

47. House Diary, Dec. 6, 1917; John J. Pershing, *My Experiences in the World War* (New York, 1931), I, 255–57.

48. House Diary, Dec. 6, 8, 1917; House to Wiseman, Dec. 7, 1917, House Papers.

49. House Diary, Dec. 8, 11, 12, 1917; Fowler, *Wiseman,* 106–7; Woodward, *Trial by Friendship,* 119–21.

50. House Diary, Dec. 11, 1917.

51. House Diary, Dec. 12, 1917.

52. House Diary, Dec. 17, 1917; Edith Bolling Wilson, *My Memoir* (Indianapolis, Ind., 1939), 154.

53. House Diary, Dec. 17, 18, 1917; Wiseman to House, Dec. 15, 1917, Lloyd George to House, Dec. 15, 17, 1917, House Papers; Woodward, *Trial by Friendship,* 121–22.

54. Woodward, *Trial by Friendship,* 122–24; "A Memorandum of an Interview with William Howard Taft," Dec. 12, 1917, in Arthur S. Link, ed., *The Papers of Woodrow Wilson* [*PWW*], 68 vols. (Princeton, N.J., 1966-93), XXXXV, 272–74; House Diary, Jan. 1, 1918.

55. House Diary, Dec. 18, 1917; Lippmann to House, Dec. 19, 1917, House Papers.

56. House Diary, Dec. 18, 1917; Zieger, *America's Great War,* 71; Cooper, *Wilson,* 404–05.

57. House Diary, Dec. 19, 30, 1917; in her memoir Edith claims that House behaved indecisively on the railroad question. He allegedly told her that he disagreed with the president's policy toward the railroads, but when Wilson

appeared, claimed that he had reconsidered his position and agreed "with every word" of his friend's proposed address. "I do not," she concludes, "like people to change their minds so quickly, and was never able to forget this little scene." It seems unlikely that this exchange ever took place, since House supported Wilson's takeover of the railroads. Moreover, he often argued, up to a point, with the president. Edith Bolling Wilson, *My Memoir*, 154–56; House Diary, Dec. 30, 1916; Phyllis Lee Levin, *Edith and Woodrow: The Wilson White House* (New York, 2001), 202–4.

CHAPTER 26

1. House Diary, Dec. 31, 1917, Jan. 4, 1918; House to Wilson, Jan. 1, 1918, Wilson to House, Jan. 2, 1918, House Papers; Auchincloss Diary, Jan. 5, 1918.

2. House Diary, Jan. 9, 1918; House to Balfour, Jan. 5, 1918, House Papers; Lawrence E. Gelfand, *The Inquiry: American Preparations for Peace, 1917–1918* (New Haven, Conn., 1963), 135–53.

3. House Diary, Jan. 9, 1918; William Phillips, *Ventures in Diplomacy* (London, 1955), 43; August Heckscher, *Woodrow Wilson* (New York, 1991), 471; John Milton Cooper Jr., *Woodrow Wilson: A Biography* (New York, 2009), 421–24; the editor of *The Papers of Woodrow Wilson,* who scrutinized House's account, concludes that "it is correct in all its important details." Arthur S. Link, ed., *The Papers of Woodrow Wilson* [*PWW*], 68 vols. (Princeton, N.J.), 1966–93, XXXXV, 476–77.

4. Thomas J. Knock, *To End All Wars: Woodrow Wilson and the Quest for a New World Order* (New York, 1992), 142–47; David Stevenson, *Cataclysm: The First World War as Political Tragedy* (New York, 2004), 318–20; Erez Manela, *The Wilsonian Moment: Self–Determination and the International Origins of Anticolonial Nationalism* (New York, 2007), 39–47; Trygve Throntveit, "The Fable of the Fourteen Points: Woodrow Wilson and National Self–Determination," *Diplomatic History*, 35, 3 (June, 2011), 445–81.

5. "An Address to a Joint Session of Congress," Jan. 8, 1918, in *PWW*, XXXXV, 434–39; George Sylvester Viereck, *The Strangest Friendship in History: Woodrow Wilson and Colonel House* (New York, 1932), 213–16.

6. House Diary, Jan. 9, 1918; House to Wilson, Jan. 11, 1918, House Papers; Knock, *To End All Wars,* 144–47; Stevenson, *Cataclysm,* 320; Manela, *The Wilsonian Moment,* 53.

7. Seward W. Livermore, *Politics Is Adjourned: Woodrow Wilson and the War Congress, 1916–1918* (Middletown, Conn., 1966), 62–78; Paul A. C. Koistinen, *Mobilizing for Modern War: The Political Economy of American Warfare, 1865–1919* (Lawrence, Kans., 1997), 221–29; Robert H. Ferrell, *Woodrow Wilson and World War I, 1917–1921* (New York, 1985), 106.

8. Livermore, *Politics Is Adjourned,* 79–104; Chamberlain to Wilson, Jan. 21, 1918, "A Press Release," Jan. 21, 1918, in *PWW*, XXXXVI, 53–56.

9. Livermore, *Politics Is Adjourned,* 69, 86–104; Robert H. Zieger, *America's Great War: World War I and the American Experience* (Lanham, Md., 2000), 69–70; David R. Woodward, *Trial by Friendship: Anglo-American Relations, 1917–1918* (Louisville, Ky., 1993), 154–55; Cooper, *Wilson,* 425–31; House urged the president to appoint a "War Board" and meet with it once a week. House Diary, Feb. 25, 1918.

10. Polk Diary, Jan. 8, 1918; House Diary, Jan. 9, 1918; House failed in his efforts to push Baker aside.

11. House Diary, Jan. 9, 1918.

12. House Diary, Jan. 17, 1918; S. R. Bertron to House, Jan. 18, 1918, House Papers.

13. House Diary, Jan. 17, 18, 19, 20, 1918; Louis D. Brandeis to House, Jan. 9, 1918, Thomas N. Perkins to House, Jan. 15, 22, 1918, S. R. Bertron to House, Jan. 18, 1916, House Papers.

14. House Diary, Jan. 26, 28, 1918.

15. House Diary, Jan. 24, 29, 1918; Edith Wilson to House, Jan. 30, 1918, Wilson to House, Jan. 30, 1918, House Papers; Wiseman, "Notes on Interview with the President," Jan. 23, 1918, in *PWW,* XXXXVI, 85–88.

16. House Diary, Feb. 1, 2, 3, 4, 22, 1918; Felix Frankfurter to House, March 12, 24, 1918, House Papers; Robert C. Bannister Jr., *Ray Stannard Baker: The Mind and Thought of a Progressive* (New Haven, Conn., 1966), 177.

17. Stevenson, *Cataclysm,* 320; House Diary, Jan. 29, 1918; House to Wilson, Jan. 31, Feb. 1, 1918, House Papers; Carl W. Ackerman to House, Feb. 4, 1918, House Papers.

18. House Diary, Feb. 8, 9, 10, 1918.

19. House Diary, Feb. 11, 1918; "An Address to a Joint Session of Congress," *PWW,* XXXXVI, 318–24.

20. House Diary, Feb. 24, 28, 1918; Stevenson, *Cataclysm,* 320; House to Balfour, Feb. 24, March 1, 1918, Balfour to House, Feb. 27, 1918, House Papers.

21. House Diary, Feb. 24, 1918.

22. House Diary, Feb. 19, 24, 25, 27, 1918.

23. House Diary, Feb. 28, 1918.

24. House Diary, Feb. 26, 28, 1918.

25. Roger Chickering, *Imperial Germany and the Great War, 1914–1918,* 2nd ed. (New York, 2004), 157–69; Holger H. Herwig, *The First World War: Germany and Austria-Hungary, 1914–1918* (London, Eng., 1997), 346; Minnie Paget to House, Jan. 28, 1918, House Papers.

26. Herwig, *The First World War,* 356–82.

27. Chickering, *Imperial Germany and the Great War,* 166; Stevenson, *Cataclysm,* 320–22.

28. Herwig, *The First World* War, 384; Chickering, *Imperial Germany and the Great War,* 166; Stevenson, *Cataclysm,* 322–24.

29. John Keegan, *The First World War* (New York, 1999), 392–95; Herwig, *The First World War*, 392–95.

30. Stevenson, *Cataclysm*, 325–33; Herwig, *The First World War,* 351.

31. John Grigg, *Lloyd George: War Leader, 1916–1918* (London, Eng., 2002), 378–405; John Turner, *British Politics and the Great War: Coalition and Conflict, 1915–1918* (New Haven, Conn., 1992), 265–70; J. P. Harris, *Douglas Haig and the First World War* (New York, 2008), 425.

32. Robert Rhodes James, *The British Revolution, 1880–1939* (New York, 1977), 379–84; Grigg, *Lloyd George*, 411–24; Woodward, *Trial by Friendship*, 130–40; Harris, *Haig*, 432–35.

33. Woodward, *Trial by Friendship,* 141–48; George F. Kennan, *Russia Leaves the War* (Princeton, N.J., 1956), 282–329, 460–516.

34. House to Herman Bernstein, Jan. 1, 1918, House Papers; House Diary, Jan. 2, 9, 1918; David W. McFadden, *Alternative Paths: Soviets and Americans, 1917–1920* (New York, 1993), 39–45; Lincoln Steffans to House, Feb. 1, 1918, House Papers.

35. McFadden, *Alternative Paths*, 39–54; Kennan, *Russia Leaves the War*, 264; House Diary, Feb. 25, 28, March 2, 3, 1918; House to Wilson, Feb. 2, March 3, 1918, to Balfour, March 4, 1918, House Papers; "A Memorandum by Sir William Wiseman," March 9, 1918, in *PWW,* XXXXVI, 590–91.

36. House to Wilson, March 10, 1918, House Papers; "To the Fourth All–Russia Congress of Soviets," March 11, 1918, in *PWW,* XXXXVI, 598; Kennan, *Russia Leaves the War,* 510–12; In mid–February House briefly considered American recognition of the Bolsheviks but did not pursue the idea. Wiseman to Reading, Feb. 12, 1918, in *PWW,* XXXXVI, 333–34; Wiseman memorandum for Reading, Feb. 14, 1918, House Papers.

37. Keegan, *The First World War,* 369–404; Herwig, *The First World War,* 392–411.

38. Woodward, *Trial by Friendship*, 149–60; Grigg, *Lloyd George,* 442–64.

39. House to Wilson, March 23, 24, 1918, House Papers; Auchincloss Diary, March 24, 1918; Edith Wilson to House, March 20, 1918, Wilson to House, March 20, 22, 1918, House Papers; House Diary, March 23, 24, 28, 29, 30, April 9, 1918; W. B. Fowler, *British-American Relations, 1917–1918: The Role of Sir William Wiseman* (Princeton, N.J.,1969), 140.

40. House Diary, March 31, April 9, 1918; Auchincloss Diary, April 1, 1918.

41. Wiseman to Foreign Office, March 28, 1918, in *PWW,* XXXXVII, 184–85; Woodward, *Trial by Friendship*, 153–55; House to Wilson, April 9, 1918, to Pershing, April 27, 1918, to Wiseman, May 12, 1918, House Papers.

42. Stevenson, *Cataclysm*, 336–41; Herwig, *The First World War,* 412–16.

43. Martin Gilbert, *The First World War: A Complete History* (New York, 1994), 412–29.

44. Gilbert, *The First World War*, 416–21; Donald Smythe, *Pershing: General of the Armies* (Bloomington, Ind., 1986), 112–17; David F. Trask, *The AEF and Coalition Warmaking, 1917–1918* (Lawrence, Kans., 1993), 61–68.

45. Ferrell, *Wilson and World War I*, 48–52; Meiron and Susie Harries, *The Last Days of Innocence: America at War, 1917–1918* (New York, 1997), 113–16.

46. David M. Kennedy, *Over Here: The First World War and American Society* (New York, 1980), 171–77.

47. Harris, *Haig*, 474; Gilbert, *The First World War*, 421; Smythe, *Pershing*, 116–18; House Diary, May 20, 23, 1918; House to Wilson, May 20, 1918; Wiseman to Drummond, May 30, 1918, in *PWW*, XXXXVIII, 203–6.

48. House to Wilson, May 12, 26, June 3, 1918, House Papers; House Diary, May 25, 1918.

49. House Diary, Jan. 21, 1918; examples of this coverage are "The E. M. House Mystery," *New York Times*, Dec. 16, 1917, and "Col. House Abounds in Facts but Few Persons Know Them," *Los Angeles Times*, Dec. 30, 1917.

50. House Diary, Jan. 25, Feb. 5, 14, 1918; Howden Smith to House, May 1, 1918, House Papers; House realized, however, that "No life of me that would be worth while can be written until some of my important papers can be divulged." House Diary, Feb. 20, 1918.

51. House Diary, April 9, 15, May 14, 22, 1918; House to Edith Wilson, May 5, 1918, *PWW*, XXXXVII, 534; House to Howden Smith, April 30, 1918, House Papers; Wilson to House, May 6, 1918, Edith Wilson to House, May 6, 1918, House Papers; Lippmann to House, May 21, 1918, House Papers; Arthur D. Howden Smith, *Mr. House of Texas* (New York, 1940), 270–72; Phyllis Lee Levin, *Edith and Woodrow: The Wilson White House* (New York, 2001), 211–13.

52. Arthur D. Howden Smith, *The Real Colonel House* (New York, 1918), 13, 21, 274–85: Howden Smith to Dr. Broadman, May 16, 1931, House Papers.

53. Edith Wilson to House, May 1, 1918, Wilson to House, May 6, 1918, House Papers; House Diary, May 17, 1918; in early May, House intervened in the tangled and bitter controversy over the failure of the administration's aircraft production program. To prevent the passage of a Senate resolution authorizing an investigation, House shrewdly suggested that the president appoint Charles Evans Hughes as a special investigator, in effect undercutting Republican support for the resolution. House, who understood the value of bipartisanship, explained to Wilson that "if you use Taft, Root, Hughes and other republicans as you are doing, people will begin to understand that there is some reason why Col. Roosevelt is not available. I have been doing my best to help bring about a [s]chism between such republicans as Taft, Root and Hughes on the one hand and such republicans as Sherman, Brandegee, Penrose and their ilk on the other and it looks as if it might be done." House Diary, May 4, 12, 15, 17, 1918; House to Wilson, May 7, 9, 1918, House Papers; Livermore, *Politics Is Adjourned*, 125–34; Cooper, *Wilson*, 430, 434.

54. House Diary, May 17, 1918.

55. House Diary, May 2, 17, 18, 1918; "An Address in New York on Behalf of the American Red Cross," in *PWW,* XXXXVIII, 53–57; House to Wilson, May 24, 1918, House Papers.

56. House Diary, May 17, 19, 20, 1918; Auchincloss Diary, May 18, 20, 1918; McAdoo to House, May 20, 1918, House Papers.

57. House Diary, May 26, June 5, 1918; Grayson to House, May 14, 1918, McAdoo to House, May 31, 1918, June 3, 1918, House Papers; House to McAdoo, June 6, 1918, House Papers.

58. McAdoo to House, June 14, 1918, House Papers.

CHAPTER 27

1. Janet Auchincloss to Loulie House, Sept. 7, 1918, House Papers; House Diary, June 5, 8, 9, 14, July 23, 1918.

2. Pershing to House, June 19, 1918, House Papers; House to Wilson, June 23, 1918, to Thomas Nelson Page, July 1, 1918, to Pershing, July 4, 1918, House Papers.

3. David R. Woodward, *Trial by Friendship: Anglo-American Relations, 1917–1918* (Lexington, Ky., 1993), 170–84; David French, *The Strategy of the Lloyd George Coalition, 1916–1918* (Oxford, Eng., 1995), 253–59.

4. George F. Kennan, *The Decision to Intervene* (Princeton, N.J., 1958), 365–81; Norman E. Saul, *War and Revolution: The United States and Russia, 1914–1921* (Lawrence, Kans., 2001), 287–88, 301–3; Kennan, *Russia and the West under Lenin and Stalin* (Boston, Mass., 1960), 101–3; Woodward, *Trial by Friendship,* 179.

5. Auchincloss Diary, June 12, 13, 1918; House Diary, June 11, 12, 13, 14, 1918; House to Wilson, June 13, 21, 1918, House Papers; Wiseman to Drummond, June 14, 1918, House Papers; Kennan, *Decision to Intervene,* 385–88.

6. House Diary, June 13, 17, 1918; George H. Nash, *The Life of Herbert Hoover: Master of Emergencies, 1917–1918* (New York, 1996), 463–69. Wilson, however, would not appoint Hoover.

7. House to Wilson, June 21, 1918, House Papers; House Diary, June 26, 1918; House to Norman Hapgood, June 15, 1918, in Saul, *War and Revolution,* 295.

8. Kennan, *Decision to Intervene,* 394–97; Robert Lansing, "Memorandum of a Conference at the White House in Reference to the Siberian Situation," in Arthur S. Link, ed., *The Papers of Woodrow Wilson* [*PWW*] 68 vols. (Princeton, N.J., 1966–93), XXXXVIII, 542–43; David S. Foglesong, *America's Secret War against Bolshevism: U. S. Intervention in the Russian Civil War, 1917–1920* (Chapel Hill, N.C., 1995), 158–64.

9. Wilson to House, July 8, 1918, House Papers; Reading to Balfour, June 25, 1918, in *PWW,* XXXXVIII, 429–31; "Memorandum," July 17, 1918, in *PWW,* XXXXVIII, 640–43; Wiseman to Arthur Cecil Murray, July 4, 1918, in *PWW,* XXXXVIII, 523–25.

10. Kennan, *Decision to Intervene*, 405–22; Charles E. Neu, *The Troubled Encounter: The United States and Japan* (New York, 1975), 95–96.

11. House Diary, July 9, 11, 19, 1918; Phillips Diary, July 23, 1918.

12. Holger H. Herwig, *The First World War: Germany and Austria-Hungary, 1914–1918* (London, Eng., 1997), 416–20; Michael S. Neiberg, *Fighting the Great War: A Global History* (Cambridge, Mass., 2005), 330–31; David F. Trask, *The AEF and Coalition Warmaking, 1917–1918* (Lawrence, Kans., 1993), 97.

13. Robert B. Bruce, *A Fraternity of Arms: America and France in the Great War* (Lawrence, Kans., 2003), 254; David Stevenson, *With Our Backs to the Wall: Victory and Defeat in 1918* (Boston, Mass., 2011), 112–27; Gordon A. Craig, *Germany, 1866–1945* (New York, 1978), 395; Herwig, *The First World War*, 424; Lamar Cecil, *Wilhelm II: Emperor and Exile* (Chapel Hill, N.C., 1996), 294–96.

14. Trask, *The AEF*, 92–93; Meirion and Susie Harries, *The Last Days of Innocence: America at War, 1917–1918* (New York, 1997), 319–21.

15. Donald Smythe, *Pershing: General of the Armies* (Bloomington, Ind., 1986), 161–62; House Diary, June 20, 1918; House to Pershing, July 4, 1918, to Bliss, July 30, 1918, House Papers; as early as July 1 House felt confident of an Allied victory. House to Clemenceau, July 1, 1918, to Thomas Nelson Page, July 1, 1918, House Papers.

16. Smythe, *Pershing*, 162–65; House Diary, Aug. 17, 1918; House to Pershing, Aug. 21, 1918, to Lloyd Griscom, Sept. 6, 1918, House Papers; Bliss to House, Sept. 12, 1918, House Papers.

17. Erez Manela, *The Wilsonian Moment: Self-Determination and the International Origins of Anticolonial Nationalism* (New York, 2007), 43–45; George W. Egerton, *Great Britain and the Creation of the League of Nations: Strategy, Politics, and International Organization, 1914–1919* (Chapel Hill, N.C., 1978), 63–69; Drummond to Wiseman, Feb. 9, 1918, House Papers; Cecil to House, Feb. 16, 1918, House Papers.

18. John Milton Cooper Jr., *Breaking the Heart of the World: Woodrow Wilson and the Fight for the League of Nations* (New York, 2001), 26–28; Thomas J. Knock, *To End All Wars: Woodrow Wilson and the Quest for a New World Order* (New York, 1992), 148–50; Lowell to House, March 13, 1918, House Papers; House to Wilson, March 8, 21, 1918, House Papers.

19. Cooper, *Breaking the Heart of the World*, 25–28; Wilson to House, March 20, 22, 1918, House Papers.

20. "A Memorandum by William Howard Taft," March 29, 1918, in *PWW*, XXXXVII, 198–203; August Heckscher, *Woodrow Wilson* (New York, 1991), 477–78.

21. House Diary, April 11, 1918; Lansing to House, April 8, 1918, House to Lansing, April 13, 1918, House Papers.

22. House Diary, June 11, 20, 24, 1918; House to Cecil, June 25, 1918, to Wilson, June 25, 1918, House Papers; Cecil to House, July 22, 1918, House Papers.

23. Reading to Wilson, July 3, 1918, in *PWW,* XXXXVIII, 501–3; House to Wilson, July 6, 8, 11, 1918, Wilson to House, July 8, 1918, House Papers; House Diary, July 11, 1918; Wiseman to Cecil, July 18, 1918, in *PWW,* XXXXIX, 11–14.

24. House Diary, July 13, 14, 15, 16, 1918; House to Wilson, July 14, 1918, House Papers.

25. House to Wilson, July 16, 1918, House Papers; "Suggestion for a Covenant of a League of Nations," July 15, 1918, House Papers; Knock, *To End All Wars,* 152; House Diary, July 22, 28, 30, Aug. 4, 1918.

26. House Diary, Aug. 14, 1918; Auchincloss Diary, Aug. 10–19, 1918; Edith Wilson to House, July 1, 1918, House to Edith Wilson, July 30, 1918, House Papers.

27. Joseph E. Garland, *Boston's Gold Coast: The North Shore, 1890–1929* (Boston, Mass., 1981), 192, 239; Phyllis Lee Levin, *Edith and Woodrow: The Wilson White House* (New York, 2001), 213; Wiseman to Murray, Aug. 30, 1918, in *PWW,* XXXXIX, 397–99; House Diary, Aug. 15, 16, 17, 18, 19, 1918.

28. House Diary, Aug. 15, 1918; Cooper, *Breaking the Heart of the World,* 29–30.

29. Wiseman to Reading, Aug. 16, 1918, House Papers; House Diary, Aug. 15, 1918; John Milton Cooper Jr., *Woodrow Wilson: A Biography* (New York, 2009), 439–41.

30. House Diary, Aug. 15, 1918; on August 18 House received a tedious, long-overdue letter from Root, outlining his views on international organization. House gave the letter to the president, who read it out loud and concluded that Root "has the wrong idea." House felt he could in time "bring him around to our view"; if not, Root could not be a member of the peace commission. Root to House, Aug. 16, 1918, House to Root, Aug. 23, 1918, House Papers; House Diary, Aug. 18, 1918.

31. House Diary, Aug. 16, 1918; Oswald Garrison Villard to House, Feb. 14, 1918, Samuel Blythe to House, April 9, 1918, A. W. Ricker to House, April 25, 30, 1918, House Papers.

32. House Diary, Aug. 18, 1918.

33. House Diary, Aug. 16, 19, 1918.

34. House Diary, Aug. 19, 1918; Wilson to Jessie Sayre, Aug. 22, 1918, in *PWW,* XXXXIX, 318–19; Edith Wilson to Alice Gordon Grayson, Aug. 30, 1918, Grayson Papers.

35. Martin Gilbert, *The First World War: A Complete History* (New York, 1994), 450–59; Neiberg, *Fighting the Great War,* 345–47; J. P. Harris, *Douglas Haig and the First World War* (Cambridge, Eng., 2008), 499–500; Reading to Wiseman, Sept. 12, 1918, House Papers.

36. House Diary, Aug. 25, 1918; House to Wilson, Sept. 3, 1918, House Papers. Wilson had considered making a trip to California, leaving at the end of September, to support the Fourth Liberty Loan Campaign. McAdoo urged him to go, reminding the president that "You have not been in the West

since you became President, and I think there is a feeling out there that you are inclined to forget your friends in the West." By September 9, Wilson, worried about a prolonged absence from Washington, decided not to make the trip. McAdoo to Wilson, Aug. 27, 1918, in *PWW*, XXXXIX, 361–62; Grayson to Alice Gordon Grayson, Aug. 30, Sept. 4, 1918, Grayson Papers; "A Statement," Sept. 9, 1918, in *PWW*, XXXXIX, 490; Cooper, *Breaking the Heart of the World*, 25.

37. House Diary, Sept. 7, 8, 1918; Edith Wilson to House, June 14, July 1, 1918; House to Edith Wilson, June 23, 1918, House Papers.

38. House Diary, Sept. 8, 1918; earlier in the summer Wilson had tried to reassure his counselor: "I hail your letters with deep satisfaction and unspoken thanks go out to you for each one of them, whether I write or not, most affectionate appreciation of all that you do for me." Wilson to House, July 8, 1918, House Papers.

39. Lippmann to Mezes, Sept. 5, 1918, House Papers.

40. House Diary, Sept. 10, 13, 1918; House to Wilson, Sept. 9, 13, 1918, House Papers.

CHAPTER 28

1. House Diary, Sept. 21, 24, 1918.

2. John M. Blum, *Joe Tumulty and the Wilson Era* (Boston, Mass., 1951), 157–58; David M. Kennedy, *Over Here: The First World War and American Society* (New York, 1980), 233–45; Thomas J. Knock, *To End All Wars: Woodrow Wilson and the Quest for a New World Order* (New York, 1992), 169.

3. House Diary, Sept. 24, 1918; Seward W. Livermore, *Politics Is Adjourned: Woodrow Wilson and the War Congress, 1916–1918* (Middletown, Conn., 1966), 135, 181–82.

4. House Diary, Sept. 27, 1918; House to Wilson, Sept. 25, 1918, House Papers; Thomas H. Hartig, *Robert Lansing: An Interpretive Biography* (New York, 1982), 280–81.

5. House Diary, Sept. 27, 1918; Knock, *To End All Wars*, 162.

6. "An Address in the Metropolitan Opera House," Sept. 27, 1918, in Arthur S. Link, ed., *The Papers of Woodrow Wilson* [*PWW*], 68 vols. (Princeton, N.J., 1966–93), LI, 127–33.

7. House Diary, Sept. 27, 1918; House to Wilson, Sept. 30, 1918, House Papers.

8. "President Says War Must Achieve a Peace Based on Equal Justice for All Peoples," *New York Times*, Sept. 28, 1918; Knock, *To End All Wars*, 163–65; "A Memorandum of a Conversation by Thomas William Lamont," Oct. 4, 1918, in *PWW*, LI, 220–26.

9. Holger H. Herwig, *The First World War: Germany and Austria-Hungary, 1914–1918* (New York, 1997), 423–26; David Stevenson, *Cataclysm: The First World War as Political Tragedy* (New York, 2004), 348–71; Robert B. Asprey, *The*

German High Command at War: Hindenburg and Ludendorff Conduct World War I (New York, 1991), 459–71.

10. House Diary, Oct. 6, 1918; House to Wilson, Oct. 6, 1918, House Papers.

11. Auchincloss Diary, Oct. 8, 1918; House Diary, Oct. 9, 1918; Klaus Schwabe, *Woodrow Wilson, Revolutionary Germany, and Peacemaking, 1918–1919: Missionary Diplomacy and the Realities of Power* (Chapel Hill, N.C., 1985), 30–41.

12. Note no. 7 in *PWW*, LI, 277–78; Tumulty to House, Oct. 7, 1918, House Papers; Tumulty to Wilson, Oct. 8, 1918, in *PWW*, LI, 265–68; House Diary, Oct. 9, 1918.

13. "The Penultimate Draft of a Note to the German Government," October 8, 1918, in *PWW*, LI, 264–65; Schwabe, *Woodrow Wilson*, 44–47; Binoy Kampmark, " 'No Peace with the Hohenzollerns': American Attitudes on Political Legitimacy towards Hohenzollern Germany, 1917–1918," *Diplomatic History*, 14, 5 (Nov. 2010), 769–91.

14. House Diary, Oct. 9, 13, 1918.

15. Schwabe, *Woodrow Wilson*, 47–50; Asprey, *The German High Command*, 472–73.

16. House Diary, Oct. 15, 1918; "A Draft of a Note to the German Government," Oct. 14, 1918, in *PWW*, LI, 333–34; Schwabe, *Woodrow Wilson*, 50–55.

17. David R. Woodward, *Trial by Friendship: Anglo-American Relations, 1917–1918* (Lexington, Ky, 1993), 208–13; G. R. Conye, *Woodrow Wilson: British Perspectives, 1912–21* (New York, 1992), 138–45; John Grigg, *Lloyd George: War Leader, 1916–1918* (London, Eng., 2002), 619–30; Stevenson, *Cataclysm*, 387–88.

18. House Diary, Oct. 15, 1918; "A Memorandum by Sir William Wiseman," Oct. 16, 1918, in *PWW*, LI, 347–52; Wilson, "To Whom It May Concern," Oct. 14, 1918, House Papers; British naval intelligence had no trouble breaking House's "childish code." Patrick Beasly, *Root 40: British Naval Intelligence, 1914–1918* (New York, 1982), 213, 293.

19. House to Wilson, Oct. 16, 1918, Edith Wilson to House, Oct. 15, 1918, House Papers.

20. "A Memorandum by Sir William Wiseman," Oct. 16, 1918, in *PWW*, LI, 347–52; House Diary, Oct. 22, 1918; Auchincloss Diary, Oct. 18, 19–23, 1918; Auchincloss to Polk, Oct. 24, 1918, House Papers; Joseph C. Grew, *Turbulent Era: A Diplomatic Record of Forty Years, 1904–1945* (Boston, Mass., 1952), I, 331–39.

21. Schwabe, *Woodrow Wilson*, 54–68.

22. House Diary, Oct. 24, 28, 1918; Inga Floto, *Colonel House in Paris: A Study of American Policy at the Paris Peace Conference 1919* (Princeton, N.J., 1980), 38–42.

23. House Diary, Oct. 25, 1918; "A Memorandum by Homer Stille Cummings," Oct. 20, 1918, in *PWW*, LI, 389–93; "An Appeal for a Democratic Congress," Oct. 19, 1918, in *PWW*, LI, 381–82; John Milton Cooper Jr., *Woodrow Wilson: A Biography* (New York, 2009), 445–46.

24. House Diary, Oct. 26, 1918; Auchincloss Diary, Oct. 19–23, 26, 1918.

25. "From the Diary of Josephus Daniels," Oct. 17, 1918, in *PWW*, LI, 372; Meirion and Susie Harries, *The Last Days of Innocence: America at War, 1917–1918* (New York, 1997), 405–12; Donald Smythe, *Pershing: General of the Armies* (Bloomington, Ind., 1986), 190–237; House also received reports, however, indicating that Wilson had tremendous support among "liberal and socialist forces" in Europe. Elmer Roberts to House, Nov. 1, 1918, Ray Stannard Baker to House, Nov. 1, 1918, House Papers.

26. Niall Ferguson, *The Pity of War* (New York, 1998), 337; Bliss to Baker, Oct. 23, 1918, in *PWW*, LI, 583–87; David French, *The Strategy of the Lloyd George Coalition, 1916–1918* (Oxford, Eng., 1995), 273–77; Woodward, *Trial by Friendship*, 214–15.

27. House Diary, Oct. 26, 27, 1918; House to Wilson, Oct. 27, 1918; W. B. Fowler, *British-American Relations, 1917–1918: The Role of Sir William Wiseman* (Princeton, N.J., 1969), 223–24.

28. House to Wilson, Oct. 29, 1918, House Papers; House Diary, Oct. 29, 1918; Ronald Steel, *Walter Lippman and the American Century* (Boston, Mass., 1980), 149–50.

29. Charles Seymour, *The Intimate Papers of Colonel House* (Boston, Mass., 1928), IV, 97–99.

30. Auchincloss Diary, Oct. 28, 1918; House to Wilson, Oct. 29, 1918, House Papers; "Notes of a Conversation in M. Pichon's Room at the Quai d'Orsay, Paris, on Thursday, Oct. 29, 1918, at 3 p. m.," House Papers; Stephen Roskill, *Hankey: Man of Secrets, 1877–1918* (London, Eng., 1970), I, 622–23; Fowler, *Wiseman*, 225; Stephen Bonsal, *Unfinished Business* (Garden City, N.Y., 1944), 1–4.

31. House to Wilson, Oct. 29, 30, 1918, Wilson to House, Oct. 29, 30, 1918, House Papers; Auchincloss Diary, Oct. 30, 1918; House Diary, Oct. 29, 30, 1918; Internal evidence suggests that the diary entry for Oct. 29, 1918 was, in fact, dictated after the morning meeting on October 30. Floto, *Colonel House*, 285.

32. House Diary, Oct. 29, 30, 1918; House to Wilson, Oct. 30, 1918, House Papers; Roskill, *Hankey*, 623–24; "Notes of a Conversation in M. Pichon's Room at the Quai d'Orsay, on Wednesday, October 30, 1918, 3 p. m.," House Papers.

33. House to Wilson, Oct. 27, 30, 1918, Wilson to House, Oct. 29, 1918, House Papers; Schwabe, *Woodrow Wilson*, 87–91; Baker to Pershing, Oct. 27, 1918, in *PWW*, LI, 470–71.

34. House to Wilson, Oct. 30, 31, 1918, Wilson to House, Oct. 31, 1918, House Papers.

35. Elizabeth, Greenhalgh, *Foch in Command: The Forging of a First World War General* (Cambridge, Eng., 2011), 471–78; House Diary, Nov. 1, 1918; Auchincloss Diary, Nov. 2, 1918; "Notes on a Conversation at the residence of Colonel House, 78, Rue de l'Université, Paris, on Friday, November 1, 1918, at 11 a. m.," House Papers; Smythe, *Pershing*, 221–22; Pershing to House,

Oct. 30, 1918, to SWC, Oct. 30, 1918, House to Wilson, Oct. 31, 1918, House Papers; Pershing Diary, Oct. 30, Nov. 2, 1918; House Diary, Oct. 30, Nov. 2, 1918.

36. House Diary, Nov. 2, 1918; Auchincloss Diary, Nov. 2, 1918.

37. House Diary, Nov. 3, 4, 1918; Auchincloss Diary, Nov. 3, 1918; House to Wilson, Nov. 3, 1918, House Papers; Roskill, *Hankey*, 626–27; "Notes on a Conversation at the residence of Colonel House, 78, Rue de l'Université, Paris, on Friday, November 3, 1918, at 3 p. m.," House Papers; Lloyd George to House, Nov. 3, 1918, House Papers.

38. House Diary, Nov. 4, 1918; Auchincloss Diary, Nov. 5, 1918; Auchincloss to Polk, Nov. 10, 1918, House Papers; Lippmann to House, Nov. 7, 1918, House Papers.

39. House to Wilson, Nov. 5, 1918, House Papers.

40. Woodward, *Trial by Friendship*, 218–19; Grigg, *Lloyd George*, 637.

41. Harries, *Last Days of Innocence*, 412–14; Floto, *Colonel House*, 57–60; Arthur Walworth, *America's Moment: 1918, American Diplomacy at the End of World War I* (New York, 1977), 72–73; Cooper, *Wilson*, 449–53; Thomas J. Knock, "Wilsonian Concepts and International Realities at the End of the War," in Manfred F. Boemeke, Gerald D. Feldman, and Elisabeth Glaser, eds., *The Treaty of Versailles: A Reassessment After 75 Years* (New York, 1998), 111–129; Throughout the pre-armistice negotiations, House, Clemenceau, and Lloyd George avoided any discussion of Italian reservations to the Fourteen Points. But on October 30, House had a tense meeting with Orlando. Confronted with the Italian prime minister's emotional rhetoric, House gave him the substance of the concessions granted in the Treaty of London. He did not mention this conversation in his diary or report it to Wilson. In another conversation with Orlando on November 3, House reassured the prime minister that Wilson, when he arrived in Europe, would consider Italian territorial claims "in the most sympathetic spirit." Italian leaders concluded that the United States supported their nation's ambitions in the Adriatic region. Floto, *Colonel House*, 54; "Conversation between Senior Orlando and Colonel House, November 3rd, 1918, 5 p. m.," House Papers; House Diary, Nov. 3, 9, 1918; Daniela Rossini, *Woodrow Wilson and the American Myth in Italy: Culture, Diplomacy, and War Propaganda* (Cambridge, Mass., 2008), 169–76, 249.

42. Daniel D. Stid, *The President as Statesman: Woodrow Wilson and the Constitution* (Lawrence, Kans., 1998), 136–50; Knock, *To End All Wars*, 184–89; David Burner, *The Politics of Provincialism: The Democratic Party in Transition, 1918–1932* (New York, 1968), 33–40; Cooper, *Wilson*, 447–48; Villard to Tumulty, Nov. 8, 1918, in *PWW*, LI, 646; "A Memorandum by Homer Stille Cummings," Nov. 8 or 9, 1918, in *PWW*, LI, 646–48; Cobb to House, Nov. 8, 1918, House Papers; House Diary, Nov. 6, 1918.

43. Evelyn Princess Blucher, *An English Wife in Berlin* (New York, 1920), 253; Herwig, *The First World War*, 427–28, 440–46.

44. Harries, *Last Days of Innocence*, 415–16; Gilbert, *The First World War*, 500.

45. George F. Kennan, *The Decline of Bismark's European Order: Franco-Russian Relations, 1875–1890* (Princeton, N.J., 1979), 3; Neiberg, *Fighting the Great War*, 362–64; David Stevenson, *With Our Backs to the Wall: Victory and Defeat in 1918* (Cambridge, Mass., 2011), 509–45.

46. House Diary, Nov. 10, 11, 1918; House to Wilson, Nov. 11, 1918, House Papers.

47. Edith Bolling Wilson, *My Memoir* (Indianapolis, Ind., 1939), 170–71; House to Wilson, Nov. 10, 1918, House Papers; "An Address to a Joint Session of Congress," Nov. 11, 1918, in *PWW*, LIII, 35–43; Ray Stannard Baker, *American Chronicle: The Autobiography of Ray Stannard Baker* (New York, 1945), 364.

CHAPTER 29

1. Arno J. Mayer, *Politics and Diplomacy of Peacemaking: Containment and Counterrevolution at Versailles, 1918–1919* (New York, 1967), 253–54; John Milton Cooper Jr., *Pivotal Decades: The United States, 1900–1920* (New York, 1990), 320; Ronald Steel, *Walter Lippmann and the American Century* (Boston, Mass., 1980), 152.

2. House to Wilson, Oct. 28, 30, House Papers; House Diary, Oct. 29, 1918.

3. Wilson to House, Oct. 29, Nov. 8, 1918, House to Wilson, Nov. 9, 1918, House Papers; House Diary, Nov. 8, 9, 1918.

4. House Diary, Aug. 15, Nov. 12, 1918; David Dutton, ed., *Paris 1918: The War Diary of the 17th Earl of Derby* (Liverpool, Eng., 2001), 327; Summary of Talk between Colonel House and Lord Derby, Nov. 12, 1918, House Papers.

5. John Milton Cooper Jr., *Breaking the Heart of the World: Woodrow Wilson and the Fight for the League of Nations* (New York, 2001), 32–33; Charles E. Neu, "Woodrow Wilson and His Foreign Policy Advisers," in William N. Tilchin and Charles E. Neu, eds., *Artists of Power: Theodore Roosevelt, Woodrow Wilson, and Their Enduring Impact on U. S. Foreign Policy* (Westport, Conn., 2006), 77–94; Wilson never responded to House's cable of November 5, 1918, declaring the pre-armistice agreement a great triumph of American diplomacy.

6. Thomas J. Knock, *To End All Wars: Woodrow Wilson and the Quest for a New World Order* (New York, 1992), 190–92; Key Pittman to the President, Nov. 15, 1918, in Arthur S. Link, ed., *The Papers of Woodrow Wilson* [*PWW*], 68 vols. (Princeton, N.J., 1966-93), LIII, 93–95; "From the Diary of Josephus Daniels," Nov. 12, 1918, in *PWW*, LIII, 65; "An Annual Message on the State of the Union," Dec. 2, 1918, in *PWW*, LIII, 274–86.

7. "A Memorandum by Frank Irving Cobb," Nov. 4, 1918, *PWW*, LIII, 590–91; House to Wilson, Nov. 14, 1918, Wilson to House, Nov. 16, 19, 1918, House Papers.

8. House Diary, Nov. 16, Dec. 3, 1918; House to Wilson, Nov. 19, 1918, House Papers; McAdoo was eager to join House at the peace conference. House

Diary, Oct. 13, 1918; McAdoo to House, Dec. 14, 1918, Jan. 13, 1919, House to McAdoo, Dec. 18, 1918, House Papers.

9. House Diary, Aug. 15, Oct. 6, 13, 15, 16, 1918.

10. Wilson to House, Nov. 14, 1918, House Papers; Baker to Wilson, Nov. 23, 1918, in *PWW*, LIII, 182–83; "A Press Release," Nov. 29, 1918, in *PWW*, LIII, 243; House Diary, Dec. 1, 1918.

11. Cooper, *Breaking the Heart of the World*, 34–38; John Milton Cooper Jr., *Woodrow Wilson: A Biography* (New York, 2009), 456–58.

12. House to Wilson, Nov. 8, 9, 12, 16, 20, 1918, Wilson to House, Nov. 22, 1918, House Papers.

13. Arthur Walworth, *America's Moment: 1918, American Diplomacy at the End of World War I* (New York, 1977), 210–30; House Diary, Dec. 12, 13, 19, 26, 1918, Jan. 4, 1919.

14. George H. Nash, *The Life of Herbert Hoover: The Humanitarian, 1914–1917* (New York, 1988), 365–78.

15. Janet Auchincloss Diary, Dec. 19, 1918; House Diary, Feb. 16, 1915, Dec. 19, 1918.

16. Inga Floto, *Colonel House in Paris: A Study of American Policy at the Paris Peace Conference 1919* (Princeton, N. J., 1980), 62–67; House to Wilson, Oct. 22, Nov. 15, 21, 23, 1918, House Papers; House Diary, Nov. 15, 19, Dec. 7, 1918.

17. Fanny Denton to her mother, Nov. 17, 1918, House Papers; Stephen Bonsal, *Unfinished Business* (New York, 1944), 5–6; Auchincloss to Polk, Nov. 15, 21, 1918, House Papers; Auchincloss Diary, Nov. 21, 22, 23, 25, 28, 29, 1918; House Diary, Nov. 30, 1918; House to Polk, Nov. 20, 1918, to Wilson, Nov. 30, 1918, to Joseph N. Nye, Dec. 8, 1918, House Papers.

18. Cooper, *Wilson*, 460–62; Lawrence E. Gelfand, *The Inquiry: American Preparations for Peace, 1917–1919* (New Haven, Conn., 1963), 168–74; House Diary, Dec. 9, 1918.

19. "From the Diary of Dr. Grayson," Dec. 13, 1918, in *PWW*, LIII, 378–79; Auchincloss Diary, Dec. 13, 1918; House to Wilson, Dec. 12, 1918; House Diary, Dec. 4, 13, 1918.

20. "From the Diary of Raymond Blaine Fosdick," Dec. 14, 1918, in *PWW*, LIII, 384–85; Edith Wilson to her Family, Dec. 15, 1918, in *PWW*, LIII, 396–99.

21. House Diary, Dec. 14, 1918; Floto, *Colonel House in Paris*, 68–69; Auchincloss Diary, Dec. 15, 1918.

22. House Diary, Dec. 14, 1918; Auchincloss Diary, Dec. 14, 1918; Auchincloss to Polk, Dec. 15, 1918, House Papers.

23. House Diary, Dec. 15, 1918; Wiseman to Foreign Office, Dec. 15, 1918, in *PWW*, LIII, 394–96.

24. House Diary, Dec. 15, 1918; Derby to Balfour, Dec. 16, 1918, in *PWW*, LIII, 409–10.

25. House Diary, Dec. 16, 17, 18, 1918.

26. House Diary, Dec. 18, 19, 1918; Derby to Balfour, Dec. 20, 1918, in *PWW*, LIII, 456–57; Derby was also unimpressed with Wilson, reporting that "nobody can

help liking him but at the same time his views seem to me of the most visionary character." Derby to Balfour, Dec. 22, 1918, in *PWW*, LIII, 470–71.

27. House Diary, Dec. 19, 21, 1918; Auchincloss Diary, Dec. 21, 1918; House to R. M. Johnston, Jan. 5, 1919, House Papers.

28. House Diary, Dec. 20, 21, 1918; Daniela Rossini, *Woodrow Wilson and the American Myth in Italy: Culture, Diplomacy, and War Propaganda* (Cambridge, Mass., 2008), 179; Mayer, *Politics and Diplomacy of Peacemaking*, 197–204.

29. House Diary, Dec. 9, 12, 15, 17, 18, 20, 1918; Auchincloss to Polk, Dec. 20, 1918, House Papers.

30. Clemenceau told House on Dec. 5, 1918, that the peace conference could not begin before the first of January 1919. House Diary, Dec. 5, 1918; Balfour to House, Dec. 13, 1918, House Papers.

31. House Diary, Dec. 17, 1918; House to William E. Dodd, Jan. 6, 1919, House Papers; Cooper, *Wilson*, 464–65; House made no secret of his dislike of Lloyd George, telling Derby that "there would be no differences between Great Britain and the United States provided we had to deal with such men as Balfour, Grey, himself or any number of Englishmen I could name. In other words, I made it clear that Lloyd George was the stumbling block." House Diary, Dec. 11, 1918.

32. House Diary, Dec. 24, 25, 1918; Derby to Balfour, Dec. 24, 1918, in *PWW*, LIII, 498–99; Auchincloss to House, Dec. 25, 1918, House Papers; Auchincloss Diary, Dec. 20, 1918.

33. Auchincloss to House, Dec. 25, 1918, House Papers; House to Thad A. Thomson, Dec. 24, 1918, to Wilson, Dec. 25, 1918, House Papers; Auchincloss Diary, Dec. 24, 25, 1918.

34. G. R. Conye, *Woodrow Wilson: British Perspectives, 1912–21* (New York, 1992), 149–54; George W. Egerton, *Great Britain and the Creation of the League of Nations: Strategy, Politics, and International Organization, 1914–1919* (Chapel Hill, N.C., 1978), 105–09; Imperial War Cabinet Memorandum, Dec. 30, 1918, in *PWW*, LIII, 558–69.

35. John Turner, *British Politics and the Great War: Coalition and Conflict, 1915–1918* (New Haven, Conn., 1992), 317–33; Mayer, *Politics and Diplomacy of Peacemaking*, 133–66; Robert Rhodes James, *The British Revolution, 1880–1939* (New York, 1977), 390–92.

36. Auchincloss Diary, Dec. 25, 26, 27, 28, 30, 1918; House Diary, Dec. 27, 28, 1918; Floto, *Colonel House in Paris*, 85–86.

37. Mayer, *Politics and Diplomacy of Peacemaking*, 179–86; Henry Blumenthal, *Illusion and Reality in Franco-American Diplomacy, 1914–1945* (Baton Rouge, La., 1986), 71.

38. House Diary, Dec. 30, 31, 1918; Derby to Balfour, Jan. 6, 1919, in *PWW*, LIII, 633–34.

39. Mayer, *Politics and Diplomacy of Peacemaking*, 194–226; Rossini, *Wilson*, 179–80; Ray Stannard Baker to House, Dec. 6, 1918, House Papers.

40. House Diary, Jan. 3, 4, 6, 7, 1919; Auchincloss Diary, Jan. 9, 1919.

41. House Diary, Jan. 7, 8, 1919; Knock, *To End All Wars*, 201–8.

CHAPTER 30

1. Gregor Dallas, *1918: War and Peace* (New York, 2001), 324–35; August Heckscher, *Woodrow Wilson* (New York, 1991), 513–14.

2. Margaret MacMillan, *Paris 1919: Six Months That Changed the World* (New York, 2001), xxvi–xxvii, 26–27; Erez Manela, *The Wilsonian Moment: Self–Determination and the International Origins of Anticolonial Nationalism* (New York, 2007), 59: Elsa Maxwell, *R.S.V.P.: Elsa Maxwell's Own Story* (Boston, Mass., 1954), 135.

3. Janet Auchincloss Diary, Jan. 12, 1919; Gordon Auchincloss Diary, Jan. 11, 12, 13, 1919; Arthur Walworth, *Wilson and His Peacemakers: American Diplomacy at the Paris Peace Conference of 1919* (New York, 1986), 29.

4. House Diary, Jan. 21, 23, 1919; House to Thomas Nelson Page, Jan. 28, 1919, to Lord Northcliffe, Feb. 7, 1919, House Papers.

5. Heckscher, *Wilson*, 514–15; MacMillan, *Paris 1919*, 53–57; Grayson to Alice Gordon Grayson, Jan. 13, 1919, Grayson Papers.

6. House Diary, Jan. 21, 22, 1919; McCormick Diary, Jan. 29, 1919; Inga Floto, *Colonel House in Paris: A Study of American Policy at the Paris Peace Conference of 1919* (Princeton, N.J., 1980), 100.

7. MacMillan, *Paris 1919*, 85–86; Thomas J. Knock, *To End All Wars: Woodrow Wilson and the Quest for a New World Order* (New York, 1992), 209; "Protocol of a Plenary Session of the Inter-Allied Conference for the Preliminaries of Peace, Jan. 25, 1919," in Arthur S. Link, ed., *The Papers of Woodrow Wilson* [*PWW*], 68 vols. (Princeton, N.J., 1966–93), LIV, 264–71; Note from House to Wilson, Jan. 25, 1919, House Papers; House Diary, Jan. 25, 26, 1919.

8. Zara Steiner, *The Lights That Failed: European International History, 1919–1933* (Oxford, Eng., 2005), 26–34; Patrick O. Cohrs, *The Unfinished Peace after World War I: America, Britain and the Stabilisation of Europe, 1919–1932* (Cambridge, Eng., 2006), 40–45.

9. MacMillan, *Paris 1919*, 37–38; Lord Robert Cecil, *A Great Experiment: An Autobiography* (New York, 1941), 67.

10. Steiner, *The Lights That Failed*, 4; MacMillan, *Paris 1919*, 43–49; Knock, *To End All Wars*, 211–13; House Diary, Jan. 27, 28, 29, 30, 1919.

11. House Diary, Jan. 30, 1919.

12. House Diary, Feb. 3, 1919; MacMillan, *Paris 1919*, 91.

13. George W. Egerton, *Great Britain and the Creation of the League of Nations: Strategy, Politics, and International Organization, 1914–1919* (Chapel Hill, N.C., 1978), 114–26; House Diary, Jan. 21, 27, 30, 31, Feb. 3, 1919; Cecil Diary, Feb. 3, 1919, in *PWW*, LIV, 460–61.

14. House Diary, Feb. 3, 4, 6, 7, 8, 9, 10, 11, 12, 13, 1919; Knock, *To End All Wars*, 217–21; on February 4, the day before the League of Nations Commission got

under way, Baron Makino and Viscount Chinda, the Japanese delegates on the commission, visited House and proposed adding a racial equality clause to the covenant. House seemed sympathetic, telling the Japanese representatives how much he "deprecated race, religious or other kinds of prejudice" and suggested that they "prepare two resolutions, one which they desired, and another which they would be willing to accept in lieu of the one they prefer." He sought to find a compromise, but soon learned that Balfour, Cecil, and the rest of the British empire delegation were opposed to any sort of clause. On February 13, the day before the League of Nations Commission finished its work, Makino and Chinda agreed to withdraw their amendment. The issue of racial equality was, in fact, postponed rather than resolved. Even so, House was relieved, noting that "it has taken considerable finesse to lift the load from our shoulders and place it upon the British, but happily it has been done," House Diary, Feb. 4, 6, 9, 12, 13, 1919; Knock, *To End All Wars*, 223–24.

15. Steiner, *The Lights That Failed,* 20–26; Cohrs, *The Unfinished Peace,* 48–51; MacMillan, *Paris 1919,* 31–35.

16. Knock, *To End All Wars,* 221–23; House Diary, Feb. 11, 1919; Grayson Diary, Feb. 12, 1919, in *PWW,* LIV, 94.

17. House Diary, Feb. 9, 11, 1919.

18. "An Address to the Third Plenary Session of the Peace Conference," Feb. 14, 1919, in *PWW,* LIV, 164–78; Knock, *To End All Wars,* 225–26; House Diary, Feb. 14, 1919; House to Wilson, Feb. 14, 1919, Wilson to House, Feb. 14, 1919, House Papers.

19. John Milton Cooper Jr., *Woodrow Wilson: A Biography* (New York, 2009), 467, 474–75; "An Address to the Third Plenary Session of the Peace Conference," Feb. 14, 1919, in *PWW,* LIV, 164–78; Steiner, *The Lights That Failed,* 40–43.

20. House Diary, Feb. 14, 1919; Floto, *Colonel House in Paris,* 103; Stephen Bonsal, *Unfinished Business* (Garden City, N.Y., 1944), 49–50.

21. House Diary, Feb. 14, 1919; Andrew J. Peters to House, Feb. 25, 1919, House Papers; Wilson to Tumulty, Feb. 14, 1919, House Papers; House told Bonsal that "in my judgment you can never look over the probable field of battle too soon, and a man in my confidence has been making a tally of the probable vote on ratification of the unfinished treaty in the Senate. It is clear to me that not nearly as many Senators, as the President thinks, are 'sold' on the Treaty and the Covenant, but if he plays his cards well he will win. So today in our talk I told him I was already counting noses, and as that made him laugh I went into details." House believed that "the President could best direct future negotiations from Washington. There he would be in a calmer atmosphere and have the advantage of enjoying close contact with developing American opinion." Bonsal, *Unfinished Business,* 59.

22. House Diary, Feb. 14, 1919; Bonsal Diary, Feb. 15, 1919, in Bonsal, *Unfinished Business,* 58; Edith Wilson to House, Feb. 15, 1919, House Papers. Two days after Wilson left Paris, House received more evidence of his friend's high

regard for him. One of his many friends, Lady Johnstone, told him of a talk with the president in which she had challenged him to name a great man "in the world today." Wilson responded: "I think Colonel House is such a man, and that he is equal to the task." House was not aware, however, of doubts about him that were growing among some members of Wilson's inner circle. Grayson observed that "the bacillus of Ego has badly infected G. A. [Gordon Auchincloss]," while Edith complained to her husband that his counselor had misjudged Clemenceau. Grayson noted that "Colonel House made a big mistake in his estimate of him [Clemenceau] to the President," and also noted that "Mrs. House is getting in worse all the time with W. W. and E. B. W." House Diary, Feb. 16, 1919; Grayson to Alice Gordon Grayson, Jan. 22, 29, 1919, Grayson Papers; Benham Diary, Feb. 9, 1919, in *PWW*, LV, 40–41; Grayson Diary, Feb. 8, 1919, in *PWW*, LV, 3.

23. Knock, *To End All Wars*, 228; Floto, *Colonel House in Paris*, 104.

24. Cooper, *Wilson*, 476–79; Grayson Diary, Feb. 24, 26, 1919, in *PWW*, LV, 267; Polk to Auchincloss, Feb. 24, 1919, House Papers.

25. Wilson to Edward William Bok, Feb. 27, 1919, in *PWW*, LV, 303; John Milton Cooper Jr., *Breaking the Heart of the World: Woodrow Wilson and the Fight for the League of Nations* (New York, 2001), 55–71; Knock, *To End All Wars*, 233–45.

26. William Phillips to House, March 4, 1919, House Papers; "An Address at the Metropolitan Opera House," March 4, 1919, in *PWW*, LV, 413–21.

27. Ray Stannard Baker, *American Chronicle* (New York, 1945), 369; Lloyd Griscom, *Diplomatically Speaking* (Boston, Mass., 1940), 359; William L. Westermann Diary, Dec. 18, 1918, Columbia University; James T. Shotwell, *The Autobiography of James T. Shotwell* (Indianapolis, Ind., 1961), 81; Shotwell Oral History Interview, 85–90.

28. David Lloyd George, *Memoirs of the Peace Conference* (New Haven, Conn., 1939), I, 157–58; Harold Nicolson, *Peacemaking 1919* (London, 1964), 15; Arthur James Balfour, *Retrospect: An Unfinished Autobiography* (London, 1930), 244; Cecil Diary, Feb. 6, 1919, in *PWW*, LIV, 514; Cecil, *A Great Experiment*, 64.

29. Gregor Dallas, *At the Heart of a Tiger: Clemenceau and His World, 1841–1929* (New York, 1993), 516; Wythe Williams, *The Tiger of France: Conversations with Clemenceau* (New York, 1949), 184–85; MacMillan, *Paris 1919*, 18.

30. George Creel, *Rebel at Large: Reflections of Fifty Crowded Years* (New York, 1947), 242; Bernard M. Baruch, *Baruch: The Public Years* (New York, 1960), 141.

31. MacMillan, *Paris 1919*, 64–74; George F. Kennan, *Russia and the West under Lenin and Stalin* (Boston, Mass., 1960), 121–25.

32. David W. McFadden, *Alternative Paths: Soviets and Americans, 1917–1920* (New York, 1993), 191–98.

33. Floto, *Colonel House in Paris*, 108–9; McFadden, *Alternative Paths*, 198–209.

34. McFadden, *Alternative Paths,* 205, 213; House Diary, Feb. 15, 1919; House to William E. Dodd, Jan. 6, 1919, House Papers; Wilson to the American Commissioners, Feb. 19, 1919, House Papers.

35. Martin Gilbert, *Winston S. Churchill: The Stricken World, 1916–1922* (Boston, Mass., 1975), IV, 255; House Diary, Feb. 16, 17, 18, 1919; House to Wilson, Feb. 17, 1919, Wilson to House, Feb. 23, 1919, House Papers.

36. Floto, *Colonel House in Paris,* 105–15; McFadden, *Alternative Paths,* 218–26; Bullitt to House, Jan. 19, 30, Feb. 11, 1919, House Papers; Note, in *PWW,* LV, 541; Will Brownell and Richard N. Billings, *So Close to Greatness: A Biography of William C. Bullitt* (New York, 1987), 78–82.

37. Floto, *Colonel House in Paris,* 102–4; House to Dodd, Jan. 6, 1919, House Papers; MacMillan, *Paris 1919,* 143.

38. Maurice Hankey to House, Feb. 19, 1919, House Papers; "Draft Resolution Proposed by Mr. Balfour," Feb. 19, 1919, House Papers.

39. House Diary, Feb. 19, 20, 21, 1919; House to Wilson, Feb. 19, 20, 21, 1919, Wilson to House, Feb. 23, 1919, House Papers.

40. House Diary, Feb. 22, 1919; House to Wilson, Feb. 23, 1919, House Papers; Stephen A. Schuker, "The Rhineland Question: West European Security at the Paris Peace Conference of 1919," in Manfred F. Boemeke, Gerald D. Feldman, and Elisabeth Glaser, eds., *The Treaty of Versailles: A Reassessment after 75 Years* (New York, 1998), 275–96.

41. MacMillan, *Paris 1919,* 173–74; House Diary, Feb. 9, 11, 29, 1919; McCormick Diary, Feb. 23, 1919; House to Wilson, Feb. 24, 1919, House Papers.

42. House Diary, Feb. 23, 26, 27, 1919; Auchincloss to Polk, Feb. 27, 1919, House Papers; House to Wilson, March 1, 1919, to McAdoo, March 8, 1919, House Papers; in many talks with journalists during Wilson's absence, House indiscreetly emphasized his own diplomatic skills and suggested that the conference was proceeding more quickly because of the absence of Wilson and Lloyd George. Walworth, *Wilson and the Peacemakers,* 149, 161–62.

43. House Diary, Feb. 27, March 2, 1919; McCormick Diary, March 2, 1919; Floto, *Colonel House in Paris,* 128–30; for an impassioned defense of House, see Arthur Walworth, "Considerations on Woodrow Wilson and Edward M. House: An Essay Letter to the Editor," *Presidential Studies Quarterly,* 24, 1(Winter 1991), 79–86; House to Wilson, Feb. 27, 1919, Wilson to House, March 4, 1919; Note, in *PWW,* LV, 305; Egerton, *Great Britain and the Creation of the League,* 150–51.

44. Floto, *Colonel House in Paris,* 139–40; MacMillan, *Paris 1919,* 150; Auchincloss Diary, March 7, 1919; House Diary, March 3, 1919. After recovering from his illness in January, House seemed to tolerate the grueling pace of the conference fairly well. Only occasionally did he complain about the workload. On March 10, however, one observer found him very weary, sunk low in his chair, and speaking in a "listless voice." Janet Auchincloss Diary, Feb. 4, 1919; House Diary, Feb. 16, March 7, 12, 1919; House to Edward S. Martin, Feb. 7,

1919, to C. P. Scott, March 10, 1919, House Papers; Arthur Sweetser Diary, March 10, 1919.

45. House Diary, March 4, 1919; House to Wilson, March 4, 1919, House Papers.

46. Floto, *Colonel House in Paris*, 150–52; House Diary, March 6, 1919; Auchincloss Diary, March 11, 1919.

47. House Diary, March 6, 7, 1919.

48. House Diary, March 7, 10, 1919; Auchincloss Diary, March 10, 11, 1919; House to Wilson, March 7, 1919, House Papers; Wilson to House, March 10, 1919, House Papers; Note, in *PWW*, LV, 477–78.

49. House Diary, March 10, 11, 1919; Auchincloss Diary, March 10, 12, 1919; Both Clemenceau and Lloyd George hoped that House would attend the Council of Four meetings, but he doubted that he would do so. House Diary, March 10, 12, 1919.

50. House Diary, March 12, 1919; Note, in *PWW*, LV, 480; Grayson Diary, March 12, 1919, in *PWW*, LV, 479–82; Auchincloss Diary, March 14, 1919.

CHAPTER 31

1. House Diary, March 12, 14, 1919; Auchincloss Diary, March 19, 1919.

2. Grayson Diary, March 13, 1919, in Arthur S. Link, ed., *The Papers of Woodrow Wilson* [*PWW*], 68 vols. (Princeton, N.J., 1966-93), LV, 486–88.

3. Edith Bolling Wilson, *My Memoir* (Indianapolis, Ind., 1939), 245–6; Note, *PWW*, LV, 488.

4. Phyllis Lee Levin, *Edith and Woodrow: The Wilson White House* (New York, 2001), 280–85; Inga Floto, *Colonel House in Paris: A Study of American Policy at the Paris Peace Conference of 1919* (Princeton, N.J., 1980), 164–70; August Heckscher, *Woodrow Wilson* (New York, 1991), 546; Edmund Starling, Wilson's secret service agent, remembered that House emerged from Wilson's compartment "looking disturbed and walking rapidly . . . . I saw the President standing, his eyes fixed on me but showing no recognition, his arms hanging loosely at his side . . . . His face was pale and seemed drawn and tired. His whole figure expressed dejection." Edmund W. Starling, *Starling of the White House* (New York, 1946), 135; Grayson, in an article written in 1926 but published in 1964, explained that "It was upon Mr. Wilson's return to France that he found to his amazement that Colonel House had consented to a plan for the separation of the Peace Treaty from the covenant of the League of Nations. He had assented to Premier Clemenceau's wishes and suggestions about this matter. He had also agreed to the establishment of a Rhenish republic that would act as a buffer state between Germany and France, the creation of which would have been in absolute contradiction to President Wilson's Fourteen Points. So President Wilson had no sooner arrived in France than he found it necessary to repudiate practically everything that had been done during his absence . . . . From that time on, the relationship between the President

and the Colonel ceased to be close and confidential." Cary T. Grayson, "The Colonel's Folly and the President's Distress," *American Heritage*, 15 (Oct. 1964), 4–7, 94–101.

5. Heckscher, *Wilson*, 547; House Diary, March 15, 1919; Grayson Diary, March 15, 1919, in *PWW*, LV, 529–31.

6. David Robin Watson, *Georges Clemenceau* (London, Eng., 2008), 87–89; Margaret MacMillan, *Paris 1919: Six Months that Changed the World* (New York, 2001), 194–95; Michael S. Neiberg, *Foch: Supreme Allied Commander in the Great War* (Washington, D.C., 2003), 96.

7. Zara Steiner, *The Lights that Failed: European International History, 1919–1933* (Oxford, Eng., 2005), 48–50; Cecil Diary, March 18, 1919, in *PWW*, LVI, 81–82.

8. "A Memorandum by David Lloyd George," March 25, 1919, in *PWW*, LVI, 259–70; "Mantoux's Notes of a Meeting of the Council of Four," in *PWW*, LVI, 208–9; MacMillan, *Paris 1919*, 261–64.

9. Watson, *Clemenceau*, 95–99; Baker Diary, in *PWW*, LVI, 577–78.

10. House Diary, March 14, 22, 1919; Thomas Nelson Page to House, March 31, 1919, House Papers.

11. House Diary, March 24, 1919; Floto, *Colonel House*, 173–75.

12. House Diary, March 16, 18, 24, April 11; John Milton Cooper Jr., *Breaking the Heart of the World: Woodrow Wilson and the Fight for the League of Nations* (New York, 2001), 71–74; George W. Egerton, *Great Britain and the Creation of the League of Nations: Strategy, Politics, and International Organization, 1914–1919* (Chapel Hill, N.C., 1978), 153–63.

13. House Diary, March 20, 24, 1919; Floto, *Colonel House*, 178–82; Arthur Walworth, *Wilson and His Peacemakers: American Diplomacy at the Paris Peace Conference, 1919* (New York, 1986), 297–98.

14. Will Brownell and Richard N. Billings, *So Close to Greatness: A Biography of William C. Bullitt* (New York, 1987), 86–94; Bullitt to House, March 16, 1919, House Papers; House Diary, March 25, 26, 1919; "Notes of a Conversation between Signor Orlando and Colonel House," March 26, 1919, House Papers.

15. House Diary, March 26, 1919; Steiner, *The Lights That Failed*, 138–42; David W. McFadden, *Alternative Paths: Soviets and Americans, 1917–1920* (New York, 1993), 233–43; Auchincloss Diary, March 26, 28, 31, 1919.

16. House Diary, March 27, 29, 1919; McFadden, *Alternative Paths*, 244–54; George F. Kennan, *Russia and the West under Lenin and Stalin* (Boston, Mass., 1960), 136–50; John M. Thompson, *Russia, Bolshevism and the Versailles Peace* (Princeton, N.J., 1966), 204–5.

17. House Diary, April 1, 2, 1919; House also became involved in tense negotiations with the British over the naval terms of the treaty, especially the fate of Germany's surface fleet. After considerable wrangling between Josephus Daniels, Admiral Benson, and British naval officials, House and Cecil worked out a compromise in which the United States agreed to modify its naval

building program and the two governments agreed to consult with each other in the future. MacMillan, *Paris 1919*, 176–79; House Diary, March 28, 30, 31, April 8, 9, 10, 1919; Cecil to House, April 8, 1919, House to Cecil, April 9, 1919, Cecil memorandum, April 10, 1919, House Papers.

18. House Diary, April 2, 1919.

19. House Diary, April 3, 4, 1919; Lloyd George asked that House, rather than Lansing, replace the president. Grayson Diary, April 4, 1919, in *PWW*, LVI, 584–85; the secretary of state was "surprised and humiliated" by Wilson's decision. "Colonel House as the President's Substitute on the Council of Four," April 8, 1919, Lansing Papers; after Wilson's return to Paris, House did not comment on his health. But one of his protégés, Stephen Bonsal, noted that "the change for the worse in the President's physical condition since his return from America is increasingly noticeable and is being generally remarked upon. The tic on his left cheek that is so disfiguring and to me so alarming has become almost chronic. Evidently the President is in a highly nervous condition and the confidence that animated him as he left for Washington is gone." Bonsal, *Suitors and Suppliants: The Little Nations at Versailles* (New York, 1946), 263.

20. Grayson Diary, April 3, 4, 1919, in *PWW*, LVI, 554–57; Grayson to Tumulty, April 7, 1919, in *PWW*, LVII, 235–36; Note, *PWW*, LVI, 557–58.

21. House to Frank Trumbull, March 28, 1919, House Papers; Auchincloss to Polk, April 10, 1919, House Papers; House Diary, April 4, 5, 1919; in the official minutes, House states "that the moment has come to take a decision, and that it is possible to do it quickly." Arthur S. Link, ed., *The Deliberations of the Council of Four (March 24–June 28, 1919): Notes of the Official Interpreter, Paul Mantoux* (Princeton, N.J., 1992), 144–45.

22. House Diary, April 8, 1919; Heckscher, *Wilson*, 556–57; Note, *PWW*, LVII, 63–65; House, who was not consulted about the summoning of the *George Washington*, foolishly sought to belittle the decision. Grayson Diary, April 7, 1919, in *PWW*, LVII, 62–67; Notes, *PWW*, LVII, 63–65; Floto, *Colonel House*, 202.

23. Heckscher, *Wilson*, 558–59; MacMillan, *Paris 1919*, 200–203.

24. Heckscher, *Wilson*, 560; MacMillan, *Paris 1919*, 180–93.

25. Heckscher, *Wilson*, 561; House supported generous boundaries for the new Poland and saw his friend Paderewski, who was now prime minister, often during the peace conference. As he wrote Paderewski, "Your cause is very dear to my heart and here in Paris I am doing everything I can to make your work easier." House Diary, April 6, 14, 15, May 2, June 4, 22, 23, 1919; House to Paderewski, March 24, 1919, House Papers; MacMillan, *Paris 1919*, 207–28; Anita Prazmowska, *Ignacy Paderewski: Poland* (London, Eng., 2009), 61–97.

26. House Diary, April 8, 12, 13, 14, 15, 1919.

27. Baker Diary, March 27, April 3, 7, 1919, in *PWW*, LVI, 337–38, 577–78, LVII, 68–71.

28. Wilson also observed that "he had found Clemenceau to be exactly the opposite of everything that House had said he was." Grayson Diary, April 7, in *PWW*, LVII, 62–67.

29. Bonsal noted that "Whenever the Colonel appears on the scene Mrs. Wilson's by no means sunny countenance looks like a thunder cloud." Bonsal Diary, undated, 1919; Edith Bolling Wilson, *My Memoir*, 250–52; Edith gave a slightly different version of this conversation in a talk with Ray Stannard Baker on May 25, 1921. Baker Diary, May 25, 1921, in *PWW*, LVII, 288–94; Grayson Diary, April 21, 1919, in *PWW*, LVII, 531–33; Note, *PWW*, LVII, 533–34; Admiral Gary T. Grayson, "The Colonel's Folly and the President's Distress," *American Heritage*, 99–101; many years later House recorded his version of the conversation: "I went to see the President and while waiting for him talked to Mrs. Wilson. She had been reading a copy of the *Washington Post* in which the Steed article had been published. What she said was: 'Have you read this article by Wickham Steed? It is very unkind to Woodrow but complimentary to you.' I told her I had read it in the *Mail* when it came out and that I did not think he meant it unkindly or in criticism of the President. That was all of our conversation on the subject." Untitled memo, Oct. 3, 1930, House Papers.

30. Edith Bolling Wilson, *My Memoir*, 252; Edith Wilson to House, May 26, 1919, House Papers.

31. McAdoo to House, April 1, 1919, House Papers; John M. Blum, *Joe Tumulty and the Wilson Era* (Boston, Mass., 1951), 169–99; see, for example, Grayson Diary, March 31, April 9, 12, May 2, 4, 1919, in *PWW*, LVI, 436–40; LVII, 145–47, 284; LVIII, 330–33, 422.

32. "Ray Stannard Baker," in John A. Garraty and Mark C. Carnes, eds., *American National Biography* (New York, 1999), II, 30–32; Charles L. Ponce De Leon, *Self Exposure: Human Interest Journalism and the Emergence of Celebrity in America, 1890–1940* (Chapel Hill, N.C., 2002), 123; Robert C. Bannister Jr., *Ray Stannard Baker: The Mind and Thought of a Progressive* (New Haven, Conn., 1966), 69–187.

33. "Bernard Mannes Baruch," *American National Biography*, II, 299–300; Jordan A. Schwarz, *The Speculator: Bernard M. Baruch in Washington, 1917–1965* (Chapel Hill, N.C., 1981), 31–49; Meirion and Susie Harries, *The Last Days of Innocence: America at War, 1917–1918* (New York, 1997), 278–79.

34. Wilson to Baruch, Dec. 7, 1918, in *PWW*, LIII, 334; Arthur Krock, *Memoirs: Sixty Years on the Firing Line* (New York, 1968), 53.

35. Walworth, *Wilson and His Peacemakers*, 300; Grayson Diary, April 5, 20, May 8, June 15, 1919, in *PWW*, LVII, 3–4, 512–13; LVIII, 534; LX, 569–70; Grayson to Alice Gordon Grayson, April 16–17, April 27, May 9–10, May 15, May 20–22, June 6, 1919. Grayson Papers.

36. In 1914, House had used Baruch, who was a trustee of City College, to secure the appointment of Sidney Mezes as president, and in 1917 to convince the board to pay Mezes a full salary during his leave of absence as director of the

Inquiry. Schwarz, *The Speculator*, 43–49, 58–60; House to Wilson, June 16, 1916, House Papers; House Diary, May 27, 1917, Sept. 23, 1917, Feb. 18, June 25, 1919.

37. Steiner, *The Lights That Failed*, 86–87; Mark Thompson, *The White War: Life and Death on the Italian Front, 1915–1919* (London, Eng., 2008), 371–82.

38. Steiner, *The Lights That Failed*, 88–90; MacMillan, *Paris 1919*, 279–305; John Milton Cooper Jr., *Woodrow Wilson: A Biography* (New York, 2009), 490–91.

39. Daniela Rossini, *Woodrow Wilson and the American Myth in Italy* (Cambridge, Mass., 2008), 144–48; House Diary, March 12, April 2, 3, 15, 18, 19, 20, 21, 1919.

40. Baker Diary, April 19, 20, 1919, in *PWW*, LVII, 508–09, 527–28; Grayson Diary, April 24, 1919, in *PWW*, LVIII, 53–56.

41. House Diary, April 22–24, 26, May, 2, 3, 5, 10–12, 13–17, 31, 1919; Auchincloss Diary, May 12, 15, 1919; House to Thomas Nelson Page, April 22, 1919, House Papers; Wilson to House, April 7, 1919, House to Wilson, April 19, 1919, House Papers; Rene Albrecht-Carrie, *Italy at the Paris Peace Conference* (New York, 1938), 167–83.

42. MacMillan, *Paris 1919*, 306–44; Charles E. Neu, *The Troubled Encounter: The United States and Japan* (New York, 1975), 98–99; Wilson to Bryan, April 14, 1915, *PWW*, XXXII, 520–21.

43. Neu, *The Troubled Encounter*, 92; House Diary, April 26, 1919; MacMillan, *Paris 1919*, 337–38.

44. Baker Diary, April 25, 29, 30, May 1, 1919, in *PWW*, LVIII, 142–43, 229–30, 270–71, 327; Grayson Diary, April 30, 1919, in *PWW*, LVIII, 244–45; House Diary, April 28, 1919; House to Wilson, April 29, 1919, House Papers; Lansing, who vehemently opposed a deal with Japan, believed that "House is at the bottom of it. I said to him today," he recorded, "that to give Kiau Chau to Japan was to barter away a great principle. He replied, 'We have done it before.' I answered with some heat: 'Yes, it has been done and it is the curse of this conference that that method has been adapted.' He made no reply." Lansing memo, April 28, 1919, in *PWW*, LVIII, 185.

45. MacMillan, *Paris 1919*, 459–64; Ellis Dresel to House, April 21, 29, 1919, House Papers; House Diary, May 7, 1919.

46. Heckscher, *Wilson*, 568–69.

47. House Diary, April 28, 30, May 2, 5, 10, 19, 24, 25, 1919; House to H. H. Kohlsatt, May 3, 1919, to Randolph Tucker, May 12, 1919, House Papers; Orpen found House "a charming man, very calm, very sure of himself, yet modest." Robert Upstone and Angela Weight, eds., *William Orpen: An Onlooker in France* (London, Eng., 2008), 204.

48. House Diary, March 29, April 11, 12, 14, 28, 30, May 2, 5, 25, 1919; House to McAdoo, May 9, 1919, House Papers; Wiseman to House, May 25, 1919, House Papers.

49. House Diary, April 26, 28, May 2, 6, May 30, 31, 1919.

50. Steiner, *The Lights That Failed*, 62–64; MacMillan, *Paris 1919*, 465–70; Baker Diary, May 26, 1919, in *PWW*, LIX, 480.

51. MacMillan, *Paris 1919*, 470–71; Steiner, *The Lights That Failed*, 64–66; "A Discussion with the American Delegation," June 3, 1919, in *PWW*, LX, 45–71.

52. House Diary, May 30, June 1, 2, 3, 4, 8, 1919.

53. House Diary, June 10, 1919; Cooper, *Wilson*, 501; House now worried that his earlier judgment of Wilson—that he would be viewed as a "great orator rather than as a great statesman"—was too harsh. On further reflection, he "meant that his power of expression was his greatest asset."

54. Frank Trumbull to Janet Auchincloss, March 11, 1919, House Papers; House Diary, June 11, 12, 20, 1919; Janet Auchincloss Diary, June 22, 23, 1919.

55. MacMillan, *Paris 1919*, 472–74; Grayson Diary, June 23, 1919, in *PWW*, LXI, 77–79; Harry Harmer, *Friedrich Ebert: Germany* (London, Eng., 2008), 100–12.

56. House Diary, June 23, 1919.

57. House Diary, June 28, 1919; MacMillan, *Paris 1919*, 474–77; Loulie, who was only 5'5", stood so she could "see my lamb sign." Levin, *Edith and Woodrow*, 303.

58. House Diary, June 28, 1919; Auchincloss Diary, June 28, 1919.

59. House Diary, June 28, 29, 1919; Grayson Diary, June 28, 1919, in *PWW*, LXI, 302–6.

60. House Diary, June 29, 1919.

61. Wilson to Smuts, May 16, 1919, in *PWW*, LIX, 187–88.

62. MacMillan, *Paris 1919*, 465; Steiner, *The Lights That Failed*, 68; Henry Kissinger, *Diplomacy* (New York, 1994), 242.

63. Patrick O. Cohrs, *The Unfinished Peace after World War I: America, Britain and the Stabilisation of Europe, 1919–1932* (Cambridge, Eng., 2006), 62–67; MacMillan, *Paris 1919*, 480–83; Steiner, *The Lights That Failed*, 68–70.

CHAPTER 32

1. House Diary, July 14, 1919; House to Edward Martin, July 15, 1919, to Sidney Mezes, July 15, 1919, House Papers; Auchincloss to Frank Polk, July 26, 1919, House Papers.

2. House Diary, July 14, 24, 28, Aug. 7, 22, 1919.

3. House to Paul Cruger, July 15, 1919, to Thomas C. Dunn, Aug. 27, 1919, House Papers; T. W. Gregory to House, Aug. 6, 1919, House Papers.

4. House Diary, July 14, 1919; Elmer Bendiner, *A Time for Angels: The Tragicomic History of the League of Nations* (New York, 1975), 133–38; Zara Steiner, *The Lights That Failed: European International History, 1919–1933* (Oxford, Eng., 2005), 349–54.

5. House Diary, July 8, 24, Aug. 27, 1919; House to Wilson, July 10, 14, Aug. 6, 1919, House Papers; Wilson to House, July 18, Aug. 23, 1919, House Papers.

6. House Diary, Aug. 22, 1919; House to Wilson, July 30, 1919, House Papers.

7. House to Wilson, July 30, Aug. 8, 1919, House Papers; House Diary, July 28, Aug. 7, 12, 16, 22, Sept. 12, 14, 1919; Grey memo, Aug. 11, 1919, Grey to House, Aug. 12, 1919, House Papers; Note 2, in Arthur S. Link, ed., *The Papers of Woodrow Wilson* [*PWW*], 68 vols. (Princeton, N.J., 1966-93), LXII, 255–56; Keith Robbins, *Sir Edward Grey: A Biography of Lord Grey of Fallodon* (London, Eng., 1971), 351–52.

8. Wilson to House, July 18, Aug. 11, 15, 23, 1919, House Papers.

9. Wiseman to House, July 19, 1919, House Papers; on Aug. 7, Lansing noted in his diary: "Tumulty on Col. House and Prest's loss of faith in him. Also Prest's dislike of Auchincloss and Mrs. House." Lansing Diary, Aug. 7, 1919, in *PWW*, LXII, 20; A few days before Wilson left on his speaking tour, Wiseman lunched at the White House and talked about House with the president. Wiseman noted that "Colonel House is trusted by all the statesmen of Europe." Wilson replied: "And rightly, for he is trustworthy." The president knew, of course, that Wiseman was one of House's protégés. Charles Seymour, ed., *The Intimate Papers of Colonel House: The Ending of the War* (Boston, Mass., 1928), IV, 515–16; House Diary, Aug. 22, 28, Sept. 4, 1919; Note 1, in *PWW*, LXII, 574; House to Wilson, Aug. 26, 28, 1919, Wilson to House, Aug. 29, 1919, House Papers.

10. House to Wilson, Aug. 26, 1919, Wilson to House, Aug. 28, 1919, House Papers; Auchincloss to House, Aug. 28, 1919, House Papers.

11. House Diary, Sept. 4, 1919; House to Wilson, Aug. 31, Sept. 3, 1919, House Papers.

12. House Diary, Sept. 4, 8, 12, 14, 1919; House to Frank Trumbull, Sept. 11, 1919; Auchincloss to House, Aug. 12, 1919, House Papers.

13. John Milton Cooper Jr., *Woodrow Wilson: A Biography* (New York, 2009), 506–9; "An Address to the Senate," July 10, 1919, in *PWW*, LXI, 426–36.

14. John Milton Cooper Jr., *Breaking the Heart of the World: Woodrow Wilson and the Fight for the League of Nations* (New York, 2001), 111–20; Thomas J. Knock, *To End All Wars: Woodrow Wilson and the Quest for a New World Order* (New York, 1992), 256–59.

15. McAdoo to House, Aug. 20, 1919, House Papers; John Milton Cooper Jr., *Pivotal Decades: The United States, 1900–1920* (New York, 1990), 321–29.

16. August Heckscher, *Woodrow Wilson* (New York, 1991), 584–90; Lansing memo, Aug. ll, 1919, in *PWW*, LXII, 258–59.

17. Cooper, *Wilson*, 518–19; Note 2, in *PWW*, LXII, 507–8; House to Wilson, Aug. 30, 1919, House Papers; Robert Alexander Kraig, in *Woodrow Wilson and the Lost World of the Oratorical Statesman* (College Station, Tex., 2004), 141–85, argues that Wilson's tour, if viewed within the context of his belief in the power of rhetorical leadership, made good sense.

18. Cooper, *Wilson*, 520–29; "An Address in the Denver Auditorium," Sept. 25, 1919, in *PWW*, LXIII, 490–500.

19. John M. Blum, *Joe Tumulty and the Wilson Era* (Boston, Mass., 1951), 208–13; Grayson Diary, Sept. 6, 25, 26, 1919, in *PWW*, LXIII, 63–66, 487–90, 518–21; "A News Report," Sept. 26, 1919, in *PWW*, LXIII, 522–24.

20. Heckscher, *Wilson*, 611–14; Irwin Hood Hoover, "The Facts about the President's Illness," undated, in *PWW*, LXIII, 632–38.

21. Kristie Miller, *Ellen and Edith: Woodrow Wilson's First Ladies* (Lawrence, Kans., 2010), 186–95; Phyllis Lee Levin, *Edith and Woodrow: The Wilson White House* (New York, 2001), 337–70.

22. William Phillips to House, Sept. 13, 1919, enclosing telegram from Carl Ackerman, House Papers; House Diary, Sept. 14, 15, 21, 30, 1919; Auchincloss Diary, Sept. 24, 1919; House to Auchincloss, Sept. 15, 19, 21, 1919, to Wilson, Sept. 15, 19, 1919, House Papers.

23. House Diary, Sept. 21, 22, 1919.

24. House to Wilson, Sept. 29, 30, 1919, House Papers; House Diary, Sept. 15, Oct. 3, 1919.

25. House Diary, Oct. 4, 5, 21, 1919; House to Clemenceau, Sept. 25, 1919, House Papers.

26. House Diary, Oct. 21, 1919; Auchincloss Diary, Oct. 12, 1919.

27. Cooper, *Breaking the Heart of the World*, 205–33.

28. Note 1, in *PWW*, LXIV, 45; Cooper, *Breaking the Heart of the World,* 234–70; Cooper, *Wilson,* 542–45; Knock, *To End All Wars,* 263–68.

29. House Diary, Oct. 21, 1919; Edith Wilson to Loulie House, Oct. 17, 1919, House Papers; House to Edith Wilson, Oct. 22, 1919, Edith Wilson to House, Oct. 23, 1919, House Papers.

30. House Diary, Oct. 21, 29, 1919; House to Lodge, Oct. 14, 1919, to Commander Allen D. McLean, Oct. 22, 1919, to Grayson, Oct. 24, 1919, House Papers; Lodge to House, Oct. 18, 1919, Grayson to House, Oct. 22, 1919, McLean to House, Oct. 22, 1919, Breckinridge Long to House, Oct. 17, 1919, House Papers; in late October, House sent Bonsal to Washington to explain to Lodge that House's ill health prevented him from testifying for some time before the Senate Foreign Relations Committee. In the course of two conversations with Lodge—who had no desire for House to testify—the senator seemed in a mood to compromise, making handwritten notes on a copy of the covenant. Bonsal sent the document to House, but it has not survived and it is not clear if House ever sent it, or a letter summarizing its contents, to the White House. A thorough discussion of this tangled affair is in Cooper, *Breaking the Heart of the World*, 252–57; Bonsal memo for Colonel House, Nov. 1, 1919, House Papers; John A. Garraty, *Henry Cabot Lodge: A Biography* (New York, 1953), note 8, 377–78; Stephen Bonsal, *Unfinished Business* (New York, 1944), 270–79.

31. House Diary, Oct. 21, 1919; House to Edith Wilson, Nov. 17, 1919, to Wilson, Nov. 17, 1919, Edith Wilson to House, Nov. 18, 1919, House Papers.

32. Baker Diary, Nov. 18, 1919, in *PWW*, LXIV, 61–62.

33. House Diary, Nov. 5, 13, 1919; Bonsal to Fanny Denton, Nov. 9, 1919, House Papers; Raymond Fosdick to House, Nov. 7, 1919, House Papers; House to George D. Herron, Nov. 15, 1919, House Papers; House also realized that "some of our 'good friends' [have been] quietly gunning for me. I hear it from all sides. It is not done openly, and apparently they 'love me' as much as ever." House to Hugh Wallace, Nov. 15, 1919, House Papers.

34. House Diary, Nov. 20, 1919.

35. Cooper, *Breaking the Heart of the World*, 285–89; "A Statement," Dec. 14, 1919, in *PWW*, LXIV, 187.

36. Cooper, *Breaking the Heart of the World*, 284, 290–96; House Diary, Nov. 27, 1919; Auchincloss Diary, Nov. 26, Dec. 1–7, 1919; House to Edith Wilson, Nov. 24, 27, 1919, to Wilson, Nov. 24, 27, 1919, House Papers; Levin, *Edith and Woodrow*, 388.

37. Gregory to House, Nov. 25, 28, 1919, House Papers; Fosdick to House, Nov. 25, 1919, House Papers; House Diary, Nov. 27, Dec. 2, 1919; Tom Shachtman writes, without citing a source, that in late 1919 Margaret Wilson visited House in New York and told him how she thought his behavior had offended her father. House replied that he had only acted out of concern for Wilson's basic goals. When Margaret told Wilson about the conversation, he sighed and said that "House hadn't stood up to the pressure, wasn't the man Wilson had once thought him to be. Rather, he was closer to what Edith had thought of him from the first, a sycophant of small caliber. Could they meet and be friends again? The president thought not; it would be embarrassing for them both." If such a conversation took place, House makes no mention of it in his diary. Tom Shachtman, *Edith and Woodrow: A Presidential Romance* (New York, 1981), 233.

38. House Diary, Dec. 5, 11, 1919, Jan. 3, 11, 1920; House to Grayson, Dec. 25, 1919, House Papers; Jordan A. Schwarz, *The Speculator: Bernard M. Baruch in Washington, 1917–1965* (Chapel Hill, N.C., 1981), 175–76.

39. Heckscher, *Wilson*, 616; Miller, *Ellen and Edith*, 193–95; Levin, *Edith and Woodrow*, 388–95.

40. House Diary, Dec. 11, 1919; Auchincloss Diary, Dec. 8–14, 1919; "The New York World's Attack on Colonel House," Dec. 9, 11, 1919, Lansing Papers.

41. House Diary, Dec. 11, 12, 13, 22, 27, 31, 1919; House to Wickham Steed, Dec. 13, 1919, House Papers; on December 20 Daisy Harriman, House's friend and well-connected Democratic Party activist, reported on the "chaos" in Washington. "The business of Government," she told House, "was in the hands of Mrs. Wilson, Baruch, and Grayson." When she pressed Grayson on the reasons for the House-Wilson break, the clever physician avoided the question. But Harriman also confronted House, telling him that he had taken too many "friends and relatives to Europe" and had also "set up a rival estab-lishment to that of the President." Once again House refused to admit any

serious errors, claiming that he was "content and happy to be away from the confusion in Washington. . . through no fault of my own." House Diary, Dec. 20, 1919.

42. House Diary, Jan. 3, 4, 5, 11, 1920; "A Jackson Day Message," Jan. 8, 1920, in *PWW*, LXIV, 257–59; Bonsal to House, Dec. 28, 1919, House Papers.

43. House Diary, Jan. 27, 1920: House to Dear Clementine, Feb. 11, 1920, to Allison Mayfield, Jan. (undated) 1920, to Auchincloss, Jan. 15, 20, 1920, House Papers; *Houston Post*, Jan. 14, 18, 1920; *Austin American*, Jan. 18, 19, 20, 22, 23, 1920.

44. House Diary, Jan. 27, 1920; Cooper, *Wilson*, 550–52; Tumulty to Edith Wilson, Jan. 15, 1920, in *PWW*, LXIV, 276–77.

45. Cooper, *Wilson*, 552–56; Thomas H. Hartig, *Robert Lansing: An Interpretive Biography* (New York, 1982), 308–10.

46. Cooper, *Breaking the Heart of the World*, 330–75; Tumulty to Wilson, Feb. 27, 1920, in *PWW*, LXIV, 479–80; Wilson to Hitchcock, March 8, 1920, in *PWW*, LXV, 67–71; Grayson memo., March 25, 26, 1920, in *PWW*, LXV, 123–25.

47. House Diary, Jan. 31, 1920; Gregory to House, Feb. 19, 1920, James C. McReynolds to House, Feb. 23, 1920, House Papers; Note 2, in *PWW*, LXIV, 348.

48. House Diary, Feb. 3, 9, 18, 22, March 2, 1920; Edwin A. Weinstein, *Woodrow Wilson: A Medical and Psychological Biography* (Princeton, N.J., 1981), 367–70.

49. House to Edith Wilson, March 11, 1920, to Wilson, March 8, 1920, Wilson to House, March 11, 1920, House Papers; House Diary, March 7, 14, 1920.

50. House Diary, March 28, 1920.

CHAPTER 33

1. House Diary, Aug. 3, 7, Nov. 5, 30, Dec. 11, 1919, Jan. 31, Feb. 18, 25, March 2, 7, 14, 16, 17, 28, April 11, 16, May 11, 1920.

2. House Diary, Feb. 18, 25, March 17, 1920; Kendrick A. Clements, *The Life of Herbert Hoover: Imperfect Visionary, 1918–1928* (New York, 2010), 49–65.

3. House Diary, May 11, 27, 1920.

4. House Diary, Jan. 31, 1920; Grayson memos, March 25, April 1, 1920, in Arthur S. Link, ed., *The Papers of Woodrow Wilson* [*PWW*], 68 vols. (Princeton, N.J., 1966-93), LXV, 123–24, 149; The president confided to Grayson that "Colonel House's going wrong has greatly distressed me. I once thought he was too good to be true. In Paris I first realized the change that had taken place when he suggested that I turn everything over to him and let him run things. That was my first indication that he was going wrong and had swelled up. He succumbed to flattery and to his son-in-law, Auchincloss. The latter I never trusted." Grayson memo, April 13, 1920, in *PWW*, LXV, 179–80; in June, Wilson continued to ponder his break with House, telling Grayson that "I hope no more of my friends will turn out like House. He is not the House I used to know. It darkens my life." Grayson memo, June 22, 1920, in *PWW*, LXV, 443–44.

5. August Heckscher, *Woodrow Wilson* (New York, 1991), 633–35; Douglas B. Craig, *After Wilson: The Struggle for the Democratic Party, 1920–1934* (Chapel Hill, N.C., 1992), 30–35.

6. John Milton Cooper Jr., *Woodrow Wilson: A Biography* (New York, 2009), 567–69; James M. Cox, *Journey through My Years* (New York, 1946), 241–44.

7. Robert K. Murray, *The Harding Era: Warren G. Harding and His Administration* (Minneapolis, Minn., 1969), 32–70; John Milton Cooper Jr., *Pivotal Decades: The United States, 1900–1920* (New York, 1990), 362–66.

8. House Diary, May 27, 1920; House to Gregory, June 6, 1920, Gregory Papers; House to Auchincloss, June 18, 23, 1920, House Papers.

9. House to Wilson, June 7, 1920, Wilson to House, June 10, 1920, House Papers.

10. House Diary, June 25, 30, July 15, 19, 23, 26, 30, Aug. 1, 1920; House to Auchincloss, June 23, 1920, to Martin, June 24, 1920, to Mezes, July 3, 1920, House Papers; Hugh Purcel, *Lloyd George* (London, Eng., 2006), 89–93.

11. House to Auchincloss, June 29, 1920, House Papers; House Diary, July 12, 15, 19, 23, 1920; Norman and Jeanne MacKenzie, eds., *The Diary of Beatrice Webb, 1905–1924* (Cambridge, Mass., 1984), III, 360.

12. House Diary, July 12, 1920; Auchincloss to House, July 9, 1920, House Papers; House to Whitlock, June 26, 1920, to Auchincloss, June 16, 1920, to Wallace, July 12, 1920, to Cox, July 12, 1920, House Papers.

13. House Diary, July 25, 26, Aug. 1, 1920; House to Paul Cruger, July 12, 1920, to John J. Spurgeon, July 1, 27, 1920, House Papers; 1920; Ackerman, "London Notes, 1920–21," Ackerman Papers.

14. House Diary, July 23, 26, 30, 1920; Zara Steiner, *The Lights That Failed: European International History, 1919–1933* (Oxford, Eng., 2005), 146–52, 182–83, 256–60; Elmer Bendiner, *A Time for Angels: The Tragicomic History of the League of Nations* (New York, 1975), 162; House to Robert Underwood Johnson, July 8, 31, 1920, to Grey, Aug. 1, 1920, to Polk, Aug. 3, 1920, House Papers.

15. House to Mezes, July 20, 1920, to Kohlsaat, July 20, 1920, to Whitlock, Aug. 4, 1920, to Cruger, July 12, 1920, House Papers.

16. House Diary, Aug. 8, 15, 16, 22, 28, Oct. 5, 1920; House to Mezes, Aug. 15, 1920, to Gregory, Aug. 15, 1920, to Woolley, Aug. 24, 1920, to Cruger, Sept. 13, 1920, to Wiseman, Sept. 14, 1920, House Papers.

17. Auchincloss to House, Sept. 14, 1920, Woolley to House, Sept. 14, 29, 1920, House Papers.

18. Cox to House, Aug. 6, 1920, House Papers; House to Cox, Sept. 13, 1920, to Baker, Aug. 24, 1920, House Papers.

19. House Diary, Oct. 5, 1920; House to Johnson, Oct. 8, 1920, House Papers.

20. Woolley to House, Oct. 21, 1920, House Papers; House to Wallace, Oct. 16, 1920, to Fanny Denton, Oct. 20, 1920, to Woolley, Oct. 25, 1920, House to Wilson, Oct. 29, to Ackerman, Nov. 3, 1920, 1920, Wilson to House, Nov. 1, 1920, House Papers; House Diary, Nov. 13, 1920.

21. Cooper, *Pivotal Decades*, 365–76; Craig, *After Wilson*, 21–29; David Burner, *The Politics of Provincialism: The Democratic Party in Transition, 1918–1932* (New York, 1968), 65–73.

22. Baker Diary, Nov. 28, 1920, in *PWW*, LXVI, 435–36; Ray Stannard Baker, *American Chronicle: The Autobiography of Ray Stannard Baker* (New York, 1945), 481.

23. Edith Wilson to House, Nov. 15, 1920, House Papers; House Diary, Nov. 30, Dec. 14, 1920.

24. House Diary, Nov. 13, 22, 30, Dec. 14, 1920, Jan. 23, 30, Feb. 7, 22, 1921; House to Auchincloss, Aug. 30, 1920, to Fanny Denton, Oct. 13, 15, 16, 1920, to Cyrus H. K. Curtis, Nov. 11, 1920; Edward Mandell House and Charles Seymour, eds., *What Really Happened at Paris: The Story of the Peace Conference, 1918–1919* (New York, 1921).

25. House Diary, Nov. 13, 30, 1920, Jan. 23, 30, March 4, 1921; Clements, *Hoover*, 101–3.

26. Cooper, *Wilson*, 577–78; House to Fanny Denton, March 7, 1921, House Papers.

27. Baker, Diary, Feb. 12, 1921, May 25, 1921, in *PWW*, LXVII, 129–30, 288–94.

CHAPTER 34

1. House Diary, May 15, 1921; House to Auchincloss, May 15, 1921, House Papers.

2. House Diary, May 15, 20, June 3, 6, 9, July 3, 7, 21, 22, Aug. 19, 1921; House to Wiseman, July 13, 20, 1921, to Mezes, July 28, 1921, to Auchincloss, June 3, July 29, Aug. 12, 1921, House Papers.

3. House Diary, Aug. 31, Sept. 22, 1921.

4. Arthur D. Howden Smith, *Mr. House of Texas* (New York, 1940), 356–58; Hamilton Fish Armstrong, *Peace and Counterpeace: From Wilson to Hitler* (New York, 1971), 227–31, 445–46; House Diary, Dec. 21, 1921.

5. House Diary, Oct. 7, 14, 1921.

6. House Diary, Oct. 14, Nov. 29, Dec. 21, 1921; Gregory to House, June 23, 1921, House to Gregory, July 9, 1921, House Papers; "A News Item," Oct. 13, 1921, in Arthur S. Link, ed., *The Papers of Woodrow Wilson* [*PWW*], 68 vols. (Princeton, N.J., 1966-93), LXVII, 419.

7. House Diary, Oct. 28, Nov. 29, 1921; House to Arthur Sweetser, Aug. 19, 1921, House Papers; Zara Steiner, *The Lights That Failed: European International History, 1919–1933* (Oxford, Eng., 2005), 375–78.

8. Baker's *What Wilson Did at Paris* (New York, 1919) came out in the fall of 1919, Tumulty's *Woodrow Wilson as I Know Him* (New York, 1921), in 1921, the serialization of Burton J. Hendrick's *The Life and Letters of Walter Hines Page* (New York, 1922), in 1921, while the serialization of Baker's *Woodrow Wilson and the World Settlement* (3 vols., New York, 1922), began in January

1922. Robert C. Bannister Jr., *Ray Stannard Baker: The Mind and Thought of a Progressive* (New Haven, Conn., 1966), 200–203; House Diary, Nov. 19, Dec. 6, 21, 31, 1921.

9. House Diary, Dec. 31, 1921; House continued, however, to dictate occasional diary entries in 1922, 23, 24, and 25, until he finally brought his great project to an end in the summer of 1926.

10. Warren I. Cohen, *Empire without Tears: America's Foreign Relations, 1921–1933* (New York, 1987), 45–55; House to Balfour, Feb. 8, 1922, House Papers; "The Democratic Senators and the Washington Conference Treaties," March 3, 1922, Seymour Papers.

11. House Diary, Dec. 31, 1921; "Charles Seymour," in John A. Garraty and Mark C. Carnes, eds., *American National Biography* (New York, 1999), IX, 686–87; "Charles Seymour, 1885–1963," in Seymour Papers.

12. House Diary, June 10, 1922; House to Mezes, June 14, 1922, to Auchincloss, June 26, 1922, House Papers; Ackerman Diary, May 10–12, 1921.

13. House Diary, June 10, 11, Aug. 25, 29, 1922; House to McAdoo, June 27, 1922, to Auchincloss, July 8, Aug. 19, 31, Sept. 4, 1922, to Mezes, June 23, July 12, 26, Aug. 6, 29, 1922, to Balfour, July 25, 1922, to Gregory, July 16, 1922 House Papers; Auchincloss to House, June 16, 1922, Balfour to House, July 17, 1922, House Papers; Arthur Murray to House, March 17, 1922, Sweetser to House, March 22, 1922, Wiseman to House, April 5, 1922, House Papers; J. F. V. Keiger, *Raymond Poincaré* (Cambridge, Eng., 1997), 272–94.

14. Auchincloss to House, June 16, 1922, House Papers; House to Mezes, June 23, July 26, Aug. 6, 1922, to Balfour, July 25, 1922, House Papers; Balfour to House, July 17, 1922, House Papers; during his stay in London House learned that the political career of Charles Culberson, one of the original members of "our crowd," had finally come to an end. In 1922 he finished third in the Democratic primary. Earlier House had warned Culberson not to make the race, and on learning of his defeat, could only urge him to write a history of Texas politics in the 1890s; Norman D. Brown, *Hood, Bonnet, and Little Brown Jug* (College Station, Tex., 1984), 89–110; D. W. Jurney to House, March 2, 1922, House Papers; House to Culberson, Aug. 16, 1922, to Allison Mayfield, Aug. 16, 1922, House Papers.

15. House to McAdoo, June 27, 1922, to Sherman L. Whipple, July 26, 1922, to Cox, Sept. 16, 1922, House Papers; McAdoo to House, Sept. 21, Oct. 30, 1922, House Papers.

16. David Burner, *The Politics of Provincialism: The Democratic Party in Transition, 1918–1932* (New York, 1968), 103–6; note, in *PWW*, LXVIII, 180; House to Breckinridge Long, Nov. 23, 1922, House Papers.

17. Keiger, *Poincaré*, 297–99; Stephen A. Schuker, *The End of French Predominance in Europe: The Financial Crisis of 1924 and the Adoption of the Dawes Plan* (Chapel Hill, N.C., 1976), 14–28.

18. House to D. H. Heineman, Feb. 20, 1923, House Papers; in early January 1923, after an absence of only three years, House left for Texas, where he spent time in Houston and Galveston. In the early 1920s his income, along with Loulie's, totaled $31,000, not enough to cover his expenses. House hoped that if only he could lease a valuable piece of land on the Houston ship channel, his "financial worries would be over." Despite his intensive efforts during his stay in Houston, he was not able to close a deal on the land. Income figures from small black notebooks, unnumbered, House Papers; House to Wiseman, July 7, 13, 1921, to Fanny Denton, Jan. 11, 14, 1923, House Papers; Houston Post, Jan. 11, 14, 17, 1923.

19. House Diary, June 11, July 8, 23,1923; House to Kohlsaat, June 7, 18, 1923, to Auchincloss, June 7, July 12, 1923, House Papers; House to Wiseman, June 18, 1923, House Papers; Hugh Purcell, *Lloyd George* (London, Eng., 2006), 93–97.

20. Robert Rhodes James, *The British Revolution: 1880–1939* (New York, 1977), 443–63; Anne Perkins, *Baldwin* (London, Eng., 2006), 31–39.

21. House Diary, June 11, July 23, 1923; House to Auchincloss, June 7, 1923, to Heineman, June 13, 1923, to Wiseman, June 18, 1923, House Papers; House outlined his foreign policy views in "The Running Sands," *Foreign Affairs*, 1 (June 15, 1923), 1–8.

22. House Diary, July 8, 23, 31, 1923; House to Frederick H. Allen, June 14, 1923, memo for Poincaré, June 20, 1923, to Auchincloss, July 12, 1923, to Clifton Williamson, July 12, 1923, to Richard Childs, July 17, 1923, to Gregory, Aug. 2, 1923, House Papers; Allen to House, June 12, 17, July 8, 1923, House Papers; James H. Hyde Diary, July 30, 1923, Hyde Papers.

23. House Diary, Aug. 5, 7, 10, 19, 1923; House to Heineman, Aug. 10, 1923, House Papers; Gregor Dallas, *At the Heart of a Tiger: Clemenceau and his World, 1841-1929* (New York, 1993), 592–94.

24. House to Auchincloss, Aug. 19, 1923, to T. W. House Jr., Aug. 19, 1923, to Mezes, Aug. 19, 1923, House Papers; *Houston Post*, Aug. 19, 1923.

25. Burner, *Politics of Provincialism*, 107; House to Long, May 20, 1923, to David Hunter Miller, July 18, 1923, House Papers; Bonsal to House, Feb. 16, 1923, House Papers.

26. House to Long, Aug. 20, 1923, House Papers; Gregory to House, Aug. 13, 1923, Bonsal to House, Sept. 13, 1923, House Papers.

27. House Diary, Nov. 20, 23, 26, Dec. 14, 1923; House to McAdoo, Aug. 26, 1923, House Papers; McAdoo to House, Dec. 5, 31, 1923, House Papers; Douglas A. Craig, *After Wilson: The Struggle for the Democratic Party, 1920–1934* (Chapel Hill, N.C., 1992), 30–46.

28. David Greenberg, *Calvin Coolidge* (New York, 2006), 49–53; Craig, *After Wilson*, 37–50; Burner, *Politics of Provincialism*, 107–11.

29. House Diary, Feb. 9, March 8, 1924; House to George W. Anderson, Feb. 5, 1924, House Papers; conversation with Seymour, Feb. 1, 1924, Seymour Papers.

30. Conversation with Seymour, Feb. 1, 1924, Seymour Papers; House Diary, Feb. 9, 1924; Long to House, Feb. 7, 1924, House Papers; John M. Blum, *Joe Tumulty and the Wilson Era* (Boston, Mass., 1951), 264; John Milton Cooper Jr., *Woodrow Wilson: A Biography* (New York, 2009), 595–98; Cooper claims that Edith "had word sent to House that there would not be room for him." None of the documentation in the House collection supports this conclusion. After the services in Washington were over, House learned that his name was on a list put together by Cathedral authorities. Certainly Edith had not forgiven House. When Cyrus McCormick wrote to her about restoring the friendship of the two men, she replied that "the present status. . . [was] the only possible one." Cooper, *Wilson*, 597; House Diary, Feb. 9, 1924; Long to House, Feb. 7, 1924, House Papers; McCormick to Edith Wilson, Jan. 13, 1924, Edith Wilson to McCormick, Jan. 13, 1924, in *PWW*, LXVIII, 528–29.

31. House Diary, Feb. 9, 1924; *New York Times*, Feb. 7, 10, 1924.

32. House Diary, March 8, 10, 12, 1924; Seymour to House, May 14, 1924, House Papers.

33. House Diary, March 23, April 10, 23, 1924; House to Sweetser, March 6, 1924, House Papers; "John William Davis," in John A. Garraty and Mark C. Carnes, eds., *American National Biography* (New York, 1999), VI, 209–10.

34. McAdoo to House, March 4, 27, 1924, Bonsal to House, March 14, May 8, 1924, Gregory to House, April 19, June 6, 1924, Woolley to House, May 19, 29, 1924, House Papers; House Diary, May 26, 1924; Douglas B. Craig, *Progressives at War: William G. McAdoo and Newton D. Baker, 1863–1941* (Baltimore, Md., 2013), 261–85.

35. House Diary, April 10, May 26, 1924; Kevin Morgan, *Ramsay MacDonald* (London, Eng., 2006), 41–52.

36. House Diary, May 26, June 1, 1924; House to Gregory, May 27, 1924, to Miller, June 3, 1924, House Papers.

37. Keiger, *Poincare*, 301–17; Steiner, *The Lights That Failed*, 240–50; House to Kohlsaat, June 26, 1924, House Papers.

38. Woolley to House, June 6, 18, 24, 27, 1924, Auchincloss to House, July 4, 10, 1924, J. W. Binder to House, July 10, 1924, House Papers; House to Robert W. Bingham, July 11, 1924, House Papers; Craig, *After Wilson*, 51–63; William H. Harbaugh, *Lawyer's Lawyer: The Life of John W. Davis* (New York, 1973), 194–221; House was out of touch with sentiment within the party on the League of Nations. Despite the pleas of Newton Baker, the platform called only for an advisory referendum on American membership. Craig, *After Wilson*, 61.

39. House Diary, July 14, 1924; House to Mezes, July 11, 1924, to Armstrong, July 20, 1924, to Lippmann, July 22, 1924, to Woolley, July 22, 1924, House Papers.

40. House to Davis, July 10, 25, 1924, to Auchincloss, July 22, 31, 1924, to Hapgood, July 30, 1924, House Papers; Auchincloss to House, July 30, 1924,

House Papers; House explained his foreign policy views in "America in World Affairs: A Democratic View," *Foreign Affairs*, 2 (June 1924), 540–51.

41. House Diary, July 21, Aug. 9, 23, Sept. 12, 1924; House to Plunkett, Aug. 9, 1924, to Armstrong, Aug. 10, 1924, to Auchincloss, Aug. 12, 1924, to Mezes, Aug. 26, 1924, House Paper; Keiger, *Poincaré*, 307–17; Melvyn P. Leffler, *The Elusive Quest: America's Pursuit of European Stability and French Security, 1919–1933* (Chapel Hill, N.C., 1979), 82–112.

42. House to Auchincloss, Aug. 7, 12, 19, 24, 26, 1924. to Robert W. Bingham, Aug. 12, 1924, to Woolley, Aug. 15, 19, 1924, House Papers; Davis to House, Aug. 23, 1924, House Papers; House Diary, Oct. 15, 1924; Woolley to House, Sept. 17, 1924, Roper to House, Sept. 29, Oct. 28, 1924, House Papers.

43. Greenberg, *Coolidge*, 91–107; Robert H.Ferrell, *The Presidency of Calvin Coolidge* (Lawrence, Kans., 1998), 51–60.

44. Harbaugh, *Lawyer's Lawyer*, 221–50; Craig, *After Wilson*, 63–74; House Diary, Nov. 14, 1924.

45. House Diary, Nov. 14, 1924.

CHAPTER 35

1. House Diary, Nov. 30, 1924, Jan. 18, 1925; House to A. G. Gardiner, Jan. 2, 1925, House Papers.

2. House Diary, May 19, 30, June 4, 1925; House to David Harrell, June 8, 1925, Harrell Family Papers.

3. House Diary, June 4, 10, 1925; House to Auchincloss, June 2, 1925, to Edward S. Martin, June 11, 1925, to Wiseman, June 12, 1925, House Papers; Zara Steiner, *The Lights That Failed: European International History, 1919–1933* (Oxford, Eng., 2005), 410.

4. House Diary, June 19, 24, 1925; House to Auchincloss, June 22, 1925, House Papers; David Dutton, *Austen Chamberlain: Gentleman in Politics* (London, Eng., 1985), 230–58.

5. House to White, June 25, 1925, to Gregory, June 28, 1925, to Martin, July 1, 1925, House Papers; Allan Nevins, *Henry White: Thirty Years of American Diplomacy* (New York, 1930), 484–85.

6. House to Auchincloss, July 7, 1925, House Papers; House Diary, June 27, 28, July 28, 31, 1925; House asked his host if "there was a conscious hereafter." Grey thought there might be, since mankind "had evolved to a point of spirituality where it was easy to believe that the spirit could go on consciously," House Diary, July 31, 1925; House was in Edinburgh when he learned of Bryan's death. He wrote Mary Bryan that her husband had "played so large a part in our national life and for so long a time, that it will be difficult to realize that he has left us." House to Mrs. W. J. Bryan, July 27, 1925, House Papers.

7. House to Harrell, June 8, 1925, Harrell Family Papers, to Auchincloss, July 11, 1925, House Papers; House Diary, Aug. 14, 1925.

8. House Diary, Aug. 14, 25, Sept. 5, 10, 14, Oct. 6, 1925; House to D. N. Heineman, Sept. 15, 1925, House Papers.

9. House Diary, Oct. 17, Nov. 8, Dec. 12, 1925; House to Mrs. Hylton Young, Oct. 20, 1925, House Papers; Steiner, *The Lights That Failed*, 396–418; Anthony Adamthwaite, *Grandeur and Misery: France's Bid for Power in Europe, 1914–1940* (London, Eng., 1995), 119–23; Robert Rhodes James, *The British Revolution: 1880–1939* (New York, 1977), 478.

10. House Diary, Nov. 8, 22, 1925; Arthur D. Howden Smith, *Mr. House of Texas* (New York, 1940), 362–64.

11. White to House, Dec. 13, 1925, House Papers; House Diary, Dec. 20, 1925.

12. House Diary, Dec. 20, 1925.

13. House Diary, Dec. 20, 1925; House to Coolidge, Dec. 22, 1925, Feb. 11, 1926, House Papers; after his return to New York, House attended a luncheon that included Charles Evans Hughes and his wife. House could barely conceal his dislike of the former secretary of state and had only a brief conversation with him. House Diary, Dec. 25, 1925.

14. House Diary, Nov. 22, Dec. 12, 1925, Jan. 30, 1926; Phyllis Lee Levin, *Edith and Woodrow: The Wilson White House* (New York, 2001), 498–505; Edith Wilson to House, June 7, 1924, Dec. 2, 1925, to Seymour, Oct. 31, 1925, Dec. 2, 1925, House Papers; Edith Wilson to Seymour, Nov. 9, 1925, Seymour Papers; House to Ferris Greenslet, Nov. 9, 1925, to Auchincloss, Jan. 27, 1926, House Papers.

15. House to T. W. House Jr., Nov. 7, 1925, Jan. 22, 1926, to Edward Sammons, Jan. 22, 1926, to Auchincloss, Jan. 22, 1926; House Diary, Jan. 30, March 28, 1926.

16. House Diary, March 28, 1926; House to Auchincloss, March 10, 23, 1926, to Mezes, March 10, 21, 1926.

17. House Diary, March 28, 1926; House to Auchincloss, April 4, 1926, House Papers; Kipling to H. A. Gwynne, March 28, 1926, in Thomas Pinney, ed., *The Letters of Rudyard Kipling* (Iowa City, Ia., 2004), V, 283.

18. House Diary, March 28, 1926; Charles Seymour, ed., *The Intimate Papers of Colonel House* (Boston, Mass., 1926), I, x.

19. Seymour to Brand Whitlock, May 13, 1926, House Papers; Seymour, *Intimate Papers*, II, 121.

20. Seymour, *Intimate Papers*, I, viii, 114–150;, II, 470.

21. House Diary, March 28, 1926; House to Woolley, March 18, 1926, to Hamilton Fish Armstrong, March 20, 1926, to Auchincloss, March 21, April 17, 1926, to Gregory, March 22, 1926, to Martin, April 13, 1926, to Roger Scaife, April 14, 1926, to Shaw, April 17, 1926, House Papers; Albert Shaw, " Colonel House Breaks the Seals," *American Review of Reviews*, 73 (April 1926), 419–21; Walter Lippmann, "The Intimate Papers of Colonel House," *Foreign Affairs*, 4 (April 1926), 383–93; Oswald Garrison Villard, "The Nakedness of Colonel House," *The Nation*, 122 (April 14, 1926), 388–91; "House and Grey," *New York Times*,

May 7, 1926; Lippmann perceptively pointed out that the friendship between House and Wilson was "at some distance and always of a certain fragility" and that the "fame of House will depend of course upon the fame of Wilson"; on March 2, Senator Kenneth McKellar (Democrat, Tennessee) denounced House on the floor of the Senate for his "brazen effrontery" and for his "boot-licking proclivities." "Senate Democrats Censure Col. House," *New York Times*, March 3, 1926.

22. Long to House, April 15, 1926, Woolley to House, April 21, 1926, Auchincloss to House, May 19, 1926, Wiseman to House, May 20, 1926, Harriman to House, May 20, 1926, House Papers.

23. House to Gregory, March 22, 1926, to Auchincloss, March 30, 1926, to Mezes, April 8, May 1, 1926, to Long, April 26, 1926, to McAdoo, May 2, 1926, House Papers; Mezes to Seymour, May 20, 1926, House Papers.

24. House Diary, June 5, 1926; House to Mezes, June 25, 1926, to White, July 18, 1926, House Papers; James, *The British Revolution*, 478–90.

25. House to Paine, Aug. 12, 1926, to Mezes, Aug. 12, 21, 1926, to Greenslet, Aug. 24, 27, 1926, to McAdoo, Sept. 3, 1916, to Norman Hapgood, Sept. 1, 1916, House Papers; McAdoo to House, Aug. 10, 1926, House Papers. "My income," House informed an old friend, "is very small, not being more than $10,000 or $12,000, and it keeps me humping to make both ends meet for the reason that we live far beyond our income." House to Auchincloss, Aug. 19, 1926, to Mezes, Aug. 21, Sept. 18, 1926, to Randolph F. Tucker, Aug. 24, 1926, to Frank Andrews, Aug. 23, 1926, House Papers.

26. House to Fanny Denton, Sept. 10, 1926, House Papers.

27. House to Whitlock, Sept. 28, 1926, to Mezes, Oct. 8, Nov. 4, Dec. 3, 31, 1926, House Papers; Carl Ackerman to House, Dec. 13, 1926, House Papers.

28. House to Mezes, Nov. 4, 11, Dec. 12, 1926, to D. N. Heineman, Nov. 22, 1926, House Papers.

29. House to Guy M. Bryan, Dec. 10, 1926, to George W. Anderson, Jan. 3, 1927, to Gregory, Jan. 23, 1927, to Edward Filene, Jan. 24, 1927, House Papers.

30. Dunn to House, Dec. 14, 1926, House to Dunn, Jan. 1, 1927, House Papers.

31. House memo, Jan. 1, 1927, House Papers; House also paused to let Breckinridge Long and Frank Andrews know how much he appreciated their many "acts of friendship." House to Long, Jan. 2, 1927, to Andrews, Jan. 3, 1927, House Papers.

32. House to Gregory, May 19, 1927, to Auchincloss, May 19, June 4, 1927, to Martin, May 23, June 19, 1927, to Mezes, June 19, 1927, House Papers.

33. House to Martin, June 17, July 4, 1927, to Mezes, April 28, July 5, 1927, House Papers; Deborah Blum, *Ghost Hunters: William James and the Search for Scientific Proof of Life after Death* (New York, 2006), 161–67.

34. House to Auchincloss, July 10, 18, 1927, to Mezes, July 14, Aug. 2, 19, 1927, to Cruger, Sept. 7, 1927, House Papers.

35. House to Mezes, Aug. 19, 31, Sept. 15, 23, 1927, House Papers.

36. David Greenberg, *Calvin Coolidge* (New York, 2006), 127–39; David Burner, *Herbert Hoover: A Public Life* (New York, 1979), 190–97.

37. David Burner, *The Politics of Provincialism: The Democratic Party in Transition, 1918–1932* (New York, 1968), 142–57; Douglas B. Craig, *After Wilson: The Struggle for the Democratic Party, 1920–1934* (Chapel Hill, N.C., 1992), 80–97; House to Long, Aug. 25, 1927, to Gilbert Hitchcock, Sept. 25, 1927, to McAdoo, Sept. 25, 1927, to Whitlock, Sept. 26, Oct. 9, 1927, to Gregory, Oct. 6, 1927, House Papers.

38. House to Mezes, Dec. 5, 1927, Jan. 3, 5, 1928, to P. A. Fitzhugh, Jan. 16, 1928, House Papers.

39. Craig, *After Wilson*, 100–110; House to Roosevelt, Jan. 11, 1928, to Long, Jan. 13, 1928, to Henry Wales, March 14, 1928, House Papers.

40. House to Tucker, Jan. 19, 1928, to Mezes, Jan. 5, 26, Feb. 2, 9, March 17, 20, 1928, House Papers; Mezes appreciated House's solicitude. "You have been," he wrote, "endlessly kind, and more helpful than anyone who has come into my life. No man can ever have had a better friend." Mezes to House, Nov. 28, 1927, House Papers.

41. Burner, *Hoover*, 190–201; Craig, *After Wilson*, 92–111.

42. House to Frederick H. Allen, June 16, 1928, to Alfred E. Smith, June 30, 1928, to David Hunter Miller, July 22, 1928, House Papers; Bonsal to House, June 8, 1928, Woolley to House, July 20, 1928, House Papers.

43. Burner, *Hoover*, 201–7; William E. Leuchtenburg, *Herbert Hoover* (New York, 2009), 71–76.

44. Craig, *After Wilson*, 113–30, 158–80.

45. House to Mezes, Aug. 29, 31, Sept. 20, 27, Oct. 10, 1928, to Steed, Sept. 27, 1928, Whitlock, Oct. 1, 1928, to Sammons, Oct. 10, 1928, to Plunkett, Oct. 16, 1928, to Gregory, Oct. 20, 1928, House Papers.

46. House to Mezes, Oct. 29, 1928, to Gregory, Oct. 30, 1928, House Papers; Craig, *After Wilson*, 177–80; Burner, *Hoover*, 207–8.

47. House to Mezes, Nov. 9, 1928, to Edward H. Andrews, Nov. 20, 1928, to Anderson, Nov. 25, 1928, House Papers; Woolley to House, Dec. 20, 1928, House Papers.

CHAPTER 36

1. Charles Seymour, *The Intimate Papers of Colonel House* (Boston, Mass., 1928), III, v–vii, 15–16, 27, 174–77, 324–25; Seymour, *Intimate Papers*, IV, 3–12, 512–18.

2. House to Mezes, Nov. 9, 26, Dec. 16, 1928, to Plunkett, Nov. 11, Dec. 16, 1928, Jan. 10, 1929, to G. P. Gooch, Jan. 11, 1929, House Papers; "More Revelations of Colonel House," *The Nation*, 127 (Dec. 5, 1928), 595–98.

3. House to Mezes, Nov. 30, 1928, to Paul Cruger, Dec. 27, 1928, to DeWitt C. Dunn, Jan. 2, 1929, House Papers.

4. House to Mezes, Dec. 5, 16, 1928, Feb. 15, March 6, 27, 1929, to Randolph F. Tucker, Dec. 14, 1928, to T. W. House Jr., Dec. 26, 29, 1928, Jan. 31, 1929, to Don Hall, Jan. 7, 1929, House Papers; he read with interest Mrs. C. A. Dawson Scott's *Is This Wilson? Messages Accredited to Woodrow Wilson* (New York, 1929). Martin to House, Feb. 9, 1929, House to Martin, Feb. 21, 1929, House Papers.

5. House to Mona Tucker, March 31, 1929, House Papers; Fanny Denton to Marten A. Bailey, April 9, 1929, House Papers.

6. House memo, Aug. 23, 1929; on April 5, while House was still in the hospital, his fourth grandchild, Edward House Auchincloss, was born. *New York Times,* April 7, 1929; Fanny Denton to Margaret Wilson, April 6, 1929, to Esther Lape, April 6, 1929, to Bailey, April 9, 1929, to Bonsal, April 15, 23, 1929, House Papers; House to Randolph Tucker, May 4, 15, 22, 1929, to Mona Tucker, May 9, 12, 1929, to Mezes, May 28, 1929, to Bonsal, June 3, 1929. He was also concerned about illness among many members of his family. Mezes, who had suffered from tuberculosis for years, seemed near death in Switzerland, while Randolph Tucker, after undergoing an operation in the spring, discovered that he also had tuberculosis. He and Mona planned to spend the winter in Arizona. "What a tragedy," House complained, "the Year 1929 has been for every branch of our family." House to Mezes, July 11, 18, Aug. 20, 1929, to Bailey, July 29, 1929, to Henry Roberts, Aug. 16, 1929, to Gordon Auchincloss, Aug. 16, 1929, House Papers.

7. House to Lyons, June 11, 16, 1929, to Cruger, June 12, 1929, to Dr. A. R. Stevens, June 21, July 1, 10, 1929, to Miller, July 4, 1929, House Papers.

8. House to Mezes, July 11, Aug. 1, 1929, to Bailey, July 29, 1929, to Gordon Auchincloss, Aug. 14, 1929, House Papers.

9. House memo, March 9, 1929, House Papers; House to Mezes, July 25, 1929, to Gordon Auchincloss, July 28, 1929, to E. G. Saxton, Aug. 5, 1929, House Papers; *Memories,* p. 29.

10. House to John Hartness Brown, Sept. 22, 1929, to Randolph Tucker Jr., Oct. 22, 1929, to Mezes, Sept. 21, 26, Oct. 5, 1929, to Mona Tucker, Oct. 17, 1929, House Papers; House was proud of Janet, whom he described as a "handsome woman" with gray hair like her mother's at her age. "Her principal attraction," he wrote a Texas friend, "is her charm. She and Mona have never become spoiled and their manners are natural." House to Cruger, Oct. 31, 1929, House Papers.

11. David M. Kennedy, *Freedom from Fear: The American People in Depression and War* (New York, 1999), 35–41.

12. House to Mezes, Oct. 29, 1929, to Randolph Tucker, Oct. 30, 1929, House Papers.

13. House to Edward Sammons, Nov. 12, 1929, to T. W. House Jr., Nov. 14, 1929, to Mrs. Ottilie Caspari, Nov. 18, 1929, House Papers.

14. House to Clarence Malone, Dec. 1, 1929, to Sammons, Jan. 17, 1930, to Dudley Field Malone, Jan. 16, 1930, to T. W. House Jr., Jan. 20, 1930, House Papers.

15. "Col. House Contrasts Two Conferences," *New York Times Magazine*, Feb. 23, 1930; House to Plunkett, Feb. 9, 1930, House Papers.

16. House to Mezes, Feb. 22, 1930, to Randolph Tucker, Feb. 24, 1930, to Cruger, Feb. 28, 1930, to Auchincloss, March 22, 1930, to Albert Bigelow Paine, April 7, 1930, to Mona Tucker, April 11, 1930, to Gregory, April 13, 1930, to Lyons, April 21, 1930, House Papers.

17. House to Auchincloss, May 1, 12, 1930, to Mona Tucker, May 9, 1930, to Janet Auchincloss, May 9, 1930, to Mezes, May 9, 18, 23, 1930, to Randolph Tucker, May 23, 1930, House Papers; Fanny Denton to Will Hogg, May 25, 1930, Will Hogg Papers.

18. House to Mezes, June 9, 28, July 1, Aug. 24, 1930, to Sammons, July 9, 1930, to Gregory, Aug. 28, 1930, to Janet and Gordon Auchincloss, Sept. 1, 1930, to Dr. Albert Lamb, Sept. 3, 1930, House Papers.

19. House to Janet Auchincloss, July 31, 1930, to Will Hogg, May 29, Aug. 7, 1930; interview with Francis Denton Miller, Oct. 8–9, 1977.

20. William E. Leuchtenburg, *Herbert Hoover* (New York, 2009), 80–111; Kennedy, *Freedom from Fear*, 43–59.

21. House to Brand Whitlock, July 24, 1930, to Hapgood, Aug. 18, 1930, House Papers.

22. House to Bailey, Oct. 1, 1930, to Woolley, Oct. 6, Nov. 5, 1930, to FDR, Nov. 4, 1930, to Gregory, Dec. 10, 1930, to Whitlock, Dec. 11, 1930, House Papers; Kennedy, *Freedom from Fear*, 60; Leuchtenburg, *Hoover*, 112.

23. Kennedy, *Freedom from Fear*, 66–68; House to Whitlock, Dec. 11, 1930, to Grey, Dec. 16, 1930, to Mezes, Dec. 20, 1930, House Papers.

24. House to Hapgood, Jan. 9, 1931, to William Gibbs McAdoo, Jan. 6, 17, March 14, 1931, to Andrews, March 24, 1931, to Gregory, April 15, 1931, House Papers; House also reassured Gregory of the value of his friendship: "No one ever had a more loyal, generous and unselfish friend." House to Gregory, April 15, 1931, House Papers.

25. Frank Freidel, *Franklin D. Roosevelt: The Triumph* (Boston, Mass., 1956), 201–3; Alfred B. Rollins Jr., *Roosevelt and Howe* (New York, 1962), 314–15; James A. Farley, *Behind the Ballots: The Personal History of a Politician* (New York, 1938), 88–89; House to FDR, March 23, 1931, House Papers.

26. House to Woolley, April 30, May 4, 1931, to Robert M. Field, April 13, 1931, to Mrs. Mary Fels, April 30, 1931, to Andrews, March 24, April 30, 1931, to Gregory, May 2, 1931, House Papers; Andrews to House, March 31, 1931, Gregory to House, March 31, May 30, 1931, House Papers.

27. McAdoo to House, Jan. 10, 1931, House Papers; Douglas B. Craig, *After Wilson: The Struggle for the Democratic Party, 1920–1934* (Chapel Hill, N.C.,

1992), 219–22; Douglas B. Craig, *Progressives at War: William G. McAdoo and Newton D. Baker, 1863–1941* (Baltimore, Md., 2013), 309–15.

28. House to Andrews, March 24, 1931, to Gregory, May 2, 1931, to Mezes, May 9, 1931, House Papers; Rollins, *Roosevelt and Howe*, 314.

29. *Atlanta Constitution*, June 4, 1931; *New York Times*, June 11, 14, 1931; *Boston Globe*, June 14, 1931; House to Howe, June 8, 1931, to Mezes, June 11, 1931, to Woolley, June 14, 1931, to Field, June 14, 1931, House Papers.

30. Freidel, *Roosevelt: The Triumph*, 203–4; Rollins, *Roosevelt and Howe*, 316; Jack Beatty, *The Rascal King: The Life and Times of James Michael Curley, 1874–1958* (Reading, Mass., 1992), 295–99.

31. Woolley to House, July 2, 6, 21, Sept. 9, 1931, Field to House, Aug. 26, 31, 1931, House Papers; House to Hapgood, June 18, 1931, to Woolley, June 29, 1931, to Gregory, July 4, Aug. 24, 1931, to Mezes, July 5, 18, 22, 1931, to Andrews, July 18, 1931, to Willis J. Abbot, July 21, 1931, House Papers.

32. "Louis McHenry Howe," in John A. Garraty and Mark C. Carns, eds., *American National Biography* (Chapel Hill, N.C., 1999), XI, 335–36; Kenneth S. David, *FDR: The New York Years, 1928–1933* (New York, 1985), 209–17; H. W. Brands, *Traitor to His Class: The Privileged Life and Radical Presidency of Franklin Delano Roosevelt* (New York, 2008), 52; Frank Freidel, *Franklin D. Roosevelt: The Apprenticeship* (Boston, Mass., 1952), 148–49; Freidel, *Roosevelt: The Triumph*, 170–71; House to Howe, Aug. 14, 1931, House Papers; Howe to House, Aug. 17, 1931, House Papers.

33. "James Aloysius Farley," in John A. Garraty and Mark C. Carns, eds., *American National Biography* (Chapel Hill, N.C., 1999), VII, 716–71; Freidel, *Roosevelt: The Triumph*, 173–74; Steve Neal, *Happy Days Are Here Again* (New York, 2004), 26–32; Woolley to House, July 6, 21, Sept. 16, 1931, House Papers; Howe to House, Aug. 17, 1931, House Papers; House to Howe, Aug. 18, 1931, House Papers.

34. Kennedy, *Freedom from Fear*, 70–74; Leuchtenburg, *Hoover*, 113–16; House to William Arthur Deacon, Sept. 7, 1931, House Papers.

35. House to Mezes, June 26, Aug. 8, 27, 1931, to Auchincloss, July 15, 1931, to T. W. House Jr., Aug. 6, 1931, to Cruger, Aug. 19, 1931, to Nancy Mezes, Sept. 14, 1931, to Edward C. Wynne, Sept. 28, 1931, to E. G. Saxton, Sept. 28, 1931, House Papers.

36. House to Mezes, Sept. 9, 1931, House Papers.

37. House to Woolley, Oct. 1, 7, 1931, to Arthur D. Howden Smith, Oct. 9, 1931, to Howe, Nov. 17, 1931, House Papers; Woolley to House, Nov. 13, Dec. 2, 1931, House Papers.

38. Gregory to House, Nov. 9, 28, 1931, Woolley to House, Sept. 29, Dec. 23, 1931, House Papers; House, to Gregory, Dec. 1, 1931, to Woolley, Dec. 5, 1931, Jan. 14, 16, 1932, to Robert Washburn, Jan. 7, 12, 1931, to Roper, Jan. 26, 1932, House Papers; Freidel, *Roosevelt: The Triumph*, 245–47.

39. Whitlock to House, July 26, 1931, Wickham Steed to House, Dec. 23, 1931, House Papers; House to William Arthur Deacon, July 23, 1931, to Leon Dominion, Dec. 28, 1931, to Grey, Dec. 28, 1931, House Papers; Zara Steiner, *The Lights That Failed: European International History, 1919–1933* (Oxford, Eng., 2005), 635–38.

40. Robert C. Bannister Jr., *Ray Stannard Baker: The Mind and Thought of a Progressive* (New Haven, Conn., 1966), 270, 296; Ray Stannard Baker, *Woodrow Wilson: Life and Letters: Governor, 1910–1913* (Garden City, N.Y., 1931), III, 302–9; Baker, *Woodrow Wilson: Life and Letters: President, 1913–1914*, IV, 155; Later in the decade Baker published a fifth and sixth volume, *Neutrality, 1914–1917* (Garden City, N.Y., 1935), and *Facing War, 1915–1917* (Garden City, N.Y., 1937), both of which were critical of House and his wartime diplomacy. House made no mention of either volume in his correspondence. House to Woolley, Nov. 11, 1931, to Guy M. Bryan, Nov. 28, 1931, to William Bullitt, Dec. 28, 1931, House Papers; Charles Seymour, "Woodrow Wilson: Life and Letters," *American Historical Review*, 38 (1932), 138–42; on December 22, 1931, Mary Allen Hulbert, the infamous Mrs. Peck, visited House and laid her financial plight before him. House concluded that while she had a "good heart" she was also a "wild talker" and that "she is at the end of her tether and that from now she is apt to become vindictive and rather dangerous." House to Seymour, Dec. 22, 1931, House Papers.

41. House to T. W. House Jr., Dec. 7, 17, 1931, to Mona Tucker, Dec. 11, 1931, House Papers.

42. Freidel, *Roosevelt: The Triumph*, 240–43, 250–54; Brands, *Traitor to His Class*, 183–84.

43. House, Note on FDR's Albany Speech, February, 1932, House Papers; House to Woolley, Feb. 2, 10, 1932, to Gregory, Feb. 2, 1932, to Ellery Sedgwick, Feb. 5, 1932, to Homer Cummings, Feb. 10, 1932, to FDR, Feb. 10, 1932, to Farley, Feb. 10, 1932, to Robert M. Washburn, Feb. 12, 1932, House Papers.

44. House to Randolph Tucker, Jan. 31, 1932, to Gregory, Feb. 17, 1932, to Roper, Feb. 17, 1932, to Whitlock, March 31, 1932, House to Woolley, Feb. 24, March 11, 1932, House Papers; Woolley to House, March 15, 1932, House Papers; Freidel, *Roosevelt: The Triumph*, 242–43.

45. House to FDR, April 14, 1932, House Papers; Brands, *Traitor to His Class*, 180–81.

46. Brands, *Traitor to His Class*, 185; Craig, *After Wilson*, 210–43.

47. House to Field, Jan. 29, 1932, to T. W. House Jr., Jan. 29, June 4, 1932, to Clarence M. Malone, Jan. 18, April 12, 1932, to Sammons, Jan. 21, 1932, to Arthur Hugh Frazier, Jan. 26, 1932, to Whitlock, March 31, 1932, to P. A. Fitzhugh, March 11, 1932, to Mona Tucker, March 4, 1932, to Henry C. Roberts, March 29, 1932, to Gregory, May 13, 1932, House Papers.

48. House to E. G. Saxton, April 4, 1932, to T. W. House Jr., May 16, 1932, to Mary Louise Howze, May 29, 1932, House Papers.

49. House to Janet Auchincloss, June 14, 1932, House Papers.

50. House to Gregory, May 29, 1932, to William E. Dodd, June 2, 1932, to Field, June 2, 5, 1932, to Woolley, June 12, 16, 1932, House Papers.

51. Craig, *After Wilson*, 243–47; Brands, *Traitor to His Class*, 185–86; Kennedy, *Freedom from Fear*, 97–101; House to Whitlock, July 3, 1932, to Howden Smith, July 5, 1932, to Clarence C. Dill, July 8, 1932, House Papers.

52. Kennedy, *Freedom from Fear*, 79–94; Leuchtenburg, *Hoover*, 130–38.

53. House to Andrews, July 9, 1932, to Roper, July 12, 13, 30, 1932, to Frederick W. Wile, July 14, 1932, to Walter Lippmann, July 16, 1932, to Woolley, July 27, Sept. 1, 1932, to Robert Underwood Johnson, July 29, 1932; Freidel, *Roosevelt: The Triumph*, 357.

54. House to Wiseman, July 23, 1932, to Andrews, July 27, 1932, to Gordon Auchincloss, Sept. 13, 1932, to Cruger, Sept. 9, 1932, House Papers.

55. House to Robert J. Cromie, Sept. 6, 1932, House Papers; Brands, *Traitor to His Class*, 191–94; Kennedy, *Freedom from Fear*, 99–100.

56. House to Cruger, Oct. 7, 1932, to Mona Tucker, Oct. 7, 1932, to FDR, Oct. 4, 5, 6, 7, 20, Nov. 5, 1932, to Woolley Sept. 23, Nov. 1, 1932, House Papers; Vanderbilt to House, Sept. 26, 1932, Woolley to House, Sept. 27, 1932, House Papers.

57. House to Armstrong, July 19, 1932, to Hapgood, Aug. 23, 1932, to William R. Sweet, Oct. 25, 1932, to Long, June 4, 1932, to T. W. House Jr., Aug. 25, 1932, to Bullitt, Sept. 6, 1932, to Dodd, Oct. 17, 1932, to Roper, Nov. 6, 1932, House Papers; Armstrong to House, July 19, 1932, Woolley to House, Nov. 8, 1932, House Papers; Bullitt, who had undertaken a controversial mission to the Soviet Union during the Paris Peace Conference, spent most of the 1920s in Europe. In 1930 he moved to Vienna to pursue a psychological study of Wilson in collaboration with Sigmund Freud. House admired his young friend's talents and knowledge of European affairs and agreed to give him extracts from his diary. House urged him to write his study of Wilson "with moderation and without bias," and rather naïvely assumed—given the hostility that Bullitt and Freud had long felt toward Wilson—that their book would "throw a favorable light on the President." Fortunately House never saw the final result, since friends convinced Bullitt, who hoped for a position in the new Roosevelt administration, that it would be unwise to publish such a devastating critique of Wilson. *Thomas Woodrow Wilson: A Psychological Study*, did not appear until 1967. House to Helen M. Reynolds, July 12, 15, Aug. 7, 1930, to Bullitt, July 31, 1930, Sept. 6, 1932, to Irving Hoover, Sept. 16, 1930, House Papers; Bullitt to House, Dec. 13, 1931, Sept. 3, 1932, House Papers; Will Brownell and Richard N. Billings, *So Close to Greatness: A Biography of William C. Bullitt* (New York, 1987), 119–28.

58. Kennedy, *Freedom from Fear*, 101–8; Brands, *Traitor to His Class*, 193–99; Leuchtenburg, *Hoover*, 138–42.

59. House to Woolley, Nov. 9, 1932, House Papers; Eleanor Roosevelt to Loulie House, Nov. 11, 1932, Farley to House, Nov. 12, 1932, House Papers; House was eager to record an epitaph for Hoover, who he had hoped would run on

the Democratic ticket in 1920. "Hoover," he observed, "never knew enough about this country and its people to be a good President . . . . He was a great administrator, not even a good politician . . . . He never really learned political practice while he was in Washington." Arthur D. Howden Smith, *Mr. House of Texas* (New York, 1940), 364.

CHAPTER 37

1. David M. Kennedy, *Freedom from Fear: The American People in Depression and War, 1929–1945* (New York, 1999), 104–30; Frank Freidel, *FDR: Launching the New Deal* (Boston, Mass., 1973), 3–195.

2. *New York Times*, Nov. 10, 1932; House to William Gibbs McAdoo, Dec. 18, 1932, to Mona Tucker, Jan. 8, 1933, House Papers.

3. "Some Foreign Policy Problems of the Next Administration," *Foreign Affairs*, 11, 2 (January 1933), 211–19; "Roosevelt's Pilots—Colonel House and Colonel Howe," *Scribner's Magazine*, 93, 11 (January 1933), 1–7.

4. "Roosevelt's Pilots," 6; Kennedy, *Freedom from Fear,* 389–90; Robert Dallek, *Franklin D. Roosevelt and American Foreign Policy, 1932–1945* (New York, 1979), 3–20.

5. House to Woolley, Dec. 4, 1932, Jan. 7, 1933, Frank Andrews, Jan. 20, 1933, to James C. McReynolds, Feb. 1, 1933, to William Phillips, Feb. 28, 1933, to Brand Whitlock, March 4, 1933, to Guy M. Bryan, March 7, 1933, to T. W. House Jr., April 23, 1933, House Papers; Freidel, *FDR,* 143–60.

6. House to J. H. B. House, Dec. 17, 1932, to T. W. House Jr., Dec. 19, 1932, to Paul B. Cruger, Jan. 16, 1933, House Papers.

7. House to Mrs. Thomas Watt Gregory, Feb. 26, 1933, to Andrews, March 3, 1933, House Papers.

8. Kennedy, *Freedom from Fear,* 131–53; H. W. Brands, *Traitor to His Class: The Privileged Life and Radical Presidency of Franklin Delano Roosevelt* (New York, 2008), 263; Anthony J. Badger, *FDR: The First Hundred Days* (New York, 2008), 3–22.

9. House to Daniel Roper, June 11, 1933, to Breckinridge Long, June 25, 1933, to FDR, July 2, 1933, to Edward S. Martin, July 26, 1933, to A. H. Frazier, Oct. 2, 1933, House Papers; "Looking at Tomorrow," *Redbook Magazine* (June 1933), 42–43.

10. House to Cruger, May 28, 1933, to James J. Lyons, June 9, 1933, to Marten Bailey, June 26, 1933, to Roper, July 16, 1933, to Edward H. Sammons, July 27, 1933, House Papers.

11. Zara Steiner, *The Triumph of the Dark: European International History, 1933–1939* (Oxford, Eng., 2011), 9–21; Lord Lothian to House, April 11, 1933, House Papers; Leon Dominion to House, June 12, 1933, House Papers; Edward Roffi to House, April 8, 1933, House Papers.

12. "Issues and Men: An Open Letter to Colonel House," *The Nation*, 136, no. 353 (April 5, 1933), 362–65; Villard's critique is developed in Jim Powell, *Wilson's*

War: How Woodrow Wilson's Great Blunder Led to Hitler, Stalin, and World War II
(New York, 2005), 1–14.

13. House to D. N. Heineman, June 1, 1933, to Gordon Auchincloss, July 6, 1933, to
Edward C. Wynne, Aug. 10, 1933, Cordell Hull, Aug. 11, 1933, House Papers;
Kennedy, *Freedom from Fear*, 155–57; Freidel, *FDR*, 359–61; in November 1933
FDR dispatched another of House's protégés, William Bullitt, to Moscow as
the first American ambassador to the Soviet Union. While House and Bullitt
remained on good terms, they did not correspond regularly. Will Brownell
and Richard N. Billings, *So Close to Greatness: A Biography of William C. Bullitt*
(New York, 1987), 137–41.

14. House to Dodd, June 10, 28, Aug. 10, 30, 1933, to Bingham, June 17, Sept.
10, 1933, to Long, June 25, July 2, 13, 1933, to Wynne, June 23, Aug. 10, 1933,
to Bonsal, June 21, 1933, to Roper, July 6, 1933, to Woolley, July 29, 1933, to
Hull, Aug. 11, 1933, House Papers; Wynne to House, Aug. 15, 1933, House
Papers; Bingham to House, July 11, Sept. 22, 1933, House Papers; Long to
House, Sept. 15, 1933, House Papers; House realized that journalists overestimated his influence in the administration. George Creel, for example,
claimed that Farley, House, Howe, and Moley formed a Kitchen Cabinet of
close advisers, and that House ranked second only to Howe. "The Kitchen
Cabinet," *Collier's*, June 17, 1933.

15. House to Frazier, Oct. 2, 1933, to Mona Tucker, Oct. 12, 1933, to Wynne,
Oct. 9, 1933, to Cruger, Oct. 16, 1933, House Papers.

16. House to Bingham, Oct. 21, 1933, to Dodd, Oct. 21, 1933, to Long, Oct. 21,
1933, to Cudahy, Oct. 21, 1933, to Dodd, Oct. 21, Nov. 21, Dec. 28, 1933, April
11, 1934, to Wynne, March 10, 1934, to Dodd, April 11, 1934; Dodd to House,
Dec. 10, 28, 1933, House Papers; Erik Larson, *In the Garden of Beasts: Love,
Terror, and an American Family in Hitler's Berlin* (New York, 2011), 216–17.

17. House to Roper, Nov. 12, 1933, Feb. 9, 1934, to FDR, Nov. 27, 1933, Jan. 21,
1934, to Mona Tucker, Nov. 28, 1933, House Papers; FDR to House, Nov. 21,
1933, Jan. 21, 1934, House Papers.

18. House to William Malone, Dec. 26, 1933, to Dodd, Dec. 16, 1933, to Long,
Jan. 4, 1934, to Martin C. Miller, March 15, 1934, to William Arthur Deacon,
March 20, 1934, House Papers.

19. Larson, *In the Garden of Beasts,* 38–39, 245–47; William E. Dodd Jr. and Martha
Dodd, eds., *Ambassador Dodd's Diary, 1933–1938* (London, Eng., 1941), 23–24,
1–5; Kennedy, *Freedom from Fear*, 410–18; House to Cudahy, April 2, 1934, to
Dodd, May 25, 1934, to Roper, Feb. 25, 1934, House Papers.

20. House to William H. Thomas, Nov. 23, 1933, to Henry C. Roberts, April 19,
1934, to Mona Tucker, Nov. 28, 1933, to Hugh Frazier, Feb. 10, 1934, to T. W.
House Jr., Dec. 6, 1933, to E. G. Saxton, Dec. 2, 1933, to Robert T. Morris,
April 14, 1934, to Paul Cruger, April 16, 1934, to J. Donald Duncan, Jan. 14,
1934, to Janet Auchincloss, Feb. 25, 1934, to R. H. Cochrane, June 7, 1934,
House Papers.

21. House to Fanny Denton, June 9, 1934, House Papers.

22. Irwin H. Hoover, "The Case of Colonel House," *Saturday Evening Post,* July 14, 1934, 16–17; Irwin H. Hoover, *Forty-Two Years in the White House* (Boston, Mass., 1934), 87–96.

23. House to Arthur Howden Smith, July 10, 25, 1934, to Dodd, July 19, 1934, to Mrs. Irwin H. Hoover, Aug. 15, 1934, House Papers; Woolley to House, July 23, 1934, House Papers; *New York Times,* July 26, 1934; *Washington Post Magazine,* Aug. 19, 1934.

24. House to Bingham, Aug. 5, 1934, to Wickham Steed, Aug. 9, 1934, House Papers; Kevin Morgan, *Ramsay MacDonald* (London, Eng., 2006), 78–81.

25. House to Janet Auchincloss, July 3, 1934, to Lyons, Aug. 16, 1934, to Morris, Aug. 22, 1934, House Papers.

26. House to Mona Tucker, Oct. 4, 1934, to Mrs. Edwin A. Alderman, Sept. 19, 1934, to Bingham, Sept. 23, Oct. 18, 1934, to Frank W. Buxton, Sept. 23, 1934, to Jesse I. Straus, Oct. 6, 1934, to Roper, Oct. 7, 10, 25, 27, 1934, to Dodd, Oct. 8, 1934, House Papers; *New York Times,* Nov. 5, 1934.

27. Kennedy, *Freedom from Fear,* 216–17.

28. House to Straus, Oct. 6, 19, 1934, to FDR, Oct. 9, 1934, to Lothian, Dec. 13, 1934, House Papers; Lothian to House, Nov. 20, 1934, House Papers.

29. Kennedy, *Freedom from Fear,* 95–97; House to Straus, Feb. 4, 1935, to Wynne, Feb. 11, 1935, to Dodd, March 18, 1935, to Arthur Sweetser, Feb. 17, 1935, to Steed, March 13, 1935, House Papers; Wynne to House, Feb. 9, 1935, House Papers.

30. Steiner, *The Triumph of the Dark,* 83–98; FDR to House, April 10, 1935, House Papers; Bingham to House, April 1, 23, 30, 1935, House Papers; House to FDR, April 20, 1935, House Papers.

31. FDR to House, Feb. 16, March 20, 1935, House Papers; Kennedy, *Freedom from Fear,* 213–78.

32. Roper to House, April 1, 1935, House Papers; William Wiseman to House, April 1, 3, 1935, House Papers; House to Roper, April 4, May 1, 1935, to Bingham, June 14, 1935, House Papers.

33. House to Saxton, July 30, 1935, to Long, July 14, 1935, to Frederick H. Allen, July 14, 1935, House Papers.

34. House to Bingham, July 4, 1935, to Auchincloss, July 11, 1935, to Long, July 14, 1935, to Robert M. Washburn, July 18, 1935, House Papers; Auchincloss to House, July 3, 10, Aug. 2, 1935, House Papers; Arthur D. Howden Smith, *Mr. House of Texas* (New York, 1940), 369; Michael Hiltzik, *The New Deal: A Modern History* (New York, 2011), 195–200.

35. House to Ottilie Caspari, July 2, 1935, to William P. Hobby, Sept. 13, 1935, House Papers; *New York Times,* Sept. 15, 1935; "Wanted—A New Deal among Nations" *Liberty* magazine, Sept. 14, 1935.

36. Steiner, *The Triumph of the Dark,* 100–13; *New York Times,* Oct. 16, 1935.

37. Steiner, *The Triumph of the Dark*, 113–26; Kennedy, *Freedom from Fear*, 395–96; Ruth Henig, *The League of Nations* (London, Eng. 2010), 154–73.

38. House to Mona Tucker, Jan. 16, Feb. 26, 1936, to Cudahy, Nov. 9, Dec. 16, 1935, Jan. 22, 1936, to Bingham, Nov. 8, 22, 1935, to Roper, March 17, 1936, to Sweetser, April 3, 1936, to Long, April 3, 1936, House Papers; Roper to House, March 14, 1936, House Papers; House followed the deliberations of the Senate Munitions Committee, led by Senator Gerald P. Nye (Republican, North Dakota) with a measured contempt. He had no intention of testifying before the committee, which he felt had turned into an investigation of his and Wilson's activities during World War I. House to Frank W. Buxton, Dec. 12, 1935, Jan. 19, 1936, House Papers; *New York Times,* Jan. 16, Feb. 8, 1936; Wayne S. Cole, *Senator Gerald P. Nye and American Foreign Relations* (Minneapolis, Minn., 1962), 87–91.

39. Steiner, *The Triumph of the Dark*, 136–50, 167; Ian Kershaw, *Hitler, 1936–45: Nemesis* (New York, 2000), xxxvi–xlvi; Cudahy to House, April 17, 1936, House Papers.

40. House to Long, April 3, 1936, House Papers; Bingham to House, Oct. 15, 1935, House Papers; Viereck to House, March 13, 1936, House Papers; Elmer Gertz, *Odyssey of a Barbarian: The Biography of George Sylvester Viereck* (Buffalo, N.Y., 1978), 204; early on the morning of April 11, 1936, Randolph Tucker Jr., who was twenty-one, was killed when his car struck the rear of a gasoline truck near El Centro, California. He was driving from Chihuahua City, Mexico, to Beverly Hills, California, where Mona and Randolph were spending the winter. House no doubt wrote Mona and Randolph about this family tragedy, but most of his handwritten notes to family and friends have not survived. Mona Tucker told the author that she threw his letters away. *New York Times*, April 12, 1936; interview with Mona and Randolph Tucker, Aug. 25, Oct. 15, 1966.

41. House to Bingham, Aug. 18, 1936, to Lyons, July 9, 1936, to Joseph Grew, June 16, 1936, House Papers.

42. Brands, *Traitor to His Class*, 338–39.

43. Brands, *Traitor to His Class*, 338–39; Kennedy, *Freedom from Fear*, 278–86.

44. House to FDR, June 28, 1936, to Woolley, July 4, 1936, House Papers; Woolley to House, July 1, 1936, House Papers; throughout the 1930s House followed closely "the Far Eastern question," talking frequently with Japanese diplomats and government leaders. He learned about various factions within the Japanese military and concluded by early 1934 that the military party was in control of the government and was imbued with a "spirit of adventure." When House learned that Stephen Bonsal planned to travel to Japan, he urged him to "tell our friends" there that "the feeling in the United States is friendly to them. We recognize the fact that they are a great nation and are attempting to modernize the East. However, they must bear in mind that the world is undergoing a social revolution, and the things that England, Germany,

France and the United States did fifty years ago could not be done now."
House to FDR, March 28, 1933, to Dodd, Jan. 7, 1934, to Bonsal, June 21,
1934, to Lothian, Dec. 13, 1934, to Bingham, Nov. 8, 1935, to Straus, Nov. 9,
1935, House Papers.

45. Kennedy, *Freedom from Fear*, 381–84.

46. Kennedy, *Freedom from Fear*, 284–86; Brands, *Traitor to His Class,* 339.

47. House to Bingham, Sept. 16, Oct. 27, 1936, to Roper, Oct. 12, 1936, to Dodd,
Nov. 16, 1936, House Papers; Roper to House, Sept. 15, 26, 1936, House
Papers; FDR to House, Aug. 25, 1936, House Papers.

48. Woolley to House, Nov. 5, 1936, House Papers.

49. House to Mona Tucker, Feb. 4, 18, March 8, April 10, 1937, House Papers.

50. Steiner, *The Triumph of the Dark*, 180–358; Robert Rhodes James, *The British
Revolution, 1880–1939* (New York, 1977), 525–34.

51. Cudahy to House, Dec. 30, 1936, House Papers; House to Cudahy, Jan. 18,
1937, to Viereck, May 15, 1937, House Papers.

52. Kennedy, *Freedom from Fear*, 287, 323–41; Brands, *Traitor to His Class,* 340–41.

53. House to FDR, Dec. 22, 1936, to Washburn, Feb. 9, 1937, to Woolley, May
13, 1937, to Field, May 22, 1937, to Bingham, May 27, 1937, House Papers;
Woolley to House, May 12, 1937, House Papers.

54. *New York Times*, June 12, 1937; *New York Herald Tribune*, June 12, 1937; House
to FDR, June 13, 1937, to Bingham, June 18, 1937, to Woolley, June 25, 1937,
House Papers; FDR to House, June 16, 1937, House Papers.

55. House to Viereck, July 8, Sept. 3, 1937, to Roper, July 11, 1937, to Auchincloss,
July 16, 1937, to Alderman, Aug. 26, 1937, House Papers.

56. House to Mona Tucker, Sept. 26, 1937, to Allen, Oct. 10, 1937, to Martin, Oct.
27, 1937, House Papers.

57. Kennedy, *Freedom from Fear*, 404–5; Woolley to House, June 22, July 14, 26,
Aug. 25, Sept. 16, 1937, House Papers; FDR to House, Oct. 19, 1937, House
Papers.

58. House to Mrs. Roy Needham, Nov. 27, 1937, to T. W. House Jr., Dec. 15,
1937, Fanny Denton to Sawyer, Dec. 12, 1937, House to Mona Tucker, Dec.
15, 1937, to Cudahy, Dec. 16, 1937, to Washburn, Dec. 26, 1937, House Papers;
New York Times, Nov. 25, 1937.

EPILOGUE

1. Seymour memo, Jan. 5, 1938, Seymour Papers; House was proud of his relationship with Wilson's family. He was close to Margaret Wilson and Helen
Bones, and visited with McAdoo whenever he came to New York. House
to Helen Bones, Jan. 5, 1937, to Joseph Tumulty, Jan. 9, 1938, House Papers;
Helen Bones to House, Dec. 28, 1936, House Papers.

2. House to Robert Washburn, Jan. 12, 1938, to Mona Tucker, Feb. 9, 1938,
House Papers; Fanny Denton to T. W. House Jr., Feb. 26, 1938, House Papers;

New York Times, March 29, 1938; Sara Roosevelt to Loulie House, Feb. 4, 1935, House Papers.

3. Fanny Denton to T. W. House Jr., Feb. 26, 1938, House Papers; *New York Times*, March 29, 30, 1938; *Austin Statesman*, March 31, 1938; *Houston Post*, March 31, 1938.

4. *New York Times,* March 29, 1938; *New York Herald Tribune*, March 31, 1938.

5. Bernard M. Baruch, *Baruch: The Public Years* (New York, 1960), 131–34; Raymond Fosdick, *Chronicle of a Generation* (New York, 1958), 196–97.

6. Edward Auchincloss to Charles Seymour, Sept. 17, 1950, House Papers; interview with Frances Denton Miller, Oct. 8–9, 1977; William G. McAdoo, *Crowded Years: The Reminiscences of William G. McAdoo* (Boston, Mass., 1931), 511; *New York Herald Tribune,* March 31, 1938; George F. Kennan, "Comments on the Paper Entitled *Kennan versus Wilson* by Professor Thomas Knock," in John Milton Cooper Jr. and Charles E. Neu, eds., *The Wilson Era: Essays in Honor of Arthur S. Link* (Arlington Heights, Ill., 1991), 327–30.

ACKNOWLEDGMENTS

1. Arthur S. Link to author, May 3, 1966.

2. Leon Edel, *Henry James: The Master* (New York, 1972), 20.

3. W. Barksdale Maynard, *Woodrow Wilson: Princeton to the Presidency* (New Haven, Conn., 2008), 99.

Sources

MANUSCRIPTS

Austin History Collection, Austin Public Library, Austin, Texas

Margaret Cunningham Scrapbooks
David Harrell Papers
House Papers
House–Barkley Papers
House Cornerstone Contents
Mary Thorton Scrapbooks
WPA Interviews

Baker Library, Harvard Business School, Cambridge, Mass.

Thomas Jefferson Coolidge Jr. Papers

Dolph Briscoe Center for American History, University of Texas, Austin, Texas

Lula Mary Bewley Papers
Harry Y. Benedict Papers
Thomas M. Campbell Papers
Benajah Harvey Carroll Jr. Papers
Charles A. Culberson Papers
Mrs. B. S. Given Papers
Mark L. Goodwin Papers
M. R. Gutsch Papers
Thomas S. Henderson Papers
James Stephen Hogg Papers
William Clifford Hogg Papers
Edward M. House Papers
Loulie Hunter House Papers
Thomas William House Papers
Thomas William House Jr. Papers
R. W. Hudson Papers
Mrs. Percy V. Pennybacker Papers
Joe Pate Smyer Papers
James B. Wells Papers

Cambridge University Library, Cambridge, England

Kathleen Scott (Lady Kennet) Papers

Columbia University Library, New York, N.Y.

Mrs. August Belmont Papers
Benjamin W. Heubsch Papers
Sidney E. Mezes Papers
William L. Westermann Papers
Henry White Papers
Henry Parker Willis Papers

Columbia University Oral History Collection, New York, N.Y.

Norman Angell
Adolf A. Berle Jr.
Charles C. Burlingham
Waldo Chamberlin
James W. Gerard
Florence J. Harriman
Burton J. Hendrick
Walter Lippmann
Eugene Meyer
John Lord O'Brien
Lithgow Osborne
William Phillips
Louis H. Pink
George Rublee
Francis B. Sayre
James T. Shotwell
William H. Wadhams
James W. Wadsworth
James P. Warburg
Stanley Washburn
James T. Williams

Department of Manuscripts and Archives, Cornell University, Ithaca, N.Y.

Deceased alumni records

Houghton Library, Harvard University, Cambridge, Mass.

David F. Houston Papers
Walter Hines Page Papers
William Phillips Diary

Manuscript Division, Library of Congress, Washington, D.C.

Chandler P. Anderson Papers
Carl W. Ackerman Papers
Ray Stannard Baker Papers
Newton Baker Papers
William S. Benson Papers
Tasker H. Bliss Papers
Stephen Bonsal Papers
Albert C. Burleson Papers
Josephus Daniels Papers
Henry P. Fletcher Papers
Thomas Watt Gregory Papers
Charles E. Hamlin Papers
Florence J. Harriman Papers
Irwin H. Hoover Papers
Robert M. Lansing Papers
Breckinridge Long Papers
William Gibbs McAdoo Papers
David Hunter Miller Papers
John Bassett Moore Papers
Henry S. Morgenthau, Sr. Papers
John J. Pershing Papers
Arthur Sweetser Papers
Joseph Tumulty Papers
Stanley Washburn Papers
Henry White Papers
Brand Whitlock Papers
Edith Bolling Wilson Papers
Robert Woolley Papers

New York Historical Society, New York, N.Y.

James H. Hyde Papers

Peabody Essex Museum, Salem, Mass.

North Shore Breeze

San Jacinto Museum of History, Houston, Tex.

Mary Ann McDowall, "A Little Journey through Memory's Halls."
Edith R. House Scrapbook

Southwest Collection, Texas Tech University, Lubbock, Tex.

Louis Hamilton Hill Papers

Woodrow Wilson Presidential Library, Staunton, Va.

Cary T. Grayson Papers

Manuscript and Archives, Yale University, New Haven, Conn.

Gordon Auchincloss Papers
Frances B. Denton Papers
Edward M. House Papers
Vance C. McCormick Papers
Sidney E. Mezes Papers
Frank L. Polk Papers
Charles Seymour Papers
George S. Viereck Papers
William Wiseman Papers

Interviews and Correspondence with Author

Edward and Janet Auchincloss, Dec. 29, 1966, New York, N.Y.
Mrs. Robert M. Blaine, April 20, 1977, Houston, Tex.
Adolph A. Berle, Jr., June 2, 1969, New York, N.Y.
Mrs. Allston Boyer, April 25, 1969, New York, N.Y.
Mrs. Milton Gutsch, June 22, 1970, Austin, Tex.
Mrs. James P. Hart to author, Nov. 4, 1977
Ima Hogg, Oct. 13, 1967, Houston, Tex.
Edward M. House, June 11, 1970, telephone interview
Walter Lippmann, Dec. 17, 1970, New York, N.Y.
Judge James W. McClendon, Austin, Tex., Sept. 7, 1966
Frances Denton Miller, Oct. 8–9, 1977, Chestertown, Md.
Mrs. Roy M. Needham, June 17, 1970, Houston, Tex.
Mrs. Jane Prendergast, telephone conversation, April 6, 1970 and interview, January 4, 1979, San Diego, Calif.
Mrs. Charles Seymour, Aug. 15, 1969, Chatham, Mass.
Mrs. George Shelley, June 22, 1970, Austin, Tex.
Mona and Randolph Tucker, August 25, October 15, 1966, September 5, 1967 (with Janet Auchincloss).
Mona Tucker to author, Aug. 19, Sept. 15, Oct. 10, Dec. 8, 1966, July 19, 1967, June 23, 1968.

THESES

Grover, Henry Cushing, "The Dissolution of T. W. House and Company" (M. A. Thesis, University of Houston, 1962).
Ferren, John M., "Edward Mandell House: The Preparation" (Honors Essay, Harvard College, 1959).

Toprani, Anand, "Extraordinary Diplomacy: Edward M. House and Harry L. Hopkins as Presidential Foreign Policy Advisors & Special Envoys to Europe during the Period of American Neutrality in the First & Second World Wars, 1914–1916 & 1940–1941" (M. Phil., Oxford University, 2006).

BOOKS AND ARTICLES

Adamthwaite, Anthony, *Grandeur and Misery: France's Bid for Power in Europe, 1914–1940* (London, Eng., 1995).

Adams, R. J. Q., *Balfour: The Last Grandee* (London, Eng., 2007).

Afflerbach, Holger, and Stevenson, David, eds., *An Improbable War? The Outbreak of World War I and European Political Culture before 1914* (New York, 2007).

Albrecht–Carrie, Rene, *Italy at the Paris Peace Conference* (New York, 1938).

Allhands, J. L., *Boll Weevil: Recollections of the Trinity & Brazos Valley Railway* (Houston, Tex., 1946).

Anderson, John Q., ed., *Tales of Frontier Texas, 1830–1860* (Dallas, Tex., 1966).

Anders, Evan, *Boss Rule in South Texas: The Progressive Era* (Austin, Tex., 1982).

Andrew, Christopher, *Her Majesty's Secret Service: The Making of the British Intelligence Community* (New York, 1986).

Armstrong, Hamilton Fish, *Peace and Counterpeace: From Wilson to Hitler* (New York, 1971).

Arnold, Peri E., *Remaking the Presidency: Roosevelt, Taft, and Wilson, 1901–1916* (Lawrence, Kans., 2009).

Arthur, Sir George, translator, *The Memoirs of Raymond Poincaré* (New York, 1975), 12.

Asprey, Robert B., *The German High Command at War: Hindenburg and Ludendorff Conduct World War I* (New York, 1991).

Axson, Stockton, *Brother Woodrow: A Memoir of Woodrow Wilson*, Arthur S. Link, ed., (Princeton, N.J., 1993).

Badger, Anthony, *FDR: The First Hundred Days* (New York, 2008).

Baker, Ray Stannard, *American Chronicle: The Autobiography of Ray Stannard Baker* (New York, 1945).

Baker, Ray Stannard, *Woodrow Wilson and the World Settlement*, 3 vols. (New York, 1922).

Baker, Ray Stannard, *Woodrow Wilson*, 7 vols. (Garden City, N.Y., 1927–39).

Balfour, Arthur James, *Retrospect: An Unfinished Autobiography* (London, Eng., 1930).

Bannister, Robert C. Jr., *Ray Stannard Baker: The Mind and Thought of a Progressive* (New Haven, Conn., 1966).

Barkley, Mary Starr, *History of Travis County and Austin, 1839–1899* (Waco, Tex., 1963).

Barnes, Donna A., *Farmers in Rebellion: The Rise and Fall of the Southern Farmers Alliance and People's Party in Texas* (Austin, Tex., 1984).

Barr, Alwyn, *Reconstruction to Reform: Texas Politics, 1876–1906* (Austin, Tex., 1971).

Baruch, Bernard M., *Baruch: The Public Years* (New York, 1960).

Beatty, Jack, *The Lost History of 1914: Reconsidering the Year the Great War Began* (New York, 2012).

Beatty, Jack, *The Rascal King: The Life and Times of James Michael Curley, 1874–1958* (Reading, Mass., 1992).

Beckett, Ian F. W., *The Making of the First World War* (New Haven, Conn., 2012).

Bedichek, Roy, *Karankaway County* (Garden City, N.Y., 1950).

Bendiner, Elmer, *A Time for Angels: The Tragicomic History of the League of Nations* (New York, 1975).

Bessly, *Room 40: British Naval Intelligence, 1914–18* (New York, 1986).

Berghahn, V. R., *Germany and the Approach of War in 1914* (New York, 1993).

Berry, Margaret C., *The University of Texas: A Pictorial Account of Its First Century* (Austin, Tex., 1980).

Bishop, Morris, *A History of Cornell* (New York, 1962).

Blucher, Evelyn Princess, *An English Wife in Berlin* (New York, 1920).

Blum, Deborah, *Ghost Hunters: William James and the Search for Scientific Proof of Life after Death* (New York, 2006).

Blum, John M., *Joe Tumulty and the Wilson Era* (Boston, Mass., 1951).

Blumenthal, Henry, *Illusion and Reality in Franco-American Diplomacy, 1914–1945* (Baton Rouge, La., 1986).

Manfred F. Boemeke, Gerald D. Feldman, and Elisabeth Glaser, *The Treaty of Versailles: A Reassessment after 75 Years* (Washington, D. C., and Cambridge, Eng., 1998).

Bond, Richard W., "The Residence of E. M. House: Texas Historical Architecture," *Texas Architect*, 18 (June 1968), 12–17.

Bonsal, Stephen, *Unfinished Business* (Garden City, N.Y., 1944).

Bonsal, Stephen, *Suitors and Suppliants: The Little Nations at Versailles* (New York, 1946).

Brands, H. W., *Traitor to His Class: The Privileged Life and Radical Presidency of Franklin Delano Roosevelt* (New York, 2008).

Brinnin, John Malcolm, *The Sway of the Grand Saloon: A Social History of the North Atlantic* (New York, 1971).

Brock, Michael, and Brocke, Eleanor, eds., *Letters of H. H. Asquith to Venetia Stanley* (New York, 1982).

Broesamle, John J., *William Gibbs McAdoo: A Passion for Change, 1863–1917* (Port Washington, N.Y., 1973).

Brown, Norman, *Hood, Bonnet, and Little Brown Jug* (College Station, Tex., 1984).

Brown, Richard Maxwell, *Strain of Violence: Historical Studies of American Violence and Vigilantism* (New York, 1975).

Brownell, Will, and Billings, Richard N., *So Close to Greatness: A Biography of William C. Bullitt* (New York, 1987).

Bruce, Robert B., *A Fraternity of Arms: America and France in the Great War* (Lawrence, Kans., 2003).

Burner, David, *The Politics of Provincialism: The Democratic Party in Transition, 1918–1932* (New York, 1968).

Burner, David, *Herbert Hoover: A Public Life* (New York, 1979).

Burton, David H., *Cecil Spring Rice: A Diplomat's Life* (Cranbury, N.J., 1990).

Bushman, Richard L., Harris, Neil, Rothman, David, Soloman, Barbara Miller, and Thernstrom, Stephen, eds., *Uprooted Americans: Essays in Honor of Oscar Handlin* (Boston, Mass., 1979).

Campbell, Randolph B., *Gone to Texas: A History of the Lone Star State* (New York, 2003).

Carrigan, William D., *The Making of a Lynching Culture: Violence and Vigilantism in Central Texas, 1836–1916* (Urbana, Ill., 2004).

Cassar, George H., *Kitchener's War: British Strategy from 1914 to 1916* (Washington, D.C., 2004).

Cassar, George H., *Asquith as War Leader* (London, Eng., 1994).

Cassar, George H., *Lloyd George at War, 1916–1918* (London, Eng., 2011).

Cecil, Lamar, *Wilhelm II*, 2 vols. (Chapel Hill, N.C., 1989, 1996).

Cecil, Lord Robert, *A Great Experiment: An Autobiography* (New York, 1941).

Chambers, John Whiteclay II, *To Raise an Army: The Draft Comes to Modern America* (New York, 1987).

Chickering, Roger, *Imperial Germany and the Great War, 1914–1918*, 2nd ed. (Cambridge, Eng., 2004).

Clark, Christopher, *The Sleepwalkers: How Europe Went to War in 1914* (New York, 2013).

Clark, Christopher, *Kaiser Wilhelm II* (London, Eng., 2000).

Clark, James A., and Halbouty, Michel T., *Spindletop* (New York, 1952).

Clemenceau, Georges, *Grandeur and Misery of Victory* (New York, 1930).

Clements, Kendrick A., *The Life of Herbert Hoover: Imperfect Visionary, 1918–1928* (New York, 2010).

Coffman, Edward M., *The War to End All Wars: The American Military Experience in World War I* (New York, 1968).

Coffman, Edward M., *The Regulars: The American Army, 1898–1941* (Cambridge, Mass., 2004).

Cohen, Warren I., *Empire without Tears: America's Foreign Relations, 1921–1933* (New York, 1987).

Cohrs, Patrick, *The Unfinished Peace after World War I: America, Britain, and the Stabilisation of Europe, 1919–1932* (Cambridge, Eng., 2006).

Cole, Wayne S., *Senator Gerald P. Nye and American Foreign Relations* (Minneapolis, Minn., 1962).

Coletta, Paolo E., *William Jennings Bryan*, 3 vols., (Lincoln, Neb., 1964–69).

Conyne, G. R., *Woodrow Wilson: British Perspectives, 1912–21* (New York, 1992).

Cooper, John Milton Jr., and Neu, Charles E., *The Wilson Era: Essays in Honor of Arthur S. Link* (Arlington Heights, Ill., 1991).

Cooper, John Milton Jr., *Pivotal Decades: The United States, 1900–1920* (New York, 1990).

Cooper, John Milton Jr., *Breaking the Heart of the World: Woodrow Wilson and the Fight for the League of Nations* (New York, 2001).

Cooper, John Milton Jr., *Reconsidering Woodrow Wilson: Progressivism, Internationalism, War, and Peace* (Washington, D.C., 2008).

Cooper, John Milton Jr., *Woodrow Wilson: A Biography* (New York, 2009).

Cooper, John Milton Jr., *The Warrior and the Priest: Woodrow Wilson and Theodore Roosevelt* (Cambridge, Mass., 1983).

Cooper, John Milton Jr., *Walter Hines Page: The Southerner as American, 1855–1918* (Chapel Hill, N.C., 1977).

Cotner, Robert C., *James Stephen Hogg: A Biography* (Austin, Tex., 1959).

Conye, G. R., *Woodrow Wilson: British Perspectives, 1912–1921* (New York, 1992).

Cox, James M., *Journey through My Years* (New York, 1946).

Craig, Douglas B., *After Wilson: The Struggle for the Democratic Party, 1920–1934* (Chapel Hill, N.C., 1992).

Craig, Douglas B., *Progressives at War: William G. McAdoo and Newton D. Baker, 1863–1941* (Baltimore, Md., 2013).

Craig, Gordon, *Germany, 1866–1945* (New York, 1978).

Craig, Lee H., *Josephus Daniels: His Life and Times* (Chapel Hill, N.C., 2012).

Creel, George, *Rebel at Large: Reflections of Fifty Crowded Years* (New York, 1947).

Crunden, Robert M., *Ministers of Reform: The Progressives' Achievement in American Civilization, 1889–1920* (New York, 1982).

Dallas, Gregor, *1918: War and Peace* (New York, 2001).

Dallas, Gregor, *At the Heart of a Tiger: Clemenceau and His World, 1841–1929* (New York, 1993).

Dallek, Robert, *Franklin D. Roosevelt and American Foreign Policy, 1932–1945* (New York, 1979).

Dallek, Robert, *Democrat and Diplomat: The Life of William E. Dodd* (New York, 2013).

Davidson, Jo, *Between Sittings: An Informal Autobiography* (New York, 1951).

David, Kenneth S., *FDR: The New York Years, 1923–1933* (New York, 1985).

Davis, Julia, and Fleming, Dolores A., *The Ambassadorial Diary of John W. Davis: The Court of St. James, 1918–1921* (Morgantown, W.Va., 1993).

Davis, Thomas B. Jr., *Chronicles of Hopkins Grammar School, 1660–1935* (New Haven, Conn., 1938).

Dawley, Alan, *Changing the World: American Progressives in War and Revolution* (Princeton, N.J., 2003).

Devlin, Patrick, *Too Proud to Fight: Woodrow Wilson's Neutrality* (New York, 1975).

Digby, Margaret, *Horace Plunkett: An Anglo-American Irishman* (Oxford, Eng., 1949).

Dodd, William E. Jr., and Dodd, Martha, *Ambassador Dodd's Diary, 1933–1938* (London, Eng., 1941).

Doerries, Reinhard R., *Imperial Challenge: Ambassador Count Bernstorff and German–American Relations, 1908–1917* (Chapel Hill, N.C., 1989).

Doughty, Robert, *Pyrrhic Victory: French Strategy and Operations in the Great War* (Cambridge, Mass., 2005).

Douglas, William O. *Farewell to Texas: A Vanishing Wilderness* (New York, 1967),

Dugdale, Blanche E. C., *Arthur James Balfour, 1906–1930* (New York, 1937).

Dugdale, E. T. S., *German Diplomatic Documents, 1871–1914*, 4 vols. (New York, 1969).

Dutton, David, *Austen Chamberlain: Gentleman in Politics* (London, Eng., 1985).

Dutton, David, ed., *Paris 1918: The War Diary of the 17th Earl of Derby* (Liverpool, Eng., 2001).

Edel, Leon, *Henry James: The Master, 1901–1916* (New York, 1972).

Egerton, George W., *Great Britain and the Creation of the League of Nations: Strategy, Politics, and International Organization, 1914–1919* (Chapel Hill, N.C., 1978).

Eksteins, Modris, *Rites of Spring: The Great War and the Birth of the Modern Age* (Boston, Mass., 1989).

Erikson, Erik H., *Young Man Luther: A Study in Psychoanalysis and History* (New York, 1958).

Esposito, David M., "Imagined Power: The Secret Life of Colonel House," *Historian*, 60 (1998).

Farley, James A., *Behind the Ballots: The Personal History of a Politician* (New York, 1938).

Farwell, Bryon, *Over There: The United States in the Great War, 1917–1918* (New York, 1999).

Ferguson, Niall, *The Pity of War* (New York, 1998).

Ferguson, Niall, *The War of the World: Twentieth Century Conflict and the Descent of the West* (New York, 2006).

Ferrell, Robert H., *Woodrow Wilson and World War I* (New York, 1985).

Ferrell, Robert H., *The Presidency of Calvin Coolidge* (Lawrence, Kans., 1998).

Flanagan, Maureen A., *America Reformed: Progressives and Progressivism, 1890s–1920s* (New York, 2007).

Floto, Inga, *Colonel House in Paris: A Study of American Policy at the Paris Peace Conference 1919* (Princeton, N.J., 1980).

Foglesong, David S., *America's Secret War against Bolshevism: U. S. Intervention in the Russian Civil War, 1917–1918* (Chapel Hill, N.C., 1995).

Foley, Robert T., *German Strategy and the Path to Verdun: Erich von Falkenhayn and the Development of Attrition* (Cambridge, Eng., 2005).

Fosdick, Raymond, *Chronicle of a Generation: An Autobiography* (New York, 1958).

Fornell, Earl Wesley, *The Galveston Era: The Texas Crescent on the Eve of Secession* (Austin, Tex., 1961).

Foulke, William Dudley, *The Life of Oliver P. Morton*, 2 vols. (Indianapolis, Ind., 1899).

Fowler, W. B., *British–American Relations, 1917–1918: The Role of Sir William Wiseman* (Princeton, N.J., 1969).

Fox, Stephen, *Transatlantic: Samuel Cunard, Isambard Brunel, and the Great Atlantic Steamships* (New York, 2003).

Frank, Waldo, et al., eds., *America and Alfred Stieglitz: A Collective Portrait* (New York, 1934).

Freidel, Frank, *Franklin D. Roosevelt*, 4 vols. (Boston, Mass., 1952–73).

French, David, *British Strategy and War Aims, 1914–1916* (London, Eng., 1986).

Friedrich, Thomas, *Berlin between the Wars* (New York, 1991).

Fromkin, David, *Europe's Last Summer: Who Started the Great War in 1914?* (New York, 2004).

Fry, Michael G., *Lloyd George and Foreign Policy: The Education of a Statesman, 1890–1916* (Montreal, Canada, 1977).

Garland, Joseph E., *Boston's North Shore: Being an Account of Life among the Noteworthy, Fashionable, Wealthy, Eccentric and Ordinary, 1823–1890* (Boston, Mass., 1978).

Garland, Joseph E., *Boston's Gold Coast: The North Shore, 1890–1929* (Boston, Mass., 1981).

Garraty, John A., *Right-Hand Man: The Life of George W. Perkins* (New York, 1960).

Garraty, John A., *Henry Cabot Lodge: A Biography* (New York, 1953).

Garraty, John A., and Carnes, Mark C., *American National Biography*, 24 vols. (New York, 1999).

Gelfand, Lawrence E., *The Inquiry: American Preparations for Peace, 1917–1919* (New Haven, Conn., 1963).

George, Alexander L. and George, Juliette L., *Woodrow Wilson and Colonel House: A Personality Study* (New York, 1956).

Gerard, James W., *My Four Years in Germany* (New York, 1917).

Gertz, Elmer, *Odyssey of a Barbarian: The Biography of George Sylvester Viereck* (Buffalo, N.Y., 1978).

Gilbert, Martin, *The First World War: A Complete History* (New York, 1994).

Gilbert, Martin, *Winston S. Churchill: The Stricken World, 1916–1922* (Boston, Mass., 1975).

Gilderhus, Mark T., *The Second Century: U.S.-Latin American Relations since 1889* (Wilmington, Del., 2000).

Gilderhus, Mark T., *Diplomacy and Revolution: U.S.-Mexican Relations under Wilson and Carranza* (Tucson, Ariz., 1977).

Glass, Carter, *An Adventure in Constructive Finance* (New York, 1927).

Goodwyn, Lawrence, *Democratic Promise: The Populist Movement in America* (New York, 1976).

Gorlitz, Walter, ed., *The Kaiser and His Court* (New York, 1961).

Gould, Lewis L., ed., *The Progressive Era* (Syracuse, N.Y., 1974).

Gould, Lewis L., *Four Hats in the Ring: The 1912 Election and the Birth of Modern American Politics* (Lawrence, Kans., 2008).

Gould, Lewis L., *Reform and Regulation: American Politics from Roosevelt to Wilson* (Prospect Heights, Ill., 1996).

Gould, Lewis L., *Progressives and Prohibitionists: Texas Democrats in the Wilson Era* (Austin, Tex., 1973).

Gould, Lewis L., *The Modern American Presidency* (Lawrence, Kans., 2003).

Grant, James, *Bernard M. Baruch: The Adventures of a Wall Street Legend* (New York, 1997).

Grayson, Cary T., *Woodrow Wilson: An Intimate Memoir* (New York, 1960).

Grayson, Cary T., "The Colonel's Folly and the President's Distress," *American Heritage* (Oct. 1984), 5–7, 94–101.

Greenberg, David, *Calvin Coolidge* (New York, 2006).

Greenhalgh, *Foch in Command: The Forging of a First World War General* (Cambridge, Eng., 2011).

Grew, Joseph C., *Turbulent Era: A Diplomatic Record of Forty Years, 1904–1945*, 2 vols. (Boston, Mass., 1952).

Grieb, Kenneth J., *The United States and Huerta* (Lincoln, Neb., 1969).

Grigg, John, *Lloyd George: From Peace to War, 1912–1916* (Berkeley, Calif., 1985).

Grigg, John, *Lloyd George: War Leader, 1916–1918* (London, Eng., 2002).

Griscom, Lloyd, *Diplomatically Speaking* (Boston, Mass., 1940).

Gwynn, Stephen, ed., *The Letters and Friendships of Sir Cecil Spring Rice: A Record*, 2 vols. (Boston, Mass., 1929).

Haley, James L., *Passionate Nation: The Epic History of Texas* (New York, 2006).

Hamilton, John Maxwell, and Mann, Robert, eds., *A Journalist's Diplomatic Mission: Ray Stannard Baker's World War I Diary* (Baton Rouge, La., 2012).

Harbord, James G., *Leaves from a War Diary* (New York, 1925).

Harbaugh, William H., *Lawyer's Lawyer: The Life of John W. Davis* (New York, 1973).

Harmer, Harry, *Friedrich Ebert: Germany* (London, Eng., 2008).

Harries, Meirion and Harries, Susie, *The Last Days of Innocence: America at War, 1917–1918* (New York, 1997).

Harriman, Mrs. J. Borden, *From Pinafores to Politics* (New York, 1923).

Harris, J. P., *Douglas Haig and the First World War* (New York, 2008).

Hart, John Mason, *Revolutionary Mexico: The Coming and Process of the Mexican Revolution* (Berkeley, Calif., 1987).

Hart, John Mason, *Empire and Revolution: The Americans in Mexico since the Civil War* (Berkeley, Calif., 2002).

Hart, Katherine, et al., *Austin and Travis County: A Pictorial History, 1839–1939* (Austin, Tex., 1975).

Hartig, Thomas H., *Robert Lansing: An Interpretive Biography* (New York, 1982).

Heckscher, August, *Woodrow Wilson* (New York, 1991).

Hendrick, Burton J., *The Life and Letters of Walter H. Page*, 3 vols. (New York, 1924–26).

Henig, Ruth, *The League of Nations* (London, Eng., 2010).

Herwig, Holger H., *The First World War: Germany and Austria-Hungary, 1914–1918* (New York, 1997).

Herwig, Holger H., *The Marne, 1914: The Opening of World War I and the Battle that Changed the World* (New York, 2009).

Hewitson, Mark, *Germany and the Causes of the First World War* (New York, 2004).

Higonnet, Patrice, *Paris: Capital of the World* (Cambridge, Mass., 2002).

Hiltzik, Michael, *The New Deal: A Modern History* (New York, 2011).

Hinsley, F. H., ed., *British Foreign Policy under Sir Edward Grey* (Cambridge, Eng., 1977).

Hochschild, Adam, *To End All Wars: A Story of Loyalty and Rebellion, 1914–1918* (Boston, Mass., 2011).

Hoff, Joan, *A Faustian Foreign Policy: From Woodrow Wilson to George W. Bush* (New York, 2008).

Hoover, Irwin H., *Forty–two Years in the White House* (Boston, Mass., 1934).

House, Edward M., and Charles Seymour, *What Really Happened at Paris: The Story of the Peace Conference, 1918–1919* (New York, 1921).

Houston, David F., *Eight Years with Wilson's Cabinet, 1913 to 1920* (New York, 1926).

Huebsch, B. W., "From a Publisher's Commonplace Book," *American Scholar*, 33 (1963).

Hyde, H. Montgomery, *Lord Reading: The Life of Rufus Isaacs, First Marquess of Reading* (New York, 1967).

Ikenberry, G. John, Knock, Thomas J., Slaughter, Anne–Marie, and Smith, Tony, *The Crisis of American Foreign Policy: Wilsonianism in the Twenty–first Century* (Princeton, N.J., 2009).

James, Robert Rhodes, *The British Revolution: 1880–1939* (New York, 1977).

Jarausch, Konrad H., *The Enigmatic Chancellor: Bethmann Hollweg and the Hubris of Imperial Germany* (New Haven, Conn., 1973).

Jenkins, Roy, *Asquith: Portrait of a Man and an Era* (New York, 1964).

Jenson, Billie Barnes, "Philip Dru: The Blueprint of a Presidential Adviser," *American Studies*, 12 (1971).

Johnson, Niel M., *George Sylvester Viereck: German-American Propagandist* (Urbana, Ill., 1972).

Jones, Colin, *Paris: Biography of a City* (New York, 2004).

Katznelson, Ira, *Fear Itself: The New Deal and the Origins of Our Time* (New York, 2013).

Katz, Friedrich, *The Secret War in Mexico: Europe, the United States, and the Mexican Revolution* (Chicago, Ill., 1981).

Katz, Friedrich, *The Life & Times of Pancho Villa* (Stanford, Calif., 2008).

Kazin, Michael, *A Godly Hero: The Life of William Jennings Bryan* (New York, 2006).

Keegan, John, *The First World War* (New York, 1999).

Keiger, J. F. V., *Raymond Poincaré* (Cambridge, Eng., 1997).

Keller, Morton, *Affairs of State: Public Life in Late Nineteenth Century America* (Cambridge, Mass., 1977).

Keller, Morton, *Regulating a New Economy: Public Policy and Economic Change in America, 1900–1933* (Cambridge, Mass., 1990).

Kelley, Brooks Mather, *Yale: A History* (New Haven, Conn., 1974).

Kennan, George F., *Russia and the West under Lenin and Stalin* (Boston, Mass., 1960).

Kennan, George F., *Russia Leaves the War* (Princeton, N.J., 1956).

Kennedy, David, *Over Here: The First World War and American Society* (New York, 1980).

Kennedy, David, *Freedom from Fear: The American People in Depression and War* (New York, 1999).

Kershaw, Ian, *Hitler, 1936–45: Nemesis* (New York, 2000).

Kissinger, Henry, *Diplomacy* (New York, 1994).

Knock, Thomas J., *To End All Wars: Woodrow Wilson and the Quest for a New World Order* (New York, 1992).

Koenig, Louis W., *Bryan: A Political Biography* (New York, 1971).

Koistinen, Paul A. C., *Mobilizing for Modern War: The Political Economy of American Warfare, 1865–1919* (Lawrence, Kans., 1997).

Kousser, J. Morgan, *The Shaping of Southern Politics: Suffrage Restriction and the Establishment of the One-Party South, 1880–1910* (New Haven, Conn., 1974).

Kraig, Robert Alexander, *Woodrow Wilson and the Lost World of the Oratorical Statesman* (College Station, Tex., 2004).

Kramer, Alan, *Dynamic of Destruction: Culture and Mass Killing in the First World War* (New York, 2007).

Krock, Arthur, *Memoirs: Sixty Years on the Firing Line* (New York, 1968).

Kuehl, Warren F., ed., *Biographical Dictionary of Internationalists* (Westport, Conn., 1983).

Lampert, Nicholas A., *Planning Armageddon: British Economic Warfare and the First World War* (Cambridge, Mass., 2011).

Lasch, Christopher, *The New Radicalism in America, 1889–1963* (New York, 1965).

Lately, Thomas, *The Mayor Who Mastered New York: The Life and Opinions of William J. Gaynor* (New York, 1969).

Leapman, Michael, ed., *The Book of London: The Evolution of a Great City* (New York, 1989).

Leffler, Melvyn P., *The Elusive Quest: America's Pursuit of European Stability and French Security, 1919–1933* (Chapel Hill, N.C., 1979).

Lenox, Lady Algernon G., ed., *The Diary of Lord Bertie of Thame, 1914–1918*, 2 vols. (London, Eng., 1924).

Levin, Phyllis Lee, *Edith and Woodrow: The Wilson White House* (New York, 2001).

Leuchtenburg, William E., *Herbert Hoover* (New York, 2009).

Link, Arthur S., and McCormick, Richard L., *Progressivism* (Arlington Heights, Ill., 1983).

Link, Arthur S., *Woodrow Wilson*, 5 vols. (Princeton, N.J., 1947–67).

Link, Arthur S., ed., *The Papers of Woodrow Wilson*, 68 vols. (Princeton, N.J., 1966–93).

Link, Arthur S., ed., *The Deliberations of the Council of Four (March 24–June 28, 1919): Notes of the Official Interpreter, Paul Mantoux* (Princeton, N.J., 1992).

Livermore, Seward W., *Politics Is Adjourned: Woodrow Wilson and the War Congress, 1916–1916* (Middletown, Conn., 1966).

Lloyd George, David, *War Memoirs of David Lloyd George, 1915–1916*, 6 vols. (Boston, Mass., 1933–37).

Love, Frances Taylor, *My Home Is Austin Texas* (Lafayette, La., 1958).

MacDonogh, Giles, *The Last Kaiser: The Life of Wilhelm II* (New York, 2000).

MacKenzie, Norman, and MacKenzie, Jeanne, eds., *The Diary of Beatrice Webb, 1905–1924* (Cambridge, Mass., 1984).

Manela, Erez, *The Wilsonian Moment: Self-Determination and the International Origins of Anticolonial Nationalism* (New York, 2007).

Masur, Gerhard, *Imperial Berlin* (New York, 1970).

Massie, Robert K., *Dreadnought: Britain, Germany, and the Coming of the Great War* (New York, 1991).

Maxwell, Elsa, *R.S.V.P.: Elsa Maxwell's Own Story* (Boston, Mass., 1954).

Mayer, Arno J., *Politics and Diplomacy of Peacemaking: Containment and Counterrevolution at Versailles, 1918–1919* (New York, 1967).

Maynard, W. Barksdale, *Woodrow Wilson: Princeton to the Presidency* (New Haven, Conn., 2008).

May, Ernest R., *The World War and American Isolation* (Cambridge, Mass., 1959).

McAdoo, William G., *Crowded Years: The Reminiscences of William G. McAdoo* (Boston, Mass., 1931).

McCallum, Jack, *Leonard Wood: Rough Rider, Surgeon, Architect of American Imperialism* (New York, 2006).

McComb, David G., *Houston: A History* (Austin, Tex., 1981).

McComb, David G., *Galveston: A History* (Austin, Tex., 1986).

McCombs, William F., *Making Woodrow Wilson President* (New York, 1931).

McCraw, Thomas K., *Prophets of Regulation: Charles Francis Adams, Louis D. Brandeis, James M. Landis, Alfred E. Kahn* (Cambridge, Mass., 1984).

McFadden, *Alternative Paths: Soviets and Americans, 1917–1920* (New York, 1993).

McMeekin, Sean, *The Russian Origins of the First World War* (Cambridge, Mass., 2011).

McKeekin, Sean, *July 1914: Countdown to War* (New York, 2013).

Miller, Kristie, *Ellen and Edith: Woodrow Wilson's First Ladies* (Lawrence, Kans., 2010).

Milner, Violet, *My Picture Gallery, 1886–1901* (London, Eng., 1951).

Mombauer, Annika, *The Origins of the First World War: Controversies and Consensus* (London, Eng., 2002).

Moore, R. Laurence, *In Search of White Crows: Spiritualism, Parapsychology, and American Culture* (New York, 1977).

Mordacq, General J. J. H., *Le Ministere Clemenceau* (Paris, France, 1930–31).

Morgan, Kevin, *Ramsay MacDonald* (London, Eng., 2006).

Morrison, Joseph L., *Josephus Daniels: The Small–d Democrat* (Chapel Hill, N.C., 1966).

Morris, Robert T., *Fifty Years a Surgeon* (New York, 1935).

Mulligan, William, *The Origins of the First World War* (New York, 2010).

Murray, Robert K., *The Harding Era: Warren G. Harding and His Administration* (Minneapolis, Minn., 1969).

Nackman, Mark E., *A Nation within a Nation: The Rise of Texas Nationalism* (Port Washington, N.Y., 1975).

Nasaw, David, *The Chief: The Life of William Randolph Hearst* (New York, 2000).

Nash, George H., *The Life of Herbert Hoover: Master of Emergencies, 1917–1918* (New York, 1996).

Neal, Steve, *Happy Days Are Here Again* (New York, 2004).

Neiberg, Michael S., *Fighting the Great War: A Global History* (Cambridge, Mass., 2005).

Neiberg, Michael S., *Dance of the Furies: Europe and the Outbreak of World War I* (Cambridge, Mass., 2011).

Neiberg, Michael S., *Foch: Supreme Allied Commander in the Great War* (Washington, D.C., 2003).

Neu, Charles E., *The Troubled Encounter: The United States and Japan* (New York, 1975).

Nevins, Allan, *Henry White: Thirty Years of American Diplomacy* (New York, 1930).

Nichols, Christopher McKnight, *Promise and Peril: America at the Dawn of a Global Age* (Cambridge, Mass., 2011).

Nugent, Walter, *Progressivism: A Very Short Introduction* (New York, 2010).

O'Connor, Richard. *O. Henry: The Legendary Life of William S. Porter* (Garden City, N.Y., 1970).

Olmsted, Frederick Law, *A Journey through Texas; or a Saddle-Trip on the Southwestern Frontier* (New York, 1857).

Olson, Keith W., *Biography of a Progressive: Franklin K. Lane, 1864–1921* (Westport, Conn., 1979).

Paine, Albert Bigelow, *Captain Bill McDonald, Texas Ranger: A Story of Frontier Reform* (New York, 1909).

Park, Bert Edward, *The Impact of Illness on World Leaders* (Philadelphia, Penn., 1986).

Parsons, Kermit Carlyle, *The Cornell Campus: A History of Its Planning and Development* (Ithaca, N.Y., 1968).

Perkins, Anne, *Baldwin* (London, Eng., 2006).

Perman, Michael, *Pursuit of Unity: A Political History of the American South* (Chapel Hill, N.C., 2009).

Perman, Michael, *Reunion without Compromise: The South and Reconstruction, 1865–1868* (Cambridge, Eng., 1973).

Perman, Michael, *Struggle for Mastery: Disfranchisement in the South, 1868–1908* (Chapel Hill, N.C., 2001).

Perman, Michael, *The Road to Redemption: Southern Politics, 1869–1879* (Chapel Hill, N.C. 1984).

Pershing, John J., *My Experiences in the World War*, 2 vols. (New York, 1911).

Phillips, Charles J., *Paderewski: The Story of a Modern Immortal* (New York, 1934).

Phillips, *Ventures in Diplomacy* (London, Eng., 1955).

Philpott, William, *Three Armies on the Somme: The First Battle of the Twentieth Century* (New York, 2010).

Pinney, Thomas, ed., *The Letters of Rudyard Kipling* (Iowa City, Ia., 2004).

Polakoff, Keith Ian, *The Politics of Inertia: The Election of 1876 and the End of Reconstruction* (Lawrence, Kans., 2008).

Polsky, Andrew J., *Elusive Victories: The American Presidency at War* (New York, 2012).

Ponce De Leon, Charles L., *Self Exposure: Human-Interest Journalism and the Emergence of Celebrity in America, 1890–1940* (Chapel Hill, N.C., 2002).

Porter, Roy, *London: A Social History* (Cambridge, Mass., 1994).

Postel, Charles, *The Populist Movement in America* (New York, 2007).

Powell, Jim, *Wilson's War: How Woodrow Wilson's Great Blunder Led to Hitler, Lenin, Stalin & World War II* (New York, 2005).

Prazmowska, Anita, *Ignacy Paderewski* (London, Eng., 2009).

Procter, Ben H., *Not without Honor: The Life of John H. Reagan* (Austin, Tex., 1962).

Purcell, Hugh, *Lloyd George* (London, Eng., 2006).

Quirk, Robert E., *An Affair of Honor: Woodrow Wilson and the Occupation of Vera Cruz* (Lexington, Ky., 1962).

Reed, S. G., *A History of Texas Railroads* (Houston, Tex., 1941).

Reid, Edith Gittings, *Woodrow Wilson: the Caricature, the Myth, and the Man* (New York, 1934).

Richardson, Rupert Norval, *Colonel Edward M. House: The Texas Years, 1958–1912* (Abilene, Tex., 1964).

Rifkind, Robert S., *"The Colonel's Dream of Power," American Heritage*, 10 (Feb. 1959).

Robbins, Keith, *Sir Edward Grey: A Biography of Lord Grey of Fallodon* (London, Eng., 1971).

Rodgers, Daniel T., *Atlantic Crossings: Social Politics in a Progressive Era* (Cambridge, Mass., 1998).

Rollins, Alfred D. Jr., *Roosevelt and Howe* (New York, 1962).

Roper, Daniel C., *My Fifty Years of Public Life* (Durham, N. C., 1941).

Rose, Gideon, *How Wars End: Why We Always Fight the Last Battle* (New York, 2010).

Roskill, Stephen, *Hankey: Man of Secrets, 1877–1918* (London, Eng., 1970).

Rossini, Daniela, *Woodrow Wilson and the American Myth in Italy: Culture, Diplomacy, and War Propaganda* (Cambridge, Mass., 2008).

Rudolph, Frederick, *The American College and University: A History* (New York, 1962).

Samuels, Ernest, *Henry Adams: The Major Phase* (Cambridge, Mass., 1964).

Sanders, Elizabeth, *Roots of Reform: Farmers, Workers, and the American State, 1877–1917* (Chicago, Il., 1999).

Sarasohn, David, *The Part of Reform: Democrats in the Progressive Era* (Jackson, Miss., 1989).

Saul, Norman E., *War and Revolution: The United States and Russia, 1914–1921* (Lawrence, Kans., 2001).

Saunders, Frances Wright, *Ellen Axson Wilson: First Lady between Two Worlds* (Chapel Hill, N.C., 1985).

Schuker, Stephen A., *The End of French Predominance in Europe: The Financial Crisis of 1924 and the Adoption of the Dawes Plan* (Chapel Hill, N.C., 1976).

Schuster, David G., *Neurasthenic Nation: America's Search for Health, Happiness, and Comfort, 1869–1920* (New Brunswick, N.J., 2011).

Schwabe, Klaus, *Woodrow Wilson, Revolutionary Germany, and Peacemaking, 1918–1919: Missionary Diplomacy and the Realities of Power* (Chapel Hill, N.C., 1985).

Schwarz, Jordan A., *The Speculator: Bernard M. Baruch in Washington, 1917–1965* (Chapel Hill, N.C., 1981).

Schwarz, Jordan A., *The New Dealers: Power Politics in the Age of Roosevelt* (New York, 1993).

Scott, C. A. Dawson, *Is This Wilson? Messages Accredited to Woodrow Wilson* (New York, 1929).

Senior, Ian, *Home before the Leaves Fall: A New History of the German Invasion of 1914* (Oxford, Eng., 2012).

Seymour, Charles, *The Intimate Papers of Colonel House*, 4 vols. (Boston, Mass., 1926–28).

Seymour, Charles, "End of a Friendship," *American Heritage*, 14, 5 (1963).

Shachtman, Tom, *Edith and Woodrow: A Presidential Romance* (New York, 1981).

Sharp, Alan, *The Versailles Settlement: Peacemaking after the First World War, 1919–1923* (New York, 2008).

Shotwell, James T., *The Autobiography of James T. Shotwell* (Indianapolis, Ind., 1961).

Smith, Arthur D. Howden, *Mr. House of Texas* (New York, 1940).

Smith, Arthur D. Howden, *The Real Colonel House* (New York, 1918).

Smith, Leonard V., Audoin–Rouzeau, Stephane, and Becker, Annette, *France and the Great War, 1914–1918* (New York, 2003).

Smith, Neil, *American Empire: Roosevelt's Geographer and the Prelude to Globalization* (Berkeley, Calif., 2003).

Smith, Tony, *America's Mission: The United States and the Worldwide Struggle for Democracy in the Twentieth Century* (Princeton, N.J., 1994).

Smythe, Donald, *Pershing: General of the Armies* (Bloomington, Ind., 1986).

Spate, Virginia, *Claude Monet: Life and Work* (New York, 1922).

Spratt, John Stricklin, *The Road to Spindletop: Economic Change in Texas, 1875–1901* (Dallas, Tex., 1955).

Starling, Edmund W., *Starling of the White House* (New York, 1946).

Steel, Ronald, *Walter Lippmann and the American Century* (Boston, Mass., 1980).

Steiner, Zara, and Neilson, Keith, *Britain and the Origins of the First World War* (New York, 2003).

Steiner, Zara, *The Lights that Failed: European International History, 1919–1933* (Oxford, Eng., 2005).

Steiner, Zara, *The Triumph of the Dark: European International History, 1933–1939* (Oxford, Eng., 2011).

Stevenson, David, *Cataclysm: The First World War as Political Tragedy* (New York, 2004).

Stevenson, David, *With Our Backs to the Wall: Victory and Defeat in 1918* (Cambridge, Mass., 2011), 112–127.

Stid, Daniel D., *The President as Statesman: Woodrow Wilson and the Constitution* (Lawrence, Kans., 1998).

Strachan, Hew, *The First World War, Volume I: To Arms* (Oxford, Eng., 2001).

Strachan, Hew, *The First World War* (New York, 2004).

Thompson, J. Lee, *Politicians, the Press, and Propaganda: Lord Northcliffe and the Great War, 1914–1919* (Kent, Ohio, 1999).

Thompson, John A., *Woodrow Wilson* (London, Eng., 2002).

Thompson, John M., *Russia, Bolshevism, and the Versailles Peace* (Princeton, N.J., 1966).

Thompson, Mark, *The White War: Life and Death on the Italian Front, 1915–1919* (London, Eng., 2008).

Tilchin, William N., and Neu, Charles E., eds. *Artists of Power: Theodore Roosevelt, Woodrow Wilson, and Their Enduring Impact on U. S. Foreign Policy* (Westport, Conn., 2006).

Tinsley, James A., ed., *Letters from the Colonel: Edward M. House to Frank Andrews* (Houston, Tex., Dec. 1960).

Tomes, Jason, *Balfour and Foreign Policy: The International Thought of a Conservative Statesman* (New York, 1997).

Trask, David F., *Captains & Cabinets: Anglo–American Naval Relations, 1917–1918* (Columbia, Mo., 1972).

Trask, David F., *The AEF and Coalition Warmaking, 1917–1918* (Lawrence, Kans., 1993).

Traxel, David, *Crusader Nation: The United States in Peace and the Great War, 1898–1920* (New York, 2006).

Trevelyan, George Macaulay, *Grey of Fallodon: The Life and Letters of Sir Edward Grey, afterwards Grey of Fallodon* (Boston, Mass., 1937).

Tucker, Robert W., *Woodrow Wilson and the Great War: Reconsidering America's Neutrality, 1914–1917* (Charlottesville, Va., 2007).

Tumulty, Joseph P., *Woodrow Wilson as I Know Him* (New York, 1921).

Turner, John, *British Politics and the Great War: Coalition and Conflict, 1915–1918* (New Haven, Conn., 1992).

Tyler, Ron, ed., *The New Handbook of Texas*, 6 vols. (Austin, Tex., 1996).

Ullman, Richard H., *Anglo–Soviet Relations, 1917–1921*, 3 vols. (Princeton, N.J., 1961–1972).

Upstone, Robert, and Weight, Angela, eds., *William Orpen: An Onlooker in France* (London, Eng., 2008).

Urofsky, Melvin I., *Louis D. Brandeis: A Life* (New York, 2009).

Utley, Robert M., *Lone Star Justice: The First Century of the Texas Rangers* (New York, 2002).

Vandiver, Frank E., *Black Jack: The Life and Times of John J. Pershing*, 2 vols. (College Station, Tex., 1977).

Viereck, George Sylvester, *The Strangest Friendship in History: Woodrow Wilson and Colonel House* (New York, 1932).

Viscount Grey of Fallodon, *Twenty-Five Years, 1892–1916*, 3 vols. (New York, 1925).

Walworth, Arthur, *America's Moment: 1918, American Diplomacy at the End of World War I* (New York, 1977).

Walworth, Arthur, *Wilson and His Peacemakers: American Diplomacy at the Paris Peace Conference of 1919* (New York, 1986).

Watson, David Robin, *Clemenceau* (London, Eng., 2008).

Weinstein, Edwin A., *Woodrow Wilson: A Medical and Psychological Biography* (Princeton, N.J., 1981).

Weiss, Harold J. Jr., *Yours to Command: The Life and Legend of Texas Ranger Captain Bill McDonald* (Denton, Tex., 2009).

Wesser, Robert F., *A Response to Progressivism: The Democratic Party and New York Politics, 1902–1918* (New York, 1986).

West, Rachael, *The Department of State on the Eve of the First World War* (Athens, Ga., 1978).

Wheeler, Kenneth W., *To Wear a City's Crown: The Beginnings of Urban Growth in Texas, 1836–1865* (Cambridge, Mass., 1968).

Willert, Arthur, *The Road to Safety: A Study in Anglo-American Relations* (New York, 1953).

Willert, Arthur, *Washington and Other Memories* (Boston, Mass., 1972).

Williams, Joyce Grigsby, *Colonel House and Sir Edward Grey: A Study of Anglo–American Diplomacy* (Lanham, Md., 1984).

Williams, Wythe, *The Tiger of France: Conversations with Clemenceau* (New York, 1949).

Williamson, Roxanne Kuter, *Austin, Texas: An American Architectural History* (San Antonio, Tex., 1973).

Wilson, Edith Bolling, *My Memoir* (N.Y., 1939).

Wilson, Keith, ed., *Decisions for War, 1914* (New York, 1995).

Winter, Jay, and Robert, Jean-Louis, eds., *Capital Cities at War: Paris, London, Berlin, 1914–1919* (Cambridge, Eng., 1997).

Winter, Jay, ed., *The Legacy of the Great War: Ninety Years On* (Columbia, Mo., 2009).

Woodward, C. Vann, *Reunion and Reaction: The Compromise of 1877 and the End of Reconstruction*, 2nd ed. (Garden City, N.Y., 1956).

Woodward, C. Vann, *Origins of the New South: 1877–1913* (Baton Rouge, La., 1951).

Woodward, David R., *Trial by Friendship: Anglo-American Relations, 1917–1918* (Lexington, Ky., 1993).

Wright, Gordon, *France in Modern Times: From the Enlightenment to the Present* (New York, 1995).

Yellin, Eric S., *Racism in the Nation's Service: Government and Workers and the Color Line in Woodrow Wilson's America* (Chapel Hill, N.C., 2013).

Young, Louisa, *A Great Task of Happiness: The Life of Kathleen Scott* (London, Eng., 1995).

Young, Robert J., *An American by Degrees: The Extraordinary Lives of French Ambassador Jules Jusserand* (Montreal, Canada, 2009).

Zieger, Robert H., *America's Great War: World War I and the American Experience* (Lanham, Md., 2000).

Ziegler, Jesse A., *Wave of the Gulf: Ziegler's Scrapbook of the Texas Gulf Coast Country* (San Antonio, Tex., 1938).

Index